MW01629362

Teacher's Manual

Consumer Education & Economics

Ross E. Lowe

Charles A. Malouf

Annette R. Jacobson

New York, New York Columbus, Ohio Chicago, Illinois Peoria, Illinois Woodland Hills, California

The McGraw-Hill Companies

Glencoe

Send all inquiries to:
Glencoe/McGraw-Hill
4400 Easton Commons
Columbus, OH 43219

ISBN: 978-0-07-876781-4 Teacher Annotated Edition
MHID: 0-07-876781-4 Teacher Annotated Edition

ISBN: 978-0-07-876780-7 Student Edition
MHID: 0-07-876780-6 Student Edition

Printed in the United States of America

3 4 5 6 7 8 9 10 DOW 13 12

Consumer Education & Economics

Consumer Education & Economics is a complete program that teaches students economic principles, how to manage family and personal finances, and how to make well-informed purchasing decisions. The student edition and other program components provide teaching ideas and tools for your many classroom needs.

STUDENT EDITION

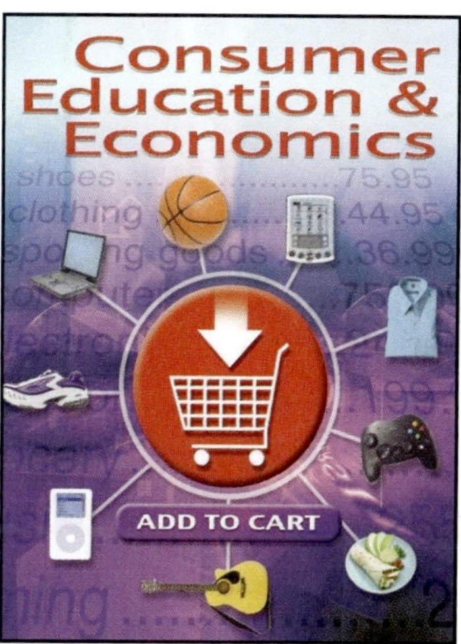

These are key features of the student edition:

- **Accurate.** The student edition has been carefully reviewed by technical experts and current educators to ensure accurate, dependable information.
- **Up-to-Date.** Topics for today's Internet generation include online shopping, online banking and bill payment, identity theft, financial software, and choosing Internet service.
- **Clear.** Complex economic principles are understandable.
- **Practical.** Everyday skills are emphasized, including financial planning, saving, budgeting, and credit use. Special features focus on resource identification and money management tips.
- **Thorough.** Need-to-know topics include investing, buying insurance, understanding warranties, estate planning, and smart shopping.
- **Skill-Based.** Students learn and practice management, decision making, and critical thinking skills.
- **Appealing.** Photos, design, and special features support content visually.
- **Organized.** The student edition has 23 chapters divided among six units. Each chapter opens with a list of the sections within and a "Reading with Purpose" activity. Objectives and key terms are listed on each section opener.

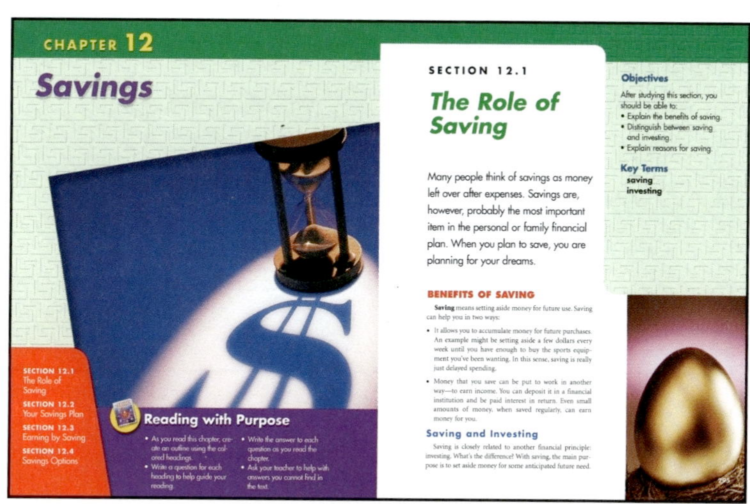

CHAPTER 12

Savings

SECTION 12.1 The Role of Saving
SECTION 12.2 Your Savings Plan
SECTION 12.3 Earning by Saving
SECTION 12.4 Savings Options

Reading with Purpose

- As you read this chapter, create an outline using the colored headings.
- Write a question for each heading to help guide your reading.
- Write the answer to each question as you read the chapter.
- Ask your teacher to help with answers you cannot find in the text.

SECTION 12.1

The Role of Saving

Many people think of savings as money left over after expenses. Savings are, however, probably the most important item in the personal or family financial plan. When you plan to save, you are planning for your dreams.

Objectives

After studying this section, you should be able to:
- Explain the benefits of saving.
- Distinguish between saving and investing.
- Explain reasons for saving.

Key Terms
saving
investing

BENEFITS OF SAVING

Saving means setting aside money for future use. Saving can help you in two ways:

- It allows you to accumulate money for future purchases. An example might be setting aside a few dollars every week until you have enough to buy the sports equipment you've been wanting. In this sense, saving is really just delayed spending.
- Money that you save can be put to work in another way—to earn income. You can deposit it in a financial institution and be paid interest in return. Even small amounts of money, when saved regularly, can earn money for you.

Saving and Investing

Saving is closely related to another financial principle: investing. What's the difference? With saving, the main purpose is to set aside money for some anticipated future need.

Student Edition (continued)

Objectives. Clear goals for learning.

Key Terms. Vocabulary list on the section opener, in the "Glossary," and highlighted and defined at first use in text.

Objectives
After studying this section, you should be able to:
- Describe information to gather when shopping for a vehicle.
- Explain how to evaluate a vehicle.
- Give guidelines for negotiating and finalizing the purchase of a vehicle.

Key Terms
book value
invoice price
base price
options
MSRP
sticker price
lemon laws

SECTION 19.3

Shopping for a Vehicle

Whether you're looking for a used car or a new one, gather as much information as you can. An informed consumer is more likely to get the right vehicle at the right price.

SETTING PRIORITIES

As you consider what type of vehicle you'll buy, think about how you'll use it. If you'll mainly travel between home and school or work, look for an economical and reliable vehicle. If you plan to carpool regularly or if you have a large active family, you'll want something roomier.

Consider where you live, too. Driving on snow-covered mountain roads requires a vehicle designed for such conditions. Extremely hot weather calls for powerful air-conditioning. There are vehicles to meet every want and budget, from traditional sedans and coupes to minivans to SUVs and pickup trucks. Determine which will best suit your budget and priorities.

New or Used?

Should you shop for a used vehicle or a new one? If you're like most people, you'll start with a used vehicle and perhaps eventually buy a new one. Used vehicles are generally less expensive than new ones. For the same amount of money, you might be able to choose between a small, cheaply made new car and a larger three-year-old car that

490

Photos and Drawings. Visuals that support content.

Captions. Explanations that often include questions for thought and discussion.

Section Reviews. Questions to assess comprehension; activities for learning.

Tables and Charts. Information presented visually for better understanding.

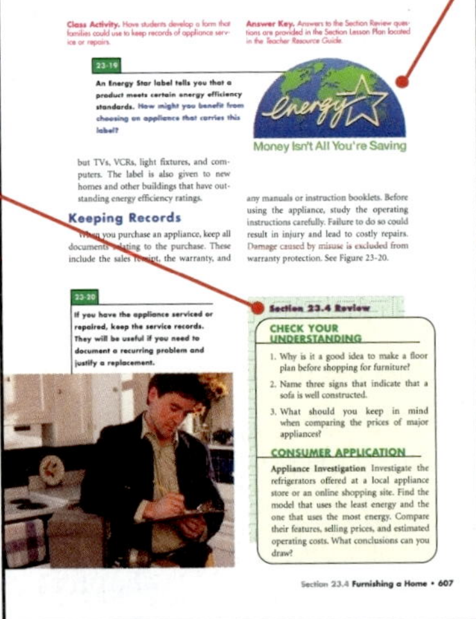
Class Activity. Have students develop a form that families could use to keep records of appliance service or repairs.

Answer Key. Answers to the Section Review questions are provided in the Section Lesson Plan located in the Teacher Resource Guide.

23-19 An Energy Star label tells you that a product meets certain energy efficiency standards. How might you benefit from choosing an appliance that carries this label?

but TVs, VCRs, light fixtures, and computers. The label is also given to new homes and other buildings that have outstanding energy efficiency ratings.

Keeping Records

When you purchase an appliance, keep all documents relating to the purchase. These include the sales receipt, the warranty, and any manuals or instruction booklets. Before using the appliance, study the operating instructions carefully. Failure to do so could result in injury and lead to costly repairs. Damage caused by misuse is excluded from warranty protection. See Figure 23-20.

23-20 If you have the appliance serviced or repaired, keep the service records. They will be useful if you need to document a recurring problem and justify a replacement.

Section 23.4 Review

CHECK YOUR UNDERSTANDING

1. Why is it a good idea to make a floor plan before shopping for furniture?
2. Name three signs that indicate that a sofa is well constructed.
3. What should you keep in mind when comparing the prices of major appliances?

CONSUMER APPLICATION

Appliance Investigation Investigate the refrigerators offered at a local appliance store or an online shopping site. Find the model that uses the least energy and the one that uses the most energy. Compare their features, selling prices, and estimated operating costs. What conclusions can you draw?

Section 23.4 Furnishing a Home • 607

Reviewing Key Terms and Ideas. Questions about chapter content and vocabulary.

Chapter Summary. Brief recap of each section in the chapter.

The Savvy Consumer. Scenarios for analysis.

Thinking Critically. Questions for discussion, including highlighted questions about economic concepts.

Building Consumer Skills. Varied application activities.

Consumer Connections. Activities related to family and community.

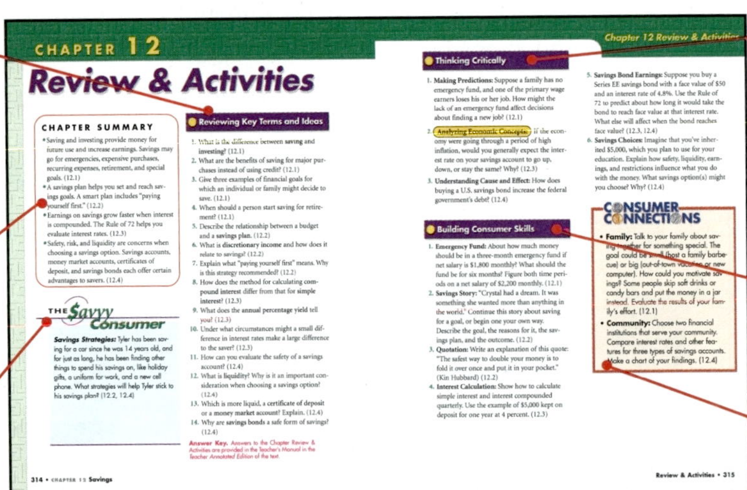
CHAPTER 12

Review & Activities

CHAPTER SUMMARY

- Saving and investing provide money for future use and increase earnings. Savings may go for emergencies, expensive purchases, recurring expenses, retirement, and special goals. (12.1)
- A savings plan helps you set and reach savings goals. A smart plan includes "paying yourself first." (12.2)
- Earnings on savings grow faster when interest is compounded. The Rule of 72 helps you evaluate interest rates. (12.3)
- Safety, risk, and liquidity are concerns when choosing a savings option. Savings accounts, money market accounts, certificates of deposit, and savings bonds each offer certain advantages to savers. (12.4)

THE Savvy Consumer

Savings Strategies: Tyler has been saving for a car since he was 14 years old, and for just as long, he has been finding other things to spend his savings on, like holiday gifts, a uniform for work, and a new cell phone. What strategies will help Tyler stick to his savings plan? (12.2, 12.4)

Reviewing Key Terms and Ideas

1. What is the difference between saving and investing? (12.1)
2. What are the benefits of saving for major purchases instead of using credit? (12.1)
3. Give three examples of financial goals for which an individual or family might decide to save. (12.1)
4. When should a person start saving for retirement? (12.1)
5. Describe the relationship between a budget and a savings plan. (12.2)
6. What is discretionary income and how does it relate to savings? (12.2)
7. Explain what "paying yourself first" means. Why is this strategy recommended? (12.2)
8. How does the method for calculating compound interest differ from that for simple interest? (12.3)
9. What does the annual percentage yield tell you? (12.3)
10. Under what circumstances might a small difference in interest rates make a large difference to the saver? (12.3)
11. How can you evaluate the safety of a savings account? (12.4)
12. What is liquidity? Why is it an important consideration when choosing a savings option? (12.4)
13. Which is more liquid, a certificate of deposit or a money market account? Explain. (12.4)
14. Why are savings bonds a safe form of savings? (12.4)

Answer Key. Answers to the Chapter Review & Activities are provided in the Teacher's Manual in the Teacher Annotated Edition of the text.

314 • CHAPTER 12 Savings

Chapter 12 Review & Activities

Thinking Critically

1. Making Predictions: Suppose a family has no emergency fund, and one of the primary wage earners loses his or her job. How might the lack of an emergency fund affect decisions about finding a new job? (12.1)
2. Analyzing Economic Concepts: If the economy were going through a period of high inflation, would you generally expect the interest rate on your savings account to go up, down, or stay the same? Why? (12.3)
3. Understanding Cause and Effect: How does buying a U.S. savings bond increase the federal government's debt? (12.4)

Building Consumer Skills

1. Emergency Fund: About how much money should be in a three-month emergency fund if net salary is $1,800 monthly? What should the fund be for six months? Figure both time periods on a net salary of $2,200 monthly. (12.1)
2. Savings Story: "Crystal had a dream. It was something she wanted more than anything in the world." Continue this story about saving for a goal, or begin one your own way. Describe the goal, the reasons for it, the savings plan, and the outcome. (12.2)
3. Quotation: Write an explanation of this quote: "The safest way to double your money is to fold it over once and put it in your pocket." (Kin Hubbard) (12.2)
4. Interest Calculation: Show how to calculate simple interest and interest compounded quarterly. Use the example of $5,000 kept on deposit for one year at 4 percent. (12.3)
5. Savings Bond Earnings: Suppose you buy a Series EE savings bond with a face value of $50 and an interest rate of 4.8%. Use the Rule of 72 to predict about how long it would take the bond to reach face value at that interest rate. What else will affect when the bond reaches face value? (12.3, 12.4)
6. Savings Choices: Imagine that you've inherited $5,000, which you plan to use for your education. Explain how safety, liquidity, earnings, and restrictions influence what you do with the money. What savings option(s) might you choose? Why? (12.4)

CONSUMER CONNECTIONS

- Family: Talk to your family about saving together for something special. The goal could be small (host a family barbecue) or big (out-of-town vacation or new computer). How could you motivate savings? Some people skip soft drinks or candy bars and put the money in a jar instead. Evaluate the results of your family's effort. (12.1)
- Community: Choose two financial institutions that serve your community. Compare interest rates and other features for three types of savings accounts. Make a chart of your findings. (12.4)

Review & Activities • 315

Special Student Edition Features

Reading with Purpose

To guide students in reading chapters, point them to these features on chapter openers. Students are asked to outline, write definitions, compose questions, find answers, summarize in writing, and visualize as they read.

InfoSource

Finding reliable information is an essential consumer skill. These features help students discover both print and online resources.

DOLLARSandSENSE

The practical tips provided in these features can help students make the most of their money.

Economic Impact & Issues

Economic principles affect the day-to-day lives of consumers. In turn, consumer actions affect the economy. Through these features, students relate chapter topics to the larger world of economics.

FIGURE IT OUT

Discussion questions and activities in "Figure It Out" encourage further exploration.

TEXTLINK

These cross-references help you and your students find related topics in other locations of the student edition.

TEACHER ANNOTATED EDITION

Look for these aids in the "Teacher's Manual" that you are now reading:

- **Content Themes Guide.** Major themes woven throughout the student edition.
- **Correlations.** Student edition links to standards developed by the Jump$tart Coalition for Personal Financial Literacy and to the Family and Consumer Sciences National Standards for "Consumer and Family Resources" and "Career, Community, and Family Connections."
- **Answer Key.** Answers for "Chapter Review & Activities."

Annotations suggest ideas for activities and discussion. Categories are:

Activity. Four types of activity annos that focus on research, teamwork, in-class work, and community involvement.

Discussion. Questions for class discussion.

Critical Thinking. Questions that promote original thinking.

Point Out. Information to stress.

Dollars and Sense, Economic Impact & Issues, and InfoSource. Teaching ideas related to special features.

Caption Answer. Answers to caption questions.

Jump$tart. Activities tied to Jump$tart standards in the areas of income, money management, spending and credit, and saving and investing.

FCCLA. Project ideas related to Family, Career, and Community Leaders of America, Inc., programs.

TEACHER RESOURCE GUIDE

This component contains:

- Section lesson plans with activity ideas and answers to section reviews.
- Section quizzes and answer keys.
- Performance assessment activities and rubrics for all chapters.

STUDENT ACTIVITY MANUAL

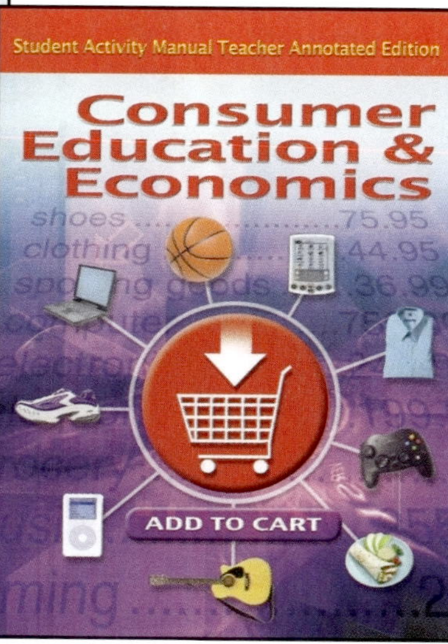

The *Student Activity Manual* contains:

- Attitude inventories that check understanding before and after reading;
- Chapter study guides;
- Activity worksheets for every chapter.

The *Student Activity Manual Teacher Annotated Edition* has answers printed in color on each page.

VOCABULARY PuzzleMaker™ CD-ROM

With this CD, you can create crossword, word search, and jumble puzzles in a printable form or for use on the computer. Answer files are included.

ExamView® ASSESSMENT SUITE CD-ROM

For streamlined assessment, you can use this CD to build comprehensive tests with Test Generator, administer tests with Test Player, and analyze results with Test Manager.

TEACHING & LEARNING RESOURCES

This resource box contains six reproducible booklets that can be used to reinforce and expand chapter information and personalize the program to fit course needs.

- **Math for Consumers.** Students focus on math skills as they balance a budget, compute finance charges, and more. With math refreshers, they brush up on basic math skills.
- **Financial Simulations.** Students face financial decisions and challenges by working through case studies.
- **Consumer Advertising.** Students analyze many forms of advertising as they react to a topic, read and reflect on it, and then conduct investigations.
- **Inclusion in the Consumer Classroom.** Activity ideas for every chapter are accompanied by ways to accommodate them for students with special needs.
- **Financial Literacy.** A how-to approach provides information and tips on financial topics, followed by questions for analysis and application.
- **Consumer Savvy.** Students explore attitudes and thoughts about financial topics with these scenario-based activities.

Content Themes Guide

This chart shows how major themes are woven throughout *Consumer Education & Economics.* You can use this information to plan a course or emphasize particular themes.

Content Themes	Unit 1 Preparing for Consumer Choices	Unit 2 Understanding Economic Principles	Unit 3 Managing Your Money	Unit 4 Building Financial Security	Unit 5 Becoming a Smart Shopper	Unit 6 Making Spending Decisions
	Sections in the Student Edition:					
Consumer Awareness & Safety	1.3, 1.4, 1.5, 2.4, 3.1, 3.2, 3.3	5.3	10.2, 11.1, 11.2, 11.3, 11.4, 11.5	13.3, 14.1, 14.2, 14.4	15.1, 15.2, 15.3, 16.2, 16.4	17.2, 17.3, 18.4, 19.3, 22.1, 22.2, 23.4, 23.5
Consumer Decisions	1.1, 2.1, 2.3, 3.1, 4.1, 4.3	5.1	9.2, 9.3, 9.5, 10.1, 10.3, 11.1, 11.3, 11.4	12.2, 14.2, 14.3, 14.4, 14.5	15.2, 15.3, 16.3	17.1, 17.2, 17.3, 17.4, 18.1, 18.4, 19.1, 19.2, 20.3, 21.1, 21.4, 22.3, 22.4, 23.1, 23.2
Consumer Purchasing	1.1, 1.5	5.2, 5.4, 6.2, 6.3, 7.1, 7.2	10.4, 11.3, 11.4	14.2, 14.3	15.2, 15.3, 16.1, 16.3, 16.4	17.1, 17.2, 17.3, 17.4, 18.2, 18.4, 19.3, 20.2, 21.3, 22.2, 23.3, 23.4
Consumer Resources	1.2, 1.3, 1.4, 1.5, 2.2, 2.4, 3.3, 4.1, 4.2, 4.3, 4.4	5.1, 5.3, 6.1, 7.1	8.3, 9.3, 9.5, 10.1, 11.2, 11.5	12.4, 13.1, 13.2, 13.3, 14.1	16.1, 16.3, 16.4	17.2, 17.4, 18.1, 18.4, 19.1, 19.3, 20.2, 20.3, 21.1, 21.3, 22.2, 22.4, 23.1, 23.2, 23.3, 23.4
Economic Concepts	2.1, 2.2, 4.2	5.1, 5.2, 5.3, 5.4, 6.1, 6.2, 6.3, 7.1, 7.2	8.1, 9.1, 10.1, 11.1	12.2, 12.3, 12.4, 13.1, 13.3, 13.4	15.1	17.1, 20.2, 21.2, 23.3
Government & Laws	1.2, 1.3, 1.4, 1.5, 2.4, 3.1, 3.2, 3.3, 4.1, 4.3, 4.4, 4.5	5.1, 5.3, 5.4, 6.1, 6.2, 6.3	8.1, 8.2, 8.3, 10.1, 10.2, 11.2, 11.3, 11.5	13.2, 13.3, 13.4, 14.3, 14.4, 14.5	15.1, 15.2, 15.3, 16.1, 16.2, 16.4	18.4, 19.3, 21.3, 22.2, 23.2, 23.3, 23.4
Planning & Management	1.1, 2.1, 2.4, 4.2, 4.5		9.1, 9.3, 9.4, 10.3, 11.3, 11.5	12.1, 12.2, 13.2, 13.5, 14.1	16.3	17.1, 18.1, 18.3, 19.4, 20.1, 20.2, 20.3, 21.1, 21.2, 22.1, 22.4, 23.5
Skill Building	1.1, 2.1, 2.4, 4.2, 4.5		8.3, 9.3, 9.4, 10.2, 10.3, 11.3	12.3, 13.1	15.2, 16.3	21.2, 21.4, 23.4, 23.5
Trends & Technology	1.1, 1.3, 1.4, 2.3, 4.2, 4.5	5.2, 6.1, 7.2	8.2, 8.3, 9.2, 10.1, 10.2, 10.4	13.3	16.1	17.1, 17.2, 17.3, 17.4, 18.4

Jump$tart Standards Correlation

The Jump$tart Coalition for Personal Financial Literacy, a coalition of nonprofit organizations, government agencies, and corporations, seeks to improve the financial skills of young adults by evaluating their financial literacy; developing, disseminating, and encouraging the use of standards for grades K–12; and promoting the teaching of personal finance. Visit their Web site at http://www.jumpstartcoalition.org.

Assisted by educators from throughout the United States, Jump$tart developed Personal Finance Standards and their corresponding benchmarks covering four key areas: income, money management, spending and credit, and saving and investing. Each standard identifies specific skills and concepts that Jump$tart believes students should learn before graduating from high school to ensure that they can take responsibility for their financial well-being.

The following chart shows how the ***Consumer Education & Economics*** textbook meets Jump$tart's Personal Finance Standards.

Jump$tart Personal Finance Standards	*Consumer Education & Economics Sections*
Income — Students will be able to:	
1. Identify sources of income.	8.1
2. Analyze how career choice, education, skills, and economic conditions affect income.	4.1, 4.3, 6.1
3. Explain how taxes, government transfer payments, and employee benefits relate to disposable income.	5.3, 5.4, 8.1, 8.3
Money Management — Students will be able to:	
1. Explain how limited personal financial resources affect the choices people make.	2.2
2. Identify the opportunity cost of financial decisions.	2.2, 2.3
3. Discuss the importance of taking responsibility for personal financial decisions.	9.1
4. Apply a decision-making process to personal financial choices.	2.3
5. Explain how inflation affects spending and investing decisions.	6.1
6. Describe how insurance and other risk-management strategies protect against financial loss.	14.1
7. Design a plan for earning, spending, saving, and investing.	9.1, 9.3
8. Explain how to use money-management tools available from financial institutions.	9.5, 10.1, 10.2, 10.3, 10.4
Spending and Credit — Students will be able to:	
1. Compare the benefits and costs of spending decisions.	2.3, 16.3, 16.4
2. Evaluate information about products and services.	2.4, 16.3, 16.4
3. Compare the advantages and disadvantages of different payment methods.	10.3, 10.4, 11.1
4. Analyze the benefits and costs of consumer credit.	11.1
5. Compare sources of consumer credit.	11.1, 11.3, 11.4
6. Explain factors that affect creditworthiness and the purpose of credit records.	11.2
7. Identify ways to avoid or correct credit problems.	11.5
8. Describe the rights and responsibilities of buyers and sellers under consumer protection laws.	1.2
Saving and Investing — Students will be able to:	
1. Explain the relationship between saving and investing.	12.1
2. Describe reasons for saving and reasons for investing.	12.1, 13.1
3. Compare the risk, return, and liquidity of investment alternatives.	13.1
4. Describe how to buy and sell investments.	13.3, 13.4
5. Explain how different factors affect the rate of return of investments.	13.1, 13.3
6. Evaluate sources of investment information.	2.4, 13.1, 13.3, 13.4
7. Explain how agencies that regulate financial markets protect investors.	13.3

FACS National Standards Correlations: Consumer and Family Resources

COMPREHENSIVE STANDARD 2.0

EVALUATE MANAGEMENT PRACTICES RELATED TO THE HUMAN, ECONOMIC, AND ENVIRONMENTAL RESOURCES.

Content Standard 2.1: DEMONSTRATE MANAGEMENT OF INDIVIDUAL AND FAMILY RESOURCES, INCLUDING FOOD, CLOTHING, SHELTER, HEALTH CARE, RECREATION, AND TRANSPORTATION.

COMPETENCIES	TEXT SECTIONS
2.1.1 Apply management and planning skills and processes to organize tasks and responsibilities.	2.2
2.1.2 Examine how individuals and families make choices to satisfy needs and wants.	2.3
2.1.3 Implement decisions about providing safe and nutritious food for individuals and families.	21.1, 21.2, 21.3, 21.4
2.1.4 Implement decisions about purchasing, creating, and maintaining clothing.	18.1, 18.2, 18.3
2.1.5 Implement decisions about housing and furnishings.	23.1, 23.2, 23.3, 23.4, 23.5
2.1.6 Examine information about procuring and maintaining health care to meet the needs of individuals and family members.	22.1, 22.2, 22.3, 22.4
2.1.7 Implement decisions about recreational needs.	20.1, 20.2, 20.3
2.1.8 Apply consumer skills to acquire and maintain transportation that meets the needs of individuals and family members.	19.1, 19.2, 19.3, 19.4

Content Standard 2.2: ANALYZE THE RELATIONSHIP OF THE ENVIRONMENT TO FAMILY AND CONSUMER RESOURCES.

COMPETENCIES	TEXT SECTIONS
2.2.1 Determine individual and family responsibility in relation to the environmental trends and issues.	3.3
2.2.2 Examine environmental trends and issues' effect on families and future generations.	3.3
2.2.3 Examine behaviors that conserve, reuse, and recycle resources to maintain the environment.	3.3
2.2.4 Investigate government regulations for conserving natural resources.	3.3

Content Standard 2.3: ANALYZE POLICIES THAT SUPPORT CONSUMER RIGHTS AND RESPONSIBILITIES.

COMPETENCIES	TEXT SECTIONS
2.3.1 Examine state and federal policies and laws providing consumer protection.	1.2
2.3.2 Investigate how policies become laws related to consumer rights.	1.2
2.3.3 Examine skills used in seeking information related to consumer rights.	1.2

Content Standard 2.4: EVALUATE THE IMPACT OF TECHNOLOGY ON INDIVIDUAL AND FAMILY RESOURCES.

	COMPETENCIES	TEXT SECTIONS
2.4.1	Review types of technology that impact family and consumer decision-making.	2.3, 17.1
2.4.2	Examine how media and technological advances impact family and consumer decisions.	2.3, 17.1
2.4.3	Assess the use of technology and its impact on quality of life.	1.1, 1.3, 2.3, 17.1

Content Standard 2.5: ANALYZE INTERRELATIONSHIPS BETWEEN THE ECONOMIC SYSTEM AND CONSUMER ACTIONS.

	COMPETENCIES	TEXT SECTIONS
2.5.1	Examine the use of resources in making choices that satisfy needs and wants of individuals and families.	2.3
2.5.2	Examine individual and family roles in the economic system.	5.2
2.5.3	Examine economic impacts of laws and regulations that pertain to consumers and providers of services.	5.3, 6.3, 7.2
2.5.4	Determine practices that allow families to maintain economic self-sufficiency.	4.2, 4.3, 4.4, 4.5, 9.1, 9.3, 10.3, 12.1, 12.2, 12.3, 12.4

Content Standard 2.6: DEMONSTRATE MANAGEMENT OF FINANCIAL RESOURCES TO MEET THE GOALS OF INDIVIDUALS AND FAMILIES ACROSS THE LIFE SPAN.

	COMPETENCIES	TEXT SECTIONS
2.6.1	Examine the need for personal and family financial planning.	9.1
2.6.2	Apply management principles to individual and family financial practices.	9.1
2.6.3	Apply management principles to decisions about individual and family insurance.	14.1, 14.2, 14.3, 14.4, 14.5
2.6.4	Obtain personal and legal documents related to managing individual and family finances.	9.4

Career, Community, and Family Connections

COMPREHENSIVE STANDARD 1.0

INTEGRATE MULTIPLE LIFE ROLES AND RESPONSIBILITIES IN FAMILY, WORK, AND COMMUNITY SETTINGS.

Content Standard 1.1: ANALYZE STRATEGIES TO MANAGE MULTIPLE INDIVIDUAL, FAMILY, CAREER, AND COMMUNITY ROLES AND RESPONSIBILITIES.

COMPETENCIES	TEXT SECTIONS
1.1.1 Examine policies, issues, and trends in the workplace and community that impact individuals and families.	4.1
1.1.2 Analyze the impact of social, economic, and technological change on work and family dynamics.	4.1
1.1.3 Analyze ways that individual career goals can enhance the family's capacity to meet goals for all family members.	4.1
1.1.4 Analyze the potential impact of career path decisions on balancing work and family.	4.1
1.1.5 Determine goals for life-long learning and leisure opportunities for all family members.	4.1, 4.3
1.1.6 Determine skills and knowledge needed to develop a life plan for achieving individual, family, and career goals.	4.1

Content Standard 1.2: DEMONSTRATE TRANSFERABLE AND EMPLOYABILITY SKILLS IN COMMUNITY AND WORKPLACE SETTINGS.

COMPETENCIES	TEXT SECTIONS
1.2.1 Examine potential career choices to determine the knowledge, skills, and attitudes associated with each.	4.2
1.2.2 Demonstrate job seeking and job keeping skills.	4.4, 4.5
1.2.3 Apply communication skills in community and workplace settings.	4.5
1.2.4 Demonstrate teamwork skills in community and workplace settings.	4.5
1.2.5 Examine strategies to manage the impact of changing technologies in workplace settings.	4.5
1.2.6 Demonstrate leadership skills and abilities in the workplace and community.	4.5
1.2.7 Examine factors that contribute to maintaining safe and healthy work and community environments.	3.2, 3.3, 4.5
1.2.8 Demonstrate work ethics and professionalism.	4.5

Content Standard 1.3: ANALYZE THE RECIPROCAL IMPACT OF INDIVIDUAL AND FAMILY PARTICIPATION IN COMMUNITY ACTIVITIES.

COMPETENCIES	TEXT SECTIONS
1.3.1 Examine goals that support individuals and family members in carrying out community and civic responsibilities.	3.2
1.3.2 Arrange a plan for individuals and families to select and develop skills in community activities.	3.2
1.3.3 Determine skills that provide beneficial services to the community.	3.2
1.3.4 Examine community resources and systems of formal and informal support available to individuals and families.	2.2
1.3.5 Examine the impact of public policies, agencies, and institutions on the family.	4.1, 5.3

Student Edition Answer Key
Chapter Review & Activities

Chapter 1

To the Teacher: Some review items are not listed when answers or project results will vary. Possible answers are provided as a guide in some cases.

Reviewing Key Terms and Ideas

1. Consumer—user of goods and services. Worker—producer of goods and services. Citizen—user and funder of public services.
2. To use goods and services.
3. Technology gives the consumer instant access to the marketplace but also may make it easier to buy on impulse.
4. Any six from Figure 1-5 on page 30.
5. A consumer affairs department tells customers about their rights and needs. Consumer action panels are formed by trade associations to address consumer complaints.
6. Media are channels of mass communication that keep customers informed about fraud and hazardous products.
7. Any four: Safeguard Social Security number. Handle mail with care. Store personal information safely. Protect information on your computer. Be careful about giving out personal information. Use secure Web sites. Get security from Internet provider. Shred financial papers.
8. A cookie allows a Web site to "remember" information about you and use it to send back information you might like to have. Some people consider this an invasion of privacy. If you eliminate cookies, you may lose the convenience of online shopping.
9. Doing so protects personal information from theft during transmission.
10. It protects your primary email address from being revealed, thereby preventing online harassment.
11. A pyramid scheme uses members to recruit more members, promising large profits. However, one person's "profit" is actually the contributions of other members. Eventually, the pyramid collapses due to insufficient members, and most members lose their investment.
12. Break the "chain" by not sending it to others.
13. Start by contacting the local merchant for a possible return. If that doesn't work, contact the manufacturer by telephone, email, or mail to explain the problem; request a solution; and find out what to do next.
14. If initial contacts produce no results.
15. Small claims court does not require a lawyer, and rules are less strict than those in a regular court.

Savvy Consumer

Meeting an online friend is not safe. Leah doesn't really know whether Madison is who she says she is. Predators fake their identity and friendship. Leah should talk to a parent, who might agree to help her verify Madison's identity and go with her for a first meeting.

Thinking Critically

1. The marketplace would be seriously affected because not only do teens spend their own money, but they are also a big factor in their family's purchases.
2. When consumers buy products, a business profits. As a result, it can pay workers and perhaps increase its work force, thereby creating more consumers with money to spend.

Chapter 2

Reviewing Key Terms and Ideas

1. A need should be a higher priority than a want.
2. Values strongly affect the priorities you set. Standards are levels of quality or quantity for which you strive.
3. Possible examples: saving to buy boots (short-term goal); pursuing a career (long-term goal).
4. Because of scarcity, consumers lack the resources to satisfy all their wants. Therefore, they must give up some wants (paying an opportunity cost) to get others.
5. Possible resources include money, time, and various material, technological, and natural resources. Management strategies should reflect the concepts on text pages 59–62.
6. Any four: stay focused; identify time wasters; get organized; plan ahead; make to-do lists; take action; make use of free time; value other people's time.
7. Planning helps control impulse buying based on factors other than value.
8. Evaluate the decision. Its importance lies in the opportunity to learn to do better the next time.
9. Families are different sizes, at different stages of life, and have different customs and lifestyles, all of which affect financial decisions.
10. The desire to stand out from the crowd and to impress others.
11. Critical thinking can help a consumer detect bias by noticing that source of information is not impartial but is instead slanted to the interests of an advertiser or owner.

12. Any four: consumer protection agencies, professional advisors, media sources, package information, advertising, salespeople, other consumers. Most likely to be biased include package information, advertising, and salespeople.
13. You will be better able to discuss the product with salespeople.

Savvy Consumer

Dan may want to please and help his friend. He should use available resources to compare different monitors in order to get the best buy. He might say, "Thanks for the tip. I'll do some checking and let you know what I decide to get."

Thinking Critically

2. Possible answers: saving gas by walking; using public transit or carpooling; not eating out; buying less expensive foods; renting movies instead of going to the theater.
3. Positive ways: products are improved and costs may be reduced. Negative ways: tempting products may cause overspending; some innovations may carry still unknown problems.

Chapter 3

Reviewing Key Terms and Ideas

1. By not handling food items in a way that damages them or makes them unappealing to other customers.
2. Shoplifting violates the ethical principle of honesty.
3. May result in higher prices.
4. Possible answer: whether to buy from a company that mistreats its workers or harms the environment.
5. The process by which a foreign-born person becomes a citizen.
6. Jury members play the important role of reaching an unprejudiced verdict based on evidence.
7. It can by contributing to higher taxes, increased crime, community members' fear, and sometimes injury and death.
8. Volunteering for a group to assist that group's efforts to improve the community; or volunteering for a specific cause that you believe is important.
9. Volunteering may provide opportunities to observe, learn, and practice leadership skills.
10. Acquiring cooperation, teamwork, and leadership skills will help you get along and work well with others on the job, in social activities, and in family life.
11. Ecology involves the study of the impact of the misuse of natural resources and the disturbance of natural cycles.
12. They are nonrenewable because they cannot replace themselves through a natural cycle.
13. The proper disposal of waste helps keep the environment safe. The amount of waste threatens the capacity of the nation's landfills.
14. Such substances decompose naturally in the environment, thereby saving landfill space.
15. Protects valuable natural resources to ensure their quality and longevity.
16. To protect human health and to safeguard the natural environment.
17. Reduce: limit the amount of waste sent to landfills. Reuse; use products more than once. Recycle: save products with materials that can be recycled into other products.

Savvy Consumer

Paul should read what the Web site says about use. To be legal, the site should have a statement that says so. If no statement is present, it probably isn't legal to take that music, and Paul should not download anything from the site.

Thinking Critically

1. a) Give the frozen package to an employee. b) Walk into the hallway for your conversation so you don't bother people sitting in the waiting room. c) Pick them up and hang them on hangers or return them to a salesperson. Don't walk on them.
2. Safely report the incident to authorities. Confronting the person could put you in danger. Ignoring the incident entirely would itself be a violation of ethical principles.
3. They can take personal steps to decrease pollution in their own environment, encourage others to do the same through writing and projects, and write to legislators about concerns. Answers should take into account the economic impact of organized consumers.

Building Consumer Skills

4. 12 gallons per day or 4,380 gallons per year. By cutting back on usage, the total would be 1,095 gallons, for a savings of 3,285 gallons.

Chapter 4

Reviewing Key Terms and Ideas

1. Your career choices will largely determine your income potential over the years. Income and other benefits will determine the kinds and quality of goods and services you can afford.
2. The number of hours you put in, night and weekend work, travel, and being on call all influence when and how you relate to family members.
3. Flextime allows workers to work the hours that best fit their schedule.
4. Planning helps you control your future rather than just letting your career happen by chance.
5. Any two: interests, personality, aptitudes, abilities.
6. By assisting and educating consumers and helping individuals, families, or businesses manage their finances and other resources.
7. Pros (any two): possess great control; financial rewards can be great; very satisfying if successful. Cons (any two): large initial investment; risk of losing all the investment; income is uncertain; long hours usually required.
8. Your career goals determine what type of education or training is needed.
9. Internship: work experience is gained and the business is observed first-hand. Apprenticeship: combines classroom instruction with paid on-the-job experience under a skilled worker.
10. Answer should describe Coverdell Education Savings Accounts, prepaid tuition, and 529 plans (page 108).
11. References are people who will recommend you on the basis of your character or ability if contacted by an employer. Listing them on a résumé makes that information available to prospective employers.
12. Direct benefits: health insurance, vacations, training opportunities, retirement plan. Indirect benefits: location, commute, work environment, and company reputation.
13. Descriptions of any three: technical, interpersonal, management, and leadership.
14. A mentor employs leadership skills in being a guide or informal teacher of new employees.
15. A strong work ethic involves key employee attributes that lead to success: getting to work on time, working a full day, and meeting deadlines.
16. Give at least two weeks notice so that a replacement can be found.

Savvy Consumer

An interviewer should not ask about age, marital status, religion, national origin, race, or credit rating. If Reggie was asked such information, he did the right thing by giving general answers. He could relay his concerns to the EEOC office in his area for help.

Thinking Critically

1. Answers should include issues on pages 94–96.
2. A candidate's dress, manner, and actions during an interview are considered a prediction of what the person will be like on the job. First impressions count because an interviewer typically has little time and limited information when making a decision.
3. In a slow economy, someone might accept a less desirable job because of the difficulty of finding employment.

Building Consumer Skills

2. Answers should be realistic concerning the opportunities available.
3. Interview questions should not include private information unrelated to the job.
4. Presentations should show knowledge of the law as well as a well-managed team effort.
5. Skills and qualities for success may be combined in a ranked master list.

Consumer Connections

2. Help students understand the impact of strong customer service. Have students who work in service jobs share their experiences.

Chapter 5

Reviewing Key Terms and Ideas

1. To provide a way for society to use resources to satisfy people's needs and wants.
2. To solve the problem of scarcity, when there aren't enough resources to provide for unlimited wants.
3. Traditional: key economic decisions are based on a society's traditional customs and beliefs. Command: such decisions are made by a central government. Market: such decisions are made by individuals acting in self-interest. Mixed: combination of the command and market economies.
4. Descriptions of these goals: growth, efficiency, stability, justice, security.
5. When individuals are free to own and control businesses.
6. The desire to make money (make a profit) motivates the producers of goods and services.

7. Factors of production are basic types of resources needed to produce goods and services. They are land, labor, capital, entrepreneurship, and technology.
8. Descriptions of individual proprietorships, partnerships, and corporations.
9. A greater demand for a limited supply will tend to raise a product's price. An oversupply and limited demand for a product will tend to lower its price.
10. Competition leads to higher quality products, lower prices, and better service.
11. Goods and services provide widespread benefit and would be largely unavailable without government provision. Examples (any three): national defense; police and fire protection; courts and correctional institutions; public parks; street, highway, and bridge construction and maintenance; public education; public transportation.
12. To regulate unfair business practices that reduce competition.
13. Fiscal policy and monetary policy.
14. Any three: to fund public goods and services; to influence behavior; to stabilize the economy; to redistribute income.
15. Descriptions of any four: income tax, Social Security taxes, sales tax, excise taxes, property taxes, estate and gift taxes, business or license taxes, and customs duties and tariffs.
16. Benefit principle: those who benefit from a public service should pay for it. Ability-to-pay principle: more taxes should be paid by those who can afford to pay more.
17. Proportional: takes the same percentage from everyone's income. Progressive: takes a larger percentage of income from high-income people than from low-income people. Regressive: takes a larger percentage of income from low-income people than from high-income people.

Savvy Consumer

They might lower their prices slightly to increase sales, bake fewer items to create more demand, or find ways to cut costs.

Thinking Critically

1. Answers might include that traditional economic systems are less efficient than others because of lack of specialization.
2. Through ingenuity, people come up with new ideas, which can spur an economy. A market economy might expand through ingenuity since it relies on individuals to make decisions and act.
3. Answers should include the idea that as market demand increases, more workers will be needed.

Chapter 6

Reviewing Key Terms and Ideas

1. Contraction: business activity slows down. Expansion: the economy begins to recover through more spending, greater demand, and higher employment.
2. A recession is a period of significant decline in the economy. Workers are laid off and consumers cut back on spending.
3. The Great Depression occurred in the 1930s. The stock market crashed and many people were out of work.
4. High consumer confidence encourages consumer spending and business hiring. Low consumer confidence lowers spending and helps to cause a recession.
5. Economic indicators are measurements used to monitor the health of the economy. Three are gross domestic product, unemployment rate, and the consumer price index.
6. Gross domestic product measures the total dollar value of goods and services produced in a country in a year. The consumer price index measures the change in prices over time of a specific group of goods and services.
7. A budget helps a government keep planned spending from exceeding projected revenue.
8. Budget surplus is the amount by which revenue exceeds spending. Budget deficit is the amount by which spending exceeds revenue.
9. War and recession. In wartime, the government increases defense spending. During a recession, the government spends more on programs to assist the unemployed while receiving less in income taxes.
10. The government borrows money when there is a budget deficit. Continued deficits and borrowing increase the national debt.
11. Interest paid on the national debt might have been used for education, health care, public transportation, and public safety.
12. They have the same goal of stabilizing the economy. They differ in that fiscal policy uses taxing and spending policies, while monetary policy uses regulation of the money supply.
13. The Federal Reserve System is the central bank of the United States. It sets monetary policy, provides services to the banking industry and government, and regulates banks.

14. Lowering the discount rate encourages banks to borrow more money from the Federal Reserve Bank, thereby increasing the money supply. Lowering the reserve requirement also increases the money supply.
15. Fed policies regulate the money supply, thereby affecting the interest rates on loans and credit card balances.

Savvy Consumer

Economic trends and indicators can tell him whether the economic situation looks good for the summer season. If it does, that might mean people will have money to hire him rather than do their own lawn care.

Thinking Critically

4. The federal funds rate is a bank's cost of borrowing money. The laws of demand and supply dictate that when demand exceeds supply, prices tend to rise; when supply exceeds demand, prices tend to fall. (See page 137 in Section 5.2.) Thus, when the money supply decreases, the federal funds rate goes up; when the money supply increases, the rate goes down.

Building Consumer Skills

4. Students should correctly identify the member of Congress who represents them.

Chapter 7

Reviewing Key Terms and Ideas

1. Import: product brought in for sale from a foreign country. Export: product sent to a foreign country for sale there.
2. Any two: consumer choices; increased competition; expanded markets; international relations; prosperity and peace.
3. To allow businesses with different currencies to convert one currency to the other.
4. As a currency's value goes down, exports tend to increase. As the currency's value goes up, exports tend to decrease.
5. An accounting of all its financial transactions that involve other countries during a particular time period.
6. A trade deficit results when a country spends more on imports than it receives for exports.
7. Pros: sign of prosperity, since U.S. consumers have more money to spend on imports; rising level of imports goes along with rising domestic production and low unemployment. Cons: leads to foreign investment in and ownership of U.S. real estate and businesses; increases unemployment as jobs are lost to foreign producers.
8. A tariff is a tax on imports that raises their price and hence discourages their purchase. A quota limits the amount of a product that can be imported, thereby tending to make its price higher.
9. A government order prohibiting trade in a particular product or with a particular country.
10. Protectionism is a policy that uses trade restrictions to protect domestic businesses from foreign competition. Free trade is a policy of minimizing trade restrictions.
11. Explanation of any two: national security, job security, protecting infant industries, environmental protection, preventing unfair advantages.
12. Explanation of any two: positive effect on exports, positive effect on consumers, benefits of specialization, benefits of competition, use of alternative strategies.
13. GATT is the General Agreement on Tariffs and Trade by which member nations agree to rules that guarantee certain trade rights and also agree to lower trade barriers.
14. The United States, Canada, and Mexico.
15. Due to technology, the world is getting smaller and communication is much faster and easier. Media increase awareness of cultures around the world. Many companies do business in other countries and maintain offices and factories in them.

Savvy Consumer

She might suggest that they sell food other vendors don't sell and that they check other vendor prices to keep their own prices in line.

Chapter 8

Reviewing Key Terms and Ideas

1. Wages for employees who do piecework are based on the number of items produced. Employees who work on commission receive a percentage or portion of profit in exchange for making a sale. Piecework and commission are similar in that the more the employee produces or sells, the more he or she is paid.

2. Under the provisions of the Fair Labor Standards Act, employers are not allowed to pay one person less than another for the same work. The minimum wage is the lowest hourly rate an employer can legally pay most workers. Compensation for overtime beyond 40 hours a week must be at least 1.5 times the regular rate of pay.
3. Descriptions of any two: health insurance, other insurance, savings plans, retirement plans, paid holidays, paid vacation, sick leave, education and training, maternity leave, money toward adoption expenses or child care.
4. Full-time employees, unlike temporary employees, can usually take part in employer-sponsored benefits plans and usually earn higher wages and salaries.
5. Direct deposit involves having your pay electronically transferred directly into your bank account.
6. Identification: name, address, dates of work, employee number, Social Security number. Earnings: regular and overtime hours, pay rate, current gross pay, year-to-date gross pay. Deductions: current and year-to-date amounts for tax withholding, benefits, and other deductions. Totals and net pay: current and year-to-date amounts for total earnings, total deductions, and net pay.
7. Complete Form W-4 to make sure correct tax is withheld from paycheck. File a tax return every year and pay any additional tax owed.
8. To increase the amount of tax withheld.
9. It shows your total earnings and total amount of taxes withheld for the year.
10. A tax deduction is subtracted from your income and reduces the amount of income that is taxed. A tax credit is subtracted directly from the amount of tax you owe.
11. Itemized deductions are the amounts spent on tax-deductible expenses during the year.
12. Listing them would be to your advantage if they total more than the standard deduction.
13. It ensures that you don't pay too little or too much tax and helps you take advantage of incentives in the tax code to reduce your tax obligation.

Savvy Consumer

If he doesn't earn enough money, the friend won't have to pay income tax, but he is still required by law to file a tax return. His earnings will give him credit toward Social Security benefits. The employer may be avoiding legal requirements and paperwork by paying in cash.

Thinking Critically

1. Employer-provided benefits could reduce the amount of take-home pay if the employer pays only a portion of the benefit and the employee makes a contribution. Also, the employer's cost of providing certain benefits might indirectly reduce the amount that the company pays its workers (exchanging one form of compensation for another).
2. You don't have to go to the bank to cash a check. Your pay is more secure because money is automatically deposited and cannot get lost in the mail or be subject to fraud.
3. As your income increases, more money is withheld from your paycheck for Social Security and federal income tax. These contributions are in turn used to redistribute income to others in the form of government insurance programs, such as Social Security, Medicare, and unemployment benefits, as well as such entitlement programs as food stamps and housing assistance.

Chapter 9

Reviewing Key Terms and Ideas

1. Any three: Live within income. Identify financial priorities. Clarify financial goals. Pay expenses. Reduce buying on credit. Be prepared for expenses. Reduce anxiety about financial health. Meet financial goals. Develop financial independence. Stay in control of financial matters.
2. Identify financial goals. Assess current finances. Analyze spending habits. Plan for financial goals.
3. By finding the difference between your assets, or what you own, and your liabilities, or what you owe.
4. To achieve financial goals you need a plan, and a budget is a plan for spending and saving your money based on income and expenses.
5. Possible answer: Marriage requires partners to figure out a way of sharing expenses and may result in both people having to change the financial plans they had before marriage.
6. You can assign expense categories to transactions as you enter them into an electronic register and then generate reports to show how you spent your money.
7. A way to pay bills electronically over the Internet instead of mailing payments, which can save postage costs. Payments are received more quickly, and you can schedule payments to be made on a specific date.

8. It helps you avoid running out of money between paychecks, evaluate your spending habits and make better choices, set aside savings for unexpected expenses, and work toward financial goals.
9. Fixed expenses are regular payments that don't vary. Variable expenses increase or decrease. Discretionary expenses are items that are not absolutely necessary. If you have trouble balancing your budget, examine discretionary expenses first.
10. Any three: identification documents, legal documents, tax records, income and expense records, financial transactions, reference documents, medical records. Answers about how long to keep specific records should be based on Figure 9–11 on page 226. Best storage systems should be based on the information on page 227.
11. You would archive documents that can be kept in a less accessible area because they are not current.
12. They will tell you what licenses, certifications, or degrees the person received and whether the person is qualified to perform a certain service.
13. Students should choose three from among CFPs, ChFCs, accountants, insurance agents, attorneys, and stockbrokers. Descriptions of expertise should be based on the information on pages 230 and 231 and should indicate an understanding of the distinctions between them.

Savvy Consumer

She could ask: Why do I want this item? Are my reasons sound? How often do I, or would I, use this item? Could I function just as well without it? Could I cut back on the amount I spend in this budgeted area? How?

Thinking Critically

1. The process of budgeting involves many opportunity cost evaluations. Example: The opportunity cost of buying a new family vehicle may be that the family cannot budget for a vacation that year.
2. A budget actually helps you determine what you want the most and makes sure you can get those things by allowing for that spending. It helps you avoid spending money frivolously, which can prevent you from getting what you really want.

Building Consumer Skills

3. Since savings are to account for 10% of the budget, then all other expenses combined represent 90% of the budget. Therefore, students should multiply each percentage shown in the chart on page 222 by 90% to get approximate percentages. Savings: 10% ($4,500). Housing: 29% ($13,050). Transportation: 16% ($7,200). Food (at home): 7% ($3,150). Food (away from home): 5% ($2,250). Personal insurance and pensions: 10% ($4,500). Health care: 5% ($2,250). Entertainment: 5% ($2,250). Apparel and services: 4% ($1,800). Other: 9% ($4,050).

Chapter 10

Reviewing Key Terms and Ideas

1. By lending depositors' money to borrowers. The interest paid by borrowers is greater than the interest paid to depositors.
2. Any two: Commercial banks—owned by shareholders and operated for profit. Mutual savings banks—operated by trustees for the benefit of depositors; profits paid to depositors as interest or held in reserve. Savings and loans—may be owned by shareholders or depositors; provide variety of financial services. Credit unions—nonprofit institution owned by its members.
3. Whether the institution has deposit insurance, what services are offered, and how convenient are the offices.
4. The movement of funds from one account to another by electronic means. Can be initiated at a teller machine, by telephone, or over the Internet.
5. To protect the security of your accounts.
6. Advantages (one required): transaction is faster than paying by check; don't need to carry checkbook or ID. Disadvantage: money is immediately deducted from account.
7. Possible answers: direct deposit, automated transfer between accounts, automated loan payments, automated payments to third party. Guidelines for all types of transfer should include setting up the transfer date and making sure adequate funds are available in the account.
8. Protects consumers who use certain forms of electronic banking; says banks must provide a record or receipt for all computer transactions and must investigate errors within ten days of being notified of a problem.
9. Because it has been stamped and perforated by a bank to show that it's been paid.

10. An overdraft occurs when you have insufficient funds in your account to cover the amount of a check that you have written. With overdraft protection, the bank automatically transfers money from savings to checking to cover the check so that it won't bounce.
11. Checks are more secure than cash; canceled checks provide proof of payment.
12. Provides a record of what your signature looks like; helps prevent checks from being forged.
13. Outstanding transactions are reflected in your check register balance but not in the bank statement balance. You will not be able to get the two balances to agree unless you make note of the outstanding transactions.
14. Purchase the money order for the amount of the bill, and send the money order to the payee through the mail.
15. They function as cash but can be replaced if lost or stolen.
16. You pay for products and services in advance and receive the card in exchange. Each time you buy something with the card, the purchase amount is deducted from the card's balance.
17. Payments are quick and easy. They reduce the need to share credit card numbers and other personal information with each payee.

Savvy Consumer

He should think about how he would use each service and then determine whether it is needed.

Thinking Critically

1. During the 1920s and 1930s (the time of the Great Depression), money in banks wasn't insured and many banks failed, causing serious losses for people. The FDIC came about in response to that situation.
2. The individual would not know how much money is actually in the account and runs the risk of overdrawing, which could result in substantial fees and a poor credit reference.

Building Consumer Skills

2. Effective in 2004, Check 21 allows a substitute check to be produced from a digital image of the original check, resulting in faster check clearance and processing.
3. Current checkbook balance minus service charge ($127.47 – $3.30) equals $124.17. Bank closing balance minus total outstanding checks ($223.56 – $99.39) also equals $124.17.
4. Comparisons should include discussion of personal, certified, and cashier's checks as well as various types of money orders.
5. a) Report it to the financial institution within two days to be liable for no more than $50 when the card is used by someone else. b) Contact the bank to stop payment on the checks. c) Report the saved numbers of the missing checks to the company that issued them. They will stop payment on the ones issued to you and reissue new ones.

Chapter 11

Reviewing Key Terms and Ideas

1. A creditor extends credit, either in money, goods, or services, to a borrower. Each party trusts the other to carry out the agreement. The borrower repays the amount borrowed, plus interest, according to a schedule the parties agree on.
2. Property pledged to guarantee repayment of a loan. A creditor might require it in order to have assurance that a loan will be repaid.
3. Single-payment: borrower pays the entire amount due in a single payment. Installment: borrower pays a set portion of the entire amount at regularly scheduled intervals.
4. Interest and fees, increased cost of merchandise, and opportunity cost.
5. Credit history shows whether you have a record of paying past debts on time and in full.
6. A credit score is a numerical rating of a person's level of credit worthiness. It may be included in a credit rating, which is an evaluation of a person's credit history.
7. Establish (any two): Open checking and savings accounts. Put a utility in your name and pay bills on time. Apply for a store credit card. Apply for a secured credit card. Maintain: Pay bills on time. Avoid excess debt.
8. Private label: can be used only at a single retailer. General purpose: can be used at millions of businesses and can often be used to obtain cash from ATMs.
9. Any three: annual fee, APR, whether APR is fixed or variable, computation method, minimum payment, grace period, minimum finance charge, other fees, credit limit, special features and services.
10. The grace period gives consumers time to pay off the credit card balance without incurring finance charges.
11. By setting a limit for how much you want to charge each month and slowing down when you get close to the limit.

12. The act made it easier for consumers to understand the terms of credit and loan agreements.
13. Interest causes your bill to increase so that it may take many years to pay the account off.
14. A clause that allows additional purchases to be added to an installment contract, using earlier purchases as security for later ones.
15. Apply for loan. Wait for credit check and approval. Carefully read and then sign the contract, making sure all provisions are as agreed. Make payments on schedule.
16. A court imposes a judgment that makes a claim upon property to satisfy a debt.
17. Debt consolidation gives opportunity to solve debt problems by combining debts to make payments more manageable. Bankruptcy should be a last resort because of serious damage to credit rating.

Savvy Consumer

She should compare the transactions to receipts she has kept. If she determines that she didn't make those purchases, her credit card number may have been stolen. She should report the problem to the credit card company immediately and follow up with a letter detailing the situation.

Thinking Critically

1. Answers should balance convenience, cash-flow benefits, and possible bonus rewards of using credit against drawbacks of building a large credit balance and having to pay interest on the debt.
2. You might have very little time to get the account paid before a late fee is charged. Some time is used up while the bill is in the mail and your payment is returned. If needed, the grace period could be discussed with the credit card company. Setting up an automatic payment can also solve this problem.
3. As interest rates decrease, consumers can buy more for the same monthly payment over the same period of time or buy the same amount for less money. Conversely, as interest rates increase, purchasing power decreases.
4. Charts should compare the length of the loan, interest rate, and other loan provisions offered by financial institutions.

Building Consumer Skills

1. Letters should show awareness that errors in a credit report can have serious consequences.
3. Banks offer a variety of loans, including home loans, home equity loans, home improvement loans, vehicle loans, personal lines of credit, and education or student loans. Consumer finance companies specialize in making small or personal loans and usually charge more for their loans than banks do. Pawnbrokers give customers money in exchange for an item, hold the item, and then allow the customer to buy the item back at a higher price.
4. 36-month loan: monthly payment is $517.05; total cost is $20,114. 48-month loan: monthly payment is $402.81; total cost is $20,835. 60-month loan: monthly payment is $334.56; total cost is $21,574. Students should balance cost of borrowing money against amount of monthly payments.
5. Diary entries should include dangers, as listed on page 286; warning signs, as described on 288–289; and suggestions for recovering from debt, as described on 289–290.

Chapter 12

Reviewing Key Terms and Ideas

1. Saving involves setting aside money for an anticipated future use. Investing involves committing money for the purpose of making a profit over time.
2. When you use credit, you must pay interest on the money you borrow. Savings earn interest while they grow. Saving for an item gives you time to decide whether it's really important to you.
3. Possible answers: college fees, down payment on home, travel.
4. When you are young, because it takes a long time to build up the money needed.
5. Savings should be part of a budget. The amount you plan to save must fit within your budget; otherwise it will be difficult to follow your plan.
6. Discretionary income is the amount of available income after taxes and necessary spending for food, clothing, and shelter. The percentage of income that can go toward savings depends on the amount of discretionary income.
7. "Paying yourself first" means setting aside part of your income for savings and then spending what's left. This strategy is recommended because it is more effective than spending first and saving what's left.
8. Compound interest is calculated on the entire account balance, including prior interest earned. Simple interest is calculated only on the amount deposited.

9. Tells you the actual annual rate at which interest is earned, including the effects of compounding.
10. When the money is being saved for a long period of time, the difference could be significant due to the long-term effects of compound interest.
11. Find out whether the account is insured by the FDIC or NCUA.
12. The ease with which savings or investments can be turned into cash. Important when choosing a savings option if you want the ability to withdraw money whenever you need it.
13. A money market account is more liquid because it allows you to write checks or make withdrawals. If you withdraw money from a certificate of deposit before the end of its term you must pay a penalty.
14. They are backed by the federal government.

Savvy Consumer

Set and follow a budget. Keep his savings goal in mind. Use automatic savings. Resist temptation. Put the savings into a form that he can't get to as easily, such as CDs that earn money and mature when he wants to purchase the car.

Thinking Critically

1. Lack of an emergency fund might cause a person to take the first job offered, instead of holding out for a better paying, more secure, or otherwise more desirable position.
2. During a period of high inflation, you would expect the interest on your savings account to go up. The Fed would likely raise interest rates to encourage consumers and businesses to cut back on spending and increase savings, thus slowing economic growth and helping to bring inflation under control.
3. When you buy a savings bond, you loan money to the government, which increases the government's debt.

Building Consumer Skills

1. $1,800 at three months: $5,400. $1,800 at six months: $10,800. $2,200 at three months: $6,600. $2,200 at six months: $13,200.
3. The quotation makes the point that to double your money, you need to save it rather than spend it.
4. 4% per annum = 1% each quarter. Simple interest on $5,000 will thus be $50 per quarter, or $200 for the year. Compound interest will be $50 for the first quarter, then $50.50, then $51.01, and finally $51.52, for a total of $203.03 for the year.
5. If the interest rate stayed at 4.8%, it would take about 15 years to reach face value. Interest rates can be adjusted every 6 months, so it might take a shorter or longer time for the bond to reach face value, but it's guaranteed to take no longer than 17 years.

Chapter 13

Reviewing Key Terms and Ideas

1. Generally, the greater the promised return on an investment, the higher the degree of risk you assume.
2. Inflation reduces the effective return on an investment by reducing the purchasing power of investment earnings. In some cases it can take away purchasing power faster than the investment earns money.
3. Descriptions of income, growth, and tax reduction (page 321).
4. By making a variety of investments, you reduce your exposure to risk.
5. Any four: by using reliable media sources; by taking courses in financial planning; by joining an investment club; by working with a professional advisor.
6. A 401(k) plan is offered by employers and involves employer and employee contributions. An IRA is a personal investment plan.
7. Most employers no longer offer traditional pension plans, so you need to take responsibility for planning your retirement and ensuring that you enjoy financial stability after you retire.
8. Set your goals. Make estimates and calculations. Adjust your plan if needed.
9. People bid on a stock, offering the price they want to pay. If someone who owns the stock is willing to sell it at the offered price, the transaction is made.
10. To provide a central location where stocks can be sold on a trading floor.
11. You earn dividends, or payments to shareholders, by investing in stocks that pay dividends.
12. Consider stocks as long-term investments. Diversify your investments. Research stocks or hire someone to do it. Avoid focusing on day-to-day ups and downs in stock prices.

13. Corporate bonds are issued by corporations; can be purchased through brokers or banks, usually in minimum amounts of $1,000; and have a higher rate of return than municipal bonds, but carry more risk. Municipal bonds are issued by local or state governments; can be purchased through brokers or dealers; and have lower returns, but interest earnings are free from federal tax and, in some cases, from state and local taxes.
14. Because mutual funds are a simple way to achieve diversification, which reduces risk, and are professionally managed.
15. A contract that is purchased from an insurance company and guarantees regular payments in the future.
16. It is easy to lose money because the risk is high.
17. To identify an executor; to identify a guardian for children, if needed; to give instructions for liabilities; to give instructions for assets.
18. State law determines how the estate is to be settled, which can be time consuming and expensive, and the outcome may not reflect the deceased person's wishes.
19. To grant someone the right to act on your behalf if you become incapable of making decisions.

Savvy Consumer

The stock could be showing a temporary spike. They have no history to go by so should be cautious, do research on the company, and perhaps wait to see how it performs over time.

Thinking Critically

2. They may feel they can't spare the income or that they will join later. The longer they wait, the less money they will be building for future security.
3. Online trading is quicker and cheaper, but people might make decisions without having all the necessary information. Using a broker takes more time and involves paying a fee, but the broker may be able to offer advice and prevent a client from making an unwise investment.
4. When people buy Treasury securities, they are loaning money to the government. This adds to what the government owes, thus increasing the national debt.

Building Consumer Skills

1. Income—bonds, bond funds, equity income funds, blue chip stocks. Growth—growth stocks, growth funds, aggressive growth funds. Tax reduction—Treasury securities, municipal bonds, IRA, 401(k).

Chapter 14

Reviewing Key Terms and Ideas

1. It spreads financial risk among a large group of people.
2. An endorsement is an attachment to a standard insurance contract that adds or takes away coverage. An exclusion is a specific risk not covered by a policy.
3. Advantage: reduces the need to engage in expensive court cases. Disadvantage (any one): not all medical conditions resulting from accidents are covered; has strict monetary limit on claims; since negligent drivers cannot be sued for causing an accident, they may have no incentive to change their driving habits; actual rates have tended to be higher under no-fault laws.
4. Any three: Collision coverage—pays for repair or replacement of own vehicle after accident. Comprehensive physical damage coverage—protects own vehicle against risks unrelated to traffic accidents. Liability coverage—protects against injury or damage caused to other people or their property. Medical payments coverage or PIP—covers medical expenses if you are injured in auto accident. Uninsured/underinsured motorists coverage—covers injury or damage caused by driver without adequate insurance.
5. Depreciation is loss in value over time caused by age, normal wear and tear, and the fact that used items are less valuable than new ones. Depreciation affects the amount of insurance needed and the amount the insurance company will pay in the event of a claim.
6. $50,000 limit for the injuries of any one person. $100,000 limit for all injured parties (two or more). $25,000 limit for property damage.
7. Replacement coverage pays the cost of replacing items with comparable new ones.
8. An appraisal, or estimate of value made by a qualified person, would determine how much insurance you'd need to buy, which in turn affects rates.
9. Personal liability, medical payments, and physical damage.
10. Descriptions of deductible, local firefighting capability, construction materials, and preventive measures (page 374).
11. Descriptions of any three: medical benefits, major medical coverage, dental benefits, vision benefits, disability insurance, long-term care insurance (page 377).
12. Group policies, COBRA, individual policies, government programs.

13. Fee-for-service: patient is charged a fee for each medical service received, and insurance plan pays a portion of that fee. Managed care: patient chooses from network of selected health care providers who agree to provide care for specified fees.
14. Descriptions of any two, noting the differences: Medicare, Medicaid, Social Security disability benefits (pages 382–383).
15. Refers to a policy's investment aspect. Each premium includes, besides the cost of coverage, an additional amount that is invested. The invested amount grows over time and is called the policy's cash value.
16. Premiums are lower and the additional money can be placed in investments that the consumer can control.

Savvy Consumer

She needs to know what is covered under each plan and where she must go for services. She should consider her own health and circumstances and the costs involved for each plan.

Thinking Critically

2. Answers may suggest that young people have less driving experience and sometimes the attitude that nothing will happen to them. More education about safe driving might help. The age for getting a license could be raised.
3. Answers may focus on the role of the primary care physician in determining which patients need to be seen by a specialist, the control of fees and costs, and the emphasis on wellness and preventive care.
4. Competition among managed care companies might result in lower costs and/or in more services or choices being offered.

Building Consumer Skills

6. Checklists might include age, marital status, health history, number of dependents, occupation, and hobbies.

Chapter 15

Reviewing Key Terms and Ideas

1. Any five: print ads in such publications as newspapers and magazines; direct mail; radio and television commercials; infomercials; ads on Web pages; billboards and signs. (Other examples may be acceptable.) Advertisers choose the form or forms that effectively reach the right audience.
2. Infomercials resemble regular radio or television programming, but they are entirely under the control of the advertiser for commercial purposes.
3. Any two: advertising lets consumers compare prices and find out about sales, provides information for better choices, introduces new types of products, and lists store hours to prevent wasted trips.
4. Some ads may be annoying. Some ads may prod people to buy items they don't need or want through persuasive techniques and sometimes deception.
5. The FTC monitors ads, especially those with health or safety claims and those directed at children. It has the power to order companies to withdraw ads with false or inaccurate claims.
6. Puffery refers to exaggerated claims used by advertisers to increase a product's appeal or reputation.
7. The fact that the endorser has a connection to the seller; the fact that the "ordinary consumer" in the ad is actually an actor portraying a consumer.
8. Consumers might be inclined to favor a product or service because a celebrity, expert, or consumer endorses it by making a positive statement about the product or by allowing his or her name, likeness, or signature to be used in the ad.
9. Bandwagon: join the crowd in buying the product. Trendsetter: be one of the few who try something new. They both appeal to the customer's ego and sense of importance in order to persuade the consumer to buy.
10. Any two: an infomercial that looks like a talk show; a magazine ad that appears to be an article; a newspaper ad that resembles an editorial; advertising that seems to be part of a Web page.
11. A marked-down item may be flawed or damaged and cannot be returned for a refund. It might not be covered by the product's regular warranty.
12. An item priced below the retailer's cost in order to attract customers to the store.
13. The consumer mails in a form and proof of purchase of the product. In return the consumer receives a check for the rebate amount.
14. Ask these questions: Is the sweepstakes entrant required to make a purchase or pay a fee? Must you spend money to claim a prize? Are the terms and rules clearly disclosed?
15. A higher-priced item is pushed for sale rather than the lower-priced one you are already considering.
16. Consumers have three business days to cancel purchases of $25 or more made in their homes or outside of the seller's normal place of business.

Savvy Consumer

There are better ways to determine what the best product is for your money, such as Consumer Reports or recommendations from people you know well. Celebrities are simply earning money and don't necessarily know or care what the best products are. These shoes may be fine, but you might be able to get a pair that's just as good for less money.

Thinking Critically

1. a) An ads objective may be brand recognition, and that may often work, but smart consumers look for useful information about products. b) Opinions will vary.
2. Without evidence, this is opinion. In practice, the FTC would be unlikely to require proof of such a claim, unless the ad included wording such as "Studies show" or "Guaranteed to cut your time and effort in half."
3. A clearance sale is an example of the principle that when supply is greater than demand, prices tend to fall. The clearance sale will probably draw consumers who are willing to buy at the lower price, showing that when a price is lowered, demand goes up. Eventually demand will equal supply. At that point the product will have reached its equilibrium price.

Building Consumer Skills

1. Examples will vary. The FTC's advertising policy statements and guidelines can be found at http://www.ftc.gov/bcp/guides/guides.htm.

Chapter 16

Reviewing Key Terms and Ideas

1. You would have to save more than the cost of your membership.
2. Factory seconds are products that have slight defects that do not affect performance or appearance. They are likely to be found at outlet stores.
3. Any four: guard against impulse buying; assess the reliability of the company; study product descriptions carefully; compare prices; determine return and refund policy and delivery terms; pay by credit card if possible; record your transaction; check the shipment on arrival; contact the company if shipment is late.
4. Guarantee of the soundness of a product or service.
5. An implied warranty is created by state law but is not in written form. It includes merchantability (product does what it is intended to do) and fitness for a particular purpose.
6. Clear description of what is covered; what will be done in case the product is defective; who is eligible; effective date and term; steps owner must take to get product repaired or replaced; what the owner should do if he or she has a complaint about the warranty.
7. A service contract is a service agreement that provides protection beyond warranty coverage. Unlike a warranty, a service contract is optional and costs extra.
8. Identify needs and wants; consider your budget; plan when to shop.
9. You may be able to find the same product or a better product at a lower price than you would otherwise pay.
10. Visit local stores to compare brands and prices. Check ads and catalogs. Search Internet retail sites. Make comparisons on quality, style, and price.
11. National brand products are nationally advertised; generic products are not. Consequently, national brands generally cost more because the cost of national advertising is passed on to the consumer.
12. Basic information about the provider, description of work to be done, estimated start and completion date, total cost and payment method, warranties or guarantees, verbal promises.
13. Any two: The price of services will be harder to determine, making comparison shopping difficult. Quality may be harder to determine because of the variable factors involved. Transaction involves estimates and contracts.
14. Contact the service provider and explain the problem. If not resolved, contact local or state consumer protection office for advice.

Savvy Consumer

The difficulty of the project and the family's skills are both factors. Also, are they willing to shop around for supplies in order to get the best prices? They might also do some cost comparing, and they should consider the budget they have in mind for the project.

Thinking Critically

3. An extended warranty might not be worthwhile on a small item, especially one that has a limited life. The overall cost of the warranty should be considered.
4. Answers should include various types of retailers and shopping methods such as local stores, Internet, and catalogs.

5. It might cause people to spend less money and therefore be a hardship for some businesses. Where bartering is common, the effect would be less.

Building Consumer Skills

5. The ones from the local store. Total cost of the purchase at the discount store is $62 ($48 + $8 + $6), more than the price at the local store. Moreover, you would have lost time by traveling to the discount store.

Chapter 17

Reviewing Key Terms and Ideas

1. Some crave every new gadget as it is developed; others are overwhelmed and give up on learning the new developments.
2. When it's so out of date that it's no longer useful.
3. Any four: How will it improve my life? How often will I use it? Do I want it just because my friends do? What are some potential drawbacks of owning this product? Are the benefits worth the costs? What are the alternatives to buying this product?
4. Select models that do not include unneeded features. Select user-friendly designs. Read product reviews. Visit Web sites to view comments from other customers.
5. Any three: included minutes, roaming and home coverage, long distance charges, special features, one-time fees.
6. Analog service has been around longer and costs less. Digital service has grown in popularity, is secure, has better voice quality, and supports Internet features.
7. Roaming charges apply when the user of a wireless phone is outside a specific area. Long distance charges apply when the wireless phone is being used to talk to a person who is outside the local calling area.
8. You may be able to choose from providers other than the local telephone company for local toll service.
9. Slamming is switching a consumer's phone service to a different company without permission. Consumers can ask their phone company to send a form stating their service cannot be changed without written permission.
10. A modem enables a personal computer to send and receive data over telephone or other communication lines.
11. Broadband access is available by cable, digital subscriber line, or wireless system; is active whenever the computer is on; and allows more data to be transmitted at a time. Dial-up access is achieved through a regular telephone connection, requires waiting for a connection to be made, and has slower connection speeds.
12. Cost, extra services, dial-up access numbers, reliability, technical support.
13. Call the Internet service provider to report the problem. Check your plan regarding possible refunds.
14. An electronic circuitry that tells the computer how to process information (the brains of the computer).
15. RAM determines the computer's ability to run complex programs and to have several programs open at the same time. It also affects how quickly programs run.
16. Any three: use free computers, rent computer time, buy used equipment, lease equipment, upgrade current equipment.

Savvy Consumer

She must weigh the desire for connection to her friends against the cost. Perhaps one close friend would help her find a way to stay in the loop without the expense.

Thinking Critically

1. Negative: High-tech toys might restrict imagination and be used instead of physical play. Positive: Such toys might teach dexterity and promote some types of learning.
3. When restrictions and regulations are removed. The breakup of the AT&T monopoly occurred in 1984, and the Telecommunications Act went into effect in 1996.
4. Software has continued to become increasingly sophisticated and feature-laden, requiring computers with more memory, faster processor speed, and greater storage capacity.

Chapter 18

Reviewing Key Terms and Ideas

1. Accessories are items that complete an outfit, such as jewelry and belts. They are a basic part of the wardrobe, along with clothing and shoes.
2. Sort garments. Identify problems. Find solutions. Clear out unwanted garments. Identify items to add.
3. Because classics are fashions that don't go out of style, they will last from year to year.
4. Try on the garment and walk, sit, stretch, and bend to determine how well it fits.

5. Natural fibers come from plants or animals. Manufactured fibers are made from such substances as wood pulp and petroleum.
6. After fibers are twisted into yarns, two sets of yarns can be interlaced to make a woven fabric, or yarns can be looped together in interlocked rows to make a knitted fabric.
7. Finishes are treatments applied to fabrics to produce a particular look or feel. Some add color, design, and texture. Some help the fabric resist wrinkles, flames, or stains.
8. Identification of the manufacturer or store or brand name, percentage of fiber content, country of origin, care instructions.
9. Check care labels. Sort items. Treat stains. Load and set the machine. Add cleaning agents.
10. Dry cleaning uses special liquids instead of water.
11. Making repairs right away saves making larger repairs later. It also keeps the garment wearable.
12. Proper storage keeps garments in good shape and ready to wear.
13. Grooming products that claim to affect the structure or function of the body are regulated as drugs by the FDA. Such products must be proven safe and effective before they can be sold. Other products are treated as cosmetics. Cosmetics can use ingredients without approval and do not have to prove their performance claims.
14. It suggests that the product is less likely to cause an allergic reaction.
15. Any three from the list on page 477.

Savvy Consumer

He might investigate what colors and styles look best on him. He could choose one or two accessories, such as a unique hat that appeals to him, to give himself a look that's different but uniquely him.

Thinking Critically

1. The prices for fad items are likely to fluctuation more than for classics.
3. Answers might include such situations as a job interview and special occasions.

Building Consumer Skills

3. Selection guidelines should address such factors as safety, comfort, and ease of getting dressed.
4. Clothing should be sorted by water temperature, wash cycle, color, amount of soil, and lint potential.

Chapter 19

Reviewing Key Terms and Ideas

1. Advantages (any two): economy, convenience, energy savings, less pollution, less congestion. Disadvantages (any two): need to fit the system's schedule; facilities may be dirty and crowded; perception that crime is more common at transit centers.
2. Advantages (any two): requirement of the job, comfort, independence, no wait for trains or buses. Disadvantages (any two): expenses (including insurance and parking), more stressful, traffic jams and road repairs, need to stay alert.
3. Using mass transit reduces the number of vehicles driven. When fewer vehicles are driven, exhaust emissions are reduced.
4. Distance to places most often visited, cost of transportation, location of mass transit stations, parking options, safety concerns, available alternatives.
5. Buying is for new or used vehicles; leasing is only for new vehicles. When the loan is repaid on a purchased vehicle, it belongs to the buyer and can be kept or sold; a leased vehicle must be turned in at the end of the lease period. Monthly lease payments will likely be lower than monthly loan payments, but in the long run leasing may be more expensive.
6. Any two: whether you want a new or used car, overall cost, expected wear and tear, expected miles driven, how long you plan to keep the vehicle.
7. The title is a legal document showing ownership, and the lender owns the vehicle until the loan is fully paid.
8. Someone leasing a car may pay a capitalized cost reduction payment to lower the monthly lease fee.
9. Evaluation of features, such as handling and braking, acceleration, fuel economy, convenience and comfort; information about how older vehicles have performed (including specific problems and frequency-of-repair reports).
10. Invoice price: price the dealer pays the manufacturer. Sticker price: the dealer's initial asking price.
11. Any five of the items described under "Evaluating a Vehicle" on pages 494–497.
12. Lemon laws protect buyers of vehicles with serious defects.
13. Because the manufacturer has discovered a problem with your vehicle model and is instructing owners to bring their vehicles in for repair.

14. Any three: know and obey traffic rules; stay focused/avoid distractions; stay sharp; buckle up; drive smoothly.

Savvy Consumer

She would be wise to have it checked by a mechanic whom she trusts. She should test-drive it herself and could also have a friend or family member look at the car with her. It would be good to ask for information about the car, such as how many owners it has had and who were the drivers. She should look the car over carefully, checking for signs of prior accidents that could affect the car's condition and paying attention to the car's mileage so far.

Thinking Critically

1. People would save money and have it to spend elsewhere. The demand for gas would lessen, and wear on the roads would decrease. Safety on the roads would likely increase since fewer vehicles would be in use. With fewer vehicles on the road, the pollution caused by them would lessen.
2. The indication is that a significant number of consumers have purchased vehicles with serious defects and that these consumers had little or no recourse before the laws were passed.
3. People might be looking for more fuel-efficient cars, which could increase those sales but reduce the sale of others. Prices on fuel-efficient cars would likely go up. Car dealers with fewer of these cars to sell might not do as well. Since the health of the auto industry affects the economy, any time that industry suffers, the economy suffers as well.
4. If you are knowledgeable about what you want, you are more likely to realize when someone is being deceptive. A person who makes you uncomfortable, is condescending, pressures you, or doesn't listen to what you say should be avoided.

Building Consumer Skills

1. Cost should be similar, but decisions will vary.
3. To evaluate effectiveness, students might talk with people who have used the Internet when buying a car.

Chapter 20

Reviewing Key Terms and Ideas

1. Recreation is any activity you find pleasurable and rejuvenating. It offers benefits for mental health, physical health, and social health.
2. Any three: interests (including hobbies), abilities, profession, budget, schedule, goals. Examples will vary.
3. Examples may include sewing, hiking, gardening, reading, cooking, or other hobbies.
4. Balance passive recreation that includes active, mental activities with physical, solitary time that includes social activities.
5. Since such resources as time and money are limited, choosing certain recreational activities requires giving up others. The value of an alternative that is given up is the opportunity cost.
6. Season tickets enable you to attend a series of events for a lower cost per ticket.
7. Any two: Public facilities are run by a governmental unit, and private facilities are run by private groups or businesses. Public facilities are supported by taxpayer dollars, and private facilities are not. Public facilities are open to all in the community, and private facilities may have restricted membership. Public facilities are usually free or low-cost, and private facilities may have substantial fees.
8. Visit at the time you would use the club, and check the quantity and condition of equipment. Check the hours of operation. Get information about the trainers. Check on fees. Call the BBB and ask friends about the club.
9. Borrowing equipment, renting equipment, buying used equipment.
10. Special attractions; special events; accommodations and their cost; least crowded and least expensive times of year; typical weather; availability of public transportation. If going to another country, local laws, customs, and currency.
11. Estimate costs. Set savings goals. Then deposit money from each paycheck into an interest-earning savings account. Create a budget and stick to it.
12. A privately owned home that offers lodging with the morning meal included in the price.
13. Because hostels are an inexpensive form of lodging.
14. An itinerary maps out the route or schedule of a trip. Reservations guarantee you will have travel accommodations and lodgings on the dates desired.
15. In your carry-on luggage so that you'll have them even if checked luggage is lost or destroyed.

Savvy Consumer

Plans should allow for each family member's wishes to be included in the schedule.

Building Consumer Skills

1. Have students use this activity to generate ideas for hobbies.
2. Help students see that leisure time should include relaxation. Not every moment in life must be filled with activity. In balance with other endeavors, a little time taken to think and daydream can be useful.

Chapter 21

Reviewing Key Terms and Ideas

1. Any four: advertising, family, friends, cultural heritage, available time, available money, knowledge of healthful choices, personal eating habits.
2. The process of using food to nourish your body.
3. Carbohydrates: main source of energy; milk, fruits, grains. Proteins: maintenance of cells and tissues; meat, poultry. Fats: healthy skin and normal growth; meat, margarine. Vitamins: help fight disease; fruits, vegetables. Minerals: a necessary part of bones and teeth; milk products, whole grain breads. Water: helps keep body temperature in normal range; plain water, fruit juice.
4. Grain Group; Vegetable Group; Fruit Group; Milk Group; and Meat and Beans Group.
5. Nutrient density compares nutrients in a food to its amount of calories. Choosing foods with high nutrient density will supply the body with a significant amount of several nutrients, such as vitamins and minerals, in relation to the amount of calories.
6. At least 60 minutes of physical activity every day.
7. Convenience foods are foods processed in ways that make them easier to use.
8. If the supply of a food product is reduced while demand remains high, its price will rise. A plentiful supply can produce lower prices.
9. Number of family members, family income, individual priorities, food shopping knowledge, raising food in a garden.
10. Supermarkets offer the convenience of a wide range of goods in one location. A specialty food store may provide choices that are not available at a supermarket.
11. Net weight is the weight of the product and its liquid, but not the weight of the container. Daily Values are nutrient reference amounts set by the FDA: the label shows what percentage of the Daily Values for specific nutrients one serving of the food provides.
12. The pull date is the last day the manufacturer recommends that the item be sold. The expiration date is the last day that a product should be eaten.
13. Store brands are priced lower than national brands and may be identical in quality.
14. Any two: Limit portion sizes. Ask for broiled or grilled foods. Control high-fat toppings. Choose carefully at the salad bar. Choose milk, water, or juice instead of a soft drink. Share a dessert instead of eating it all yourself. Have low-fat frozen yogurt or fresh fruit for dessert.
15. Order only the amount and items that you want. Look for lower-cost items. Take note of beverage prices. Consider tax and tip when ordering.
16. The gratuity is a tip offered to a server for the service performed. Customers in most restaurants are expected to include it with their payment.

Savvy Consumer

She may be missing out on nutrients she needs by narrowing her food intake so drastically. She might not be getting enough fiber, which is vital for proper human digestion. Foods are thought to contain many additional substances that may also play a role in health.

Thinking Critically

1. Remind students of the discussion of leadership in Chapter 3.
2. Specialization and international trade are discussed in Chapter 7.

Building Consumer Skills

4. You may wish to have the class study the displays and draw conclusions in writing.

Chapter 22

Reviewing Key Terms and Ideas

1. Wellness involves making a conscious effort to achieve an overall state of well-being. It should be a priority because it can help you look and feel better, have more energy and a better outlook, and experience fewer health problems.
2. Any three: Take care of yourself physically (eat well, stay active, get plenty of sleep). Be realistic about how much you can do (allow time to relax, make a to-do list, set priorities). Develop a support system of family and friends (talk with people you trust). Keep things in perspective.
3. Any two: Buckle up at all times. Never ride with a driver who has been drinking or using drugs. Wear a helmet when on a bicycle or motorcycle.

4. Read the information on the package to determine what the product is for, how it should be used, and who should not use it. If unsure which over-the-counter medication to use, talk to the pharmacist.
5. They are less expensive.
6. Dietary supplements are products taken by mouth to increase one's intake of nutrients or other dietary substances. Reasons to be cautious: They are not tightly regulated. Too much of some nutrients can cause unpleasant side effects or serious health problems. They may be a waste of money, can cause allergic reactions, and can interfere with prescription drugs.
7. Find out from reliable sources whether you really need to lose weight. Check with a physician about use of weight loss drugs or supplements. Avoid plans that promote losing more than 2 pounds per week or eating fewer than 1,500 calories per day, unless physician approved. Make sure the plan follows healthful eating guidelines. Avoid plans with exaggerated claims. Check qualifications of people involved.
8. A primary care physician provides general medical care and coordinates overall health care. A specialist is a professional with training and experience in a specific type of care.
9. At a student health center.
10. Determine what your health care plan covers regarding choice of providers. Ask friends and neighbors for recommendations. Call the office manager to make a date to visit and ask pertinent questions.
11. Before your visit, prepare a list of questions you want to ask. Take notes during your visit or ask a family member or friend to take notes for you. Ask for clarification if you do not understand the information. Before leaving, review your questions to make sure all were asked and answered, and repeat advice you were given to be sure it was understood.
12. Any three: In-home care—caregiver comes to or lives in the child's home. Family child care—child goes to the provider's home. Child care center—setting similar to a small school. Corporate child care—provided by a corporation to its employees. Preschool—for children three to five years old; typically two or three days a week for two to four hours. Parent co-op—child care center or preschool at which parents are volunteer aides. School-age child care—provides care before and after school.
13. Credentials of the establishment, accreditation of individual workers, general environment, kinds of activities, ratio of staff to children, number of children, staff training and experience, cleanliness and safety.
14. A flexible spending account allows a set amount of money from each paycheck to be set aside for dependent care or other qualified expenses. The money is not subject to income tax.
15. Help with medications or other health-related services.
16. Assisted living facilities provide help with day-to-day activities. In retirement communities, residents live independently.

Savvy Consumer

He might say that all doctors who have a person's health in mind are likely to bring up these issues. If people are too defensive, they might ignore worthwhile advice.

Thinking Critically

2. Possible answer: Some consumers assume that herbal supplements are safe because they are "natural." This assumption is not justified since herbal supplements can cause allergic reactions and other side effects and can interfere with the effectiveness of prescription medications.
3. People who can get medical help for their health problems are more likely to be productive citizens. They contribute to the economy through work and earning money to take care of themselves and their families. When large numbers of people are unhealthy and unproductive, a society suffers with less productivity and struggles to deal with people's needs.
4. A co-op would be less expensive but would require volunteer hours.

Chapter 23

Reviewing Key Terms and Ideas

1. Any five: number of people in the family; stage in the family life cycle; how people prefer to spend time; location of workplace; desire for services; preferences for location, style of home, and so on; income and savings; other resources.

2. Similar: All three involve units that are typically attached to each other at the sides or one above the other. Different: Townhouses are part of a multiple-family complex, while duplexes and row houses are not; a duplex consists of two attached units, while a set of row houses or townhouses is typically more than two units. (Students may note other differences.)
3. Traditional ownership includes both building and land, and owners are responsible for upkeep and maintenance of both. Condominium ownership involves shared ownership of common areas, such as hallways and exterior grounds. Maintenance of those areas is the responsibility of the condominium association.
4. Advantages of owning: investment opportunity, tax deductions. Disadvantages of owning: cost of maintenance, unplanned expenses. Advantage of renting: predictable costs. Disadvantages of renting: monthly rent does not lead to ownership, no tax benefits, possibility of rent increases.
5. To determine whether the unit is in suitable condition and to ask that unsatisfactory conditions be repaired.
6. A legal contract that specifies the rights and responsibilities of tenant and landlord. For five examples of information included, see points on page 588.
7. Landlord rights (any two): receive regular rent; enter the property to make repairs and inspections; evict the tenant if lease is broken. Landlord responsibilities (any two): make sure property meets government standards; ensure that basic systems work properly; keep common areas clean, safe, and free of pests; provide garbage cans; provide enough hot water; make sure heat is available during cold weather. Tenant rights: live in the unit; privacy. Tenant responsibilities: keep unit clean and safe; avoid disturbing other tenants with excess noise.
8. Conventional mortgage: interest rate remains the same for the life of the loan. Adjustable rate mortgage: interest rate changes to reflect changes in the economy.
9. Establish price range, what characteristics to look for, and areas to consider. Search for possibilities through classified ads, open houses, the Internet, and/or real estate agent. View possible homes, evaluate them, and narrow down the choices.
10. To prove to the seller that they are serious about purchasing the home.
11. Yes, as the two parties continue to exchange offers in working toward agreement.
12. Total cost can be higher than the cost of buying. Quality of the items may be lower.
13. Determine what furnishings you already have. Consider budget, savings, and savings plan. Set priorities for items to purchase. Consider how each room will be used and the look you want to achieve. Gather information and ideas. Develop a floor plan and use it to try out furniture placement.
14. Examples may include tables, dressers, desks, or other furniture without padding, fabric, springs, or covering.
15. Regular cleaning and preventive care. Benefits: a clean and pleasant environment, a healthy and safe environment, reduced wear and tear, and a more valuable home.
16. Any three: Buy energy efficient appliances. Install weather stripping. Wrap water heater in an insulating jacket. Insulate the attic. Install programmable thermostats. Use a humidifier in winter. (Other examples are possible.)

Savvy Consumer

She might like to see the identical apartment since the other one isn't in show condition. However, it would be best to also see the one she will rent in order to evaluate its location and condition in other ways besides paint. She could request to see both. She could say she wants to see the apartment when the painting is done and before she signs a lease.

Thinking Critically

1. Location is an important part of buying a home, and that includes the condition of nearby property. If areas near a house are not well kept, the house may be harder to sell, necessitating a lower selling price.
3. a) Might choose a location that has qualities of both; could agree to spend vacations in country setting. b) Could talk to a financial professional to get guidance on what is affordable. c) Could choose an appropriate time to bring up the subject, not in an angry moment, and negotiate for shared responsibilities.

Building Consumer Skills

1. Checklists will likely include such factors as safety, transportation, and proximity to shopping, work, and schools.
4. Diagrams should include at least the following steps: submitting an offer to purchase, reaching an agreement, completing loan application, and attending the closing.

Consumer Education & Economics

Sixth Edition

Ross E. Lowe

Charles A. Malouf

Annette R. Jacobson

New York, New York   Columbus, Ohio   Chicago, Illinois   Woodland Hills, California

BRAND DISCLAIMER

Publisher does not necessarily recommend or endorse any particular company or brand name product that may be discussed or pictured in this text. Brand name products are used because they are readily available, likely to be known to the reader, and their use may aid in the understanding of the text. Publisher recognizes that other brand name or generic products may be substituted and work as well or better than those featured in the text.

The McGraw·Hill Companies

Send all inquiries to:
Glencoe/McGraw-Hill
4400 Easton Commons
Columbus, OH 43219

ISBN: 978-0-07-876780-7 Student Edition
MHID: 0-07-876780-6 Student Edition

Printed in the United States of America

6 7 8 9 10 DOW 13 12 11

Contents in Brief

Teacher Reviewers

Lynn Beard
Family and Consumer Sciences Teacher
Everett High School
Lansing, Michigan

Janet T. Cole
Academy of Finance Instructor
Waipahu High School
Waipahu, Hawaii

Phillip M. D'Amico
Academy of Finance Director
William T. Dwyer Community High School
Palm Beach Gardens, Florida

Gail M. Dughi, B.S., M.Ed., Past President of Illinois Family and Consumer Sciences
FCS Instructor, Retired
Woodstock High School
Woodstock, Illinois

Shannon H. Farrell
Academy of Finance Instructor
William T. Dwyer Community High School
Palm Beach Gardens, Florida

Susan M. McCauley
Social Science Teacher and Department Coordinator
Quaker Valley High School
Leetsdale, Pennsylvania

Jay P. McKinstrey
Business Education Instructor
Pella High School
Pella, Iowa

Gail McMillon, Ed.D.
Assistant Professor
Family and Consumer Sciences
Southeastern Louisiana University
Hammond, Los Angeles

Brenda Barrington Mendiola
Superintendent
Irion County Independent School District
Mertzon, Texas

Cindy A. Miller, M.A.
Business Teacher
Murungu Unified School District
Yucca Valley High School
Yucca Valley, California

Ruth Patterson
Family and Consumer Sciences Teacher
Williamstown High School
Williamstown, New Jersey

Therese M. Peters
Family and Consumer Sciences Teacher
Warren High School
Downey, California

Deborah R. Reed
Business and Family and Consumer Sciences Teacher
Maria High School
Chicago, Illinois

Maxine H. Rooks
Family and Consumer Sciences Teacher, Retired
Virgil Grissom High School
Huntsville, Alabama

Michael Shoopman
Family and Consumer Sciences Teacher
Star Spencer High School
Spencer, Oklahoma

Technical Reviewers

David M. Blitzer, Ph.D.
Managing Director and
Chairman of the Index Committee
Standard & Poor's
New York, New York

STANDARD
&POOR'S

Michael Mandel, Ph.D.
Chief Economist
BusinessWeek
New York, New York

Mark Morrison
National Correspondent
BusinessWeek
Austin, Texas

Holly Anderson
Director of Communications
National Consumers League
Washington, DC

Nancy I. Brown
Economics Education Specialist and
Instructional Designer
Brown & Associates, LLC
Colorado Springs, Colorado

Holly Cherico
Vice President, Communications
Council of Better Business Bureaus
Arlington, Virginia

Joanne R. Dempsey
President/Executive Director
Illinois Council on Economic Education
Northern Illinois University
DeKalb, Illinois

Rod Griffin
Manager, Public Education
Experian
Allen, Texas

Mary J. Pickard, Ph.D., CFCS, CFLE
Associate Professor
East Carolina University
Greenville, North Carolina

Gwen M. Reichbach, Ph.D.
Executive Director
National Institute for Consumer Education
Eastern Michigan University
Ypsilanti, Michigan

Rhonda W. Roberson, J.D.
President/CEO
Wall Street Institute, Inc.
Washington, DC

Diane E. Rolfsmeyer
Certified Financial Planning Professional
Lincoln, Nebraska

Marlene G. Spears, R.N.
Health Science Technology Teacher, Retired
Bristol, Tennessee

Contents

Unit 1
Preparing for Consumer Choices

Contents

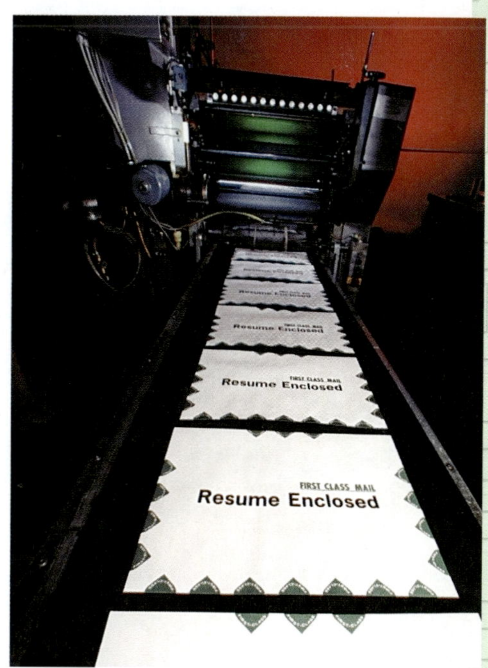

Contents

Unit 2
Understanding Economic Principles

Chapter 5 The U.S Economic System 126

Contents

Contents

Unit 3 Managing Your Money

Contents

Contents

Unit 4 Building Financial Security

Contents

Contents

Unit 5
Becoming A Smart Shopper

Contents

Unit 6
Making Spending Decisions

Contents

Contents

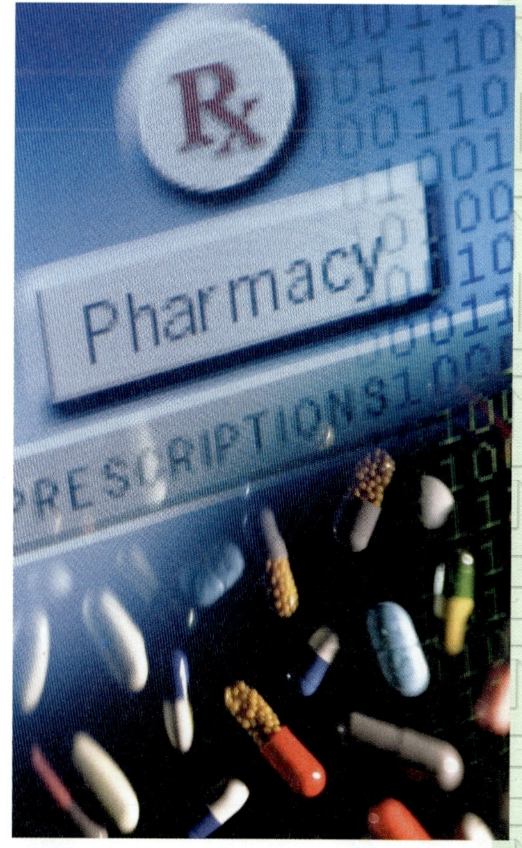

Contents

Special Features

Economic Impact & Issues

InfoSource

Special Features

Tables, Charts, and Graphs

Special Features

DOLLARSandSENSE

CHAPTER 1

Consumer Powers and Protections

Reading with Purpose

- Read the title of this chapter and describe in writing what you expect to learn from it.
- Write down each key term, leaving space for definitions.
- As you read the chapter, write the definition beside each term.
- After reading the chapter, write a paragraph describing what you learned.

SECTION 1.1

The Power of Consumers

Being a consumer goes way beyond just shopping. Your actions as a consumer cause a ripple effect, like throwing a stone into a pond.

Objectives

After studying this section, you should be able to:

- Identify the economic roles of individuals.
- Describe ways that consumers influence the marketplace.
- Analyze the impact of technology on consumers.
- Explain effective uses of consumer skills.

Key Terms

consumer
goods
services
marketplace
retailers

YOU'RE A CONSUMER

One day you're clicking around on a company's Web site and see a link to information for consumers. The next day you turn on the TV and hear a news report—"Annual consumer spending is now more than 8 trillion dollars." Who are these consumers you're hearing about? Everyone is a consumer—including you!

A **consumer** is someone who uses goods and services. **Goods** are physical objects that are produced, such as radios, chocolate chip cookies, and magazines. **Services** are actions that are performed for someone, such as repairing a car, serving a meal, or caring for a child. When you eat a meal, listen to a CD, or ride on a bus, you're a consumer.

Your Economic Roles

Right now, you are someone's classmate. You're also a teen and a friend. Someday you may be a husband or wife and a parent. These are roles you fulfill in your personal life.

You also have roles in your economic life—the part of life concerned with earning, spending, and managing money. Consumer, worker, and citizen are the three major economic roles that most people play.

Critical Thinking. ***Ask:*** How are the roles of consumer, worker, and citizen interrelated? How might one person fill all three roles on a daily basis?

- **Consumer.** You're a consumer when you use goods and services, even if you're not the one who pays for them. Even babies are consumers, using up diapers and milk as soon as they're born!
- **Worker.** You're a worker if you earn money at any kind of job, or even if you do volunteer work. Workers produce goods and perform services.
- **Citizen.** As a citizen, you use public services such as schools and roadways. Citizens pay taxes in order to pay for public services, and they have the right to vote for elected leaders.

As you continue in this course, you'll have the opportunity to learn about all three of these economic roles. Mainly, though, your studies will focus on how to be an effective consumer.

Class Activity. Have students create a diagram that illustrates how decisions made by individual consumers affect the marketplace.

CONSUMERS HAVE POWER

You may not think your choice of which movie to see or which brand of soap to buy matters to anyone else. For individual consumers, that may be true. Collectively, however, the purchasing decisions made by consumers have an impact. They affect which goods are produced and which services are offered. That means that as a group, consumers have power to influence the **marketplace**—all of the goods and services available for sale to the general public. See Figure 1-1.

Furthermore, consumers play a vital role in this country's economic system. When lots of consumers buy a business's products, that business profits. It continues paying its workers and may hire more of them. As a result, the workers, who are also consumers, have more money to spend on goods and services. The economy grows with this cycle of consumer activity.

Meanwhile, thriving businesses, in order to please present customers and attract new ones, develop new and better products. As the number of available goods and services

1-1

When you choose to buy one product over another, your decision directly affects the marketplace. How can consumers more consciously use this power?

Community Activity. Instruct students to interview someone who owns or works at a retail store in their community. Have them ask about how the store strives to please its customers through its products, services, and atmosphere. Invite students to share and discuss their findings in class.

increases, so does the competition for the consumer dollar. Marketing experts, those professionals who define what a product is and how it is sold, work to determine what the consumer wants and will buy. **Retailers**, those who sell goods and services directly to consumers, strive to offer the right mix of products and to provide helpful service. Pleasing the customer is the key to business success.

Teens Are Important Consumers

It's probably no secret to you that teens are very active consumers. In recent years, total spending by teen consumers reached over $170 billion annually.

In addition to spending their own money—from allowances, gifts, or part-time jobs—teens also play a role in family buying decisions. Just as parents may rely upon teens for the care of younger brothers and sisters, they increasingly depend upon teens to do household shopping. Teens provide input for everything from grocery purchases to entertainment choices to vacation destinations and activities. The opinions of teens matter, and those who sell goods and services know it. See Figure 1-2.

Jump$tart. Jump$tart is a coalition of agencies, organizations, and corporations that promote financial literacy in the areas of income, money management, spending and credit, and savings and investing. The coalition has set up standards to guide K-12 educational programs. The Jump$tart annotations in this text are tied to these standards.

TECHNOLOGY AND THE CONSUMER

Consumers have been buying goods and services for thousands of years. While some things haven't changed much in all that time, one thing that has changed is the technology available for communicating, accessing information, and purchasing goods and services. Instead of going to a local store to shop, you might see a product demonstrated on TV and buy it over the phone. You can use Web sites to learn about different products, read customer recommendations, compare prices, ask questions, and make purchases.

Technology such as television and the Internet puts information at your fingertips.

1-2

Given their power to affect the economy, teens can benefit from learning consumer skills. How could you help your family make wise buying decisions?

Class Activity. Organize the class into five groups. Assign each group one of the characteristics of an effective consumer and have the group design a poster or display that illustrates this characteristic. Combine all posters to create one large bulletin board display for the classroom.

It allows you to make more informed choices about where to spend your money. On the other hand, instant access to so much information can present challenges. How will you sort through all the information available? How many options should you consider? How do you know when you have enough information to make a decision?

Technology can also challenge consumers by making it easier to buy on impulse. Being able to buy with a phone call or the click of a mouse can tempt you to purchase items you don't really need and may not be able to afford. To face these and other challenges, you need strong consumer skills.

EFFECTIVE CONSUMERS

By mastering the consumer skills described throughout this book, you can make the best use of your power as a consumer. What are some of the characteristics of an effective consumer?

- **Effective consumers set goals.** They decide what they want and how they can best carry out a plan. They place priorities on how they spend their time, energy, and money. They plan for a career and for the education or training they will need.
- **Effective consumers think critically.** They make decisions based on careful consideration of alternatives and their possible outcomes. They avoid acting on impulse. They maintain a realistic perspective when encountering persuasive advertising or aggressive salespeople.
- **Effective consumers do their research.** They read, observe, and ask questions about the many options available to them. They search for reliable businesses. They compare prices, quality, features, and customer service policies.
- **Effective consumers manage everyday finances.** They handle their income, expenses, taxes, banking, and credit in a responsible way.
- **Effective consumers plan for financial security.** They set up plans for savings, investing, and insurance, calling upon qualified professionals for help as needed.

Section 1.1 Review

CHECK YOUR UNDERSTANDING

1. Explain the differences between the roles of consumer, citizen, and worker.
2. How has technology such as the Internet changed the marketplace?
3. Why is it important to use consumer skills wisely when making financial decisions?

CONSUMER APPLICATION

Your Impact Consider the ways that you spend your money. How do your decisions as a consumer impact businesses, workers, and other consumers in your area? Explain your answer.

Answer Key. Answers to the Section Review questions are provided in the Section Lesson Plan located in the *Teacher Resource Guide*.

SECTION 1.2

Protecting Consumers' Rights

Through history, consumers have often faced unfair treatment. Thanks to the efforts of many, they have also continued to gain protection.

Objectives

After studying this section, you should be able to:

- Explain consumer rights and responsibilities.
- Identify laws that protect consumers.
- Describe sources of consumer information and protection.

Key Terms

consumer advocates
redress
consumer affairs departments
consumer action panels
media

THE CONSUMER MOVEMENT

At first, consumers had little voice in issues that affected them. The development of the consumer movement changed that. The consumer movement is based on the idea that the power of consumers as a group can balance the economic and political power of business and industry.

The consumer movement has been led by many **consumer advocates**, people or organizations who work on behalf of consumers. At the state and national levels, they have worked to investigate business practices, expose unfair or dangerous situations, and encourage the passage of laws protecting consumers.

While progress in the consumer movement has been continual, many important advances took place in the early decades of the 1900s and again in the 1960s. These consumer advocates might be considered pioneers of the consumer movement:

- Harvey Wiley, a medical doctor, proved that adding certain chemicals to foods and drugs was dangerous. His campaign against mislabeling led to the passage of the Food and Drug Act of 1906.

Discussion. *Ask:* How might your shopping experiences be different had it not been for the efforts of consumer advocates?

- Upton Sinclair's novel *The Jungle* exposed filthy conditions in meat packing plants, leading to the passage of the Meat Inspection Act of 1906.
- Stuart Chase and F. J. Schlink published *Your Money's Worth* in 1927, a book demonstrating how misleading advertising affects consumers.
- In 1962 Rachel Carson published *Silent Spring*, a book that revealed the damaging effects of insecticides and other pesticides. Her work inspired many environmental laws. See Figure 1-3.
- Ralph Nader published *Unsafe at Any Speed* in 1965, demonstrating that many highway deaths were caused by defects in cars. Since then Nader, along with members of several groups that he has founded or headed, has worked on behalf of consumers in many areas including air travel, food safety, the environment, health care, insurance, and others.

Critical Thinking. *Ask:* What new issues can you think of that must be addressed to protect consumers in the marketplace today?

CONSUMER RIGHTS AND RESPONSIBILITIES

An important result of the consumer movement has been the recognition that consumers have certain rights. Four basic rights of consumers were identified by President John F. Kennedy in a message to Congress in 1962. Later presidents expanded on this "Consumer Bill of Rights." Like any other rights, those of a consumer are paired with important responsibilities. Figure 1-4 describes several consumer rights and some responsibilities that accompany them.

GOVERNMENT PROTECTION

The actions of governments can help define and enforce the rights and responsibilities of consumers. For example, one of the rights of consumers is the right to **redress**, remedy for a wrong or a loss. Because governments have passed consumer protection laws, consumers can seek legal remedy when the laws are violated. Consumer protection is provided by both laws and government agencies at federal, state, and local levels.

1-3

Rachel Carson, a biologist and writer, testified before Congress about the damage inflicted to the ecosystem by misuse of chemicals. Why do consumer advocates still have a role to play in protecting and educating consumers?

Team Activity. Have students work in small groups to create visual aids that illustrate one of the consumer rights or responsibilities listed here.

Point Out. Explain how consumers can encourage ethical business practices by supporting companies that care for their workers and for the environment.

Consumer Rights and Responsibilities

CONSUMER RIGHTS	CONSUMER RESPONSIBILITIES
Right to safety. Consumers should be protected against products that are hazardous to health or life.	**Responsibility to use products safely.** Consumers should use products as they were meant to be used.
Right to be informed. Consumers should be protected against dishonest advertising, labeling, or sales practices. They should be given the facts needed to make informed choices.	**Responsibility to use information.** Consumers should look for information about products they plan to buy and use it to compare and evaluate different brands and models.
Right to choose. Consumers should be assured access to a variety of goods and services at competitive prices.	**Responsibility to choose carefully.** Consumers should use their buying power intelligently to encourage ethical business practices and safe, reliable products.
Right to be heard. Consumers should know that their interests will be considered in the making of laws.	**Responsibility to speak up.** Consumers should let public officials know their opinions about consumer issues.
Right to redress. Consumers are entitled to swift and fair remedies for wrongs that are done.	**Responsibility to seek redress.** Consumers should pursue remedies when products and services do not meet expectations.
Right to consumer education. Consumers should have the opportunity to learn how to be effective consumers.	**Responsibility to learn.** Consumers should take advantage of every opportunity to develop consumer skills.
Right to service. Consumers have the right to expect convenience, courtesy, and responsiveness from businesses.	**Responsibility to reward good service.** Consumers should be courteous and responsive to businesses in return. They should show their appreciation for good service by patronizing businesses that provide it.

1-4 President Gerald Ford promoted the right to consumer education, expressing his hope that it would become "an integral part of regular school instruction." Discuss the impact that this right and its corresponding responsibility have on you.

Class Activity. Have students complete this sentence in writing: "I showed consumer responsibility when I . . ." Share and discuss responses in class.

Jump$tart. Have each student research one of the federal consumer protection laws listed here and design a brochure explaining it for consumers. *(Spendig & Credit)*

Discussion. ***Ask:*** Have you ever observed one of these federal consumer protection laws in action? If so, under what circumstances?

Federal Laws

Over the years, the U.S. Congress has passed a number of laws, or *statutes*, to protect consumers. Figure 1-5 lists some of them. Several of these, as well as other consumer protection laws, are discussed in later chapters.

Selected Federal Consumer Protection Laws

FEDERAL LAW	WHAT IT DOES
Fair Packaging and Labeling Act	Requires truth in packaging to help consumers compare goods
Food, Drug, and Cosmetic Act	Assures consumers of the safety and purity of food products, drugs, and cosmetics
Federal Hazardous Substances Labeling Act	Requires warning labels on all products that might be hazardous
Child Protection and Toy Safety Act	Bans the shipment and sale of goods intended for use by children, including toys, that may be dangerous to children
Automobile Information Disclosure Act	Requires that manufacturers label cars with specific information, such as suggested retail price
Textile Fiber Products Identification Act	Requires manufacturers of textiles and fabrics to provide labels listing fiber content and other information
Magnuson-Moss Warranty Act	Governs consumer product warranties (guarantees)
Truth in Savings Act	Requires financial institutions to provide figures such as interest rates in standard forms
Truth in Lending Act	Requires creditors to report all credit charges and interest rates to the consumer
Equal Credit Opportunity Act	Protects people who apply for credit from discrimination
Fair Credit Billing Act	Provides a procedure for consumers to follow in having billing errors corrected
Fair Credit Reporting Act	Controls how a person's credit history is kept, used, and shared
Financial Services Modernization Act	Requires financial institutions to notify customers about the kinds of information they collect about them, how that information may be used, and their privacy rights

1-5 **These laws both protect consumers and place responsibilities on them.** **Choose one of the laws and explain what these responsibilities might be.**

Research Activity. Have students find the name of a current piece of consumer legislation in Congress. Have them write a summary of this bill's purpose.

Federal Agencies

Having laws on the books is not enough—there must be a way to enforce them. Government agencies are created to watch over specific areas or industries. They set up rules and regulations to ensure that individual businesses comply with the laws and to prosecute those that do not.

At the federal level, dozens of agencies have a direct responsibility to consumers. Here are a few of them.

- **Federal Trade Commission (FTC)** enforces laws against dishonest advertising. It also helps protect consumer rights in the areas of credit transactions, product labeling, and privacy.
- **Consumer Product Safety Commission (CPSC)** works to protect the public against unreasonable risks and to develop safety standards for many household products.
- **United States Department of Agriculture (USDA)** inspects and sets standards for meat, poultry, and canned fruits and vegetables.

InfoSource. Instruct students to use one or more of the sources listed to create a directory of state and local consumer protection agencies in your area.

- **Food and Drug Administration (FDA)** enforces laws and regulations on the purity, quality, and labeling of food, drugs, and cosmetics.
- **Federal Communications Commission (FCC)** regulates interstate and international communications by radio, television, wire, satellite, and cable. It provides consumer information and addresses consumer complaints related to these areas.
- **National Telecommunications and Information Administration (NTIA)** works to provide consumers with more choices and better quality telecommunications products and services, such as Internet, cellular, and cable service, at lower prices.
- **Federal Consumer Information Center (FCIC)** provides information to consumers on a wide range of topics through low-cost publications, a Web site, and toll-free phone assistance.

Some of these agencies protect businesses as well as consumers. For example, when the FTC prosecutes businesses that cheat or mislead consumers, it promotes fair competition that benefits honest businesses.

InfoSource

Consumer Protection

To find state and local consumer protection agencies:

- Check the government listings in the phone book.
- Visit the Federal Consumer Information Center's Consumer Action Web site. You can access many state and local offices through this site.
- Look for links to state and local offices at the Web sites of the National Association of Attorneys General and the National Association of Consumer Agency Administrators.

Community Activity. Have students visit the Web site of your state attorney general to learn about what specific measures the attorney general's office takes to protect consumers in the state. Have them write a paragraph describing one specific way the state attorney general protects consumers.

State and Local Laws and Agencies

Legislators at the state and local levels also have passed many laws that benefit consumers. In addition, more than 300 state, county, and local governments have set up consumer protection agencies or offices. Their names and responsibilities vary. In most states, the attorney general's office oversees state consumer protection.

OTHER CONSUMER ASSISTANCE

Government agencies are not the only source of consumer assistance. Many private organizations and businesses also work on behalf of consumers.

Consumer Groups

Consumer groups are organizations that are focused on consumer education, protection, and advocacy. Although their interests and membership vary, the groups share a common belief: Only through organized group action will consumers' voices be heard and their power felt.

Examples of consumer groups operating at the national level include the National Consumers League, Public Citizen, and Consumer Action. Many state and local consumer groups are active as well. They work toward a variety of causes such as forcing down unfair prices, ending deceptive business practices, and fighting rate increases by public utilities.

Consumer Testing Agencies and Publications

Consumers Union (CU) is an independent consumer testing agency that has long been a champion of consumer rights. Staff members buy products from stores, test them, and report the results in the agency's magazine, *Consumer Reports.* By reading the magazine in print or on the Web, you can find out what tests were conducted, what criteria were used, and how the researchers rated each product. Another independent consumer testing agency is Consumers' Research, founded in 1928, which publishes *Consumers' Research* magazine.

Business and Industry Groups

A wide range of business and industry groups works to assist consumers. The best-known example is the Better Business

1-6

Your local Better Business Bureau is supported by local businesses that have agreed to conform to ethical business practices. Only members of the BBB may display this symbol. Why should you look for this symbol when choosing a merchant?

Class Activity. Have each student assume the role of a consumer reporter and write a story about a fictitious consumer complaint.

Bureau (BBB). Its offices throughout the U.S. and Canada provide reliability reports on local businesses and allow consumers to file a complaint in the event of a problem. The main BBB Web site can help you find the local office for your area. See Figure 1-6.

Many businesses have full-time **consumer affairs departments** that communicate with customers about their rights and needs as consumers. Many of the larger firms have toll-free numbers that consumers can use when they need information or want to make a complaint. See Figure 1-7.

Companies in a particular industry, such as garment manufacturers or health care providers, sometimes form trade associations to look after their common interests. **Consumer action panels** are groups formed by trade associations to address consumer complaints. The panels also keep their member businesses up to date on consumers' opinions.

News Media

Media are channels of mass communication, such as newspapers, magazines, radio, television, and related Web sites. The news media play a vital role in warning consumers about local scam artists who try to cheat consumers. If a company issues a recall of a hazardous product, the media help alert consumers and tell them what to do. Media outlets also offer useful advice on investing, health, housing, and other topics of interest to consumers. Hundreds of local newspapers and radio and television stations have consumer columns or programs.

The media can also help resolve consumer complaints. Because they want to avoid bad publicity, businesses that might ignore a consumer acting alone often respond fast and favorably when a consumer reporter gets involved.

Answer Key. Answers to the Section Review questions are provided in the Section Lesson Plan located in the *Teacher Resource Guide.*

1-7 Manufacturers test their products to ensure they meet standards of quality and safety. How else do businesses help support consumers' rights?

Section 1.2 Review

CHECK YOUR UNDERSTANDING

1. What is the underlying principle shared by advocates of the consumer movement?
2. Explain two consumer rights and their corresponding responsibilities.
3. Name and describe two federal laws that regulate product labeling.

CONSUMER APPLICATION

Consumer Laws Using online resources or personal interviews, find out how consumer rights policies become laws. Create a flowchart to summarize the process.

Objectives

After studying this section, you should be able to:

- Describe ways to protect yourself from identity theft.
- Identify laws protecting consumer privacy.
- Explain guidelines for preventing online harassment.

Key Terms

identity theft
Social Security number
secure site
online profiling
cookies

SECTION 1.3

Safeguarding Your Privacy

How many people have access to your personal and financial information? Take steps to safeguard your privacy and to ensure that information you voluntarily provide remains secure.

IDENTITY THEFT

One of the most significant threats to personal security is **identity theft**, the illegal use of an individual's personal information. Dishonest people who find out your date of birth, bank account or credit card numbers, Internet passwords, or other information can use them in ways that cause you serious financial harm. Figure 1-8 on the next page explains several ways an identity thief can obtain information about you and use that information.

Your Social Security Number

An important piece of personal information is your **Social Security number**—the unique nine-digit number used by the Social Security Administration to keep track of your earnings. It can be used to access bank and credit card accounts as well as other personal information. For this reason, don't give out your Social Security number unless absolutely necessary. If someone requests it, ask why. Some businesses use the number simply as a convenient way to

Class Activity. Have students write a diary entry from the viewpoint of a victim of identity theft. Have them read their entries aloud in class.

Point Out. Make sure students understand that some agencies and businesses that request their Social Security number have no right to do so.

Identity Theft: How Does It Happen?

HOW IDENTITY THIEVES OBTAIN INFORMATION

- They steal wallets and purses containing your ID, credit cards, or checkbook.
- They steal your mail, which may include bank, credit card, payroll, and tax information.
- They complete a change of address card to have your mail sent to another location.
- They go through your trash, or the trash of businesses that accept credit cards, for account numbers.
- They find personal information in your home.
- They steal personal information you have volunteered on the Internet.
- They pose as representatives of banks, Internet service providers, or government agencies to get you to reveal identifying information on the telephone or by email.
- They look over your shoulder when you write checks in stores or use teller machines.

HOW THEY USE THAT INFORMATION

- They open a bank account in your name and write bad checks on that account.
- They forge checks and drain your bank account.
- They order phone or wireless services in your name.
- They run up charges on your credit card account.
- They open a new credit card account using your name.
- They run up bills for which you could be responsible. You might never see the bills, but failure to pay them could harm your financial reputation.

1-8 **Identity theft, also known as true name fraud, contributes to the loss of millions of consumer dollars each year.**

identify people, but you can ask them to use a different type of identification number instead. Don't carry your Social Security card in your wallet or have the number printed on your checks.

Preventing Identity Theft

In addition to safeguarding your Social Security number, you can take other steps to protect yourself from identity theft.

- Handle your mail with care. Deposit outgoing mail in post office boxes or at the post office. Promptly remove mail from your mailbox once it has been delivered.
- Keep items with personal information in a safe place, such as a locked drawer.
- Safeguard sensitive information on your computer or online with passwords that include both numbers and letters. Avoid easily guessed combinations, such as your birthday. Don't share your passwords, and don't write them down where others can see them.
- Don't give out personal information over the phone, through the mail, by email, or on the Web unless you initiated the contact or are otherwise certain that the recipient is legitimate.
- Before sending sensitive data to a Web site, be sure it's a **secure site**, one that uses safeguards to protect information from

Research Activity. Ask students to visit the Web sites of at least five Internet retailers and note which of these sites are secure.

theft during transmission. A Web address that begins with either "shttp://" or "https://" indicates that the site is secure.

- If you have an Internet connection at home, ask the service provider about its security measures. Find out what steps you should take to protect your computer and its data.
- Before you discard charge receipts, credit applications, or bank statements and checks, tear or shred them. Also cut up expired credit cards. These steps will deter an identity thief who may pick through your trash. See Figure 1-9.

If Your Identity Is Stolen

Even if you have been very careful, an identity thief can strike. If you suspect that someone is taking advantage of your identity for his or her own gain, take action immediately.

- File a report with the police.
- Notify your bank and credit card companies. Close any accounts that may be tampered with.
- Call the three major credit reporting agencies—Equifax, Experian, and Trans Union. Ask that they put a fraud alert on your file and that no new accounts be opened without your approval.

Point Out. Explain that victims of identity theft can simplify the reporting process by filing an ID Theft Affadavit, available from the FTC.

- Call the FTC or visit its Web site for information about resolving identity theft problems.

DATA COLLECTION AND PRIVACY ISSUES

Sometimes there is a legitimate need to provide personal information to financial institutions, health care providers, insurance companies, and so on. You might also choose to share information when you buy or register a product. How various information is used and with whom it is shared have become important issues for consumers.

Suppose you order a computer game from a catalog. To place the order, you give your name, address, and credit card number. Later, when you send your product registration to the software company, you complete a short survey that asks your age and

1-9

A paper shredder can be used to destroy unwanted papers that include sensitive information. What other steps should you take to prevent identity theft?

Class Activity. Ask students to make a chart comparing the advantages and disadvantages of having personal information used in each of the ways listed. (For instance, having a credit card on file might make it easier to place future orders, but it might also increase the risk of identity theft.)

whether you have a pet, like to garden, or frequently purchase magazines. What might these companies do with the information they gathered about you? That can vary, but here are some typical uses.

- Some information, such as your credit card number, is needed only to process your order. Reputable businesses keep credit card numbers secure and don't share them with anyone. See Figure 1-10.
- The catalog company will probably keep your name, address, and purchasing history in its customer database for its own marketing purposes. For instance, it may send you additional catalogs or promotional emails in the hopes that you'll buy more products.
- The company might sell your name and address to other retailers, either directly or through data-collection companies. That explains why you may suddenly begin receiving catalogs or emails from businesses that you've never purchased from.
- Your responses to the product registration survey will probably be combined with those of other customers and analyzed to reveal patterns. The company may want to find out how many of its customers are teens, for example, or whether people who buy computer games also tend to buy books about computers.

Protecting Your Privacy

Many companies and organizations voluntarily give consumers choices about how their personal information is used. In addition, laws addressing concerns about consumer privacy are being developed. For example, a provision included in the Financial Services Modernization Act, passed in 1999, requires companies involved in financial activities to send privacy notices to customers. These notices must explain company policy regarding the sharing of customers' personal information with other businesses. Customers can choose to limit the sharing of some of this information.

Another safeguard is the Children's Online Privacy Protection Act of 1998. It requires Web sites directed to children under

1-10

When you order from a reputable company by phone or mail, you can feel secure that your credit card number will not be shared with other businesses. **What would you do if you received an unsolicited request for your credit card number?**

Discussion. *Ask:* How do you feel about Web sites' use of cookies to remember information about you? Do you consider this a useful feature or an invasion of privacy? Is it worth the inconvenience to set your Web browser to reject cookies? Why or why not?

the age of 13 to post their privacy policy through a link on their home page and anywhere personal information is being collected. In many cases, parental consent must be given before this information may be collected. Parents must be able to review the information and can later revoke their consent if they choose. Privacy provisions of both acts are overseen by the FTC.

Before giving out personal information, investigate the company's privacy policy. If you don't receive it in the mail or find it posted on the company's Web site, call the company and ask for it. Read the policy carefully to understand your rights and responsibilities.

Under many policies, you have the right to "opt out" of having your information shared or used in certain ways. To "opt out," you notify the company that you do not want the information shared. If you do nothing, the company assumes it may share the information. An "opt in" policy works the opposite way. For example, some companies pledge not to use your email address to send you promotional materials unless you "opt in," or specifically give your consent.

Online Profiling

Computer technology continues to give companies greater ability to gather and use data about consumers. One example is **online profiling**—a practice in which companies collect information about the Web sites a consumer visits, and then use that information to predict what the consumer may buy in the future.

Typically, online profiling is done by companies that specialize in Internet advertising. They use **cookies**, small files that are stored on your computer's hard drive when you visit a site. A cookie enables a Web site to "remember" information about you. For example, suppose you go to a Web site and enter "snowboarding" as a search term. Your search might be recorded in a cookie, which is then stored on your computer. Later, when you return to the same site, the site retrieves the cookie. The banner on the Web page now shows an ad for a ski resort, which has replaced the former ad for a job-hunting service. Using the cookie, the Web site tailored the advertisement to your interest in snowboarding. See Figure 1-11.

1-11

Online profiling raises issues of privacy. **Do you think it also offers benefits for consumers? Why or why not?**

Class Activity. Ask students whether they know someone who has been a victim of cyber-stalking. Have them relate incidents without giving names.

If you want to prevent online profiling, you can set your Web browser not to accept cookies. However, this can be an inconvenience because it eliminates all cookies, including ones used for other purposes. For instance, a Web site may use a cookie to keep track of the items stored in your online "shopping cart." If you disable cookies, you won't be able to shop at that site. You must weigh your privacy concerns against the convenience of online shopping.

INTERNET SAFETY

Keeping your personal information private is important in many other Internet situations, including chat rooms, forums, and instant messages. Remember, information that you put on the Internet is available to practically anyone. Most Internet users are honest and trustworthy, but some are not.

Each year, thousands of people report that they have been the victims of online harassment, sometimes called "cyber-stalking." Online harassment can take many forms. For example, a cyber-stalker could use the Internet to spread false information about you, along with your email address. As a result, you could be bombarded with obscene or threatening email messages from around the world. If the cyber-stalker gains access to personal information—such as your real name, address, or phone number—the harassment can spread to the offline world as well.

Harassment, online or not, is illegal. You can take steps to prevent online harassment and to deal with it if it occurs.

- Reveal as little personal information online as possible. Use gender-neutral screen names and email addresses. Don't put your picture on your personal Web site.

On the board, list the actions the victims took and the effects of those actions. Have students identify positive actions. Mark them with a plus sign.

- Share your primary email address only with trusted friends and family. Get an alternate email address to use for other online activity, such as chat rooms.
- Watch what you say online. Avoid creating enemies.
- Use the preference options to block transmission of mail, chat, or instant messages from anyone who persists in bothering you.
- If someone is harassing or threatening you, save the communications as proof. Tell a parent or other trusted adult. Contact the appropriate service provider, such as the administrator of the chat room or your email provider, and local law enforcement agencies.

Answer Key. Answers to the Section Review questions are provided in the Section Lesson Plan located in the *Teacher Resource Guide*.

Section 1.3 Review

CHECK YOUR UNDERSTANDING

1. Why should you guard your Social Security number?
2. How does the Financial Services Modernization Act affect consumer privacy?
3. List three steps you can take to prevent online harassment.

CONSUMER APPLICATION

Shopping Dilemma You find an item you want at an online store that accepts credit cards, but it doesn't use a secure site. What are the potential risks of buying from this merchant? How could you reduce them? Would you make the transaction? Why or why not?

Objectives

After studying this section, you should be able to:

- Recognize examples of deception and fraud.
- Explain how to report deception and fraud.

Key Terms

deceptive advertising
bait and switch
fraud
pyramid scheme
chain letter

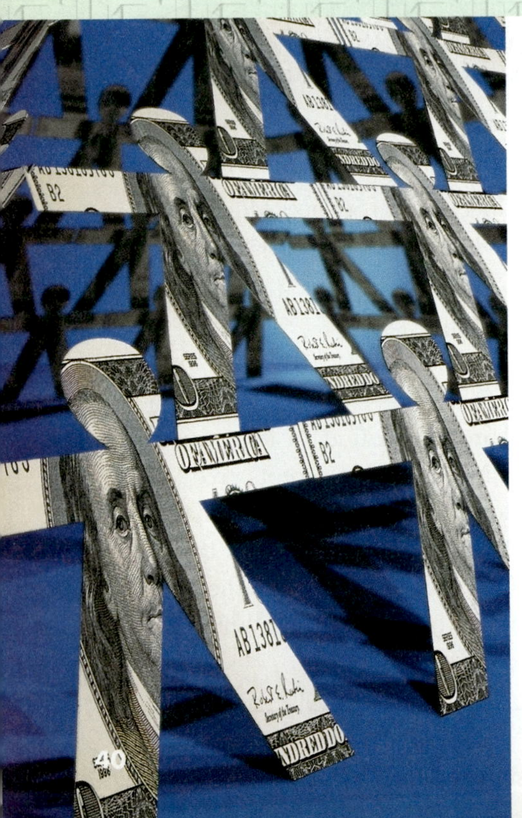

SECTION 1.4

Recognizing Deception & Fraud

A well-known Latin phrase is commonly used to advise consumers. *Caveat emptor* means "let the buyers beware." Being a skilled consumer includes recognizing dishonest, illegal approaches used in some sales and advertising and protecting yourself against them.

DECEPTIVE ADVERTISING

Most advertisers are honest, but some try to take unfair advantage of consumers. **Deceptive advertising** is advertising that is likely to mislead consumers through false statements, omitted information, or other unfair means. Deceptive advertising is illegal, and the Federal Trade Commission is empowered to stop it. Nevertheless, as a consumer, you should be on guard. Examples of deceptive advertising include:

- **Bait and switch.** If a retailer advertises a product that it has no intention of selling, hoping to persuade customers to buy another product at a higher price, it is engaging in the deceptive practice known as **bait and switch**. For example, suppose a store advertises "25-inch color TV! Only $99!" In reality, the retailer never intended to sell TVs for that price. This nonexistent bargain item is the "bait" used to lure customers into the

Team Activity. Have pairs of students role-play scenes featuring a salesclerk and a customer responding to a deceptive ad. Scenes should show how the customer responds to learning that the store will not deliver on its promise and whether the outcome is positive or negative.

store. When the customer asks about the advertised item, the retailer claims that the $99 model is "sold out" and steers customers toward a more expensive TV.

- **False promise of free gifts.** When a store advertises a "free" gift, the gift must actually be free, with no strings attached. If customers must buy an item in order to receive the gift, an advertisement that says "free" is deceptive. To avoid deception, the ad could use wording such as "gift with purchase."

TEXTLINK

Advertising is discussed further in Section 15.2.

- **Deceptive pricing.** Advertising a "sale" price that is actually no better than the product's everyday price is deceptive. The word *sale* implies a bargain—lower prices than usual. To avoid deception, the store must have sold the item regularly and recently at the nonsale price. Similarly, when a business claims that its prices are lower than a competitor's, it must be able to provide proof.
- **Hidden catches.** Suppose an ad for low-cost "spring break" airline tickets involves extra charges, such as processing fees, and hidden restrictions, such as a requirement to stay at a specific hotel in order to take advantage of the deal. If the ad does not clearly disclose these details, it is deceptive. See Figure 1-12.

FRAUD

Fraud is deceitful conduct designed to manipulate another person for some gain. The deceit may take the form of lying, repeating something that ought to have been known to be false, or concealing a fact that might have saved the other party from being cheated.

Suppose you give money to a person who says your contribution will go to charity. If the person keeps the money instead, you've been a victim of fraud. Fraud also occurs when consumers are led to buy a good or service that the seller knows, or should know, is unlikely to perform as claimed or to meet the consumer's needs as promised.

Although it's against the law, fraud is very much a part of the consumer's world. According to the U.S. Department of Justice, more than 24 million people become victims of fraud each year in the United States.

1-12

Before you sign up for a "dream vacation," check the fine print carefully. If you suspect deception, contact the FTC or another consumer protection agency.

Research Activity. Have students search the Web site of the FTC for more information about the difference between multilevel marketing plans and pyramid schemes. Have them write a report explaining what distinguishes a pyramid scheme from a legitimate plan.

Pyramid Schemes

A common example of fraud is the **pyramid scheme**, an illegal get-rich-quick plan. Each person who participates pays a sum of money to join, then recruits several other people. Those people in turn pay a fee and recruit others, and so on. Supposedly, each participant will eventually receive money from people who join later.

Pyramid schemes are fraudulent and illegal because they get people to contribute money based on false promises. The scheme is impossible to sustain in the long run. For example, a system in which each participant recruits six new members would soon require the participation of thousands, then millions, of people, as shown in Figure 1-13. Long before then, the pyramid will collapse due to failure to bring in enough new recruits. No matter how large or small the pyramid is at that point, most of the people in it are at the bottom level and lose their money. Only the few at the top of the pyramid (generally those who started the scheme) make money.

Promoters of pyramid schemes often try to disguise them. Some refer to the scheme as a "gifting club" and the cash payments as "gifts," but that doesn't make it legal. Others try to pass off a pyramid scheme as a legitimate form of business known as a *multilevel marketing plan*. In legitimate multilevel marketing plans, distributors sell a product to consumers and receive income based on the amount of those sales. If, however, distributors receive money not from selling products but from recruiting other distributors, the plan is really an illegal pyramid scheme.

Chain Letters

A variation on the pyramid scheme is a **chain letter**, a message sent by postal mail or email that instructs the recipient to send copies to a certain number of other people. Chain letters are fraudulent and illegal when

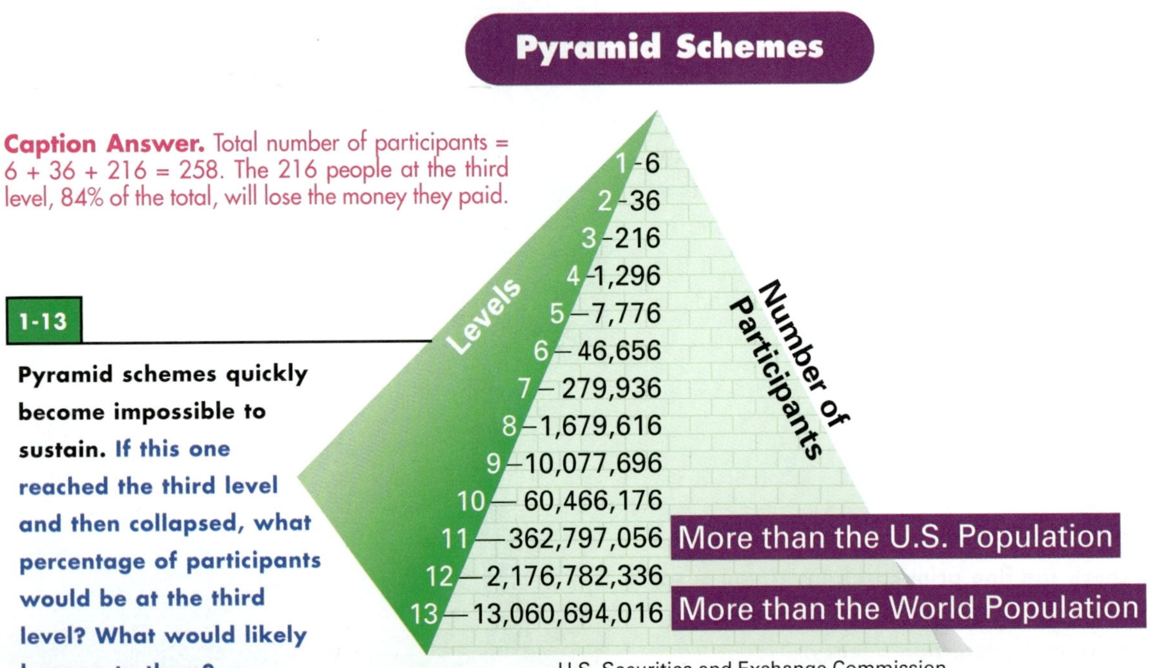

Caption Answer. Total number of participants = 6 + 36 + 216 = 258. The 216 people at the third level, 84% of the total, will lose the money they paid.

1-13

Pyramid schemes quickly become impossible to sustain. If this one reached the third level and then collapsed, what percentage of participants would be at the third level? What would likely happen to them?

Research Activity. Have students search for FTC "teaser sites" online. Ask them to visit one of these sites and compare it to real ads they have seen.

Dollars and Sense. Have each student find an ad containing one or more warning signs of deception and fraud and share it with the class.

they include instructions to send money or an item of value to someone and make promises that participants will receive money or valuables in return. A typical chain letter might tell you to send $5 to the first person on an enclosed list of names and addresses. You're supposed to then remove that name, add your own name to the bottom of the list, and send copies of the letter to several friends.

The obvious appeal of chain letters is the promise of big payoffs to anyone who participates. Theoretically, when your name reaches the top of the list, hundreds of later recipients will be sending you money or valuables. However, like pyramid schemes, chain letters don't work in the long run because they're impossible to sustain. By the time they collapse, only a few people at the beginning of the chain have been paid. Most of the people who sent money or valuables get nothing in return.

If you start such a chain letter, or even send one, you are committing a federal crime. The best thing you can do if you receive a chain letter is to break the chain by not sending it to others.

Fraud and Technology

Fraud has been around for centuries, but technology has added new wrinkles. Chain letters often utilize email, and pyramid schemes have sprung up on Web sites. In addition, new types of fraud have been developed that are unique to the Internet. For example, some people have tried to sell worthless Internet domain names.

Technology can also be used to combat fraud, as the FTC has done by posting "teaser sites" on the Web. These sites are similar to ones that a dishonest person or company might create. Visitors to the sites click on the links they find there, expecting to learn about miracle products or money-making opportunities. Instead, they are taken to a page that warns them about fraud. In this way, the FTC hopes to educate people who are likely to become fraud victims.

DOLLARSandSENSE

Warning Signs of Deception and Fraud

Many deceptive and fraudulent offers have characteristics that give them away. Be wary of:

- Individuals or businesses that won't reveal their physical address (city and state).
- Requirements that you pay up front in order to receive information about products, services, or money-making opportunities.
- High-pressure sales tactics requiring immediate, "today only" acceptance.
- Anything that fits the description of an illegal pyramid scheme or chain letter—even if the person who recruits you insists that this one is legal.
- Exaggerated claims that seem too good to be true.

Discussion. ***Ask:*** Why do you think so many people fall for get-rich-quick schemes? What can consumers do to avoid being scammed?

BUYER BEWARE

The variety of deceptive and fraudulent practices is endless. For example:

- A sweepstakes sends notification that you have won a "valuable prize," but asks that a $50 processing fee be paid up front. You send the money, and months later receive a cheap radio that you could have bought at a discount store for a few dollars.
- An earn-money-at-home opportunity promises wages up to $15 per hour for simply responding to email. Before you can start work, however, you must purchase $800 worth of software. Once you make this payment, the materials never arrive.
- You're the winning bidder in several online auctions. Your check is cashed, but you never receive one of the auction items. An item finally arrives, but instead of the valuable item described on the auction site, you get a different item worth much less.

If a situation seems suspicious, take steps to protect yourself. Get the company's name, address, and phone number, then check it out by contacting your local Better Business Bureau or your state attorney general.

Team Activity. Have students work in small groups to invent fraudulent offers. Each team should make up a print or Internet ad for an offer like those discussed in this chapter. Have each team present its ad to the class. Ask the rest of the class to point out the warning signs that the offer is fraudulent.

Answer Key. Answers to the Section Review questions are provided in the Section Lesson Plan located in the *Teacher Resource Guide.*

Reporting Deception and Fraud

If you suspect deception or fraud—whether or not you actually fell victim to it—report your suspicions. By doing so, you can help prevent others from being victimized. At the FTC's Web site, consumers can find information about deception and fraud and a Consumer Complaint Form for reporting suspected cases. The National Consumers League operates the National Fraud Information Center, which has a toll-free phone number and a Web site. Other ways to report deception and fraud include contacting your local consumer protection agency, the Better Business Bureau, your state attorney general's office, your local post office (if the fraudulent offer was received in the mail), or the local media.

Section 1.4 Review

CHECK YOUR UNDERSTANDING

1. Explain the strategy behind the bait and switch tactic.
2. What are two signs that a sales offer may be fraudulent?
3. How can you report suspected cases of fraud?

CONSUMER APPLICATION

Chain Letters Create a poster or pamphlet that educates consumers about chain letters that ask for money and explains what they should do if they receive one.

SECTION 1.5

Resolving Consumer Problems

Consumers expect good quality, safety, and service when they buy. Sometimes, however, what seems like a routine purchase turns out to be a source of frustration. When consumer problems arise, speaking up for your rights will help you resolve the problem.

Objectives

After studying this section, you should be able to:

- Demonstrate how to make an effective consumer complaint.
- Identify sources of assistance for resolving consumer problems.

Key Terms

mediation
arbitration
small claims court
class action suit

REGISTERING A COMPLAINT

Any number of problems can occur after a purchase. You put a couple of books in the backpack you just bought, and the strap breaks. The sweater you purchased from a catalog finally arrives, but it's not the size and color you ordered. You get your car back from the shop, but the original problem hasn't been fixed, and now the oil is leaking.

In order to register a complaint, you must be able to state the problem clearly. In addition, decide what sort of outcome you desire. Do you want to exchange the faulty backpack, or do you want your money back?

Next, gather up any receipts and product information related to the purchase. If you want to return or exchange an item, be sure you know the store's policies. For example, what reasons for a return are allowed? How long after the purchase can you return an item? Must it be in the original packaging?

Research Activity. Ask students to visit a company's Web site to find out and report on how the company handles complaints.

Critical Thinking. *Ask:* How does taking notes make it more likely that your complaint will be satisfactorily resolved?

Contacting the Merchant

The way in which you make your initial contact with the merchant will depend on the situation. If your complaint is about a service, talk to the person who did the work. If it's about an item purchased in a local store, you might talk to the salesperson who assisted you with the purchase or to an employee at the customer service desk. If you made a purchase over the phone or on the Internet, you may need to contact the merchant by phone or email. The merchant's Web site may provide instructions for what to do if you experience a problem. You might also find information on the Web site that can help you with your problem, such as a list of frequently asked questions (FAQs).

Whatever form of communication you choose, be polite. While frustrating, most problems between consumers and businesses can be resolved fairly easily. Merchants want to keep their customers happy, since satisfied customers result in repeat business and a good reputation. See Figure 1-14.

If your initial contact is by phone, take careful notes. Record the name of the person you spoke with, the date of your conversation, and what actions or remedies were discussed. You may need this record later if there is no action on the problem. Similarly, keep a record if you speak to someone in person but the problem is not resolved on the spot.

If after a reasonable amount of time your problem has not been resolved to your satisfaction, you may need to make a follow-up inquiry. If you initially spoke with a sales clerk or a customer service representative, ask to speak with a manager when you follow up. Continue to be polite as you clearly explain the problem.

1-14

Customers who explain their problem clearly and politely are more likely to receive a satisfactory response. How would you initially approach a merchant if you discovered that a purchase was defective?

Critical Thinking. *Ask:* Would you ever write a letter to compliment a business that provides high-quality goods or services? Why or why not?

Writing a Letter of Complaint

If your first attempts at resolving the problem don't succeed, you may need to write a formal letter of complaint. How you direct your letter will depend on the situation, but typically you might write to the store manager or the customer service department. The letter should be honest, polite, and to the point. An example is shown in Figure 1-15.

Along with your letter, enclose copies—not originals—of your sales receipt and any other supporting documents. Keep copies of the letters you write and those you receive so that you have a record of what has happened in the case.

If you don't receive satisfaction, be persistent. Write to the person again or to someone at a higher level in the company. State all the steps you've taken to solve the problem. Send a copy of your letter to the local office of the Better Business Bureau and the local or state government office responsible for consumer protection.

Discussion. *Ask:* Do you think mediation or arbitration would be a more effective way to resolve disputes? Explain why.

DISPUTE RESOLUTION

If after writing several letters you are still not satisfied, consider using a dispute resolution program. Two types are mediation and arbitration. **Mediation** is a process in which two parties try to resolve a dispute with the help of a neutral third party. The third party, or *mediator*, helps the two sides communicate and work out a solution. If the mediator suggests a remedy, the two sides can choose whether to accept it.

Arbitration is a procedure in which a neutral person or panel listens to both sides of a dispute, weighs the evidence, and reaches a decision. In *binding arbitration*, both parties agree in advance that the arbitrator's decision will be final. Once you decide to participate in binding arbitration, you must abide by the decision. Some types of arbitration are nonbinding, and some are binding on the business but not the consumer. Both mediation and arbitration are less costly alternatives than going to court.

InfoSource

Mediation and Arbitration

The Better Business Bureau provides mediation and arbitration services. To find out what other dispute resolution services are available in your area, contact local or state consumer protection agencies, your state attorney general, trade associations, or local bar associations.

InfoSource. Have students consult one of the sources listed to find dispute resolution services in your area. Have them write a "Yellow Pages" type advertisement for one of the available services.

Class Activity. Have students write a letter of complaint to a store manager or customer service department about a fictitious problem with a product. Instruct them to follow the guidelines provided in Figure 1-15 when writing their letters.

Letter of Complaint

Kim Reilly
4000 W. Hudson Ave.
Beeville, IL 61000

October 2, 20—

Teresa Perez, Store Manager
Electronics Superstore
2030 N. Main St.
Beeville, IL 61000

Dear Ms. Perez:

On September 1, I purchased a Brand X car stereo system, Model no. X1234Q for $204.16 from the Electronics Superstore. It was the display model. I was given the User's Guide and the warranty.

I installed the system in my car and used it for several weeks. However, on September 30, I inserted a CD and the error message "Err 8" was displayed on the LED. I haven't been able to eject the CD from the player. The radio works, but the CD won't play.

I reported the problem to the Electronics Superstore on October 1 and was told by your salesperson Sam Frank that by installing the system myself, I had voided the warranty. The warranty doesn't make such a statement, but Mr. Frank insisted that the store policy supersedes the warranty. He said the store's repair department could fix the system for a minimum charge of $50.00. When I purchased the system, Mr. Frank didn't give me a copy of the store policy.

The system is still under warranty, and I was not informed of the store policy. I ask that the Electronics Superstore either repair the system or replace the system at no charge, including installation by October 30. If either does not occur by then, I will seek third-party assistance. Please contact me at the above address or by phone at (400) 555-5555. Thank you for your assistance.

Sincerely,

Kim Reilly

Kim Reilly

Enc: Photocopies of sales receipt and Brand X warranty

Salutation Address your letter to the appropriate person at the right level.

Opening Identify the product and problem clearly. Give the date and place of purchase, the model number, and the price. Remember to enclose photocopies of receipts and other relevant documents.

Body Explain steps you have taken and how you want the situation to be resolved. Make your request reasonable and polite, not threatening.

Close Set a time for resolution to occur before you will seek other assistance. Be sure to include your address, phone number, and email address if appropriate.

1-15 Follow these tips when writing a letter of complaint. Why should you include copies of your sales receipt and other documentation?

LEGAL ACTION

If all else fails, you may need to take legal action. At this point it's essential to have a written record of all steps taken to resolve the matter, since you must be able to document your case. Your options for legal action include:

- **Small claims court.** In most states, you can take your case to **small claims court**. This is a court of law in which disputes involving sums under a certain amount are resolved by a judge. The monetary limit varies from state to state, but typically

Discussion. *Ask:* When might it be worthwhile to take legal action to settle a consumer dispute? When would it not be worthwhile?

Answer Key. Answers to the Section Review questions are provided in the Section Lesson Plan located in the *Teacher Resource Guide.*

1-16

The judge at small claims court resolves complaints involving relatively small amounts of money. Give an example of a dispute that might be resolved at small claims court.

might be $1,000 or $5,000. The procedural rules in small claims court are less strict than in a normal court, and you don't need a lawyer. Although there is a filing fee, usually it is small. See Figure 1-16.

- **Lawsuit.** Another option is to hire a lawyer and file a lawsuit in regular court. Going to court is expensive and time consuming, but may be worthwhile if your claim is valid and large. If you need the services of a lawyer and can't afford one, check with your local legal aid office. Look in the Yellow Pages under "legal aid" or "legal services."
- **Class action suit.** A lawsuit filed on behalf of a group of people who all have the same complaint is called a **class action suit**. For example, if a particular make and model of automobile is discovered to have faulty brakes, and the manufacturer has been unwilling to resolve the problem, a class action suit against the manufacturer might be filed on behalf of all affected consumers. Rules for bringing class action suits vary in different states.

Section 1.5 Review

CHECK YOUR KNOWLEDGE

1. Describe what type of information to include in a letter of complaint.
2. How are mediation and arbitration different?
3. When would it be appropriate to take a dispute to small claims court?

CONSUMER APPLICATION

Complaint Options Suppose that you feel that an auto body shop which charged you $500 to repair your car did poor work. However, the auto body shop refuses to correct the problem or resolve your complaint. What options are available for resolving your complaint? What factors should you consider when deciding which option to choose?

CHAPTER 1

Review & Activities

CHAPTER SUMMARY

- Consumers have the power to influence the marketplace. You must develop and master skills to be an effective consumer. (1-1)
- As a consumer, you have rights and responsibilities. Laws, agencies, and organizations protect consumers' rights. (1-2)
- Consumers need to protect themselves from identity theft. Technology creates opportunities for the invasion of privacy. (1-3)
- Learn to protect yourself against deception and fraud. To alert other consumers, report cases of deception and fraud. (1-4)
- You can learn to resolve consumer problems effectively. There are many sources of assistance for resolving problems. (1-5)

THE $avvy Consumer

Meeting Online "Friends": Leah enjoys communicating with Madison, whom she "met" in an Internet chat room for teens. They share tastes in music, food, and sports. Madison wrote that her family will be visiting Leah's town and suggested they get together. Is it safe for Leah to meet with Madison? What does Leah *not* know for sure? If she wants to meet Madison in person, who should she talk to first? What safety precautions are essential to take? (1.3)

Reviewing Key Terms and Ideas

1. Summarize the three economic roles that individuals play. (1.1)
2. What is the role of **consumers** in the **marketplace**? (1.1)
3. Describe the impact—both good and bad—of technology on consumers. (1.1)
4. Name and explain six consumer protection laws. (1.2)
5. What is the difference between a **consumer affairs department** and a **consumer action panel**? (1.2)
6. What are the **media** and how do they protect consumers? (1.2)
7. What are four steps you can take to prevent **identify theft**? (1.3)
8. Compare positive and negative effects of **cookies**. (1.3)
9. Why should you purchase only from **secure sites** on the Internet? (1.3)
10. Why is it wise to use an alternate email address for chat rooms? (1.3)
11. Explain how a **pyramid scheme** works. (1.4)
12. What should you do if you receive a **chain letter** asking for money? (1.4)
13. Suppose you buy a DVD player that doesn't work. Explain how you would handle this problem. (1.5)
14. In what circumstances might you consider using **mediation**? (1.5)
15. What are the advantages of taking a problem to **small claims court**? (1.5)

Answer Key. Answers to the Chapter Review & Activities are provided in the Teacher's Manual in the *Teacher Annotated Edition* of the text.

Thinking Critically

1. **Identifying Cause and Effect:** Suppose the teens in your community begin a campaign to save money rather than spend it. How might the lack of teen purchases affect the local marketplace? (1.1)
2. **Analyzing Economic Concepts:** Investigate how consumer spending affects the economy. Why is consumer spending essential for recovery after an economic downturn? (1.1)
3. **Supporting Your Position:** Choose one of the consumer protection laws listed in Figure 1-5. Do you think taxpayer money should be used to provide this protection? Support your argument. (1.2)

Building Consumer Skills

1. **Consumer Skills:** A commercial for exercise equipment has nearly convinced you to order it, particularly since the seller offers an easy payment plan. Discuss how using effective consumer skills can help you decide whether to buy the equipment. (1.1)
2. **Educating Others:** Create an educational pamphlet that explains consumers' rights and responsibilities by providing specific examples of each. (1.2)
3. **Safeguarding Privacy:** Investigate a privacy issue, such as online profiling or cyberstalking. Develop ten guidelines to help teens safeguard their privacy. (1.3)
4. **Fraud and Deception.** Collect advertisements from different sources. Examine the ads, looking for examples of deception or fraud. Describe one ad for the class, explaining your analysis of it. (1.4)
5. **Seeking Redress:** Select a consumer problem you or someone you know has experienced. Outline a plan of action to seek redress. (1.5)
6. **Letter of Complaint:** Write a letter of complaint based on the consumer problem in "Seeking Redress." (1.5)

CONSUMER CONNECTIONS

- **Family:** Talk with family members about practices that put them at risk for identity theft. Based on your discussion, prepare a checklist that members of your family can use to protect themselves. (1.3)
- **Community:** Share examples in class of retailers that have done business in your community for a long time and any that have gone out of business. Discuss what effect consumers may have had upon the success and failure of these businesses. (1.1)

CHAPTER 2

Consumer Management Skills

Reading with Purpose

- Write down the colored headings in this chapter.
- As you read the text under each heading, visualize what you are reading.
- Reflect on what you read by writing a few sentences under each heading to describe it.
- Reread your notes.

SECTION 2.1

Setting Priorities and Goals

As a consumer, what kind of future life do you envision for yourself? A comfortable place to live, the latest gadgets, exotic travel? The quality of your life—whether it's dreamy or disappointing—will depend on you. The ability to set priorities and goals can help.

Objectives

After studying this section, you should be able to:

- Analyze how needs, wants, values, and standards affect priorities and goals.
- Distinguish between different types of goals.
- Explain guidelines for setting and reaching goals.

Key Terms

priorities
needs
wants
values
standards
goals
family life cycle

WHAT'S MOST IMPORTANT?

The choices you make as a consumer depend in part on your **priorities**—your judgments about the relative importance of alternatives. In other words, what's most important to you? Priorities affect many types of decisions—how to spend and save your money, which products and services to buy, what career path to follow. To better understand where your priorities come from, it helps to look at the interrelated concepts of needs, wants, values, and standards.

Needs and Wants

If you were marooned on a deserted island, what would you wish for? A diary to chronicle your adventures? A mountain bike to climb sand dunes? Your favorite beach towel? Chances are, you'd desire basic stuff—water and food to sustain you; shelter and clothing to protect you

Class Activity. Write the word *success* in the middle of the board. Ask students what they associate with success, and list their ideas on the board. Then have students vote on which aspects of success are most important. Use the results to come up with a general definition of success.

from the elements. These are **needs**, things you must have in order to live. The diary, bike, and beach towel are **wants**—things you desire but that are not necessary to live. Everyone has similar needs, but wants vary from person to person.

Needs must be met before wants, so distinguishing between them is the first step in setting priorities. The difference between needs and wants is clear when the backdrop is a deserted island. It's not always so clear in everyday life. A need can be met in many different ways—food can be pizza, barbecue, tacos, or hundreds of other possibilities. Your choice will depend on your wants as well as your needs. In fact, consumer choices are seldom, if ever, based on needs alone. See Figure 2-1.

Values

Values are strongly held beliefs and principles about what is worthwhile. Most people share a core set of common values. They include honesty, respect, kindness, courtesy, and fairness. These values lead you to balance your own needs and wants with those of others.

Values can vary based on culture, religious beliefs, family upbringing, and other factors. For example, some cultures tend to value cooperation more highly than individual achievement, while in other cultures the opposite is true. Within the same culture, such things as education, comfort, and economy might be more highly valued by some people than others. The values you hold strongly affect the priorities you set.

Standards

People who share the same values may have very different standards. **Standards** are established levels of quality or quantity to measure against. For instance, most people value success rather than failure—but what is success? The standard is different for everyone. To one person, success means building up a certain amount of wealth. For someone else, success is reaching a position of leadership in a profession or in the community. Others might define success as doing interesting and enjoyable work, maintaining strong ties with family and friends, or making a contribution to society that feels personally meaningful.

Setting Priorities

Needs, wants, values, and standards all enter into the process of establishing priorities. Members of one family may decide that

2-1

A car is a transportation need for many families. Which car to buy depends on a family's wants. What are some of the wants that might influence this purchasing decision?

Critical Thinking. ***Ask:*** Suppose you had a long-term goal to attend a specific college. What short-term goals might help you reach this long-term goal?

this year, saving up for college expenses takes priority over replacing their old car. To make this decision, they consider both the value they place on education and their standards about what kind of car is acceptable to drive. In another family, buying a car may be a higher priority, since a reliable car is needed for the sales job that is a major source of income. You and your family must set your own priorities.

The priorities of individuals and families change over time. As you pass through different stages of your life span—from your teen years to early, middle, and late adulthood—your changing priorities will affect the decisions you make.

GOALS: TARGETS FOR ACTION

By setting priorities, you identify what's important to you. By setting **goals**—targets for what you want to accomplish—you begin to translate your priorities into action. Goals give you direction. They help you focus on the things you want to achieve and take the necessary steps to make them a reality. See Figure 2-2.

Types of Goals

Goals can be short-term or long-term, depending on how long they'll take to accomplish. A short-term goal may be to save up for a pair of boots you've been admiring. A long-term goal might be to pursue a career in medical technology.

Team Activity. Have students work in groups to create collages illustrating typical goals for a person or family at a particular stage of the life cycle.

Sometimes a long-term goal that looks overwhelming just needs to be broken down into short-term goals. If saving up enough money to buy a computer seems impossible, try putting aside a certain amount from each paycheck. Over time, you'll meet your larger goal.

How Goals Change

Your goals change as you do. For example, many people change careers several times. Each time, they set new goals and let go of old ones.

Goals vary throughout the **family life cycle**—the series of stages through which a family passes. Each family is different, and not all families go through the same stages in the same order. However, many families experience stages such as the beginning of a marriage, the birth of children, the parenting years, the time when children leave home, and retirement.

2-2

The goal of reaching the summit is what keeps a mountain climber going through many difficulties. How can goals motivate you to do your best?

Discussion. ***Ask:*** What factors might make it difficult to achieve a goal you had set? What could you do to overcome these difficulties?

People in similar life stages may have similar goals. Families in the beginning stage often have financial goals related to career advancement, paying off debts, and establishing a home. Parents focus on providing for their children. Health care and retirement planning become increasingly important priorities in later years.

Achieving Goals

If you've ever failed to keep a New Year's resolution, you know that achieving a goal is a lot harder than setting one. Here are some strategies that can help you reach your goals.

Class Activity. Have students interpret this statement: "The road to success is almost always under construction."

2-3

People who achieve goals aren't stopped by the hurdles in their way. They are determined to get past them. Give an example of a hurdle you surmounted to meet a goal.

Answer Key. Answers to the Section Review questions are provided in the Section Lesson Plan located in the *Teacher Resource Guide.*

- **Set goals with care.** Well-chosen goals reflect your priorities. They should also be realistic—a goal that can't possibly be met is discouraging. Avoid setting goals that are too easy, though. Goals should challenge you to take a risk and to stretch and grow.
- **Prepare to deal with difficulties.** Expect obstacles, but don't let them stop you in your tracks. Anticipate problems and think of solutions. For example, if you're saving up for a future purchase, avoid hanging out in malls where you'll be tempted to spend. See Figure 2-3.
- **Enlist the support of others.** If your goal is to improve your math grade, join a study group or ask your teacher to refer you to a tutor.
- **Acknowledge your successes and failures.** If you meet your goal, you can feel good about your accomplishment. If you don't achieve a goal, learn from your mistakes.

Section 2.1 Review

CHECK YOUR UNDERSTANDING

1. What is the difference between wants and needs?
2. What do people consider when determining their priorities?
3. What strategies can help you reach goals?

CONSUMER APPLICATION

Identifying Goals Name one of your priorities. Describe one or more goals that relate to this priority. Identify whether they are short-term or long-term goals.

SECTION 2.2

Managing Limited Resources

Think about a goal that you successfully achieved. How did you go about reaching it? Whether you realized it or not, you did it by managing your resources.

Objectives

After studying this section, you should be able to:

- Identify types of resources.
- Explain the relationship between scarcity and opportunity cost.
- Describe strategies for managing resources.

Key Terms

resources
scarcity
opportunity cost
bartering
management
procrastinate

TYPES OF RESOURCES

Resources include anything that is useful or helpful in the process of achieving goals or solving problems. Many types of resources are available to you as a consumer.

- **Human resources** are those found within people. They include personal energy, knowledge, experience, skills, talents, and qualities such as imagination and determination.
- **Time** is a resource as well. By making the best use of the time you have, you can accomplish more than you may have thought possible.
- **Financial resources** have to do with money. Income, savings, investments, and credit are among the financial resources that can help you reach goals.
- **Material and technological resources** include useful items such as food, clothing, a home, books, tools, appliances, cars, telephones, computers, and the Internet.

TEXTLINK

Resources that societies use to produce goods and services are discussed in Sections 5.1 and 5.2.

Class Activity. Ask students to make a graphic organizer illustrating the various types of resources available to them.

Community Activity. Have students use local bulletin boards, Web sites, or phone listings to make a list of resources found in their community.

- **Community resources** are provided by governments and private organizations. Agencies such as the Red Cross, for example, provide assistance to people in need. Other community resources include police and fire departments, hospitals, public transportation, parks and recreational facilities, community centers, churches, schools, libraries, and museums. See Figure 2-4.
- **Natural resources** include air, water, trees, and minerals. Everyone who benefits from these resources shares in the responsibility to use them wisely, as explained in Section 3.3.

SCARCITY AND OPPORTUNITY COST

While consumers' wants are often unlimited, their resources are not. Economists talk about the problem of **scarcity**—the fact that because of limited resources, an economic system can't possibly produce all the goods and services that people want. Therefore, choices must be made about how the limited resources will be used. You'll learn more about this concept in Chapter 5.

The concept of scarcity refers to societies, but it's an idea that consumers can personally relate to. If you had an infinite amount of time and money, what would you spend them on? You can probably come up with a very long list. Unfortunately, you don't have unlimited resources—no one does. Therefore, you must set priorities.

As you decide which items on your "wish list" are most important, you also decide—consciously or not—to cross other items off the list. You give up some wants in order to fulfill others. Economists have a term for what you give up when you decide to use resources one way rather than another. They call it **opportunity cost**.

Suppose you have $100 to spend on clothes. You have your eye on shoes that cost $90, jeans that cost $40, and a jacket that costs $55. If you buy the shoes, you won't have enough money left over to buy anything else. The opportunity cost of the shoes is whatever you think the next best choice would have been—either the jeans and the jacket *or* two pairs of jeans.

All decisions involve opportunity cost. It may be measured in time, energy, or some other resource besides money. If you join the

2-4

The benefits provided by community resources such as libraries are sometimes taken for granted. What community resources have you used in the last week? Would you have been able to accomplish your goals without them?

Team Activity. Have students work in small groups. Ask each group to brainstorm a list of ways that students could expand, conserve, substitute, or exchange resources while preparing for the senior prom. Have them apply the strategies to such needs as clothing, transportation, and so on.

swim team, which has after-school practices, part of the opportunity cost is the time you might have spent hanging out with your friends after school. If you decide to be with your friends, you give up the opportunity to be on the swim team. Weigh decisions in terms of opportunity cost to focus on what's most important to you.

USING RESOURCES EFFECTIVELY

Since resources are limited, it's a good idea to increase their benefit by using them wisely.

- **Expand resources.** In some cases, you can take steps to increase the resources available to you. For instance, paying attention in class can increase your knowledge. Putting money in a savings account instead of a shoebox means it will grow as it earns interest.
- **Conserve resources.** Using less, or conserving, makes limited resources last longer. There are many examples. Turning off lights when they're not needed saves electricity and money. Combining several errands in one trip saves time and energy. Buying a used car instead of a new one saves money, and proper care will help the car last longer. See Figure 2-5.
- **Substitute resources.** When some of your resources are in short supply, look for ways to use others to accomplish the same goal. Suppose you don't have enough money to buy your friend a birthday present. You could make one instead, using time, personal energy, skills, and creativity. When you lack time and personal energy, you might substitute money or technological resources, such as a computer, to accomplish a goal.
- **Exchange resources.** Sharing resources with someone else is another option. When his vacuum cleaner quits working, your neighbor asks to borrow yours. In return, he gives you a container of homemade soup. **Bartering**, which means exchanging goods or services with another person, makes it possible to satisfy needs and wants without spending money.

Jump$tart. Ask students to evaluate the opportunity costs of the following choices: spending a day at the beach; buying a new pair of athletic shoes; getting an after-school job. Ask them whether they think the choice is worth the opportunity costs in each case. *(Money Management)*

2-5

Resources are limited and must be preserved. How does proper maintenance conserve resources?

Critical Thinking. *Ask:* Which step in the management process do you think is the most important? Explain why.

Dollars and Sense. As a class, brainstorm a list of things many people assume they "need" that they could actually live without.

DOLLARS and SENSE

Living Simply

Another way to use resources wisely is simply to do without some things. For example, instead of living in the most expensive place they can afford and filling it up with gadgets, some people prefer a modest, uncluttered home. They may do without cable television, cut back on magazine subscriptions, and use public transportation instead of automobiles. In addition to saving money, consumers who choose a simpler way of life often feel they reap other benefits, such as reduced stress and more free time.

MANAGEMENT SKILLS

The strategies you've just read about are examples of good **management**, the process of using resources effectively to reach goals. By developing management skills, you can get the most out of the resources that are available to you, your family, or groups to which you belong.

The Management Process

When trying to reach a goal, many people follow a four-step management process. The same process can be used whether you are managing time, energy, money, or other resources.

1. **Planning.** Begin by taking a look at the situation. What is your goal? What problems must be solved? Identify the resources that are available and brainstorm ways to use them effectively. Start a list of the tasks that must be accomplished. Which ones have highest priority?
2. **Organizing.** Put the steps you must take to reach your goal in sequential order. Make a schedule, setting a target date or time for the completion of each step. Gather your resources and get them ready to use. Obtain any personal and legal documents you may need. If other people will be involved in your plan or affected by it, communicate with them and coordinate your efforts.
3. **Implementing.** To *implement* your plan means to carry it out. Follow the schedule you set for achieving the goal. Track your progress—for example, check off steps as they are completed. If necessary, adjust your plan as circumstances change or as you encounter setbacks.
4. **Evaluating.** After implementing your plan, evaluate how well it worked. Did you reach your goal? Are you satisfied with the result? What problems developed along the way? What did you learn from this experience?

Managing Money

As a consumer, one of the most important resources for you to manage is money. Developing money management skills helps families live within their income, get the most value for what they spend, achieve financial goals, gain a sense of financial security, and build for the future. Later chapters provide advice for handling the elements of money management, including:

Research Activity. Challenge students to adopt one of the stragegies listed here for managing time and energy. Have them keep a log for one week, indicating which strategy they chose and recording the results. Invite them to share their results with the class.

- Estimating income and making a spending plan.
- Paying taxes and keeping financial records.
- Using banking services and managing the use of credit.
- Saving and investing to meet long-term and short-term goals.
- Buying insurance protection.
- Shopping for the best buys on goods and services.

Managing Time and Energy

Like any other resources, time and personal energy can be planned and managed. Here are some strategies:

- **Stay focused.** Identify your priorities and goals. Make time for activities that support them.
- **Identify time wasters.** Do you spend hours browsing aimlessly on the Internet, talking on the phone, or watching reruns? These activities probably don't enrich your life or fulfill your goals. Identify time wasters, then either eliminate them or set limits.
- **Get organized.** How much time and energy do you waste looking for misplaced items? Take time to organize your closet, locker, and desk. The payoff is more time and less frustration.
- **Plan ahead.** Use a planner or assignment book. Write down assignments and due dates, your work schedule, appointments, and other commitments. See Figure 2-6.
- **Make to-do lists.** Each day, make a list of what you need or want to accomplish. Consult the list throughout the day and check off items as you complete them.
- **Take action.** A to-do list does no good if you **procrastinate**, or put off taking action. If a task seems overwhelming, identify one small step you can take to get started. Then do it.

2-6

What time was my time management seminar, anyway? Using a planner—print or electronic—can save time and reduce frustration.

Critical Thinking. ***Ask:*** What are some different ways you might put your free time to productive use? **Discussion.** ***Ask:*** Which influences on management are generally positive? Which are negative? What steps might you take to control negative influences?

- **Make use of free time.** If you're going to spend time standing in line or riding the bus, take along a reading assignment or an interesting article.
- **Value other people's time.** If you agree to meet at a certain time, be there so the other person doesn't have to wait. When you notice that someone is concentrating on a task, try not to distract or interrupt. Your consideration will be appreciated.

2-7 **Just getting out the door in the morning can be a challenge for busy families. What other challenges do working parents face? What resources might be helpful to them?**

Answer Key. Answers to the Section Review questions are provided in the Section Lesson Plan located in the *Teacher Resource Guide.*

Influences on Management

Social and economic trends can affect how consumers manage time, energy, and money. For example, the increase in the number of working parents is a trend that creates challenges for managing a household. See Figure 2-7. In addition, the population is increasingly mobile. That makes it more likely that relatives such as grandparents, aunts, and uncles—who might have served as a resource by offering help with child care, for example—live across the country instead of across town. Families and communities must recognize these and other challenges, identify resources that can help, and use them to the fullest.

Section 2.2 Review

CHECK YOUR UNDERSTANDING

1. Describe three types of resources.
2. Explain the problem of scarcity and how it results in opportunity cost.
3. What are the steps of a management plan?

CONSUMER APPLICATION

Identifying Opportunity Cost Browse print or online catalogs to identify three items you would like to purchase that cost less than $150. Identify the opportunity cost for each item. Based on opportunity cost, which item would you choose to buy? Explain your decision.

SECTION 2.3

Making Consumer Decisions

As a consumer, you make dozens of decisions every day. How you make those choices affects the quality of your life and whether or not you satisfy your goals. Examining the way you make decisions can help you to be a more effective consumer.

Objectives

After studying this section, you should be able to:

- Describe the importance of making planned decisions.
- Explain decision-making steps.
- Analyze factors that influence consumer decisions.

Key Terms

impulse purchase
fads
status symbols
conspicuous consumption

HOW DO YOU DECIDE?

Chances are, some of your consumer decisions are made without much thought. A purchase made on a whim, without planning, is called an **impulse purchase**. Marketers encourage impulse purchases. For instance, they design brightly colored, appealing packages and position eye-catching displays near the checkout counter.

Making a small impulse purchase once in a while is not a problem. In fact, sometimes it's smart, such as when you unexpectedly find a needed item on sale. However, when it happens too often or for major purchases, buying on impulse often results in overspending.

Another way of making consumer decisions is on the basis of habit. People get into the habit of buying a certain product or shopping at a certain store. Habit is not necessarily a poor basis for decision making. Used for minor or routine purchases, it can simplify your life. At times, however, habit can keep you from considering other possibilities that may be better.

Discussion. *Ask:* What types of products are you most likely to buy on impulse? How do these kinds of purchases affect your spending?

Point Out. Recreational shopping—shopping without a purpose or a list—often leads to impulse purchases.

What's the alternative? Instead of letting impulse or habit guide your choices, base your consumer decisions on thought and planning. Planned decisions are more likely to bring positive results. Making successful decisions not only helps you reach your goals, but also gives you a sense of control and self-confidence.

DECISION-MAKING STEPS

When faced with a complex decision, it's sometimes hard to know where to start. Following these seven steps can help you make informed, rational choices.

1. **Identify the decision.** What's the issue or problem? What are your goals for the outcome? Who else needs to be involved in making this decision?
2. **Identify resources and collect information.** Take stock of your resources that relate to the situation. For instance, how much time and money can you spend? Also consider what types of information would help you make this decision. Then get the facts from reliable sources.
3. **Identify the options.** List as many possible solutions as you can. The more options you think of, the more likely it is that you'll find a satisfying solution. See Figure 2-8.
4. **Weigh the options.** Think about the pros and cons of each option. How well does it meet your goals? What consequences will it have for you and others?
5. **Choose the best option.** After weighing all the options, choose the one that seems best based on everything you've considered. Keep in mind that there may not be a perfect solution. However, if no option seems acceptable, go over the preceding steps again.
6. **Take action.** Once you've made your choice, carry it out. Making a decision without acting on it accomplishes nothing.
7. **Evaluate the decision.** Ask yourself whether you got the results you expected. How did your decision affect others? What might you do differently next time? If you made a poor choice, accept responsibility and learn from it.

2-8

Starting with a list of possible solutions and then narrowing your options will help you make effective decisions.

Class Activity. Ask students to think of a decision they have made recently. Have them write a report explaining what factors influenced this decision.

FACTORS AFFECTING CONSUMER DECISIONS

Decisions are not made in a vacuum. Many factors come into play and influence the choices you make. Some influence your decision making directly; others shape the world within which you act as a consumer. Becoming aware of these factors will help you make better decisions.

- **Personal factors.** You've already learned that needs, wants, values, and standards affect your priorities and goals, and therefore your decisions. Your physical and emotional state is also a factor. Being tired, hungry, or bored, for example, can lead you to spend more money or make different consumer choices than you would otherwise.

Discussion. *Ask:* What are some popular status symbols? What kind of message might people be trying to send by owning these things?

- **Family factors.** Family customs and lifestyles affect financial priorities and decisions. Family size and stage of life have impact, too. For example, young couples with no children make different financial decisions than families with children and retired couples. See Figure 2-9. Adults in families often work together to reach agreement and choose what is best for all. Sometimes parents teach children and teens about making financial choices by involving them in certain decisions.
- **Culture.** Consumer decisions can also be influenced by culture. Traditions, religious beliefs, family roles, language and communication styles, and other cultural factors might lead one family to make different consumer choices than another.
- **Social factors.** People often make consumer choices to fit in with a group. They can be influenced by **fads**—interests, products, or styles that people take up with exaggerated enthusiasm for a brief time. On the other hand, sometimes consumers want to stand out from the crowd. Social factors lead some people to acquire **status symbols**, possessions or activities by which social or economic prestige is measured. Depending on the group, status symbols can range from a certain brand of athletic shoes to expensive cars, jewelry, and vacation homes. Another term for this type of consumer behavior is **conspicuous consumption**, purchasing goods or services to impress others.

2-9

Stage of life affects purchasing decisions. This young family needs a range for their first new home. What other items might they need?

Critical Thinking. ***Ask:*** In what ways can advances in technology be beneficial to consumers? In what ways can they be harmful?

- **Societal and demographic factors.** Consumer decisions are affected by trends in society. Examples include increased mobility, longer work hours, and the movement of people and jobs from urban centers to outlying areas. Another factor is demographic trends. *Demographic* refers to population statistics. For instance, the average age of the population is increasing, and the number of single-person households is rising. Both societal and demographic factors can affect the way consumers earn, save, and spend money.

- **Economic factors.** Financial resources, such as income level, clearly affect consumer decisions. In addition, so does the economic outlook on a local and national level. Even economic conditions on the other side of the world can affect U.S. consumers and businesses.

- **Technology.** Advances in technology impact consumers in many ways. New or improved products and services—such as powerful computers, dirt-repellent fabrics, and more accurate medical tests—can benefit consumers by improving their quality of life. Technological breakthroughs sometimes make it possible to produce goods at lower cost, saving consumers money. On the other hand, consumers may be tempted to spend more as they feed their desire for increasingly sophisticated gadgets. Technological advances such as Internet shopping can change the way that buyers and sellers interact to do business. Some innovations, such as genetically engineered foods, raise complex issues that consumers must confront.

- **Media.** Through print, sound, and images, the media are an ever-present influence on consumer consciousness. Ranging from expert advice to advertising, information presented by the media exerts a profound influence on consumers' decisions about what, when, where, and how much to purchase.

Answer Key. Answers to the Section Review questions are provided in the Section Lesson Plan located in the *Teacher Resource Guide.*

- **The marketplace.** Slick and sophisticated advertising and promotional methods compete for consumers' attention, as do attractive packaging and the allure of products themselves. Often, the marketplace creates consumer desire for goods and services that may not be needed.

- **Legal and moral factors.** Government laws and regulations, such as those dictating product safety and banking practices, protect consumers and provide them with information upon which to base sound purchasing decisions. Being a responsible consumer might involve refusing to buy from companies that exploit workers, animals, or the environment.

Section 2.3 Review

CHECK YOUR UNDERSTANDING

1. Why should you avoid making impulse purchases?
2. Describe the steps of the decision-making process.
3. Choose three factors that affect consumer decisions and explain their impact.

CONSUMER APPLICATION

Purchasing Decision Think of a specific purchase you would like to make now or in the future. Apply the decision-making process to that purchase by describing how you would carry out each step.

SECTION 2.4

Evaluating Information Sources

Information is the basis of all consumer decisions. Wise consumers know how to think critically, where to find reliable consumer information, and how to use it effectively.

Objectives

After studying this section, you should be able to:

- Evaluate the reliability of information sources.
- Identify sources of consumer information.
- Explain ways to use consumer information effectively.

Key Terms

critical thinking
credentials
bias

THINKING CRITICALLY

Do you believe everything you read and hear? Smart consumers examine information carefully before deciding whether to accept it as true. Making judgments about the reliability of information requires skill in critical thinking. **Critical thinking** means applying reasoning strategies in order to make sound decisions. These strategies include evaluating information sources, distinguishing between fact and opinion, and drawing conclusions.

EVALUATING INFORMATION

Keeping up with constantly changing information can be a challenge for consumers. Sometimes you may seek out consumer information, as when researching a major purchase. Other times you simply come across information—you might see a product demonstrated on TV or pick up a magazine with an article about investments. No matter how you obtain consumer information, evaluate it carefully before allowing it to influence your judgment.

Jump$tart. Have students find an ad or a consumer article and evaluate the information in it using the questions listed. *(Saving & Investing)*

Reliable information can help you make better consumer decisions. Unreliable information could steer you in the wrong direction—perhaps even leading you to be taken in by fraud. To determine the reliability of information you encounter, ask yourself these questions.

- **What is the source of the information?** It's not enough to say that you read it in a magazine, saw it on TV, or found it on the Internet. Look for an identification of the actual source. For example, who wrote the article? Does the author cite specific sources of information? What person or group runs the Web site? Be wary of information that seems anonymous.
- **What authority or expertise does the source have?** Anyone can create a Web site, claim to be an expert, or make up a name for a nonexistent organization. Look for signs that the source is legitimate. If an organization is unfamiliar to you, find out more about it. If an individual is cited as an information source, look

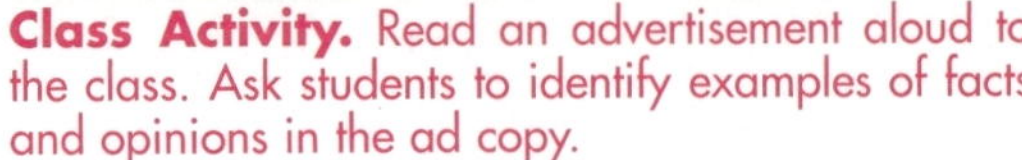

Class Activity. Read an advertisement aloud to the class. Ask students to identify examples of facts and opinions in the ad copy.

for details about his or her background. In many fields, legitimate experts have **credentials**—licenses, certifications, or degrees that indicate knowledge and experience in a certain subject area. For example, the letters "M.D." after a name indicate that the person has a Doctor of Medicine degree. Consider whether a source's credentials are relevant to the type of information being offered. See Figure 2-10.

- **Is the source biased? Bias** is a preference that might prevent impartial judgment. It can sometimes be created by a financial or business interest. For example, many magazines run product reviews. The writers and editors do their best to provide fair and accurate information. However, because most magazines depend on money from advertisers, the product reviews might be biased toward making favorable comments about an advertiser's products. Advertising itself is a biased source of information because its purpose is to sell a product.
- **Is the information fact or opinion?** "This computer is easy to use" is someone's opinion. In contrast, "People who buy this computer are entitled to toll-free telephone support for one year" is a factual statement.

Point Out. Magazines sometimes run advertisements dressed up to look like unbiased articles. Only the words "special advertising section," usually in very small letters at the top, identify them as ads.

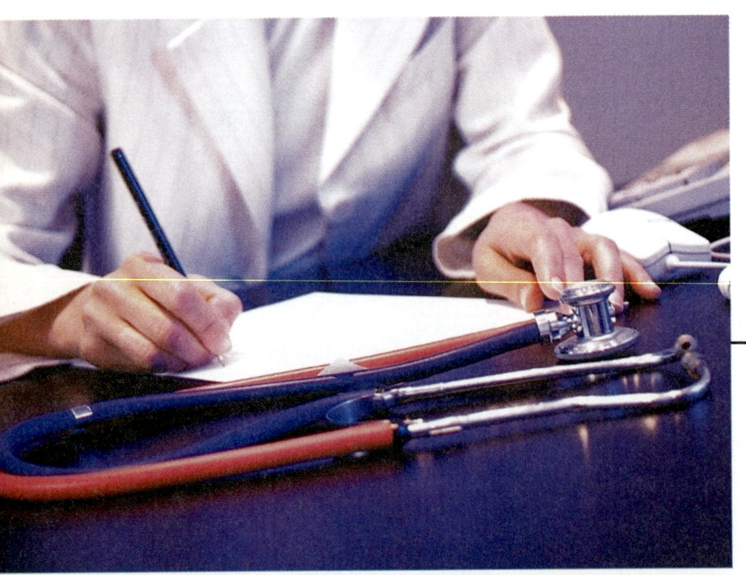

2-10

It takes more than wearing a white coat or using the title "Dr." to be a reliable medical expert. For what types of information would you consider a medical doctor to be a reliable source?

Research Activity. Challenge students to collect three news articles that report the results of research studies. Have students evaluate whether each article seems to be oversimplifying the study results. Have them follow up by reading one of the studies and comparing it to what was reported in the article.

Often, consumer information includes a mixture of fact and opinion. It's up to you to recognize the difference.

- **How can I confirm the information?** If information is factual, try to confirm it by checking other sources. Even if the information was accurate at one time, it might be out of date.
- **Is it suspicious?** Does the "special investment opportunity" promise to make you rich with no risk or effort on your part? Is the "miraculous" weight loss product supposed to melt away pounds while you eat as much as you want? Remember, if something seems too good to be true, it probably is. Review the warning signs of deception and fraud listed on page 43.

Research Studies

Sometimes an article, ad, or news report cites scientific research—for example, "A recent study shows that..." The mention of a scientific study tends to lend an air of authority to information. However, you should think critically about research studies, just as you would about other sources.

Look for an explanation of who conducted the research. What are their scientific credentials? Who paid for the study? If a study on preventing gum disease was sponsored by a toothpaste company, you should consider the possibility that the study was biased.

Often, headlines and news reports oversimplify the results of studies. Look for details about how the study was conducted. Remember, too, that suggesting a possible link between two factors—such as a food and a disease—is not the same as proving cause and effect. In any case, scientists know that one study is not enough to prove or disprove any theory. The results must be verified by the work of other researchers. See Figure 2-11.

SOURCES OF CONSUMER INFORMATION

Whether you realize it or not, you're surrounded by sources of consumer information. All can be useful in different ways. Turn to sources that are appropriate for the kind of information you're looking for.

Class Activity. Have students write statements related to information in the chapter, making at least one factual and another opinion. Ask each student to read one statement aloud, and have the class determine whether it's fact or opinion, and why.

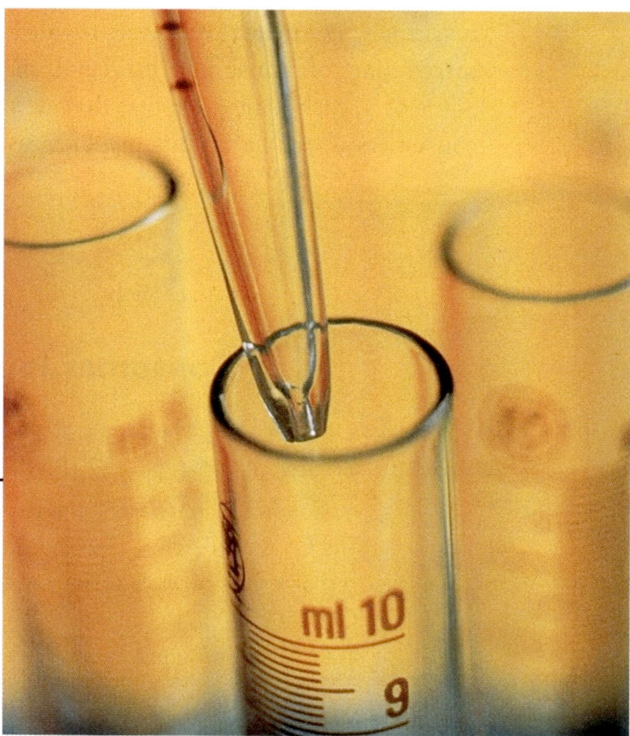

2-11

Legitimate researchers publish information about their studies in reputable scientific journals. Other scientists then review their methods and try to duplicate the results. **Why is this process essential?**

InfoSource. Have students research a consumer topic, using the three sources listed, and compare the information available from each source.

- **Consumer protection agencies and organizations.** Many of the sources of consumer protection described in Section 1.2 are also reliable sources of consumer information. These include government agencies such as the Federal Trade Commission, the Federal Consumer Information Center, and your state attorney general's office; consumer groups such as the National Consumers League; consumer testing agencies and publications such as Consumers Union and *Consumer Reports*; and the Better Business Bureau.
- **Professional advisors.** Some people hire professionals to advise them on financial matters such as taxes, insurance, and investments. It's important to make sure that any advisors you work with have the proper credentials and are worthy of your trust. Guidelines for choosing a qualified financial professional are explained in Section 9.5.
- **Media sources.** TV, radio, newspapers, magazines, and media Web sites provide a mixed bag of consumer information. Some of it, such as news reports that alert consumers about hazardous products, is reliable and even essential. Some articles and programs focus on opinion rather than fact, and information from some sources may be biased or unreliable.

Discussion. *Ask:* Can you recall any situations in which a salesperson provided you with useful information about a product?

- **Package information.** Labels and package inserts often identify what a product is made of and give directions for using it properly. As you'll learn in Section 16.2, some products and services come with guarantees or warranties. Studying this information carefully can help you to choose products that are right for you and to get the most out of your purchases.
- **Advertising.** Advertisements and other marketing materials can keep you up to date on available products and help you compare prices, features, and services. Remember, however, that advertising is biased toward persuading you to buy. Section 15.2 will help you learn to distinguish between persuasive and informative messages in ads.
- **Salespeople.** If you have questions about a product, salespeople and customer service representatives can often help. However, some salespeople are more knowledgeable than others. Some may be

InfoSource

Consumer Information

Check out these reliable sources of free or low-cost consumer information.

- A Web site called FirstGov for Consumers is a gateway to online consumer information from the federal government.
- The Consumer Action Handbook provides advice and a directory of consumer resources. It's availble online or by mail from The Federal Consumer Information Center.
- The FCIC's Consumer Information Catalog lists hundreds of publications of interest to consumers.

Critical Thinking. *Ask:* Would you base a purchasing decision solely on another consumer's opinion? Why or why not?

more interested in making a sale than in providing accurate information.

- **Other consumers.** You may want to seek an informed opinion from consumers who have used a particular product or service. You might talk to a friend about his new camera, or ask a family member to recommend an auto mechanic. Some Web sites let you view product ratings and comments that have been posted by dozens or hundreds of people. Keep in mind, though, that other consumers might not have the same needs, wants, and standards as you.

2-12 **Make efficient use of the consumer information that's available to you. How has the Internet made product research easier? More difficult?**

Answer Key. Answers to the Section Review questions are provided in the Section Lesson Plan located in the *Teacher Resource Guide.*

USING INFORMATION EFFECTIVELY

Information isn't of much value unless you put it to use. Depending on the situation, you might use consumer information to shop for a product or service, plan your finances, resolve a problem with a merchant, steer clear of fraudulent offers, or in any number of other ways.

Organizing the information you find can help you make better use of it. For example, if you've done some research on several competing products, you might list the pros and cons of each or make a table comparing their features. You could put your list or table in a file folder along with product ratings, advertisements, and a list of questions you want to ask salespeople. Refer to this information when you shop.

The amount of information available on some topics may seem almost limitless. It's impossible to take it all in. Gather as many facts and opinions as you need, then make a choice and take action. See Figure 2-12.

Section 2.4 Review

CHECK YOUR UNDERSTANDING

1. Why do consumers need critical thinking skills?
2. Describe three sources of consumer information.
3. Name two ways you can use consumer information effectively.

CONSUMER APPLICATION

Information Search Suppose you're researching music systems for a future purchase. Where would you look for information and why? Explain how you would evaluate the reliability of the information you find.

CHAPTER 2

Review & Activities

CHAPTER SUMMARY

- Needs, wants, values, and standards affect priorities and goals. Goals give you a sense of direction and help you achieve what's important to you. (2.1)
- You can increase the benefit you get from limited resources by using them effectively. Developing management strategies will help you get the most out of your resources. (2.2)
- A variety of personal, social, economic, and other factors influence consumer decisions. Using decision-making steps will help you make informed consumer choices. (2.3)
- Consumers have access to numerous sources of information about products and services. Consumer information should be evaluated to determine whether it's reliable. (2.4)

THE $avvy Consumer

Recommendation From a Friend: Dan needs a new computer monitor. His friend Anthony recommended the model he just bought, adding, "If you give them my name and buy a monitor, I'll get 20 percent off my next buy." Dan likes the monitor but has not taken time to shop around. Why might Dan feel pressure to follow Anthony's recommendation? How can Dan use resources to make the best buying decision? What should he say to Anthony? (2.4)

Reviewing Key Terms and Ideas

1. Why do you need to distinguish between **needs** and **wants** when setting **priorities**? (2.1)
2. How do your **values** and **standards** shape the **goals** you set? (2.1)
3. Give an example of a long-term goal and a short-term goal. (2.1)
4. What is the relationship between **scarcity** and **opportunity cost**? (2.2)
5. Give an example of a limited **resource** and suggest steps for managing it. (2.2)
6. What are four strategies for managing time and energy? (2.2)
7. How can making planned consumer decisions help you obtain better value for the money you spend? (2.3)
8. Identify the last step of the decision-making process and explain why it is important. (2.3)
9. Why do different families make different financial decisions? (2.3)
10. Describe factors that encourage **conspicuous consumption** by the purchase of **status symbols.** (2.3)
11. How can **critical thinking** help a consumer detect **bias** in an information source? (2.4)
12. Name four sources of written consumer information and identify those that are most likely to be biased. (2.4)
13. Why is it a good idea to take your product research information with you when you shop? (2.4)

Answer Key. Answers to the Chapter Review & Activities are provided in the Teacher's Manual in the *Teacher Annotated Edition* of the text.

Thinking Critically

1. **Analyzing Economic Concepts:** Give two examples of decisions you made recently that involved the use of time or money. What was the opportunity cost of each decision? Did you factor in the opportunity cost when you made these choices? (2.2)
2. **Identifying Alternatives:** Suppose a young single person is laid off from a job and has to live off limited savings for a few weeks. Identify ways to conserve and substitute resources to get through the period. (2.2)
3. **Understanding Cause and Effect:** In what positive and negative ways do advances in technology affect consumer decisions? (2.3)

Building Consumer Skills

1. **Achieving Goals:** In writing identify one of your long- or short-term goals. Explain how it reflects your needs, wants, values, standards, and priorities. Then write an action plan to achieve the goal, including tasks, timelines, resources needed, and barriers anticipated. (2.1, 2.2)
2. **Decision Making:** Ask members of your family to identify items they would like to buy if they could spend about $100. As a family, follow the steps of the decision-making process to agree, hypothetically, on which item to buy. Think about the process. How did shared decision making work for your family? (2.3)
3. **Influences on Teens:** List several categories of purchases you and many teens make on a regular basis, such as snacks and tickets to events. For each category, list factors that affect the choices. Rank them according to how much you think each factor influences teen consumer decisions. Compare your list with those of other classmates. (2.3)
4. **Evaluating Criteria:** Create a list of criteria to use in evaluating consumer information. With your class, narrow the list to the ten most important. Post the criteria in the classroom for use throughout the course. (2.4)

CONSUMER CONNECTIONS

- **Family:** With your family, write down some of the members' personal short-term and long-term goals. Discuss ways the entire family can be involved in achieving these goals. (2.1)
- **Community:** With a group of classmates, poll community members about how to use limited funds to support community resources. Interview at least ten teens and ten adults. Ask: (a) Which services or facilities should receive more money? (b) Which should receive less money? Create a chart to show your results in percentages. Compare your results with those of other groups. (2.2)

CHAPTER 3

Responsible Choices

SECTION 3.1
Consumer Ethics

SECTION 3.2
Responsible Citizenship

SECTION 3.3
Environmental Awareness

Reading with Purpose

- As you read this chapter, create an outline using the colored headings.
- Write a question for each heading to help guide your reading.
- Write the answer to each question as you read the chapter.
- Ask your teacher to help with answers you cannot find in the text.

SECTION 3.1

Consumer Ethics

As a consumer, you expect the businesses you deal with to be honest and to treat you with respect and fairness. In return, you have an obligation to be honest, respectful, and fair toward businesses, their employees, and other consumers.

Objectives

After studying this section, you should be able to:

- Explain the meaning of ethics.
- Give guidelines for consumer courtesy.
- Describe the costs of shoplifting.
- Analyze the role of ethics in consumer decisions.

Key Terms

ethics
shoplifting

THE MEANING OF ETHICS

Every society has general principles that define what is good and right. Guidelines for human behavior based on principles about what is right and wrong are called **ethics**. Examples of ethical principles include honesty, trustworthiness, respect, fairness, concern for the welfare of others, and responsibility for one's actions and their consequences.

Ethical behavior involves the ability to tell right from wrong and the commitment to do what is right. What is right is not necessarily what is easiest or most convenient for you. In fact, it may be the opposite. Returning an empty shopping cart to its designated place, rather than leaving it where it blocks traffic, may seem like a nuisance—but it shows respect and responsibility.

Consumers make decisions based on ethics every day. These decisions reflect the type of people they are. What do your actions say about you? Your behavior with salespeople and fellow consumers is a good place to look for answers.

Community Activity. Ask students to visit one or more businesses in their community and observe the behavior of the other customers. Have them note whether the customers were courteous or discourteous and what results their behavior had.

CONSUMER COURTESY

Treating others with respect requires being courteous and considerate. Basic courtesy at any time includes honoring the rules of the establishment, not using foul language, and waiting your turn. In particular, show courtesy to retail staff and customer service personnel, whether you interact with them in person, on the phone, or by email. If you have a request or complaint, don't raise your voice or use threats or insults. You're much more likely to get the results you want by being calm and respectful.

Here are some other courtesy guidelines for common situations. How does your behavior measure up? What other guidelines can you add?

- **The supermarket.** Would you want to buy a jar of pickles that another shopper had opened and sampled? How about fruit that had been squeezed and tossed around roughly, or ice cream that someone had left on a shelf to melt? Items that are damaged by careless shoppers must be thrown away, which wastes food and leads to price increases.
- **Public transportation.** When you buy a ticket to ride a bus, train, or ferry, you're entitled to one seat. Piling shopping bags on empty seats, especially while other passengers are forced to stand, is selfish. If you see a person standing who is older, pregnant, or disabled, offer your seat. Being loud and disruptive is not only rude, it can distract the driver and cause an accident. See Figure 3-1.
- **The salon.** Suppose you had a haircut scheduled, but you couldn't keep the appointment. What would you do? You should call—preferably at least 24 hours ahead—and cancel. If you don't, you deprive your hairdresser of earnings. You also deprive other clients who may have wanted your time slot.

Team Activity. Have students work in pairs. Each pair should act out a scene showing what happens when a customer does not behave courteously in one of the situations described here. Then they should act out the same scene a second time showing what happens when the customer does show courtesy.

3-1

Treating others with respect includes being courteous and considerate. How can you practice courtesy when using public transportation?

Critical Thinking. ***Ask:*** How might people attempt to justify their dishonest actions? What do such actions say about their character?

- **The clothing store.** When trying on clothes, do you follow the fitting room rules? Leaving clothing in a heap on the floor can damage the items and is inconsiderate to other customers and store employees.

- **The restaurant.** Good table manners will be appreciated by your fellow diners. In a fast-food place, clear the table when you're through so others can use it. In a sit-down restaurant, remember to leave a tip for the server.

DISHONEST PRACTICES

When was the last time a sales clerk gave you back too much change? What did you do? It certainly can be tempting to keep the extra money. However, that would be dishonest because the money belongs to the store. Dishonesty is a violation of other people's trust. Consumers who are dishonest create hardship for everyone.

Shoplifting

Merchants lose millions of dollars each year to **shoplifting**, the theft of merchandise from stores. In addition to the direct losses, merchants must spend large sums on theft-prevention measures such as inventory tracking systems, merchandise tags, cameras, and security guards. See Figure 3-2. Because of these losses and expenses, retailers sometimes have to lay off employees or freeze new hiring. Some retailers are forced out of business.

Research Activity. Have students read an article about shoplifting and write a paragraph summarizing the facts that surprised them most.

Every consumer is harmed by shoplifting, too. The average family pays hundreds of dollars a year in the form of higher prices charged by merchants to make up for retail theft. Customers must also put up with security procedures that can be inconvenient. For example, bags may have to be checked at the front desk, and limits may be set on dressing room items.

Shoplifting carries a high price for those who try it. When shoplifters are caught, the consequences can include arrest, fines, jail time, and a criminal record. Just as shattering can be the damage to one's reputation and the shame and embarrassment caused to oneself, family, and friends.

3-2

Some businesses install complex security systems to prevent theft. Do you think store owners are justified in monitoring shoppers? Why or why not?

Class Activity. Have students write about one of the dishonest practices described on this page. Ask them to explain how this practice directly or indirectly affects businesses and honest consumers. They should note who ends up footing the bill for dishonest shoppers.

Other Dishonest Practices

Shoplifting is not the only dishonest practice that harms businesses and consumers. Other examples include:

- **Snacking in the grocery store.** The grapes may look juicy and delicious. Should you pop a few into your mouth? Eating food you haven't paid for is the same as shoplifting. Don't sample food in grocery stores unless the store invites you to. See Figure 3-3.

Discussion. ***Ask:*** Have you ever observed any of these dishonest practices? If so, what did you do? Explain your action.

- **Returning used goods.** Imagine someone returning a dress to the store for a refund after she's already worn it to the prom. Would you want to be the person who pays top dollar for this used dress?
- **Price switching.** A jacket is on sale for $90. What happens if a dishonest customer takes the sale tag and puts it on another jacket that costs $150? Either the store or the next shopper—who could be you—is cheated out of $60.
- **Fare beating.** Sneaking into trains, buses, or theaters without paying is dishonest and results in higher prices for everyone. Unpaid fares reduce the amount of money available to run public transportation systems, so service may have to be cut back. People who are caught fare beating are often charged with a crime.
- **Using copyrighted material without permission.** Music files, pictures, articles, and other materials you find on the Internet or elsewhere are not necessarily free for the taking. Copyright laws give control over their use—and the right to profit from them—to the people and companies who invested time, effort, and money in producing and distributing these materials. "Sharing" creative works is really stealing, and it could prevent someone from making a living.

3-3

Bulk food bins are a convenience and provide cost savings for consumers. They're not an invitation to sample the merchandise. Why is snacking in the store the same as shoplifting?

Critical Thinking. ***Ask:*** What effects might large consumer boycotts have on a company's business practices?

3-4 **Some consumers boycott—refuse to buy from—companies whose actions concern them. For example, if an environmental group believes that a company's policies contribute to the destruction of rainforests, a boycott might be organized against the company's products.**

Class Activity. Have students choose one of the practices listed on page 78 and respond to this in writing: Predict what would happen if the occurrence of this dishonest practice tripled in the next month. Compare responses in class.

Answer Key. Answers to the Section Review questions are provided in the Section Lesson Plan located in the *Teacher Resource Guide.*

ETHICAL ISSUES FOR CONSUMERS

Consumers sometimes face another kind of ethical decision. Suppose one day you read an article that's critical of a particular company's business practices. Perhaps the article says the company's workers aren't being treated fairly or that the company isn't doing as much to protect the environment as it should. It just so happens that this company makes one of your favorite products.

What would you do in this situation? How would you feel about continuing to buy the product? If you disagree with the company's policies, how could you help bring about change in an ethical way? On the other hand, what if the article omits or distorts facts to paint an unfair picture? Thoughtfully examining issues such as these is not always easy, but it's part of being an ethical consumer. See Figure 3-4.

Section 3.1 Review

CHECK YOUR UNDERSTANDING

1. Define ethics and give examples of ethical principles.
2. Explain three guidelines for consumer courtesy.
3. How does shoplifting hurt others?

CONSUMER APPLICATION

An Ethical Decision Write a brief skit or story in which a consumer chooses to act ethically rather than unethically. Explain why the person's actions demonstrate ethical consumer behavior.

Objectives

After studying this section, you should be able to:

- Explain civic duties and responsibilities of citizenship.
- Describe ways to be of service to your community.
- Analyze the benefits of cooperation, teamwork, and leadership skills.

Key Terms

naturalization
citizenship
vandalism
volunteer
leadership

SECTION 3.2

Responsible Citizenship

Besides being a consumer, you're also a citizen—of a community, a country, and the world. Being a citizen gives you both privileges and obligations. What are these obligations? What does it mean to be a responsible citizen?

THE MEANING OF CITIZENSHIP

Being a citizen means giving allegiance to a government in return for protection by it. One can become a citizen of a nation by birth (by being born in that country) or through **naturalization**, the process by which a foreign-born person becomes a citizen. In addition to being a citizen of your country, you are a citizen of your state and community. You also share common needs and goals with many people around the world.

Citizenship means more than simply being a citizen. It refers to the way you respond to being a member of a community or other group. Citizenship is an active process. Good citizens fulfill social responsibilities and act in an ethical manner. They care about others and contribute to their well-being. When people give something beneficial to society, they feel connected to others in their communities.

Class Activity. Ask students whether they know anyone who has tried to get out of jury duty. Ask them what would happen if everyone called for jury duty tried to avoid it. On the board, list the possible consequences of such a decision. Then ask students to explain why jury duty is an important civic duty.

Good citizens don't expect their positive actions to always be noticed or rewarded. What matters to them most is that they strive to make the world better.

PERFORMING CIVIC DUTIES

U.S. citizenship carries with it certain civic obligations. Some are required, while others are voluntary. Nevertheless, they are all part of being a good citizen.

- **Respect the law.** Laws are designed to protect citizens and ensure fair treatment. You are obligated to follow laws even if you don't agree with them.

- **Pay taxes.** Taxes are imposed by the government to pay for the services it provides to citizens. Citizens have the obligation to pay their full share of taxes.
- **Vote.** Voting is a privilege. In many parts of the world, people can't vote in free elections and therefore have no voice in their government. To participate in elections, U.S. citizens must be at least 18 years old and registered to vote. See Figure 3-5.
- **Stay informed.** Voters have a responsibility to be well informed. To decide intelligently on an issue, they must assess the arguments on all sides. To choose political leaders who will represent their views, they must learn where candidates stand on the issues.
- **Perform jury duty when called.** Jurors play a vital role in the justice system. They listen to the evidence presented in a trial and then reach a verdict based on that evidence. Citizens who are at least 18 years old, understand the English language, and have not been convicted of a felony are eligible for jury duty.
- **Serve in the military if called.** In times of war or crisis, citizens may be called on to help provide national defense. The Selective Service System, an agency of the U.S. government, maintains a list of names from which to draw in case Congress and the President call for rapid expansion of the armed forces. Most

3-5

Registering to vote is the first step to participation in elections. Find out where and how people in your community can register to vote.

Point Out. Men who don't register for the draft can be prosecuted, fined up to $250,000 and jailed for up to five years.

young men are required to register with the Selective Service within 30 days of their 18th birthday.

TAKING RESPONSIBILITY

As a member of your community, you are one of its "owners." You have a responsibility to care for public property, to use public services wisely, and to help keep your community safe, clean, and healthy.

- **Observe community regulations.** Follow the rules posted at parks and swimming pools to protect everyone's safety. Obey all traffic laws.
- **Cooperate during a crisis.** For example, during a drought, citizens might be asked or told to refrain from watering their lawns or washing their cars. Everyone's cooperation is needed.
- **Respect public service employees.** Give way to emergency vehicles such as ambulances, fire trucks, and police cars. Slow down and give highway workers plenty of room.
- **Report maintenance problems.** If you see unsafe playground equipment or a broken streetlight, for example, contact city authorities so they can be repaired.
- **Take responsibility for pets.** Clean up after your pet and obey leash laws. Report stray animals to animal control officers. See Figure 3-6.

Community Activity. Challenge students to take one of the steps to care for their community. Have them describe the results in an essay.

- **Clean up public property.** Join in a community cleanup to beautify your community and to keep it safe.

Vandalism

Vandalism is the deliberate destruction of property. Graffiti, broken windows, defaced public restrooms, and missing traffic signs contribute to higher taxes, increased crime, community members' fear, and sometimes injury and death. You can participate in or help start a neighborhood watch program to reduce the incidence of vandalism.

Internet vandalism includes actions such as releasing computer viruses, breaking into confidential databases, and shutting down Web sites. These actions take their toll on the economy due to lost income and added costs for businesses and other organizations.

3-6

Protect your pet and other people and animals by observing community leash laws. Name some other ways you can be a responsible member of your community.

Research Activity. Have students search online to find out how much Americans gave to charity last year and how this amount varied by income level.

SERVING OTHERS

Reaching out to provide service offers an extra opportunity to make a difference in your community. Many Americans routinely donate a portion of their income to worthy causes. They support nonprofit organizations that serve the needy, provide public services, promote education or the arts, or fund medical research, for example. In addition to money, many groups need material goods. You can donate furniture and appliances to homeless shelters, clothing and books to overseas aid organizations, and bags of groceries to food banks.

FCCLA. Have students plan and present an assembly on responsible citizenship. Choose a theme, such as "You Can Make a Difference" (volunteering) or "Counting on You" (civic duties) and present it through skits, demonstrations (voting machines), guest speakers, or testimonies (student volunteers). This project could be developed as an FCCLA Community Service Program.

Discussion. ***Ask:*** What benefits might you receive from volunteering? What benefits might others receive as a result of your help?

Volunteer Service

One of the most rewarding ways to help others is to donate your time, skills, and talents by volunteering. A **volunteer** is a person who offers services to a worthwhile cause for no pay. Each year more than 100 million Americans, including millions of teens, do volunteer work. See Figure 3-7.

Volunteering your time and service requires commitment, so do careful research to determine where you'd most like to volunteer. Consider whether you want to work with a particular group of people or for a specific cause that you're passionate about. Also think about what skills you have and how they could be used to benefit someone. Finally, consider your schedule. Whether you decide you can volunteer two hours each week or each month, follow through with your commitment.

Finding the right place to volunteer isn't difficult. Ask your teachers or other adults you know. Look in the newspaper, telephone book, or on the Internet for organizations or groups in your area that do the kind of work that interests you. Then just pick up the phone and ask whether they could use another volunteer.

3-7

You can take responsibility for your neighborhood by organizing a group of volunteers to clean up graffiti and pick up litter.

Critical Thinking. ***Ask:*** How can developing teamwork and leadership skills help you in your future career?

Answer Key. Answers to the Section Review questions are provided in the Section Lesson Plan located in the *Teacher Resource Guide.*

3-8

In times of trouble, effective leaders pull people together to solve problems and renew community spirit. Who is your leadership role model? Why?

TEAMWORK AND LEADERSHIP SKILLS

Being involved in your community will provide you with plenty of opportunities to develop skills in cooperation, teamwork, and leadership. When you participate in a group venture, you and other members cooperate with one another to achieve the group's goals. Teamwork—with each team member doing his or her part to reach those goals—is essential to success. At times you must be willing to compromise, giving up some of what you want for the good of the group.

You might, in some cases, assume a leadership role. **Leadership** involves the ability to inform and guide others. Effective leaders identify group goals and commit to achieving them. They confidently direct decision making, listen to ideas and concerns, and work to solve conflicts. They build team spirit by showing their appreciation for all who contribute. See Figure 3-8.

Leadership qualities can be learned. Look around you for someone who personifies good leadership and make this person your role model. To give your leadership skills a jump-start, consider getting involved in student government or becoming an officer in a school club. Family, Career and Community Leaders of America (FCCLA) is a national organization that provides many opportunities to build leadership skills. You can read more about FCCLA on page 120.

Section 3.2 Review

CHECK YOUR UNDERSTANDING

1. Why is voting important?
2. Describe three ways to use public property or services responsibly.
3. How do the qualities of a good leader benefit the group?

CONSUMER APPLICATION

Volunteer Opportunities Compile a list of professional and youth organizations that welcome the help of teen volunteers. What are their purposes and functions? What are their specific needs? Share the list with other students in your school.

SECTION 3.3

Environmental Awareness

Do you consciously think about the land you walk on, the water you drink, and the air you breathe? Because you depend on these and other precious natural resources in life, it makes sense to value and protect them.

Objectives

After studying this section, you should be able to:

- Evaluate the impact of environmental issues.
- Describe the role of government and consumers in protecting the environment.
- Explain ways to conserve natural resources.

Key Terms

ecology
renewable resources
nonrenewable resources
fossil fuels
biodegradable
conservation

ENVIRONMENTAL CONCERNS

Ecology is a science that deals with the relationships between living things and the environment. Ecologists study what happens when natural resources are misused and natural cycles are disturbed. Ecologists and other scientists agree that a number of environmental issues pose serious challenges to health, safety, quality of life, and the economy. They include:

- **Depleting nonrenewable resources.** Natural resources fall into two categories. **Renewable resources**, such as plants, trees, water, soil, and air, replace themselves by natural cycles over time. **Nonrenewable resources** are natural resources that cannot replace themselves. Once they are gone, there will never be any more. **Fossil fuels**—energy sources formed in the earth, such as coal, oil, and natural gas—are one form of

Point Out. One cause of global warming is deforestation. Trees help absorb carbon dioxide, the main gas involved in global warming.

Dollars and Sense. Have students research the costs of one of the environmental problems listed and prepare a presentation with visuals for class.

nonrenewable resource. Heavy use of fossil fuels increases the chance that the supply will be depleted, or used up, before alternatives are found.

- **Water pollution.** Although water is a renewable resource, its supply is limited. Only 1 percent of the world's water is freshwater. Most of it comes from groundwater located deep in the earth. This water supply is increasingly being contaminated by *toxic*, or poisonous, chemicals from factories, pesticides, and other sources. The contamination is difficult and costly to clean up.
- **Air pollution.** Each day tons of dust and chemicals are dumped into the air you breathe. Air pollutants have been linked to cancer, birth defects, and lung and nervous system damage in humans, as well as to disease and death in animals and plants. Air pollution can lead to other environmental problems such as acid rain, global warming, and depletion of the ozone layer.
- **Waste disposal.** Millions of tons of garbage wind up in landfills and incinerators each year. While some substances are **biodegradable**, which means they can decompose naturally in the environment, many items in landfills remain intact for hundreds of years. Landfills in some areas are rapidly filling up with waste, and land for such use is becoming scarce. In addition, some waste products—such as motor oil, pesticides, household cleaners, batteries, and paints—release poisons into the land, air, and water supply.

GOVERNMENT'S ROLE

Finding solutions to environmental problems is a challenge that requires the coordinated efforts of people all over the world. There are many approaches to **conservation**, the careful management and protection of valuable natural resources to ensure their quality and longevity. Both governments and consumers have a role to play. Federal, state, and local governments can act to protect the environment using means such as:

- **Restrictions and penalties.** For example, the Clean Water Act and the Clean Air Act regulate the amount of pollutants that can be discharged into the water and air. Fines can be imposed on polluters.

DOLLARSandSENSE

The Costs of Environmental Problems

Environmental problems are costly to consumers. Cleaning up polluted water, land, and air costs taxpayers millions of dollars every year. It also creates costs for industries, leading to higher consumer prices for manufactured goods. As resources such as water and fossil fuels become scarce, their prices rise too. The more waste piles up, the higher the costs of disposal and handling. Thus, when you make environmentally responsible choices, you're being economically wise as well.

Discussion. *Ask:* Have you taken any of these actions to help solve environmental problems? Can you think of any other actions you could take?

- **Incentives.** The government can offer monetary incentives, such as tax credits, to businesses and consumers that implement energy conservation measures.
- **Funding.** Lawmakers can provide money for projects that help the environment. For example, they can use taxpayers' money to fund research and development of alternative energy sources such as solar, geothermal, hydroelectric, and wind power.
- **International efforts.** The government works with other countries to create agreements to limit waste and pollution.
- **Agency coordination.** The Environmental Protection Agency (EPA), an independent agency within the U.S. government, was established in 1970. Its mission is to protect human health and to safeguard the natural environment. It enforces environmental laws and assists states in environmental protection efforts. It also conducts scientific research and education to advance the nation's understanding of environmental issues.

InfoSource. Have students visit the Web site of one of the agencies listed and create an FAQ list about the environmental issues it addresses.

WHAT YOU CAN DO

Consumers play a role in creating environmental problems, and therefore have a personal responsibility to help solve them. Every individual must do his or her part. Consumers can work with their government and community to conserve resources. They can become informed about environmental threats and what steps they can take to reduce them. They can also vote for government leaders who are committed to conservation.

Many consumers work actively for environmental causes. Teens have been at the forefront of the environmental movement for decades. They've started ecology clubs and created recycling programs in their communities. They've cleaned up trash-clogged rivers and lobbied government officials to pass tougher laws to protect the earth.

Even simple, everyday habits can help protect the environment. Here are just a few ideas—you can probably come up with more.

Community Activity. Encourage interested students to write a letter to one of their legislators about an environmental issue. Their letters should explain the problem that concerns them and ask the legislator to take a specific action to help solve it.

InfoSource

Environmental Issues

For more information about environmental issues, you can contact a number of agencies and organizations. Find their addresses at the library or visit their official Web sites.

- *Federal agencies:* Environmental Protection Agency, Natural Resources Conservation Service, U.S. Forest Service, U.S. Fish and Wildlife Service, Bureau of Land Management, National Park Service.
- *Environmental groups:* Audubon Society, National Wildlife Federation, Nature Conservancy, Sierra Club, and others.

Team Activity. Have students work in groups to generate additional ideas for conserving energy. Then have groups share their ideas with the class.

Conserve Energy

Many environmental problems result from the use of fossil fuels. Cutting back on energy consumption is one of the best things you can do to help the environment.

- **Use less heat and air conditioning.** Set the thermostat lower during heating season and higher during cooling season. Close vents and registers in unused rooms and keep the doors closed.
- **Use less hot water.** Turn your water heater temperature down. Wash clothes in warm or cold water and rinse in cold. Run dishwashers only with full loads.
- **Use lights wisely.** Remember to turn off lights when they're not needed. Try compact fluorescent bulbs—they last longer than standard incandescent bulbs and use less electricity.

Research Activity. Challenge students to calculate their daily personal water usage. They may use online calculators and other resources to help them.

- **Drive less.** Walk, ride a bike, carpool, or use public transportation when you can.

TEXTLINK

You can find additional ideas for conserving energy in Section 23.5.

Conserve Water

People who live in areas affected by water shortages have learned to become more aware of their water use. No matter where you live, you can do your part by using only as much water as you need. For example, don't run water the entire time you're brushing your teeth or washing dishes. Every minute a faucet runs, two gallons of water go down the drain. Fix leaky faucets, especially if they are leaking hot water. Take quick showers instead of baths—you'll use one-fifth the water. Many families install faucet flow restrictors and low-flow showerheads to conserve both water and energy. See Figure 3-9.

Cut Down on Waste

Families and individuals can cut down on the amount of waste sent to landfills. Follow the three R's:

- **Reduce.** When you purchase and use products, reduce waste right from the start. Some people call this *precycling*. For instance, avoid products packaged in unnecessary layers of material. Cut down on food waste. Reduce your use of disposable products, such as paper cups.

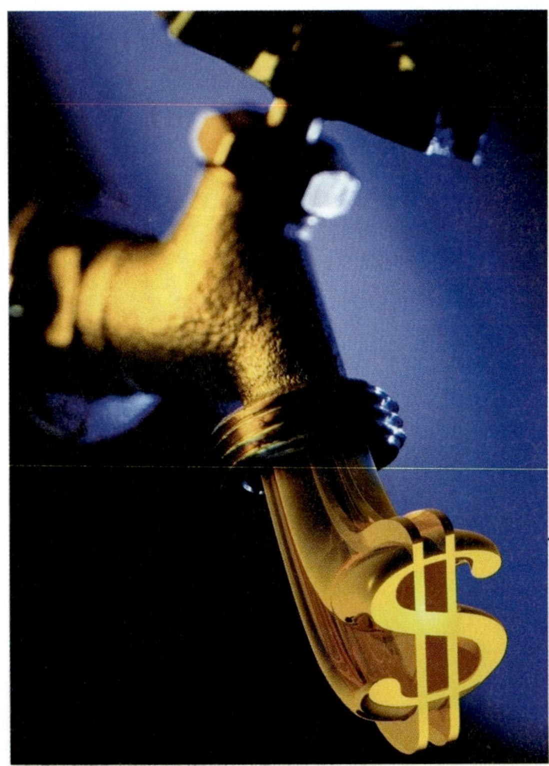

3-9

Besides wasting water and energy, leaving the faucet on sends your money down the drain in the form of higher power, water, and sewer bills. What else can you do to cut back your water use?

Class Activity. Have students design posters with examples of ways to reduce, reuse, and recycle. Display their posters around the school.

Answer Key. Answers to the Section Review questions are provided in the Section Lesson Plan located in the *Teacher Resource Guide.*

3-10

This symbol indicates that a product is made at least partly of recycled materials. A similar symbol, three arrows that are not inside a circle, means that the product can be recycled.

- **Reuse.** Using products and containers more than once cuts down on the need to discard and replace items. Save used printer paper—you can print or write on the back of it. Instead of buying containers to store leftovers, use empty glass jars that you've washed out.
- **Recycle.** Make use of your community's recycling programs for paper, aluminum, plastics, and glass. Buy products that are made of recycled materials. See Figure 3-10.

Be Cautious with Chemicals

Many household products, ranging from cleaning agents to paint to batteries, can contaminate the environment and pose a hazard to health and safety. You can help reduce this problem by making responsible choices. For household cleaning, products such as vinegar and baking soda are safe, inexpensive alternatives to harsh chemicals. Use organic fertilizers and nonchemical pest controls in the lawn and garden. If you must use chemicals, buy only as much as you need and will use up. Store products properly, and take care to avoid spills.

Certain products, including spent batteries, empty paint cans, and some household cleaner containers, cannot be disposed of in landfills because of the danger they pose to the environment. Contact your community's waste disposal company to find out about safe disposal.

Section 3.3 Review

CHECK YOUR UNDERSTANDING

1. Explain two environmental concerns associated with the use of fossil fuels.
2. Describe two ways in which the government acts to protect the environment.
3. Choose an environmental problem. List three things consumers can do to help reduce it.

CONSUMER APPLICATION

Conservation Essay What do you do that wastes natural resources? What changes can you make to conserve these resources? What responsibility do you feel to others—including future generations—to conserve resources? Write a one-page essay answering these questions.

CHAPTER 3

Review & Activities

CHAPTER SUMMARY

- Ethical principles include respect, responsibility, honesty, and courtesy. Consumer dishonesty harms businesses and consumers. (3.1)
- Performing civic duties and taking responsibility in your community are part of being a good citizen. Serving the community is a good way to develop cooperation, teamwork, and leadership skills. (3.2)
- Environmental issues affect all people, life forms, land, air, and water. Both governments and consumers have roles in conserving resources and protecting the environment. (3.3)

THE $avvy Consumer

A Sour Note? One of Paul's friends tells him about a Web site where he can download music files by some of his favorite groups for free. Paul visits the site and suspects the downloads are illegal. How can he learn whether his suspicions are correct? What action should he take if they are? (3.1)

Reviewing Key Terms and Ideas

1. How can you be a courteous consumer when shopping in a supermarket? (3.1)
2. How does **shoplifting** violate consumer **ethics**? (3.1)
3. How might fare beating affect paying consumers? (3.1)
4. Give an example of an ethical issue that consumers might face. (3.1)
5. What is **naturalization**? (3.2)
6. Why is it important to serve on a jury when called? (3.2)
7. Does **vandalism** in another part of town affect your family? Explain. (3.2)
8. Describe two types of **volunteer** service and explain how they help the community. (3.2)
9. How can you develop **leadership** skills as a volunteer? (3.2)
10. How could cooperation, teamwork, and leadership skills benefit you? (3.2)
11. What environmental issues are brought up when studying **ecology**? (3.3)
12. Why are **fossil fuels** considered **nonrenewable resources**? (3.3)
13. Why is waste disposal becoming a matter of increasing concern? (3.3)
14. What is the advantage of using **biodegradable** substances? (3.3)
15. How does **conservation** help the environment? (3.3)
16. What is the mission of the Environmental Protection Agency? (3.3)
17. Explain the three R's of waste reduction. (3.3)

Answer Key. Answers to the Chapter Review & Activities are provided in the Teacher's Manual in the *Teacher Annotated Edition* of the text.

Thinking Critically

1. **Consumer Courtesy:** How would you respond in these situations and why? a) In the supermarket, you see a customer leave a frozen package on a cereal shelf. b) You receive a cellphone call in a medical waiting room. c) You walk into a fitting room and see two garments lying on the floor. (3.1)
2. **Making Judgments:** What should you do if you see someone shoplifting or vandalizing property? Is it your business or not? Should you confront the person or report the incident? Explain your answer. (3.1, 3.2)
3. **Analyzing Economic Concepts:** How can consumers use their power and influence to decrease the amount of environmental pollution? (3.3)

Building Consumer Skills

1. **Intellectual Property:** Research intellectual property issues, such as plagiarism or copyright violation. Create a personal code of ethics regarding the use of intellectual property. Place it where you will see it when you do your homework. (3.1)
2. **Organization Investigation:** Using online resources, identify a youth or professional organization in an area of interest to you, such as 4H or Future Teachers of America. What are the roles and responsibilities of its members? What is its purpose and function? Report your findings. (3.2)
3. **Community Resources:** Contact a person in charge of a community resource, such as a public swimming pool or library. Inquire about the effects of vandalism on the facility, including cleanup, repair, and prevention costs; whether vandalism discourages public use; and what citizens can do to remedy the problem. Report your findings. (3.2)
4. **Calculating Water Waste:** Suppose you brush your teeth for two minutes with the water running. Each minute, two gallons of water go down the drain. Assuming you brush three times a day, how many gallons of water are used each year while you brush? How many gallons would you save each year if you ran the water for only half a minute? (3.3)

CONSUMER CONNECTIONS

- **Family:** Observe the ways your family members use water and energy and create waste for three days. As a family, discuss what you observed. Could resources have been reduced, reused, or recycled? Develop a plan to conserve resources more effectively. (3.3)
- **Community:** With your class, choose a community organization that provides valuable services. Using the FCCLA Planning Process, plan and implement a volunteer event for the organization. (3.2)

CHAPTER 4

Career Decisions

Reading with Purpose

- Read the title of this chapter and describe in writing what you expect to learn from it.
- Write down each key term, leaving space for definitions.
- As you read the chapter, write the definition beside each term.
- After reading the chapter, write a paragraph describing what you learned.

SECTION 4.1

Balancing Life Goals

Decisions you make about your working life affect other parts of your life, such as family relationships. Career goals must be balanced with other goals that are important to you.

Objectives

After studying this section, you should be able to:

- Analyze the impact of career decisions.
- Explain strategies for balancing multiple roles.
- Discuss workplace policies affecting families.

Key Terms

career
standard of living
flextime
telecommute

THE IMPACT OF CAREER CHOICES

A career is more than just a job. A **career** is a series of related jobs or achievements through which a person progresses in a particular field. Someone who chooses to enter the field of aviation, for example, might work at a variety of jobs within that field. Starting as a reservation agent, the person might move to the position of gate agent and then receive training as a flight attendant. Someone else working in the same field could follow a completely different career path, earning a degree in business and managing an airline.

Most people have more than one career in their lifetime. When people decide to start a new career, they generally do so to obtain personal satisfaction in the changing workforce.

Pursuing a well-chosen career path is one of the most valuable gifts that you can give yourself. Your quality of life—your resources and lifestyle, personal satisfaction, and even family life—will depend on the wisdom of your choices.

Class Activity. Draw three columns on the board: "Financial Resources," "Personal Satisfaction," and "Family Life." Take a poll of students to find out how much importance, on a scale of 1 to 10, they would assign each of these factors in choosing a career. Ask them to explain their reasons.

Financial Resources

The career path you choose will define your financial resources and your standard of living for years to come. The term **standard of living** refers to the way you live as measured by the kinds and quality of goods and services you can afford. A minimal standard of living provides little more than basic needs. With higher standards of living, people are able to fulfill goals such as home ownership, travel, or other wants based on their priorities. See Figure 4-1.

Of course, your income will change as you advance along your career path, depending on the specific jobs you hold. In general, however, certain career areas tend to have more income potential than others. Although money isn't everything, it's wise to evaluate the earnings potential in career fields you are considering. The cost of living in your area may affect what career you choose. If you enter a particular field, how likely is it that you'll reach the standard of living you desire? If the answer is "not very likely," you'd be wise to either re-examine your goals and priorities or to consider other career options.

4-1

The path you choose when planning your career will determine your standard of living. **What kind of standard of living is important to you?**

Personal Satisfaction

Financial rewards are important, but people are also motivated by personal satisfaction, or the psychological rewards of their jobs. These rewards can include enjoying the way you spend your workday, being challenged and stimulated by your job, and working with interesting people. Doing a job well also brings a sense of accomplishment and pride. For most people, this sense of accomplishment is magnified when they do work that they consider meaningful—that in some small way makes the world a better place. When your work reflects your goals and priorities, you have a strong sense of purpose in your life.

Family Life

The career path you choose will affect not only you personally, but also members of your current and future family. Think about the impact that working in a particular field might have on your family relationships. For instance, some jobs are more likely than others to require that you put in long hours, work nights or weekends, travel frequently, or be on call to handle emergencies. How might family members feel about those

Team Activity. Have students work in teams to make collages that illustrate the roles of family member, employee, and community member.

requirements? How would you feel about missing out on family activities because of your job?

BALANCING ROLES

A demanding career can consume so much energy and time that you have little left. At the same time, what's happening in your personal and family life can affect your work performance. Learning how to balance multiple roles—as a family member, an employee, and a community member—is an essential skill. Here are some strategies that can help you to balance your roles.

- **Develop a clear sense of priorities.** If you have one set of priorities in your work life and another in your home life, your roles are likely to conflict. Weigh what's important in *all* areas of your life. For instance, when deciding whether to seek a promotion, think about the impact not only on your career, but also on your family and personal life. See Figure 4-2.
- **Learn to say no.** The more roles you have, the more demands will be made on your time and energy. Make choices based on your own priorities, not the expectations of others.
- **Set realistic goals and standards.** Accept the fact that you may not be able to fulfill all your roles as perfectly as you'd like. Trying to be perfect will only frustrate and exhaust you.

Discussion. ***Ask:*** What challenges have members of your family faced when balancing their roles? How did they resolve these challenges?

- **Ask for and accept help.** Family members can work as a team to take care of household responsibilities. Coworkers can assist you if a project proves overwhelming. Community resources can be part of your support system.

WORKPLACE POLICIES

Many employers establish policies that make it easier for workers to balance multiple roles in the family, workplace, and community. The policies benefit employers as well. They are able to attract and retain the best workers, and their workforce is more productive.

- **Flextime** is offered by many employers. A system that allows flexible work hours, **flextime** enables employees to work the hours that suit them best. For example, one employee might choose to work from

4-2

When balancing roles, you need a clear sense of your priorities. Would you accept a promotion if it meant moving away and missing family activities? Why or why not?

Community Activity. Have students contact businesses in the community and inquire about what family-friendly policies they offer.

Answer Key. Answers to the Section Review questions are provided in the Section Lesson Plan located in the *Teacher Resource Guide.*

6:00 A.M. until 3:00 P.M. to be home with children after school. Another might prefer a schedule of 10:00 A.M. to 7:00 P.M.

- **Job sharing** is a system in which employers allow two part-time workers to share one position. One medical receptionist might work mornings and another afternoons; one cashier might work three days a week and another two.
- **Work-at-home options** eliminate or reduce the need to commute to an office each day. Technology makes it possible to **telecommute**, or work from home using communication links to the workplace. Workers can communicate by telephone, email, and fax, for example. Some can log onto office computer networks from home.
- **Employee assistance programs** make free or low-cost counseling available. Employees can confidentially seek help with many types of difficulties, such as workplace stress, problems in personal relationships, the illness or death of a family member, or substance abuse.
- **The Family and Medical Leave Act** (FMLA) requires most employers to grant workers leave for certain family and medical reasons. Eligible workers can take up to 12 weeks of unpaid leave each year for the birth or adoption of a child, the need to care for a family member with a serious health condition, or a serious health problem of their own. See Figure 4-3.

4-3 **When a worker takes leave under the FMLA, health benefits and job security are preserved. What other workplace policies could benefit a family with young children? How?**

Section 4.1 Review

CHECK YOUR UNDERSTANDING

1. In what ways do a person's career choices impact his or her life?
2. What are some of the strategies that people use to balance their multiple roles?
3. Describe two workplace policies that affect families.

CONSUMER APPLICATION

Labor Unions Organizations that represent workers for the purpose of increasing pay and improving working conditions are known as labor unions. Use online sources to investigate the labor union movement, the types of unions in the United States, and their pros and cons.

SECTION 4.2

Choosing a Career Path

Many people have fulfilling careers because they're good detectives. They were able to track down clues that pointed them to a satisfying career—and so can you.

Objectives

After studying this section, you should be able to:

- Explain the benefits of career planning.
- Identify factors to consider in choosing a career path.
- Describe consumer and management career opportunities.
- Analyze the risks and rewards of entrepreneurship.

Key Terms

aptitudes
entrepreneur

THE NEED FOR A CAREER PLAN

Some people never plan their career; they only look for a job. Their sole focus is having a steady income for the immediate future. They don't stop to consider what they want their working life to be like in 5, 10, or 20 years.

Other people have lofty ambitions—perhaps to be a wealthy corporate executive, an engineer working in the space program, or an award-winning musician. However, they don't have a plan for how to get there. They spend their life wishing for a lucky break that will somehow propel them straight to their dream.

What both types of people need is a career plan. Setting your goals, charting your career path, and staying on that path will put you in control of your future. High school is an especially good time to begin planning for your career. You have time to explore options and investigate different fields. You can take courses that relate to possible career goals and fine-tune the skills you need to succeed.

Critical Thinking. *Ask:* Why is a career plan necessary? What do you think might happen to someone who does not make a career plan?

Changing Course

Having a career plan doesn't lock you into your choices for life. In fact, it's essential that your plan be flexible. People switch careers about three times on average. Sometimes it's because of circumstances they can't control, such as a slowdown in their industry. In other cases, people find that their priorities and interests shift as they move into a new stage of life.

Changing careers often requires personal and financial sacrifices. People who change careers may have to juggle work with part-time classes or give up their income while they go back to school. They may have to start over at a low-paying position and work their way back up. Putting careful thought and research into your career plan doesn't guarantee you'll never switch careers, but it reduces the chances that you'll do so out of dissatisfaction. See Figure 4-4.

Workplace Trends

A variety of factors combine to create a dynamic, changing workplace. In the future, your career might be affected by these and other factors.

- **Technology.** Sometimes jobs are eliminated by automation. On the other hand, new positions have been created in technology fields, and demand for workers with technical skills has increased. Technology has also changed the way workers communicate and manage.
- **Outsourcing.** Driven by the need to cut operating costs, many organizations use a strategy called *outsourcing*—paying independent contractors to perform functions that were previously handled by employees. For example, accounting tasks might be contracted to an outside individual or firm. This trend eliminates jobs within the company, but creates expanding opportunities for small businesses and self-employed people.
- **Cultural diversity.** The United States is a multicultural nation and is becoming more so. In addition, many companies sell products and services around the world, and some have offices abroad. As a result, workers increasingly interact with people from a wide variety of cultures. Cultural sensitivity is essential in this economic climate. Speaking more than one language is an asset in most jobs and a requirement in some.

Research Activity. Ask students to read and summarize an article on technology, outsourcing, or cultural diversity in the workplace. Discuss how these trends might affect their future career plans.

Discussion. *Ask:* What are some ways to keep your career plan flexible? In what situations might this flexibility prove useful?

4-4

An interest in art and history could lead to a job in a museum. What are some of your interests? What career fields might they relate to?

Team Activity. Have each student fold a sheet of paper into quarters and use these four sections to list their interests, personality traits, aptitudes, and abilities. Then have students form small groups and discuss each other's assessments. Have them suggest careers that might fit each person.

CREATING A CAREER PLAN

Making a career plan involves identifying short-term and long-term career goals. First, however, you need to take a look at your personal qualities, identify possible career areas, and learn more about them.

Know Yourself

Taking time to examine your personal qualities may help lead you to a fulfilling career. Think about your:

- **Interests.** Make a list of your hobbies, favorite school subjects, volunteer work, and other interests. Look for common elements and themes that might suggest a career field.
- **Personality.** Do you prefer working with a team of people or on your own? Do you want a job that lets you express your creativity? Would you thrive in a fast-moving work environment? You'll be more satisfied with an occupation that's a good fit with your personality.
- **Aptitudes.** Natural talents are called **aptitudes**. If you're good at working with numbers, for instance, you have numerical aptitude. You might have an aptitude for building things, visualizing images, or expressing ideas in words.
- **Abilities.** There's a difference between aptitudes and abilities, which are learned skills. Someone could have an aptitude for music, yet not have the ability to play the piano. However, that ability can be developed through instruction and practice. See Figure 4-5.

Dozens of tests have been developed to help people gain insight into their interests, personality traits, aptitudes, and abilities. Examples include the Kuder Occupational Interest Survey, the General Aptitude Test Battery, and the Armed Services Vocational Aptitude Battery. Your school counselor may have information about these and other tests. It may be possible to take such tests at your school, on the Internet, or at a nearby community college.

Discussion. ***Ask:*** What summer jobs or volunteer work might give you experience in a field that interests you?

4-5

You may want to capitalize on your aptitudes by developing them further. By learning and practicing new skills, you'll gain abilities that can help you in your career.

InfoSource. Tell students to study these references at your library or on the Internet and explain how each one could aid them in making career decisions.

Research Activity. Have students research a specific career that interests them and answer the questions listed on this page about the career.

Identify Possible Career Areas

The next step is to match up your personal qualities with related career options. For example, if you enjoy math and have an aptitude for art, perhaps architecture would appeal to you. Many of the tests that assess personal qualities suggest suitable career areas and occupations based on your responses. In addition, books and Web sites on career planning can help you match your personal qualities to possible career choices.

Whether you use tests, books, or Web sites as a source of career advice, remember that these tools are only guides. They can be especially useful when they point out career options that you hadn't considered before. However, each makes career suggestions based on a narrow range of factors. You'll need to combine information from many different sources and weigh it according to your priorities.

Research Career Areas

Finding out which career fields or occupations might suit you personally is a good start, but it's only part of the story. To make informed decisions, you'll need to learn more about your options. Research can help you answer many questions about career areas and occupations, such as:

- What are the specific occupations within this career field?
- Are job opportunities expected to grow, shrink, or remain steady in the future? See Figure 4-6.
- Which geographic areas have the most job opportunities?
- What education or training is required for specific occupations?
- What level of pay can be expected?
- What is a typical workday like for a person in this occupation?
- What are some possible paths of advancement within this field?

Your school guidance office can provide you with advice and resources for researching career fields and job trends. Available resources include books, business and professional magazines, and online job banks and databases.

InfoSource

Career Information

The U.S. Department of Labor collects statistics and information about the job market and the workforce. Look for these references at your library or on the U.S. Department of Labor's Web site.

- *O*NET, the Occupational Information Network.* Includes information on skills, abilities, and interests associated with occupations.
- *Occupational Outlook Handbook.* Contains detailed information on over 250 occupations. Revised every two years.
- *Occupational Outlook Quarterly.* Supports the OOH by providing updated information four times per year.

Community Activity. Ask students to interview three employed aduts about the pros and cons of their occupations. Students should record each subject's job, its main benefits, and its major drawbacks. Have students report their findings in class.

A good way to learn about the real pros and cons of a particular occupation is to make contact with people already working in it. If you attend a career fair, you can speak with people in a variety of occupations. Informational interviews are another option. Most experienced workers are glad to answer questions and talk about what they enjoy most, and least, about their work. Your school may have a job shadowing program that allows students to observe workers throughout a day on the job.

You can also gain exposure to a job and job setting through volunteer work and summer jobs. You'll learn a lot and make valuable contacts.

Job Trends

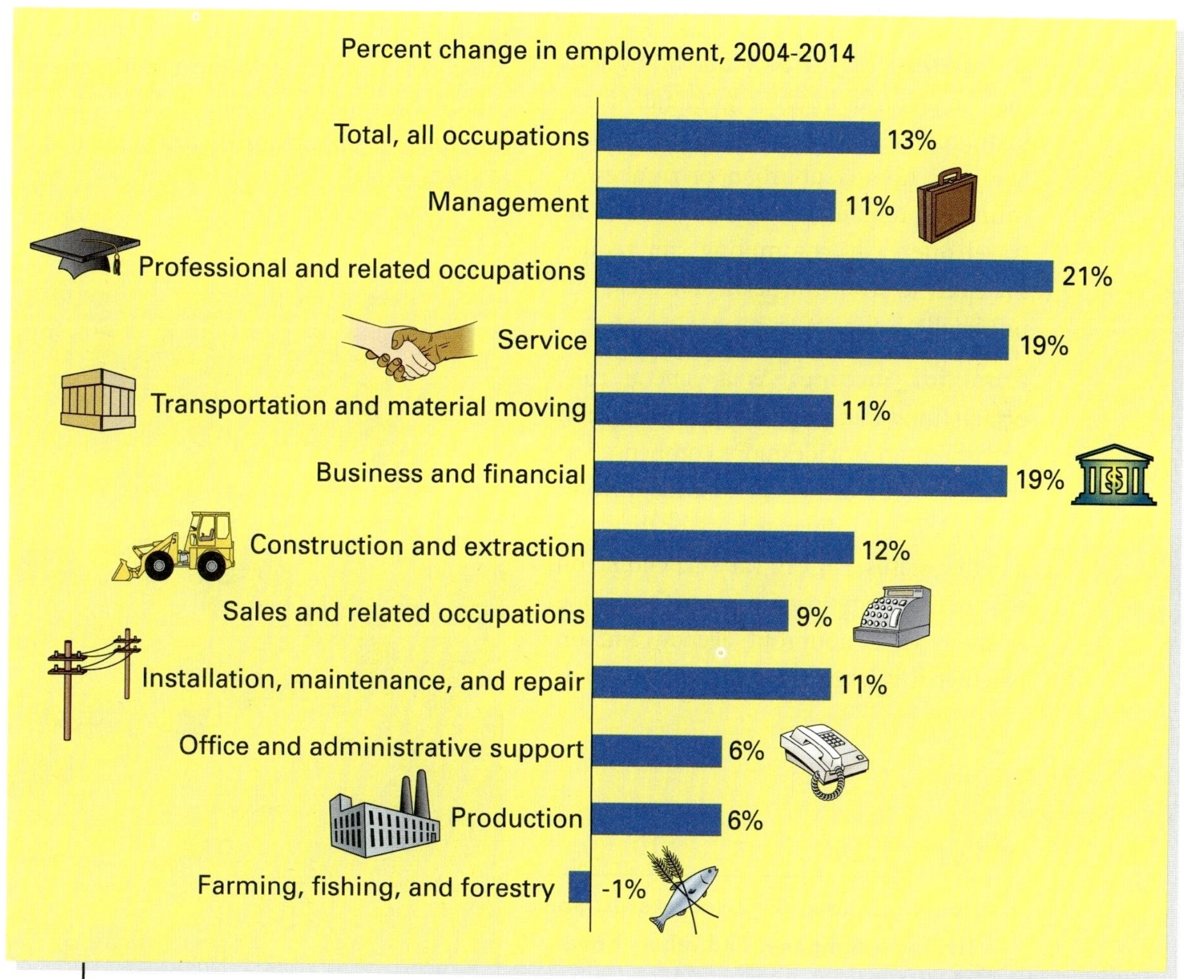

Source: Bureau of Labor Statistics

4-6 **This graph shows the projected change in employment areas over a ten-year period.** **Which areas look promising? Which would you probably avoid pursuing?**

Critical Thinking. *Ask:* Aside from the factors listed here, what else might you consider when evaluating career options?

Evaluate Options

Many factors enter into your choice of a career area and the specific career goals you set. In addition to considering whether you'll find an occupation interesting and rewarding, think about practical considerations such as:

- **Job availability.** As the economy and technology change, occupational patterns tend to shift as well. New career areas are created, and others that have been secure in the past may no longer exist. You may want to think twice about entering a career field in which jobs are scarce or expected to decline in the future.
- **Geographical influences.** Some jobs may be plentiful in one region and scarce in another. Consider whether you want to live in an urban, suburban, or rural environment, remain near your family, or travel often. Telecommuting can reduce the need to live in a particular area, but not in all cases.
- **Potential income.** As a general rule, occupations that require more education and training provide more compensation than others. So do occupations that involve more physical or financial risk or that have a higher status. Pay can vary depending on whether the employer is a profit-making business or a nonprofit agency, and on whether it is large or small. A shortage or surplus of workers in an occupation can influence potential income. So can current economic conditions in an industry.

Point Out. Remind students that their education and training will affect their level of employment. In some fields, workers can advance with experience.

CONSUMER AND MANAGEMENT CAREERS

As you review your career options, you may want to consider the field of consumer services and resource management. People in this field work to assist and educate consumers and to help individuals, families, or businesses manage their finances and other resources. See Figure 4-7.

Like any occupations, those in consumer services and resource management can be categorized according to the amount of education and training needed. Figure 4-8 gives examples of opportunities available at each of these levels:

4-7

Accountants keep financial records. Some work for a company, and others have their own business. What kind of training might you need for this occupation?

Point Out. Jobs in the field of consumer services and resource management may also require math skills.

- **Entry-level.** For most entry-level positions, you will need a high school education, vocational training, or both.
- **Technical.** At this level, you will need either on-the-job training, such as an apprenticeship, or an associate (two-year) degree from an accredited college. Some positions require both.
- **Professional.** For a professional position, you will need at least a four-year college degree and possibly advanced training in your field.

If you're interested in the consumer services and resource management field, what personal qualities and skills can help you succeed? As in any career field, qualities such as cooperation, integrity, motivation, and respect for others are important. Most jobs in this field also require tact and confidence. Willingness to travel is an asset in some occupations.

Critical Thinking. *Ask:* Do you think you have the right qualities for a job in consumer services and resource management? Why or why not?

Developing strong interpersonal, communication, time management, and organizational skills is of particular importance in the consumer and management field. Computer skills are a requirement or asset in most positions. Some jobs may require additional technical, writing, planning, research, problem-solving, fundraising, or sales skills. Knowledge of consumer laws and rights is essential in some consumer occupations. Managers also need leadership, supervision, and coaching skills.

Consumer and Management Employment Opportunity Examples

	ENTRY LEVEL	TECHNICAL	PROFESSIONAL
Business	Customer Service Representative	Public Relations Representative	Consumer Affairs Director
Finance	Bank Teller	Bookkeeper	Financial Planner
Manufacturing	Product Demonstrator	Product Representative	Product Research and Development
Consumer Organization	Consumer Assistant Technician	Consumer Products Tester	Consumer Arbitrator
Communications	Advertising Sales Representative	Consumer Newswriting Intern	Consumer Newscaster
Government	Consumer Aide	Consumer Consultant	Consumer Safety Inspector
Education	Teacher Assistant	Family and Consumer Counselor	Family and Consumer Sciences Educator

4-8 **These are just a few of the occupations in the field of consumer services and resource management. What other occupations might be included in this career area?**

Class Activity. Hold a class debate on the pros and cons of being an entrepreneur. Have two teams debate whether the rewards outweigh the risks.

4-9

The small but growing businesses of entrepreneurs have created most of the new jobs in the United States since the 1960s. What kind of business might you like to start?

Class Activity. Have students name ways they have earned money, and list them on the board. What other ideas have friends and family members used? Explore teen entrepreneurship by asking what services they might provide to earn money.

ENTREPRENEURSHIP

Have you ever thought of turning your passion into a business? An **entrepreneur** (on-truh-pruh-NOOR) is someone who owns a business or assumes the financial risk for a business. In the consumer and management field, an entrepreneur might own a bookkeeping business or write consumer articles on a freelance basis, for example.

- **Risks.** Entrepreneurs often have to invest a substantial amount of their own money and convince others to invest theirs. They risk losing it all if the business doesn't succeed. Income is often uncertain and can be nonexistent at first. Many entrepreneurs put in long hours, especially during the startup of a business.
- **Rewards.** On the plus side, entrepreneurs have a tremendous amount of control. They decide what their business will sell, whom to hire, and when to work. If the business succeeds and grows, the financial rewards can be great. The satisfaction of turning an interest into a thriving business venture can be very rewarding.

Successful entrepreneurs are goal-oriented, self-motivated, and self-disciplined. They get along well with a variety of personalities and are good at motivating and persuading others. Entrepreneurs must be adaptable, willing to take risks and make sacrifices, and able to learn from their mistakes and move forward. You could be a successful entrepreneur if you develop these traits. See Figure 4-9.

Answer Key. Answers to the Section Review questions are provided in the Section Lesson Plan located in the *Teacher Resource Guide*.

Section 4.2 Review

CHECK YOUR UNDERSTANDING

1. Why do you need a career plan?
2. Identify personal qualities you need to consider when making a career plan.
3. What are the risks and rewards of being an entrepreneur?

CONSUMER APPLICATION

Consumer Careers Research the effect of consumer affairs careers on local, state, and national economies and rate the importance of these careers. How might economic growth affect consumer careers? Share your ideas with the class.

SECTION 4.3

Investing in Education

Once you have a career goal in mind, you'll need to obtain knowledge, skills, and training. Education—whether it takes place in a school, in a workplace, or at home—is the answer.

Objectives

After studying this section, you should be able to:

- Analyze the relationship between education and career opportunities.
- Give guidelines for selecting among educational opportunities.
- Explain ways to manage education costs.

Key Terms

internship
apprenticeship
distance education programs
accredited

WHY INVEST IN EDUCATION?

As you learned in the previous section, jobs at all levels—entry level, technical, and professional—require skills and knowledge. To acquire knowledge and develop skills, you need some form of education or training. Government statistics show that people with less education are more likely to have trouble finding jobs. Education makes it easier for people to weather changes in the labor market and ensures greater career opportunities.

Education is an investment in *you*, and like all good investments, it pays dividends. In recent years, for every $100 earned by a full-time male worker who is a high school dropout, a high school graduate earned about $130 and a college graduate earned more than $200. For female workers, the difference is slightly greater. Imagine that difference over a year's salary and then over your lifetime income!

Jump$tart. Ask students to assume that a high school dropout can earn $206 per week working at a minimum-wage job. Have them calculate how much more that worker could earn by completing high school and by attending college. *(Income)*

Point Out. Many internships are unpaid. People need to weigh the value of the experience they will gain against the income they are giving up.

Community Activity. Have students choose a type of educational opportunity and find out where such opportunities are available in their community.

EDUCATIONAL OPPORTUNITIES

The type of education or training that you choose will depend on what preparation is needed for the occupations and career areas that interest you. Some education and training opportunities are work-based, some are classroom-based, and others use a combination of approaches.

- **Internships.** An **internship** is a paid or unpaid short-term job offered to a student who is interested in entering a particular field. The employer gains a temporary worker; the student gains work experience and the chance to observe the business or industry firsthand.
- **Apprenticeships.** An **apprenticeship** is a training program that combines classroom instruction with paid on-the-job experience under the guidance of a skilled worker. Apprenticeships are common in many skilled trades, such as carpentry or culinary arts. Labor groups, employers, associations, and some career and technical schools offer apprenticeships.
- **Armed forces.** The armed forces provide training in many fields, such as computer programming, engineering, and public relations.
- **Career and technical institutions.** These schools and colleges train students to become licensed or certified in skilled occupations, ranging from computer-assisted design to health care occupations. Programs can usually be completed in one to three years.
- **City or community colleges.** Similar training programs can sometimes be found here. In addition, these schools offer two-year academic programs leading to an associate degree. Credits can usually be transferred to a four-year college or university.
- **Colleges and universities.** These institutions offer four years of academic courses leading to bachelor's degrees, as well as graduate programs leading to advanced degrees.
- **Distance learning.** If it's not possible to attend traditional classes, you can take advantage of the **distance education programs** offered by many institutions.

4-10

Distance education programs serve many students who might not otherwise be able to attend school. **Give some examples of people who might take advantage of distance learning.**

Discussion. ***Ask:*** What factors would you consider when choosing a school? How might the school you choose affect your future career?

These programs use various methods—such as the Internet, videotape, audio and video conferencing, and print materials—to teach students who are not present on campus. See Figure 4-10.

Choosing a School

In the United States, there are about 4,000 degree-granting colleges, universities, and community colleges, plus thousands of other schools that provide specialized training programs. Give yourself plenty of time to consider what you want in a school and then to research your options.

Program quality is an important consideration. Find out which schools have the best reputation in your area of interest. Investigate the credentials of faculty members. Be sure the schools and departments you're considering are **accredited**—officially recognized as maintaining standards that will qualify students for additional education or for work in their chosen profession. Other factors to consider include the size, location, and setting of schools; the resources and services they offer; and the costs for tuition, fees, and living expenses. See Figure 4-11.

Guidebooks comparing information about many different schools can be found at the library, at your school guidance office, and on the Internet. Review school catalogs, brochures, and Web sites. If possible, visit prospective schools. Plan your visit when classes are in session so you can get a sense of whether or not you would feel comfortable there.

Point Out. Emphasize the need to start early when applying to schools. Those who put it off may miss deadlines for admission or financial aid.

Applying to Schools

You should begin researching schools in your junior year so that you'll be ready to send applications during your senior year. Contact schools by phone or mail, or check their Web sites for application procedures, forms, and deadlines. The criteria used to determine whether or not you'll be admitted vary from place to place. If you choose the college or university route, your grades, class rank, and entrance-exam scores will be of vital importance.

Many schools consider factors other than grades and test scores—they look at the whole person. If the application process includes writing an essay, you'll have a chance to provide a glimpse into your personality, priorities, and goals. You also may have to submit one or more letters of recommendation from adults who know you well.

4-11

Success in college depends partly on choosing the right school. Would you prefer a big campus with classes held in large lecture halls, or is a small campus more appealing?

Research Activity. Have students research one of these programs for financing education and make a chart comparing its pros and cons.

If a school wants to interview you, make every effort to attend. This is your chance to sell yourself and to highlight the strengths of your application. Many of the job interview tips in Section 4.4 can be applied to a school admissions interview.

PAYING FOR YOUR EDUCATION

College costs have been rising at a rate of about 5% a year. Whether you choose to attend a college, career or technical school, or other institution, think about how you'll pay for your education.

Saving and Investing

It's never too late to start saving for your education beyond high school. However, the earlier you and your family begin to put money aside, the more money you'll have when you start school.

TEXTLINK

You can read more about saving and investing in Chapters 12 and 13.

Money put aside for education will accumulate faster if it's allowed to grow tax-free or tax-deferred. Special programs make that possible.

Dollars and Sense. Ask students to brainstorm other ways they might reduce or offset the costs of college for themselves and their families.

- **Coverdell Education Savings Accounts.** Formerly known as an Education IRA, a Coverdell ESA is a special savings account set up for a person under 18 to be used for future higher education expenses. Depending on your household income, your family may be able to deposit up to $2,000 a year into such an account. Earnings accumulate tax-free, and withdrawals that don't exceed education expenses are also tax-free.
- **Prepaid tuition.** Most states sponsor prepaid tuition plans that enable a family to pay for tuition credits at today's rates, rather than at future inflated prices.
- **529 plans.** These investment plans, named after the section of the tax code that governs them, enable families to save for future college costs and are more flexible than prepaid tuition plans. The investment grows tax-free, and distributions are free of federal taxes.

These plans can have some drawbacks, including reducing your chances of getting financial aid. Carefully research each option and consider its pros and cons. Consult guidebooks that provide advice on paying for your education.

DOLLARS and SENSE

Cutting College Costs

If college is in your plans, keep these cost-cutting tips in mind.

- Get good grades! Students with the highest GPAs and test scores often receive scholarships or substantial financial aid packages.
- Take advanced placement courses in high school. Success in these courses can translate into college credits and save you money.
- If you're heading to a university, keep in mind that tuition is generally lowest at state schools in your home state.

Research Activity. Have students search the FTC Web site for information about phony scholarship scams. Have them discuss their findings in class.

Financial Aid

Most full-time college undergraduates receive financial aid of some kind. Financial aid can come from a combination of sources.

- **Grants and scholarships** do not have to be repaid. Grants are given on the basis of need. Many scholarships are awarded partly or entirely according to achievement, such as academic excellence or outstanding athletic skill. Governments, private foundations, colleges, service organizations, and other entities award grants and scholarships.
- **Loans** must be repaid after you graduate or leave school. They are offered by governments, colleges, and financial institutions. Most educational loans have a lower interest rate than regular loans. Several Web sites can help you calculate how much debt you can afford given your anticipated career and earnings.
- **The Federal Work-Study Program** provides jobs for students with financial need. Students who qualify receive federal funds for doing part-time community service work or tasks related to their field of study.

When you're searching for financial aid, it pays to investigate as many possibilities as you can. Start by asking for information from your school guidance office and the financial aid offices of the schools you're interested in attending. At the U.S. Department of Education's Web site, you can fill out the Free Application for Federal Student Aid (FAFSA). To learn about state-awarded aid, contact your state's higher education office. The Web sites of banks, colleges, businesses, and other organizations may have information about loans and scholarships.

Answer Key. Answers to the Section Review questions are provided in the Section Lesson Plan located in the *Teacher Resource Guide*.

You can become eligible for special sources of financial aid by serving your country. For example, young people who join AmeriCorps, a volunteer service program, earn education awards of over $4,000 for a year of service. Those who serve in the military may be eligible for various kinds of educational assistance offered under the program known as the GI Bill.

As you gather information about financial aid, watch out for phony scholarship scams. Beware of seminars, contests, and other offers that guarantee you'll receive a scholarship if you pay a fee in advance. You could pay the fee and receive nothing in return. Some companies do provide assistance in finding financial aid, but you might be able to find the same information yourself for free. Check out any such offers carefully before handing over your money.

Section 4.3 Review

CHECK YOUR UNDERSTANDING

1. Explain the statement: Education is an investment.
2. Name several factors to keep in mind when you are choosing schools.
3. What are some sources of financial aid for full-time students?

CONSUMER APPLICATION

Financial Aid Identify a school that provides training and education in a profession that interests you. Check the school's Web site to find out about available grants, scholarships, and loans. Summarize your findings in a brief report that you can share with a parent or guardian.

Objectives

After studying this section, you should be able to:

- Describe effective job search skills.
- Explain how to evaluate job offers.
- Identify federal laws that promote fair hiring.

Key Terms

résumé
references
interview

SECTION 4.4

Getting a Job

When you embark on a job search, much of your success will depend on your effort, resourcefulness, persistence, and salesmanship. Yes, you are selling something—yourself.

STARTING YOUR SEARCH

When you're ready to take a job in your chosen career area, you have reason to be excited about the possibilities. Although a job search takes time and can be hard work, landing the right job will make it all worthwhile. Follow these steps carefully and be thorough at each step. Bring the same discipline to your job search as you would to a job.

Preparing a Résumé

A **résumé** (REH-zuh-MAY) is a personal data sheet that describes you to prospective employers. It includes details about your education and experience and outlines the special qualifications you'll bring to a job. Preparing a résumé helps to organize your thoughts and reminds you that you have a lot to offer an employer.

When you prepare your résumé, you can choose from several acceptable formats. One example is shown in Figure 4-12. Books and Web sites about preparing résumés can show you other formats and help you decide which one is best for your situation.

Discussion. ***Ask:*** Why should you always let your references know that you have listed their names on your résumé?

Class Activity. Have students prepare their own résumés, using Figure 4-12 as a model. Remind them to proofread their résumés and check spellings.

Sample Résumé

4-12

Keep your résumé short, simple, and neat. Ask an adult—a parent or teacher—to review it for you.

Sandra Diaz
35 Oak Ridge Road
St. Louis, Missouri 63133
317-555-2162
diaz@serviceprovider.com

OBJECTIVE:	To become a manager in an environmental research setting dedicated to consumer safety.
EXPERIENCE:	
July 2000-Present	Assistant Consumer Safety Officer, Southside Laboratories, St. Louis, Missouri. Performed toxicology testing on food additives, recorded data results, and ordered supplies.
1998-2000	Receptionist, Westside Physicians Clinic, St. Louis, Missouri. Answered phone, scheduled appointments, greeted patients, and processed billings.
1997-1998	Sales Assistant, Women's Fine Apparel, Florissant, Missouri. Assisted with customer service, displayed inventory, and cashiered.
EDUCATION:	Associate in Applied Science degree, 2000, Morris Community College, St. Louis, Missouri. High school diploma, 1998, Brodecker High School, St. Louis, Missouri.
SKILLS:	Good organizational skills Knowledge of laboratory procedures Fluent in Spanish Word processing, spreadsheets, databases
HONORS:	National Honor Society, 1996-1998 Women in Sciences Scholarship, 1998-2000
CERTIFICATION:	American Society of Clinical Pathologists
MEMBERSHIP:	Family, Career and Community Leaders of America (FCCLA)

References available on request.

FCCLA. Have students use Career Connection to investigate career fields and choose a field that they think is suited to their personal interests, skills, and goals. Have them map out a career plan aimed at getting a job in this field, including a series of long-term goals for education and work experience and short-term goals that will help them work toward each long-term goal. Have them organize their plans in the form of a time line, map, or blueprint.

Successful résumés are neat, well organized, and brief—usually no more than one or two pages. Don't be modest—highlight your experience and accomplishments, but don't exaggerate. Be honest. If you haven't been employed previously, highlight experience you have gained through other means, such as volunteer work, student government, and neighborhood jobs. Use strong action verbs such as *organized*, *created*, and *developed*. Spell-check and carefully proofread your résumé. Errors make you look careless.

On your résumé or on a separate sheet, include the names and contact information for your references. **References** are people who will recommend an applicant to an employer on the basis of character or ability. As a courtesy, let the people you list as references know that you have given their names.

Class Activity. Have students create a networking graphic organizer. They may use a design such as a web diagram, a pyramid, or a tree diagram to show the names of people they know who might have job leads, people who are known to those people, and so on.

Finding Job Leads

Once you've prepared your résumé, you're ready to look for job openings. There are many ways to find them. Here are a few ideas.

- **Schools.** Businesses that want to hire young people often contact local schools. Visit the guidance office at your school or at other educational institutions. See Figure 4-13.
- **Networking.** Most jobs are filled by word of mouth, so tell everyone you know that you're job hunting. They may be aware of openings at their own workplaces or through other contacts in the community. Go to job fairs and make contacts. Expand your network by joining a job-related email list server or an Internet newsgroup.
- **Online job banks.** Some Web sites list hundreds of thousands of jobs. You can search by location, company, job category, and other qualifiers. You can also post your résumé for thousands of employers to see. If you're a minor (which in most states means under age 18), check with a parent or guardian before posting your address and phone number on the Internet.
- **Newspapers.** The "Help Wanted" section of the classified ads announces available jobs.
- **Employers.** Try contacting employers directly. Many of them post job openings on their Web sites or help-wanted signs at their place of business. Even if there are no current job openings, they may become available in the future. You might ask to meet with a representative of the organization to learn more about their needs.
- **Government employment offices.** If you're seeking a job with the federal government, check with the Office of Personnel Management. It publicizes government job openings through printed materials, automated telephone systems, and on its Web site. For city, county, or state jobs, check the governmental unit's department of human resources.
- **Employment agencies.** These organizations help people find jobs by matching applicants' qualifications with those needed by employers with job openings. Public agencies are funded by the government and offer free services. Private agencies charge fees that can be substantial but that are often paid for by the employers.

4-13

Businesses may send recruiters to schools to find suitable applicants for employment or internships. Talk to your school guidance counselor about this possibility.

Class Activity. Have each student write a cover letter expressing interest in a specific job. Have students exchange and critique each other's letters.

- **Other sources.** Check the library, unions and apprenticeship councils, and professional or trade journals and newsletters.

Approaching Prospective Employers

When you find an opening that interests you, contact the employer. Send your résumé with a *cover letter*, a short letter of introduction that highlights your qualifications for the position. The letter should be brief and clear, neatly typed, and free of errors. Address it to the appropriate person by name and job title. If a name is not given in a job ad, call the employer and ask to whom you should address the letter.

The body of the letter should give a brief description of your qualifications and refer to the résumé. End the letter by offering to discuss your qualifications for the job in person.

At some point after you make contact, the employer may ask you to fill out a job application. Even though it may ask for some of the same information as your résumé provides, the application is a necessary part of the process. Fill it out neatly, completely, and accurately.

Dollars and Sense. Have students visit the FTC's Web site to learn more about job scams. Ask them to describe examples of specific scams.

INTERVIEWING SUCCESSFULLY

Many applicants will be eliminated from consideration on the basis of their letters or résumés. The applicants might not be qualified, or their letters and résumés might be poorly written or supply incomplete information. From the remaining applicants, the employers choose the most promising candidates. Only those few will be asked to come in for an **interview**, a formal meeting that employers use to evaluate prospective employees. During the interview, you have just a few minutes to make a good impression, so you'll want to be well prepared.

Prepare Yourself

There are several things you can do to prepare for a job interview. Review your résumé to remind yourself of your strong points. Look for weak areas in your education or employment history, then prepare explanations in the event that the interviewer questions them.

Find out all you can about the company. Doing some research will show the interviewer that you're interested in working for the company and will help you discuss the

DOLLARSandSENSE

Beware of Job Scams

Have you seen newspaper ads and posters telling you that you can make thousands of dollars a month working from home? Have you noticed ads guaranteeing a federal or postal position, or a high score on an entrance exam? Many of these ads are fraudulent. If you contact the organization, you'll be asked to send money. It's likely that you'll receive little in return, least of all a job. If it sounds too good to be true, it probably is. For more information on job scams, check the Federal Trade Commission's Web site.

Team Activity. Have students work in pairs to practice answering the interview questions below. Have partners critique one another's answers.

InfoSource. Challenge students to visit the Web site of a company where they would like to work and use it to write a description of the company.

job intelligently. Be prepared to suggest contributions you can make to fill the company's needs.

List questions you might want to ask during the interview. Job duties, work schedules, employee evaluations, work areas and equipment, corporate history, and opportunities for advancement are all possible topics for discussion.

Finally, rehearse. Think of questions you might be asked and decide how to answer them. Here are some possible questions.

- Why do you want to work here?
- What qualifications do you have for the job?
- What are your goals for the future—say, five or ten years from now?
- Why did you leave your last job?
- What would you say are your greatest strengths and weaknesses?

Certain questions are illegal in a job interview. For example, an interviewer is not supposed to ask about your age, marital status, religion, national origin, race, or credit rating. However, the interviewer might forget to follow these restrictions or may be unaware of them. You don't have to answer illegal questions. It's usually best to simply redirect the conversation to another topic.

The Interview

Be sure to be clean, well groomed, and appropriately dressed for the interview. For most jobs, a neat, conservative appearance is best. Wear clean, pressed clothing similar to, or a little more formal than, what you would wear on the job. If you're not sure, go to the job site and observe how workers dress.

Arrive for the interview on time—or better yet, a few minutes early. Being late sends the message that you're irresponsible and uninterested. Bring extra copies of your résumé in case you'll be meeting with several people. Make sure you have all the information you might need to fill out an application, such as your Social Security number. See Figure 4-14. Don't bring friends or distractions. If you carry a wireless phone or pager, turn it off.

During the interview, be courteous but friendly. Follow these tips:

- **Watch your nonverbal signals.** Display good posture and maintain eye contact. Return a handshake with a firm grip. Don't fidget, play with your hair, or chew gum.

InfoSource

Researching Companies

To learn more about a company before your job interview:

- Check the company's Web site.
- Look for Web sites or print resources that list financial information about companies, including quarterly and annual reports.
- Plug the company name into an online search site and see if any other information comes up. Perhaps the company has waged an extremely successful sales campaign, or it's been commended for providing outstanding community service.

Class Activity. Have pairs of students role-play job interviews in front of the class. Afterward, have the rest of the class comment on the strengths and weaknesses shown by the job applicant. Ask them to note how well each applicant followed the tips listed on these pages.

- **Sell yourself.** Look for openings in the conversation that allow you to talk about your accomplishments, particularly those that pertain to the job. Be positive about yourself and your abilities without bragging. Don't ramble—be clear and concise.
- **Be positive.** Bad-mouthing a previous boss or coworker won't score points with an interviewer, and neither will talking about your personal problems.
- **Ask questions.** If necessary, refer to the list you prepared in advance. Unless the interviewer brings it up, avoid asking about pay—that will come later, if you're offered the job.
- **End on a positive note.** Before leaving, emphasize your interest in the position. If the interviewer doesn't mention it, ask when you can expect a decision. Ask for a business card so that you'll have the interviewer's correct name, title, and address. Thank the interviewer.

Follow Up

Within a few days of the interview, send a follow-up letter thanking your interviewer for taking the time to see you. This is an important step because it gives you the opportunity to add to the interviewer's good impression of you. Include a reminder of some positive point in your discussion and restate your interest in the job. If you forgot to make an important point during the interview, the letter gives you a second chance.

Also follow up by evaluating your own performance. What did you do well? Is there anything you want to do differently next time? What could you have done to be better prepared?

Class Activity. Gather magazine photos of teens in various outfits. Show them one at a time to the class, and ask whether the teen is dressed suitably for a job interview.

4-14

Arriving on time for an interview and being well prepared shows that you are responsible. What else can you do to show your interest in a job?

Critical Thinking. ***Ask:*** Suppose you receive two job offers. One job pays more, but the other has better benefits. Which would you take? Why?

EVALUATING JOB OFFERS

Although it may take many tries, eventually you'll be offered a job. Whether the offer comes during the interview or weeks later, you don't have to make a decision on the spot. Ask for time to think it over. Before you accept a job offer, make sure you understand the conditions of employment, such as your start date, work schedule, and job duties.

Benefits such as health insurance, paid vacations, training opportunities, and a retirement plan add value to a job offer.

4-15

Being offered a job is an exciting moment, but accepting the job is even more so. You've made the decision to begin a new stage of your life.

Research Activity. Have students investigate the pay rate typically offered to entry-level workers in a particular field and report their findings in class.

Besides these direct benefits, you should also consider factors such as the location and commute, the work environment, and the company's reputation.

In many cases, you and the employer will negotiate pay. Do research ahead of time to determine what should be reasonable for the employer and acceptable to you. You might talk to others who have done similar work, or check job search Web sites and the *Occupational Outlook Handbook.* When discussing pay, don't be too demanding, yet don't sell yourself short. After agreement is reached, ask the employer to put it in writing. See Figure 4-15.

If a deal is not made or if you decide to refuse the job, thank the employer, in person and by letter, for the offer. Try to leave the door open for the future.

EMPLOYMENT PROTECTIONS

Several federal laws protect against discrimination in hiring and in the workplace. These laws were passed to ensure that everyone is judged on his or her ability to do the job. For example:

- The Equal Employment Opportunity Act forbids discrimination by employers,

Critical Thinking. ***Ask:*** Why do you think the government has found it necessary to pass these laws protecting applicants and employees?

Community Activity. Ask students to locate the EEOC office for their area and find out its office hours and contact information.

Federal 5-in-1 Labor Law Poster®

This posting includes all employee notices required by the federal government.

ISSUE DATE 10/96

▼ CONSOLIDATED EEO

Equal Employment Opportunity is THE LAW

Employers Holding Federal Contracts or Subcontracts

Applicants to and employees of companies with a Federal government contract or subcontract are protected under the following Federal authorities:

RACE, COLOR, RELIGION, SEX, NATIONAL ORIGIN

Executive Order 11246, as amended, prohibits job discrimination on the basis of race, color, religion, sex or national origin, and requires affirmative action to ensure equality of opportunity in all aspects of employment.

INDIVIDUALS WITH DISABILITIES

Section 503 of the Rehabilitation Act of 1973, as amended, prohibits job discrimination because of a disability and requires affirmative action to employ and advance in employment qualified individuals with disabilities who, with reasonable accommodation, can perform the essential functions of a job.

VIETNAM ERA AND SPECIAL DISABLED VETERANS

38 U.S.C. 4212 of the Vietnam Era Veterans Readjustment Assistance Act of 1974 prohibits job discrimination and requires affirmative action to employ and advance in employment qualified Vietnam era veterans and qualified special disabled veterans.

Any person who believes a contractor has violated its nondiscrimination or affirmative action obligations under the authorities above should contact immediately:

The Office of Federal Contract Compliance Programs (OFCCP), Employment Standards Administration, U.S. Department of Labor (DOL), 200 Constitution Avenue, N.W., Washington, D.C. 20210 or call (202) 219-9368 (DOL's toll-free TDD number for individuals with hearing impairments is (800) 326-2577), or an OFCCP regional or district office, listed in most telephone directories under U.S. Government, Department of Labor.

Private Employment, State and Local Governments, Educational Institutions

Applicants to and employees of most private employers, state and local governments, educational institutions, employment agencies and labor organizations are protected under the following Federal laws.

RACE, COLOR, RELIGION, SEX, NATIONAL ORIGIN

Title VII of the Civil Rights Act of 1964, as amended, prohibits discrimination in hiring, promotion, discharge, pay, fringe benefits, job training, classification, referral, and other aspects of employment, on the basis of race, color, religion, sex or national origin.

DISABILITY

The Americans with Disabilities Act of 1990, as amended, protects qualified applicants and employees with disabilities from discrimination in hiring, promotion, discharge, pay, job training, fringe benefits, classification, referral, and other aspects of employment on the basis of disability. The law also requires that covered entities provide qualified applicants and employees with disabilities with reasonable accommodations that do not impose undue hardship.

AGE

The Age Discrimination in Employment Act of 1967, as amended, protects applicants and employees 40 years of age or older from discrimination on the basis of age in hiring, promotion, discharge, compensation, terms, conditions or privileges of employment.

SEX (WAGES)

In addition to sex discrimination prohibited by Title VII of the Civil Rights Act (see above), the Equal Pay Act of 1963, as amended, prohibits sex discrimination in payment of wages to women and men performing substantially equal work in the same establishment.

Retaliation against a person who files a charge of discrimination, participates in an investigation, or opposes an unlawful employment practice is prohibited by all of these Federal laws.

If you believe that you have been discriminated against under any of the above laws, you immediately should contact:

The U.S. Equal Employment Opportunity Commission (EEOC), 1801 L Street, N.W., Washington, D.C. 20507 or an EEOC field office by calling toll free (800) 669-4000. For individuals with hearing impairments, EEOC's toll free TDD number is (800) 669-6820.

Programs or Activities Receiving Federal Financial Assistance

RACE, COLOR, NATIONAL ORIGIN, SEX

In addition to the protection of Title VII of the Civil Rights Act of 1964, Title VI of the Civil Rights Act prohibits discrimination on the basis of race, color or national origin in programs or activities receiving Federal financial assistance. Employment discrimination is covered by Title VI if the primary objective of the financial assistance is provision of employment, or where employment discrimination causes or may cause discrimination in providing services under such programs. Title IX of the Education Amendments of 1972 prohibits employment discrimination on the basis of sex in educational programs or activities which receive Federal assistance.

INDIVIDUALS WITH DISABILITIES

Section 504 of the Rehabilitation Act of 1973, as amended, prohibits employment discrimination on the basis of a disability in any program or activity which receives Federal financial assistance. Discrimination is prohibited in all aspects of employment against persons with disabilities who, with reasonable accommodation, can perform the essential functions of a job.

If you believe you have been discriminated against in a program of any institution which receives Federal assistance, you should contact immediately the Federal agency providing such assistance.

EEOC - P/E-1

4-16 **By law, a notice like this must be placed somewhere in the workplace so that employees will have easy access to the information.** **Why are employers required to post this information?**

employment agencies, and unions on the basis of race, color, religion, sex, or national origin. See Figure 4-16.

- The Americans with Disabilities Act and the Rehabilitation Act protect people with physical or mental disabilities from discrimination.
- The Age Discrimination Act makes it illegal to discriminate against anyone over 40 in hiring or while on the job.
- The Equal Pay Act protects men and women who perform substantially equal work in the same workplace from gender-based wage discrimination.

The U.S. Equal Employment Opportunity Commission enforces these laws. If you feel you may have been discriminated against, contact the EEOC office in your area. You can also go to your union, if you're a union member, or see an attorney who specializes in employment issues.

Section 4.4 Review

CHECK YOUR UNDERSTANDING

1. Describe a résumé. What does it include?
2. What factors should you consider when evaluating a job offer?
3. What is the overall purpose of federal employment protection laws?

CONSUMER APPLICATION

Applying for a Job Select a job you would like to apply for. Write a résumé and a cover letter to introduce yourself to the employer and highlight your qualifications for the position. Exchange letters with a classmate. Ask if he or she would interview you and why.

Answer Key. Answers to the Section Review questions are provided in the Section Lesson Plan located in the *Teacher Resource Guide.*

Objectives

After studying this section, you should be able to:

- Describe skills that contribute to success on the job.
- Explain appropriate employee behavior.
- Give guidelines for leaving a job.

Key Terms

mentor
work ethic
severance package
unemployment insurance

SECTION 4.5

Succeeding on the Job

In today's rapidly changing workplace, you need to be flexible and ready to learn new skills. To be successful, you also need to get along with others and accept increasing levels of responsibility.

SKILLS FOR SUCCESS

You are developing skills now that will serve you later in your career. Solid reading, writing, math, and thinking skills, resource management skills, and technical skills are as necessary for success in the workplace as they are for success in school.

Technological, demographic, and work culture changes all contribute to the increasing demand for new skills in the workplace. To be successful in a rapidly changing job climate—or simply to keep a job—workers must be able to switch gears and quickly learn new skills. Take advantage of on-the-job training, continuing education courses, and adult education courses.

Technical Skills

As the impact of technology is felt in every sphere of life, workers will need to develop their technical skills and update them on a regular basis. All workers should know how to use a computer and be familiar with at least the basics of word processing. Many also need to use spread-

Team Activity. Have pairs of students role-play on-the-job scenarios in which they demonstrate one of the interpersonal skills listed here.

Point Out. A majority of employers rate good interpersonal skills as the single most important qualification for an employee.

sheet, database, and scheduling programs. You should be comfortable navigating the Internet and sending and receiving email.

Interpersonal Skills

The rising stars in any organization are often distinguished by their excellent interpersonal skills.

- **Communication skills.** Being a good listener shows respect for coworkers and allows you to analyze customer needs and wants. To present ideas clearly, improve your speaking and writing skills. Develop good electronic communication skills, such as using email appropriately and preparing effective computer presentations. Practice assertiveness. Learn to become comfortable speaking to groups.
- **Conflict resolution skills.** If you have a disagreement with someone, don't lash out or avoid that person. Instead, work to resolve the problem. Negotiation skills can help prevent conflicts from occurring.
- **Teamwork skills.** Teamwork includes recognizing and working toward organizational goals, fulfilling your obligations, and helping to ensure that your talents and skills mesh with those of other team members. Learn to develop mutually helpful relationships with others. See Figure 4-17.
- **Tolerance.** Become comfortable interacting with people who are different from you. Learning another language or taking workshops on cultural differences can help you to better understand others. Diversity enriches a workplace.

4-17

Developing interpersonal skills is crucial for success on the job. How can developing teamwork skills help you master other interpersonal skills?

Community Activity. Have students interview classmates who are involved in student organizations, such as student government or after-school clubs. Tell students to ask their subjects about how they think participating in these groups has helped them develop leadership skills.

Management Skills

Workers at any level need management skills. Management involves planning, controlling, and evaluating the use of resources to achieve goals. Here are some examples:

- **Time.** Use time wisely to meet deadlines. Don't get sidetracked by time-wasting activities, such as workplace gossip. Set priorities that enable you to juggle tasks.
- **Money.** Work within the budget for your project or department by carefully using supplies, for example.
- **Human resources.** Delegate tasks to others when appropriate. Learn to gauge their strengths and weaknesses and assign tasks that maximize their growth and productivity. See Figure 4-18.

Leadership Skills

In order to get ahead in most workplaces, you'll need leadership skills. The best way to develop those skills is to take on roles of increasing responsibility. You may need to begin outside the workplace—for example, by running for office in a student organization.

The workplace will offer many opportunities for leadership growth. You may be able to volunteer for a committee, organize a special event, or take on a leadership role in a professional organization. If you're in a union, consider becoming a union officer. Once you've been on the job for some time, you can become a **mentor**, an experienced coworker who acts as a guide or informal teacher for new employees.

You can start developing leadership skills now by joining Family, Career and Community Leaders of America (FCCLA). This national student organization offers a variety of projects that help young men and women become leaders. Projects focus on character development, thinking skills, communication skills, and vocational preparation. Members have opportunities to learn leadership skills in their specific career area and take charge of their future.

Class Activity. Draw three columns on the board, labeled "Time," "Money," and "Human Resources." Ask students to brainstorm specific strategies for managing each type of resource. List their responses on the board. Ask students to point out which of these strategies they could apply in their daily lives. Mark these strategies with a star.

4-18

Tasks are often delegated to make use of individual skills and talents. What is another benefit of delegating tasks?

Research Activity. Ask students to find and read a recent news story about someone who exhibited unprofessional behavior on the job. Have them write a paragraph summarizing the story and describing the consequences of the person's behavior. Ask students to share their summaries in class.

BEHAVIOR ON THE JOB

Your success also will be determined by your behavior in the workplace. Employers notice how employees present themselves, how well they follow rules, and how conscientious they are.

Policies and Procedures

When you start a new job, you'll be expected to learn and follow the policies and procedures of your workplace. Your employer may provide an employee manual that explains them in detail. If you attend a new-employee orientation, take notes and ask questions.

Professionalism

Professionalism refers to suitable conduct on the job. People who are professional exhibit skill in their work and live up to the highest standards of their profession. See Figure 4-19.

- **Develop a strong work ethic.** A **work ethic** is a sense of responsibility to do a job well. It's reflected in behavior such as getting to work on time, working a full day, and meeting deadlines. Goofing off, wasting time, and abusing telephone or Internet privileges show lack of work ethic.
- **Take responsibility for your actions.** Only by accepting responsibility for your mistakes can you learn from them. Your employer and coworkers will respect you for honestly admitting a mistake, but lying or blaming others will cost you respect and possibly your job.
- **Acknowledge the contributions of others.** Just as you want the credit for your own ideas and work, so do your coworkers. The good relationships you build as a result of acknowledging others' contributions will earn you credit as a good team player and potential leader.
- **Be courteous and respectful.** Return phone calls and emails promptly. Give others a chance to talk at meetings without belittling their ideas. Keep your emotions under control with coworkers, clients, and customers. Avoid distracting others.
- **Present an appropriate appearance.** Practice good hygiene and grooming. If your employer has a dress code, honor both its words and its intent. In the absence of a dress code, think about the image the organization wants to project. Remember, you represent your employer.

4-19

Showing courtesy and respect to others at meetings is a sign of professionalism. **Why can your professional reputation be one of your most valuable assets?**

Critical Thinking. *Ask:* Why is it a good idea to find a new job before resigning from your old one? How might being employed affect your search for a new job? Under what circumstances would you consider leaving a job before you have found a new job?

Job Safety

The Occupational Safety and Health Administration (OSHA) is a federal agency that sets and enforces on-the-job safety standards. OSHA standards and workplace inspections have prevented many injuries, illnesses, and deaths. However, workers also bear a responsibility for job safety.

Learn and follow the safety procedures at your workplace. For example, use machinery as instructed and wear protective equipment if necessary. See Figure 4-20. If you are injured on the job, notify your supervisor and get medical treatment.

Notify your employer of safety problems or health hazards. If the problem is not eliminated, file a report with OSHA. You have a right to refuse to work under conditions that can lead to serious injury or death. It's against the law for your employer to retaliate against you for reporting safety violations.

LEAVING A JOB

In your career, it's likely that you'll work for several employers. Reasons for leaving a job include:

- **Resigning.** You might choose to resign because you find a better opportunity elsewhere. If you're unhappy in your job, resist the urge to quit before you find a new one. Instead, start a job search during nonwork hours. Prospective employers are more interested in applicants who are currently employed.
- **Layoffs.** A *layoff* is a temporary or permanent reduction in a company's workforce. Layoffs can occur for many reasons. Workers in seasonal jobs, such as landscaping, might be laid off for several months each year. Permanent layoffs can occur when two companies merge or when a business cuts back financially.
- **Termination.** Employees can be terminated (fired) for poor job performance. The employee is usually warned during previous performance reviews that he or she must show improvement. If you receive such a warning, work with your supervisor to learn what the specific problem is and how you can overcome it. Workers can also be terminated for gross misconduct, such as dishonesty, theft, or violence. In this case, the employee is asked to leave immediately.

4-20

Whether or not your job requires protective equipment, follow all safety procedures in the workplace and be mindful of the safety of others.

Class Activity. Have students write a journal entry from the viewpoint of a worker who has just left a job, describing what he or she plans to do next.

Answer Key. Answers to the Section Review questions are provided in the Section Lesson Plan located in the *Teacher Resource Guide.*

Termination is illegal in certain circumstances. For example, it's illegal to fire employees because of race, gender, age, or disability, or to retaliate against a worker for reporting unsafe or illegal business practices. Information about illegal termination can be found on the U.S. Department of Labor's Web site or on consumer law Web sites.

Rights and Responsibilities

Regardless of your reason for leaving, you will have certain responsibilities toward your employer. In turn, your employer will have responsibilities toward you.

- **Show respect for your employer.** If you resign, give your employer at least two weeks notice so that a replacement can be found. If you're asked to finish a project before you go, do your best work. Leave your work area neat. Take home personal items, but don't discard files or other work-related items unless you're told to. Return company property such as security badges, manuals, books, and work-issued clothing or equipment.
- **Make good use of your exit interview.** On your last day, you may be asked to have a final discussion with a company representative. Answer questions honestly, but don't use the interview as an opportunity to speak disrespectfully about the company or your coworkers. Maintain your professionalism, both out of consideration and self-interest—you'll want to use this employer as a reference in the future.
- **Make sure you receive what you are due.** This may include a final paycheck, bonus or commission checks, and money for unused vacation time. Ask about your options regarding health coverage and any other plans you participated in, such as a retirement plan. You may want to consult a financial advisor as well. If you were laid off, you may be offered a **severance package**—bonus pay or special benefits offered to laid-off workers. For example, career counseling or job search assistance may be among the benefits.
- **Apply for unemployment benefits if you qualify. Unemployment insurance** is a joint federal and state plan designed to provide income to workers who have lost their jobs. Eligibility for benefits varies from state to state. In many states, people must have worked for a certain length of time, be unemployed for a certain length of time, and be unemployed through no fault of their own. Recipients must also be able and available to work and must actively seek work.

Section 4.5 Review

CHECK YOUR UNDERSTANDING

1. Describe three interpersonal skills that can help you succeed in the workplace.
2. Explain how to apply your work ethic on the job.
3. Name three responsibilities you have when you leave a job.

CONSUMER APPLICATION

Workplace Safety Choose an industry and research job safety hazards. Create a poster for workers in that industry that explains the hazards and what employees and employers can do to prevent them.

CHAPTER 4

Review & Activities

CHAPTER SUMMARY

- Career choices affect your ability to meet other goals. Career goals should be balanced with other goals in life. (4.1)
- Knowing yourself, investigating career areas, and planning your career helps you control your future. (4.2)
- Education opens the door to more and better career opportunities. You can learn how to manage the costs of education. (4.3)
- Job search skills range from preparing a résumé to interviewing. A job offer should be evaluated carefully before you accept it. (4.4)
- Skill development and professional and ethical behavior contribute to success on the job. (4.5)

Was It Discrimination? During a job interview, Reggie was asked some questions that seemed very personal. Not wanting to appear uncooperative, he gave some general answers. Later, he wondered about the purpose of the questions and whether his responses would hurt his chances. How can Reggie determine whether the questions were appropriate? What should he do if he decides they were not? (4.4)

Reviewing Key Terms and Ideas

1. How do **career** choices influence **standard of living**? (4.1)
2. How can the career you choose affect your family relationships? (4.1)
3. How does **flextime** help workers balance multiple roles? (4.1)
4. How will you benefit from planning your career? (4.2)
5. Describe two factors to consider when creating a career plan. (4.2)
6. How do workers in consumer service careers help consumers? (4.2)
7. Explain two pros and two cons of being an **entrepreneur**. (4.2)
8. How might your choice of career affect the type of education you choose? (4.3)
9. Explain the career preparation benefits of **internship** and **apprenticeship** programs. (4.3)
10. Describe three ways to save for your education beyond high school. (4.3)
11. Why would you include **references** in your **résumé**? (4.4)
12. Besides salary, what should you consider in evaluating a job offer? (4.4)
13. Describe three types of skills that help you succeed on the job. (4.5)
14. How does being a **mentor** help you build leadership skills? (4.5)
15. How can a strong **work ethic** contribute to success on the job? (4.5)
16. How much notice should you give when you resign from a job? Why? (4.5)

Answer Key. Answers to the Chapter Review & Activities are provided in the Teacher's Manual in the *Teacher Annotated Edition* of the text.

Thinking Critically

1. **Understanding Cause and Effect:** How might family responsibilities affect work performance or choice of career? How might work responsibilities or choice of career affect a person's ability to meet family responsibilities? (4.1)
2. **Recognizing Assumptions:** What assumptions might a prospective employer make based on a candidate's appearance and behavior during a job interview? How important is it to make a good first impression? (4.4)
3. **Analyzing Economic Concepts:** How might the state of the economy affect how you evaluate job offers? (4.4)

Building Consumer Skills

1. **Career Pathways:** Investigate a career area that interests you. Identify entry-level, technical, and professional jobs. Outline the education and experiences you would need to qualify for a job at each of these levels. (4.2)
2. **Financing Education:** Investigate two ways to finance education and training after high school. Outline a plan of action to finance your education, incorporating at least one of the ways you researched. (4.3)
3. **Job Interview:** With a partner, simulate a job interview for the class. Incorporate suggestions for improvement in a repeat performance. (4.4)
4. **Management Skills:** Work with a team to learn more about one antidiscrimination law. Create and give a presentation for the class. Assess team members' knowledge and skills before dividing up tasks. After the presentation, evaluate team performance and individual contributions. (4.4)
5. **Skills for Success:** Working with a team, list ten diverse careers that people in your community have. Discuss the work involved in each career, and identify what the team believes are the top three skills or personal qualities needed for success in each career. Compare team conclusions in class. (4.5)

CONSUMER CONNECTIONS

- **Family:** Survey family members about their careers. Ask these questions: Did you plan your career path? How many career changes have you had? Why? What do you wish you had done differently in preparing for your career? From your survey, what do you conclude? (4.1)
- **Community:** For a week, observe customer service in businesses you visit. Share observations in class. What effective skills did employees show? How were these helpful in solving any customer problems? How do company policies affect the way customer complaints are handled? (4.5)

CHAPTER 5

The U.S. Economic System

Reading with Purpose

- Write down the colored headings in this chapter.
- As you read the text under each heading, visualize what you are reading.
- Reflect on what you read by writing a few sentences under each heading to describe it.
- Reread your notes.

SECTION 5.1

Comparing Economic Systems

Objectives

After studying this section, you should be able to:

- Explain why economic systems develop.
- Distinguish between traditional, command, market, and mixed economies.
- Describe goals and characteristics of the U.S. economy.

Key Terms

economics
economic system
traditional economy
command economy
market economy
mixed economy
free enterprise

Does the word "economy" make you think of Wall Street, corporate tycoons, and other things that seem a world away? You may not realize it, but the economy plays a central role in your life every day.

WHAT IS ECONOMICS?

If you've read the first few chapters in this book, you're already aware of some basic economic concepts. You know that as a consumer, you purchase and use *goods*—such as shoes, pizza, and toothpaste—and *services*—such as public transportation, haircuts, and music lessons. You also know that you must use your limited resources wisely to meet your needs and wants. *Needs* are necessities such as food, basic clothing, and shelter. *Wants* are things people desire that are not necessary, such as a new computer or the latest fashions.

Problems of needs, wants, and resources are the realm of economics. **Economics** is the social science that examines how societies use scarce resources to produce and distribute goods and services that satisfy peoples' wants and needs. Simply stated, economics is the study of choices about using resources. A specialist in the field of economics is an *economist.*

Class Activity. Ask students to name economic choices a society might make. List their responses on the board. Ask students to identify the opportunity costs of each choice. Write the costs next to each choice. Then ask students which choices they think are worth the cost.

The study of economics includes two branches. *Macroeconomics* is economics on a national and global scale, concerned with the economic decisions made by governments. *Microeconomics* focuses on economic decisions made by individual people and businesses. However, the two are interrelated. As a consumer, you both affect the national economy and are affected by it. Understanding basic principles of economics can help you make better consumer decisions.

THE NEED FOR ECONOMIC SYSTEMS

An **economic system** is the way a society uses resources to satisfy its people's needs and wants. Economic systems develop in response to the problem of limited resources.

Economic Resources

As a consumer, your resources include many things that you may use to reach your goals—money, time, skills, personal energy, tools, community agencies, and so on. Societies also have resources with which to meet their goals. Their economic resources include such things as land and natural resources; power, communication, and transportation systems; factories and equipment; productive workers; and money with which to fund government programs or trade with other nations. See Figure 5-1.

Societies vary widely in the amount of resources available to them. Some have little, while others are comparatively wealthy. Still, no society has an unlimited supply of resources.

Scarcity and Opportunity Cost

The resources of a society are limited, but people's wants are unlimited. Therefore, a society can't possibly provide everything that its people want. This economic concept is called *scarcity*, and it's the fundamental problem that all economic systems try to solve.

Because there aren't enough resources to satisfy all wants, choices must be made. Choosing one option means giving up another. Every economic choice has an *opportunity cost*, the value of the best alternative given up. For example, land on which

5-1

Economic resources include productive farmland. How might the U.S. economy be different if this resource were not so abundant?

Class Activity. Have each student create a large table that contrasts traditional, command, and market economies. Tables should show how each type of economy answers the three basic economic questions (what goods and services are produced, who produces them, and who uses them).

a factory is built can't be used for growing crops. The opportunity cost of using the land for the factory is the value of the crops that could have been produced instead. See Figure 5-2.

Three Basic Questions

Because of limited resources and the problem of scarcity, every society must make choices that affect the lives and comfort of its people. It must resolve three basic questions.

- What goods and services will be produced?
- How will these goods and services be produced?
- Who should share the goods and services that are produced?

How a particular society answers these questions—what will be produced, how, and for whom—determines what kind of economic system it has.

5-2

As the need for housing grows, more homes are built. What is the opportunity cost of a new home development?

TYPES OF ECONOMIC SYSTEMS

Economists have identified four basic types of economic systems. Three of them—traditional, command, and market economies—are really theoretical models, since it's thought that no "pure" example of any of them exists in the world today. Most of the world's economies fit into the fourth category, mixed economies.

Traditional Economy

In a **traditional economy**, decisions about what to produce, how, and for whom are based on traditional customs and beliefs of the society. People hunt, fish, farm, and live in the way their ancestors did. Families or tribes are self-sufficient, producing most of their own food, clothing, shelter, and other items. The economy thus consists of many small independent economic units. Access to technological advancements is limited. Another term for a traditional economy is *subsistence economy*.

Societies that follow the traditional economic system to a significant degree are very rare today. A few exist in rural, nonindustrial areas in various parts of the world.

Critical Thinking. ***Ask:*** Would it be possible for a modern society to follow the traditional economic system? Why or why not?

Discussion. *Ask:* What are some examples of societies (past or present) with traditional, command, market, and mixed economies?

Command Economy

In a **command economy**, decisions about what to produce, how, and for whom are decided by a central government. Another name for this system is a *controlled economy*. Government leaders control all the economic resources and make all the economic decisions. They decide the quantity and costs of goods and services that are produced and where they will be sold. Individuals who live in a command system have nothing to say about what is produced or how it is produced. They may not even be allowed to choose their role in the production process.

Critical Thinking. *Ask:* What are the advantages and disadvantages of each type of economy? Is there one best type of economy?

Instead, the government may decide what jobs people are allowed to have and who will be trained for them.

Market Economy

In a **market economy**, decisions about what to produce, how, and for whom are decided by individuals acting in their own self-interest. Individuals and private companies own and control economic resources such as businesses, factories, and farms. They decide for themselves what goods to make and what services to offer. In this sense, a market economy is the opposite of a command economy. Another term for this type of economy is a *capitalist* system.

An essential characteristic of a market economy is the existence of free markets. A *market* is a mechanism that brings potential buyers and sellers together to exchange goods and services. A market can be big, like the stock market, or small, such as a neighborhood where teens offer to wash cars or walk dogs for a fee. See Figure 5-3.

Mixed Economy

A **mixed economy** is a combination of the command and market economic systems. The idea of a free market is combined with some degree of government control. Most of the world's economies fall into this category. However, there can be great differences

5-3

At this example of a market—an auction—buyers and sellers come together and set prices. Give another example of a market.

Discussion. *Ask:* How well do you think the U.S. economy succeeds in meeting each of the economic goals listed here?

among mixed economies. For example, in the People's Republic of China, the command system is more prominent than the market system. In the U.S. economy, the market system dominates.

THE U.S. ECONOMIC SYSTEM

Just as you set goals for what you want to achieve, so do nations. The economic goals of the United States include:

- Growth—an increase in the amount of goods and services produced over time.
- Efficiency—wise use of limited resources.
- Stability—a steady level of economic well-being, without wild ups and downs.
- Justice—an economic system that treats all citizens fairly.
- Security—support systems for citizens who face economic hardship through no fault of their own.

In addition to these goals, a number of characteristics are fundamental to the U.S. economy. They include:

- **Private property.** Individuals and groups are allowed to own economic resources such as land and businesses. Consumers own the goods that they purchase.
- **Freedom of choice.** In the U.S. economy, consumers freely choose how to spend their money. Choices made by you and other consumers determine which products succeed and fail in the marketplace.

Answer Key. Answers to the Section Review questions are provided in the Section Lesson Plan located in the *Teacher Resource Guide.*

- **Freedom of enterprise.** The U.S. economy is often called a system of *private enterprise* or **free enterprise**. These terms emphasize that individuals are free to own and control business enterprises.
- **Limited government control.** In a free enterprise system, businesses are allowed to compete for profit with a minimum of government regulation. Governmental control over economic matters is limited because individual economic freedom is so highly valued.

The U.S. economy is also influenced by the principles of profit, competition, and supply and demand. You'll learn about those principles, and how they affect consumers, in the next section.

Section 5.1 Review

CHECK YOUR UNDERSTANDING

1. Each economic system must answer three questions. What are they?
2. How does a command economy differ from a market economy?
3. Describe three characteristics of the U.S. economy.

CONSUMER APPLICATION

Changing Economic Systems Use online or print resources to identify several nations that are currently changing from a command to a market economy. What are some key reasons for the change? What challenges does the transition create?

Objectives

After studying this section, you should be able to:

- Describe factors that motivate and influence production.
- Explain forces that determine prices in a free market.
- Discuss the roles of producers and consumers in the U.S. economy.

Key Terms

profit
capital
productivity
corporation
shareholders
demand
law of demand
supply
law of supply
competition

SECTION 5.2

Producers and Consumers

No single person or group coordinates the U.S. economy. Yet amazingly, you and millions of other consumers can get almost anything you need or want—if you pay the price. How is this possible? It's because of the interaction of producers and consumers in the free enterprise system.

PRODUCING GOODS AND SERVICES

Producers make goods and provide services. They operate in a variety of areas—manufacturing, agriculture, transportation, construction, and so on. No matter what they specialize in, producers in the U.S. economy have much in common, beginning with their motivation.

The Profit Motive

In a market economy, producers of goods and services are motivated by the desire to make money. They want to maximize their **profit**, or earnings after all costs of production have been paid. Suppose a recording company agrees to release a CD by a new singing group. The company spends money to produce and manufacture the CD, distribute it to stores and radio stations, and advertise it.

Critical Thinking. ***Ask:*** What are the advantages of having profit as a motive for producers? Are there other factors aside from profit that might motivate producers? What might be lost in the marketplace if maximizing profit is the producers' only motivation?

The company has calculated how many CDs it must sell in order to recover its costs and break even. Any additional sales result in profit.

What does this mean for you as a consumer? With some exceptions, only the goods and services that generate profit will be available to you. If the CD in the previous example resulted in a satisfactory profit, the recording company would probably be willing to produce another CD by the same group. However, if sales were disappointing, the recording company would rather use its resources in other ways more likely to generate profit.

Factors of Production

It's not possible to produce goods and services without having resources to work with. Economists have identified basic types of resources needed to produce goods and services. They are often referred to as *factors of production.*

- **Land.** In economics, land refers to natural resources. It includes not only bodies of land and water, but also the resources found on or in them, such as fish, animals, trees, and mineral deposits. Many types of goods can be produced from these raw materials.
- **Labor.** The work that people do is a human resource. The contributions of all types of workers—from teachers and construction workers to airline pilots and artists—result in the production of goods and services.
- **Capital.** As a factor of production, **capital** refers to machines and technology used in the production of goods and services. Examples include factories, farming equipment, and roads. See Figure 5-4.
- **Entrepreneurship.** The U.S. economy encourages individuals to become entrepreneurs by owning their own businesses. Entrepreneurs acquire and organize other resources to produce goods and services. They often start new ventures and develop new products. The U.S. Small Business Administration has information to help entrepreneurs get started. Loans and grants are available for people who qualify.

FCCLA. Challenge students to work in groups to develop a plan for a small business that relates to an area of Family and Consumer Sciences education, such as culinary arts (for example, a catering business) or child care (a babysitting service). Have each group enter its plan as an Entrepreneurship STAR event.

5-4

Machines used to build cars are capital, but the cars themselves are not unless they're used to produce services. What type of car or other vehicle would be considered capital?

Class Activity. Have students create posters or diagrams illustrating the process of specialization and its effects on productivity.

- **Technology.** Some economists add technology, or applied science, as a fifth factor of production. Technological advances—such as the birth of the Internet—make it possible to develop new types of goods and services or new ways of producing and distributing existing ones.

Productivity

Productivity is a measure of the efficiency with which goods and services can be produced. Productivity can be increased through the use of technology and entrepreneurship, as well as by educating and training the labor force. See Figure 5-5.

Another practice that improves productivity is *specialization*. This means that people focus on producing a particular good or service that they are able to produce well. Without specialization, all members of society would have to grow their own food, make their own clothing, and build their own homes. It's much more efficient for people and businesses to specialize. One person might become trained as a carpenter, while another writes songs or studies medicine. They obtain other goods and services by trading or purchasing.

Critical Thinking. *Ask:* Is it always possible to identify which type of ownership a business has without doing research? Why or why not?

Business Organizations

Businesses bring together factors of production to create goods and services in order to make a profit. Almost every product you use—from skateboards and jeans to sodas and braces—is produced by a business.

Businesses are often classified by the way they are organized. By law, there are three types of business organizations in the United States.

- **Individual proprietorship.** This type of business is owned and controlled by one person, known as the *proprietor*. The owner is rewarded with all of the profits if the business is successful, but also bears unlimited risk. If the business fails, the owner may lose all the money he or she

Team Activity. Organize the class into small groups. Assign each group a specific industry, or have groups choose for themselves. Have each group create a chart or diagram showing how the five factors of production apply to its industry. Have groups share their work with the class.

5-5

Teaching employees new skills can increase their productivity. **How does maintaining a productive labor force serve the economy?**

Critical Thinking. ***Ask:*** Why is having limited liability a major advantage for corporations? What will happen to shareholders if a corporation fails?

Research Activity. Ask students to track the value of a company's stock over the course of a week. Have them show the results in a line graph.

has invested in it. The owner may even be forced to sell other assets, such as a home, to repay business debts.

- **Partnership.** This type of firm is owned and controlled by two or more people. The partners share in decision making, profits, and risks. Like individual proprietors, people in partnerships bear unlimited risk if the business fails.
- **Corporation.** A **corporation** is an organization that is owned by many people but treated by law as a single entity separate from its owners. The owners of a corporation are called **shareholders**. They are people who have purchased shares of stock, which are units of ownership in the company. If a corporation does well, profits may be divided among shareholders according to how many shares of stock they own. If it does poorly, shareholders may lose money. However, they can't lose more money than they invested. The personal assets of shareholders are protected because the corporation is a separate legal entity. This limited liability of owners is a major benefit of corporations compared to other business organizations.

TEXTLINK

You can learn more about shares of stock by reading Section 13.3.

PRICES IN A FREE MARKET

How are prices determined? You might assume that someone—perhaps a store manager—simply decides how much to charge for a shirt, a can of beans, or a bicycle. That's partly true, but it's far from the whole story. Would it surprise you to learn that *you* help determine prices?

Demand

To a great extent, prices in a market economy depend on the interaction of demand and supply. **Demand** is the quantity of a particular good or service that consumers are willing and able to buy at a given price. See Figure 5-6. If you'd like to buy a certain brand and style of jeans and have the money to pay for them, you're contributing to consumer demand for those jeans.

5-6

These young entrepreneurs are hoping to profit from consumer demand. What factors might affect the demand for lemonade?

Class Activity. Ask students how many of them would be willing to pay $100 for a pair of jeans. List the number on the board. Then ask how many would pay $95. Keep lowering the price by $5 and listing the number who would pay it. Discuss how this exercise illustrates the law of demand.

You might enjoy a cruise around the world, but unless you're willing and able to pay for one, you're not adding to the demand for world cruises.

Demand for a product is not a fixed number. It goes up or down depending on the price at which the product is offered during a given time period. According to the **law of demand**, when the price of a product goes down, demand for that product will generally go up. When the price goes up, demand will generally go down. All other factors being equal, consumers will be willing and able to purchase more pairs of jeans at $35 than at $50.

Supply

Supply is the quantity of a particular product that producers are able and willing to make available for sale. It, too, depends on the price of the product at any given time. According to the **law of supply**, when the price of a product goes up, the supply will generally go up. When the price goes down, the supply will generally go down. Why? When a company is able to sell a product for a higher price, it can make more profit. The profit motive provides an incentive to increase the supply.

Notice that as the price of a product changes, demand and supply move in different directions. See Figure 5-7.

Interaction of Demand and Supply

So far, you've learned how changes in prices affect demand and supply. The opposite is also true. A change in demand or supply can cause the price of a product to go up or down.

Caption Answer. The quantity demanded goes up while the quantity supplied goes down.

5-7

These graphs show how price is related to the quantity demanded or supplied. When the price goes down, what happens to the quantity demanded? What happens to the quantity supplied?

Demand and Supply Curves

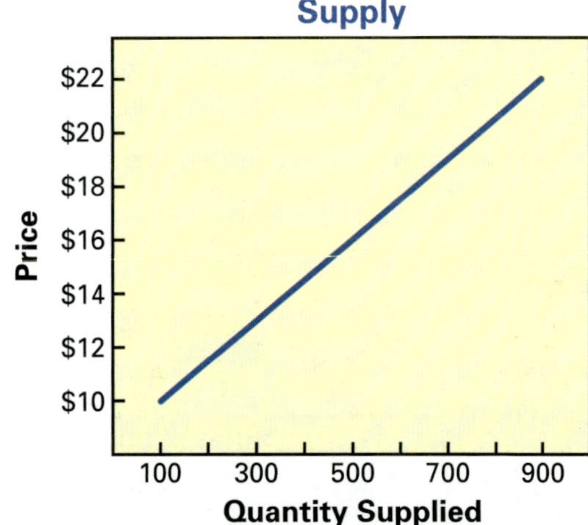

Discussion. *Ask:* Can you think of a product that was popular for only a short time? What happened to the availability of the product when demand fell?

Suppose that because of unusually mild weather, fewer people than expected are buying winter coats. As a result, stores have a *surplus*, or excess quantity, of coats. They want to get rid of them to make room for other merchandise, so they cut prices to attract shoppers. When supply is greater than demand, prices tend to fall.

On the other hand, suppose a heavily advertised video game becomes the must-have gift during the holiday shopping season. The game manufacturer can't produce it quickly enough, resulting in a shortage. In this situation—when demand exceeds supply—prices tend to rise. Some consumers, desperate to own the game, will be willing to pay more for it.

Remember, however, that once prices change, the quantity of games sold will change in response. Due to the law of supply, the video game manufacturer will be willing to produce more games at the higher price. Due to the law of demand, fewer consumers will be willing and able to buy the game when the price goes up. Supply will increase and demand will decrease. As a result, the price will begin to come down again. Eventually supply will equal demand, and the price will become stable.

As these examples show, the interaction of supply and demand largely determines how much of a product will be made and at what price it will be sold. For every product, there is a price at which demand will equal supply. Economists call this the *equilibrium price*. At this price, consumers are willing to buy exactly the same quantity of the product as producers are willing to make. See Figure 5-8.

Class Activity. Have students create a visual illustrating the effects of an increase in oil prices on the economy as a whole.

Production Costs

Besides demand and supply, what else influences prices? Naturally, the price of an item is affected by the cost of producing it. Thus, changes in the cost of production factors can cause prices to move up or down. For example, a rise in oil prices sends a ripple effect through the economy. Since fuel is made from oil, the cost of operating a car or truck goes up. Airfares climb because airlines must pay more for jet fuel. The prices of food and other goods rise because the cost of transporting goods increases.

The cost of labor has a significant effect on prices. If a company finds that it must increase the pay it gives workers, it may have to charge consumers more for its products.

5-8

When the equilibrium price is achieved, both consumers and producers benefit.

Finding the Equilibrium Price

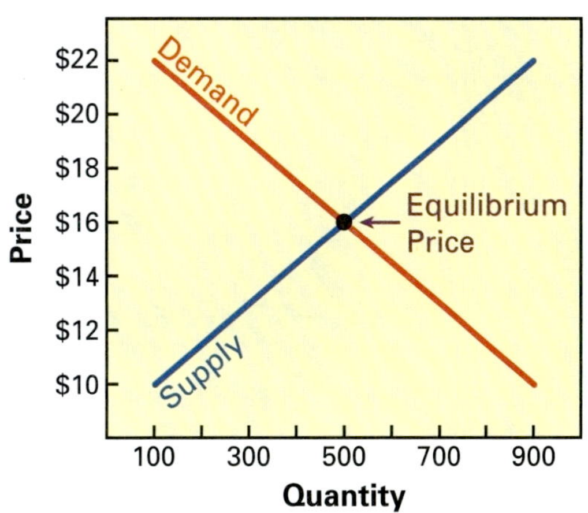

Critical Thinking. *Ask:* How does the work of labor unions affect production costs? Why might some businesses resist the formation of unions?

Why might a company need to pay workers more? One reason is that the laws of supply and demand apply to the labor market. Workers who have skills that are in demand usually command the highest salaries. If there's a shortage of skilled workers, employers must compete for them by offering higher pay or better benefits.

Some businesses might be tempted to reduce their labor costs by paying workers unfairly low wages or making them work under unsafe conditions. Laws and government agencies help prevent such abuses. Additional protection is provided by labor unions. A *labor union* is an organization that represents workers for the purpose of bringing about better pay and working conditions.

Community Activity. Have students interview a local business owner about what steps he or she takes to gain an edge over the competition.

Through a process called *collective bargaining*, unions and employers negotiate an employment contract that addresses issues such as pay, benefits, working hours, safe working conditions, and job security. See Figure 5-9.

Competition

Another factor that affects prices is the presence or absence of competition. **Competition** is rivalry between two or more businesses that offer similar goods or services. Each tries to win a larger share of the market.

The rival companies know that consumers have the option of buying another product or shopping at another store. Therefore, they compete for consumers' dollars. One way to do this is by offering the product at a lower price. Companies can also compete by offering higher quality products, more useful features, better service, and so on. No matter which company wins the most business, consumers are the real winners.

5-9

Labor unions and employers work to address fair practices through a system of negotiation and contracts. Name some groups in the workforce that are represented by labor unions.

Point Out. Businesses that offer a unique product or service have no competition. This allows them to set their prices higher.

Dollars and Sense. Have students write a paragraph explaining how they exercise their power as consumers.

Answer Key. Answers to the Section Review questions are provided in the Section Lesson Plan located in the *Teacher Resource Guide*.

DOLLARS and SENSE

Use Your Consumer Power

As a consumer, you have a powerful influence on what goods and services are produced and at what prices they're offered. Make the most of this opportunity.

- Shop around for the best quality and price. By doing so, you vote with your dollars.
- Avoid buying products or services that you feel are overpriced or that don't meet your needs and wants.
- Write to companies that offer unsatisfactory products or services. In a polite way, let them know why you're not a satisfied customer.

Competition is also good for the economic system as a whole. That's because competition encourages efficient use of resources. Businesses want to lower the prices of their goods and services to compete with their rivals, yet they still want to make a profit. Increased efficiency lets them do both.

CONSUMERS IN THE MARKETPLACE

As you can see, consumer spending has a major impact. The lure of profit based on consumer sales motivates businesses to produce goods and services. Consumer demand influences what products will be produced, how many will be offered for sale, and at what price. Competition for consumer dollars encourages businesses to improve their products and their productivity. All this is evidence of the controlling influence of consumers, which is called *consumer sovereignty*.

Consumers can band together to exert pressure on businesses or political leaders. For example, they can engage in a *boycott*, which is an organized refusal to purchase particular goods or services. Consumers who are unhappy with a company's business practices might start a campaign encouraging other consumers to stop buying that company's products. If enough consumers join the boycott, the company has a powerful motive to address consumers' concerns.

Section 5.2 Review

CHECK YOUR UNDERSTANDING

1. Explain what motivates businesses to produce goods and services.
2. How are prices determined in a free market?
3. In what ways do consumers influence the U.S. economy?

CONSUMER APPLICATION

Technology Use Research how technology is used in one of the following fields: communications, the arts, engineering, science, health, human services, or business.

Objectives

After studying this section, you should be able to:

- Give examples of public goods and services.
- Describe government programs for redistributing income.
- Explain why the government regulates economic activity.
- Identify two ways in which the government can stabilize the economy.

Key Terms

Social Security
Medicare
monopoly
antitrust laws

SECTION 5.3

The Government's Roles

A market economy is a powerful and efficient system, but not a perfect one. Meeting economic goals such as security, stability, efficiency, and justice can sometimes be difficult. The government steps in to help further these goals, playing a limited but vital role in the U.S. economy.

LEVELS OF GOVERNMENT

The United States has three levels of government: federal, state, and local. The federal government operates on the national level, dealing with matters that affect the country as a whole. Rights and powers not granted to the federal government are held by state governments. At the local level, government bodies such as counties, townships, cities, towns, and boroughs work to meet the needs of citizens.

Each level of government performs important economic functions. Some of these functions enable the economy to operate more smoothly. Others help to create a more just society. In general, governmental bodies have four major roles to play in the U.S. economy: providing public goods and services, regulating economic activity, redistributing income, and ensuring economic stability.

Community Activity. Have students produce a list of specific public goods and services provided by their local government. They may rely on their own knowledge or consult community bulletin boards, Web sites, and other local resources for information.

PROVIDING PUBLIC GOODS AND SERVICES

Public goods and services are those that federal, state, and local governments provide to citizens. Examples include:

- National defense.
- Police and fire protection.
- Courts and correctional institutions.
- Public parks.
- Street, highway, and bridge construction and maintenance.
- Public education.
- Public transportation.

These goods and services provide widespread benefit. In many cases, they would be impractical or unprofitable for private individuals or groups to provide. See Figure 5-10.

REDISTRIBUTING INCOME

In a market economy, society's resources are distributed to the people who have money to pay for them. While this system has many advantages, it can result in problems for people who lack sufficient income due to illness, age, unemployment, or other circumstances. Some of them face difficulty in meeting the basic needs of food, clothing, shelter, and health care. The government works to reduce economic inequality by redistributing income. Money collected from taxpayers is used to fund programs that assist people in need.

Social Security and Medicare

Social Security is an insurance program that is sponsored by the federal government and pays benefits to qualified people. The benefits are paid for by a required tax on the earnings of most workers. Those workers and their families are then eligible to receive benefits under certain circumstances. The Social Security system provides a range of benefits, most of which are based on previous earnings.

- **Retirement benefits.** When they reach a certain age and retire, workers who have paid Social Security taxes become eligible to receive monthly benefits.
- **Survivors' benefits.** When an insured worker dies, the surviving spouse and any children are paid benefits to replace lost income.

Caption Answer. Public transportation can help those without private transportation get to a job, which increases the local labor force.

5-10

Public transportation is paid for by taxpayers. How might public transportation benefit a local economy?

Discussion. ***Ask:*** How do programs that redistribute income serve the goals and ideals of the United States?

- **Disability benefits.** Workers who develop physical or mental conditions that prevent them from working may receive these benefits.

> **TEXTLINK**
> More information about Social Security benefits can be found in Sections 13.2, 14.4, and 14.5.

Another part of the Social Security system is **Medicare**, a program that pays some of the costs of medical and hospital care for people who are 65 and older. It also provides care for some people under 65, such as those who are disabled.

Unemployment Insurance

As you may recall from Chapter 4, unemployment insurance provides income to eligible workers who are unemployed through no fault of their own. The program was established by federal law but is operated separately by each state. Funding comes mainly from a tax paid by employers.

Public Assistance Programs

Public assistance programs provide aid to individuals based on need, regardless of whether they have paid taxes into the program. Programs have been established to provide assistance in the areas of income, nutrition, health, and housing. Here are some examples.

InfoSource. Have students visit the Social Security Administration's Web site to learn more about how Social Security benefits them.

- **Temporary Assistance to Needy Families (TANF).** This state-run program uses federal and state funds to provide low-income families with cash payments and job opportunities.
- **Supplemental Security Income (SSI).** This program provides cash for food, clothing, and shelter to the elderly, disabled, and their families. The Social Security Administration administers the program, which uses federal and state funds.
- **Food stamps.** People who are unemployed, on public assistance, or homeless, and those with low incomes, may qualify to receive assistance to purchase food. They receive paper coupons or electronic cards that can be used like cash to buy food. The program is administered by the U.S. Department of Agriculture (USDA) and state agencies.

InfoSource

Social Security Benefits

To find out what Social Security benefits you're entitled to:

- Look for your annual benefits statement. Once you begin earning wages, the Social Security Administration should mail a statement to you each year. It includes an estimate of what your monthly Social Security benefits might be, based on what you've earned so far.
- You can also request specific information about your benefits through the Social Security Administration's Web site.

Research Activity. Have each student choose one of the public assistance programs listed here. Ask students to consult library and Internet resources for more information about the benefits the program provides. Have them summarize the program in a paragraph and share their findings in class.

- **Supplemental Food Program for Women, Infants and Children (WIC).** This program provides nutritious food and nutrition counseling to women who are pregnant or have just given birth. It also provides food to infants and children up to age five who are nutritionally at risk. The program is administered by the USDA through state health departments.

- **National School Lunch and School Breakfast Programs.** The federal government provides schools with surplus food, as well as money for school lunches and breakfasts. See Figure 5-11.

- **Food Distribution Program.** This USDA program distributes food to nursing homes, day care centers, homeless shelters, food banks, and low-income individuals and families.

- **Medicaid.** This health insurance program, jointly funded by federal and state governments, provides health-related services to low-income and needy people.

- **State Children's Health Insurance Program.** Children from low-income families who don't have health insurance and don't qualify for Medicaid can receive health insurance through this program.

- **Housing programs.** The Department of Housing and Urban Development (HUD) provides several types of programs to help people rent or buy affordable housing.

REGULATING ECONOMIC ACTIVITY

A third economic function of government is regulation. Economic activities often have a bystander effect. That is, a person or group of people may be unintentionally hurt or helped as a result of the activity. The government tries to prevent economic activities from causing harmful side effects.

Caption Answer. Other ways the government distributes food include food stamps, WIC, and the USDA Food Distribution Program.

5-11

The federal government provides low-cost or free meals to millions of children each day. In what other ways does government provide food distribution?

Class Activity. Hold a class debate on the benefits of policing polluters. Have one team focus on the benefits to the environment and public health, while the other team stresses the effect of environmental laws on production costs, and ultimately, on consumer prices.

- **Protecting the environment.** A factory might be very productive, yet pollute the air and water. Market forces alone don't give the factory owner an incentive to stop the pollution. Therefore, the government steps in. The Environmental Protection Agency sets standards for pollutants and takes action against polluters. See Figure 5-12.
- **Protecting consumers.** Government regulations ensure that unsafe products are taken off the market. They also limit the sale of potentially misused products such as alcohol and prescription drugs.
- **Protecting workers.** The government protects workers from being exploited by employers. It sets a minimum wage that most workers must be paid. Child labor laws regulate the employment of children. Employers are expected to provide a safe work environment. They are not allowed to discriminate on the basis of race, ethnic origin, religion, gender, disability, or other factors.

Promoting Competition

As you have read, competition is good for consumers and for the economy as a whole. For a business, however, lack of competition would be more profitable. Federal and state governments have therefore enacted laws designed to promote competition.

Many of these laws focus on preventing unfair monopolies. A **monopoly**, sometimes called a *trust*, is a situation in which a single company controls the supply of a good or service for which there is no close substitute. A monopoly gives a company a great degree of control over price. If only one store in town sells light bulbs, for example, the store can raise the price of light bulbs without fear of losing business to competitors.

5-12

The EPA works to control the level of pollutants in the environment. Why is protecting the environment important?

Critical Thinking. ***Ask:*** Why is the federal government in the best position to take measures that maintain economic stability?

There can be legitimate reasons why a monopoly exists. Perhaps no other company chooses to compete because the cost of doing business is too high or the potential for sales is too low. A company that invents a new product might be given the exclusive right to sell it for a certain number of years.

However, sometimes companies try to eliminate competition by using unfair methods. A firm might try to merge with its only competitor, for instance, or erect barriers that prevent others from selling a similar product. **Antitrust laws** are designed to regulate unfair business practices that reduce competition. Antitrust laws are enforced by

5-13

Corporate mergers require government approval. Why?

Answer Key. Answers to the Section Review questions are provided in the Section Lesson Plan located in the *Teacher Resource Guide.*

the Federal Trade Commission, the Antitrust Division of the Department of Justice, and state agencies. See Figure 5-13.

ENSURING ECONOMIC STABILITY

One of the goals of the U.S. economy is stability. When the economy becomes unstable, both businesses and consumers suffer. There may be widespread unemployment. Prices for goods and services may suddenly climb steeply or drop sharply. The economy may enter a serious decline.

The federal government uses two basic approaches to try to maintain economic stability. One method, called *fiscal policy*, involves adjusting its policies about taxing and spending. The other method, called *monetary policy*, involves regulating interest rates and the money supply. You can learn more about both methods in Chapter 6.

Section 5.3 Review

CHECK YOUR UNDERSTANDING

1. List five public goods and services provided by governments.
2. What is a monopoly? Why does the government try to prevent the creation of monopolies?
3. What methods can the federal government use to stabilize the economy?

CONSUMER APPLICATION

Redistributing Income Use online or print resources to learn more about one of the government programs for redistributing income. Who is eligible to participate? How do people apply to the program?

Objectives

After studying this section, you should be able to:

- Explain the purposes of taxation.
- Describe taxes paid by U.S. consumers.
- Explain principles of tax fairness.
- Identify major government spending categories.

Key Terms

tax
revenue
proportional tax
progressive tax
regressive tax

SECTION 5.4

Principles of Taxation

It happens all the time—an extra $3, $5, or $10 is tacked on to the price of your purchase. Taxes again! Why are taxes necessary? Where does the money go?

PURPOSES OF TAXATION

A **tax** is a required payment to a local, state, or national government. Contrary to what you might think, taxes don't exist just to annoy you. Governments use taxes and the tax system for several purposes.

- **To fund public goods and services.** Providing public goods and services—from road repair to national defense—is costly. Taxes are the main source of **revenue**, money collected or received by a government for public use. The government also borrows money to fund goods and services.
- **To influence behavior.** Taxes on tobacco and alcohol, for example, discourage people from using these products by effectively raising their prices. Tax breaks are offered for home ownership, charitable giving, and other behavior that the government wants to encourage.
- **To stabilize the economy.** As you'll learn in the next chapter, the economy goes through cycles of growth and decline. The government can raise or lower taxes to help stabilize these cycles.

Class Activity. Have students write an essay ranking the purposes of taxation in order of importance and giving reasons for their rankings.

Discussion. ***Ask:*** Who pays each of the taxes described? Which forms of taxation are direct and which are indirect?

- **To redistribute income.** The tax system allows governments to redistribute income by increasing the tax burden on some groups and decreasing it for others. Taxes taken from the wealthy can be spent on programs to help the needy.

THE TAXES PEOPLE PAY

During your life you may be subject to many types of taxes, depending on where you live and your economic activities. Here are some of the taxes paid, directly or indirectly, by consumers.

- **Income tax.** Income that you earn—whether from a job or other sources, such as interest on savings accounts—is subject to income tax. The Sixteenth Amendment to the Constitution authorizes Congress to tax business and personal incomes. Federal income tax is collected by a government agency called the Internal Revenue Service (IRS). Some state and local governments also collect income tax. Personal income tax paid by individuals is the federal government's main source of revenue. See Figure 5-14.
- **Social Security taxes.** These taxes pay for the Social Security programs described in the previous section. Social Security taxes are based on wages earned and are withheld from paychecks. They are sometimes called FICA taxes because their collection is authorized by the

5-14

Most of the federal government's revenue comes from individuals.

Federal Government Revenue

Actual revenue for fiscal year 2005
Total: $2,154 billion

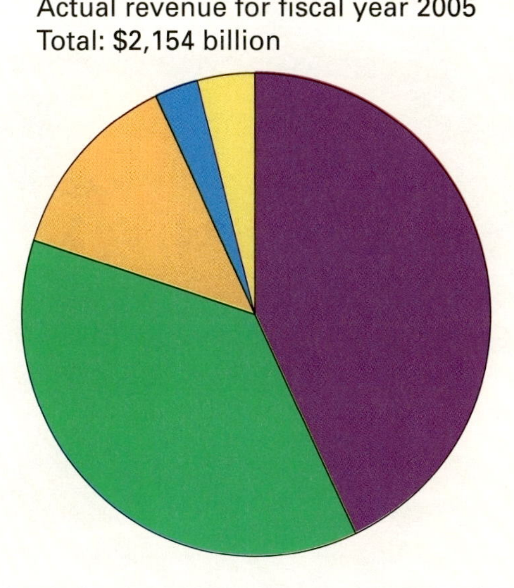

Individual income taxes (purple)	43%
Social Security and retirement revenue (green)	37%
Corporate income taxes (gold)	13%
Excise taxes (blue)	3%
Estate and gift taxes, customs duties, and other revenue (yellow)	4%

Source: Office of Management and Budget

Research Activity. Research one of the taxes described. Why was it originally enacted? How has it changed over time?

Community Activity. Instruct students to interview a CPA or tax attorney in their community. Have them ask about estimating estate taxes.

Federal Insurance Contributions Act (FICA). Employers and employees pay equal amounts of Social Security tax. Self-employed people pay the entire amount.

- **Sales tax.** In most states, consumers pay sales tax on the value of the goods and services they purchase. General sales tax is the leading source of revenue for many state governments. In many cases, food and prescription drugs are not taxed or are taxed at a lower rate.
- **Excise taxes.** An excise tax is a tax on the manufacture or sale of certain goods and services. It's included in the price paid by consumers. Examples of goods and services subject to federal or state excise taxes include motor fuel, alcohol, tobacco, firearms, air transportation, and telephone service.
- **Property taxes.** Most property taxes are based on the value of land and buildings owned. Property taxes are collected by state and local governments at rates that vary greatly from place to place. They are the main source of revenue for local governments. Your school is funded largely by local property taxes. See Figure 5-15.
- **Estate and gift taxes.** Estate tax is based on the value of a person's property after his or her death, if the value exceeds a certain amount. Gift tax may be charged to someone who gives a gift exceeding a certain dollar value. A tax relief act passed by Congress in 2001 reduced gift taxes and provided for gradually phasing out the federal estate tax.
- **Business or license taxes.** People pay license fees to drive a car, own certain pets, hunt, and fish. License fees are also paid by members of some professions, such as doctors, lawyers, electricians, and teachers, who must pass certification tests in order to have the right to work in a particular state. License fees help pay for record keeping and other costs.

Caption Answer. The property in some areas has greater value than property in other areas; therefore, it generates more tax revenue.

5-15

Property taxes help pay for public playgrounds and parks. Why do some districts take in more tax revenue than others?

Caption Answer. Students might answer that taxes are generally increased when the nation goes to war.

- **Customs duties and tariffs.** The federal government places these taxes on goods imported from other countries. If you go to a local shop and buy an item that was made in France or Japan, the price you pay may include customs duties and tariffs.

TEXTLINK

Section 7.2 explains why tariffs are imposed.

Critical Thinking. ***Ask:*** Which taxes do you believe are unfair and why? How would you propose that the services they pay for be funded?

The U.S. tax system developed gradually over time. Figure 5-16 describes some key dates in the history of federal taxation.

TAXES AND FAIRNESS

Are you familiar with the phrase "No taxation without representation"? It was a rallying cry for American colonists in the 1760s who opposed paying taxes to the British government. Because the colonists had no representation in that government, they felt the taxes were unfair.

Americans have debated questions about tax fairness ever since. It's not always easy to determine the best method for distributing the tax burden fairly. However, two principles are often followed.

5-16

During the Great Depression, the government enacted social programs to assist the millions of people who had lost their jobs. What other events in the twentieth century led to increased taxation?

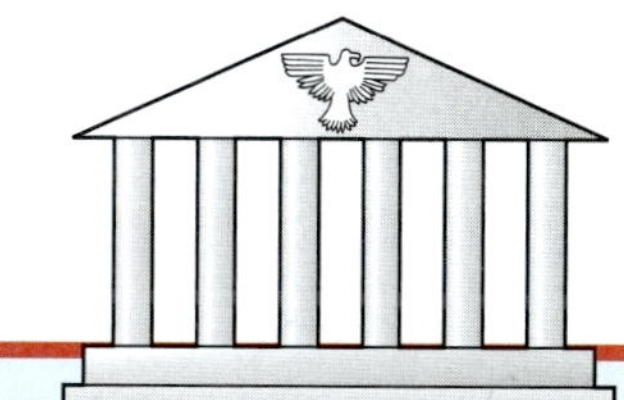

The Growth of Federal Taxation

DATE	EVENT
1789	The Constitution gives Congress the power to levy taxes for the first time. The first taxes are tariffs and excise taxes.
1794	President George Washington orders troops to put down a rebellion by corn and rye farmers who oppose the whiskey tax because it cuts their profits.
1863	To finance the Civil War, the federal government collects income taxes for the first time.
1872	Income tax ends.
1895	An attempt to impose an income tax fails when the Supreme Court rules it unconstitutional.
1913	The Sixteenth Amendment to the Constitution allows the government to collect income taxes.
1930s	During and after the Great Depression, the government increases taxes to pay for social programs.

Class Activity. Make two columns on the board. Label one "Benefit principle" and the other "Ability-to-pay principle." Ask students which types of taxes are based on each principle. Have them explain their answers. List responses in the appropriate columns.

- **Benefit principle.** This principle holds that those who benefit from a public service should pay for it. For example, in most communities, taxes on motor vehicles and gasoline are used to build and maintain roads. People who own more vehicles or drive them more often pay more of these taxes, but also benefit more from the roads they help fund.
- **Ability-to-pay principle.** According to this principle, more taxes should be paid by people who can afford to pay more. As you'll see, this principle influences the way some tax rates are set.

Tax Rates

The tax rate is the percentage that is charged in tax. In the case of a *flat tax*, the rate is the same for everyone who pays the tax. For example, if the state income tax rate is 4% for all taxpayers, no matter how large or small their income, that's a flat tax.

With a *graduated tax*, different rates are applied. The federal income tax is an example. People with higher incomes are taxed at a higher rate. People with lower incomes are taxed at a lower rate. People whose income falls below a certain level pay no federal income tax at all.

Relationship of Taxes to Income

Taxes of all kinds take a bite out of everyone's income. However, some taxes affect high-income people to a greater degree than they affect low-income people. The reverse is also true. Looked at from this perspective, a tax can be described as proportional, progressive, or regressive.

Federal Government Spending

Actual expenditures for the fiscal year 2005.

FUNCTION	AMOUNT	PERCENTAGE
Social Security	$519 billion	21%
Defense	$473 billion	19%
Medicare	$294 billion	12%
Medicaid and SCHIP*	$187 billion	8%
Homeland security	$30 billion	1%
Net interest on national debt	$184 billion	7%
Other payments	$785 billion	32%
Total	**$2,472 billion**	**100%**

*SCHIP (State Children's Health Insurance Program)

Source: U.S. Office of Management and Budget

Jump$tart. Ask students which forms of taxation are progressive and which are regressive. Discuss why some taxes might be useful even though they are regressive. *(Income)*

5-17

Together, national defense and programs that assist individuals claim about three-fourths of each federal dollar.

Research Activity. Have students find out how tax revenues are spent in your state. Have them illustrate their findings in a pie chart.

- A **proportional tax** takes the same percentage out of everyone's income. The flat state income tax described earlier is a proportional tax. People who make $25,000 a year pay a tax amounting to 4% of their income, and so do people who make $100,000 a year.
- A **progressive tax** takes a larger percentage of the income of high-income people than of low-income people. The federal income tax is progressive. People who make $25,000 a year might pay federal income tax amounting to 10% of their income. For a family with an income of $100,000 a year, the tax bite would be larger—perhaps around 18% of their income, for example.
- A **regressive tax** takes a larger percentage of the income of low-income people than of high-income people. This situation can occur even though the actual tax rate may be flat. For instance, suppose a family with an income of $25,000 and one with an income of $100,000 both spend $8,000 a year on food. If food is subject to a flat 5% sales tax, both families will pay the same amount of tax on food: $400. However, that $400 represents 1.6% of $25,000 income and only 0.4% of a $100,000 income. The tax takes a larger bite out of the lower-income family's budget.

Regressive taxes are generally viewed as unfair. However, people may disagree about whether a particular tax is regressive. Progressive taxes, in contrast, are based on the ability-to-pay principle. Therefore, many people believe that they contribute to tax fairness.

Answer Key. Answers to the Section Review questions are provided in the Section Lesson Plan located in the *Teacher Resource Guide*.

HOW TAXES ARE SPENT

Every year, people elected to government office must decide how to spend the money collected in taxes. At the federal level, a large portion of government spending goes to pay for social programs such as Social Security, public assistance, and health care. See Figure 5-17.

In general, state and local governments spend the largest portion of their revenue—about one-third—on education. Other major areas of state and local spending include public assistance, transportation, public safety, and health care.

Citizens should stay informed about how their tax dollars are being spent. The revenues and expenditures of federal, state, and local governments are a matter of public record. To find out more about government spending, contact your elected officials or visit government Web sites.

Section 5.4 Review

CHECK YOUR UNDERSTANDING

1. How does society benefit from having a tax system?
2. Describe the difference between property tax and estate tax.
3. How do major spending categories for the federal government differ from those for state and local governments?

CONSUMER APPLICATION

Sales Tax Investigate your state and local sales tax. Compute each tax for items costing $100, $500, and $1,000. How might sales tax affect your decision to make a costly purchase?

CHAPTER 5 Review & Activities

CHAPTER SUMMARY

- The problem of scarce resources is addressed differently by traditional, command, market, and mixed economies. The U.S. economic system is a mixed economy with specific goals and characteristics. (5.1)
- Factors such as profit, resources, and productivity influence production in the U.S. economy. The interaction of demand and supply has a major impact on prices in a free market. (5.2)
- Governments provide public services, redistribute income, and regulate economic activity, including competition. (5.3)
- The various taxes that people pay fulfill several basic purposes. Questions of tax fairness are often debated. (5.4)

THE $avvy Consumer

Muffin Market: The high school band has been holding a bake sale every Friday at lunchtime to raise money for a trip. The muffin business has dropped off, however, and band members are now spending more on supplies than they're taking in. How can they apply some laws of the marketplace to boost sales? (5.2)

Reviewing Key Terms and Ideas

1. Why do **economic systems** develop? (5.1)
2. What fundamental problem do all economic systems try to solve? (5.1)
3. Describe the basic differences between a **traditional**, a **command**, a **market**, and a **mixed economy**. (5.1)
4. Describe five goals of the U.S. economy. (5.1)
5. What is **free enterprise**? (5.1)
6. Explain how **profit** motivates production. (5.2)
7. What is meant by "factors of production"? Name five of these factors. (5.2)
8. Describe three types of business organizations in the U.S. (5.2)
9. Explain how **demand** and **supply** interact to determine prices in a free market. (5.2)
10. Why does **competition** among businesses benefit consumers? (5.2)
11. Why does the government provide certain goods and services? Give three examples. (5.3)
12. Why does the U.S. government have **antitrust laws**? (5.3)
13. What two policies can the government use to stabilize the economy? (5.3)
14. Explain three purposes of taxation. (5.4)
15. Describe four types of **taxes** paid by U.S. consumers. (5.4)
16. Explain two basic principles of tax fairness. (5.4)
17. How do **proportional**, **progressive**, and **regressive taxes** differ? (5.4)

Answer Key. Answers to the Chapter Review & Activities are provided in the Teacher's Manual in the *Teacher Annotated Edition* of the text.

Thinking Critically

1. **Understanding Cause and Effect:** What are some possible reasons why few traditional economies are found in the world today? (5.1)
2. **Identifying Relevance:** What role do you think ingenuity plays in the development of a strong economy? In which type of economic system might ingenuity be most prevalent? Why? (5.1)
3. **Analyzing Economic Concepts:** Explain how the laws of supply and demand apply to the job market. (5.2)
4. **Making Predictions:** What if the U.S. economy were strickly a market economy and not regulated by the government? Predict how the lack of regulation might affect the environment, consumers, and workers. (5.3)

Building Consumer Skills

1. **Economic Roles:** With a partner, prepare a skit in which one of you represents producers and the other consumers. Use the skit to demonstrate the vital role each of you plays in the U.S. economy. (5.2)
2. **Product Development:** With a team, develop a product that you could sell as a business. Conduct market research to determine consumers' needs, design your product, and test it for usability. Analyze the test results, make necessary changes to the product, and then create a label for it. Determine a selling price, considering the cost of creating the product. Demonstrate your product for the class and ask for feedback. (5.2)
3. **Government Aid:** Create a pamphlet describing various income redistribution programs available in your community. Include information about the purpose of each program, who is eligible, and where people can go to apply or obtain more information. (5.3)
4. **Tax Rates:** Learn how corporate and individual tax rates compare around the world. Summarize what you discover in a report to the class. (5.4)
5. **Paying Taxes:** Some people complain about paying taxes, and others feel that it is their civic duty to do so. Write some reasons that might explain each attitude. Then compare ideas in class. (5.4)

CONSUMER CONNECTIONS

- **Family:** Discuss with family members how they are affected by taxes, as well as which government services they need and use. Ask whether they would like to see any changes in tax laws or government services. (5.3, 5.4)
- **Community:** Research a business in your community that uses advanced computer operations to design, develop, and maintain its products or services. Visit the business to see how the technology is used. Write a newspaper feature on the technology. (5.2)

CHAPTER 6

The Health of the Economy

SECTION 6.1
Economic Ups and Downs

SECTION 6.2
Deficits and Debt

SECTION 6.3
Stabilizing the Economy

Reading with Purpose

- As you read this chapter, create an outline using the colored headings.
- Write a question for each heading to help guide your reading.
- Write the answer to each question as you read the chapter.
- Ask your teacher to help with answers you cannot find in the text.

SECTION 6.1

Economic Ups and Downs

Throughout U.S. history, there have been periods of wealth and periods of want. The ups and downs of the economy have a major impact on the standard of living and the quality of people's lives.

Objectives

After studying this section, you should be able to:

- Describe the phases of the business cycle.
- Analyze the effects of economic conditions on consumers.
- Discuss factors that affect the state of the economy.
- Explain measurements used to gauge the state of the economy.

Key Terms

business cycles
recession
depression
inflation
interest
economic indicators
gross domestic product
consumer price index

THE BUSINESS CYCLE

Did you know that you've lived through an unparalleled period in U.S. history? The decade between 1991 and 2001 was the longest uninterrupted period of economic growth in the United States. During this time, the great majority of people who wanted to work were able to find jobs. The stock market soared to all-time highs. Despite increased prosperity, prices for most goods and services did not increase significantly.

Just think how different your life may have been if you were living in the 1930s. During that decade, the economy went into a severe decline. Factories and businesses closed down. Many Americans couldn't find jobs. Many were homeless and hungry.

The ups and downs of the economy are called **business cycles**. Many economists believe that these fluctuations follow a pattern—peak, contraction, trough, and expansion—as illustrated in Figure 6-1 on the next page.

Class Activity. Explain that in a recession, people cut back on expenditures. Draw two columns on the board: "essentials" and "extras." Ask students what expenses they would put into each category, and list their responses. Then ask them which things they would cut if they had no income.

The Business Cycle

The business cycle has four phases. The length of time of each cycle is irregular.

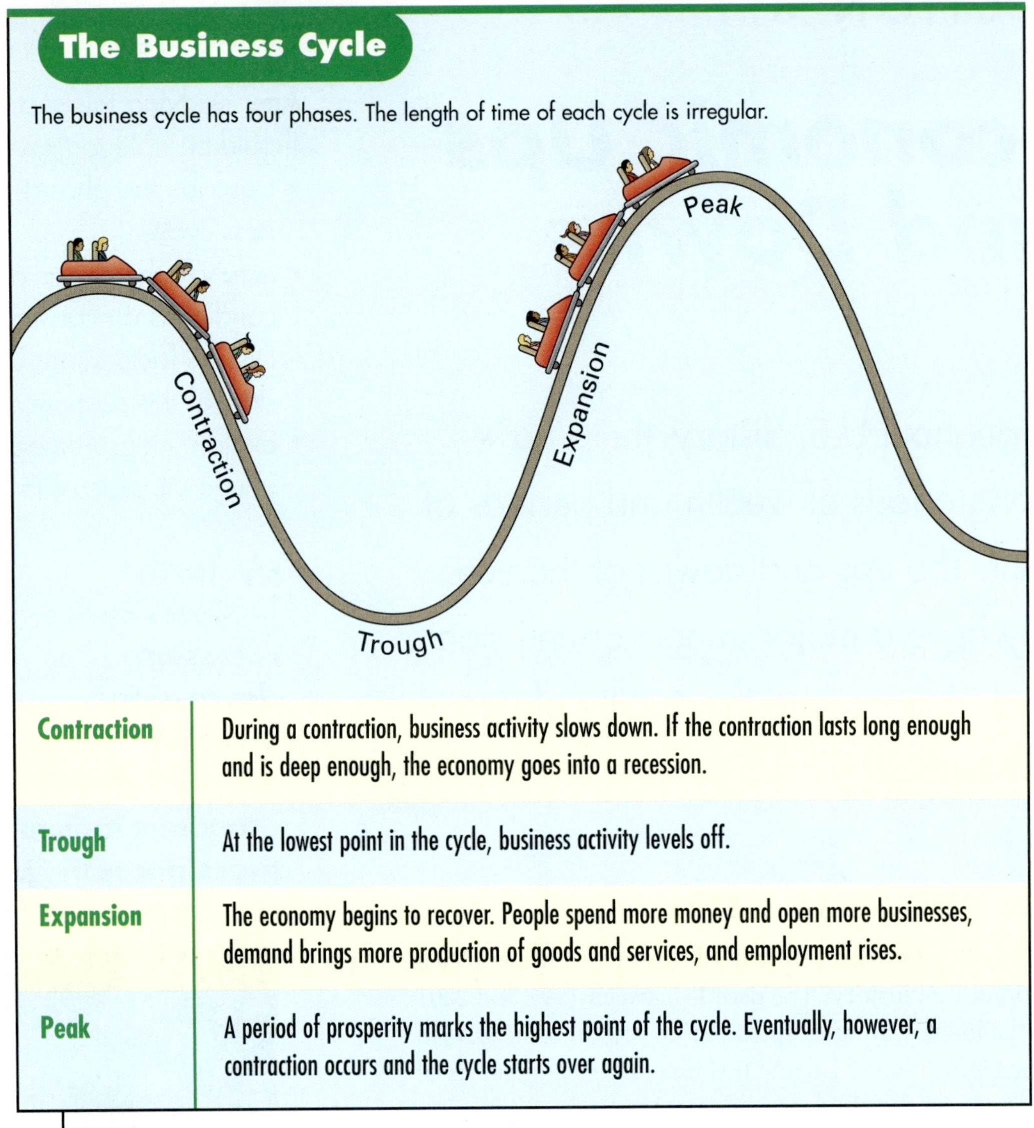

Contraction	During a contraction, business activity slows down. If the contraction lasts long enough and is deep enough, the economy goes into a recession.
Trough	At the lowest point in the cycle, business activity levels off.
Expansion	The economy begins to recover. People spend more money and open more businesses, demand brings more production of goods and services, and employment rises.
Peak	A period of prosperity marks the highest point of the cycle. Eventually, however, a contraction occurs and the cycle starts over again.

6-1 **Business cycles are not as regular as shown in this illustration, but the peaks and troughs can seem like a roller-coaster ride.** **What can you do to prepare for these economic ups and downs?**

ECONOMIC EXTREMES

Mild ups and downs in the economy are to be expected, and they don't cause serious problems. More extreme fluctuations, however, can cause hardships for businesses and consumers.

Recession

A **recession** is a period of significant decline in the economy. It usually lasts six months to a year. During a recession, the economy produces more than people can consume. Business profits go down, so businesses

Community Activity. Have students interview someone who lived through the Great Depression. They should ask questions about what conditions were like and what strategies people used to cope with economic hardships. Have students compare what they learned in class.

cut back on production and lay off workers. Since laid-off workers don't have paychecks, consumers cut back on their spending. Decreased demand causes business profits to go down even more, and the cycle continues.

Recessions have been a recurrent problem for the U.S. economy. The 1980s started out with a recession that turned into the most serious economic slowdown since World War II. Before the boom of the 1990s, the decade began with a mild recession. Another began in March of 2001.

Depression

During a recession, the economy is in a downward spiral. If the negative factors are strong, they can lead to a **depression**—a major economic slowdown, longer lasting and more serious than a recession. During a depression, demand decreases sharply, prices plummet, many businesses fail, and unemployment soars.

The Great Depression dominated the world economy in the 1930s. See Figure 6-2. The economic decline began in August 1929. In late October of that year, the stock market crashed. However, many economists believe that the seriousness of the depression was due not to the crash itself, but to poor policy decisions by the government. The depression lasted until the advent of World War II. Controls are now in place to prevent some factors that led to the Great Depression.

Inflation

You might think that a growing economy is always good news. However, too-rapid growth during an economic expansion can lead to inflation. **Inflation** is a general, prolonged rise in the prices of goods and services. It doesn't necessarily mean that all prices rise, but the average price of goods and services goes up.

Jump$tart. Ask students how a recession might affect wages for those who keep their jobs. Help them by pointing out that in a recession, the supply of available workers is higher than the demand. *(Income)*

6-2

During the Great Depression, one out of every four people in the workforce couldn't find a job. What types of consumer and management skills do you think Depression-era families needed?

Critical Thinking. ***Ask:*** Which do you believe is a more serious problem—recession or inflation? Why? Who is hurt most by each?

Inflation affects consumers by reducing their purchasing power. When prices rise sharply, your dollar buys fewer goods and services than before. For example, suppose your employer gives you a 4% increase in pay, but the inflation rate—the rise in the average price of goods and services—is 6%. Even though your pay went up, you actually experienced a 2% drop in purchasing power. See Figure 6-3.

Inflation also affects consumers who borrow, lend, or invest money. They need to consider how inflation relates to **interest**, the fee paid for the opportunity to use someone else's money over a period of time. Consumers earn interest when they deposit money in a savings account; they pay interest when they borrow money. If the rate of inflation is 4%, money in a savings account that earns only 3% interest is losing purchasing power. On the other hand, inflation can benefit someone who has borrowed money at a fixed interest rate that is lower than the rate of inflation.

Discussion. ***Ask:*** During a period of high inflation, is it better to be a saver or a borrower? Why?

FACTORS AFFECTING UPS AND DOWNS

Some economists believe that economic ups and downs are an unavoidable part of a market economy. However, after studying business cycles over long periods, economists have identified many factors external to the economy that seem to trigger the ups and downs. They include:

6-3

Inflation is especially hard on those with fixed incomes, such as many retired people. Their income stays the same over time, but each year it buys less and less.

Community Activity. Have students design and conduct a survey to measure consumer confidence in your area. As a class, brainstorm a list of questions about people's level of optimism, spending habits, and saving habits. Have each student survey at least three people and report results in class.

- **Consumer confidence.** The economy is affected by psychological factors. If people anticipate economic prosperity, consumers may increase their spending and businesses may hire new workers. This behavior makes prosperity more likely to happen. If Americans feel gloomy about the future, they will cut back spending and help bring about recession.
- **Technological innovation.** Some business cycles were spurred by inventions such as the automobile, the airplane, and the computer. Technological innovation can create new markets where none existed before. They can transform the economy, the workplace, and the culture. After the economy has absorbed the change, it may slow down again. See Figure 6-4.
- **Government policies.** As you'll learn in Section 6.3, government actions—tax cuts, spending, and regulation of the money supply—cause fluctuations in business cycles. Government policies can either help or hurt the economy.
- **War.** During wartime, demand for goods and services associated with the war effort increases. For example, troops need uniforms, weapons, medical care, food, and transportation. Government spending for national defense pumps billions of dollars into the economy. Therefore, war is associated with economic expansion.

Discussion. *Ask:* How has the war on terrorism affected the economy? Who has benefited from it? Who has suffered financially?

MEASURING THE ECONOMY'S PERFORMANCE

How the economy is doing will affect everything from government policy on interest rates to how much of a raise an employee gets. Economists keep an eye on the economy by measuring its performance throughout the year. Measurements used to monitor the health of the economy are called **economic indicators**.

6-4

In the 1990s, the growth of the Internet created a "dot-com" boom. New Internet-based businesses seemed to spring up overnight, but many eventually failed. How do you think the economy was affected?

Point Out. The GDP includes the value of exports (goods and services sold to other countries) minus imports (items purchased from other countries).

InfoSource. Have students use the sources listed to learn how GDP, unemployment, or the consumer price index has changed over the past year.

Economists track many types of economic indicators. Among the most widely reported are measurements of production, unemployment, and inflation. Understanding their significance, and paying attention when they change, can help you make informed consumer decisions.

Gross Domestic Product

The **gross domestic product**, commonly called the GDP, is the total dollar value of goods and services produced in a country during the year. Goods are counted in the GDP only when they are new. Only final products are included so that the same goods are not counted twice. For example, tires that are shipped to an auto assembly plant are not counted separately. Their value is included in the value of the new cars that roll off the assembly line.

The GDP is the broadest measure of the economy. It provides a way of comparing what was produced in one year with what was produced in another year. When the GDP increases too quickly, inflation may become a problem. When it increases too slowly, unemployment may rise. Dividing the GDP by the size of the population (GDP per capita) reveals a national standard of living that can be compared from one nation to another. You may also see the term *real GDP*, which refers to GDP figures that have been adjusted for inflation.

Unemployment Rate

News of the monthly unemployment rate is often on the front pages of newspapers or is the lead story in their business sections. This statistic is the percentage of the civilian labor force that is without a job but actively looking for work.

A high unemployment rate is a sign that the economy is ailing. When large numbers of people are without work, productive resources are being wasted. Unemployment can also drain government resources, as unemployed workers often need state and federal financial assistance to pay for basic needs. In addition, the personal ravages of unemployment are easy to see. Being out of work can disrupt family life and cause one to lose feelings of worth and self-respect. Maintaining a low unemployment rate is a priority for government officials. Employed people are more able to be self-sufficient, which helps to stabilize the economy.

Since World War II, the unemployment rate has mostly stayed between 3% and

InfoSource

Current Economic Indicators

To find out the current values of major economic indicators, such as the unemployment rate, GDP, and consumer price index, try these sources:

- The business section of your local newspaper.
- Business publications such as *BusinessWeek* and *The Wall Street Journal.*
- Web sites of the Bureau of Labor Statistics, the Bureau of Economic Analysis, and the Federal Reserve Board.

Research Activity. Have students use Internet resources to find out what goods and services the CPI market basket contains. Have them use this information to create a visual illustrating the market basket. Ideas include a table, a chart, or a drawing with labels.

11%. Economists generally consider the economy to be at full employment when the nation's unemployment rate is below 5.5%. This figure accounts for the fact that at any given time, there will always be some people experiencing short-term unemployment. Unemployment may vary from area to area, so rates are also figured for states and municipalities (cities and towns).

Consumer Price Index

An important measure of inflation is the **consumer price index**, or CPI. It measures the change in prices over time of a specific group of goods and services. The group of items, called a market basket, includes over 200 categories of goods and services that the average household uses. Represented in the market basket are food and beverages, housing, apparel, transportation, medical care, recreation, education and communication, and other goods and services.

The consumer price index is not the dollar value of the market basket items. Rather, it is a number that relates the current price of the market basket to the price during a specific time period in the past. The price during that past period is assigned a CPI value of 100. If the current CPI is 180, for example, that means the price of the market basket is 80% higher than it was during the comparison period.

Each month, the percentage change in the CPI is reported by the Bureau of Labor Statistics. If the CPI was 180 last month and is 181 this month, the monthly change is around +0.5%.

Answer Key. Answers to the Section Review questions are provided in the Section Lesson Plan located in the *Teacher Resource Guide.*

LOCAL, NATIONAL, AND GLOBAL ECONOMIES

Economic conditions can vary from one part of the country to another. Climate changes, natural disasters, population shifts, the availability of workers, local government policies, and the fortunes of local businesses are a few of the factors that cause variations. For example, farmers in one region may go bankrupt after a severe drought even though the national economy is booming. Residents of a small community might increase their wealth when a large business opens its doors and creates jobs.

Local economies and the U.S. economy are not insulated from the rest of the world. The economies of every nation are becoming increasingly interdependent. A recession in the United States can trigger economic slowdowns around the globe. A rise in oil prices overseas can register as increased inflation here. You can read more about the issues of global economics in Chapter 7.

Section 6.1 Review

CHECK YOUR UNDERSTANDING

1. What are the phases of a business cycle?
2. How are consumers affected by inflation?
3. How might technological innovation affect the economy?

CONSUMER APPLICATION

Economic Indicators Look up the current values of the three economic indicators described in this section. Explain how these measurements might affect consumer purchasing decisions.

Objectives

After studying this section, you should be able to:

- Distinguish between a budget surplus and a budget deficit.
- Identify reasons for deficit spending by governments.
- Analyze the effects of the national debt on consumers.

Key Terms

budget
budget surplus
deficit spending
budget deficit
national debt

SECTION 6.2

Deficits and Debt

Balancing the budget, deficit spending, the national debt—you may have heard or read the terms in news reports about the economy. What do they mean for consumers, including you?

THE BUDGET PROCESS

Section 5.4 explained where the government gets its money and how that money is spent. Taxes, especially personal income taxes, provide most of the federal government's revenue. Almost half of this money is spent on a combination of Social Security, Medicare, and income security programs that help people in need. The federal government also spends money for national defense and other purposes.

Like individuals, governments create budgets to manage their spending. A **budget** is an estimate of anticipated income and expenses for a certain period of time. Each year, budgets are created by government officials on the federal, state, and local levels.

The federal budget is based on a *fiscal year* that begins on October 1 each year. Long before then, the Office of Management and Budget, part of the Executive Branch, begins work on a budget proposal. After reviewing and approving the proposed budget, the President submits it to Congress for debate. Throughout the budget process, the goal is to balance the budget so that planned spending does

Class Activity. Hold a mock budget process. Tell students to pretend they have $100 to spend, but a majority of them must agree on a plan to spend it. Have students propose ideas for using the money. List their suggestions on the board. Then hold a vote on how to spend the money.

not exceed projected revenue. Priorities must be weighed and compromises struck. Eventually, the House of Representatives approves the final budget and it becomes law.

After the fiscal year ends on September 30, the actual amounts of revenue and spending are reviewed and compared. If more money was collected than spent, the result is a **budget surplus**. It's far more common, however, for the amount spent to exceed the revenue collected.

DEFICIT SPENDING

The practice of spending more money than was received in revenue is called **deficit spending**. The amount by which spending exceeds revenue is the **budget deficit**. Figure 6-5 shows the historical pattern of budget deficits and surpluses.

The causes of budget deficits vary. Wars tend to trigger deficit spending as the government spends billions of dollars on defense. Deficit spending also tends to occur during a recession—the government increases spending to provide benefits for people who are out of work, while receiving less revenue from income taxes. Budget deficits can also occur because of policy decisions by Congress and the President.

Caption Answer. The economy was doing very well, and unemployment and inflation remained low.

6-5

The federal budget had a deficit every year from 1970 to 1997. What might account for the budget surpluses in the late 1990s?

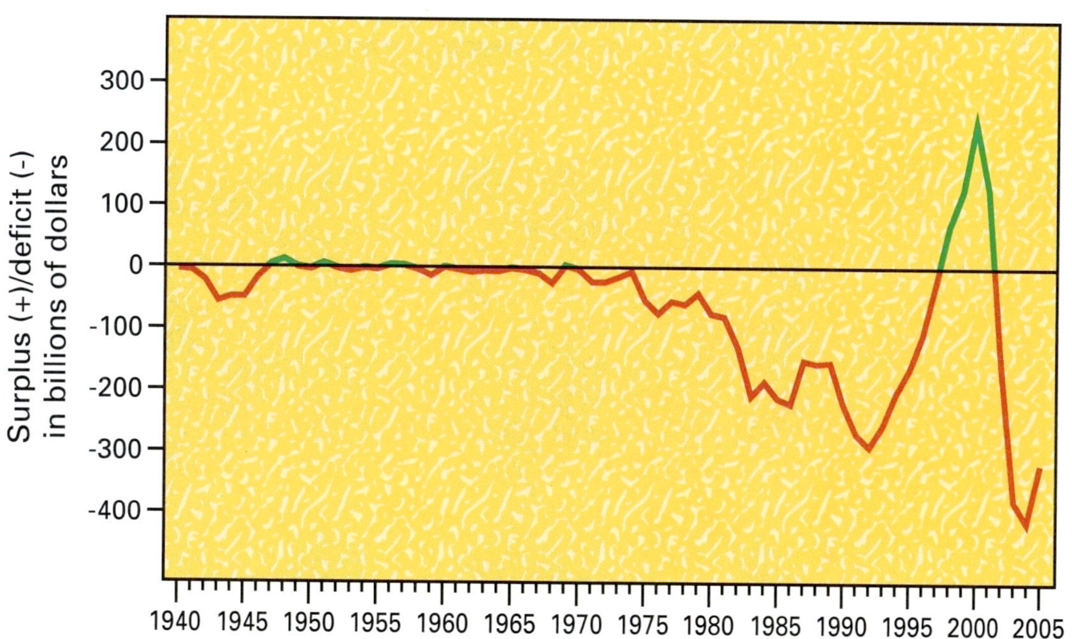

Point Out. Some of the public debt is owed to U.S. citizens who have bought securities. Other parts are owed to foreign investors, banks, and corporations.

THE NATIONAL DEBT

When consumers choose to spend more than they earn, they borrow money by using a credit card or getting a loan. When the government has a budget deficit, it must borrow money too. It does this by selling various types of securities, such as savings bonds and Treasury bills, to individuals, corporations, and financial institutions.

Someone who buys a savings bond is loaning money to the government for a certain period of time. The government agrees to pay back the original amount plus interest. Thus, a savings bond is not only an investment option for the person who buys it, but also a way for the government to finance its programs during periods of deficit spending. See Figure 6-6.

Each year that the government has a budget deficit, it borrows an additional amount, adding to what it owes. The total

Research Activity. Research the types of securities the government uses to borrow money. How is each security sold?

amount of money that the federal government owes is the **national debt**, also known as the public debt. Due to the large and consistent deficits that occurred in the past, the national debt has grown to enormous size. By early 2006, it totaled more than $8 trillion.

During the prosperous 1990s, some experts said that the national debt would be eliminated as the economy continued to grow. They anticipated continued budget surpluses that could be used to pay back much of the debt. However, deficit spending again became necessary when the United States went to war in late 2001.

What's the Impact?

Some policymakers and economists are not worried about the national debt. They say that if it's expressed as a percentage of

Caption Answer. The bonds provided the money needed to fund the national defense and were repaid during the years after the war.

6-6

During World War II, First Lady Eleanor Roosevelt was among the many public figures who encouraged Americans to buy bonds. How did purchasing bonds aid the war effort?

Research Activity. Research the current level of the national debt. Has the debt increased or decreased in the past year? Why?

Answer Key. Answers to the Section Review questions are provided in the Section Lesson Plan located in the *Teacher Resource Guide*.

6-7

Budgeting and spending decisions made by the President and Congress affect the size of the national debt. How can citizens stay informed about these decisions? How can they influence them?

Caption Answer. Citizens can stay informed by paying attention to national news. They can influence decisions by contacting their legislators.

gross domestic product, the national debt actually *decreased* from World War II to the present.

However, the national debt is of concern to many people. They point out that interest on the national debt eats up a significant portion of the federal budget each year. This takes away money that could otherwise be spent on government services and programs such as education, health care, public transportation, and public safety. In recent years, for example, interest paid on the national debt has exceeded what the federal government spends on education.

If citizens are concerned about the national debt, what can they do? Voters elect the politicians who create budgets and deficits. By studying the issues and using their voting power, consumers can help shape responsible government policies. See Figure 6-7.

Section 6.2 Review

CHECK YOUR UNDERSTANDING

1. How does the government determine whether there is a budget deficit or a budget surplus?
2. Identify two reasons the federal government might engage in deficit spending.
3. How does the national debt affect consumers?

CONSUMER APPLICATION

Federal Budget Research the federal budget for the current fiscal year. Is a deficit or a surplus projected? What reasons are given for the deficit or surplus? Explain how you, as a consumer, might use this information.

Objectives

After studying this section, you should be able to:

- Compare and contrast fiscal and monetary policy.
- Explain the role of the Federal Reserve System.
- Analyze how the Fed's actions affect consumers.

Key Terms

fiscal policy
money supply
monetary policy
Federal Reserve System
Federal Reserve Board
federal funds rate
dicount rate
reserve requirement

SECTION 6.3

Stabilizing the Economy

Consumers benefit when prices are stable and economic growth is steady. By working to stabilize the economy, the government hopes to minimize both inflation and unemployment. The tools at its disposal include fiscal policy and monetary policy.

FISCAL POLICY

Fiscal policy refers to the federal government's use of taxing and spending policies to help stabilize the economy. The President and Congress can raise or lower taxes and increase or decrease government spending. Each of these actions has an effect on the economy.

For example, if economists see a possible recession on the horizon, one way to give the economy a boost might be to cut personal taxes. Putting more money into consumers' hands allows them to buy more goods and services, increasing demand and spurring the economy. Another approach might be a tax break for businesses, making it easier for them to invest in capital goods, expand production, and create new jobs.

Still another possibility is to increase government spending. In a recession, businesses cut back on their spending—they shut down factories, lay off workers, and so on. The government might try to offset this decline by

Research Activity. Ask students to read and summarize a recent news article about the use of fiscal policy, such as tax cuts or spending.

Critical Thinking. *Ask:* What should the government do when the goals of fiscal policy conflict with other goals of government? Why?

funding a major construction project that would create jobs and keep money flowing in the economy. See Figure 6-8.

When the economy is booming, there's a danger that too-rapid growth will lead to high inflation. Raising taxes siphons off money consumers and businesses would otherwise spend, keeping growth in check. The government might also limit economic growth by decreasing its own spending.

Many economists believe that fiscal policy, if used wisely, can be a powerful tool for managing the economy. However, it's an imprecise tool. The economy is complex, and it can take months for fiscal policy to have an effect.

Fiscal policy has other drawbacks as well. At times, the goals of fiscal policy can conflict with other goals of government, such as to improve education, strengthen national defense, or make health care available to the needy. In addition, political leaders—wary of angering taxpayers and special interest groups—may be reluctant to raise taxes or cut spending.

MONETARY POLICY

Fiscal policy is not the only tool for stabilizing the ups and downs of the economy. Another approach is to regulate the **money supply**, which is the total amount of money in circulation at any given time. Efforts to stabilize the economy by regulating the money supply are known as **monetary policy**. Whereas fiscal policy is carried out by the President and Congress, monetary policy is carried out by the nation's central bank.

The Federal Reserve System

The **Federal Reserve System** is the central bank of the United States. The Fed, as it's often called, provides financial services to the banking industry and the government. It also regulates banks to make sure that they follow the law. However, the primary responsibility of the Fed is to set monetary policy.

6-8

Federal projects, such as building a new hydroelectric dam, can pump money into the economy. Who would benefit directly from such a project? Who benefits indirectly?

Class Activity. Have students create a cause-and-effect graph or other visual to show how changes in the money supply affect the economy.

The governing body of the Federal Reserve System is the Board of Governors, commonly known as the **Federal Reserve Board**. Its seven members are nominated by the President and confirmed by the Senate. These seven people, along with five presidents of district Federal Reserve Banks, make up a group called the Federal Open Market Committee (FOMC). The FOMC monitors the health of the economy and decides whether changes in monetary policy are needed.

Eight times a year, the FOMC holds its regularly scheduled meetings. After each meeting, the committee releases a statement announcing its actions and explaining the reason for them. In addition, the chairperson of the Federal Reserve Board meets with Congress twice a year to give updates on the economy's health and the Fed's monetary policy goals. Investors pay close attention to Fed announcements and reports. The stock market often rises or falls depending on whether the Fed's outlook seems optimistic or pessimistic. See Figure 6-9.

Research Activity. Have students read a summary of the last FOMC meeting and write a paragraph explaining what actions the group took and why.

The Fed and the Money Supply

The Fed sets monetary policy by taking action to increase or decrease the money supply. The money supply is significant because it affects the availability of credit. In turn, the availability of credit affects business expansion and consumer purchasing, on which the growth of the economy depends.

When the Fed increases the money supply, credit becomes more available and less costly. This enables consumers to spend more and businesses to borrow money for expansion. New jobs are created and output is raised. Because it promotes economic growth, increasing the money supply can head off a recession or make an existing one shorter and less severe.

On the other hand, when the Fed decreases the money supply, credit becomes harder to get and more expensive. As a result, consumers and businesses cut back on spending and investing. Curbing economic growth in this way can help to control inflation.

6-9

This is the trading floor of the New York Stock Exchange. Actions by the Fed can have strong impact on the stock market.

Dollars and Sense. Ask students what changes a family might make in its budget to take advantage of changing interest rates.

The Fed can manipulate the money supply in three ways. It can engage in open market operations, raise or lower the discount rate, and adjust the reserve requirement.

Open Market Operations

The Fed can affect the money supply by selling or buying government securities—stocks, bonds, and other financial assets—in the open market. This is the most important and frequently used tool the Fed has at its disposal.

If the Federal Open Market Committee decides to decrease the money supply, it directs the Federal Reserve Bank of New York to sell some of its holdings of government securities. On the open market, anyone can buy these securities, including banks and other financial institutions, individuals, and big corporations. To pay for the government securities, buyers typically write checks to the Fed, which takes money out of circulation. On the other hand, if the FOMC wants to increase the money supply, it directs the Fed bank to buy securities. In so doing, the Fed pumps money into the economy.

Research Activity. Have students investigate how the federal funds rate has changed over the past five years. Have them show their findings in a graph.

Open market operations have an effect on the **federal funds rate**. This is the interest rate at which banks lend money to one another overnight. The federal funds rate, although not directly controlled by the Fed, is strongly influenced by the Fed's actions. When the Fed decreases the money supply by selling securities, the federal funds rate goes up. When the Fed increases the money supply by buying securities, the federal funds rate goes down. The Federal Open Market Committee periodically sets and announces a target level for the federal funds rate. At the same time, it takes action that will cause the rate to move in the desired direction.

Changes in the federal funds rate tend to trigger changes in the interest rates that financial institutions charge consumers and businesses. A higher federal funds rate leads to higher interest rates for consumers, encouraging them to save. A lower federal funds rate leads to lower rates for consumers, encouraging them to borrow and spend.

Discussion. ***Ask:*** If the bank offered you 2 percent interest on your money, would you be more likely to put your money in the bank or spend it? What if the bank offered you 6 percent interest?

DOLLARSandSENSE

Take Advantage of Interest Rates

If you stay informed about the Fed's actions, you can take advantage of current interest rates.

- When the Fed lowers interest rates, it may be a good time to borrow money, as long as your employment is secure and your earnings are not changing.
- When the Fed raises interest rates, it's a time to curb additional spending and put more money into savings.

Critical Thinking. ***Ask:*** What might happen if a bank loaned 100 percent of the money it took in?

The Discount Rate

Sometimes banks borrow money from the Federal Reserve Bank. Like consumers who take out loans, banks pay interest when they borrow money. The interest rate that banks pay to the Fed is called the **discount rate**. The Fed has the power to directly set the discount rate.

If the Fed thinks the economy is slowing down, it might lower the discount rate. This would encourage banks to borrow more money from the Fed, increasing the money supply. On the other hand, if the economy is threatened by inflation, the Fed may raise the discount rate. This discourages banks from borrowing from the Fed and shrinks the money supply.

However, the direct effect of changes in the discount rate on the money supply is usually small. Often the real purpose of changing the discount rate is to signal a major change in the Fed's monetary policy. As with the federal funds rate, changes in the discount rate tend to trigger corresponding changes in interest rates that affect consumers.

Critical Thinking. ***Ask:*** Why do banks pay less interest to borrow money than individuals do?

Reserve Requirement

When you make a deposit into a checking or savings account, your money doesn't just sit in a vault. The bank may lend your money to a new business or to a family buying a home. However, by law, financial institutions cannot lend out all of the money that they take in. They must hold a portion of it in reserve.

The Fed sets the **reserve requirement**—the percentage of a bank's deposits that it must keep on hand. If a bank's customers have deposited $100 million and the reserve requirement is set at 10%, the bank must hold $10 million in reserve. See Figure 6-10.

Holding money in reserve takes it out of circulation. Thus, raising the reserve requirement decreases the money supply. Lowering the reserve requirement increases the money supply, since banks have more money available to lend to consumers and businesses. However, since the Fed's ability to adjust reserve requirements is limited, this policy tool is rarely used.

6-10

A bank's reserves may be stored in its vault or kept on deposit at a Federal Reserve Bank. Why do you suppose banks are required to keep reserves?

Class Activity. Have students create charts showing what actions the Fed can take and how each one affects consumers.

Answer Key. Answers to the Section Review questions are provided in the Section Lesson Plan located in the *Teacher Resource Guide.*

6-11

Actions taken by the Federal Reserve Board affect the everyday lives of consumers. How does the Fed control inflation?

Effects on Consumers

Like fiscal policy, monetary policy can sometimes misfire. However, everyone benefits from Fed policies that allow the economy to operate more smoothly and efficiently. Fed policies impact several areas of your life, such as:

- **What you'll pay for goods and services.** The Fed keeps a watchful eye on inflation. When prices creep up, the Fed often acts to prevent them from rising too fast. See Figure 6-11.
- **Your ability to get credit and the interest rates you will pay.** Since Fed policies regulate the money supply, they impact your ability to get credit and the interest rates you will pay for loans and credit card balances.
- **What you'll earn in interest.** Fed policies affect interest rates that financial institutions must pay you for savings accounts, certificates of deposit, and other investments.
- **Your job stability and the wages you are paid.** By increasing the money supply, the Fed encourages the creation of new jobs. Decreasing the money supply can have the opposite effect. When there are plenty of jobs, wages tend to increase as employers try to attract and retain workers. When jobs are scarce, wages tend to fall.

Section 6.3 Review

CHECK YOUR UNDERSTANDING

1. What is fiscal policy? Give an example of how it's used.
2. What group carries out monetary policy?
3. Name four ways in which monetary policy actions affect the lives of individual consumers.

CONSUMER APPLICATION

Tax Credit In 2001, the federal government cut taxes and sent a credit of several hundred dollars to most taxpayers in the middle of the year. What was the government's purpose in doing so? What would you have done with such a refund?

CHAPTER 6

Review & Activities

CHAPTER SUMMARY

- The U.S. government regularly measures the state of its economy. The economy goes through phases of ups and downs called the business cycle. (6.1)
- Government spending practices create budget surpluses or budget deficits. The size of the national debt affects how revenues are spent. (6.2)
- The U.S. government's fiscal policy helps to stabilize the economy. The Federal Reserve Board, an agency of the U.S. government, tries to stabilize the economy by regulating the money supply. (6.3)

THE $avvy Consumer

Greener Pastures: Frank is anticipating another brisk season in the lawn-mowing business. He's thinking of buying a riding mower so that he can cut more lawns more quickly. However, he'll have to take out a loan to afford one. How can looking at economic trends and indicators help him decide whether to make this investment? (6.1)

Reviewing Key Terms and Ideas

1. What happens during the contraction phase of the **business cycle**? The expansion phase? (6.1)
2. What is a **recession**? How are consumers affected by it? (6.1)
3. Describe the economic event that happened in the 1930s. (6.1)
4. Explain how consumer confidence affects the state of the economy. (6.1)
5. What are e**conomic indicators**? Give three examples of these indicators. (6.1)
6. Explain what the **gross domestic product** and the **consumer price index** each measure. (6.1)
7. How can creating a **budget** help a government manage its spending? (6.2)
8. How does a **budget surplus** differ from a **budget deficit**? (6.2)
9. Name two situations that often lead to **deficit spending**. Explain why they have that effect. (6.2)
10. What causes the **national debt** to increase? (6.2)
11. Explain a negative effect of the national debt on consumers. (6.2)
12. How are **fiscal policy** and **monetary policy** alike? How are they different? (6.3)
13. What is the **Federal Reserve System**? What are its responsibilities? (6.3)
14. What could the **Federal Reserve Board** achieve by lowering either the **reserve requirement** or the **discount rate**? (6.3)
15. Explain how Federal Reserve actions can affect the cost of credit to consumers. (6.3)

Answer Key. Answers to the Chapter Review & Activities are provided in the Teacher's Manual in the *Teacher Annotated Edition* of the text.

Thinking Critically

1. **Understanding Cause and Effect:** How do interest groups affect local, state, and federal budgets? Do these influences differ at each level? (6.2)
2. **Drawing Conclusions:** Why do you think budget deficits are more common than budget surpluses? (6.2)
3. **Making Predictions:** The Federal Reserve Board is independent of the President and Congress. How might its monetary policy decisions be affected if it were under the control of one or the other? Why? (6.3)
4. **Analyzing Economic Concepts:** Using the laws of demand and supply, explain why the Fed's open market operations affect the federal funds rate the way they do. (6.3)

Building Consumer Skills

1. **Inflation Calculation:** Determine the cost of ten products your family buys. Using CPI data or an online inflation calculator, learn how much the items cost in the year you were born and also ten years before that. Chart the comparisons. (6.1)
2. **GDP Analysis:** Use online resources to determine three factors that affect the gross domestic product. How do the factors affect the GDP? Summarize results in writing. (6.1)
3. **Unemployment Rates:** Compare recent unemployment rates in the country's states. Which states have the lowest and highest rates? How might you account for the differences? What is the unemployment rate in your state? How has it changed in recent years? (6.1)
4. **Letter to a Lawmaker:** Write a letter that you might send to your U.S. representative expressing your views about the national debt and government fiscal policy. Support your opinion with facts and figures obtained from reliable sources. (6.1, 6.2)
5. **Effects of a Rate Change:** Choose one of the following: banks, consumers with large savings accounts, consumers who have just taken out a home loan, or consumers who are about to apply for a home loan. Write a scenario that shows how that group might be affected if the Fed lowers the discount rate. (6.3)

CONSUMER CONNECTIONS

- **Family:** Discuss how your family might be affected by such conditions as high inflation or recession. Consider how the effects might differ if your family income came from different types of sources. (6.1)
- **Community:** Research and report on your local (or state) government's budget. Who is involved in creating and approving it? Does deficit spending ever occur? Why or why not? What happens if there is a deficit? (6.2)

CHAPTER 7

Global Economics

SECTION 7.1
Trade Between Nations

SECTION 7.2
Trade Restrictions and Agreements

Reading with Purpose

- Read the title of this chapter and describe in writing what you expect to learn from it.
- Write down each key term, leaving space for definitions.
- As you read the chapter, write the definition beside each term.
- After reading the chapter, write a paragraph describing what you learned.

SECTION 7.1

Trade Between Nations

Was the alarm clock that woke you this morning made in Japan? Did you have a banana from the Caribbean for breakfast? Whether or not you realize it, international trade affects American consumers every day.

Objectives

After studying this section, you should be able to:

- Describe how international trade benefits consumers.
- Explain the significance of currency exchange rates.
- Analyze the impact of the U.S. trade deficit.

Key Terms

import
export
exchange rate
balance of trade
trade deficit
balance of payments

A WORLD OF TRADE

The U.S. economy is not isolated, but part of a larger world market. In the global market, the exchange of money, goods, and services flows across international borders. The United States plays a major role in this exchange. Knowing something about how international trade works and how it affects you is part of being an informed citizen and consumer.

Imports and Exports

A product brought in for sale from a foreign country is an **import**. Imports can be manufactured goods, such as wireless phones, that consumers will use. They can be producer goods—manufactured items to be used in making other products—such as semiconductors for computers and parts for automobiles. They can be agricultural products, such as bananas, or raw materials, such as petroleum. Even services, such as transportation or accounting, can be imported in the sense that they are purchased from a business based in another country.

Community Activity. Have students take an informal poll of family and friends to find out what products they use on a regular basis that are imported from other countries. Have them make a list of products used and the countries they come from. Compile results in class to form a master list.

A product sent to a foreign country for sale there is an **export**. Like imports, exports can be consumer goods, producer goods, agricultural products, raw materials, or services. Figure 7-1 gives examples of goods that the U.S. imports and exports.

Why Nations Trade

Why might one nation want to trade with another? Often, one country has natural resources that another country lacks or has in short supply. For example, the United States has very little of the mineral bauxite, which is essential for making aluminum. Almost all of the bauxite used in the United States today is imported.

Even when a country can produce enough of a product to meet its needs, it may choose to import it instead. Adam Smith, an eighteenth-century Scottish economist, showed that a nation can increase its productivity and wealth by specializing in what it produces most efficiently and trading for goods it produces less efficiently.

For example, suppose that much of the available land in a small nation is rocky. When farmers try growing grain for food, they can't produce enough for their nation's needs. However, if they give up growing grain and instead use the land to raise sheep, they can produce lots of wool. The surplus wool can be exported to other countries, and the money received in exchange can be used to buy imported grain. In turn, this enables other countries that are relatively efficient at growing crops to specialize, too. They can devote their resources to producing grain instead of trying to raise sheep. When every nation specializes in the goods they can produce most efficiently, the total amount of production in the world increases.

Team Activity. Form small groups. Give each group a deck of cards. Explain that each student's goal is to have seven different cards. Have each group shuffle and deal the cards, then record how many students have seven different cards in their hands. Then have students exchange cards with each other. Any student is free to offer and free to refuse any trade. Have students trade for ten minutes and then record the results. How many students have seven different cards now? Discuss what this exercise shows about the benefits of trade.

U.S. Exports and Imports

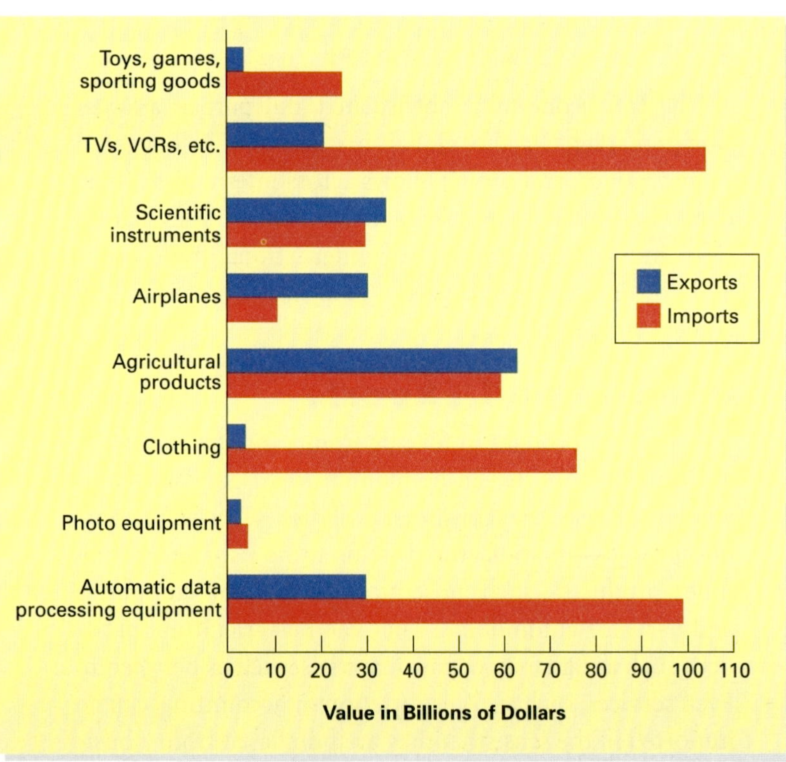

Source: U.S. Bureau of Economic Analysis, for 2005.

7-1

This graph includes just a few of the products that the U.S. imports and exports. What reasons might there be for both importing and exporting a particular type of product?

Class Activity. Have students create posters or other visuals that illustrate the benefits of trade between nations.

Benefits of Trade

Life would be very different if the U.S. did not trade with other nations. In general, what are some of the ways in which international trade benefits you and others?

- **Consumer choices.** Some consumer goods would not be available unless they were imported. International trade gives consumers a broader range of choices.
- **Increased competition.** Foreign trade brings additional competitors to the marketplace. As a rule, competition benefits consumers by encouraging producers to offer better products at lower prices.
- **Expanded markets.** Businesses that produce goods and services for export to other countries benefit from an expanded market for their products. In turn, this benefits the workers they employ.
- **International relations.** Countries that export many goods and services to the United States are likely to want to promote good relations with the U.S. government. Consumers in other countries may look more favorably on the United States when they are exposed to U.S. products and culture. See Figure 7-2.

Discussion. *Ask:* What kinds of U.S. jobs have been lost due to foreign competition? Were new jobs created to replace those jobs?

- **Prosperity and peace.** When U.S. consumers buy imports, they send dollars abroad. If this money is spread around to the people in other countries, those people become more prosperous. Prosperity tends to maintain a more peaceful world.

On the other hand, international trade sometimes has drawbacks. The overall benefits of trade are small consolation to a worker who loses his or her job to foreign competition. As you'll read in Section 7.2, there can be good reasons to restrict trade in specific situations. Still, trade between nations is, without a doubt, a vital part of the world in which you live.

7-2

American-style fast food is available the world over, just as the food of many nations can be found in the United States.

Research Activity. Have students do research to find out how the demand for a particular nation's currency has changed over a given period of time. Ask them to write a paragraph describing the factors that may have affected the currency's value.

CURRENCIES AND TRADE

Importers and exporters don't simply exchange one good for another. They use money or credit when trading internationally, just as you use money or credit when you buy from a store. However, countries don't all use the same *currency*, or form of money. In the United States, the currency is the dollar; in Russia, the ruble; in Ethiopia, the birr; and so on.

When two countries with different currencies want to do business with one another, the buyer must convert its money to the seller's currency. For example, a hospital in Mexico that wants to buy medicine from a U.S. company would exchange its currency, pesos, for U.S. dollars. A financial institution would perform the currency exchange, charging a fee for this service. See Figure 7-3.

Flexible Exchange Rates

The cost of one currency expressed in terms of another currency is called the **exchange rate**. Suppose the exchange rate for converting euros to U.S. currency is 89 U.S. cents for each euro. You can think of the exchange rate as the price of buying a particular currency. In this case, if you wanted to buy a euro, it would cost you 89 cents plus the bank's fee.

At one time, currency exchange rates were fixed—they were set by governments and rarely changed. However, in the 1970s, most countries adopted flexible exchange rates. Under this system, the price of buying a particular currency rises and falls from day to day. It's determined by the market forces of demand and supply. If one day more people around the world want to exchange their own currencies for Japanese yen, the increased demand causes the price of the yen to go up. If fewer people want to buy yen, the price goes down.

For importers and exporters, flexible exchange rates can make the cost of doing business unpredictable. Suppose an importer signs a contract to purchase goods from India in six months at a certain price in

Critical Thinking. *Ask:* How would the exchange rate between two currencies affect travelers visiting foreign countries?

7-3

The separate national currencies of a dozen European countries have been replaced by a single common currency called the euro (€). How does the euro simplify trading and traveling in Europe?

Class Activity. Have students make a two-column chart comparing the advantages and disadvantages of fixed and flexible exchange rates.

InfoSource. Have students use the resources listed to find the exchange rate between the U.S. dollar and the currency of a country they would like to visit.

rupees. However, the exact price in U.S. dollars won't be known until the day of the transaction. The importer might spend more or less money than expected. Businesspeople work with banks to try to protect themselves from changes in exchange rates.

Factors Affecting Exchange Rates

When the price, or value, of a currency goes up, it is said to be strong. When its value goes down, the currency is said to be weak. Many factors affect the demand for a currency and thus whether it is strong or weak compared to another currency.

Changes in interest rates are one such factor. A country that offers high interest rates increases the demand for its currency. For example, suppose the U.S. Treasury issues bonds with a new high interest rate. Since the bonds seem like a good investment, people in Europe may want to exchange euros for dollars so they can buy the bonds. The value of the dollar compared to the euro might rise because of the increased demand for dollars.

A currency's value is also affected by economic and political stability. Investors from around the world often prefer to invest in the United States because they consider it a stable nation. When they do so, the demand for dollars increases and the dollar becomes stronger.

Although exchange rates are largely determined by market forces, many countries set an upper and a lower limit on the exchange rate. If the currency threatens to move beyond its limits, the government will intervene to keep the rate stable.

How Exchange Rates Affect Trade

The strength or weakness of a nation's currency affects the willingness of other countries to trade with that nation. If the U.S. dollar is weak, exports from the United States tend to increase. That's because other countries get a bargain rate when converting their currency to U.S. dollars. They get more for their money than if they had purchased goods from a country with a stronger currency. In contrast, if the dollar is strong, U.S. exports will probably decrease. Converting currency to U.S. dollars becomes too expensive, so countries choose to buy more of their goods elsewhere.

InfoSource

Exchange Rates

Do you need to know the current value of a Canadian dollar or a Zambian kwacha? There are several ways to find information about current exchange rates.

- Look for a currency converter at a Web site that offers financial and business news.
- Search the Web using the key words "currency exchange rates."
- Check *The Wall Street Journal* or contact a financial institution.

Research Activity. Research the current U.S. balance of trade. Is it positive or negative?

Class Activity. Have students create a visual illustrating the concept of balance of payments. Ask students to share their visuals with the class.

UNDERSTANDING THE TRADE DEFICIT

Consumers who keep up with financial and political news may hear lots of references to the trade deficit. Just what is a trade deficit, and what does it mean for the U.S. economy? Learning about trade deficits begins with two concepts: balance of trade and balance of payments.

Balance of Trade

A nation rarely, if ever, imports exactly as much as it exports. The difference between the value of a nation's exports and its imports is called its **balance of trade**.

If the value of exports is greater than the value of imports, the balance of trade is said to be positive. A negative balance of trade, or **trade deficit**, occurs if a country spends more on imports than it receives for exports. See Figure 7-4.

Balance of Payments

A country's **balance of payments** is an accounting of all its financial transactions that involve other countries during a particular time period. Money received for exports and spent on imports is recorded in the balance of payments. So are many other financial dealings, such as the purchase of stock in a U.S. company by someone in Europe or Asia.

Unlike the balance of trade, which can be lopsided, the balance of payments is designed to balance like a bookkeeping account. Transactions that result in money entering the country are balanced against transactions that lead to money leaving the country. In practice, the two columns don't balance exactly, due to small differences that can't be helped. In theory, however, the sum of inflow and outflow is zero.

When there's a trade deficit, the U.S. is paying more for imports than it is receiving as payment for exports. Therefore, if you con-

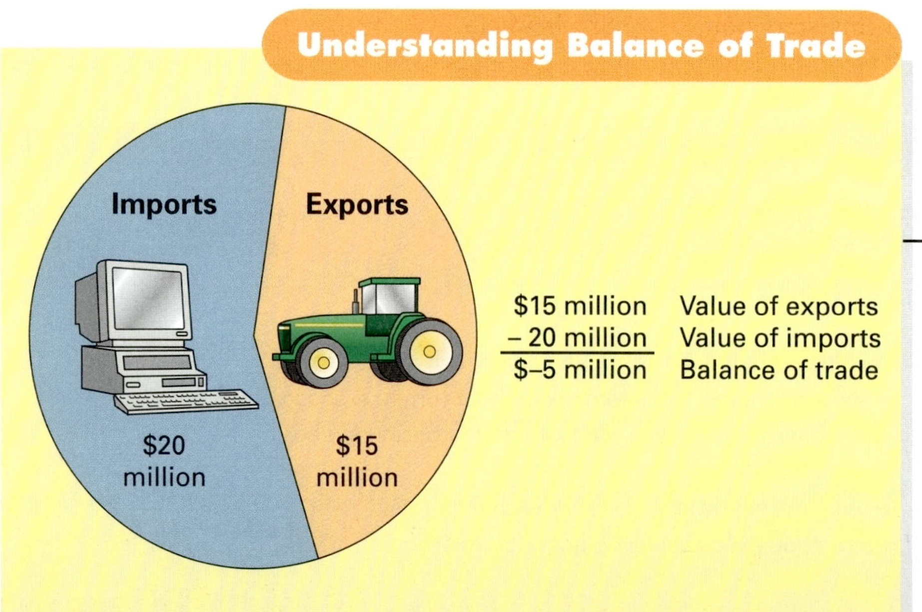

Caption Answer. The trade deficit described is $5 million.

7-4

In this example, during one year a country exports $15 million worth of tractors and imports $20 million worth of computers. If those were the only imports and exports, what is the country's trade deficit?

Caption Answer. "Net of Imports and Exports" represents the trade deficit in this example.

Class Activity. Challenge students to draw a political cartoon on the subject of the trade deficit. Have them explain their cartoons to the class.

sider only imports and exports, more money is flowing out of the country than is flowing in. This net outflow must be balanced by a net inflow on some other part of the balance of payments statement. Typically, it shows up in the area of foreign investment. See Figure 7-5.

The U.S. Trade Deficit

The United States has been running a trade deficit almost every year since the early 1970s, as shown in Figure 7-6 on the next page. One of the major reasons is heavy use of imported oil, primarily for heating, gasoline, manufacturing, and agriculture.

Some people say that a persistent trade deficit is harmful because of the increase in foreign investment that tends to come with it. They point out that foreign owners of U.S. real estate and businesses might prefer to send their profits overseas. Foreign investors might also have little loyalty to local communities or workers. If foreign investors buy U.S. government bonds, the federal government owes an increasing amount of interest to foreigners.

On the other hand, some economists see foreign investment not as a problem, but as a sign that the U.S. economy is strong enough to attract investors. In fact, some say that a large trade deficit is itself a sign of prosperity. When the economy is doing well, U.S. consumers have more money to spend on goods and services. As a result, they buy more products of all kinds, including imports. If other countries aren't experiencing a similar rise in prosperity, they won't buy more U.S. exports, so the trade deficit widens.

Many people who oppose the trade deficit are concerned about unemployment. They take the view that importing too much and exporting too little robs U.S. workers of jobs. On the other hand, some economists point out that a rise in imports doesn't necessarily lead to a rise in unemployment. Rather, both imports and domestic production go up during an economic expansion and fall during a recession.

The question of trade imbalance is a complex one. In the next section, you'll read about government policies that can reduce imports, as well as differing opinions about how often these policies should be used.

Balance of Payments

Here's a simplified example of what the U.S. balance of payments statement might look like in a fictitious year. Figures are in billions of dollars. A real balance of payments statement would include other items not shown here.

IMPORTS AND EXPORTS	INFLOW	OUTFLOW
Merchandise exports	700	
Merchandise imports		1100
Service exports	300	
Service imports		200
Net of imports and exports		**300**

INVESTMENTS	INFLOW	OUTFLOW
U.S.-owned assets abroad		400
Foreign-owned assets in the U.S.	700	
Net of investments	**300**	

7-5

Notice that the "net of imports and exports" figure is balanced by the "net of investments" figure. Which of these two figures represents the trade deficit?

Caption Answer. The trade deficit grew from $108 billion to $726 billion, an increase of $618 billion. Consumer choices and purchases increased.

Answer Key. Answers to the Section Review questions are provided in the Section Lesson Plan located in the *Teacher Resource Guide.*

United States Balance of Trade (Good and Services)

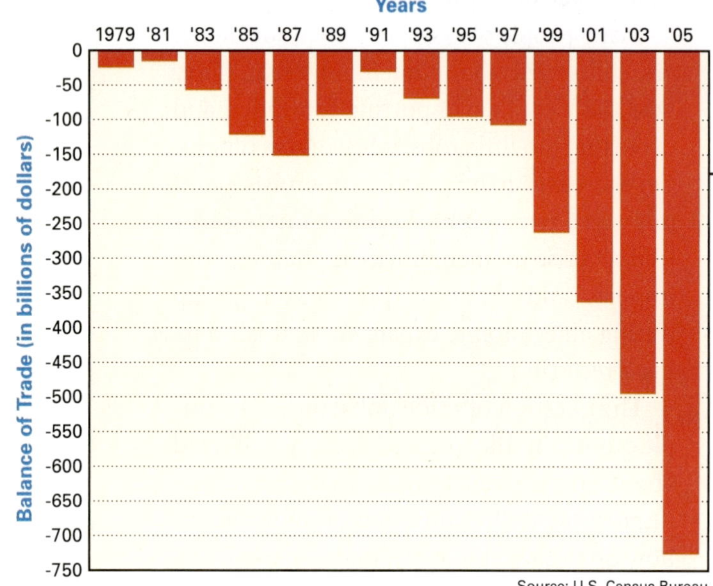

7-6

The U.S. trade deficit has increased dramatically since the late 90s. Analyze the graph. About how much did the trade deficit grow between 1997 and 2005? What does this growth suggest about consumer choices during this period?

Adam Smith

Section 7.1 Review

CHECK YOUR UNDERSTANDING

1. According to the economist Adam Smith, what are the benefits of specialization?
2. What is the flexible exchange rate system? How can it make the cost of doing business unpredictable?
3. What effect does a trade deficit typically have on foreign investment in the U.S.?

CONSUMER APPLICATION

State Exports Research the exports of your state. What are the top three types of exports? With what countries is most of the trade conducted? What was the total value of exports in a recent year? Explain how international trade benefits your state's economy.

SECTION 7.2

Trade Restrictions and Agreements

Governments regulate economic activity, including trade with other nations. As you'll see, there are several ways in which governments may restrict international trade and several reasons for doing so.

Objectives

After studying this section, you should be able to:

- Describe methods used to restrict international trade.
- Analyze arguments in favor of protectionism and free trade.
- Explain the impact of major trade agreements.

Key Terms

tariff
import quota
embargo
protectionism
free trade
WTO
NAFTA

WAYS TO RESTRICT TRADE

Governments can restrict imports or exports using several methods. The three main ones are tariffs, quotas, and embargoes.

- **Protective tariffs.** The most common type of trade restriction is a **tariff**, a tax on imports. However, not all tariffs are designed to restrict trade. Small *revenue tariffs* are intended simply as a source of government income. Larger tariffs—sometimes as high as 62%—are called *protective tariffs.* The tariff is paid by the importer, who then adds it to the price charged to consumers. The much higher price of imported goods discourages consumers from buying them.

- **Quotas.** An **import quota** is a government limit on the quantity or value of a certain imported product. In the past, the U.S. government has placed quotas on

Critical Thinking. *Ask:* If import quotas tend to raise prices for consumers, why would a nation choose to use them?

imports of peanuts, cotton, sugar, and cars, among other products. The use of quotas tends to raise consumer prices. See Figure 7-7.

- **Embargoes.** An **embargo** is a government order prohibiting trade. It might apply to a specific type of product or to trade with a specific country, and it can be used to restrict imports or exports. Embargoes are not common. When used, they are often declared for political reasons. For example, in 1986 Congress halted all trade with South Africa to

7-7

When trading with other countries, imports can be restricted by limiting the quantity or value of a product coming into the country. This is called an import quota.

Critical Thinking. *Ask:* What examples of public protest have occurred in this country? What were the effects? How are embargos similar?

protest its policies of racial discrimination. The embargo was lifted in 1993, when South Africa began to change its policies.

PROTECTIONISM VERSUS FREE TRADE

The question of how much to restrict trade is a subject of debate. Some people favor **protectionism**, a policy of using trade restrictions to protect domestic businesses from foreign competition. Others favor **free trade**, a policy of minimizing trade restrictions. See Figure 7-8.

Arguments for Protectionism

Those who favor protectionism point out several reasons for restricting trade.

- **National security.** Certain goods and services—such as oil, weapons, and shipbuilding—are vital for national security. No nation wants to become too dependent on imports from a country with which it may someday be at war. Governments also limit exports for national security reasons. In the United States, certain kinds of computers, software, and nuclear technology cannot be exported without government approval.
- **Job security.** Some imported products cost much less than those made in the United States, in part because workers in other countries are often paid far less than U.S. workers. This puts pressure on U.S. workers to accept lower wages and fewer benefits. If companies that can't compete against cheaper foreign products are forced out of business, U.S. workers lose their jobs.

Class Activity. Hold a class debate on trade policies. Have one team argue in favor of protectionism and the other in favor of free trade. Give each team a chance to respond to the other's arguments. Afterward, ask the class whether the debate swayed their personal opinions about trade.

- **Infant industries.** Suppose U.S. consumers are buying a certain product that's only available through imports. A U.S. business wants to begin making the product. As this new, or infant, industry gets started, it will have to learn by doing. It may take several years before the industry can operate efficiently. Trade restrictions against imports can protect the infant industry until it's able to compete on its own.
- **Environmental protection.** The United States has many laws and regulations to protect the environment. Some countries have few environmental laws or have problems enforcing their laws. Trade restrictions against those countries could reduce the demand for their products, thus reducing pollution.

- **Unfair advantages.** Governments sometimes restrict imports in response to what they consider unfair trade practices. For example, in 1987 the U.S. government concluded that Japanese firms had been selling computer chips in the United States at unfairly low prices—below what it cost to produce the chips. U.S. companies that made similar chips could not match these prices and might have been forced out of business. The U.S. government placed a high tariff on the imported chips, eliminating the unfair advantage.

Arguments for Free Trade

Few people would argue that trade should never be restricted under any circumstances. However, many economists believe it's wise to keep tariffs and other trade restrictions to a minimum. The following points are among those used to support a policy of free trade.

- **Effect on exports.** One of the main arguments against protectionism is that other countries often retaliate with their own trade restrictions. When other countries impose tariffs or quotas, U.S. companies can't export as many goods and services. Export industries are also hurt in another way. Fewer imports coming into the United States means less money flowing abroad. With less money to spend, people and businesses in other countries will buy fewer U.S. products.

7-8

Free trade allows people of one country to buy goods from another country. What are some advantages and disadvantages of free trade?

Research Activity. Ask students to guess what the major exports and imports of the United States are. Then have them do research to check their guesses.

Research Activity. Have students read and summarize an article about how foreign competition has affected the U.S. automobile industry.

- **Effect on consumers.** Protectionist policies drive up the consumer price of many goods. In contrast, free trade results in a greater variety of products to choose from at lower prices, so consumers can get more for their money.
- **Benefits of specialization.** As you've learned, production is more efficient when countries specialize in certain goods and services and trade for others. Efficient production is one of the nation's basic economic goals.
- **Benefits of competition.** Free trade promotes competition, another basic principle of the U.S. economy. Competition from imports can spur U.S. firms to improve their production efficiency and the quality of their products.
- **Alternatives.** Those who favor free trade suggest that market problems can best be solved by methods other than trade restrictions. For instance, the government can support domestic industries through subsidies, a form of financial assistance.

Those who favor free trade acknowledge that not every person benefits from it in the short run. Some businesses may not survive competition from abroad. However, many economists maintain that free trade results in increased prosperity that eventually benefits everyone. See Figure 7-9.

TRADE AGREEMENTS

Between World War I and World War II, many countries followed a policy of protectionism. International trade was greatly hindered as a result. Seeking to increase trade, many countries adopted a free trade policy after World War II. Since then a number of international trade agreements have been reached.

Discussion. ***Ask:*** What products are available to you as a result of free trade? How might your life change if the United States stopped trading with other countries?

7-9

Goods from almost every nation are traded each day in the international marketplace. Do you think it is in the best interest of the United States to limit international trade or to expand it? Why?

Discussion. *Ask:* How has the media influenced your knowledge of other cultures? Has it increased your interest in products from other countries?

GATT and the WTO

In 1947, to promote international trade, 90 countries signed a General Agreement on Tariffs and Trade (GATT). Many additional countries signed a new GATT in 1994. The goal of this agreement was to reduce or remove trade barriers. The GATT agreement set up a regulatory body called the **World Trade Organization (WTO)**. The WTO is an organization that governs over 140 member nations. The government of each member nation agrees to specific rules that guarantee certain trade rights and lower trade barriers.

NAFTA

The **North American Free Trade Agreement (NAFTA)** is a wide-ranging regional trade agreement between the United States, Canada, and Mexico. The agreement went into effect on January 1, 1994. It's designed to make trade between the three nations easier and to give legal protections to investors and international businesses in all three countries. Under NAFTA, trade among the three partners expanded rapidly.

European Union

The European Union (EU) is an organization of independent European nations whose goal is to create a unified and strong market. It began with cooperation between six nations in 1951. Fifty years later, 15 nations were members of the EU, with others moving toward membership. In 1993, the EU began eliminating most trade restrictions among members. In 1999, the euro was introduced as the European Union's common currency.

Answer Key. Answers to the Section Review questions are provided in the Section Lesson Plan located in the *Teacher Resource Guide.*

A GLOBAL ECONOMY

Thanks to technology, the world is getting smaller all the time. Fiber optic cables and communications satellites bridge the distances between nations. With wireless voice and Internet connections, people on the go can check currency exchange rates, stay on top of worldwide financial news, buy foreign stocks, and talk to colleagues and customers all over the world.

Media such as television and movies also have a strong influence. People around the world are exposed to American culture through news, entertainment, and advertising. As a result, they buy more U.S. products, such as blue jeans, soft drinks, and music.

Many large U.S. companies have offices or factories in other countries, and many foreign-based companies have a presence in the United States. Companies with divisions in more than two countries are called *multinationals.* In addition, firms in different countries often form alliances with one another. More than ever before, it's a global economy.

Section 7.2 Review

CHECK YOUR UNDERSTANDING

1. Explain how protective tariffs restrict trade.
2. How is the issue of job security used as an argument by protectionists?
3. What is NAFTA, and what is its purpose?

CONSUMER APPLICATION

Current Trade Restriction Learn about a trade restriction currently imposed by the U.S. government. What type of restriction is it? What is its purpose? How does it affect consumers?

CHAPTER 7

Review & Activities

CHAPTER SUMMARY

- Currency exchange rates affect trade between nations, which has benefits for nations and consumers. Economists disagree about the impact of the long-running U.S. trade deficit. (7.1)
- Governments can impose several types of restrictions on international trade. Many nations have signed trade agreements to make trading less restrictive. Some people support protectionism, while others support free trade. Factors such as technology and media have created an increasingly global economy. (7.2)

THE $avvy Consumer

Playing Fair: The local park district gave Cynthia's consumer science class permission to sell food at the district's softball games, if they can reach an agreement with the professional vendors who already have food stands at the games. A committee meets tonight to discuss what to sell and how much to charge. What suggestions can Cynthia give to help make their plan acceptable to the other vendors? (7.2)

Reviewing Key Terms and Ideas

1. What is the difference between an **export** and an **import**? (7.1)
2. Describe two ways in which consumers benefit from international trade. (7.1)
3. Why are currency **exchange rates** necessary? (7.1)
4. How does the exchange rate affect the **balance of trade**? (7.1)
5. What is a country's **balance of payments**? (7.1)
6. What creates a **trade deficit**? (7.1)
7. What are the pros and cons of a U.S. trade deficit? (7.1)
8. Compare the effects of a **tariff** and an **import quota** on international trade. (7.2)
9. What is a trade **embargo**? (7.2)
10. How does **free trade** differ from **protectionism**? (7.2)
11. Explain two arguments for protectionism. (7.2)
12. Explain two arguments for free trade. (7.2)
13. What is GATT and what is its significance? (7.2)
14. What countries are involved in **NAFTA**? (7.2)
15. What has influenced the creation of a global economy? (7.2)

Answer Key. Answers to the Chapter Review & Activities are provided in the Teacher's Manual in the *Teacher Annotated Edition* of the text.

Thinking Critically

1. **Drawing Inferences and Conclusions:** What might happen if the trade deficit continues to increase over the next 20 years? Do you think the stability of the U.S. dollar makes a difference in the effects of the trade deficit? Explain your answers. (7.1)
2. **Supporting Your Position:** Based on what you have learned so far, do you favor protectionism or free trade? Give reasons to support your opinion. (7.2)
3. **Analyzing Economic Concepts:** What are the advantages and disadvantages of international competition from the perspective of U.S. consumers, workers, and businesses? (7.1, 7.2)

Building Consumer Skills

1. **Consumer Choice:** Think of several items you and your family have purchased recently. Read the labels and note how many came from another country or contain parts, ingredients, or materials from another country. Write a paragraph summarizing how international trade affects your life and how your purchases and your family's affect international trade. (7.1)
2. **Exchange Rates:** Choose a foreign currency. Measure it against the U.S. dollar by checking a source that provides exchange rates. Select a product and calculate how much it would cost if you purchased it with the foreign currency. Keep track of the exchange rates for a week and note how they fluctuate. Which day would have been best to make your purchase? (7.1)
3. **Trade Disputes:** One role of the World Trade Organization is to settle disputes between trading countries. Research the dispute resolution and process used by the WTO. Read about an actual dispute being resolved by the WTO. Present your findings as a case study to the class. (7.2)

CONSUMER CONNECTIONS

- **Family:** With members of your family, identify imports and exports you use regularly. Ask whether family members prefer a product made in the United States over one that was imported. What are their reasons? (7.1, 7.2)
- **Community:** How has international trade affected your local economy? For example, have local manufacturers expanded as a result of foreign markets? Has a factory closed because it could not compete with less expensive imports? Check news articles and the Internet to learn more. Interview local business and government leaders. Dicuss your findings in class. (7.1)

CHAPTER 8

Income and Taxes

SECTION 8.1
Examining Pay and Benefits

SECTION 8.2
Understanding Your Paycheck

SECTION 8.3
Paying Income Taxes

Reading with Purpose

- Write down the colored headings in this chapter.
- As you read the text under each heading, visualize what you are reading.
- Reflect on what you read by writing a few sentences under each heading to describe it.
- Reread your notes.

SECTION 8.1

Examining Pay and Benefits

When you start a job, you will probably be excited to get your first paycheck. You may also receive benefits such as health insurance. Together, pay and benefits represent an employee's income. Understanding various types of income will help you weigh job opportunities and may even affect your choice of a career field.

Objectives

After studying this section, you should be able to:

- Distinguish between types of income.
- Explain regulations affecting pay.
- Give examples of benefits.
- Describe employment classifications and their effect on pay and benefits.

Key Terms

salary
wages
piecework
commission
tips
minimum wage
overtime
vested

TYPES OF PAY

When you're offered a job, be sure you understand how your rate of pay is figured. Pay can be calculated in a number of different ways.

- A **salary** is a set amount of money earned by an employee per year or other fixed length of time. For example, a salary might be set at $40,000 per year. A portion of the salary is paid at regular intervals, such as weekly or monthly. Each paycheck reflects the total salary for the year divided by the number of pay periods in the year minus deductions and taxes. Salaried employees usually can expect the same amount each pay period.

Jump$tart. Ask students whether they consider tips to be a fair way to pay employees. What are the benefits and drawbacks of relying on tips? *(Income)*

- **Wages** are employee earnings that are paid by the hour, day, or item. If you work for a wage of $10 per hour, your paycheck would be $10 multiplied by the number of hours you worked during the pay period. Instead of receiving hourly wages, some employees do **piecework**, work for which wages are based on the number of items or pieces produced. Piecework usually involves the manufacture or assembly of items.
- A **commission** is a fixed percentage or amount of profit given to an employee in exchange for making a sale. For instance, if you sell cars for an auto dealership, as shown in Figure 8-1, you might receive a certain portion of the dealership's profits from the cars you sell. Some employees earn a commission in addition to hourly wages or a salary. Others work purely on commission—their pay is based entirely on the profits from what they sell.

8-1

The income of employees paid on commission can fluctuate over time. How might the overall state of the economy affect their income?

Caption Answer. Commissions may rise and fall with the economy. When the economy declines, commissions may shrink.

- A bonus is a sum of money paid to an employee in addition to regular pay. Many employers pay bonuses when employees meet certain goals or perform their jobs especially well.
- **Tips** are money given to an employee by customers in exchange for a service. For instance, in many restaurants it's customary for you to give your server a tip based on the cost of your meal. Many workers who receive tips often aren't paid a significant hourly wage, so tips can be a substantial addition to their income.

REGULATIONS AFFECTING PAY

No matter how workers are paid, they have a right to be paid fairly. Under the Fair Labor Standards Act (FLSA), the federal government has enacted certain standards governing employee payment and compensation.

Equal Pay

The Fair Labor Standards Act includes equal pay provisions that forbid employers from paying one person less than another person for the same work. The rules apply to employees who work in the same establishment, under the same or similar conditions, doing work requiring equal skill, effort, and responsibility. The FLSA often is used to prevent discrimination against women, minorities, and older workers.

Discussion. *Ask:* As a teen, would you be willing to work for a subminimum wage? Why or why not?

Minimum Wage

To ensure that workers who earn hourly wages are paid fairly, the federal government has established provisions within the Fair Labor Standards Act for a national **minimum wage**. This is the lowest hourly rate an employer may legally pay most workers. The figure is raised periodically to help workers keep up with inflation.

The government also has established a special minimum wage, sometimes called a *subminimum wage*, which is set lower than the standard minimum wage. The special minimum wage can be applied to full-time students, employees who are younger than 20, and employees who are developmentally disabled.

Economic Impact & Issues. *Ask:* From an employee's and employer's viewpoint, which is preferable, job perks or higher salary? Explain.

Overtime

Most jobs that pay hourly wages are based on a standard 40-hour work week. According to the Fair Labor Standards Act, work in excess of 40 hours per week is classified as **overtime**. In most cases, compensation for work beyond 40 hours must be at least 1.5 times the employee's regular rate of pay. Exceptions are made for certain types of jobs.

Overtime usually is not paid to salaried employees. They are sometimes referred to as *exempt* employees, indicating that they are not subject to overtime regulations. An hourly employee who is offered a promotion to a salaried position should take the loss of overtime pay into account when weighing the offer.

Economic Impact & Issues

Employee Benefits Reflect the Marketplace

Employers are caught between two marketplace realities: the need to attract the best workers while minimizing operating costs. Pressure to meet both goals is increasing in today's competitive, global economy. One way companies have found to achieve their profit goals is to update traditional benefits packages to make them less costly. This strategy often dovetails with employees' interest in more personalized "perks."

Some "benefits" that appeal to employees are simply built-in advantages of the job. For example, technology allows many employees flexible work arrangements, like telecommuting. Unpaid leave during slow seasons is common in such fields as tourism.

Some companies reduce costs by replacing one-size-fits-all insurance plans with "cafeteria" packages that allow employees to choose benefits that are the most useful to them and their families. In place of traditional pay raises, companies might offer performance-based rewards. These perks can be a motivation for current employees and entice prospective employees to join a company.

With workers averaging more job changes over a lifetime, the idea of "portable" health insurance and pensions is gaining ground. The money or benefits workers have built up "follow" them from job to job.

FIGURE IT OUT

Ask three working adults which employee benefits they think are the most important and why. Compare results in class. Then discuss how the benefits named relate to current economic trends in your area or the nation as a whole.

Research Activity. Have students research the cost of private health insurance. Then ask them to estimate the dollar value of a company health plan.

TYPES OF BENEFITS

When choosing among different jobs, be sure to consider not only pay but benefits. A job that pays less but offers more benefits may give you a better income in the long run. Benefits can take many forms, so learn which ones the employer offers.

- **Insurance benefits.** Employees often can enroll in group health care plans offered by their employers. Such plans allow employees and their dependents access to health care at reduced costs. Other types of insurance may also be offered.

Research Activity. Have students find out how paid holidays are handled in various countries and report their findings. Discuss their reactions in class.

- **Savings and retirement benefits.** Employers offer many types of employee savings plans and retirement plans. Typically, the employer deducts money from the employee's paycheck to deposit in a savings or investment account. Some or all of the money might be deducted on a pre-tax basis, which reduces the amount of income tax the employee must pay. Some employers match a portion of the employee's contribution. After a certain amount of time, the employee becomes **vested**, or entitled to some or all of his or her money in the retirement plan when leaving the company. For example, a plan might state that employees become vested at the rate of 20% per year. An employee who leaves the company after being in the plan three years would be entitled to 60% of his or her retirement account balance.

TEXTLINK

Health insurance is explained in Section 14.4. You'll learn more about retirement plans in Section 13.2.

- **Other benefits.** Many employers offer benefits such as paid holidays, vacation, and sick leave. They might pay for additional education or job training to help employees learn new skills. Some offer paid maternity leave and money toward adoption expenses and child care. See Figure 8-2.

8-2

Child care is a concern for many employed parents. As a benefit, some companies have on-site child care, and some help financially with the costs of care.

FCCLA. Have students use the Making Money unit of Financial Fitness to compare the income and benefits they could earn in possible future careers.

EMPLOYMENT CLASSIFICATIONS

An employee's pay and benefits can depend on whether he or she is a full-time, part-time, temporary, or contract worker.

- **Full-time.** Full-time employees hold wage or salary jobs of at least 35 hours per week. They usually can take part in employer-sponsored benefits plans, including health care and savings programs. They also tend to earn higher wages and salaries than employees working in other employment classifications.
- **Part-time.** Employees who work fewer than 35 hours per week, no matter how they are paid, are usually considered part-time employees. In some companies, they are eligible to receive the same or similar benefits as full-time employees. In other companies, however, they are not eligible for benefits.
- **Temporary.** At times employers hire workers to fill temporary vacancies or to help with additional work. These temporary employees are paid by an employment agency and given short-term assignments at various companies. The employer pays the agency an hourly wage for the services of the employee. The agency pays the employee a slightly lower hourly rate and keeps the difference. Employers don't provide benefits to temporary employees. However, some employment agencies offer basic benefits, usually health care coverage.
- **Contract.** Contract employees are hired for a specified period of time to complete a particular project for an employer, usually at an hourly rate or a total project rate. Employers are not obligated to provide benefits to contract employees, but benefits sometimes are included as part of the contract.

Point Out. Contract employees must often pay income taxes directly because taxes are not deducted from their pay.

By using temporary or contract employees, employers gain several advantages. They can easily increase or decrease staffing as their needs change. Costs may be less if benefits aren't paid and costly hiring and training procedures can be avoided. Employers also have a trial period in which to evaluate potential new employees whom they may decide to hire on a permanent basis. The employment of temporary and contract employees has been on the rise.

Answer Key. Answers to the Section Review questions are provided in the Section Lesson Plan located in the *Teacher Resource Guide.*

Section 8.1 Review

CHECK YOUR UNDERSTANDING

1. Explain the difference between working for a salary and working for wages.
2. When might an employee be paid less than minimum wage?
3. How is a contract employee different from a temporary employee?

CONSUMER APPLICATION

Comparing Income You are trying to decide between two summer jobs. One pays $2 an hour above minimum wage and guarantees at least 25 hours per week, with up to 40 hours possible in busy periods. The other job pays $2 less than minimum wage. However, you'll receive tips and can work as many or as few hours as you wish. Explain how you would compare the income potential of the two jobs. What else would you take into consideration and why?

Objectives

After studying this section, you should be able to:

- Explain variations in how workers receive pay.
- Describe the information found on a pay stub.
- Identify paycheck deductions and their purposes.

Key Terms

direct deposit
gross pay
deduction
net pay

SECTION 8.2

Understanding Your Paycheck

People often talk about the benefits of receiving a "regular paycheck." Just as there are many types of employees and incomes, there are a variety of ways workers receive their pay. In fact, some workers actually choose never to receive a paycheck!

HOW EMPLOYEES ARE PAID

Companies differ in how often and when they pay employees. Some employers choose to pay their employees on a weekly basis; others pay their employees every two weeks, once a month, or twice a month. It is your responsibility to find out when you will be paid so that you can plan your personal finances.

Direct Deposit

When you receive a paycheck, you can either cash it or deposit the amount in your bank account. However, there is a way of being paid without receiving a paycheck. Through **direct deposit**, pay is electronically transferred directly into the recipient's bank account. Most employers allow employees to request direct deposit by completing and signing a form. Instead of an actual paycheck, employees receive a receipt or statement showing the amount

Community Activity. Have students contact local banks to find out whether they accept direct deposit payments.

deposited, the name of the financial institution, and the account number. Employees also receive a pay stub, just as if they were paid by check.

INFORMATION ON A PAY STUB

A pay stub provides useful information, and it's a good idea to get in the habit of looking at it each time you're paid. An error in your pay stub might cost you some of the money you worked so hard to earn. A pay stub also can help you keep track of exactly how much you're earning, how the amount was calculated, and where some of your money is going.

Figure 8-3 shows a typical pay stub. Although yours may look a little different, all pay stubs include similar types of information.

Critical Thinking. *Ask:* Why is it important for hourly employees to maintain their own record of hours worked?

Identification

Each pay stub includes your name and address and the dates for which you are being paid. Your employee number and Social Security number also might be included.

Earnings

The pay stub should show the number of hours—regular and overtime—worked during the current pay period. These figures are especially important to hourly-wage employees. Always check to be sure that the numbers are accurate. For workers who are paid a yearly salary, this section of the pay stub might be left empty or might reflect the number of regular working hours in the pay period.

Caption Answer. Errors might have been made in your employee information or in calculating your pay and deductions.

8-3

A pay stub includes important details about your pay and deductions. Why should you go over your pay stub carefully each time you're paid?

Identification

WORKER, PAT L | **Period Ending** 06/01 | **Check #** 1103503

Employee # 5678 | **Employee SSN** 000-50-1234 | **Department** 425

Earnings	Hours	Current	Year-to-Date	Deductions	Current	Year-to-Date
REGULAR RATE 7.00	54	378.00	4158.00	DENTAL FEDTAX STATE TAX FICAHI MED INS SOCSEC	5.00 23.03 4.29 5.45 16.50 7.20	55.00 253.33 47.19 59.95 181.50 79.20
Totals	54	378.00	4158.00		61.47	676.17
Net Pay		316.53				

Earnings

Deductions

Net pay

Totals

Team Activity. Have each student write down five questions about the content of this section for a "pop quiz." Then have students exchange papers and take each other's quizzes. Afterward, the student who wrote the questions should grade the quiz and correct any wrong answers.

Most workers are especially interested in the part of the pay stub labeled earnings or gross pay. **Gross pay** is the total amount of money earned for working during the pay period. For a salaried employee, gross pay will usually be the same for each pay period. If you work for an hourly wage, check your pay stub for accuracy by multiplying the number of hours worked by the hourly rate. The result should equal the gross pay.

Finally, your pay stub may show how much you've earned so far this year. Most pay stubs include a column that lists the total hours worked and gross pay for the year to date.

8-4 **The taxes you pay provide services to everyone, such as well-constructed highways that make traveling safe and convenient. In what other ways do citizens benefit from paying income tax?**

Deductions

Most paycheck stubs will include a list of deductions. On a pay stub, a **deduction** is anything that is subtracted from gross pay. As with earnings, deductions often are listed for both the current pay period and the year to date. There are several types of deductions.

- **Tax withholding.** Tax deductions can include federal, state, and local income taxes. See Figure 8-4. Also included in this section are deductions for Social Security (a federal assistance program that pays retirement, survivors, and disability benefits) and Medicare (a federal program that helps pay medical expenses for those who qualify). Social Security and Medicare deductions sometimes use the abbreviation FICA, which stands for Federal Insurance Contributions Act.

Class Activity. Have students look at Figure 8-3 and calculate what percentage of this worker's income is going toward taxes.

- **Benefits.** Contributions to employee benefit programs, such as medical, dental, and vision care plans, are included in this section.

Caption Answer. Multiply your net pay (or average net pay for several pay periods) times the number of pay periods for the year.

Answer Key. Answers to the Section Review questions are provided in the Section Lesson Plan located in the *Teacher Resource Guide*.

- **Other deductions.** Some employees also have money deducted for their employer-sponsored savings or retirement plan or for donations to charity.

8-5

Your net pay is the amount of money you'll receive each pay period. How can you determine your annual net pay?

Totals and Net Pay

Finally, the pay stub shows total earnings, total deductions, and net pay. **Net pay** is the amount of pay an employee is left with after taxes and other deductions are subtracted from the gross pay. Net pay also is called "take-home pay" because it's the amount of money that an employee actually receives.

If your pay doesn't vary from one pay period to the next, you can determine how much gross and net pay you will earn in a year. Simply multiply the figures for gross and net pay by the number of pay periods during the year. For instance, suppose you get paid every two weeks. That's a total of 26 paychecks over the course of a year. By multiplying the gross pay figures on a single check by 26, you can estimate how much money, before taxes and other deductions are subtracted, you will earn for the year. If your pay varies from paycheck to paycheck, you can estimate your annual earnings by averaging several checks. See Figure 8-5.

Section 8.2 Review

CHECK YOUR UNDERSTANDING

1. What is direct deposit?
2. What is the difference between gross pay and net pay?
3. List and explain the three categories of deductions that might appear on a pay stub.

CONSUMER APPLICATION

Estimating Pay Imagine that you've taken a summer job working at a local entertainment complex. Your hourly wage is $7.00. You'll work 40 hours per week and be paid every other week for a total of 16 weeks. Using the figures provided, estimate your gross pay for the summer and for each pay period.

Objectives

After studying this section, you should be able to:

- Identify responsibilities related to income taxes.
- Describe the purpose of various income tax forms.
- Explain the types of information included on a tax return.
- Discuss the benefits of tax planning.

Key Terms

allowances
dependent
tax deduction
itemized deductions
standard deduction
tax credit

SECTION 8.3

Paying Income Taxes

Many people don't worry about income taxes until April 1—two weeks prior to the deadline for turning in tax returns. However, you'd be smart to think ahead. By planning carefully, you can meet your tax obligations while preserving as much of your income as allowed by law.

INCOME TAX RESPONSIBILITIES

Imagine that you've just landed your first job. Along with other new responsibilities, you now have a duty to the government and to your fellow citizens to pay your fair share of income taxes. Remember, income tax is the largest source of money used by the federal government to provide services to its citizens. Some state and local governments also collect income tax.

How do you fulfill your responsibility to pay income taxes? Two main tasks are involved:

- Complete a form that allows your employer to withhold income taxes from your pay.
- File a tax return at least once a year, and pay any additional tax owed.

Critical Thinking. ***Ask:*** If no taxes were withheld from workers' pay during the year, how would government services be affected?

INCOME TAX WITHHOLDING

In most cases, your employer will *withhold*, or take out, income tax from every paycheck and send the money to the government. That way you pay taxes a little at a time throughout the year instead of all at once. The amount withheld varies from person to person. It's determined by how much you earn, how often you get paid, and the information you give your employer on Form W-4.

Form W-4

When you start a job, your employer will ask you to fill out Form W-4, Employee's Withholding Allowance Certificate, shown in Figure 8-6. The form asks for the following kinds of information:

- **Personal information.** Write in your name, address, and Social Security number, and mark whether you are single or married.

Discussion. ***Ask:*** What changes in your personal situation might require a review of your W-4 allowances?

- **Exempt status.** You may be exempt, or excused, from having income tax withheld. If you didn't have to pay taxes the previous year, and you expect to have too little income to pay taxes in the current year, you can write "Exempt" on line 7 of Form W-4.
- **Allowances.** If you're not exempt from withholding, you'll need to specify the number of allowances you're claiming. **Allowances** are factors that affect the amount of income tax withholding. The more allowances you claim, the less tax your employer will take out. Use the worksheet on Form W-4 to figure out how many you can claim. Although you should not claim more allowances than you're entitled to, you can choose to claim fewer allowances, increasing the amount of tax withheld.

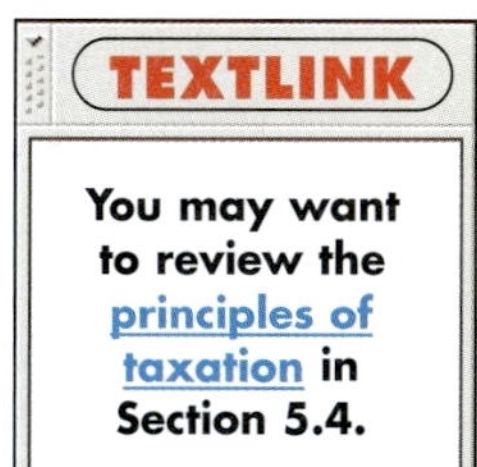

8-6

The information you provide on Form W-4 tells your employer how much tax to withhold from your paycheck.

Form **W-4** Department of the Treasury Internal Revenue Service

Employee's Withholding Allowance Certificate

▶ For Privacy Act and Paperwork Reduction Act Notice, see page 2.

OMB No. 1545-0010

1 Type or print your first name and middle initial: Chris A. | Last name: Sample | 2 Your social security number: 000 12 3456

Home address (number and street or rural route): 123 W. Main St.

3 ☒ Single ☐ Married ☐ Married, but withhold at higher Single rate.
Note: *If married, but legally separated, or spouse is a nonresident alien, check the Single box.*

City or town, state, and ZIP code: Smallville KS 66000

4 **If your last name differs from that on your social security card, check here. You must call 1-800-772-1213 for a new card.** ▶ ☐

5 Total number of allowances you are claiming (from line **H** above **or** from the applicable worksheet on page 2) | 5 | 2

6 Additional amount, if any, you want withheld from each paycheck . . . . | 6 | $

7 I claim exemption from withholding for 2001, and I certify that I meet **both** of the following conditions for exemption:
- Last year I had a right to a refund of **all** Federal income tax withheld because I had **no** tax liability **and**
- This year I expect a refund of **all** Federal income tax withheld because I expect to have **no** tax liability.

If you meet both conditions, write "Exempt" here . . . . ▶ | 7 |

Under penalties of perjury, I certify that I am entitled to the number of withholding allowances claimed on this certificate, or I am entitled to claim exempt status.
Employee's signature (Form is not valid unless you sign it.) ▶ Chris A. Sample **Date** ▶

Critical Thinking. *Ask:* Why must you file a tax return even if you are not eligible for a refund?

GETTING READY FOR TAX TIME

If you've paid taxes all year by having them withheld from your pay, why is April 15 sometimes called "income tax day"? That's the deadline by which most people need to file a tax return. The purpose of a tax return is to report your actual earnings, calculate how much tax you owe on those earnings, and compare the tax owed to the total amount withheld. If you owe more taxes than you paid during the year, you must pay the difference. If you paid more than you owe, you'll get a refund—but only if you file a return.

Federal income tax returns are sent to the Internal Revenue Service (IRS), the government agency in charge of collecting federal income tax. Your tax return must be sent to the IRS by April 15 of the year following the year for which you are filing. If you do not file your tax return or pay the taxes you owe, the IRS can charge you a penalty or late fees, or both.

Research Activity. Have students visit the Web site of the IRS to find out what categories of workers are not required to file a tax return.

Do You Need to File?

Most workers are required by law to file a tax return, but there are exceptions. People whose income falls below a certain amount are not required to pay income taxes. This minimum amount varies depending on many things, including whether you are self-employed, over the age of 65, a single adult, a child, or a married person with children.

What Materials Do You Need?

Before you can file your tax return, you must have certain information and forms. See Figure 8-7. Most people need at least the following materials:

- **Form W-2.** Your employer will send you a form showing your total earnings for the year and the total amount of taxes withheld. This form, called a Form W-2 Wage and Tax Statement, is shown in Figure 8-8. By law, it must be sent to all employees by January 31. When you receive it, make sure that your name and Social Security number are correct and that the income and taxes withheld correspond to the year-to-date figures on your last pay stub of the year.
- **Form 1099.** If you have earned interest on savings during the year, your bank will send you a Form 1099-INT, showing the amount you earned. Other 1099 forms are used for reporting other types of income. Each is also sent to the IRS.

8-7

Having all of your tax materials and financial records together before you begin will help streamline the process of completing your tax return.

Class Activity. Ask students to use the information on the W-2 form shown here to calculate this worker's take-home pay for the year.

Critical Thinking. *Ask:* Which financial records would you want to keep during the year to use in preparing your tax return?

a Control number		OMB No. 1545-0008		
b Employer identification number 123456-78			1 Wages, tips, other compensation 9,672.00	2 Federal income tax withheld 745.00
c Employeris name, address, and ZIP code ABC STORES 2001 RING ROAD LARGETOWN, NY 10001			3 Social security wages 9,672.00	4 Social security tax withheld 599.66
			5 Medicare wages and tips 9,672.00	6 Medicare tax withheld 140.24
			7 Social security tips	8 Allocated tips
d Employeeis social security number 000-98-7654			9 Advance EIC payment	10 Dependent care benefits
e Employeeis name, address, and ZIP code JESSE B. STUDENT 4567 LINCOLN ST. LARGETOWN, NY 10001			11 Nonqualified plans	12 Benefits included in box 1
			13	14 Other
			15 Statutory employee ☐ Deceased ☐ Pension plan ☐ Legal rep. ☐ Deferred compensation ☐	

16 State	Employeris state I.D. no.	17 State wages, tips, etc.	18 State income tax	19 Locality name	20 Local wages, tips, etc.	21 Local income tax
NY	00-98765	9,672.00	345.00			

Form **W-2** Wage and Tax Statement

Department of the Treasury—Internal Revenue Service

8-8 **Each employer you work for during the year must provide you with a Form W-2. Each W-2 will show your total income for that particular job.**

- **IRS instruction booklets and forms.** You must use one of three forms to file your tax return—Form 1040, 1040A, or 1040EZ. Forms 1040EZ and 1040A are simplified versions; you must meet certain criteria, such as having income below a certain level, in order to use them. Most teens living at home and working part-time can use Form 1040EZ. Forms are available at public libraries, or you can print them from the IRS Web site.
- **Personal records.** Gather your financial records from the previous year in case you need them as you prepare your tax return.

COMPLETING YOUR TAX RETURN

An instruction booklet is available from the IRS for each tax return form. The booklet gives line-by-line directions for completing the form correctly. Read the directions and follow the steps carefully. You can prepare yourself by becoming familiar with the information a return asks for and the terms you may see.

- **Filing status.** You must choose a filing status, which is based on factors such as whether you are single or married. The status you choose will have an effect on the amount of tax owed.
- **Exemptions.** Tax laws allow some income to be exempt (excused) from tax, based on the number of people in the household. Each qualified person counts as one exemption. Qualified people may include the taxpayer, a spouse, and dependents. A **dependent** is someone who is supported by a taxpayer's income.

Class Activity. Have students practice filling out a Form 1040 EZ, using the information from the sample Form W-2 on page 203.

Point Out. Most taxpayers can now file their taxes online at no cost. The IRS Web site offers links to companies that provide this service.

- **Income.** You must list your income from all sources. This information will come from your Forms W-2 and 1099. From your total income, you may get to subtract certain items, called *adjustments to income.* The result is your *adjusted gross income.*
- **Deductions.** A **tax deduction** reduces the amount of income that is taxed. Essentially, the government says that if you use part of your income for certain purposes, such as giving to charity or paying interest on a home loan, you don't owe taxes on that income. See Figure 8-9. There are two ways to take tax deductions. One is to list **itemized deductions**, or the amounts actually spent on tax-deductible expenses during the year. The other option is to take a **standard deduction**, a set amount that the IRS allows without listing any actual expenses. You can choose either method, but to list itemized deductions you must use Form 1040.
- **Taxable income.** You also can subtract an additional amount from your income based on the number of exemptions you are claiming. What's left is your *taxable income*—the portion of your income that is actually subject to income tax.
- **Tax owed.** A tax table is provided in the instruction booklet. The table will tell you how much income tax you owe for the year based on your taxable income and filing status.
- **Tax credits.** Unlike a tax deduction, which is subtracted from your income, a **tax credit** is subtracted directly from the amount of tax owed. Taxpayers who meet certain guidelines, such as paying for college tuition and child care expenses, can take tax credits.
- **Final calculations.** After finding the total tax you owe, you'll list the amount of tax withheld from your pay, as shown on your Form W-2. Finally, you'll compare the amount of tax owed with the amount paid during the year. If you overpaid, you'll get a refund; if you underpaid, you must send the remaining tax to the IRS with your return. You may pay by personal check, a money order, or authorization to charge the bill to your credit or debit card.

Caption Answer. The government allows deduction of mortgage interest as an incentive to encourage home ownership.

8-9

Owning a home offers a tax advantage by allowing you to claim the interest you pay on your mortgage loan as a tax deduction. Why would the government allow this deduction?

InfoSource. Have students use a local telephone directory to find community groups and private companies that assist with tax preparation.

Answer Key. Answers to the Section Review questions are provided in the Section Lesson Plan located in the *Teacher Resource Guide.*

InfoSource

Tax Help

If you have questions or need help filing out a tax return, try these sources of assistance.

- IRS instruction booklets, Web site, and toll-free help line.
- Community groups that offer free tax help.
- Books on tax preparation.
- Tax preparation software programs.
- Private companies that offer tax preparation services for a fee. Look in the yellow pages under "Tax Return Preparation."

Electronic Filing

Rather than mailing your income tax return, you can send it electronically through a bank, the IRS Web site, or a company whose tax preparation software you're using. The IRS can process electronic returns more efficiently and send refunds more quickly. If you're eligible to use the 1040EZ form, you can submit your return using a touch-tone telephone.

THE BENEFITS OF TAX PLANNING

Careful planning throughout the year will help you avoid surprises when you file your tax return. Review your W-4 allowances to avoid having too much or too little withheld from your paycheck. If you have too little withheld, you may end up with a big tax bill. If you have too much withheld, you will have loaned money to the government interest-free. You probably could have put this money to better use by investing it or using it to pay down debts.

Tax planning can help you take advantage of incentives, or benefits for using your money a particular way, in the tax code. For instance, increasing your contributions to charity may reduce your income tax obligation. Some investments offer better tax advantages than others. Learn about these and other potential tax breaks and how to qualify for them. Books and articles about tax planning can help, as can professional financial planners. If your income level obligates you to pay income taxes, you need not pay more than your fair share.

Section 8.3 Review

CHECK YOUR UNDERSTANDING

1. Explain the difference between Form W-2 and Form W-4.
2. How do deductions and tax credits affect the amount of tax you pay?
3. Name two ways in which you can benefit from careful tax planning.

CONSUMER APPLICATION

Tax Return Imagine that your friend has delayed filling out his tax return until April 12. Briefly list the information that your friend must organize before filing a tax return.

Review & Activities

CHAPTER SUMMARY

- Your income consists of both your pay and the benefits provided by your employer. The pay and benefits you receive depend on your employment classification (8.1)
- Pay schedules vary from employer to employer, but you should receive your pay on a regular and dependable basis. When you receive your pay, examine the pay stub to make sure your gross pay, deductions, and net pay are correct. (8.2)
- All employees share in the responsibility of paying income tax so the federal government can provide services to its citizens. Careful planning and organizing throughout the tax year will ensure that what you pay is your fair share of taxes. (8.3)

THE $avvy Consumer

Just Between Us: Ray's friend told him about his after-school job as a delivery driver for a small paint store: "I didn't fill out a W-4 form. My boss said I won't make enough to have to pay taxes since I only work part-time at minimum wage. I get paid in cash, which is a lot easier for us both." What should Ray tell his friend? (8.3)

Reviewing Key Terms and Ideas

1. What is the difference between doing **piecework** and working on **commission**? How are they similar? (8.1)
2. Give three examples of how the federal government has ensured that all employees are paid fairly. (8.1)
3. Describe two kinds of benefits an employer might offer. (8.1)
4. What are two possible advantages of being a full-time employee rather than a temporary employee? (8.1)
5. Explain how **direct deposit** works. (8.2)
6. What are the four categories of information provided on your pay stub? Name one additional type of information found in each category. (8.2)
7. What steps must you take to make sure you fulfill your income tax responsibilities? (8.3)
8. Why might a person claim fewer **allowances** than he or she is entitled to when filling out a W-4? (8.3)
9. What is the purpose of Form W-2? (8.3)
10. How do a **tax deduction** and a **tax credit** differ? (8.3)
11. What are **itemized deductions**? (8.3)
12. Why might listing itemized deductions instead of taking a **standard deduction** be to your advantage? (8.3)
13. Why is tax planning beneficial? (8.3)

Answer Key. Answers to the Chapter Review & Activities are provided in the Teacher's Manual in the *Teacher Annotated Edition* of the text.

Thinking Critically

1. **Understanding Cause and Effect:** How do employer-provided benefits affect an employee's take-home pay? (8.1)
2. **Analyzing Information:** What advantages might there be in receiving your pay by direct deposit? (8.2)
3. **Analyzing Economic Concepts:** How does an increase in your wage or salary directly affect the government's efforts to redistribute income? Refer to Section 5.3 for additional information. (8.2, 8.3)
4. **Tax Returns:** Prepare a tax return using one of the descriptions below. In class discuss the similarities and differences in preparing tax returns in each situation. (8.3)
   - Single, living at home, $15,000 annual salary, no dependents, no interest income.
   - Married, single, annual income of $26,000, renting an apartment, 1 child, $100 interest income.
   - Married, dual income of $50,000 home loan with $5,000 interest, 2 children, $2,000 charitable deductions.

Building Consumer Skills

1. **Wage Comparison:** Would you prefer to work on commission or be a salaried employee? Support your preference in writing. Then pair with a classmate who made the opposite choice. In a role-play for the class, present the two points of view. (8.1)
2. **Pay Periods:** Describe in writing the advantages and disadvantages of being paid weekly, every other week, monthly, and in a lump sum at the completion of a large project. Explain how the frequency of pay affects when bills are paid throughout a month. (8.2)
3. **Paycheck Deductions:** Ask three adults to identify the kinds of deductions taken from their paycheck. Categorize each payroll deduction as a mandatory or optional deduction based on tax laws and company policies. For optional deductions, ask the adults to explain why they chose them. (8.2)

CONSUMER CONNECTIONS

- **Family:** Ask family members who file tax returns which tax form(s) they use and why. Find out whether they file returns themselves or get assistance. Have they filed electronically? What do they recommend? (8.3)
- **Community:** Talk with a local business payroll and benefits officer. Discuss how payroll and benefit plans have changed in the past ten years. Share your information with the class. In class, identify the trends in payroll and benefits plans in your community. (8.1)

CHAPTER 9

Financial Planning

SECTION 9.1
Looking at Your Finances

SECTION 9.2
Using Financial Software

SECTION 9.3
Creating a Budget

SECTION 9.4
Organizing Your Records

SECTION 9.5
Seeking Professional Advice

Reading with Purpose

- As you read this chapter, create an outline using the colored headings.
- Write a question for each heading to help guide your reading.
- Write the answer to each question as you read the chapter.
- Ask your teacher to help with answers you cannot find in the text.

SECTION 9.1

Looking at Your Finances

If you were going on a cross-country road trip, you'd use a map to plan a route to your destination. Surprisingly, many people don't map out a plan to help them get where they want to be financially.

Objectives

After studying this section, you should be able to:

- Explain the benefits of financial planning.
- Describe steps in financial planning.
- Recognize how life stages and events can affect financial plans.

Key Terms

budget
balance sheet
assets
liabilities
net worth

BENEFITS OF FINANCIAL PLANNING

Financial planning is important to every household regardless of family size, life stage, or income level. Planning allows you to identify priorities, clarify financial goals, and determine how to reach them. It helps you pay your expenses and live within your income, reducing the need to buy on credit. Knowing that you're prepared for both everyday and unexpected expenses can reduce anxiety about financial health. Planning helps you stay in control of financial matters and develop a sense of financial independence.

Living Within Your Means

Financially sound families live within their means. That means they make smart choices about their spending based on the resources they have available. They postpone some purchases rather than going into debt to have the biggest house, fastest car, and newest clothing all at once.

Class Activity. Challenge students to draw cartoons that illustrate the concept of premature affluence and the benefits of cultivating good financial sense.

Learning to live within their means can be a challenge for teens who have their own income. Many teens don't have to pay for expenses such as groceries, electric bills, and rent. They have the freedom to spend their money on other things, such as clothing, CDs, and nights out. See Figure 9-1.

This freedom can give some teens a false sense of wealth that financial advisors call *premature affluence.* They can have difficulty adjusting when they suddenly have to take on essential living expenses as they become more independent. Teens who begin their working lives with a plan for saving and spending their money are cultivating good financial sense.

ELEMENTS OF FINANCIAL PLANNING

Financial planning is not a single process, but a combination of elements. They include:

- Making a **budget**—a plan for spending and saving your money.
- Choosing *investments* that allow your money to grow over time.
- Establishing *credit* and managing it wisely.

Jump$tart. Ask students why it is important to develop sound spending habits during their teen years. Discuss possible reasons. *(Money Management)*

Critical Thinking. *Ask:* What factors might influence a household's financial priorities?

- Obtaining adequate *insurance* to protect against loss.
- Making decisions about *retirement plan* choices and other employee benefits.
- Setting up an *estate plan* to administer your property according to your wishes.

Putting together a sound financial plan takes time. A good way to start is by identifying goals, taking stock of your current finances, and analyzing your spending habits. Then you can begin planning how to reach your financial goals.

9-1

Premature affluence causes some teens to have severe financial difficulties once they're living on their own. What financial strategies could a teen practice while living at home and working in order to avoid this problem later?

Team Activity. Have each student make a list of goals that are important to him or her. Then have pairs of students swap and compare lists. Ask them to note similarities and differences between their two lists and to explain these similarities and differences in a paragraph.

Identifying Financial Goals

Defining financial goals will help you take the right steps to reach them. Your financial goals should be guided by what's important to you and your family. Examples might be saving for a college education, moving to a neighborhood with better schools and parks, or being able to afford the supplies for your hobby.

TEXTLINK

Chapter 2 provides more details about setting goals.

Point Out. Businesses may also use balance sheets to assess their financial health.

Assessing Current Finances

Once you've defined your goals, evaluate the current state of your finances. Create a net worth statement, or **balance sheet**, which is a statement of what you own and what you owe. Items of value that you own, including money, are called **assets**. Debts or obligations owed to others are called **liabilities**. The difference between your assets and liabilities is your **net worth**. A sample balance sheet is shown in Figure 9-2.

Your net worth increases when your assets increase or your liabilities decrease. Your net worth decreases when your assets decrease or your liabilities increase. Because your net worth changes, you should update your balance sheet at least once a year and whenever your assets or liabilities change dramatically.

9-2

When you create a balance sheet, you can immediately see your net worth. Name an event that could cause your net worth to decrease.

Balance Sheet

Assets		Liabilities	
Checking account	$540	Current bills due	$1,250
Savings account	3,250	Amount owed on credit cards	4,500
Series EE savings bonds	300		
Stocks and bonds	21,720		
Current value of house	92,000	Amount owed on house mortgage	68,000
Current value of car	2,300	Other liabilities	
Total	$120,110	Total	$73,750
Net worth:			$46,360

Class Activity. Ask each student to estimate the cost of a small expense, such as a candy bar or a cup of coffee. Have them calculate how much they would spend on that item by buying it every day for a year. Then ask them what they could buy by skipping that daily purchase and saving the money.

9-3

Recording all of your expenses and saving receipts will help you analyze how you spend your money. Why is it important to analyze small expenses as well as large ones?

Analyzing Spending Habits

Analyzing your spending habits can help you better understand where your money goes. Even seemingly small expenses can add up to large amounts over time.

As an individual or a family, you can analyze your spending habits by keeping a record of all spending during a typical month. Keep receipts for purchases and record all checks in the check register. See Figure 9-3. At the end of the month, review your spending habits. Separate spending into useful categories, such as food, housing, clothing, transportation, entertainment, and so on. There are many possible ways to categorize expenses, so use what works for you.

Next, analyze your expenses. Think about why certain expenses are so high. If eating out is a major expense, a busy schedule may be part of the reason. Perhaps you can find ways to prepare food at home more often and reduce this expense.

Be on the lookout for poor spending habits. You may discover, for example, that you tend to make a lot of impulse purchases using your credit card. Awareness of poor spending habits can help you make better decisions.

Planning for Financial Goals

Once you know where you are financially and where you want to be, you're ready to plan how to get there. Later sections of this book will help you with the elements of your financial plan, starting with a budget.

Along the way, remember to use the management skills discussed in Chapter 2. Translate your general financial goals into specific ones that can be measured and achieved. Identify your resources and look for ways to use them effectively. Use the management process to create, organize, implement and evaluate your plan. Follow the decision-making steps to make wise financial choices. Above all, take personal responsibility for your own financial plan.

Team Activity. Organize the class into four groups. Assign each group one of the life stages. Have each group create a poster showing what a family's primary expenses might be during that life stage. Have each group present the poster to the class. As a class, compare the expenses of the four stages.

ADAPTING TO CHANGING NEEDS

No matter how extensive your financial planning is, you can't predict the future. You'll need to adjust your planning as personal or family circumstances, needs, and values change.

Family Life Stages

Not all families go through the life stages described below, but many do. As they move from one stage to another, family members should review and make revisions to their financial plan. Some new goals will be added, some goals might be discarded, and the financial plan may need to be altered.

- **Marriage.** Married people assume each other's assets and liabilities, and each partner's financial choices affect the other. Identifying and working toward financial goals with another person is an important key to financial health.
- **Parenthood.** As children arrive, the financial plan must reflect not only their food, clothing, furnishings, and other daily living expenses but also plans for their future. Planning for such needs as child care, summer camp, and college will change depending on the age of the children. The family may decide to become a dual income, or two-income, family. See Figure 9-4.
- **Children moving out.** When children leave home to live on their own, a family's expenses for food, utilities, and car insurance will go down.
- **Aging.** As family members grow old together, their financial needs change. A family's home loan may be paid off, eliminating a substantial expense. At the same time, some expenses, such as health insurance, may increase. Families who have planned for retirement may cash in investments to pay for their living expenses. They may choose to maintain some of their investments for future use.

9-4

College expenses require careful financial planning that should begin when the child is still young. What changes in financial planning might parents need to make once their son or daughter is in college?

Economic Impact & Issues. ***Ask:*** How might people respond to an increase in taxes for funding colleges?

Answer Key. Answers to the Section Review questions are provided in the Section Lesson Plan located in the *Teacher Resource Guide.*

Economic Impact & Issues

Why College Tuitions Rise

The cost of going to college increases every year. Why do the costs go up? The reasons are complex. State governments are large supporters of colleges and universities. When the economy slows, states often need to cut spending. One area that can lose state funding is education. States may reduce direct funding to schools as well as financial aid to students. The schools raise tuition and other costs, such as athletic fees, to make up the difference. Schools may use tuition and fees to boost scholarships and financial aid that were affected by the state's budget. In a sluggish economy, charitable contributions from alumni and corporations may also drop, further pressuring schools to raise tuition.

Some economists also see the law of supply and demand at work. Enrollments have jumped in recent years, as more people see higher education as a necessity in today's technological, specialized society. In addition to hiring faculty for increased enrollments, colleges need to expand their facilities. The costs of adding classrooms and updating laboratories may be passed on to students and their families through tuition increases. For colleges, it's a seller's market—and they're the seller.

FIGURE IT OUT

Find out how college tuitions have increased over the last twenty-five years and chart the results. What impacts do you think such changes have on young people and society? How can college students handle the rising costs of college?

Family life stages can be affected by changing demographic trends. *Demographic* means having to do with statistics about a population. For example, the average life expectancy has been increasing. This has an effect on the timing of family life stages and on the financial goals at each stage.

Family Crises

Unforeseen events like the loss of a job, divorce, death or injury of a spouse, or natural disasters can affect financial planning. Even though these changes are unexpected, families take steps to meet economic crises. These steps include keeping an emergency reserve fund of cash; having enough life, health, and home insurance; and seeking help from others to manage the financial strain.

Section 9.1 Review

CHECK YOUR UNDERSTANDING

1. How does a balance sheet help you assess your current financial situation?
2. How do financial goals help you develop a workable financial plan?
3. Name two life stages that would require changes in a family's financial planning.

CONSUMER APPLICATION

Dual-Income Families Identify reasons why some families become dual-income families. Write a paragraph explaining the advantages and disadvantages dual incomes provide a family.

SECTION 9.2

Using Financial Software

Why is an account with a negative balance "in the red"? In the days of recording financial transactions by hand, red ink indicated debts owed. Today, computer software tools may make managing your personal and family finances much easier.

Objectives

After studying this section, you should be able to:

- Describe how computer software can aid in managing personal and family finances.
- Explain guidelines for choosing and using financial management software.

Key Terms

online banking
online bill payment
online bill presentment

WHAT CAN FINANCIAL SOFTWARE DO?

You can choose from a variety of financial software tools. Some are designed for a specific task, while others offer a combination of features. Available features include:

- **Checkbook and other transactions.** You can use software to print checks, keep an electronic check register, and reconcile your check register with the bank statement. Many programs allow you to track other types of accounts as well, such as credit card and savings accounts.
- **Expense tracking.** You may be able to assign categories—such as rent, groceries, or entertainment—to transactions as you enter them into the electronic register. Once you've assigned categories, you can generate reports showing how you spent your money.

Critical Thinking. *Ask:* What are the advantages and disadvantages of using financial software? Who would be likely to benefit most from it?

- **Budgeting.** Some programs let you create and track your budget. You can compare your actual expenses with your budgeted plans and make adjustments accordingly.
- **Automatic reminders.** You may be able to set up the software so you will be reminded of regular payments, like rent or utility bills, before they are due.
- **Financial review.** You can use the software to review your current and projected future account balances and calculate your net worth.
- **Income tax planning.** Some programs can suggest tax-reducing strategies. Specialized tax software is available to help you prepare and file your return.
- **Investment tracking.** Some software packages include features for tracking the value of investments such as stocks, bonds, and retirement accounts.
- **Planning calculators.** The financial calculators included in some programs can help you calculate loan payments and payoff dates, as well as plan for college expenses or retirement.

Community Activity. Have students contact local banks to find out whether they offer online banking and bill payment and, if so, for what fee.

Online Banking Features

Financial software packages may include features that can assist you with **online banking**—conducting business with financial institutions over the Internet. For instance, you may be able to download, or transfer, transactions from a bank's Web site to the financial software, eliminating the need to enter transactions by hand.

The company that makes the financial software may also offer services for online bill payment and presentment. **Online bill payment** means paying bills electronically over the Internet rather than sending a paper check through the mail. See Figure 9-5. **Online bill presentment** means receiving bills over the Internet as well. Although you may have to pay an extra fee for these services, they can be worthwhile to

9-5

You may be able to sign up for online bill payment through a financial software company or your bank. Why might you choose to pay bills online?

Research Activity. Ask students to investigate a Web site that provides free online financial tools. Have them find out what personal information users of the site are required to provide. Then ask them to write a paragraph explaining whether or not they would be willing to use this site and why.

you. Paying bills online saves postage costs, and your payments are received and processed more quickly. You can schedule payments to be made on a future date or to be repeated every month.

SHOULD YOU USE FINANCIAL SOFTWARE?

Well-designed financial software can make it easier to organize and manage your personal finances, but it's not necessary. Consider the benefits and costs of the software before you decide whether to use it.

As long as you enter data correctly, math errors are eliminated. The ease of calling up information on your screen helps you stay in control of your finances. You may find that you review your financial plan more often because it's easy to do. See Figure 9-6.

However, purchasing and upgrading financial software can be costly. Users need good computer skills and the time to learn the specific program they choose.

As an alternative to buying financial software, you may be able to use the free online financial tools provided on some Web sites. You may have to provide personal information in exchange.

Critical Thinking. ***Ask:*** How can you predict what your future needs and wants are likely to be as far as financial software is concerned?

CHOOSING A PACKAGE

To determine which financial software package is right for you, evaluate what you want to use the software for and what features you need. Then do some research to learn about the software packages that are available. You can usually find a list of features on the product package or at the company's Web site. Some companies offer free demos that you can download and try out. In addition, look for independent reviews in magazines and on Web sites.

Think about your future needs and wants, too. A program that seems more expensive now may be the best option if it will meet your needs for a long time.

9-6

Some people feel that tracking their finances by computer is easier than dealing with piles of paper.

Critical Thinking. ***Ask:*** What problems might you encounter if you don't follow the tips listed here for using financial software?

Answer Key. Answers to the Section Review questions are provided in the Section Lesson Plan located in the *Teacher Resource Guide*.

TIPS FOR USING SOFTWARE

Once you've chosen financial software, protect your data and take full advantage of the software by following these tips.

- Make regular backups of data onto a separate disk. Store your backup disk in a safe place.
- When you're just starting to use the software, become comfortable with its basic features first instead of trying to learn it all at once. See Figure 9-7.
- Make use of any free Web-based or toll-free telephone help provided by the software company. For additional help, look for books in the library or bookstore.
- Decide how much time and effort you're willing to invest. Some programs allow you to track your finances down to the smallest details, but doing so may be a waste of time and energy. Choose the level of commitment that provides the most benefit.
- Stay aware of upgrades. Most software packages are updated regularly, and previous purchasers can often get the latest version for free or for a small fee.

9-7

Learning how to use your financial software will take time, but you'll save time in the long run. Explore the program's features to make sure you're using it effectively.

Section 9.2 Review

CHECK YOUR UNDERSTANDING

1. What are two features that many financial software packages offer?
2. What is online bill presentment?
3. What should you consider when deciding whether to use financial software?

CONSUMER APPLICATION

Online Bill Pay When you open your monthly credit card statement, you notice a flyer explaining a new program from your creditor: online bill presentment and payment for a monthly charge of $3.95. Is this a good deal? Write a paragraph explaining the potential benefits and drawbacks of the offer.

SECTION 9.3

Creating a Budget

Objectives

After studying this section, you should be able to:

- Explain the purpose and benefits of a budget.
- Describe how to create and use a budget.

Key Terms

gross income
net income
fixed expenses
variable expenses
discretionary expenses

You've finally moved into your first apartment. Everything seems great—until you pay the first stack of bills. Your checking account has barely enough left for next month's rent, and payday is two weeks away. You need a budget—fast!

WHY MAKE A BUDGET?

Budgeting often is misunderstood. Many people think that following a budget means depriving yourself of all the things you want. Some believe that budgets are only for those who have a lot of money—or very little. Some think that a budget is a plan that someone creates for you and makes you follow.

None of these beliefs is true. Rather than being dictated to you, a budget is all about making your own choices. It's simply a plan for saving and spending your money in ways that best meet your needs and wants. Furthermore, having a budget is helpful no matter how large or small your income. If it's created and used effectively, a budget can help you:

- Avoid running out of money between paychecks.
- Evaluate your spending habits and make better choices.
- Set aside savings for unexpected expenses.
- Work toward your financial goals.

Team Activity. Have students work in small groups to make a list of general categories into which personal expenses could be organized. Ask each group to share its list with the class. Compare the categories proposed by different groups. As a class, come up with a master list of categories for budgets.

SETTING UP YOUR BUDGET

Although a budget can cover any amount of time, most people create one for the year, subdivided into monthly amounts. You can use software or just pencil, paper, and a calculator. Either way, creating a budget involves three main tasks: estimating income, estimating expenses, and bringing the two into balance.

Estimate Income

The first step is figuring out how much annual income you expect to have. You can create a budget based on either gross income or net income. **Gross income** is the total amount of money you expect to earn before taxes and other paycheck deductions. **Net income** is the amount of money you expect to receive after paycheck deductions. If you use gross income in your budget, treat paycheck deductions, such as taxes, as expense categories.

If you don't know your annual income, estimate it based on several paychecks. Be sure to include an estimate of irregular income from sources such as tips, bonuses, interest from savings, and cash gifts. See Figure 9-8.

Estimate Expenses

Next, estimate your expenses. It's useful to group expenses into general categories, such as food, housing, auto, and education. These categories will help you identify whether the ways you budget and spend your money are consistent with your financial goals.

Some expenses are easy to figure into your budget because they're fixed. **Fixed expenses** are regular payments that don't vary in amount. Examples include rent or a car loan payment. In contrast, the amount you spend on groceries, clothing, or utility bills can go up or down each month.

FCCLA. Challenge students to use the Cash Control unit of Financial Fitness to track their own personal spending for a period of a month. Have them organize their expenses into categories and compare total income with expenses. Then have them make a plan for saving to meet a specific financial goal.

9-8

Estimating your income is the first step toward creating a budget. Would you rather estimate your gross income or your net income to set up your budget?

Discussion. *Ask:* Which of these three methods do you think would be most useful in estimating future expenses for individual families? Why?

Expenses that normally increase or decrease are called **variable expenses**. For these, you'll need to estimate a monthly average.

The more accurate your estimates, the more effective your budget will be. Expenses can be estimated using several methods. You may want to use a combination of them.

- **Your past spending.** If you haven't already been keeping a spending record, now is a good time to start. Bank statements, receipts, tax forms, and similar records can be helpful in identifying what you've spent in the recent past.
- **Expert recommendations.** Look in magazines and on the Web for guidelines from qualified financial experts. For instance, some financial planners recommend that for most people, food expenses should reasonably be no more than 8 to 15 percent of income. Use these types of recommendations only as a guide, adjusting them to fit your situation.
- **National averages.** One source is the *Consumer Expenditure Survey*, a survey published periodically by the Bureau of Labor Statistics that shows how consumers in the United States spend their money. See Figure 9-9 on page 222.

InfoSource. Ask students how an individual family could make use of statistics on average consumer spending in planning a budget.

Plan for Savings

Many budgeters overlook one of the most important categories: savings. Savings are sometimes thought of as money left over. However, you should treat savings just like any other expense category that must be paid. By setting aside money each month, you can build up an emergency fund to use in case of a job loss or unanticipated expense, such as a big car repair bill. Putting aside savings is also necessary in order to reach long-term financial goals.

You can read more about why and how to develop a savings plan in Chapter 12.

Balance the Budget

Once you've estimated your income and your expenses, it's time to balance your budget. Begin by adding all of your projected income for a month. Then subtract all of your projected expenses for the same month. The result should be zero. If it's a positive number, you can add the surplus to the amount you've budgeted for savings.

If the result is a negative number, then your expenses exceed your income. You'll need to adjust your budget figures. However, don't drastically reduce any expense amount on paper without making sure you have a plan for cutting back on your spending in real life.

InfoSource

Consumer Expenditures

To find current data from the Consumer Expenditure Survey:

- Look on the Web at the Bureau of Labor Statistics site.
- Check a local public, college, or university library.

Class Activity. Have students rank the expense categories shown in Figure 9-9 in order from highest to lowest. Ask them to write a paragraph explaining what this information reveals about the way most Americans spend their money and what conclusions they would draw about making budget decisions.

How U.S. Consumers Spend Their Money

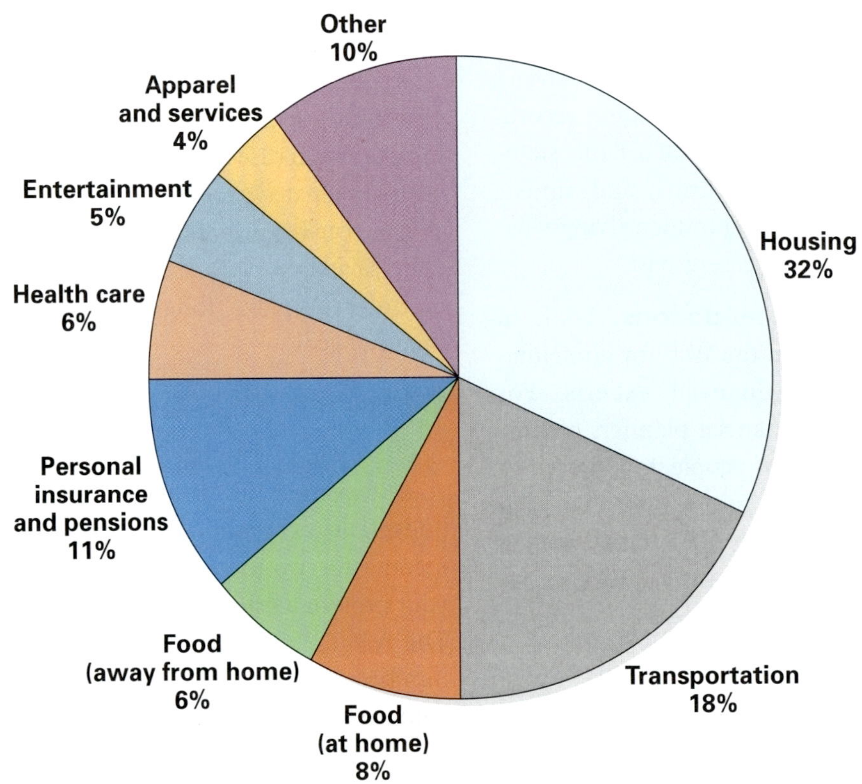

Housing: Includes rent or home loan payments, property taxes, home insurance, and maintenance and repairs.

Transportation: Includes car payments, fuel, maintenance and repairs, auto insurance, and public transportation.

Personal insurance and pensions: Includes life insurance, retirement plans, and Social Security contributions.

Health care: Includes health insurance premiums, medications, and medical services and supplies.

Source: Developed from "Consumer Expenditures in 2004," Bureau of Labor Statistics

9-9 **Statistics about average consumer spending can help you plan your budget. Note that each figure shown in this chart is a percentage of total *spending,* not a percentage of total *income.* Why is this distinction important to consider when planning your own budget?**

Class Activity. Have students refer to the list of expense categories generated in the Team Activity on page 220. Ask students to classify each expense category as necessary or discretionary. List their responses in two columns on the board. Remind them that some expenses might fit in either column.

- Start by looking at how much you've allocated for **discretionary expenses**—expense categories that are not absolutely necessary, such as vacations or entertainment. These are often easiest to cut.
- Next, think of ways to trim other variable expenses. You might be able to save money on food, for instance, by dining out less often and using more coupons when you grocery shop.
- Reducing fixed expenses usually is more difficult, but it can be done. Try shopping around for a better deal on auto insurance. Consider driving a less expensive car.
- In addition to cutting expenses, consider ways to increase income. A family member may decide to put in more hours at work, aim toward a promotion, look for a better-paying job, or take on an additional job. Keep in mind, however, that a new job may result in increased expenses for items such as clothing, transportation, and child care.

USING YOUR BUDGET

Once you've established a budget, use discipline to follow through on it, and set aside time each week to monitor it. Track your actual income and expenses and compare them to your budget. Figure 9-10 shows how budget amounts can be compared to actual expenditures.

EXPENSE	BUDGET	ACTUAL	DIFFERENCE
HOUSING, UTILITIES			
Mortgage or rent	850	850	0
Home repairs, maintenance	50	125	-75
Electricity	45	42	+3
Gas	80	92	-12
Water, garbage, sewer	75	75	0
Telephone	65	61	+4
FOOD			
Groceries	350	325	+25
Restaurant and take-out meals	100	150	-50
CHILD CARE	520	520	0
INSURANCE			
Health	150	150	0
Homeowners' or renters'	75	75	0
Automobile	84	84	0
Life	10	10	0
HEALTH CARE			
Dentist	25	0	+25
Doctor	20	35	-15
Other	50	0	+50
Prescriptions	36	45	-9
TOTALS			-54

Jump$tart. Ask students what they would do if their budget didn't balance. Which strategies would they try first to bring it into balance, and why? *(Money Management)*

9-10

This review sheet shows budgeted and actual expenses for one month. Some expenses might have been unavoidable. How might this family have reduced expenses to avoid going over budget?

Team Activity. Organize the class into small groups. Have each group brainstorm strategies for managing spending in one of the following categories: entertainment, food, transportation, or clothing. Ask groups to share their strategies with the class.

Remember that amounts can be a little over or under each month because the budgeted amount is just an average. However, if you consistently spend more than you budgeted in a particular category, you may need to adjust your spending, revise your budget amounts, or both.

- **Adjusting your spending.** If you frequently spend more than you budgeted for a certain category, analyze why. You may need to keep closer track of your spending in that category so that you can see exactly where your money goes. Do you make too many purchases on impulse? Could you save by shopping more carefully for the best buys? As when balancing your budget, think of creative ways to change your habits or make substitutions so that you can stay within your planned spending amount.
- **Revising budget amounts.** Especially in the first few months of using your budget, you may find that some of your estimates—no matter how carefully made—don't reflect real costs or needs. You may also remember additional expenses or expense categories that need to be added. If you must increase the amount of money available in some budget categories, you'll have to reduce the amount of money in other budget categories to cover the difference.

Answer Key. Answers to the Section Review questions are provided in the Section Lesson Plan located in the *Teacher Resource Guide*.

EVALUATING THE BUDGET

As you continue to use your budget, you'll naturally review and adjust it every month or so. In addition, take time once or twice a year to evaluate how well your budget is working for you. Is it meeting your needs and goals? What might you want to change about your budget system? For instance, if you don't keep up with it because it seems too complicated, perhaps you need a simpler budget or an easier way to track expenses.

Remember, too, that an effective budget is adaptable as your circumstances and goals change. Family events—a promotion, retirement or loss of a job, moving to a different home, adding to the family, and so on—should be reflected in the budget. When you allow for flexibility, your budget can continue to do its job as the engine of your financial planning for years to come.

Section 9.3 Review

CHECK YOUR UNDERSTANDING

1. List items that should be included in a budget.
2. Should you include savings in your budget? Why or why not?
3. Why might you need to adjust your budget amounts?

CONSUMER APPLICATION

Budget Categories Make a list of the categories you would use in preparing a personal budget based on your current income and expenses. Identify whether each expense category is fixed or variable.

SECTION 9.4

Organizing Your Records

Creating a budget leaves you with a financial plan in place. It can also leave you with stacks of papers and documents spread out across your work area. Now what do you do?

Objectives

After studying this section, you should be able to:

- Explain reasons for keeping certain records and documents.
- Identify types of records and documents to keep and for how long.
- Describe ways to store and organize records and documents.

Key Terms

safe deposit box
archive

WHY KEEP RECORDS?

Establishing a system for storing important records and documents not only reduces clutter; it ensures that you can find information when you need to. Here are some typical reasons to keep documents, financial records, and other records:

- **For identification.** A birth certificate, driver's license, and passport are examples of documents that can be used as proof of your identity.
- **For legal proof.** You might need a canceled check to prove that you made a payment. An automobile title proves you are the legal owner of the vehicle and have the right to sell it.
- **For loan applications.** If you want to get a car loan, for example, you'll need to document your income and assets when you apply.
- **For tax purposes.** In order to fill out your tax return properly, you need complete records of tax-related financial information, such as donations to charity.

Class Activity. Have students develop a plan for a simple home filing system. They may present their plans in the form of a list or diagram.

- **For budgeting purposes.** As you read in the previous section, records of income and expenses are essential for effective budgeting.
- **To verify transactions.** Keep records of financial transactions to ensure that billing statements, W-2 forms, and other documents are correct.
- **For reference.** Insurance contracts, an inventory of the items in your home, and a warranty are examples of documents that you may need to refer to. Keep your financial account numbers on file in case your checkbook or credit cards are lost or stolen.

Critical Thinking. *Ask:* What problems might a family encounter if they fail to keep important documents long enough?

- **For medical reasons.** Your medical records contain important details about past medical treatments, allergies, and other conditions.

HOW LONG TO KEEP RECORDS

Some records, such as your birth certificate and Social Security card, should be kept permanently. Others can safely be discarded after a time. Figure 9-11 provides guidelines for storing records. Use common sense, too. If you have a dispute with a company about a bill, for example, keep a copy of the bill until the dispute is resolved.

How Long to Keep Documents

Document	How Long to Keep
Bank statements and canceled checks	6 years
ATM receipts	Until you have used them to verify your bank statement
Credit card statements	3 years
Credit card receipts	In general, until you have used them to verify your credit card statement For large purchases, until you no longer own the item purchased
Utility bills	3 months
Repair records and warranties	For the length of the warranty
Pay stubs	Until you have used them to verify your W-2 and other withholding statements
Tax returns and related documents	7 years from filing date
Real estate and property tax documents	1 year past sale or past when the lease or rental agreement expires

9-11 The times for storing records and documents vary widely. **Give an example of a document you should keep permanently.**

Point Out. Remind students that a Social Security card should never be stored in a wallet or billfold. Doing so allows a thief to steal your identity.

STORING RECORDS AND DOCUMENTS

When choosing a storage option, balance the need to safeguard documents from fire, theft, or other dangers with the need for easy access. To help you keep track of everything, keep a list of where documents and records are stored.

- **Safe deposit box.** A **safe deposit box** is a locked box that can be rented in a secure area of a bank. See Figure 9-12. Store documents here that would be difficult to replace, such as birth certificates, car titles, and property deeds. You may wish to keep photocopies of these papers elsewhere.

Critical Thinking. *Ask:* What are the advantages and disadvantages of storing important documents in electronic form?

- **Home safe or lock box.** Although these options are less secure than a safe deposit box—a thief could simply take the entire box and open it later—documents are more convenient to access. Different sizes are available, and some are fireproof.
- **Home filing system.** Records such as bank statements, tax returns, and insurance policies can be kept in a filing cabinet or in folders or envelopes stored in crates. Your most recent records should be easiest to access. If you want to keep non-current records, you can box them up and **archive** them—put them in long-term storage in a less accessible area.
- **Electronic storage.** Financial software files, spreadsheets, and word processing files can store valuable data. If you have a scanner, you can create electronic copies of documents such as insurance policies. Copy your electronic records onto a backup disk and store it in a separate safe location.
- **Billfold.** Identification such as a driver's license should be kept in your billfold.

Team Activity. Have students work in small groups to make a list of documents that should be stored in a wallet or billfold. Have them give reasons why it might be important to have each document on hand outside your home.

9-12

When you need to access the contents of a safe deposit box, a bank employee will check your signature. Then you and the employee must each use a separate key to unlock the box. **Why are these precautions important?**

Research Activity. Have students consult the Web site of the United States Postal Service to learn the procedure for forwarding mail.

Dollars and Sense. Ask students where they would look to find contact information for each person or organization on this list.

DOLLARSandSENSE

Updating Documents

When you move, be sure to update important documents and records. Provide your new address and phone number to anyone who must be able to reach you:

- Financial institutions, creditors, insurance companies, and utilities.
- Voter registration office. You must register to vote in your new precinct.
- Your employer.
- Your state motor vehicle office to update your driver's license and car registration.
- Your previous post office so that mail will be forwarded to your new address.
- Clubs, magazine publishers, or other organizations that send you materials through the mail.
- Friends and family members.

REVIEWING RECORDS

Once a year, go through your files and review your records. The beginning of the year is a good time so that you can also gather records you'll need to prepare your tax return. Discard or archive old records. Review the contents of your safe deposit box, too. Remember to update your list of accounts and your inventory of where records are stored.

Answer Key. Answers to the Section Review questions are provided in the Section Lesson Plan located in the *Teacher Resource Guide.*

Section 9.4 Review

CHECK YOUR UNDERSTANDING

1. Explain three reasons for keeping records and documents.
2. What should you consider when deciding where to store your records and documents?
3. How often should you review your records?

CONSUMER APPLICATION

Record Storage Plan Imagine a person your age who drives to a part-time job and has a credit card. Make a list of the types of records and documents such a person would probably have. Then write a plan that describes which records and documents to store and where to store them.

SECTION 9.5

Seeking Professional Advice

Many people choose to plan and manage their finances on their own, and they succeed. Others assemble a team of financial experts. Their knowledge and advice can help consumers make wise decisions about money.

Objectives

After studying this section, you should be able to:

- Identify sources of professional financial and legal advice.
- Analyze factors to consider when seeking professional advice.

Key Terms

credentials
pro bono

WHAT HELP DO YOU NEED?

Many different kinds of financial professionals can help you plan and manage your finances in exchange for a fee. Since these fees can be high, first make sure you really want or need a financial planner. An alternative might meet your needs just as well. For example, you could take a course in financial management and learn to perform financial tasks for yourself. Also, be realistic about what a financial planner can and can't do. He or she can't make you stick to your budget, for instance—that's up to you and your family alone.

If you do decide to seek the help of a professional, have a clear idea of what kind of help you want. Are you looking for assistance with a tax return, advice about investing, or someone to check over a contract for the purchase of a home? Choose a financial planner based on the services you need.

Class Activity. Tell students to make a list of questions they would ask when looking for a financial professional who meets their needs.

Community Activity. Have students consult a local telephone directory to find the five nearest financial professionals in their community.

WHO IS QUALIFIED TO HELP?

People with no particular education or skills may advertise that they offer financial services. How can you find an expert? Look for someone with the right credentials. **Credentials** are licenses, certifications, or degrees that indicate that a person is qualified to perform a certain service.

Financial professionals may be part of a national chain, affiliated with a local bank, or independent. They may advertise themselves using a variety of general terms, such as financial planner, financial advisor, or financial consultant. While there is nothing wrong with those terms, they don't necessarily tell you what education, training, and experience the person has had. In contrast, the terms in the following list have specific meanings. If you're familiar with these professions and credentials, you'll be better able to find someone with the right qualifications to provide the services you need or want. See Figure 9-13.

- **Certified Financial Planner (CFP).** People who have earned this designation have completed specialized training and passed a rigorous examination. They also must take additional training every year and have three years of financial work experience. A certified financial planner can help you evaluate your financial status and make recommendations for ways to reach your financial goals.
- **Chartered Financial Consultant (ChFC).** This designation is awarded to CFPs who complete an additional course of study in insurance, economics, taxation, real estate, and other areas related to investing and financial planning.

9-13

Financial professionals can assist you in developing a sound financial plan, from creating a budget to choosing among investment options. How can you be sure a financial advisor is qualified?

Discussion. ***Ask:*** If you were looking for advice on how to invest your money, which type of professional would you consult? Explain why.

- **Accountant.** Accountants offer a range of services, including tax advice and preparation, investment advice, and financial planning. *Certified Public Accountants (CPAs)* must be licensed by the state in which they practice. A CPA who has experience in a range of personal finance issues and passes a comprehensive examination may be certified as a *Personal Financial Specialist (CPA/PFS)*.

- **Insurance agent.** Insurance is an important part of a sound financial plan, and some types can be a form of investment. All insurance agents must be licensed by the state in which they practice. In addition, some insurance agents have earned the credential of *Chartered Life Underwriter (CLU)*. This credential means that the agent has at least three years experience; has received additional training in areas such as retirement and estate planning; and participates in continuing education courses.

Dollars and Sense. Challenge students to locate one source of low-cost financial advice in their community.

- **Attorney.** You may want an attorney to help you prepare a will, review documents connected with a home purchase, enforce a contract, or handle complicated tax situations. Attorneys typically are more expensive than other advisors. However, some provide legal services **pro bono**—that is, at no charge—to clients who face extreme financial hardship.

- **Stockbroker.** Stockbrokers buy and sell stocks and must be licensed by the state where they practice. Stockbrokers also must be registered through the National Association of Securities Dealers (NASD) and must pass NASD-administered securities examinations.

FEES AND COMMISSIONS

Some financial professionals are paid a set fee for their services. Others earn a commission—a percentage of the dollar amount of investment products sold to the client. Still others are paid by a combination of fees and commissions.

DOLLARSandSENSE

Low-Cost Financial Advice

Well-paid advisors aren't your only option for good financial advice. Some low-cost or no-cost options are available.

- Legal aid organizations in many parts of the country offer free legal assistance to people with low incomes. Contact the American Bar Association or your state's consumer affairs bureau.
- If your employer has an Employee Assistance Program, see whether it offers financial services.
- The IRS offers the Taxpayer Advocate Service, which provides independent, professional help for taxpayers who cannot resolve problems with the IRS through normal channels.

Community Activity. Ask students to interview an adult they know who has worked with a financial professional. Have them find out what process the adult used to choose the professional and whether he or she has been satisfied with the professional's services.

For consumers, a potential problem with commissions is that they can create a *conflict of interest.* The advisor may be tempted to choose a course of action based on what would earn the most commission rather than on what's best for you. If the advisor frequently suggests that you sell your investments and buy different ones, or recommends only those investment products for which a commission is earned, a conflict of interest may be at work.

Ideally, ethical professionals always put your interests ahead of their own. Still, fee-only arrangements eliminate all questions of conflict of interest.

CHOOSING A PROFESSIONAL

Finding the right financial professional takes research and planning. Professional associations such as the Financial Planning Association, the National Association of Personal Financial Advisors, and the American Bar Association can give you names of qualified financial experts in your area. Also ask family members and friends for recommendations.

When you've identified an advisor to consider, schedule a meeting with him or her. See Figure 9-14. Ask questions such as these:

- *What is your training and experience?* Find out what specific credentials the person has. If the provider has fewer than three years' experience, ask whether a more experienced associate will review the work.
- *Will some services be provided by other staff members or outside sources?* Ask whether you can meet everyone who will be working on your plan.
- *Are you paid fees, commissions, or both?* An advisor who advertises "free" services may actually work on commission.
- *What is the estimated cost of all the services I will be receiving?* Weigh the potential benefits against the costs to make sure you're making an economical choice.

Ask for information about credentials, services, and fees in writing. Don't hire an advisor who refuses. Also ask for references from clients who have needs and financial situations similar to yours. Contact the clients to ask whether they are satisfied with the service they've received. Finally, verify the advisor's credentials by checking with the organizations that grant them. Find out

9-14

Establishing an open, trusting relationship with a financial professional is crucial. Be assertive about getting answers to your questions.

InfoSource. Have students consult the Web site of one of the organizations listed here to find out how to go about checking a professional's credentials.

Answer Key. Answers to the Section Review questions are provided in the Section Lesson Plan located in the *Teacher Resource Guide*.

InfoSource

Professional Credentials

To check the credentials of professional advisors, contact the following organizations.

- *Attorney:* Local or state Bar Association
- *ChFC* and *CLU*: American College, Bryn Mawr, PA
- *CPA*: The Board of Accountancy for your state or area
- *Insurance agent*: Your state's Department of Insurance or other state licensing agency
- *Stockbroker*: National Association of Securities Dealers

whether the advisor has ever been disciplined or has had his or her license suspended. If everything checks out, you can hire the advisor with confidence.

STAY FOCUSED ON YOUR GOALS

Once you've chosen a financial professional, remember that he or she is no more than an advisor. You should still set your own financial goals and make your own decisions. Stay informed, ask questions, and make sure you understand what the professional is doing with your money. Regularly review your financial plan with your advisor and make changes as necessary.

Also evaluate whether the advisor you have chosen continues to be right for you. The best time to assess your relationship with your financial planner is immediately after a regular review of your plan. The information will be fresh then, and you can make an informed decision.

Section 9.5 Review

CHECK YOUR UNDERSTANDING

1. Name three considerations that are important in choosing a financial planner.
2. Choose two types of financial planners. Explain how each can help with your financial plan.
3. Describe how the differences in the ways service providers are paid could affect their helpfulness in creating and maintaining your financial plan.

CONSUMER APPLICATION

Choosing an Advisor A friend of yours has decided that he needs some professional help with his finances. He is planning to visit at least three financial planners before choosing one. Write a paragraph in which you give your friend advice about choosing the right advisor.

CHAPTER 9 Review & Activities

CHAPTER SUMMARY

- A financial plan is essential for maintaining financial health and reaching goals. As personal circumstances change, so should your financial plan. (9.1)
- Financial software helps you organize and manage finances. Before purchasing software, research products carefully. (9.2)
- Control spending and saving by following a budget. Regularly evaluate your budget to make sure it's working for you. (9.3)
- Knowing which records must be kept and storing them securely and logically helps you stay organized. (9.4)
- You can turn to financial professionals for advice. Finding one who meets your needs takes research and planning. (9.5)

THE $avvy Consumer

Can't Live Without It? Leticia has been trying to reduce her spending by cutting some items from her budget. However, she's having a hard time telling needs from wants. She can make an argument for keeping everything. What questions can she ask about each item to decide whether it's really essential? (9.3)

Reviewing Key Terms and Ideas

1. List three ways you can benefit from financial planning. (9.1)
2. How would you go about setting up a financial plan? (9.1)
3. How can you determine your **net worth**? (9.1)
4. What role does a **budget** play in achieving financial goals? (9.1)
5. Identify a life stage and explain how it might require a change in your financial plan. (9.1)
6. Explain how financial software can help you track expenses. (9.2)
7. What is **online bill payment**? How can it be beneficial to consumers? (9.2)
8. How does following a budget help you control your spending and saving? (9.3)
9. Explain the differences between **fixed**, **variable**, and **discretionary expenses**. If you're having trouble balancing your budget, which should you examine first? (9.3)
10. Name three types of records to keep and specify how long to keep them. What would be the best storage system for each? (9.4)
11. Why would you **archive** some documents and records? (9.4)
12. What will a professional financial advisor's **credentials** tell you? (9.5)
13. Identify three types of financial professionals and describe their expertise. (9.5)

Answer Key. Answers to the Chapter Review & Activities are provided in the Teacher's Manual in the *Teacher Annotated Edition* of the text.

Thinking Critically

1. **Analyzing Economic Concepts:** Review the concept of *opportunity cost* in Section 2.2. How is opportunity cost involved in the budgeting process? (9.1)
2. **Supporting Your Position:** Give your opinion about this statement and support it with sound reasoning: "Using a budget limits my use of money and doesn't allow me to buy what I want." (9.1, 9.3)
3. **Recognizing Assumptions:** Find several cartoons about the use of money and financial planning. Identify the underlying assumptions and beliefs about money, budgeting, and financial planning in the cartoons. (9.1, 9.3, 9.4, 9.5)

Building Consumer Skills

1. **Spending Habits:** List the costs of items and services you have purchased in the last two weeks. Did you buy based on needs or wants? Explain whether and how you might spend your money differently if starting over. (9.1)
2. **Software Evaluation:** Obtain product demos for two financial software packages. Evaluate them according to features, ease of use, and cost. Which package would you recommend to the average consumer and why? (9.2)
3. **Budget Planning:** Create a sample monthly budget for a family of four with an annual net income of $45,000. Use the figures from the consumer spending chart on page 222 as a guide. If you wish, adjust percentages for your sample. Include a plan for savings. Show expenes as both dollar amounts and percentages. Justify your budget amounts. (9.3)
4. **Record Keeping:** As part of a personal growth plan, create a record-keeping system for your important documents, such as store receipts and school records. Use a file cabinet, storage box, or other filing equipment. Schedule a time each month to file new documents. Describe your system to the class. (9.4)
5. **Financial Planning Services:** Read two articles about choosing financial planning services. Write a summary of the guidelines. Do you consider the advice sound? Why or why not? (9.5)

CONSUMER CONNECTIONS

- **Family:** With family members discuss responsibilities they've had at each stage of life. Ask about the challenges and rewards of being a family member, including financial and emotional. List strategies family members have used to handle tough situations. How does perseverance help? (9.1)
- **Community:** Scan listings that begin with *financial* and *financing* in the Yellow Pages of a local telephone directory. Which entries would you select if looking for each of these: financial planning advice, investment services, and help with financial problems? How would you evaluate reliability? (9.5)

CHAPTER 10

Banking

Reading with Purpose

- Read the title of this chapter and describe in writing what you expect to learn from it.
- Write down each key term, leaving space for definitions.
- As you read the chapter, write the definition beside each term.
- After reading the chapter, write a paragraph describing what you learned.

SECTION 10.1

Comparing Financial Institutions

You could stash your money in an old jelly jar or hide it under the mattress. Keeping your money in a bank, however, is safer and wiser.

Objectives

After studying this section, you should be able to:

- Describe the services offered by financial institutions.
- Distinguish among various types of financial institutions.
- Explain guidelines for choosing a financial institution.

Key Terms

interest
commercial bank
mutual savings bank
savings and loan
credit union
internet bank
FDIC

HOW BANKS WORK

The term "bank," in a general sense, refers to any type of financial institution where you may deposit money. Consumers look to banks as secure places to save money, obtain credit, and withdraw cash.

When you deposit money in a bank, it doesn't just sit there. Your money is lent to borrowers who need cash for business or personal financial needs. However, you can access your money on demand.

When the bank loans some of your money to other people, those borrowers pay interest to the bank. **Interest** is a fee paid for the opportunity to use someone else's money over a period of time. If you have a savings account, the bank pays you interest for letting it use your money. Because the interest paid by borrowers is generally greater than the interest paid to savers, banks make a profit from these transactions.

In addition to providing savings accounts and loans, banks fulfill other basic functions. For example, a typical bank offers checking accounts, safe deposit boxes, and perhaps investment and financial planning services.

Research Activity. Have students visit the Web site of an Internet-only bank. Ask them to find out what services the bank offers and how its rates and fees compare to those offered at a local bank branch. Have them draw conclusions about whether Internet-only banks are a sound choice.

TYPES OF FINANCIAL INSTITUTIONS

All financial institutions must have a *charter*, a document from the federal or state government that grants them the right to operate within certain legal limitations. From the consumer's viewpoint, all financial institutions that accept deposits are similar. The main differences have to do with how they are owned and regulated. See Figure 10-1.

- **Commercial banks** are financial institutions owned by shareholders and operated for their profit. In general, banks that operate for the profit of shareholders pay lower interest rates on savings accounts and charge more for loans than nonprofit financial institutions.
- **Mutual savings banks** are state-chartered financial institutions operated by trustees for the benefit of depositors. Profits are either paid to depositors as interest or held in reserve.
- **Savings and loans** are financial institutions that originally specialized in providing funds to home buyers, but now provide a variety of financial services. Although some are owned by shareholders and operated for profit, many are owned by their depositors. Other types of savings associations, such as federal savings banks, are similar to savings and loans.
- A **credit union** is a nonprofit financial institution owned by its members. The members have a common bond, such as working for a certain employer, belonging to a labor union, or living in a certain region.
- An **Internet bank** is a financial institution that operates exclusively over the Internet using online banking. Since Internet banks do not maintain branch offices or employ tellers, they operate efficiently and can pass along their savings to customers. Thus, they may offer higher deposit rates and lower loan rates than traditional "brick-and-mortar" banks. In other respects, an Internet bank operates much the same as other financial institutions.

10-1

Banks, savings and loans, and credit unions are similar in many ways. What types of services do they offer to consumers?

Class Activity. Have students prepare a chart comparing the advantages and disadvantages of different types of financial institutions.

CHOOSING A FINANCIAL INSTITUTION

In addition to Internet banks, you may be able to choose from locally owned banks and branches of regional or national institutions. You might do all your banking at one place or become a customer of several different banks. To choose wisely, consider the following factors.

- **Deposit insurance.** In the event of bank failure, deposit insurance protects you from losing the money in your accounts. The **FDIC**, or Federal Deposit Insurance Corporation, is a federal agency that insures savings, checking, and other deposit accounts in most commercial banks, savings banks, and savings associations. If the financial institution goes out of business, the FDIC will reimburse losses in insured accounts up to a maximum amount per depositor. For credit unions, similar deposit insurance is administered by the National Credit Union Administration. Both FDIC and NCUA insurance are backed by the full faith and credit of the U.S. government, making deposit accounts safe and secure. See Figure 10-2.
- **Services and convenient access.** Find out what services are offered by the banks you're considering. Choosing one bank that offers all the services you will use may be preferable to dealing with different banks for different needs. Does the bank operate branch offices near you with convenient hours of operation? If not, can you conduct your transactions another way—such as over the phone or on the Internet—and will that type of access be sufficient?

Discussion. ***Ask:*** Would you rather bank at a locally owned bank or a branch of a regional or national institution? Why?

- **Rates and fees.** Compare interest rates, fees, and special account requirements. You can get this information from a bank employee or on the bank's Web site. Keep in mind that some financial institutions offer better terms if you maintain a certain balance or combination of accounts. You'll learn more about evaluating account terms later in this chapter.

10-2

Make sure the financial institution you choose displays one of these symbols, indicating it has federal deposit insurance. What is the advantage of having your deposits federally insured?

FCCLA. Have students use the Banking Basics unit of Financial Fitness to produce a brochure comparing different banks and financial institutions in their area. Have them investigate each bank's location and hours, the services it offers, its rates, the fees it charges, and any other information that might help consumers. Then have them summarize all this information in a booklet that consumers could use to help them choose a bank.

Answer Key. Answers to the Section Review questions are provided in the Section Lesson Plan located in the *Teacher Resource Guide.*

Economic Impact & Issues

Can Consumer Saving Sink The Economy?

Can the money you put away in a savings account affect the economy? It can—and does, for better and for worse.

As you've read, banks and other financial institutions loan consumers' savings to businesses to pay for expansion. A growing business employs more workers, buys more raw materials and services, and pays more in taxes, all of which contribute to a thriving economy. If savings are low, the bank may borrow money from another financial institution, including those in other countries. Some companies may turn to foreign investors, leaving less money available for investment in the United States. Also, potential investors worry when consumers don't save. Low savings are often associated with high spending and high debt, which can be disastrous to consumers and businesses if the economy takes a downturn.

On the other hand, extremely thrifty consumers can stall economic growth. Every dollar saved is one not spent. If people aren't buying, businesses have no reason to expand and may even fail. Employment rates may level out or drop. Meanwhile the government's tax base, the source from which it draws taxes, shrinks as revenue from sales and other taxes also flattens.

FIGURE IT OUT

Suppose automobile prices are high during one year. Then the prices go down significantly the next year as auto makers become more competitive and aim to sell more cars. What impact do you think this would have on overall consumer spending and saving? How might the economy be affected?

Financial Services Modernization Act

The Financial Services Modernization Act of 1999 transformed the banking industry by eliminating restrictions among companies in the securities, banking, and insurance industries. This change made it possible for financial institutions to consolidate the financial services they offer. For instance, banks may offer insurance investment services to customers, and insurance companies may offer traditional banking services. Therefore, you may want to consider some nontraditional sources, such as your insurance agent, when you shop for banking services.

Section 10.1 Review

CHECK YOUR UNDERSTANDING

1. Name three of the basic financial services that financial institutions provide.
2. How does a credit union differ from a commercial bank?
3. What is the FDIC and what is its purpose?

CONSUMER APPLICATION

Bank Shopping Make a checklist of questions you would want to ask when researching and comparing financial institutions.

SECTION 10.2

Banking Electronically

Objectives

After studying this section, you should be able to:

- Explain various electronic banking methods.
- Give consumer guidelines for using electronic banking.

Key Terms

electronic funds transfer (EFT)
ATM
PIN
point-of-sale transaction
debit card

Banking has reached a level of sophistication that no one could have imagined 50 years ago. Communications and computer technology give consumers the ability to withdraw cash when banks are closed, pay bills without writing a check, and view their account balances from home.

ELECTRONIC BANKING METHODS

Electronic banking allows transactions such as deposits, withdrawals, and transfers to be completed without a bank teller. Customers can perform transactions themselves or request that they occur automatically at certain times. The key process in electronic banking is the **electronic funds transfer (EFT)**, the movement of funds by electronic means. Electronic funds transfers can be made in a variety of ways, such as at a teller machine, by telephone, or over the Internet.

For financial institutions, electronic banking reduces costs. Consumers also benefit from electronic banking, especially the convenience it offers. By following a few basic guidelines for different types of electronic transactions, you can make the most of your self-service banking opportunities.

Community Activity. Have students contact a local bank to find out what fees it charges for ATM use by customers and noncustomers.

ATM Transactions

An **ATM**, or automated teller machine, is a computer terminal that gives bank customers electronic access to their accounts at any time through the use of a specially coded card. ATMs are located in public places, such as bank drive-ups and lobbies, shopping centers, and supermarkets. They are most commonly used to withdraw cash, make deposits, transfer money between accounts, and check account balances. See Figure 10-3.

Many ATMs, although owned by different banks or businesses, are part of one or more interconnected ATM networks. If your ATM card has a network logo on it, you can use the card at any teller machine displaying the same logo.

Before using an ATM card, be sure you understand when and how fees will be charged. Many banks allow their ATMs to be used by their own customers for free. Others charge a fee if you exceed a certain number of ATM transactions per month.

Point Out. Remind students not to write PIN numbers on ATM cards and not discard an ATM receipt on which the account number is visible.

If you make a cash withdrawal from an ATM not owned by your bank, you will likely be charged a fee at the point of transaction. For example, if you withdraw $50 cash, your account balance might be reduced by $52. By law, the amount of the fee must be disclosed before you complete the transaction. In addition, your own bank may add a fee to your monthly statement. Planning the time and place of your withdrawals can help you avoid excess fees.

A **PIN**, or personal identification number, is the secret code that protects the security of your accounts, allowing you alone to access them. You must enter the correct PIN in order to make a transaction. For your security, follow these guidelines when using ATMs:

- Know where your ATM card is at all times. If it is lost or stolen, notify the bank.
- Memorize your PIN and never allow anyone else to see it.

Jump$tart. Ask students to analyze the reasoning behind the guidelines for using ATMs. What are the possible risks of failing to follow each of these tips? *(Money Management)*

10-3

ATMs provide access to your accounts 24 hours a day. Why should you save your transaction receipts?

Point Out. Remind students of the importance of making sure that the site is secure when making debit card transactions online.

- When you enter your PIN, shield the screen and keypad from the view of others.
- Be aware of your surroundings. If you notice suspicious activity, use a different ATM or come back later.
- Pocket your cash immediately after making a withdrawal. Count it later when you're in a secure place.

Point-of-Sale Transactions

Many ATM cards allow you to do more than use a teller machine. You can use them to pay for a purchase in the grocery checkout lane or at a self-service gas pump, deducting the cost of your purchase directly from your bank account. This is an example of a **point-of-sale transaction**—paying for an item by making an electronic funds transfer at the place of purchase.

A card that can be used in this way is actually a **debit card**—a card that allows the user to subtract money from a bank account in order to obtain cash or make a purchase. Debit cards are also known as *check cards* or *deposit access cards.*

Dollars and Sense. Ask students what might happen if they make a payment online without having enough funds in the account to cover it.

Two types of point-of-sale transactions can be made with a debit card:

- **Online.** An *online* debit card transaction requires you to enter your PIN into a keypad. The money is deducted from your account immediately. Some merchants let you enter an amount larger than the cost of your purchase and receive the difference in cash.
- **Offline.** An *offline* debit card transaction is possible if the debit card carries the logo of a credit card network. In this case, you use the debit card just as if it were a credit card. Instead of entering your PIN, you sign a receipt. The money is not deducted from your account immediately, but usually in one to three days.

Using a debit card to make a purchase has some advantages over writing a check. The transaction is generally faster, and you don't need to carry a checkbook or present identification. The drawback of an online transaction is that the money is subtracted from your account more quickly than if you had written a check.

DOLLARSandSENSE

Tips for Electronic Banking

If you bank electronically, follow these tips to keep your accounts on track.

- Record all transactions in your check register as soon as you make or schedule them. Be sure that adequate funds are available to make electronic payments.
- Keep paper receipts of electronic transactions. Verify that transactions on your monthly bank statement match your receipts.
- Find out whether your bank charges a fee for services such as debit card transactions or online banking. Fees can vary widely.

Critical Thinking. *Ask:* Is security a more or less serious concern when using banking services now than it was in the past? Explain why.

The quick subtraction of money from your bank account is also the main difference between using a debit card and a credit card. You might view this as a disadvantage or an advantage. The money is gone sooner, but you don't incur debt on which you might have to pay interest.

As with ATM cards, keep your debit card PIN private. Be sure to keep the card number secure, too, since it provides access to your bank account.

Automated Services

At your request, banks will automatically make electronic funds transfers to or from your account. Examples include:

- **Direct deposit.** Funds are transferred from a third party into the account you designate. This is a convenient way to receive your paycheck or a government payment, such as a tax refund.
- **Automated transfers between your accounts.** For example, you can arrange for a specific amount to be transferred from checking to savings on a certain day each month.
- **Automated loan payments.** If you have a loan from the same bank, you might ask for the payment to be automatically deducted from your checking or savings account each month. This eliminates the possibility that a payment will be late, missed, or lost in the mail. You may get a better interest rate on the loan, too.
- **Automated payments to a third party.** Some utility companies, for example, let you sign up to have your monthly payments deducted directly from your bank account. Instead of a bill, you receive a notice of the next payment amount and date. See Figure 10-4.

Class Activity. Take an informal class poll to find out which of these automated services students and their families use. Make a graph of the results.

Telephone Banking

Many banks allow you to access your accounts electronically by telephone. Most such systems require you to use a touch-tone keypad to enter information, but some are voice-activated. A recorded message will ask you to enter a password or PIN, and then give you a list of options and instructions for making your choices. Typical options include finding out your account balances, making transfers between accounts, and hearing a list of previous transactions.

10-4

Paying utility bills automatically is a great convenience for consumers. How do automated payments benefit companies?

Class Activity. Have students prepare a list of practical steps they could take to prevent their ATM or debit cards from being lost or stolen.

Answer Key. Answers to the Section Review questions are provided in the Section Lesson Plan located in the *Teacher Resource Guide.*

Online Banking

Online banking is offered by many financial institutions. To use this feature, you need access to a computer with Internet capabilities. The bank may provide special software or tell you to use a Web browser with a secure connection. A log-in name and secret password help keep the account secure. Some consumers can bank online using a wireless phone or other device.

Online banking has several advantages. It allows you to see a list of recent account transactions upon request, rather than waiting for a monthly statement. You can complete many banking transactions from home at any time of day or night. You may be able to pay and receive bills over the Internet as well, which can save you time and postage. See Figure 10-5.

10-5 **Online banking offers real-time access to your accounts. What are its advantages and disadvantages compared to traditional banking?**

CONSUMER PROTECTION

The Electronic Fund Transfer Act, passed by Congress in 1978, protects consumers using some forms of electronic banking. The Act says that banks must offer consumers a record or receipt for all computer transactions. Banks also must investigate errors and report back to the consumer within ten days of being told of a problem.

If your ATM or debit card is lost or stolen, report it to the financial institution. If you do so within two business days, you are liable for no more than $50 resulting from another person's use of your card. If you wait longer, you could be liable for up to $500. If you don't report the loss within two months, you may be held liable for the entire amount. Most debit card issuers provide more protection against fraudulent use than required by law, but this varies.

Section 10.2 Review

CHECK YOUR UNDERSTANDING

1. What steps should you take to keep the PIN for an ATM card secure? Why?
2. Compare and contrast online and telephone banking.
3. If a debit card is lost, must the cardholder pay for purchases made by someone who finds the card? Explain.

CONSUMER APPLICATION

Making Payments You're taking out a car loan, and you want to be sure to make all of your payments on time. Explain how electronic banking services could help you meet this objective.

Objectives

After studying this section, you should be able to:

- Identify reasons for having a checking account.
- Describe factors to consider in selecting a checking account.
- Explain checking account procedures and responsibilities.

Key Terms

payee
canceled check
overdraft
endorsement
reconcile
outstanding

SECTION 10.3

Managing a Checking Account

A checking account keeps your money safe while giving you easy access when you need it. Whether you use it to write checks, get cash at an ATM, or pay bills online, a checking account is a basic money management tool.

HOW CHECKS WORK

With a checking account, you can pay someone by writing a check. A check is a written order that instructs a bank to pay a specific amount of money to a particular person or business. The **payee**, or the one to whom a check is made out, can take the check to his or her own bank and cash or deposit it. The check then makes its way back to your bank, which deducts the money from your checking account and cancels the check. A **canceled check** is a check that is stamped and sometimes perforated to show that it's been paid.

If you write a check for $100, you're responsible for making sure there's at least $100 in your checking account. Lack of sufficient funds to cover the full amount of a check is called an **overdraft**. If you write a check that creates an overdraft, your check will "bounce." The unpaid check—usually marked "Not sufficient funds"—is returned to the payee's bank. Both you and the payee will probably be charged a substantial fee by your respective banks. Businesses and banks penalize overdrafts because they cost

Team Activity. Have students work in pairs to rank from most to least important the five factors to consider when choosing a checking account.

time, money, and effort. Repeatedly writing bad checks is criminal behavior.

Advantages of Checks

Checks are more secure than cash, especially for sending through the mail. If cash is lost or stolen, it can be taken and used by anyone. A check, however, is usable only by the payee.

Canceled checks provide legal proof of payment. Many banks won't routinely send you canceled checks unless you request this service and pay an extra fee. However, they may send you photocopied images of the checks each month or, for a small charge, provide a copy of a specific check on request.

CHOOSING A CHECKING ACCOUNT

How do you choose a checking account that's right for you? First, get information about account terms by visiting the financial institution or its Web site. Compare several accounts to find the one that best suits your needs. Here are some items to check out.

Dollars and Sense. Ask students why a bank might charge a fee for writing checks but not for using a debit card.

- **Minimum balance.** You may have to keep a certain amount of money in the account to avoid paying a penalty. It is best to make sure you can comfortably stay above the minimum.
- **Fees.** Find out what types of fees are involved. These may include a monthly service charge, a fee for each check you write, ATM and debit card fees, and so on.
- **Transaction limits.** Some accounts limit the number of withdrawals or the number of teller-assisted transactions you can make for free each month.
- **Interest.** Checking accounts that earn interest often have more restrictions, such as a higher minimum balance. Make sure interest won't be canceled out by fees.
- **Standard overdraft protection.** The bank might automatically transfer money from savings to checking to cover a check that would otherwise bounce.

DOLLARSandSENSE

Are Your Checking Fees Too High?

Does it seem like your bank is taking more from your account than you're putting in? Try these strategies to lower your fees.

- Adjust your banking habits depending on what fees your bank charges. For instance, it may charge for writing checks but not for using your debit card.
- Meet with a customer service representative to see whether another kind of checking account could save you money.
- Avoid writing overdrafts. If your bank charges a flat fee per check or interest for your overdraft protection, take special care to keep your account from being overdrawn. If possible, keep money in a savings account and opt for standard overdraft protection that draws on your savings account to pay checks.
- Use your ATM card only at your own bank to avoid other banks' charges.

Community Activity. Have students contact a local financial institution to find out how a person under 18 years old can open a checking account.

USING A CHECKING ACCOUNT

You can open a checking account when you're 18 years old. The bank will ask you to sign a signature card—a record of how you sign your name, as shown in Figure 10-6. To verify that a signature on a check is yours, a teller can refer to this card. This helps prevent checks from being forged, or used illegally.

The bank will provide starter checks, but not all businesses accept starter checks for payment. You can order checks that are personalized with your name and address.

Making Deposits

Most banks allow you to make deposits in several ways—by mail, at an ATM, at a drive-up window, or in a face-to-face teller transaction. You'll probably be required to present a deposit slip. The slip should indicate your name, account number, the date, the amount you're depositing, and in what form (cash, checks, or both). If you're making a teller-assisted deposit and don't wish to deposit the entire amount of a check, you can specify how much cash you'd like back.

After you make a deposit, there may be a waiting period of one or more days before you can access those funds by withdrawing them or writing checks against them.

Critical Thinking. ***Ask:*** In what situations would you be most likely to choose each method of making a deposit?

The bank needs this time to verify the deposit. The length of the waiting period must comply with federal law, but varies from bank to bank. It may also vary depending on where you made your deposit, whether it was in cash or by check, the amount, and the time of day. Financial institutions must disclose their funds availability policy to customers.

Endorsing a Check

When you receive a check, you can deposit it, cash it, or transfer it to another payee. For a check to be valid, however, it needs to have an **endorsement**, a signature on the back of the check that entitles the payee to either receive payment or transfer it to someone else.

10-6

Your signature card helps to prevent others from using your checks illegally. If you have a joint account, the bank requires a signature card for each person.

Team Activity. Form small groups. Give each group a blank check register page. Tell them a starting balance to enter into the top box. Then read off a list of transactions, including dates, numbers, and amounts. Have them record the transactions and update the register, as shown in Figure 10-7.

When you endorse a check, sign your name in ink exactly as it appears on the face of the check. If this differs from your signature card, also add your correct signature. Depending on what you want to do with the check, you can endorse it in one of three ways.

- **A blank endorsement** consists of only the endorser's name. This endorsement makes the check payable to anyone who presents it for payment.
- **A special endorsement** limits payment to a particular payee. An example is "Pay to the order of Rita Neal," followed by your signature. Rita Neal then must endorse the check before cashing or depositing it.
- **A restrictive endorsement** limits the use of a check. If you write "For deposit only" above your signature, the check can be deposited only to your account. If the check is lost, the finder can't cash it.

Recording Transactions

Keeping an accurate record of transactions will help you know how much money you have in your account and avoid overdrafts. Some checkbooks make pressure-sensitive copies of each check that you write. Others have check stubs for recording information. The most common method of recording transactions is to write them in a check register kept in your checkbook, as shown in Figure 10-7.

Get in the habit of filling in the check stub or register before you write a check. Remember to also record ATM and debit card transactions, automated payments, direct deposits, and transfers between accounts.

Check Register

CHECK NO.	DATE	CHECK ISSUED TO	AMOUNT OF CHECK		√	DATE OF DEP	AMOUNT OF DEPOSIT		BALANCE	
									556	48
543	2/8	Pure & Fresh, Inc. (bottled water)	16	50	✓				16	50
									539	98
544	2/16	XYZ Center	59	95					59	95
									480	03
	2/18	Deposit					400	00	400	00
									880	03
545	2/20	City Electric	124	63					124	63
									755	40
546	2/21	123 Comm	35	96					35	96
									719	44
	2/22	ATM withdrawal	60	00					60	00
									659	44

10-7 **Recording transactions is crucial to maintaining your account accurately.**
What might happen if you forget to record a transaction?

Critical Thinking. ***Ask:*** Why is it necessary to enter a check in the checkbook if you have torn it up? What might happen if you did not enter it?

Writing a Check

Write checks in ink so that they can't be altered. If you make a mistake, you should tear up the check, enter the check number in your register, and write "VOID" next to the number. Figure 10-8 shows the correct way to write a check.

Caption Answer. The amount is written twice to ensure that it's correct. The version written in words is considered official.

When you present a check to a store clerk, you may be asked for photo identification, such as a driver's license. This helps assure the clerk that you are the person whose name is on the check.

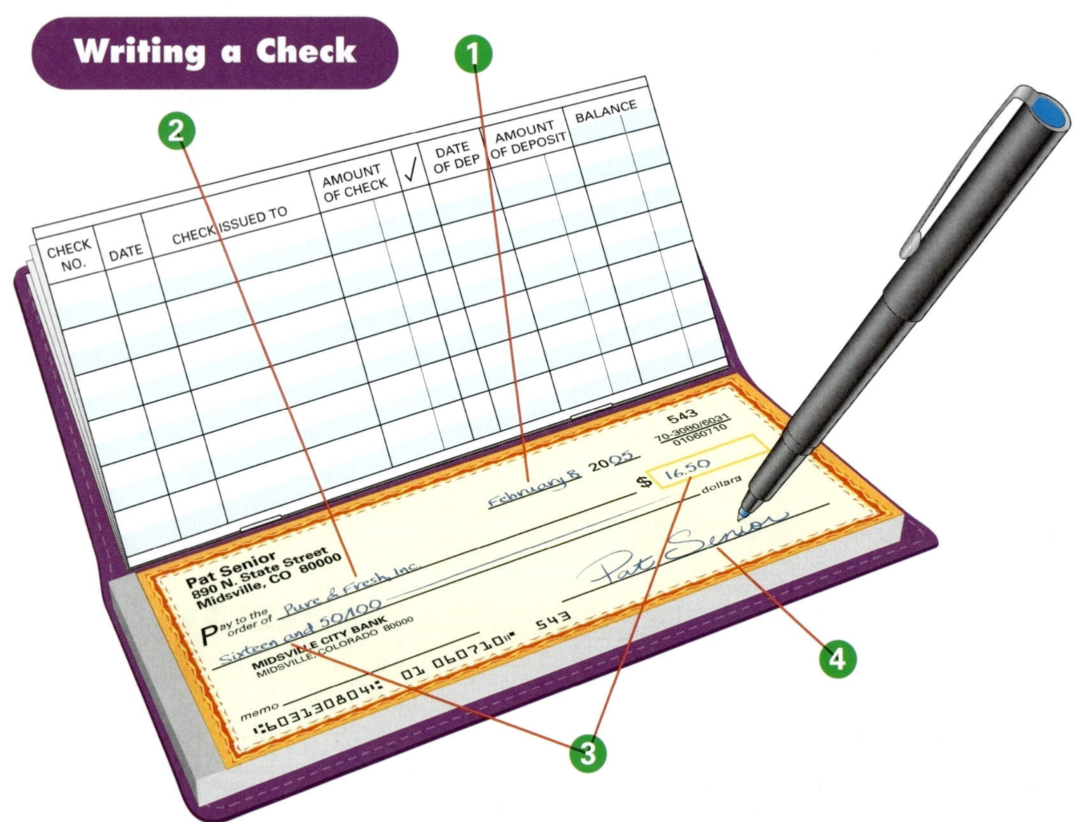

To properly write a check, you'll need to fill in the following items on the check's face:

1. Date
Write the month, day, and year you are writing the check.

2. Payee
Write the name of the payee on the line following the words "Pay to the order of."

3. Amount
Write the amount of the check twice—first in numerals, and then in words. Start writing far to the left so that no figures can be inserted by anyone else.

4. Signature
Sign all checks the way you sign your name on the account signature card.

10-8 **Be sure to write legibly when filling out a check.** **Why do you suppose the amount must be written twice?**

Point Out. Identity thieves sometimes steal printed checks from mailboxes in order to get hold of unsigned checks.

If a check is lost or stolen after you've signed it, tell your bank to stop payment on the check. That means the bank will refuse to honor it. Since there is usually a sizeable fee for this service, be careful not to lose signed checks. Unsigned checks, too, should be safeguarded. If your checkbook falls into the wrong hands, there is a risk that checks could be forged. Report a lost checkbook to your bank immediately.

Caption Answer. The total amount of withdrawals was $553.49.

Receiving Your Bank Statement

Once a month, your bank will send you a statement of your account. It shows the opening balance from the beginning of the statement period, a list of financial transactions conducted during the month, service charges, and the closing balance. If your bank does not return canceled checks, be sure to save your statements as records. An example is shown in Figure 10-9.

Bank Statement

603-130804

MIDSVILLE CITY BANK
MIDSVILLE CO 80000

MIDSVILLE CITY BANK

ACCT 060710	PAT SENIOR 890 N STATE ST MIDSVILLE CO 80000					
PAGE 1 OF 1	THIS STATEMENT COVERS: 1/16/— THROUGH 2/15/—					
MIDSVILLE CITY REWARD 603-130804	**SUMMARY**					
	PREVIOUS BALANCE		691.20	MINIMUM BALANCE		537.71
	DEPOSITS		400.00+	AVERAGE BALANCE		687.00
	INTEREST PAID		2.27+	AVERAGE RATE		4.000%
	WITHDRAWALS		553.49–			
	SERVICE CHARGES		.00–	INTEREST PAID TO DATE		3.54
	NEW BALANCE		**539.98**			
CHECKS AND WITHDRAWALS	CHECK	DATE PAID	AMOUNT	CHECK	DATE PAID	AMOUNT
	542	1/30	49.92	543	2/10	16.50
				544	2/14	387.07
EXPRESS BANKING	WITHDRAWAL #036 AT 48 ON 2/06				2/07	100.00
DEPOSITS					DATE POSTED	AMOUNT
	CUSTOMER DEPOSIT				2/03	400.00
	INTEREST PAYMENT THIS PERIOD				2/15	2.27

10-9 **Your bank statement shows the same transactions that you record in your check register. What was the total amount of withdrawals?**

Class Activity. Have students practice the steps for reconciling a bank account. For this excercise, you could distribute copies of an actual bank statement with all personal information blacked out, or you could make up a ficticious statement. Provide copies of a blank reconciliation form as well.

Reconciling Your Account

As soon as possible after receiving your bank statement, you should reconcile your account. To **reconcile** a bank account means to bring the bank statement and your own record of transactions into agreement. This process is also called balancing your checkbook. By reconciling your account promptly, you can correct any errors, whether yours or the bank's, before they cause problems with your account. For instance, if your records mistakenly show that your account has more money than it really does, your account could easily become overdrawn.

If you're using financial software to keep track of your checking account, you can follow the software's instructions for reconciling and let the computer perform the necessary calculations. However, reconciling by hand isn't difficult if you take it step by step. Start by gathering your check register (or other transaction record) and your bank statement. Most statements include a reconciliation form, usually printed on the reverse side. Figure 10-10 shows an example. If your

Reconciliation Form

DEPOSITS NOT SHOWN ON STATEMENT

DATE	AMOUNT
2/15	$ 400.00
TOTAL	$ 400.00

RECONCILE YOUR ACCOUNT

1. Ending statement balance $ 539.98
2. Total amount of deposits not shown on statement $ 400.00
3. Add line 1 and line 2 $ 939.98
4. Total amount of withdrawals $ 280.54
5. Subtract line 4 from line 3 $ 659.44

LINE 5 SHOULD BE EQUAL TO YOUR CHECKBOOK BALANCE.

WITHDRAWALS NOT SHOWN ON STATEMENT

CHECK/DATE	AMOUNT
544 2/16	$ 59.95
545 2/20	124.63
546 2/21	35.96
ATM 2/22	60.00
TOTAL	$ 280.54

10-10 **Reconciling involves making sure that you and your bank agree on how much money is in the account.** **What kind of error might the bank make?**

Point Out. Remind students that bank employees are human and can make mistakes, so they should avoid assuming that bank records are always right.

statement doesn't include one, you can use a plain sheet of paper. You'll also need a pen or pencil and a calculator.

- First, look for transactions listed on the bank statement that you have not recorded in your check register. For example, the bank statement may list a service charge, or you may have forgotten to record an ATM withdrawal. Write these transactions in your register and update the balance. However, if you think the bank statement lists a transaction in error, make a note to contact the bank about it.
- In the column of your check register headed by a √, put a checkmark next to each transaction that appears on the bank statement.
- Find any transactions in your check register that you didn't mark off. These are **outstanding** transactions—ones that were received by the bank after the closing date of your statement. On the reconciliation form or a sheet of paper, make two lists of outstanding transactions—one for deposits, the other for checks and withdrawals. Total each list.
- On your paper or the appropriate part of the form, write the new, or closing, balance from the front of your bank statement. Add your outstanding deposits to that figure. Then subtract your outstanding withdrawals. The result should agree with the ending balance in your check register. If so, you've successfully reconciled your account!

Answer Key. Answers to the Section Review questions are provided in the Section Lesson Plan located in the *Teacher Resource Guide*.

Community Activity. Have students call a local bank to find out the most common problems customers have in reconciling their statements.

If the figures do not match, check your work carefully. Sometimes the amount of the discrepancy can be a clue. For example, if your checkbook balance is $23.49 less than the figure you came up with on the reconciliation form, you may have overlooked an outstanding check in that amount. Double-check your math on the reconciliation form and in the checkbook register. If you can't find a reason for the discrepancy after going over your figures several times, take your materials to the bank for assistance.

If you suspect there's an error or other problem on the bank statement, such as an ATM withdrawal that you did not make, contact the bank according to the instructions given on the statement. To preserve your rights, you must send a letter to the correct address within 60 days of receiving the statement that has the error.

Section 10.3 Review

CHECK YOUR UNDERSTANDING

1. Why is sending a check through the mail preferable to sending cash?
2. How can you compare checking accounts to determine which one would best meet your needs?
3. When and how is a check register used?

CONSUMER APPLICATION

Proof of Payment You received a letter from the phone company informing you that you have not paid last month's bill. You are certain that you wrote a check for that bill and sent it to the phone company before it was due. How could you prove that you had made your payment?

Objectives

After studying this section, you should be able to:

- Describe alternatives to cash, personal checks, and credit cards.
- Explain possible reasons for using each form of payment.

Key Terms

certified check
cashier's check
money order
traveler's checks
wire transfer
prepaid cards

SECTION 10.4

Using Other Payment Methods

Even if you have a checking account, you might want to use other options to send money by mail or to pay for items without using cash. Several methods are available through banks and financial service companies.

GUARANTEED CHECKS

Some individuals and businesses won't accept personal checks because of the possibility of overdrafts. In that case, you might want to use either a certified check or a cashier's check. A **certified check** is a check from a personal checking account that has been stamped by the bank to guarantee that there are sufficient funds in the account to cover it. The bank puts a hold on the money in the account at the time the check is certified.

A **cashier's check** is a check issued and guaranteed by a bank. You pay the bank with cash or credit, or the bank can withdraw the money from your account. The bank then issues its own check to the payee you've named. Cashier's checks are often required for unusually large payments, such as the down payment on a home loan. Some banks charge a service fee for issuing certified and cashier's checks.

Community Activity. Ask students to find out where money orders and traveler's checks can be purchased in their area.

Caption Answer. The merchant can be sure the check is being used by the authorized person and is collectable.

MONEY ORDERS

A **money order** is a purchased certificate used to pay a specified amount to a particular payee. Money orders are a safe, convenient way to send payment through the mail as an alternative to personal checks.

Postal money orders are issued and backed by the U.S. Postal Service. You can purchase them at any post office. There are two types: domestic, which can be cashed at post offices and banks in the U.S., and international. A small, fixed fee is charged for a domestic money order. Fees for international money orders are higher.

Private companies also sell money orders for a fee. Typically, these money orders can be purchased at places such as banks, supermarkets, convenience stores, and check-cashing stores. They can be deposited into bank accounts or cashed at retail locations that accept them.

10-11 **Traveler's checks are accepted throughout the world. Why would merchants welcome payment with traveler's checks?**

TRAVELER'S CHECKS

Traveler's checks are documents that function as cash but can be replaced if lost or stolen. Because of this replacement feature, and because they are widely accepted, traveler's checks are often used on vacations and other trips. See Figure 10-11.

You can purchase traveler's checks at financial institutions in specific dollar amounts, such as $25, $50, or $100. The service charge is usually a percentage of the face amount.

When you buy traveler's checks, you sign each check in front of the selling agent. When you cash one, you sign it again in front of the payee. Thus, the payee can be sure the check is being used by the authorized person. When you use traveler's checks to make a purchase, any change due will be given to you in cash.

After buying traveler's checks, immediately record the checks' serial numbers on the accompanying form. As you cash each check, use this form to note the date and place you cashed it. Keep this record separate from the checks. If your traveler's checks are lost or stolen, immediately report the numbers of the missing checks to the company that issued them. They will make arrangements to stop payment on the lost checks and issue you new ones.

MONEY TRANSFER SERVICES

Certain companies offer money transfer services that can send funds almost anywhere in the world. Suppose a cousin in another state has an emergency need for cash

Research Activity. Ask students to investigate the costs of money orders, traveler's checks, money transfer services, and wire transfers. Have them display the results in the form of a graph. Ask them which payment method they would choose if they had to send money to someone they did not know.

and calls you for help. You could initiate an electronic money transfer by telephone, on the Web, or by going in person to a business that offers this type of service. To receive the money, your cousin would go to a designated pickup location and show identification. See Figure 10-12.

Transfers paid for with cash are usually available within minutes. If you pay with a credit card, delivery of the funds can take up to one day. Money transfer services, while helpful in an emergency, are relatively expensive. The fee for sending $100 might be $15 or more.

WIRE TRANSFERS

A **wire transfer** is a financial transaction that electronically moves funds from one bank to another. Suppose you were about to move across the country, and you wanted a quick, secure way to transfer money from your old bank to your new one. You could direct your old bank to close your account and send the balance to the new bank as a wire transfer. Most banks send and receive wire transfers several times a day. They may charge a fee for sending them, receiving them, or both.

PREPAID CARDS

Many merchants offer **prepaid cards**, cards sold in specified dollar amounts that can be used to purchase products or services. Also called *stored-value cards*, they can be a convenient alternative to cash, debit cards, and credit cards.

When you purchase a prepaid card, you pay for products or services in advance and receive the card in exchange. Information about the card's value is electronically stored on the card itself. Each time you purchase something with the card, the purchase amount is deducted from the card's balance. Some cards can be recharged when they run out of money. Phone cards, gift cards, merchandise credits, and public transit cards are typical examples of prepaid cards. See Figure 10-13.

Point Out. Some prepaid cards expire after a given period of time. Others deduct a "service fee" each month from the available balance.

10-12

To receive a money transfer, you must show identification, such as a driver's license or a state ID. Think of a situation or problem for which a money transfer might be the best solution.

Research Activity. Ask students to research a company that provides online payment services and find out what services it offers and for what fee.

Most prepaid cards can be used only for specified types of purchases. However, some carry the logo of a major credit card network and can be used to purchase items anywhere the credit card is accepted. Unlike a credit card, a prepaid card limits spending to the card's stored value.

ONLINE PAYMENT SERVICES

Since the Internet has become increasingly used for communication and shopping, many online payment services have been developed. They vary widely but have a common goal of making payments quick and easy. They also reduce the need to share credit card numbers and other personal information with each payee.

One type of service is a secure prepaid shopping account. You might set up the account by going to a certain Web site and using a credit card to create a prepaid balance. When you want to shop, you go back to that site and enter a password, then link to a merchant's Web page to make purchases. Money for the purchases is deducted from your account.

Other services are designed for person-to-person payments. For example, at the Web site of one such service, registered users can enter a password, the email address of the person they wish to pay, and the amount. The payment is either charged to their credit card or deducted from their checking account. The payee receives an email explaining how to collect the payment.

Answer Key. Answers to the Section Review questions are provided in the Section Lesson Plan located in the *Teacher Resource Guide.*

Jump$tart. What are the advantages and disadvantages of using online payment services? *(Spending & Credit)*

10-13 **People who use mass transit regularly can buy prepaid public transit cards so that they don't need to use cash each time they ride. How do prepaid cards differ from credit cards?**

Section 10.4 Review

CHECK YOUR UNDERSTANDING

1. How are cashier's checks and money orders comparable?
2. When is a traveler's check signed and why?
3. How do the reasons for using a money transfer service and a wire transfer differ?

CONSUMER APPLICATION

Sending Money Suppose you want to send $50 to a friend in another state. Investigate three of the payment methods described in this section and compare them in terms of cost and convenience for you and your friend. Which would you choose and why?

CHAPTER 10

Review & Activities

CHAPTER SUMMARY

- Financial institutions offer varied money management services. To choose a financial institution, compare services, benefits, and costs. (10.1)
- Electronic banking provides self-service and automatic transactions. (10.2)
- Compare checking accounts to find the services you need for the lowest fees. Manage an account by keeping accurate records and an adequate balance. (10.3)
- Several payment methods are alternatives to personal checks or cash. The payment method used may depend on fees and convenience. (10.4)

THE $avvy Consumer

At Your Service: Jeremy's bank offers an array of conveniences and services: ATMs, debit cards, online banking, automated transfers, overdraft protection, and more. "Why not take advantage of them all?" he wonders. What factors should Jeremy consider before enrolling in each service? (10.2)

Reviewing Key Terms and Ideas

1. How do banks make a profit even though they pay depositors **interest**? (10.1)
2. Choose two types of financial institutions and explain how they differ. (10.1)
3. What would you want to know when choosing a financial institution? (10.1)
4. What is an **electronic funds transfer**? How can you initiate an EFT? (10.2)
5. What is the purpose of a **PIN**? (10.2)
6. Give an advantage and a disadvantage of using a **debit card**. (10.2)
7. Provide an example of an automated fund transfer. Explain guidelines for setting up the transfer. (10.2)
8. What protection does the Electronic Fund Transfer Act provide? (10.2)
9. Why can a **canceled check** be offered as proof that you have paid a bill? (10.3)
10. What is an **overdraft**? Why should you consider having overdraft protection? (10.3)
11. Give two reasons for having a checking account. (10.3)
12. Why must you fill out a signature card when you open a checking account? (10.3)
13. Why should you carefully check **outstanding** transactions when you reconcile your account? (10.3)
14. How can you pay a bill with a **money order**? (10.4)
15. Why are **traveler's checks** useful? (10.4)
16. Explain how to use a **prepaid card**. (10.4)
17. What are two advantages of online payment services? (10.4)

Answer Key. Answers to the Chapter Review & Activities are provided in the Teacher's Manual in the *Teacher Annotated Edition* of the text.

Thinking Critically

1. **Analyzing Economic Concepts:** The FDIC was created in 1933. Why do you think it was started at that time? (10.1)
2. **Determining Cause and Effect:** Suppose a checking account is never reconciled. How might this affect the person's financial situation? (10.3)
3. **Applying Knowledge:** Identify two situations in which you might use each of these services: prepaid card, certified check, cashier's check, money order, traveler's check, and money transfer service. (10.4)
4. **Payment Comparisons:** Compare paying bills with checks and with money orders. What are the advantages of each? (10.3, 10.4)
5. **Taking Action:** Explain what you would do if you discover that each of the following is missing or has been stolen: **a**) ATM card; **b**) checkbook; **c**) traveler's checks. (10.2, 10.3, 10.4)

Building Consumer Skills

1. **Banking Role-Plays:** With a partner, role-play one of these situations: **a**) A banker describes three checking account options and how to open an account to a customer, while the customr comments on benefits and drawbacks. **b**) One person helps another learn how electronic banking works. (10.2, 10.3)
2. **Check 21:** Check 21 is a federal law that lets banks handle more checks electronically, making check processing faster, more efficient, and less expensive. Learn about this law and report on its impact. (10.3)
3. **Reconciling Statements:** Reconcile the checkbook balance with the bank balance, using the data shown. (10.3)
   Bank statement closing balance: $223.56
   Checkbook balance: $127.47
   Outstanding checks: $37.23, $8.72, $21.68, $25.16, $6.60
   Service charge: $3.30

CONSUMER CONNECTIONS

- **Family:** Discuss with your family how they selected their current financial institution(s). What top three considerations affected their decision? How would you choose a financial institution? (10.1)
- **Community:** When you write a check, some businesses can tell immediately whether your account has the money to cover it. Some businesses even process and return checks at the time you make a purchase. Do any businesses in your community handle checks in these ways? Investigate and report to the class. (10.3)

CHAPTER 11

Consumer Credit

Reading with Purpose

- Write down the colored headings in this chapter.
- As you read the text under each heading, visualize what you are reading.
- Reflect on what you read by writing a few sentences under each heading to describe it.
- Reread your notes.

SECTION 11.1

Understanding Credit

Credit can be a valuable tool. Like many privileges, it comes with responsibilities. With discipline and wise decision making, credit can be a strong personal asset.

Objectives

After studying this section, you should be able to:

- Explain basic principles of credit.
- Describe types of credit.
- Analyze the benefits, costs, and drawbacks of using credit.

Key Terms

credit
creditor
principal
secured credit
collateral
closed-end credit
open-end credit
installment
finance charge

THE MEANING OF CREDIT

Credit is the supplying of money, goods, or services at present in exchange for the promise of future payment. When you borrow money from a bank or use a credit card to purchase gasoline, you're using credit. The business or organization that extends the credit is the **creditor**.

Each party in any credit transaction trusts the other to carry out his or her part of the agreement. For example, a bank—the creditor—might loan a consumer $5,000 to purchase a used car. The creditor agrees to accept monthly repayments over a period of three years. The borrower agrees to repay a total of $5,724. That includes $5,000 of **principal**, which is the original amount borrowed, plus $724 interest paid for the use of the creditor's money.

Jump$tart. ***Ask:*** Are there times when credit does not benefit everyone involved? If so, give an example to illustrate your thinking. *(Spending & Credit)*

Economic Impact & Issues. Have students research consumer confidence surveys online before creating one of their own.

In this example, credit benefits everyone involved. The borrower was able to purchase the car, the seller found a willing buyer, and the bank profits by receiving interest income over time.

TYPES OF CREDIT

The credit available to consumers ranges from credit cards to bank loans to merchant finance contracts. In general, consumer credit can be categorized in the following ways.

- **Cash credit and sales credit.** If you take out a loan and receive cash, you're using cash credit. If you buy something now and wish to pay for it later, you're using sales credit.
- **Secured and unsecured credit.** **Secured credit** is backed by a pledge of property. In other words, the borrower offers something of value as assurance that the loan will be repaid. The lender has a *security interest* in the pledged property, meaning that the property can be taken by the lender if the loan is not repaid. The property that is pledged to guarantee repayment is known as security or **collateral**. Because collateral reduces the lender's risk, secured credit is generally easier to obtain than unsecured credit.

Economic Impact & Issues

Consumer Confidence and Credit

Suppose you see a new store at the mall. Is your first reaction "What do they sell?" or "How long will they last?" Your expectations for the shop's success or failure are a sign of your consumer confidence—your feelings about the future of the economy.

Detailed surveys to measure these sentiments are done by universities, corporate financial advisors, and the media. In these surveys, consumers are asked their views and predictions about selected economic factors, such as the job market and household income. Consumers' answers are given a numerical value to create a consumer confidence index.

Some surveys ask directly about using credit. In others, questions about buying "big-ticket items," such as appliances, suggest consumers' willingness to take on debt. Some surveys show an interesting trend related to credit: respondents who feel optimistic about their own incomes are apt to make large purchases, even if they feel pessimistic about the overall economy. Actual consumer spending bears this out.

Some economists question the value of consumer confidence surveys. Nonetheless, financial planning experts—fiscal policy advisors, for example—consider the public's mood when making economic predictions.

FIGURE IT OUT

Develop and use a survey on credit use among teens in your school. How often do they use credit cards? Find out what makes teens feel confident about making credit purchases. What reduces their confidence? Do income and debt have impact? Compare the influences on teens to factors that influence adults.

Class Activity. Ask students to give examples of each type of credit listed. Write their responses on the board.

- **Closed-end and open-end credit.** **Closed-end credit** is a one-time extension of credit for a specific amount and time period. The total amount of interest to be paid is known at the beginning of the loan. In contrast, **open-end credit**—sometimes referred to as a *line of credit*—can be used repeatedly. A typical credit card provides open-end credit. The cardholder makes a monthly payment of all or part of the account balance. The amount of interest that must be paid is based on the account balance at any given time.
- **Single-payment and installment credit.** Some closed-end credit agreements call for the borrower to pay the entire amount due in a single payment. More commonly, however, closed-end credit is paid in installments. An **installment** is a set portion of the loan amount that the borrower must pay at regularly scheduled intervals. For instance, a furniture store might advertise a sofa for sale in "four easy installments." A *payment schedule* specifies the dates on which installment payments are due and the amount of each installment. It may also indicate how much of each installment is applied toward principal and interest.

PROS AND CONS OF CREDIT

Credit is a privilege that benefits consumers in several ways. Its advantages include:

- **Temporary expansion of income.** Credit allows you to use goods and services before you've paid for them or while you're paying for them. This is especially helpful for unexpected expenses that can't wait, such as replacing a worn-out refrigerator. Major purchases such as a car or home might not be possible without credit.

Critical Thinking. ***Ask:*** If credit allows a temporary expansion of income, what is the effect of repaying the money borrowed?

- **Convenience.** A credit card can give you the secure feeling of being able to make purchases without carrying a large amount of cash. See Figure 11-1. You can also shop online or by telephone with a credit card. Getting a refund on returned items is usually easier if they were charged, and monthly statements of credit card purchases simplify record keeping.
- **Financial responsibility.** Good credit provides proof to others of your financial responsibility and can make it easier to obtain credit in the future.

Class Activity. Have students practice computing percentages: ***A)*** 5% (0.05) of $340 is $17; ***B)*** 7% (0.07) of $68 is $4.76; ***C)*** 8½% (0.085) of $229 is $19.47; ***D)*** 1% (0.01) of $450 is $4.50; ***E)*** 10% (0.10) of $450 is $45.00.

11-1 **When you're on a vacation, having a credit card reduces the need to carry cash. Why is this an advantage?**

Discussion. *Ask:* How do you think using credit would affect your spending habits? Would it, for instance, make you more prone to impulse buying?

The Costs of Credit

Using credit involves costs as well as benefits. These costs include:

- **Interest and fees.** The cost of using credit, including interest and any fees, is called the **finance charge**. Finance charges can usually be avoided if a credit card is paid in full each month.
- **Increased cost of merchandise.** Retailers who offer credit must pay banks to collect on their credit sales and be prepared to write off unpaid debt. To offset these costs, many businesses increase prices. Some offer a discount for paying cash.
- **Opportunity cost.** Although credit provides expansion of income at first, in the long run it reduces purchasing power. Repaying borrowed money plus interest forces consumers to give up things they want or need now and in the future. The wants and needs they give up are the opportunity cost of credit. See Figure 11-2.

Other Drawbacks of Credit

Besides its costs, the use of credit has other disadvantages. Take these into consideration when making decisions about credit.

Caption Answer. The consumer would have $1090 less available for spending in Year B compared to Year A.

- **Security concerns.** Using a credit card requires that you take precautions against the card being stolen or otherwise used without your permission.
- **Impulse buying.** The power of credit may make you more likely to buy items on the spur of the moment, without the careful consideration that a purchasing decision deserves.
- **Overspending.** Handing over a credit card instead of "real" money can make items seem almost free. However, the debt that mounts up is all too real. Consumers who consistently spend more than they can afford get into financial trouble that may take years to undo.
- **Reclaimed merchandise.** If you buy on credit and fail to pay for the items, they could be taken back by the merchant.

DECIDING WHEN TO USE CREDIT

Sometimes using credit is a wise and easy choice. Imagine how long it would take, and how difficult it would be, to save enough cash to pay the entire cost of a new car, your college education, or a home. Using credit makes these purchases possible.

Credit Affects Purchasing Power

Year A		Year B	
Disposable income earned	$12,000	Disposable income earned	$12,000
Amount borrowed at 18% interest	+500	Loan repaid with interest	-590
Available for spending	$12,500	Available for spending	$11,410

11-2 **Using credit increases your purchasing power in the present but reduces purchasing power in the future.** **How much less would a consumer have available for spending in Year B compared to Year A?**

Team Activity. Have students work in pairs to write a scenario in which a person wants to buy an expensive item. Ask them to write two possible endings: (a) the person saves up to buy the item; (b) the person buys it on credit. Have them show the consequences of each choice.

In other situations, it may be harder to decide whether to buy on credit. In general, use credit only when you can repay comfortably and not neglect your other financial obligations. See Figure 11-3.

Before using credit, consider your alternatives. Paying by cash or check helps ensure that you limit purchases to what you can afford. If you want to buy online or by phone, using a prepaid card or debit card provides the convenience of a credit card without the debt. As you'll learn in Chapter 12, saving to buy an item at a later date has several advantages. Try giving yourself time to think about purchases rather than using credit to buy on impulse. You may decide that an item you thought you "couldn't live without" is not that important to you after all.

11-3 **Many people limit their debt by never using credit for consumables such as food.** **What do you suppose is the reasoning behind this guideline?**

Answer Key. Answers to the Section Review questions are provided in the Section Lesson Plan located in the *Teacher Resource Guide.*

Section 11.1 Review

CHECK YOUR UNDERSTANDING

1. How do creditors profit by offering credit?
2. How is open-end credit different from closed-end credit?
3. How does the use of credit affect a consumer's future purchasing power?

CONSUMER APPLICATION

Cash or Credit Suppose you're buying a sofa. Using the store's credit plan, the payments would be $60 a month for 24 months. If you pay in cash, the cost is $1,200. What factors would you weigh in deciding whether to pay cash or buy on credit? How would they affect your decision?

Objectives

After studying this section, you should be able to:

- Analyze factors that affect the ability to get credit.
- Explain the significance of credit reports.
- Describe how to establish and maintain a good credit history.

Key Terms

credit history
credit bureau
credit report
credit rating
credit score
cosigner

SECTION 11.2

Qualifying for Credit

Consumers do not automatically get credit or keep it. They must take steps to build a record that shows they are financially responsible and can manage debt wisely.

WHAT LENDERS CONSIDER

Before they will extend credit, banks and other lenders want to know how much of a risk they are taking. Is the borrower likely to pay back the money on time? Since lenders don't have a crystal ball to see into the future, they focus on the borrower's present and past.

The Three C's of Credit

In deciding whether to extend credit, lenders consider the three C's—character, capacity, and capital. *Character* refers to a person's reputation, especially concerning repaying debt on time. *Capacity* is a person's earning power and ability to pay debts from regular income. *Capital* refers to items owned, or assets. The consumer who owns items of value is a better credit risk than one who does not, because assets can be sold, if necessary, to repay debt.

Class Activity. Have students create a chart listing the various items that appear on a credit application and showing which of the three C's of credit each item assesses. Remind students that some items, such as employment, may assess more than one of the three C's.

Credit History

The main way in which a consumer can demonstrate the first C—character—is by establishing a positive **credit history**, or pattern of past behavior in regard to repaying debt. Without a credit history, lenders have little information with which to evaluate the consumer's reliability. On the other hand, if the potential borrower has a record of paying past debts in full and on time, lenders feel more confident in extending credit.

The Credit Application

The questions on a credit application are designed to assess whether you are a good credit risk based on the three C's of credit. See Figure 11-4. Although applications vary, many ask for information about:

- **Employment.** You'll be asked where you work, how long you've been there, and how much you're paid. The lender will probably contact your employer to verify this information.
- **Residence.** The lender may want to know how long you've lived at your present address. Maintaining the same residence is a sign of stability.
- **Home ownership.** Owning a home is evidence of capital. Also, a homeowner is considered a more permanent resident than a person who rents.
- **Monthly housing costs.** The lender wants to know whether you're paying so much for housing that there is little left for payment of new debts.
- **Credit references.** You may be asked to list businesses with which you have dealt on a credit basis. Their records are the best indication of your bill-paying habits. If you haven't used credit before, you may be asked to give the names of personal references, such as teachers and businesspeople who can provide information about your character.
- **Collateral.** You may be asked to identify property that will serve as security for the loan.

Jump$tart. Tell students that some people are not willing to use any form of consumer credit. Ask them what the advantages and disadvantages of this choice might be. *(Spending & Credit)*

11-4

A credit application provides the lender with information about your character, capacity, and capital. Why are these factors important to the lender?

Research Activity. Have students visit the Web site of the FTC to find out steps consumers can take if they think they have been discriminated against in obtaining credit. Have them write a letter to a fictitious creditor from a consumer who has been unfairly denied credit.

- **Bank references.** Any bank you list as a reference will usually be asked how much you owe the bank and what balances you have in your checking and savings accounts.

Equal Credit Opportunity Act

The Equal Credit Opportunity Act is a federal law ensuring that all consumers are given an equal chance to obtain credit. The act protects credit applicants against discrimination on the basis of sex, marital status, race, religion, national origin, age, or income from public assistance.

CREDIT REPORTING AND RATING

In addition to the information supplied on the credit application, lenders base their credit-granting decisions on information obtained from credit bureaus. A **credit bureau**, or credit reporting agency, is a firm that collects information about the creditworthiness of consumers. Credit bureaus get their information from stores, banks, and other creditors, as well as from public records such as court judgments. In addition to local credit bureaus, there are three national credit reporting agencies: Equifax, Experian, and TransUnion.

Credit bureaus and reporting agencies compile the information into a **credit report**, a record of a particular consumer's transactions and payment patterns. The report is then sold to creditors who are evaluating applicants. A credit report includes information such as the date each credit account was opened, the balance owed, the monthly payment amount, and whether payments have been late. Figure 11-5 shows part of a sample credit report.

Credit Report

RCB Reliable Credit Bureau

Page 1 of 3

Prepared for JANE X. ANYONE | **Social Security Number** 000-10-5454 | **Date of Birth** 10/16/1979

Report Date January 5, 2— | **Report Number** 1896758

Creditor/ Account Number	Date opened/ Reported since	Date of status/ Last reported	Type/Term/ Monthly payments	Credit limit/ High balance	Recent balance/ Recent payment	Status/ Comments
Community Bank Big City, TX 125551674	6-2000/ 6-2000	12-2002/ 12-2002	Line of credit/ 18 months/ $60	$1,000/ NA	$0 as of 12-2002/ $54	Closed/ never late
First Credit Card Las Vegas, NV 5678-1234-5555-5555	10-2001/ 10-2001	12-2002/ 12-2002	Revolving/ NA/ $0	$5,000/ $2,349	$0 as of 12-2002/ $434	Open/ never late

11-5 **Information about a consumer's payment history is kept on file by credit bureaus. How is this information used by prospective creditors?**

Point Out. Explain to students that they should limit the number of credit checks they get because having too many credit checks will lower their score.

Credit Ratings and Scores

Credit bureaus and reporting agencies do not judge whether consumers deserve credit. They only provide information for lenders to interpret. When deciding whether to grant credit, a lender uses the credit report and other information to arrive at a **credit rating**, an evaluation of a consumer's credit history.

As part of their evaluation process, lenders may obtain or calculate a consumer's credit score. A **credit score** is a numerical rating, based on credit report information, that represents a person's level of creditworthiness. Individual lenders decide for themselves what scoring method to use and what score is needed to obtain approval.

Credit reporting agencies don't develop these scores, but they play a role in making them available to creditors. They also offer a service that enables consumers to view their own credit score for a fee. Along with the score, consumers receive an explanation of how it was influenced by various risk factors, such as payment history and the amount

InfoSource. Have students find out under what circumstances people are entitled to a free copy of their credit report.

currently owed. This information is actually more important to consumers than the score itself, because it helps them understand what they can do to improve their credit history over time.

Fair Credit Reporting Act

Credit bureaus work to keep their records as accurate as possible. However, errors can occur that may result in consumers being unfairly denied credit. The Fair Credit Reporting Act assures a consumer's right to access his or her credit file and dispute incorrect information.

It's a good idea to check your credit report at least once a year. If you find an error, you can request that the credit bureau reinvestigate the information. Inaccurate information must be corrected or removed from your file. You may then ask that anyone who has recently been given the incorrect information be notified. When a dispute between you and the credit bureau can't be resolved, you may request that your version of the dispute be filed and included in future reports.

Your Credit Report

To get a copy of your credit report, contact one of the three national credit reporting agencies: Equifax, Experian, or TransUnion. Creditors can put you in touch with them, or you can visit the agencies on the Web. If you wish, you can obtain your credit report online using a secure browser connection. Under certain circumstances, you are entitled to a copy of your report for free. Otherwise, there may be a small charge.

Point Out. Some marketers of secured credit cards take advantage of consumers with poor credit by charging annual fees or unusually high interest rates.

The Fair Credit Reporting Act also states that information from your credit file may be given only to those who have a legitimate need for it. An employer or prospective employer can check your credit report only if you give your written consent.

ESTABLISHING AND MAINTAINING CREDIT

Since lenders evaluate applicants by looking at credit history, you may wonder how anyone obtains credit for the first time. Actually, there are several steps you can take to establish credit.

- Open checking and savings accounts. Make regular deposits and avoid overdrawn checks.
- Put a utility, such as telephone or Internet service, in your name and pay the bills promptly. Be sure the creditor reports your payment history to a credit bureau.
- Apply for a credit card from a local store. Without a credit history, you may qualify for only a small line of credit, but it's a start. Use the card and pay the bills on time. After several months, apply for a card from another business.

Some consumers who don't qualify for credit on their own seek the help of a cosigner. A **cosigner** is a person with a strong established credit history who signs the credit application and contract along with the borrower. In the event that the applicant fails to make payments, the cosigner is responsible for making them. The new credit applicant can build a good credit history by making prompt, regular payments. Once this is done successfully, no cosigner will be needed for future credit applications.

Answer Key. Answers to the Section Review questions are provided in the Section Lesson Plan located in the *Teacher Resource Guide.*

Another way to establish credit is to apply for a *secured credit card,* one that requires you to keep a savings account as security. A disadvantage is that the money used as security is tied up so you can't use it for other purposes. In addition, you may have to pay a higher interest rate than for an unsecured card, as well as high fees. Make sure you understand the terms of a secured card before applying for one.

No matter what steps you take to establish credit, manage your new credit wisely by paying bills reliably and avoiding excess debt. You'll soon be on your way to establishing and maintaining a good credit history that will help you accomplish your financial goals throughout life.

Section 11.2 Review

CHECK YOUR UNDERSTANDING

1. What are the three C's of credit and what do they indicate to lenders?
2. Why should consumers make sure their credit reports are accurate?
3. What are five possible ways to establish credit for the first time?

CONSUMER APPLICATION

Loan Application Create your own loan application form, referring to page 267. Use fictitious information to fill in two copies of the application: one that a lender would probably turn down, and one that would likely be accepted. Explain why each application would be accepted or turned down.

SECTION 11.3

Managing Credit Cards

Credit cards are perhaps the most widely used type of credit. The terms of a credit card agreement and the way you manage your account will affect your financial health.

Objectives

After studying this section, you should be able to:

- Identify sources and types of credit cards.
- Evaluate credit card terms and conditions.
- Give guidelines for using credit cards wisely.
- Explain how to resolve credit card billing problems.

Key Terms

APR
grace period
credit limit

TYPES OF CREDIT CARDS

Consumers can choose from thousands of credit cards issued by different companies and with different features. To sort them out, two basic distinctions are especially important to consumers: where the card is accepted and when charges must be paid.

Private Label and General Purpose Cards

Some cards, called *private label cards*, can be used only at a single retailer. Many department store chains and gasoline companies, for example, offer private label credit cards.

In contrast, a *general purpose card*—also known as a bank card or major credit card—can be used at millions of different businesses across the country or around the world. The familiar logo of a card network is found on the card and can be seen at places of business that accept it. The largest card networks are each owned by an association of thousands of financial institutions. Most general purpose cards can be used not only to make purchases but also in other ways, such as to obtain cash advances from automatic teller machines.

Jump$tart. Ask students to compare the advantages and disadvantages of revolving credit cards and charge cards. *(Spending & Credit)*

Discussion. ***Ask:*** What is appealing about each of the credit card variations? Who do you think would be most likely to choose each one?

Revolving Credit Cards and Charge Cards

Some credit cards use an arrangement called *revolving credit*. On receiving a bill, the cardholder has several payment options: pay for all charges in full, make only a minimum payment, or pay any amount in between. If a balance is carried over, the cardholder must pay interest on it. Other cards do not allow a balance to be carried over. All charges must be paid in full each month. Card issuers often refer to this type as a *charge card* rather than a credit card.

Credit Card Variations

The credit card business is very competitive. Card issuers continually come up with ways to entice consumers to apply for their cards. Here are a few examples.

- *Prestige* or *status cards*, such as "gold" and "platinum" cards, offer consumers an increased line of credit and a variety of other benefits. They might charge an annual fee. These cards are highly promoted to consumers with established credit.
- *Co-branded cards* carry the name of not only a card network and possibly a bank, but also another company—a retail store, a hotel chain, or a long distance service, for example. Typically, by using the card you can earn a reward from the partner company, such as points toward a free stay at the sponsoring hotel chain.
- An *affinity card* carries the name of a non-profit or charitable organization, such as a school or an animal welfare organization. The organization receives money from the card issuer, such as a percentage of every dollar charged or a portion of the annual fees collected. See Figure 11-6.
- A *smart card* has a computer chip in it. The chip can store information used for online shopping, such as user names, passwords, and billing and shipping information. When inserted into a special card reader connected to a computer, the card makes it possible to fill out Web order forms quickly and easily. A password keeps the information secure.

COMPARING CREDIT CARD TERMS

It's wise to shop carefully for a credit card just as you would for any major purchase. Here are some of the features and costs of credit cards that you should consider.

11-6

Prestige cards and affinity cards are both designed to attract consumers. How do they differ?

Class Activity. Have each student rank the features listed here based on which he or she would consider most important in choosing a credit card.

- **Annual fee.** Few private label cards charge an annual fee, but some general purpose cards do.
- **Annual percentage rate.** The **APR**, or annual percentage rate, is the annual rate of interest that is charged for using credit. The APR of revolving credit cards can vary significantly and makes a big difference in the cost of using credit.
- **Whether the APR may change.** A *variable* rate means that the APR can go up or down depending on economic factors. The agreement must explain how a variable rate is determined and how often it may change. Even with a fixed APR, check the fine print of the agreement to see whether the rate can increase for any reason, such as if you are late making payments. Also watch out for cards that have a *teaser rate*—a low introductory rate that is in effect for only a limited time.
- **Computation method.** The agreement specifies how finance charges are computed. The method used can make a significant difference in how much interest you'll pay. Figure 11-7 on page 274 compares several common computation methods.

Dollars and Sense. Have students do research to find out the average amount of debt carried by college students when they graduate.

- **Minimum payment.** You must make at least a minimum payment by the due date. The credit agreement will state how the minimum payment is determined. It will also state what happens if you fail to make a required monthly payment when due. The creditor may, for example, require payment at once of the entire outstanding balance of your account.
- **Grace period.** Many credit cards allow a **grace period**, or period of time during which the balance may be paid in full to avoid finance charges. A grace period of 20 to 25 days is common. Check the terms carefully to see how the grace period works. For instance, it might not apply if there is an unpaid balance carried over from the previous bill.
- **Minimum finance charge.** Some cards specify that in months when you owe a finance charge, it will be at least a certain amount. For instance, if you carry over a balance of only $1, a minimum finance charge of 50 cents may apply.
- **Other fees.** The cardholder agreement may specify fees for late payments, cash advances, exceeding your credit limit, and returned checks, for example.

DOLLARSandSENSE

Campus Credit Card Lures

Many credit card companies visit college campuses to recruit new cardholders. They set up tables outside bookstores and student centers, handing out goodies and persuading students to sign up. For students who can successfully manage it, a credit card is an opportunity to build a positive credit history. However, some students quickly run up more debt than they can handle. They end up in the credit card trap—and sometimes out of school, too. For this reason, some colleges have banned on-campus credit card pitches.

Caption Answer. The computation method might result in lower finance charges.

Research Activity. Have students use credit card application forms to determine the computation methods used by three different card issuers.

Finance Charge Computation Methods

Suppose the APR is 18% and the previous balance is $400. The current billing cycle (the period of time between monthly statements) is 30 days. You made a payment of $300 on the 16th day and a purchase of $50 on the 19th day. The "Example" column shows how much you would pay in finance charges using each computation method.

METHOD	EXAMPLE
Previous Balance Method One of the most costly to the consumer. 1. The amount owed at the end of the last billing cycle is the previous balance. 2. The previous balance is multiplied by the monthly interest rate.	$6.00
Adjusted Balance Method Usually the best method for the consumer, but not common. 1. Any payments or credits made during the billing cycle are subtracted from the previous balance. This is the adjusted balance. 2. The adjusted balance is multiplied by the monthly interest rate.	$1.50
Average Daily Balance Method (excluding new purchases) Favorable to the consumer. 1. For each day in the billing cycle, payments made are deducted from the previous balance. 2. All daily balances are totaled, then divided by the number of days in the billing cycle to find the average daily balance. 3. The average daily balance is multiplied by the monthly interest rate.	$3.75
Average Daily Balance Method (including new purchases) The most common method. 1. For each day in the billing cycle, payments made are deducted from the previous balance and new purchases are added. 2. All daily balances are totaled, then divided by the number of days in the billing cycle to find the average daily balance. 3. The average daily balance is multiplied by the monthly interest rate.	$4.05
Two-Cycle Average Daily Balance Method One of the most costly to the consumer. Computed like the average daily balance method, except that the average is based on the previous billing cycle as well as the current one.	Depends on activity in previous billing cycle.

11-7 **The finance charge you pay depends on the computation method used by the creditor.** **Why might you choose a card with a slightly higher APR than another?**

Critical Thinking. *Ask:* What are the possible advantages and disadvantages of having a high credit limit? Explain why.

- **Credit limit.** The **credit limit** is the maximum amount of credit that the creditor will extend to the borrower. If the credit limit is $1,000, your unpaid charges cannot total more than that amount at any time.

- **Special features and services.** Some credit cards offer incentives such as rebates or discounts, frequent flyer miles, insurance coverage, and other special features. Be sure to weigh these benefits against other factors, such as the card's annual fee and interest rate. See Figure 11-8.

As you compare credit card offers, consider how you plan to use the card. If you think you'll carry over a balance, look for a low interest rate. If you intend to pay the balance in full every month, a card with no annual fee—regardless of its interest rate—would be a good choice.

Discussion. *Ask:* What types of credit card incentives do you believe are most likely to be useful to consumers?

Truth in Lending Act

The federal government has made it easier for consumers to understand the terms of credit and loan agreements by passing the Truth in Lending Act. The act requires creditors to adequately inform consumers about credit terms and costs. Lenders must disclose specific information such as the APR, how variable rates are calculated, when payments are due, and all fees. On most credit card applications, information required by the Truth in Lending Act is clearly labeled and easy to find. This can be very helpful as you compare the terms and costs of different cards.

Before you apply for a credit card, make sure you have read the disclosures and understand the basic terms of the account. If your application is accepted, you will receive a cardholder agreement that spells out the terms in detail. Read this information carefully. Once you begin using the card, you are legally bound by those terms.

Class Activity. Ask students to compare two cards, one with no annual fee and an 18 percent APR, the other with a $20 annual fee and an APR of 10 percent. Have students calculate how big a balance the user would have to carry to make the card with an annual fee a better deal.

11-8

When evaluating credit card incentives, consider whether you'll actually make use of them. Frequent flyer miles, for example, often have restrictions on when and how they may be used.

Class Activity. As a class, brainstorm a list of additional tips for using credit cards wisely.

USING CREDIT CARDS WISELY

Once you have a credit card, wisely managing its use will help you maintain a good credit history. Follow these pointers:

- Remember that your credit limit is a maximum, not a goal. It may be more than you want to, or can afford to, borrow.
- Save your credit card receipts. Use them to keep a running total of how much you've charged each month. You'll also want to check them against your monthly bill.
- Set your own limit for how much you want to charge each month. When you get close to the limit, slow down. If you reach the limit, put the card away in a safe place.
- Whenever possible, pay the full balance each month to avoid finance charges.
- If for some reason you can't pay the full balance, make the largest payment you can afford. If you charged $1,000 and made only the minimum payment each month, it could take you more than 20 years to pay off the balance!
- Pay bills on time to avoid late fees and protect your credit history.

Caption Answer. You can't always be sure that the person calling has given you his or her true identity. Making the call with a number you look up is safer.

Safeguarding Your Card

Credit card fraud—unauthorized use of credit cards or account numbers that have fallen into the wrong hands—is a serious problem. To protect yourself, keep your cards with you or in a safe place at all times. When you hand over a credit card to make a purchase, be sure it's returned to you before you leave. If possible, keep it in your sight. See Figure 11-9.

Remember to safeguard not only the card itself, but the number. Keep receipts and other documents containing your credit card number in a safe place, and shred them before discarding them. Don't give the number to just anyone. Know to whom you are giving it and that the reason is legitimate. Before sending your card number over the Internet, make sure you're using a secure connection.

Point Out. Tell students that one idea for those who need to slow down their credit card use is to put their cards on ice—literally. Putting the card in a container of water and freezing it makes it impossible to grab the card and spend impulsively. The card can still be thawed and used in an emergency.

11-9

Giving your credit card number over the phone can be risky. Would it be safer to give the number if you made the call or if someone called you?

Class Activity. Refer students to Figure 11-10. Point out the difference between the minimum payment due and the total balance. Ask students to calculate how much this card user would owe at the end of a year if she charged the same amount every month and made only the minimum payment.

Keep a record of your credit card numbers in a safe place separate from the cards. If a card is lost or stolen, notify the credit card company immediately. Under the Consumer Credit Protection Act, the maximum amount for which you may be held liable if someone uses the card illegally is $50. If, however, you inform the company before someone else uses the card, you have no liability at all.

REVIEWING THE MONTHLY STATEMENT

Traditionally, cardholders receive a statement, or bill, each month by mail. Many creditors also offer secure online access to account statements.

The statement lists all transactions that have been processed since the last statement date. It also shows any finance charges that have been added, the account balance, the minimum payment due, and the due date. A sample statement is shown in Figure 11-10.

As soon as you receive your statement, check the list of transactions against your receipts. Also check the interest rate shown on the statement to verify that it's the same rate that is on your credit card agreement. A detailed explanation of how the finance charge is computed usually appears on the back of the statement.

Credit Card Statement

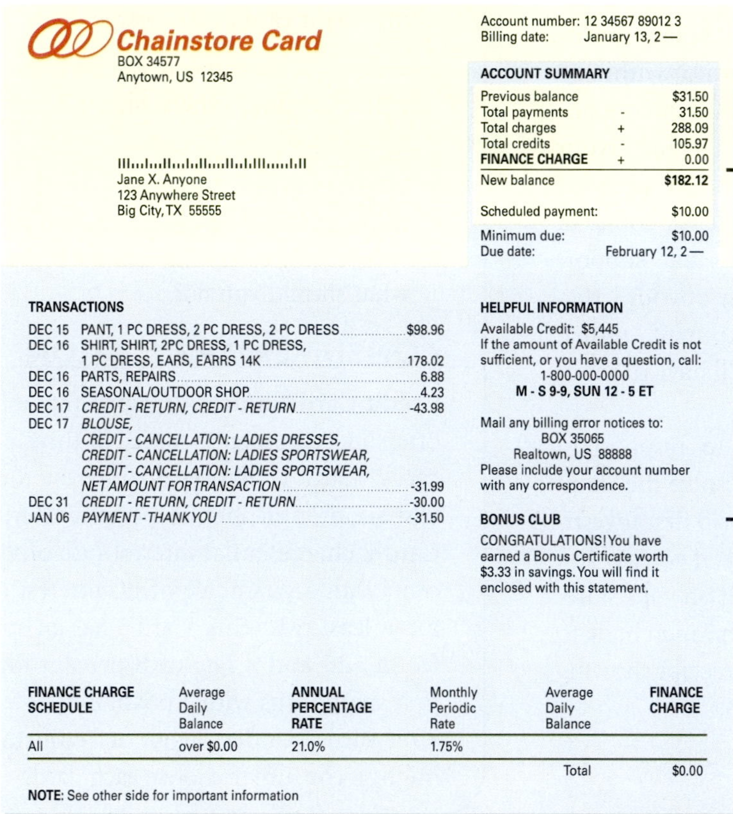

Chainstore Card
BOX 34577
Anytown, US 12345

Jane X. Anyone
123 Anywhere Street
Big City, TX 55555

Account number: 12 34567 89012 3
Billing date: January 13, 2—

ACCOUNT SUMMARY

Previous balance		$31.50
Total payments	-	31.50
Total charges	+	288.09
Total credits	-	105.97
FINANCE CHARGE	+	0.00
New balance		**$182.12**
Scheduled payment:		$10.00
Minimum due:		$10.00
Due date:		February 12, 2—

TRANSACTIONS

DEC 15	PANT, 1 PC DRESS, 2 PC DRESS, 2 PC DRESS	$98.96
DEC 16	SHIRT, SHIRT, 2PC DRESS, 1 PC DRESS, 1 PC DRESS, EARS, EARRS 14K	178.02
DEC 16	PARTS, REPAIRS	6.88
DEC 16	SEASONAL/OUTDOOR SHOP	4.23
DEC 17	*CREDIT - RETURN, CREDIT - RETURN*	-43.98
DEC 17	*BLOUSE, CREDIT - CANCELLATION: LADIES DRESSES, CREDIT - CANCELLATION: LADIES SPORTSWEAR, CREDIT - CANCELLATION: LADIES SPORTSWEAR, NET AMOUNT FOR TRANSACTION*	-31.99
DEC 31	*CREDIT - RETURN, CREDIT - RETURN*	-30.00
JAN 06	*PAYMENT - THANK YOU*	-31.50

HELPFUL INFORMATION
Available Credit: $5,445
If the amount of Available Credit is not sufficient, or you have a question, call:
1-800-000-0000
M - S 9-9, SUN 12 - 5 ET

Mail any billing error notices to:
BOX 35065
Realtown, US 88888
Please include your account number with any correspondence.

BONUS CLUB
CONGRATULATIONS! You have earned a Bonus Certificate worth $3.33 in savings. You will find it enclosed with this statement.

FINANCE CHARGE SCHEDULE	Average Daily Balance	**ANNUAL PERCENTAGE RATE**	Monthly Periodic Rate	Average Daily Balance	**FINANCE CHARGE**
All	over $0.00	21.0%	1.75%		
				Total	$0.00

NOTE: See other side for important information

Discussion. ***Ask:*** Where is a safe place to keep your record of credit card numbers?

11-10

Read your credit card statement carefully. Why should you check it against your receipts?

Class Activity. Have students write a letter to a fictitious credit card issuer describing a credit billing error.

RESOLVING BILLING PROBLEMS

Sometimes there is an error on a billing statement. The amount of a transaction may be incorrect, a charge may be listed twice, or your statement may not reflect a payment that you've made. If a charge you don't recognize appears on your statement, your credit card number may have been used without your consent.

Consumers have legal rights that protect them in case of billing errors and unauthorized use of their credit cards. Knowing what to do in case of a problem will help you preserve your rights.

Fair Credit Billing Act

The Fair Credit Billing Act outlines procedures for settling credit card billing disputes. To preserve your rights, you must write a letter to the creditor at the address the credit card statement says to use for billing errors. Your letter must reach the creditor within 60 days after you received the first bill containing the error. In the letter, include your name, account number, and a detailed description of the problem. Enclose copies of receipts or other documents that support your position, and keep a copy of your letter. Send the letter by certified mail, return receipt requested, so that you'll have proof of what the creditor received.

The creditor is required to respond in writing within 30 days and resolve the claim within 90 days. The creditor will first investigate the problem. For example, if you say you did not make a purchase listed on your statement, the creditor will ask the merchant to produce a copy of the signed receipt showing the name of the consumer who made the purchase. During the investigation, you may withhold payment on the disputed amount, but you are still obligated to pay the rest of the bill as usual.

If the investigation shows that the bill was correct, you must pay the disputed amount and any finance charges that have accumulated. However, if the error is confirmed, the creditor must credit your account for the disputed amount and remove any related finance charges.

Answer Key. Answers to the Section Review questions are provided in the Section Lesson Plan located in the *Teacher Resource Guide.*

Section 11.3 Review

CHECK YOUR UNDERSTANDING

1. What is the difference between a revolving credit card and a charge card?
2. What is APR, and why is it an important consideration when shopping for a credit card?
3. What can you do to help prevent unauthorized charges from appearing on your credit card bill? If they do appear, what should you do?

CONSUMER APPLICATION

Credit Card Choices Imagine that a bank offers its customers a choice of three credit cards. Card 1 charges no interest for the first six months, but 15 percent after that. Card 2 charges a flat interest rate of 9 percent, with a guarantee of no interest hikes for at least two years. Card 3 has an annual fee of $25 and a rate of 8 percent for the first six months with a possibility of a hike afterward. Under what circumstances might a consumer choose each card?

SECTION 11.4

Taking Out a Loan

Most consumers, at some point or another, choose to take out a loan—perhaps for a car, a house, or a major appliance. Knowing how to get and manage the right loan will help you avoid financial difficulties.

Objectives

After studying this section, you should be able to:

- Discuss sources and types of loans.
- Explain provisions that may be found in loan contracts.
- Describe the loan process from application to payment.

Key Terms

consumer finance companies
loan sharks
down payment
balloon payment
acceleration clause
add-on clause
right of rescission

SOURCES AND TYPES OF LOANS

Loans are available from a number of sources. The choice of where to borrow and what type of loan to get has an impact on the overall cost of credit. Make sure your choice is the right one.

Loans from Financial Institutions

Many consumers prefer getting a loan from a bank. Most financial institutions offer a variety of loans to meet different needs. Interest rates and other terms depend on the type of loan.

- *Home loans* are closed-end installment loans for the purchase of a home. The repayment plan is typically 15, 20, or 30 years. The home serves as security for the loan.

Jump$tart. Discuss with students the reasons why shopping carefully for a loan is as important as shopping for a major purchase. *(Spending & Credit)*

Point Out. Consumers who default on home equity loans risk foreclosure (having the lender take possession of their home).

- Consumers who already own a home may take out a *home equity loan*, using their ownership interest (equity) in their home as security. These loans can be used for a variety of purposes. Some are closed-end loans; others are an open-end line of credit, available whenever the homeowner needs or wants to use it.
- A *home improvement loan* helps the homeowner make needed repairs or improvements to a home, thus increasing its value when it comes time to sell. It's a closed-end loan, typically with a five-year term, and is usually secured by the home. See Figure 11-11.
- A *vehicle loan* is a closed-end, secured loan for the purchase of a new or used vehicle. Repayment terms vary but generally are from three to five years.
- A *personal line of credit* is an open-end, usually unsecured loan. After the loan is approved, the consumer can draw upon it when needed up to a preset limit.
- *Education or student loans*, used to pay for higher education, often have low interest rates and flexible repayment schedules.

Loans from Finance Companies

Consumer finance companies are businesses that specialize in making small or personal loans. Often, they give credit to those who cannot get it elsewhere because of a negative credit history, low income, or minimal assets. Compared to banks, finance companies usually charge more for their loans for the following reasons:

- Finance companies do not have depositors to supply the money they lend. They must borrow the money they lend and pay interest on it.

11-11

Some loans can be used for any reason, while others have a specific purpose. What type of loan might best fit this situation?

Class Activity. Have students calculate the APR on a two-week payday loan of $100 that carries $15 worth of finance charges. Ask students what these numbers reveal about the risks of payday loans as a source of consumer credit, especially for someone on a tight budget.

- With each loan, a lender incurs costs for credit investigations and record keeping. Since they make relatively small loans, finance companies can't absorb such costs as easily as banks.
- The typical borrower handled by a consumer finance company is a greater credit risk than the typical bank borrower. Thus, collection costs and bad debts are higher.

"Payday" Loans

Some check-cashing facilities, finance companies, and other establishments make small, short-term, high-interest-rate loans known as *payday loans*, or cash advance loans. Usually, a borrower writes a personal check payable to the lender for the amount he or she wishes to borrow plus a fee. The company gives the borrower the amount of the check minus the fee and holds the check until the borrower's next payday. The fee for a payday loan might be a percentage of the loan amount or a certain fee for every $50 or $100 loaned.

Wise consumers steer clear of payday loans. The APR—which must be disclosed under the Truth in Lending Act—can be extremely high. See Figure 11-12. Borrowing against the next paycheck often creates a cycle of debt that can be difficult to break. Consumers who need to borrow would be better off applying for a loan from a bank, savings and loan, or credit union.

Insurance Policy Loans

Some life insurance policies are a source of loans. The policyholder can borrow money against the amount he or she has already paid in premiums. The insurance company gives the money quickly, no credit investigation is needed, and the policy serves as the only security. The interest rate is usually lower than bank rates. However, borrowers should keep two potential drawbacks in mind:

- The main purpose of life insurance is to pay a benefit to survivors in the event of the policyholder's death. If there is an outstanding loan, the company will deduct any amount still owed before paying the benefit.

Class Activity. Have students write advice to Josh: *Josh lives from pay check to pay check, and he's low on cash this week. Driving down the street, he sees a sign on a building that says "Payday Loans." Josh has a special date this weekend and is thinking about stopping in.*

11-12

The fee for a small payday loan may not seem excessive when stated in dollars and cents. However, the actual APR could be 300% or more.

Team Activity. Have students work in pairs to write and perform skits about a person who wants to borrow money from a close relative. Possible subjects might be a teen who wants to borrow money to buy a used car or a young adult asking for help with a home loan.

- Some companies do not regularly remind the borrower to pay back the loan. The borrower often pays only the interest, allowing the loan to ride. This increases the total amount of interest that must be paid.

Private Loans

Sometimes people turn to family members or friends when they need to borrow large sums of money. While this can be a helpful option, it has the potential to cause strained relationships if the debt is not repaid. Private loans work best when these guidelines are followed:

- Keep the loan as small as possible. Remember to consider your other expenses.
- Be prepared to prove that you can pay back the loan. Provide a copy of your check stub or have the lender contact your employer to verify your salary.
- Agree with the lender on the interest rate. See Figure 11-13.
- Agree on a payment plan. Specify the date and amount of each payment.
- Be specific about the terms of the loan. Put everything in writing. Use loan forms from an office supply store, or write your own agreement.
- Pay promptly. If you lose your source of income, talk to the lender immediately about making other arrangements for the loan payments.
- Get and keep a signed receipt for each payment to prove that you paid back the loan.

Loans from Other Sources

Some consumers borrow money against their credit cards. Cash advances and "convenience checks" are available from credit card companies at interest rates that are generally as high as the original credit card agreement. Loans from other sources often cost less.

Class Activity. Tell students to assume a friend has asked to borrow money. Have them write a "no" response that is firm but friendly. Share responses in class.

11-13

Loans between friends or family members can cause problems when not handled carefully. **What might cause such problems?**

Community Activity. Have students contact a local pawnbroker to find out what types of items people are most likely to pawn.

Another costly way to get a loan is through the services of a *pawnbroker*. The consumer trades an item of value, such as jewelry, to the pawnbroker for a sum of money usually far below the item's worth. The pawnbroker holds the item for a period of time—usually 30 days—during which time the consumer has use of the money. The consumer then essentially has to buy back his or her property at a substantially higher price than the pawnbroker paid.

Consumers should avoid dealing with **loan sharks**, unlicensed lenders who operate illegally and charge excessive interest. They prey on consumers who are unable to get a loan from a legitimate creditor. If the borrower has difficulty repaying, the loan shark typically renews the loan with even less favorable terms. Soon the borrower is in an impossible financial situation.

Caption Answer. Read the installment contract carefully to look for a clause that describes a larger payment to be paid last.

LOAN CONTRACT PROVISIONS

Before you take out a loan, shop around to get the best terms you can. Because of the Truth in Lending Act, the creditor is required to clearly specify all provisions of the loan in writing. For example, the contract must state the APR, when payments are due, and whether you will be charged a penalty if you pay back the loan ahead of schedule.

If you're financing the purchase of an item, a down payment may be required. A **down payment** is a portion of a purchase price paid by cash or check at the time of purchase. For example, if you were buying furniture that cost $1,000, you might make a $100 down payment and finance (take out a loan for) the other $900. Loan contracts should spell out the amount of down payment, if any, and the amount financed.

When you apply for a loan, keep an eye out for the following clauses. Understanding them in advance will help you avoid unpleasant surprises.

Balloon Payment Clause

A final payment that is much larger than the other installments is called a **balloon payment**. Suppose you've been making weekly payments of $50 on an installment contract for an entertainment center. When you receive the final bill, you discover that the amount due is $500—ten times more than you expected. See Figure 11-14.

11-14

If you're not expecting it, a balloon payment can come as a shock. How can you find out whether a loan has a balloon payment?

Critical Thinking. *Ask:* What could you do to avoid the risk of missing a payment that would trigger an acceleration clause?

Balloon payments often lead to refinancing—that is, getting another loan, with more finance charges, to pay off the first loan. To make matters worse, the new contract may have a balloon payment clause, too. As a result, buyers find it increasingly difficult to get out of debt. If you can't avoid a balloon payment clause, be sure to plan ahead for the final payment.

Acceleration Clause

An **acceleration clause** gives the seller the right to declare the whole balance due if the buyer misses even one installment payment. For example, suppose you have made 15 payments of $75 a week and still have 15 payments remaining. If you miss the 16th payment because of illness or for any other reason, the merchant could demand immediate payment of the $1,125 balance.

If you think you may have difficulty making a payment by the required date, contact the lender as soon as possible. With advance notice, the merchant might be willing to work out a solution that is satisfactory to both of you.

Caption Answer. When you apply for a loan, have information about income, employment history, residence, debts, and credit history.

Add-On Clause

An **add-on clause** allows additional purchases to be added to an installment contract, with earlier purchases used as security for later ones. Suppose you buy a sofa on an installment contract. Before you finish paying for it, you buy a refrigerator under the contract's add-on clause. If you later stop making payments, the creditor can take back both the sofa and the refrigerator, no matter how much you had paid toward the sofa.

In some states, the consumer is protected by laws that require payments to be prorated, or divided proportionately. Each payment is applied to each item until those bought first are paid in full. Those goods that are paid for no longer serve as security for later purchases.

GETTING THE LOAN

After you've shopped for the best terms and have decided on a lender and type of loan, you are ready to apply. You may be able to apply for a loan by telephone, online, or in person. To streamline the process, be prepared to provide information about your income, employment history, residence, and credit history. See Figure 11-15.

11-15

Applying for a loan is easier if you're prepared for the questions that will be asked. What materials might you want to have with you?

Research Activity. Ask students to research the costs of credit life insurance and draw conclusions about whether it is beneficial for consumers.

Once you complete the application, you'll have to wait while the creditor runs a credit check. This can sometimes be done immediately; in other cases, you may need to wait a day or longer for approval.

After you've been approved, you'll be required to sign the loan contract. Read it carefully and make sure the terms are exactly as you agreed when you were shopping.

At this time, the lender might suggest that you purchase *credit life insurance.* This insurance, which is optional, is designed to pay off the loan in the event of your death. Keep in mind that it's expensive compared to other types of insurance. Don't feel pressured to purchase it.

Answer Key. Answers to the Section Review questions are provided in the Section Lesson Plan located in the *Teacher Resource Guide.*

If you are pledging your home as security for a loan or other credit transaction, you have the right to cancel the loan within three business days. This right, called the **right of rescission**, is provided by the Truth in Lending Act. Notice of cancellation must be given in writing.

The loan contract will outline your payment schedule. Whether you agree to pay the loan back by making monthly payments or by using another schedule, you will most likely pay in installments. Repayment options may include paying online, setting up automatic deductions from your bank account, or using a payment booklet as shown in Figure 11-16.

11-16 **A payment booklet contains dated coupons to be enclosed when you mail payments.**

Section 11.4 Review

CHECK YOUR UNDERSTANDING

1. Explain one benefit and one drawback of going to a consumer finance company for a loan.
2. What is a balloon payment clause, and how does it affect consumers?
3. In what ways can one apply for a loan?

CONSUMER APPLICATION

Comparing Rates Compare the interest rates of three different types of loans offered by one financial institution. Give possible reasons why some rates are higher than others, based on other characteristics of the loans.

Objectives

After studying this section, you should be able to:

- Analyze the consequences of excess debt.
- Identify warning signs of excess debt.
- Describe assistance and remedies for debt problems.

Key Terms

delinquent
default
repossession
collection agency
lien
garnishment
credit counseling
debit consolidation loan
bankruptcy

SECTION 11.5

Handling Debt Problems

A prospective creditor who says "no" to a request for credit may be doing the consumer a favor. Becoming overloaded with debt can lead to serious financial difficulty. For consumers who do find themselves with more debt than they can handle, help is available.

DANGERS OF EXCESS DEBT

Consumers can get into trouble with debt for a number of reasons. Crises such as the loss of a job, a serious illness, or a divorce can make it difficult for even a careful money manager to keep up with payments. In other cases, the lure of overspending leads consumers into debt. Whatever the reason, taking on too much debt can have serious effects, including:

- Inability to keep up with normal expenses from one paycheck to the next.
- Getting caught in a cycle of taking on new debt to pay off old debt.
- Stress over constant financial worries.
- Serious damage to one's credit history.
- Inability to save or invest sufficiently to reach financial goals.

Class Activity. Have students write a story about a person with a debt problem. Stories should show how the problem started, its effects, and resolution.

DEBT COLLECTION METHODS

When you sign a loan contract or credit card agreement, you are legally obligated to pay back the debt. What happens if you fail to make payments when they are due? At first, the creditor may simply send notices of your overdue, or **delinquent**, payments. By paying promptly, you may be able to avoid more serious consequences. Should payments continue to be delinquent, the creditor will probably report this information to one or more credit bureaus. You may receive a notice that you are in **default**, which means failure to fulfill the obligations of the loan, and a warning that the creditor is taking more aggressive actions toward collecting the debt.

Class Activity. Have students explain the wisdom in this quote by Thomas Jefferson: "Never spend your money before you have it."

Repossession and Shut-offs

Suppose you buy a television through store credit and fail to make payments. In most cases, the creditor can take back the TV. Taking away property due to failure to make loan or credit payments is called **repossession**. See Figure 11-17. If you fail to make payments for services, such as electricity or telephone service, those creditors may shut off or discontinue providing the service.

Collection Agencies

After exhausting its own efforts to get a consumer to make past-due payments, a creditor may turn the account over to a **collection agency**. This is a business that collects unpaid debt for others. The debtor's credit report will reflect the fact that a collection agency has been called in, seriously lowering his or her credit rating.

In most cases, agencies earn a percentage of the debt collected, giving them strong incentives for being relentless and aggressive in their collection tactics. However, the Fair Debt Collection Practices Act protects consumers against abusive practices of debt collectors, such as harassment, overcharging, and disclosing consumers' debt to third parties.

Caption Answer. The car belongs to the creditor until the loan is paid.

11-17

When a consumer doesn't keep up with car payments, the vehicle may be towed away. Why does the creditor have the right of repossession in this case?

Team Activity. Have students work in small groups to develop brochures for consumers about ways to avoid excess debt. Suggest that they start by developing a list of guidelines and then expand on the list by adding illustrations and examples. Have groups share their brochures with the class.

Judgments and Liens

If other efforts fail, a creditor may go to court and get a judgment, or court ruling, that says the debt must be paid. The consumer may be ordered to pay the creditor's attorney fees in addition to the original debt.

If the debtor owns a home, the judgment may appear on record as a lien. A **lien** (LEEN) is a claim upon property to satisfy a debt. When the home is sold, money from the sale is first used to pay any lien holders. The debtor receives only the amount that is left, if any. Judgments and liens are a matter of public record, appear on the debtor's credit report, and lower his or her credit rating.

Garnishment

Garnishment is the legal withholding of a specified sum from a person's wages in order to collect a debt. If ordered by the court, the debtor's employer must withhold part of the worker's wages and send the money to the court, which then passes it on to the creditor. Money is withheld from the worker's paycheck until the debt and all court costs are paid.

Class Activity. Read this to students and have them write advice to the person: "Several months ago, I got a loan for a big-screen television because I just had to have one. How was I to know that later my car would quit running, and I'd have a huge repair bill. I've been using my credit cards to help on expenses, but now they're after me because of some overdue payments. I'm worried, and I'm not sure what to do next."

AVOIDING EXCESS DEBT

By far the best solution to the problem of excess debt is avoiding too much debt in the first place. Individuals and families should set reasonable limits for debt, taking into consideration their income, fixed expenses, savings, and other assets. Then they must have the discipline to stay within those limits. For example, they may have to postpone or reconsider some purchases instead of charging everything they want to a credit card. Setting aside some "rainy day" savings will reduce the need to borrow when unexpected expenses come up.

Warning Signs

Consumers who constantly worry about credit cards and loans—and continue to spend more than they make—probably already know that they have debt problems. See Figure 11-18.

11-18

Financial problems can be a major source of stress.

Team Activity. Have students work in small groups to develop one-minute public service announcements about the warning signs of a debt problem and ways to get help. Suggest that they make up a character to illustrate the problem. Have groups perform their announcements for the class.

Other warning signs of a debt problem include:

- Reaching the credit limit on most credit cards.
- Skipping payments on some bills in order to pay others, or using cash advances on one credit card to pay off another.
- Using credit cards for day-to-day purchases like groceries, movie tickets, or fast food—not simply as a convenience or to earn cardholder rewards, but due to lack of cash.

CLIMBING OUT OF DEBT

If you find yourself in financial difficulty, here are some options that can help you recover.

- **Working with creditors.** Contact creditors immediately to let them know you are having problems. See whether you can adjust payment terms. Most creditors will be willing to work with you to find a mutually beneficial solution.
- **Self-help measures.** Although creditors and others can provide help, much of what needs to be done is up to you. Begin by stopping your use of credit cards. Make paying off debts your top priority. See Figure 11-19.
- **Credit counseling.** Many consumers have overcome debt problems with the help of **credit counseling**, guidance provided by trained people who help consumers learn to live within their means. Money that the consumer deposits each month with the counseling service is used to pay creditors according to a payment schedule developed by the counselor. Some credit counseling services charge little or nothing for managing the plan; others charge a monthly fee that could add up to a significant amount over time.

Community Activity. Have students search local phone directories or Internet listings to find credit counseling services available in your area. Ask them to contact one of these organizations and find out what services it offers and what fees it charges.

11-19

Recovering from excess debt is possible. Getting rid of credit cards and contacting creditors are two simple ways to begin.

Critical Thinking. *Ask:* What are the consequences of personal bankruptcy? Why should it be considered a last resort for consumers?

- **Debt consolidation loans.** A consumer who has several debts and is not able to make payments on all of them every month may find a debt consolidation loan appealing. A **debt consolidation loan** combines all existing debt into a new loan with a more manageable payment schedule. You use the money from the new loan to pay off all previous creditors. Then you can make just one payment each month to the lending agency. Before taking on a debt consolidation loan, investigate its terms thoroughly. The loan may achieve lower monthly payments by simply spreading out debt over a longer period of time, resulting in additional interest charges. Some debt consolidation loans are actually home equity loans in which the home is pledged as security.

Dollars and Sense. Have students consult the Federal Trade Commission's Web site for more information on illegal credit repair services.

Bankruptcy: A Last Resort

When all other options fail, a consumer may be forced to file personal bankruptcy. **Bankruptcy** is legal relief from repaying certain debts. The decision to file for bankruptcy is a serious one and should be given much consideration.

Two types of personal bankruptcy are commonly used by consumers. They are named after chapters of the federal Bankruptcy Code.

- **Chapter 7** requires, in most cases, the sale of all the debtor's property except that protected from bankruptcy under state or federal law. The money from the sale of the property is distributed to creditors.
- **Chapter 13** allows the debtor to keep property. The debtor proposes a plan, which must be approved and supervised by the court, to pay off some or all of the

DOLLARSandSENSE

Credit "Cures" to Avoid

Bad Credit? No Credit? No Problem! That's what the ads would have you believe. When it comes to credit repair offers, be suspicious of companies that:

- Want you to pay for credit repair services up front.
- Don't tell you your legal rights and what you can do yourself for free.
- Recommend against contacting credit bureaus directly.
- Advise you to create a "new" credit identity under a different name or identification number. This is illegal, and you could be prosecuted for fraud.

If you suspect that a business is acting in an illegal way to help you "erase" your debts, contact the Federal Trade Commission immediately.

Research Activity. Have students research the growth of personal bankruptcies over the past ten years and identify factors linked to the increase.

Answer Key. Answers to the Section Review questions are provided in the Section Lesson Plan located in the *Teacher Resource Guide.*

11-20

By practicing financial discipline, consumers can overcome debt problems and build a positive credit history.

Class Activity. Have students find what they think is the most important piece of information in this section and explain their choice.

debt over time. Debtors who have regular income and debt under a certain amount qualify for Chapter 13.

During bankruptcy proceedings, the debtor is protected from debt collection activities. After complying with all of the bankruptcy requirements, the debtor is in general relieved of the responsibility to pay any remaining prior debt. However, certain debts, such as taxes, child support, and most student loans, are still the debtor's legal obligation.

A serious disadvantage of bankruptcy is the damage to the person's credit history. A bankruptcy filing remains on a person's credit report for ten years.

Rebuilding Credit

Improving one's credit history after debt problems is largely a matter of time. By law, most delinquencies and judgments remain in a credit report for seven years. Bankruptcy remains for seven to ten years. The good news is that after that time, there will be no indication of the past debt problems.

Aside from waiting it out, consumers with a poor credit history can take several steps to improve it. Paying bills on time is the most important factor. Avoiding high balances on credit cards and resisting the temptation to open additional credit accounts will also help. See Figure 11-20. With diligence, care, and patience, consumers can overcome debt problems and make a new start.

Section 11.5 Review

CHECK YOUR UNDERSTANDING

1. Explain three actions a creditor may take to collect debt. How do they affect the debtor's credit history?
2. How can consumers recognize that they have a serious debt problem?
3. How can credit counseling help consumers?

CONSUMER APPLICATION

Credit Guidelines Assume that you are writing credit guidelines for teen consumers. List the five most important pieces of advice you would offer them for avoiding debt problems.

CHAPTER 11

Review & Activities

CHAPTER SUMMARY

- Using credit can temporarily expand purchasing power. Analyze the benefits and costs of credit carefully when you use it. (11.1)
- Lenders look at character, capacity, and capital. A good credit rating is valuable. (11.2)
- Choose a credit card wisely by comparing terms and conditions. (11.3)
- Compare loans and lenders and be sure you understand the contract before signing. (11.4)
- Avoid the dangers of excess debt by recognizing its warning signs. Options are available for recovering from excess debt. (11.5)

THE $avvy Consumer

What's That Charge? Sarah sees two charges on her credit card statement that she doesn't recall making to companies she doesn't recognize. She wonders whether someone stole her card number and made the purchases. What should she do before disputing the charges? If the charges were not hers, what action should she take? (11.3)

Reviewing Key Terms and Ideas

1. Briefly describe how **credit** works. (11.1)
2. What is **collateral**, and why might a **creditor** require it? (11.1)
3. Explain the difference between single-payment and **installment** credit. (11.1)
4. What are the costs of using credit? (11.1)
5. How can your **credit history** demonstrate that you will be a good credit risk? (11.2)
6. How is a **credit score** related to a **credit rating**? (11.2)
7. Give two examples of how to establish a good credit rating and two examples of how to maintain it. (11.2)
8. What is the difference between private label and general purpose cards? (11.3)
9. Name three types of credit card terms and conditions you would compare before choosing a card. (11.3)
10. How does having a **grace period** benefit consumers? (11.3)
11. How can you use a **credit limit** wisely? (11.3)
12. How does the Truth in Lending Act protect consumers? (11.3)
13. Why is making only minimum payments on a very large credit card bill a problem? (11.3)
14. What is an **add-on clause**? (11.4)
15. Identify the sequence of steps from the time you decide the type and source of loan you want. (11.4)
16. How does a **lien** work? (11.5)
17. Which option should you try first to solve debt problems—a **debt consolidation loan** or **bankruptcy**? Explain. (11.5)

Answer Key. Answers to the Chapter Review & Activities are provided in the Teacher's Manual in the *Teacher Annotated Edition* of the text.

Thinking Critically

1. **Drawing Conclusions:** Consumers often use credit to buy food and other items that are readily consumed. The debt remains long after the item is gone. Do you think it's wise to use credit in this way? Consider the benefits, costs, and drawbacks of using credit. (11.1)
2. **Making Predictions:** Suppose the grace period on a credit card is very short, and the company charges a late-payment fee of $25. What might happen? (11.3)
3. **Analyzing Economic Concepts:** How do interest rates influence buying decisions? (11.1, 11.3, 11.4)
4. **Making Comparisons:** Prepare a chart that you could use to compare information about two different loans. Explain how the information in the chart would be helpful. (11.4)

Building Consumer Skills

1. **Credit Report:** Imagine that your credit report mistakenly indicates you made several late payments to a creditor. Write a letter to the credit bureau requesting that the error be corrected. (11.2)
2. **Credit Card Comparisons:** Find information about three credit cards currently offered to consumers. Read the terms and conditions and note the APR of each card. Create a chart that compares the cards. (11.3)
3. **Sources and Types of Loans:** Compare the types of loans offered by the following sources: banks, consumer finance companies, and pawnbrokers. (11.4)
4. **Loan Costs:** Suppose you're making a down payment of $1,500 on a car that costs $18,000. You have the option of taking out a 36-month, 48-month, or 60-month loan at 8% interest. Using a loan calculator on a financial Web site, determine the monthly payment and total cost of the car for each loan. What factors would influence your loan choice? (11.4)
5. **Excess Debt:** Suppose someone is unable to pay the bills each month and wants to get out of debt. Write diary entries over a period of time as written by this person. Show the difficulties of the problem, including the different methods considered, such as payday loans and private loans. Through the diary, indicate how the debt problem is eventually resolved in a realistic way. (11.4, 11.5)

Consumer Connections

- **Family:** Ask an adult family member to explain his or her thoughts about cosigning a loan with you. How would the decision be affected by the purpose of the loan? The amount? What might be some reasons for and against cosigning? (11.4)
- **Community:** Survey teens about their use of credit. Include frequency of use, average amount charged per month, use of personal or parents' accounts, and pros and cons of using credit. Summarize your findings. (11.1, 11.2, 11.3)

CHAPTER 12

Savings

Reading with Purpose

- As you read this chapter, create an outline using the colored headings.
- Write a question for each heading to help guide your reading.
- Write the answer to each question as you read the chapter.
- Ask your teacher to help with answers you cannot find in the text.

SECTION 12.1

The Role of Saving

Objectives

After studying this section, you should be able to:

- Explain the benefits of saving.
- Distinguish between saving and investing.
- Explain reasons for saving.

Key Terms

saving
investing

Many people think of savings as money left over after expenses. Savings are, however, probably the most important item in the personal or family financial plan. When you plan to save, you are planning for your dreams.

BENEFITS OF SAVING

Saving means setting aside money for future use. Saving can help you in two ways:

- It allows you to accumulate money for future purchases. An example might be setting aside a few dollars every week until you have enough to buy the sports equipment you've been wanting. In this sense, saving is really just delayed spending.
- Money that you save can be put to work in another way—to earn income. You can deposit it in a financial institution and be paid interest in return. Even small amounts of money, when saved regularly, can earn money for you.

Saving and Investing

Saving is closely related to another financial principle: investing. What's the difference? With saving, the main purpose is to set aside money for some anticipated future need.

Team Activity. Have students work in small groups to write skits that illustrate different types of family emergencies. Each skit should have two different endings to show the effects of having or not having an emergency fund. Have groups perform their skits for the class.

The fact that your savings can earn money for you is a bonus. A typical example of saving is putting money in a savings account at a bank. There's practically no risk of losing your money, and you can withdraw it whenever you like.

Investing is committing money for the purpose of making a profit over time. The objective of investing is to make your money grow in the long run. Unlike saving, investing requires taking risks with your money, and you may not have easy access to it. However, investing has the potential to earn more for you.

TEXTLINK

You'll learn more about investing in Chapter 13.

Of course, before you can invest money, you need a sum of money to invest! For this reason, investing often begins with saving. You might accumulate money in a savings account until it reaches a certain amount, then invest it.

Jump$tart. Challenge students to create a visual that illustrates the difference between saving and investing and the benefits of each. *(Saving & Investing)*

REASONS FOR SAVING

You'll be more motivated to establish a savings plan if you have a specific purpose in mind. Here are some common reasons for saving money.

Emergencies

No matter how carefully families or individuals plan their spending, something may happen that they didn't expect. It might be a refrigerator that suddenly stops working, medical bills that aren't covered by insurance, or the loss of a job. To protect yourself in such situations, you and your family should have an emergency fund—money set aside in case of loss of income or unexpected major expenses. It should be used only for its intended purpose. (Wanting to buy a big-screen TV is not an emergency!) See Figure 12-1.

12-1

Even successful people can lose their jobs suddenly due to a downturn in the economy or a business that goes under. Having an emergency fund can help ease the stress.

Class Activity. As a class, brainstorm a list of recurring expenses for which a young adult might need to save. List them on the board. For each one, estimate the amount of the expense and how often it is likely to occur. Total up the amounts to figure out how much these expenses could add up to per year.

How much money should be in an emergency fund? One rule of thumb is that it should equal three to six times monthly net income. A fund this size makes it possible to keep up with daily expenses through unemployment lasting three to six months.

Recurring Expenses

You might want to save so that you can more easily meet large recurring expenses. Suppose you have your own phone and are responsible for the monthly bills. By setting aside small amounts from your weekly income, you'll have the money on hand when the phone bill arrives each month.

You may want to follow the same plan in order to purchase gifts for family and friends on birthdays and holidays. As you get older, you may acquire other recurring expenses to save for, such as real estate taxes and insurance premiums.

Future Purchases

You probably know what it's like to want something you just don't have the money for. Maybe you have your eye on an expensive new jacket, or you've been longing for an electric guitar. One way to get that special item is to save for it. See Figure 12-2.

Saving for an item means delaying your purchase until you have the money. Often, people don't want to wait. They choose to buy the item on credit instead. This approach can lead to increased spending in the long run, for three reasons:

- Using credit means you must pay interest on the money you're borrowing. In effect, this adds to the cost of the item.
- In contrast, saving *earns* interest. Money that you keep in a savings account gives you interest income. When you buy on credit, that income is lost.
- Credit makes it easy to buy anything that appeals to you at the moment. Saving for an item gives you time to decide whether it's really important to you. This helps you spend your money wisely.

12-2

Packing a lunch for school is one way to cut spending. What else can you do to save money for something special?

Research Activity. Ask students to research the life expectancy for people their age. Then ask them to calculate how many years of retirement they are likely to have and multiply this number by their estimated yearly expenses to figure out how much money they might need in retirement by today's numbers.

Financial Goals

Saving can help people achieve their financial goals, whatever they may be. Savings goals often change at different stages of the family life cycle. For example:

- Ladonna is planning to go to college in a few years. She and her family are setting aside money to help pay for college fees and the expenses of living away from home. After college, Ladonna might decide to save for other goals, such as buying a car.
- Ladonna's brother and sister-in-law are putting aside money because they hope to start a family one day. They know that with children come many additional expenses.
- Ladonna's great-aunt, who is retired, enjoys taking trips across the country. She saves money in an account she calls her "travel fund."

While their needs and goals are varied, these family members have at least one thing in common. They all know the value of saving. See Figure 12-3.

Caption Answer. This family might save for expenses related to children and to their new home. A retired couple might save for money to live on in the future or to travel.

12-3

The financial goals that families set often depend on their stage of life. How might the financial goals of this family differ from those of a retired couple?

Economic Impact & Issues. Have students research reverse mortgages. In what situations might they be appropriate?

Answer Key. Answers to the Section Review questions are provided in the Section Lesson Plan located in the *Teacher Resource Guide.*

Economic Impact & Issues

Plan Now to Save for Retirement

Financial advisors agree: saving for retirement should start early in your career. Certain economic factors, such as the stock market, housing market, and job market, shape retirement saving strategies—and may shape your own.

Most people's retirement savings rely on a healthy stock market to grow. Even when people don't invest in the market themselves, their employers often do, using money that employees contribute to employer-sponsored retirement plans.

The housing market also plays a leading role in savings. Many people count their home as a source of retirement income. After paying on their home for years, they may sell it to buy a smaller one, using the profits from the sale and money saved on smaller utility and tax bills to help meet their expenses. Other people take out loans based on the value of their home. In both cases, a strong housing market, in which homes command a high price, works in their favor.

Finally, employment trends affect a savings plan. A certain number of workers are needed to pay into Social Security so that benefits can be paid to retired workers.

FIGURE IT OUT

Economists urge people to rely more on personal planning and less on employers and the government to fund their retirement. Interview several working adults of different ages about what they are doing to save for retirement. How do their plans compare with the experts' advice?

Retirement

One important financial goal is preparing for retirement. When you're young, retirement seems far off. It takes a long time, however, for people to build up enough money to live comfortably when they retire. Most people will need a large fund built up through savings and investments to meet their expenses after they stop working. Once you have a full-time job, you need to start saving and investing for the time when you'll no longer want to or be able to work.

TEXTLINK You can read more about retirement planning in Section 13.2.

Section 12.1 Review

CHECK YOUR UNDERSTANDING

1. Explain two benefits of saving.
2. How does saving differ from investing?
3. Identify four common reasons for saving.

CONSUMER APPLICATION

Saving for Taxes Imagine that you just paid your annual real estate tax bill. This year's bill came to $1,894. You think it may be somewhat higher next year. You'd like to set aside some of your twice-monthly paycheck to save up for next year's taxes. How much would you save out of each paycheck? Why?

Objectives

After studying this section, you should be able to:

- Explain steps for reaching savings goals.
- Describe ways to establish a successful savings habit.

Key Terms

savings plan
discretionary income

SECTION 12.2

Your Savings Plan

The best way to make a habit of saving money is to have a plan. By setting reasonable savings goals, you can set aside money for future needs and put your savings to work for you.

WHY YOU NEED A PLAN

Many people hope to save money, but have trouble actually doing it. Perhaps you're one of them. Every dime you get goes for the things you want and need to buy now. There's nothing left over to set aside. "When I'm making more money," you say to yourself, "I'll start saving—but not now."

Guess what? Someday when you're making more money, you'll feel exactly the same way. The more money you have, the more you'll want to spend. If you think of savings as money left over after spending, you may never end up with more cash than you can fit in a piggy bank.

To be a successful saver, you need a **savings plan**—a step-by-step approach for putting money aside in savings. Don't expect the savings to accumulate by themselves. Take charge of your saving!

Discussion. *Ask:* How might your savings goals change over time?

FCCLA. Have students use the Financing Your Future unit of Financial Fitness to set a specific savings goal, break it into short-term goals, and create a plan for saving. Have them set benchmarks to track their progress toward this goal over a period of several months.

STEPS TO SAVING

Saving money takes time, so the sooner you begin, the better. Start by deciding on your goals for saving. Then take steps to reach your goals.

1. **Decide what you're saving for.** Is it new clothes? A car of your own? College expenses?
2. **Set a specific goal.** Decide on the amount of money you need to reach your goal and the date by which you need it.
3. **Break your long-term goal into short-term goals.** If you want to have $250 in six months, you'll need to save about $10 a week. Ask yourself whether that seems realistic. If not, you may need to revise your long-term goal.
4. **Save regularly and consistently.** Decide on specific strategies for saving.
5. **Put your savings to work.** Keep your money in an account that earns interest. You'll reach your goal that much faster.
6. **Keep your savings goals in mind.** To stay motivated, post a picture that will remind you of your long-term goal. Mark your short-term goals on your calendar and check them off as you reach them. Make a chart of your progress. Then watch your savings grow!

CONSIDER YOUR BUDGET

The amount you save must be realistic and leave enough money to pay your daily expenses. Otherwise, you'll find it hard to stick to your plan. You may need to revise your savings goals to fit within your budget. See Figure 12-4.

In a family budget, the percentage of income that can go toward savings varies. It depends on the family's **discretionary income**—the amount of available income after taxes and necessary spending for food, clothing, and shelter. A large family with a small income may have difficulty saving even a small percentage of their earnings. Necessary expenses such as housing and food take up a relatively large proportion of the family's income, leaving less available for

12-4

Some expenses, such as transportation costs, are necessary to meet daily needs. **What essential expenses do you have?**

Discussion. ***Ask:*** Why is it better to pay yourself first rather than to save whatever's left at the end of the month?

savings. In contrast, a two-income couple without children may be able to save a relatively large percentage of their income. See Figure 12-5.

Start small if you need to. How much you save isn't as important as developing the habit of saving consistently. The sooner you develop that habit, the more your savings will build over time.

PAY YOURSELF FIRST

The most effective savings plans are based on a simple principle: Pay yourself first. That means setting aside part of your income for savings first, then spending what's left. It's the opposite of what many unsuccessful savers do—they spend first and save whatever's left.

Decide how much to save out of each paycheck, based on your savings goals and your budget. You'll be more likely to stick to your system if you set a fixed amount that's easy to

Class Activity. Have students write a paragraph explaining how automatic savings systems might make it easier for a family to save.

remember and handle. However, if the amount of your earnings varies a great deal from paycheck to paycheck, you might decide to save a certain percentage of your pay instead.

Automatic Savings

Once you've decided how much to save, you can simply put that amount in your savings account when you deposit or cash your paycheck. That works fine if you have the self-discipline to stick to your plan. To make saving even easier, however, consider these techniques.

- **Automatic transfers.** One easy method of saving is to set up an automatic electronic transfer, as explained in Section 10.2. Each month, the bank transfers a specified amount from checking to savings.

Research Activity. Have students read the first chapter of *Mama's Bank Account,* by Kathryn Forbes, and write a paragraph describing mama's secret to saving.

12-5

A well-planned budget can help you establish a savings plan while also meeting necessary expenses. In making a budget, what priority would you place on savings? Why?

Dollars and Sense. Ask students to brainstorm ways teens might cut their expenses. Encourage them to try one suggestion for a week and then figure out how much they saved. Have them multiply this amount by 52 to figure out how much they could save in a year by following this strategy.

DOLLARSandSENSE

Saving Day by Day

Even saving a small amount each day can add up over time. Here are some ideas you could try.

- To cut down on spending, carry only as much cash as you need each day. Leave the rest of your weekly cash at home, along with your ATM card and any credit cards.
- At the beginning or end of each day, place all your change in a special jar. When it's full, deposit the money in your savings account.
- Look for small, painless ways to spend less. Could you rent your favorite movie instead of buying it? How about borrowing it from the public library? Spending less means saving more.

- **Direct deposit.** Many employers can electronically deposit earnings in the employee's bank account. The employee may be able to request that part of the money be deposited in a savings account and the rest in a checking account.
- **Payroll deductions.** Many employers encourage employees to save and invest by permitting payroll deductions. The employee authorizes a specific amount to be deducted from each paycheck and put into a savings plan.

STICK TO YOUR PLAN

When you "pay yourself first," saving is easy. The challenge is to make the rest of your money last until the next payday. You may have to adjust your spending habits, especially when you start a new savings plan. Resist the temptation to dip into your savings unless it becomes absolutely necessary. Keeping your goals in mind will help you succeed.

Section 12.2 Review

CHECK YOUR UNDERSTANDING

1. Describe the steps in reaching savings goals.
2. Why are families with lower incomes usually not able to save the same percentage of their income as families with larger incomes?
3. Explain three methods of saving automatically.

CONSUMER APPLICATION

Savings Goals Identify a long-term savings goal. Then describe how you could break it down into specific short-term goals.

Answer Key. Answers to the Section Review questions are provided in the Section Lesson Plan located in the *Teacher Resource Guide.*

Objectives

After studying this section, you should be able to:

- Distinguish between simple and compound interest.
- Explain the significance of annual percentage yield.
- Analyze how time impacts the growth of savings.

Key Terms

simple interest
compound interest
annual percentage yield (APY)

SECTION 12.3

Earning by Saving

When you open an account at a financial institution, your money will begin to earn interest. The higher the interest rate, the more you'll earn—right? Usually, but it's not quite that simple. It also depends on how the financial institution calculates and pays interest on your account.

CALCULATING INTEREST

Savings accounts can differ in how often interest is paid or credited to you. Many accounts pay interest monthly. That means once a month, the interest you have earned is added to your account balance. Some accounts pay interest quarterly instead of monthly.

The stated interest rate for an account is the annual rate. If interest is paid monthly, the calculation is based on one-twelfth of the annual rate. For example, suppose an account earns 3% interest, paid monthly. Each month, you are actually paid 0.25% interest. Over an entire year, that adds up to 3%.

Accounts can also differ in how the interest calculation is made. Two basic methods of calculation are simple interest and compound interest.

Class Activity. Have students calculate the difference in simple and compound interest paid monthly at 5% on savings of $10,000.

Simple Interest

Simple interest is interest calculated only on the money you've deposited, not on prior interest earned. Suppose you deposit $50 per month into an account that pays 5% simple interest. An annual interest rate of 5% equals 0.4% monthly interest (5 ÷ 12 = 0.4). Each month, the bank takes the sum of your deposits (minus any withdrawals) and multiplies this figure by 0.4% (0.004). The result is added to your account balance. Figure 12-6 shows how your account will grow if you don't make any withdrawals.

Compound Interest

Few financial institutions pay simple interest these days. Most offer compound interest to attract customers. **Compound interest** is interest calculated on both deposits made and prior interest earned. In other words, interest is paid on the interest.

Caption Answers. *Figure 12-6:* The account balance at the end of month 9 is $459. ***Figure 12-7:*** The interest for month 7 is $1.42.

Interest may be compounded daily, monthly, yearly, or as frequently as the savings institution chooses. More frequent compounding is generally better for the saver, as long as interest earned is left in the account to grow.

Again, suppose you deposit $50 a month into an account that pays 5% interest. This time, the interest is compounded monthly as well as paid monthly. Figure 12-7 shows how the interest is calculated. As you can see, for the first few months there is no difference in interest paid compared to the simple interest method. As more time goes by, however, the effects of compounding begin to be seen.

Keep in mind the difference between how often interest is compounded and how often it's paid. For example, it's possible for interest to be compounded daily and paid monthly. In that case, the interest is calculated based on daily compounding, but you don't actually receive the interest in your account until the end of the month.

Simple Interest

$50 is deposited at the beginning of each month.
The account pays 5% simple interest.

Month	Total Deposits	Interest Calculation	Interest Paid That Month	Account Balance at End of Month
1	$50	$50 × 0.004	$0.20	$50.20
2	$100	$100 × 0.004	$0.40	$100.60
3	$150	$150 × 0.004	$0.60	$151.20
4	$200	$200 × 0.004	$0.80	$202.00
5	$250	$250 × 0.004	$1.00	$253.00
6	$300	$300 × 0.004	$1.20	$304.20
...	...	...	...	...
12	$600	$600 × 0.004	$2.40	$615.60

12-6 **Simple interest is calculated only on the amount of money you've deposited.** **What would the account balance be at the end of month 9?**

Compound Interest

$50 is deposited at the beginning of each month.
The account pays 5% interest, compounded monthly.

Month	Total Deposits	Interest Calculation	Interest Paid That Month	Account Balance at End of Month
1	$50.00	$50.00 × 0.004	$0.20	$50.20
2	$100.20	$100.20 × 0.004	$0.40	$100.60
3	$150.60	$150.60 × 0.004	$0.60	$151.20
4	$201.20	$201.20 × 0.004	$0.80	$202.00
5	$252.00	$252.00 × 0.004	$1.01	$253.01
6	$303.01	$303.01 × 0.004	$1.21	$304.22
...	...	...	...	...
12	$613.37	$613.37 × 0.004	$2.45	$615.82

12-7 **Compound interest is calculated on the entire account balance, including prior interest earned.** **How much interest would be paid in month 7?**

Research Activity. Have students search online to compare the APY paid on basic savings accounts by several different financial institutions.

Annual Percentage Yield

As you've seen, two accounts that each pay 5% interest can actually earn different amounts of interest over a year. Differences in whether and how often interest is compounded can make it difficult to compare one account with another. Suppose you were trying to choose between an account that earns 8.25% simple interest and one that earns 8% interest compounded daily. Would you know which account would earn more for you?

The Truth in Savings Act, passed in 1991 and amended since then, helps consumers make such comparisons. One of its requirements is that financial institutions tell consumers the **annual percentage yield (APY)** of accounts. This figure tells you the actual annual rate at which interest is earned, including the effects of compounding. It assumes that interest remains in the account rather than being withdrawn.

With simple interest, the APY is the same as the stated interest rate. The account paying 8.25% simple interest has an APY of 8.25%. The other account, paying 8% interest compounded daily, has an APY of 8.33%. That means that if you left $100 on deposit for one year, you'd earn $8.33 in interest. You'll earn more with this account.

Critical Thinking. ***Ask:*** Why do you think the Truth in Savings Act was created?

TIME IS MONEY

In the examples so far, the amount of interest earned has been small. You may be thinking, "So what? A few pennies aren't enough to bother with."

When savings are left to grow for a long time, however, the amounts earned can be much more than a few pennies. You may have heard the old saying "Time is money." This saying has several meanings. One meaning is that when it comes to saving or investing, time is your ally. The longer you leave money on deposit to earn interest, the more quickly that interest starts to add up. See Figure 12-8.

12-8

It's often said that money doesn't grow on trees. However, when your money earns interest and you let it grow over time, you can look forward to a harvest of extra dollars in the future.

Team Activity. Have students create math problems involving compound interest. Have partners exchange and solve each other's problems.

Caption Answer. Students might say that interest rates are affected by the health of the economy, consumer savings, and risk.

The Long-Term Effects of Compounding

The effects of compound interest increase greatly over time. Suppose two families each have a $5,000 emergency fund that they wish to keep in a savings account. One family chooses an account paying 4% simple interest. The other chooses an account paying 4% compounded daily. At the end of one year, assuming both families leave their fund untouched, the second family has just $4 more than the first.

Now suppose that both families, fortunately, have no need to use their emergency fund for 20 years. At the end of that time, how much more would you guess the second family will have in their account than the first family? It's much more than $4 times 20. In fact, if the interest rates stay constant, the second family will have $2,127 more than the first!

That's what some people call "the magic of compound interest." If interest remains in the account and is compounded, your savings will grow much more.

The Long-Term Effect of Interest Rates

You've just compared the long-term effects of simple and compound interest. As you know, the difference between simple and compound interest can be expressed as a difference in annual percentage yield (APY). In the previous example, the difference in APY was only 0.08%. What effect does an even greater difference in APY have on long-term earnings?

Figure 12-9 shows the difference in investing $1,000 for 20 years at three different interest rates. As you can see, in the long run, it pays to shop around for the best rates.

Rule of 72

One quick way to evaluate an interest rate is to apply the rule of 72. Divide 72 by the interest rate. (In the case of compound interest, you would use the APY). The answer is the approximate number of years it will take to double your money.

For example, if the APY is 6%, the calculation is 72 ÷ 6 = 12. That means if you deposited $1,000, in about 12 years the account balance would reach $2,000. (This assumes that you make no further deposits or withdrawals and that the interest rate stays the same.) If the APY is 8%, you would double your money in about 9 years (72 ÷ 8 = 9). This calculation can help you see the long-term effects of different interest rates.

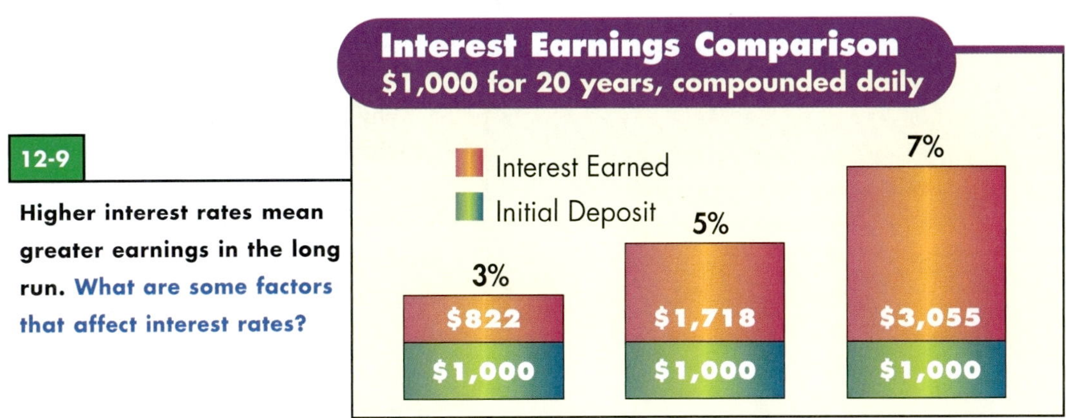

12-9

Higher interest rates mean greater earnings in the long run. What are some factors that affect interest rates?

Community Activity. Have students find out the APY offered on savings accounts at a local bank. Then have them use the Rule of 72 to calculate how long it would take for their money to double if they deposited $1,000 at that bank and made no additional deposits or withdrawals.

Small Amounts Grow Large

As you've seen, time is money. That's why it's so important to develop the savings habit early. Even small amounts, when saved regularly and put into an interest-earning account, can really add up over time. The graph in Figure 12-10 shows how just $30 a month—less than a dollar a day—can grow.

12-10

The combination of regular deposits and compound interest helps your money grow. If this were your savings account, what might you do with the money you accumulated?

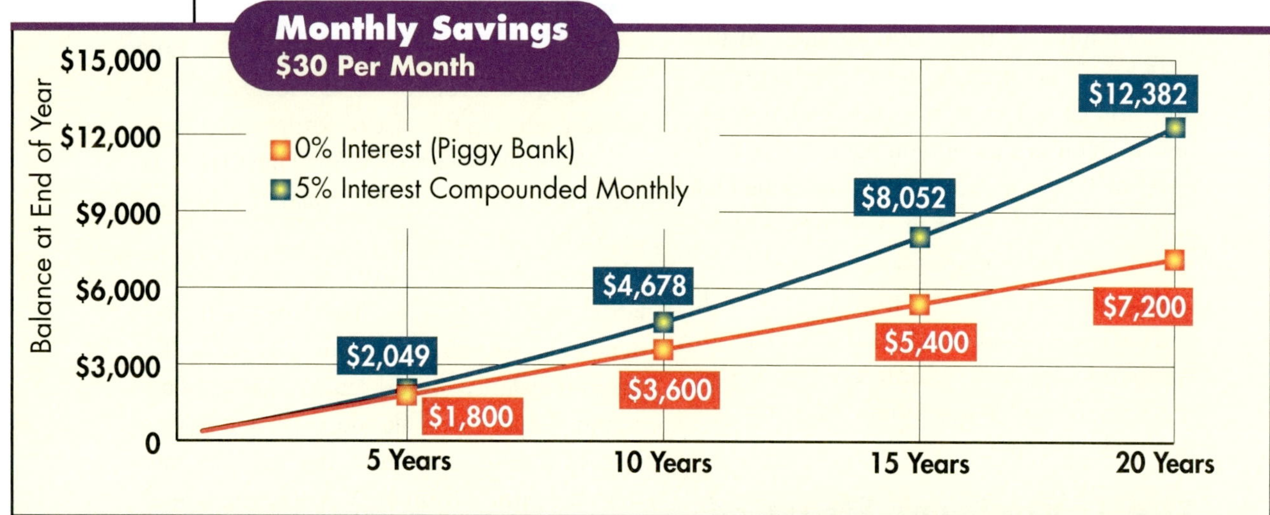

Answer Key. Answers to the Section Review questions are provided in the Section Lesson Plan located in the *Teacher Resource Guide.*

Section 12.3 Review

CHECK YOUR UNDERSTANDING

1. How is compound interest calculated?
2. Why might the stated interest rate for an account be different from the APY?
3. Why is it important to compare savings accounts to get the best interest rate?

CONSUMER APPLICATION

Rule of 72 Using the Rule of 72, calculate about how many years it would take to double your money at these annual percentage yields: 3%, 5.13%, 7.25%.

SECTION 12.4

Saving Options

To get the most out of your savings, you need to keep the money where it will earn interest. A savings account is one option, but you have many others. How can you decide which choice is best for you?

Objectives

After studying this section, you should be able to:

- Explain factors affecting the choice of savings options.
- Identify and compare various savings options.

Key Terms

liquidity
terms
money market account
certificate of deposit (CD)
savings bonds

FACTORS IN CHOOSING SAVINGS OPTIONS

Savings options differ widely. To make the right choice for your situation, compare these factors.

- **Safety and risk.** As explained in Chapter 10, deposits at most financial institutions are insured by the Federal Deposit Insurance Corporation (FDIC) or National Credit Union Administration (NCUA). This insurance is an indication of safety. However, even if you see the FDIC or NCUA sign at a financial institution, check the individual account options carefully. In addition to insured savings accounts, many savings institutions offer financial services that are not insured. These options carry more risk and are usually considered investments rather than savings plans.
- **Liquidity.** If you're saving for emergencies or recurring expenses, you want the ability to withdraw money whenever you need it. The ease with which savings or investments can be turned into cash to be spent is called

Class Activity. Have students rank the factors listed on pages 309-310 based on which they would consider most important when choosing a bank account. Ask students to share their answers with the class. Compare the answers given by different students and discuss reasons they might differ.

liquidity. Some savings accounts are highly liquid: You can withdraw money from them on the spur of the moment. Others have a fixed **term**—a period of time during which money must be kept on deposit. If you withdraw money before the end of the term, you must pay a penalty set by the bank, such as three or six months' interest.

- **Earnings.** When you check the interest rates for various types of accounts, be sure to find out the APY (annual percentage yield) as well. As you've learned, the APY includes the effects of compound interest. The higher the APY, the greater your earnings will be.

- **Taxes.** In most cases, you must pay income tax on the interest you earn from a savings account. However, some savings options offer tax advantages. For example, as you'll read later, the interest you earn on U.S. savings bonds is not subject to state and local taxes. When comparing different savings options, remember that any tax advantages let you keep more of the money you earn.
- **Restrictions.** Depending on the type of savings product you choose, you may have to comply with some restrictions. You may be required to deposit a certain amount, ranging from $5 to $2,500 or more, to open the account. You may have to maintain a certain minimum balance. You may be limited in the number of transactions you can make. By finding out about any restrictions ahead of time, you can make sure the account you choose will meet your needs.
- **Fees and service charges.** Be sure to find out about any fees that apply to each account you're considering. Is there a charge for ATM transactions? Is there a monthly maintenance fee for handling your account? What fee must you pay if your account falls below the minimum balance? Studying the account information carefully can save you money and help you avoid unpleasant surprises. See Figure 12-11.

12-11

Financial institutions provide information about their savings options in several ways. You might study a brochure, call for information by phone, or check the institution's Web site.

Class Activity. Have students create a chart comparing and contrasting savings accounts and money market accounts.

InfoSource. Ask students to "shop around" on the Web for the best savings interest rate they can find. Have them report their results to the class.

BASIC SAVINGS OPTIONS

You have a choice of savings options with differing interest rates and restrictions. In general, options with higher interest rates have more restrictions. It's common to start with a simple savings account. As more money is accumulated, some of it can be moved to higher-yielding forms of saving. Basic savings options include savings accounts, money market accounts, certificates of deposit, and savings bonds.

Savings Accounts

Generally, the most liquid savings option is an ordinary savings account. The minimum balance is usually lower than for other forms of savings, with fewer restrictions and fees. However, the interest paid on these savings accounts is generally lower as well.

In the past, deposits and withdrawals were always handled by a bank teller. They were recorded in a little book, called a passbook, that the customer brought to the bank. Today, many savings transactions are made at ATM machines, by phone, or online using home computers. Most savings account customers receive a statement at the end of the month that lists deposits, withdrawals, and interest earned.

Money Market Accounts

Another savings option is a **money market account**. This is a type of savings account in which deposits are invested by the financial institution to yield higher earnings. As a result, money market accounts generally have a higher interest rate than ordinary savings accounts. However, they also have more restrictions. For instance, most money market accounts require a higher minimum opening deposit, such as $2,500.

Unlike a savings account, a money market account usually lets you write checks—but only a few per month, such as three. Withdrawals and transfers are usually limited as well.

Money market *accounts* should not be confused with money market *funds*—a form of mutual fund (a type of investment discussed in Section 13.4). Unlike money market accounts, money market funds are not protected by FDIC or NCUA insurance.

InfoSource

Savings Interest Rates

To find out what interest rates are currently offered on savings accounts, money market accounts, and CDs:

- Call banks and other financial institutions, look at their newspaper ads, or check their Web sites.
- Visit a Web site that specializes in consumer financial advice. Look for a link to savings interest rates. Many sites let you compare the rates offered by different financial institutions across the nation or in a specific region.

Discussion. *Ask:* Under what circumstances would buying each type of bond be a good choice?

Caption Answer. Series EE and I bonds are most similar.

12-12

The three types of savings bonds are designed to meet different needs.

Which two types are most similar to one another?

Comparing Savings Bond Features

	SERIES EE	SERIES HH	SERIES I
Savings Strategy	To hold an investment that increases in value	To obtain current income in the form of interest payments	To hold an investment that's protected against inflation
How Purchased	• Through financial institutions • Online from the U.S. Treasury Dept. • Through payroll deduction	• In exchange for Series EE bonds • By reinvesting H bonds (an older type of savings bond)	• Through financial institutions • Online from the U.S. Treasury Dept. • Through payroll deduction
Smallest Denomination	$50	$500	$50
Purchase Price	50% of face value	Face value	Face value
Interest Rate	Variable rate (adjusted every 6 months)	Fixed rate	The sum of two rates (never less than zero): • A fixed rate • A variable rate based on the rate of inflation
When Interest Is Paid	When bond is cashed	Every 6 months by direct deposit to checking or savings account	When bond is cashed
Cashing the Bond	• Can be cashed after 6 months • Penalty if cashed before 5 years • Pays current value of bond (guaranteed higher than purchase price)	• Can be cashed after 6 months • Pays face value of bond	• Can be cashed after 6 months • Penalty if cashed before 5 years • Pays current value of bond (likely to be higher than purchase price)
Earnings Potential	• Increases in value every month • Guaranteed to reach face value in 17 years • May reach face value sooner, depending on interest rates • Continues earning interest for up to 30 years	• Bond itself does not increase in value • Earns interest for up to 20 years	• Generally increases in value every month (except in periods of deflation, when value could remain unchanged) • Earns interest for up to 30 years

Critical Thinking. ***Ask:*** What are the advantages and disadvantages of CDs to the depositor? To the financial institution?

Certificates of Deposit

A **certificate of deposit (CD)** is a certificate issued by a financial institution to indicate that money has been deposited for a certain term. The certificate specifies the amount deposited, the interest rate, and the length of the term.

Terms for CDs typically range from three months to five years. If you withdraw money before the end of the term, you must pay a substantial penalty, such as six months' interest. Generally, the longer the term, the higher the interest rate.

The interest rate is usually fixed until the end of the term. At that time, you can cash in the CD or renew it for another term at the current interest rate. In many cases, the CD is automatically renewed unless you notify the financial institution by a certain date.

The minimum deposit for a CD can range from $1,000 to $100,000. Although you may not be able to make additional deposits during the term of the CD, you can change the amount deposited when you renew it.

12-13

Series I savings bonds earn more in times of higher inflation. What other advantages do they offer? (Helen Keller is pictured in the sample bond below.)

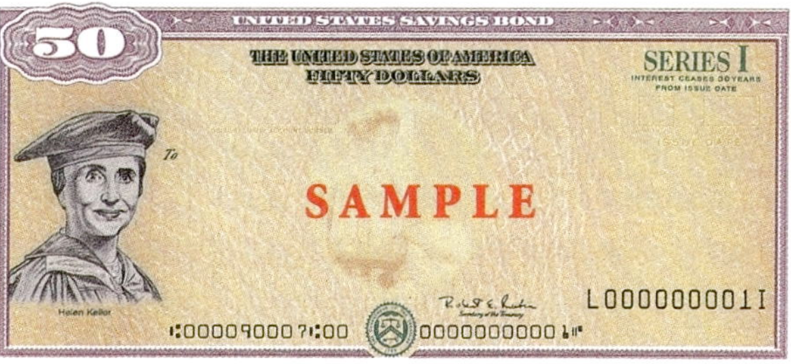

Answer Key. Answers to the Section Review questions are provided in the Section Lesson Plan located in the *Teacher Resource Guide.*

Savings Bonds

Savings bonds are nontransferable debt certificates issued by the U.S. Treasury. When you buy a savings bond, you're loaning money to the federal government, which eventually pays you back with interest.

Savings bonds are a very safe form of savings. Because they're backed by the federal government, there's no risk of losing money.

The interest earned on savings bonds is *exempt* (free) from state and local income taxes. However, it's subject to federal income tax. With most savings bonds, the federal tax can be *deferred* (postponed) until the bond is cashed in or stops earning interest.

The federal government currently issues three types of savings bonds. Figure 12-12 on page 312 shows how they are similar and different. A Series I bond is shown in Figure 12-13.

Section 12.4 Review

CHECK YOUR UNDERSTANDING

1. What factors should you consider before choosing a savings option?
2. What is the advantage of a savings option that's highly liquid? What is the disadvantage?
3. In what general circumstances might a certificate of deposit be a wise savings choice?

CONSUMER APPLICATION

Savings Bond Rates Find out the interest rates currently being paid on each type of U.S. savings bond. If a relative gave you a savings bond today, which type would you want it to be? Why?

CHAPTER 12

Review & Activities

CHAPTER SUMMARY

- Saving and investing provide money for future use and increase earnings. Savings may go for emergencies, expensive purchases, recurring expenses, retirement, and special goals. (12.1)
- A savings plan helps you set and reach savings goals. A smart plan includes "paying yourself first." (12.2)
- Earnings on savings grow faster when interest is compounded. The Rule of 72 helps you evaluate interest rates. (12.3)
- Safety, risk, and liquidity are concerns when choosing a savings option. Savings accounts, money market accounts, certificates of deposit, and savings bonds each offer certain advantages to savers. (12.4)

Savings Strategies: Tyler has been saving for a car since he was 14 years old, and for just as long, he has been finding other things to spend his savings on, like holiday gifts, a uniform for work, and a new cell phone. What strategies will help Tyler stick to his savings plan? (12.2, 12.4)

Reviewing Key Terms and Ideas

1. What is the difference between **saving** and **investing**? (12.1)
2. What are the benefits of saving for major purchases instead of using credit? (12.1)
3. Give three examples of financial goals for which an individual or family might decide to save. (12.1)
4. When should a person start saving for retirement? (12.1)
5. Describe the relationship between a budget and a **savings plan**. (12.2)
6. What is **discretionary income** and how does it relate to savings? (12.2)
7. Explain what "paying yourself first" means. Why is this strategy recommended? (12.2)
8. How does the method for calculating **compound interest** differ from that for **simple interest**? (12.3)
9. What does the **annual percentage yield** tell you? (12.3)
10. Under what circumstances might a small difference in interest rates make a large difference to the saver? (12.3)
11. How can you evaluate the safety of a savings account? (12.4)
12. What is **liquidity**? Why is it an important consideration when choosing a savings option? (12.4)
13. Which is more liquid, a **certificate of deposit** or a **money market account**? Explain. (12.4)
14. Why are **savings bonds** a safe form of savings? (12.4)

Answer Key. Answers to the Chapter Review & Activities are provided in the Teacher's Manual in the *Teacher Annotated Edition* of the text.

Thinking Critically

1. **Making Predictions:** Suppose a family has no emergency fund, and one of the primary wage earners loses his or her job. How might the lack of an emergency fund affect decisions about finding a new job? (12.1)
2. **Analyzing Economic Concepts:** If the economy were going through a period of high inflation, would you generally expect the interest rate on your savings account to go up, down, or stay the same? Why? (12.3)
3. **Understanding Cause and Effect:** How does buying a U.S. savings bond increase the federal government's debt? (12.4)
5. **Savings Bond Earnings:** Suppose you buy a Series EE savings bond with a face value of $50 and an interest rate of 4.8%. Use the Rule of 72 to predict about how long it would take the bond to reach face value at that interest rate. What else will affect when the bond reaches face value? (12.3, 12.4)
6. **Savings Choices:** Imagine that you've inherited $5,000, which you plan to use for your education. Explain how safety, liquidity, earnings, and restrictions influence what you do with the money. What savings option(s) might you choose? Why? (12.4)

Building Consumer Skills

1. **Emergency Fund:** About how much money should be in a three-month emergency fund if net salary is $1,800 monthly? What should the fund be for six months? Figure both time periods on a net salary of $2,200 monthly. (12.1)
2. **Savings Story:** "Crystal had a dream. It was something she wanted more than anything in the world." Continue this story about saving for a goal, or begin one your own way. Describe the goal, the reasons for it, the savings plan, and the outcome. (12.2)
3. **Quotation:** Write an explanation of this quote: "The safest way to double your money is to fold it over once and put it in your pocket." (Kin Hubbard) (12.2)
4. **Interest Calculation:** Show how to calculate simple interest and interest compounded quarterly. Use the example of $5,000 kept on deposit for one year at 4 percent. (12.3)

CONSUMER CONNECTIONS

- **Family:** Talk to your family about saving together for something special. The goal could be small (host a family barbecue) or big (out-of-town vacation or new computer). How could you motivate savings? Some people skip soft drinks or candy bars and put the money in a jar instead. Evaluate the results of your family's effort. (12.1)
- **Community:** Choose two financial institutions that serve your community. Compare interest rates and other features for three types of savings accounts. Make a chart of your findings. (12.4)

CHAPTER 13

Investments

Reading with Purpose

- Read the title of this chapter and describe in writing what you expect to learn from it.
- Write down each key term, leaving space for definitions.
- As you read the chapter, write the definition beside each term.
- After reading the chapter, write a paragraph describing what you learned.

SECTION 13.1

Investment Strategies

A savings account is safe and earns interest. However, someday you may be ready to consider investments that will earn more money for you in the long run.

Objectives

After studying this section, you should be able to:

- Explain factors to consider when evaluating investments.
- Describe principles for investing wisely.
- Identify ways to learn more about investing.

Key Terms

return
volatility
risk
diversification
portfolio
investment club

INVESTMENT CHARACTERISTICS

Investing is putting money to work so that it makes even more money for you over time. Investors can choose from many different kinds of investments, such as stocks, bonds, mutual funds, annuities, real estate, and others. You'll read more about them in later sections of this chapter. Before considering different types of investments, you should understand the basic characteristics by which investments are judged.

Return

Return is the income that an investment produces. Depending on the type of investment, returns can come in several forms. Some investments pay returns at regular intervals while you own them, similar to the way a savings account pays interest. Another way to gain a return is to sell an investment for a profit. For instance, if you sell an old comic book for more than your original purchase price, the increase in the comic book's value is a type of return.

Class Activity. Make three columns on the board. Label them "Liquidity," "Volatility," and "Risk." As a class, brainstorm a list of situations in which each of these factors might be important to a family. List them in the appropriate columns. Note how many situations fit in more than one column.

Tax advantages are another type of return to consider. Income from different types of investments may be subject to different rules when it comes to income tax. If two investments pay the same interest rate in a given year, the one that also saves you money on your taxes gives you a better return.

Liquidity

As explained in Chapter 12, *liquidity* is the ease with which assets can be converted to cash. If selling an investment takes several weeks or months, that investment is less liquid than one that can be sold immediately. A home, for example, is not considered a liquid investment because it might take months to sell.

Volatility

Volatility is the degree to which an investment's return or value may change. Some investments are quite volatile; their value swings up and down often, and can change suddenly and drastically. Others are relatively stable, changing in value more slowly and steadily. Compare the volatility of investments shown in Figure 13-1.

Risk

Every investment involves some degree of risk. **Risk** is the possibility of variation in the return on your investment. You might think of risk as uncertainty. Suppose, for instance, that you have an idea for starting a business. If your business succeeds, you could make a lot of money. However, you can't be certain that the business will succeed. It might fail. That's the risk you take. See Figure 13-2.

When you put your money into some other type of investment, rather than your own business, risk is still involved. Investments don't come with guarantees. You can,

Caption Answer. Allsmall Corp.

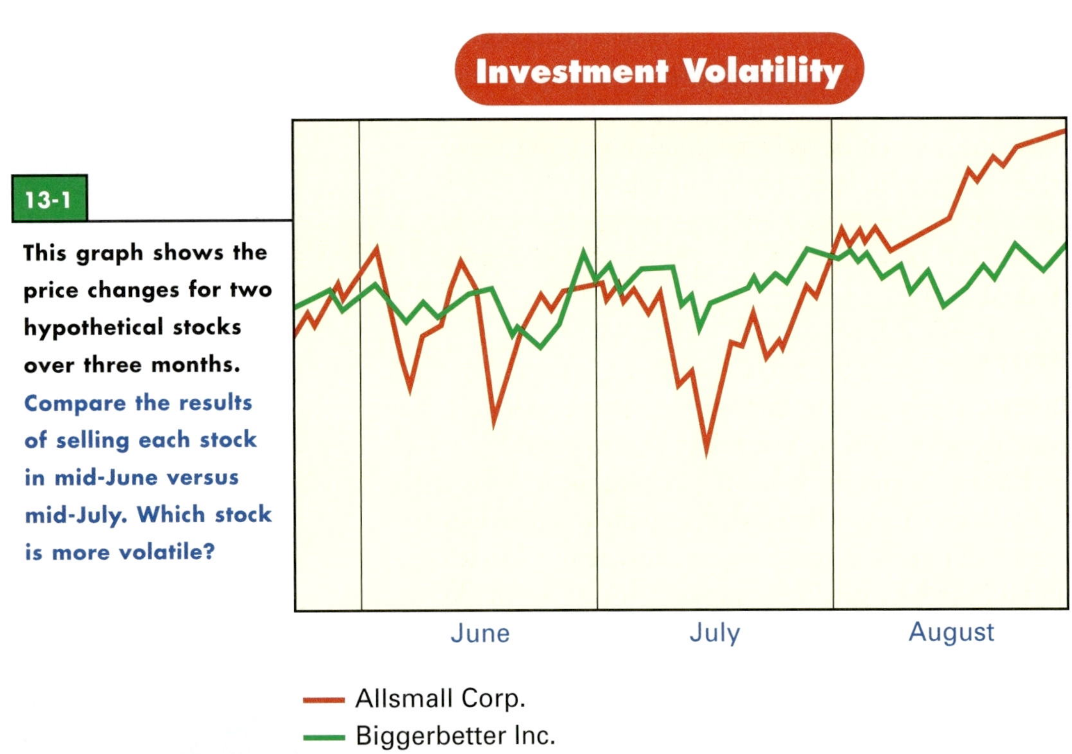

13-1

This graph shows the price changes for two hypothetical stocks over three months. Compare the results of selling each stock in mid-June versus mid-July. Which stock is more volatile?

Discussion. *Ask:* What types of investment do you think of as generally low risk? What types do you think of as high risk?

Critical Thinking. *Ask:* Why is it important to make sure the rest of your financial plan is in order before you think about investing?

13-2

If a company goes out of business, people who have invested in it lose all or part of their money. What motivates people to take the risk of investing in a business?

Class Activity. Have students interpret the meaning of this quotation from Thomas Fuller: "He that would have fruit must climb the tree."

however, make choices about how much risk you're willing to assume based on your investment goals. Some investments are considered *conservative*, or lower in risk. However, conservative investments also tend to produce lower returns. Generally, the greater the possible return an investment offers, the higher the degree of risk you must assume.

One type of risk is the chance that you'll lose everything you invested. While that possibility exists, it's rare. More often, risk means that your return may be lower than you had expected or even negative.

Risk can be related to volatility. A highly volatile investment might suddenly drop in value on the day you decide to sell it. If that happened, you wouldn't get the return you were expecting. On the other hand, volatility could work in your favor if the value suddenly goes up instead of down. That's the other side of risk—the possibility of greater returns.

Risk also may be associated with liquidity. If you're in a hurry to sell an investment, you might have to accept a low price just to complete the deal quickly. The less liquid an investment is, the higher this type of risk.

Another type of risk is *inflation risk.* Suppose an investment pays a return of 3%, but the inflation rate is 5%. In effect, you're losing money. Inflation is taking away purchasing power faster than you're earning money on your investment. Some investments that people think of as safe are actually high in inflation risk.

PRINCIPLES OF INVESTING

Before you think about investing, make sure the rest of your financial plan is in order. Do you follow a well-planned budget? Have you set aside enough savings to cover emergencies and short-term goals? Is your use of credit under control? If so, you may be ready to invest. You'll need a well-organized plan to stay on the right track.

Identify Your Objectives

Successful investing starts with a clear purpose and goals. "Getting rich" isn't specific enough! What will the money you invest and earn eventually be used for?

Team Activity. Have students work in small groups. Ask them to think of several investment objectives a family might have and come up with a time frame for achieving each objective. Then have them make a horizontal bar graph showing how the family could work toward these goals over time.

What amount can you afford to invest, and how much do you hope to end up with? What's your timeline—the length of time until the money should be available for use?

The timeline, in particular, has a significant effect on your investment choices. Generally, the shorter your timeline, the less risk you can afford to take. With a longer timeline, you can choose investments that are less liquid, more volatile, and higher in risk. Since higher-risk investments have the potential for better returns, a long timeline is to your advantage. See Figure 13-3.

Many people have more than one investment goal, each with its own target and timeline. Consider a couple in their early thirties. In another ten years, their eight-year-old child may be ready for college. They also want to build up money for retirement, which is more than 30 years away. Because each goal—college and retirement—has a different timeline, each may require a different mix of investments.

Focus on a Strategy

Knowing your financial goals and timeline can help you identify an appropriate investment strategy. Three basic types of investment strategies are income, growth, and tax reduction. They are closely related to the types of returns discussed earlier.

Jump$tart. Ask students how identifying objectives can help families make wise investment choices. *(Saving & Investing)*

13-3

This child may not be ready for college yet, but it's not too soon for his parents to begin investing for that goal. What is the advantage of starting to invest early?

Critical Thinking. ***Ask:*** For what category of investors might reducing tax obligations be a major part of their investment strategy?

- **Income.** This strategy involves putting money into investments that pay relatively dependable returns at regular intervals. They provide a source of income in the present and beyond. Someone who has retired would probably choose income investments.

- **Growth.** If you're more concerned with the future value of your investments than in receiving present income, you would probably follow a growth strategy. This means putting money into investments that may not pay returns now, but are likely to grow in value in the long run. Investing in a brand-new business is an example. The investment is unlikely to provide income right away, because businesses face a lot of expenses in their early years. In 10 or 20 years, however, the business may grow to be very prosperous and valuable.

Class Activity. Have students create a visual, such as a poster or a cartoon, illustrating the concept of diversifying investments.

- **Tax reduction.** For some people, reducing their income tax obligation is a primary goal of investing. They choose investments that offer the best tax advantages.

Diversify Your Investments

Whatever your financial goals, be sure to diversify your investments. **Diversification** is a strategy of making a variety of investments in order to reduce your exposure to risk. Suppose (just for fun) that you had a million dollars to invest, and you put it all into a single investment. If that one investment went bad, you could lose everything. By splitting your money among many different investments instead, you would greatly reduce your risk.

Wise investors develop a **portfolio**, or collection of investments, that is both diversified and well balanced. Balancing a portfolio means choosing investments with the right mix of characteristics for your situation, rather than simply diversifying at random.

DOLLARSandSENSE

Smart Investing

When making investment decisions, keep these tips in mind:

- Don't expect to make money overnight. It's reasonable to expect an overall return of 3% to 4% over the rate of inflation.
- Be wary of investments that sound too good to be true. Many people have lost their life savings in fraudulent get-rich-quick schemes.
- Update your investment plan periodically. As the years go by, the time frame for your long-term goals will become shorter, so you may need to invest more conservatively.
- Remember that it's your money, no one else's. Never rely solely on an advertisement or a friend's advice.

Research Activity. Have students do a keyword search on the Internet to find information about how age is related to asset allocation.

For instance, you'll want to balance higher-risk investments, such as stocks, with lower-risk ones, such as bonds. The right balance depends on your goals and timeline, as shown in Figure 13-4.

Asset allocation is the process of developing an overall plan for balancing an investment portfolio. With the help of a financial planner or other sources of information, you decide what percentage of your portfolio should be in different types of investments such as stocks, bonds, real estate, and liquid assets. No single asset allocation is right for everyone—it depends on your goals and timelines. Many financial experts consider asset allocation to be one of the most important factors in successful investing.

Balancing Risk

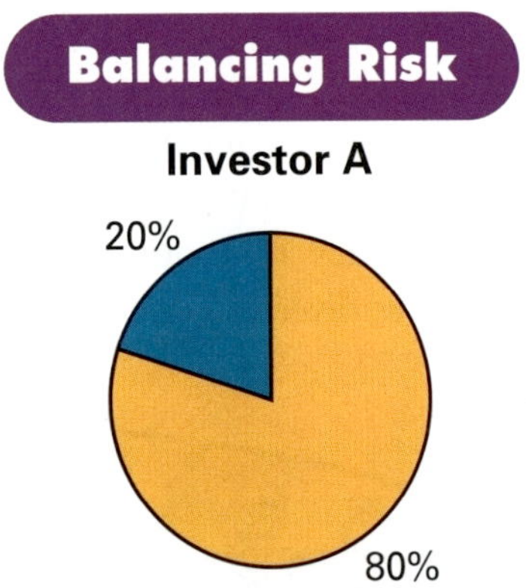

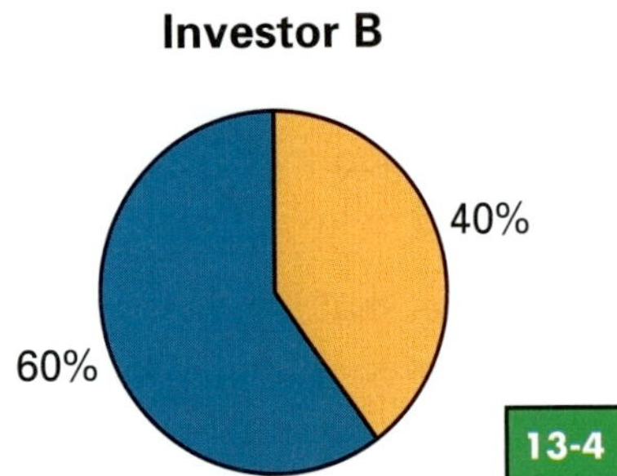

13-4

Most portfolios consist of a mixture of investments with different risk characteristics. The proportion of higher-risk to lower-risk investments varies from one investor to another. Which person is investing more conservatively? What are some possible reasons?

Jump$tart. Challenge students to develop a list of resources they could use to learn about investment options and strategies. *(Saving & Investing)*

LEARNING ABOUT INVESTING

To make intelligent decisions, you'll need to learn more about the principles of investing and gather objective information about the kinds of investments that are available. You can learn more about investment options and strategies in the following ways:

- **Reliable media sources.** A variety of books, magazines, newspapers, radio and television shows, and Web sites offer information about investing. As always, don't accept everything you read or hear as fact without investigating the source and evaluating its reliability.
- **Courses in financial planning.** Nearby colleges or universities probably offer credit and noncredit courses on investing.
- **Investment clubs.** Consider joining an **investment club**, a group of people who meet regularly to learn about investing and to make investments together. Club members pool their financial resources, sharing the risks and rewards of investing.

Caption Answer. Investor B is the more conservative investor. This investor may be older or closer to reaching his or her goals than Investor A.

Research Activity. Ask students to visit a Web site devoted to investing. Have them write a summary of the information the site offers for beginners.

Community Activity. Have students check local resources to find out about investment clubs in their area and who is eligible to join.

13-5

After sharing the information they've gathered, investment club members decide how to invest their money as a group. How might belonging to an investment club make it easier to achieve a diversified portfolio?

They usually split up the task of researching specific investments, then vote on whether to buy them and when to sell them. In this group setting, experienced investors can help newer members understand investing. For more information, contact the National Association of Investors Corporation (NAIC). See Figure 13-5.

- **Professional advisors.** Banks, brokerage firms, and independent financial planners offer investment advice. If you decide to work with an advisor, check out his or her credentials first, as explained in Section 9.5. Then evaluate all the advice you are given. After all, it's your money—you choose how you want to spend it, and you also choose how you want to invest it.

Answer Key. Answers to the Section Review questions are provided in the Section Lesson Plan located in the *Teacher Resource Guide.*

Section 13.1 Review

CHECK YOUR UNDERSTANDING

1. What are three possible ways investors can get a return on their investments?
2. Why is it important to diversify your investments?
3. How can an investment club help someone learn about investing?

CONSUMER APPLICATION

Investment Characteristics Suppose you have been saving for college, but you'd like to get a higher rate of return than the interest on a savings account. You'll need the money in two years. Discuss the characteristics you would look for in an investment. Be sure your answer includes the concepts of liquidity, volatility, and risk.

Objectives

After studying this section, you should be able to:

- Compare and contrast investment options designed for retirement planning.
- Explain the need to take an active role in retirement planning.

Key Terms

pension plan
401(k) plan
IRA
Roth IRA
Keogh plan

SECTION 13.2

Retirement Planning

Many people stay vital and active for 20 years or more after they retire. If you start planning and investing soon enough, you can spend those years enjoying yourself instead of worrying about paying the bills. It's up to you!

SOCIAL SECURITY RETIREMENT BENEFITS

Planning for retirement is easier when you understand the various types of retirement income that you might receive. One of the basic sources of retirement income is Social Security benefits. The Social Security fund is administered by the federal government and funded through a tax paid by citizens who are currently working.

The amount of Social Security retirement benefits you will receive is influenced by how long you work, your earned income, and the age at which you apply for the benefits. Once a year, workers who pay Social Security taxes receive a benefits statement from the Social Security Administration. The statement includes an estimated amount for monthly Social Security retirement benefits.

The earliest you can apply for Social Security retirement benefits is age 62. However, the amount of benefits is permanently reduced if you apply before reaching full retirement age. For anyone born after 1959, the full retirement age is 67.

Point Out. Social Security was started in the 1930s as a form of insurance against income loss. It is not meant to be the sole source of retirement funding.

PENSION PLANS

In addition to Social Security benefits, many retirees can draw money from one or more pension plans. A **pension plan** is any retirement plan offered to a company's employees. A retirement fund is set aside for each employee who participates. Money in the fund is contributed by the employer, the employee, or both, depending on the rules of the plan. The money in the fund is invested to grow over time. The contributions and earnings are not taxed until the employee draws from the account at retirement. See Figure 13-6.

Company plans are either defined-benefit or defined-contribution plans. A key difference between them is whether the employer or the employee assumes investment risk.

- **Defined-benefit plan.** In this type of plan, a company pays its retiring employees a specified amount each month, based on each employee's salary history and years of employment. The employer assumes all investment risk, since the specified benefit must be paid even if the employer's investments lose value. For this reason, defined-benefit plans are no longer common.

Critical Thinking. ***Ask:*** Why is it a disadvantage for a large percentage of pension contributions to be invested in a single company?

- **Defined-contribution plan.** In this type of plan, employees can contribute to a retirement fund that is invested on their behalf. In some cases, the employer also contributes. Upon retirement, a participating employee is eligible to receive the original contributions plus the return made on the investments. Since the amount the employee receives depends on the investment results, the employee assumes all risk.

401(k) Plans

Many employers offer a 401(k) plan as their pension plan. A **401(k) plan** is a type of defined-contribution pension plan to which the employee contributes on a pretax basis.

13-6

Pension plans help provide financial security after retirement. Funds that accumulate in the plan during the working years are subject to income tax once they are withdrawn. How does the tax deferral benefit the plan participant?

Critical Thinking. ***Ask:*** What are the advantages and disadvantages of a profit-sharing plan for employers and for employees?

Caption Answer. Immediate income tax reduction; employer's matching contribution; investment earnings that build up over time.

13-7

If someday you're given the opportunity to sign up for a 401(k), don't pass it up. Try to contribute at least as much as the employer will match. What are three ways in which a 401(k) plan can potentially benefit employees?

Class Activity. Have students write advice to Emily, who says: "I'm only 24 and working at my first job after college. Since I have my whole life to save for retirement, I don't need to start now."

By directly contributing to the plan, the employee reduces the amount of income that is subject to tax. In addition, some employers will match 401(k) contributions up to a certain percentage. Both the employee's contributions and the company's matching dollars earn an investment return. The employee may be able to choose from several investment options made available by the employer. If so, the employee must consider how assets are allocated in the plan and make adjustments when needed.

Most plans require that employees keep the money in the plan until they reach a certain age, generally 59½. Penalties are assessed for early withdrawal. However, many plans are portable, meaning that employees who leave the company can transfer, or "roll over," benefits into another retirement plan. The amount that can be moved depends on the degree to which the employee is *vested*, or entitled to keep plan benefits. Employees must generally stay with the company a certain number of years in order to become fully vested. See Figure 13-7.

403(b) Plans

A 403(b) plan is much like a 401(k) plan, except only employees of certain nonprofit organizations can participate. Teachers and other school employees, librarians, and some doctors and nurses are just a few people who can contribute to a 403(b) plan.

Other Defined-Contribution Plans

Some types of defined-contribution plans give employees a stake in the company's profitability. For example, in a *profit-sharing plan*, the employer allocates a portion of the company's annual profits to each participating employee.

An *Employee Stock Ownership Plan (ESOP)* is another example. Instead of profits, employers give participants shares of stock in their company. These shares may not be sold until the employee leaves the company or retires. If the company does well, ESOP participants share in that success through the increased value of their stock. The main disadvantage for ESOP participants is lack of diversity. It may not be wise to rely on an ESOP as the sole source of retirement income.

Class Activity. As a class, compare how much an investor will earn, after taxes, by investing $1,000 a year for 30 years in a traditional IRA and in a Roth IRA. Assume that both IRAs earn 10 percent per year and that the investor now pays 25 percent in taxes and will pay 15 percent after retirement.

PERSONAL INVESTMENTS

In addition to or instead of a retirement plan offered through your employer, you can invest for retirement on your own. These plans offer tax advantages in exchange for restrictions on when you can withdraw money prior to retirement.

Individual Retirement Accounts

An individual retirement account, or **IRA**, is a personal savings plan that enables workers and their spouses to set aside money for retirement. Contributions are limited by law to specific dollar amounts each year. Two types of IRAs are used for retirement planning.

- **Traditional IRA.** Contributions to this type of IRA may be tax-deductible. Instead of counting as taxable income in the year it's earned, money put into the IRA will be subject to tax when it's withdrawn in retirement. By then, many people have a smaller income and are taxed at a lower rate. Whether traditional IRA contributions are tax-deductible depends on your income level and whether you're covered by an employer's retirement plan. If you're not eligible for the tax deduction, you can still make nondeductible contributions. Annual contributions to an IRA can be made until age 70½. That's also the age by which withdrawals must begin. Withdrawals made prior to age 59½ are usually subject to a penalty.
- **Roth IRA.** A **Roth IRA** is an IRA in which contributions are not tax-deductible; however, earnings accumulate tax-free. After the account is at least five years old, you can make withdrawals tax-free and penalty-free if you are at least 59½ or if you use the money to become a first-time homeowner.

Keogh Plans

A **Keogh** (KEY-oh) **plan** is a federally approved, defined-contribution, tax-deferred retirement plan designed specifically for self-employed people. Individuals set up their own plans according to federal guidelines. Contributions are fully tax-deductible, and early withdrawals are generally subject to the same penalties as traditional IRAs. See Figure 13-8.

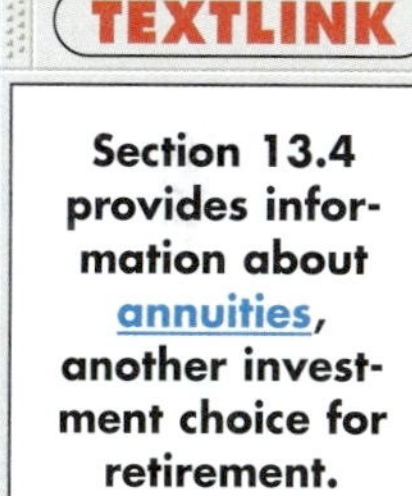

Section 13.4 provides information about annuities, another investment choice for retirement.

13-8

Keogh plans provide small business owners with a way to establish their own retirement plan.

Discussion. ***Ask:*** Why do you think so many people put off saving for retirement? What are the drawbacks of this approach?

TAKING CHARGE OF RETIREMENT PLANNING

Years ago, workers seldom needed to take an active role in planning their retirement. Most employers offered defined-benefit pension plans to which workers did not have to contribute. Between those plans and Social Security benefits, many people took it for granted that they would have an adequate income during retirement.

Caption Answer. Two other factors affecting growth are the amount invested and the rate of return.

However, that's no longer the case. Since traditional defined-benefit, employer-funded pensions are disappearing, most of the responsibility for planning your retirement falls on your own shoulders. A sound retirement plan will help ensure that you enjoy a measure of financial stability after you retire. You might even be able to retire early, giving yourself the gift of extra leisure time while you are still in good health to enjoy it. Without a retirement plan, you could face a future of financial uncertainties and hardships. Thus, it's in your best interest to take the initiative and start planning and investing for retirement—the sooner the better.

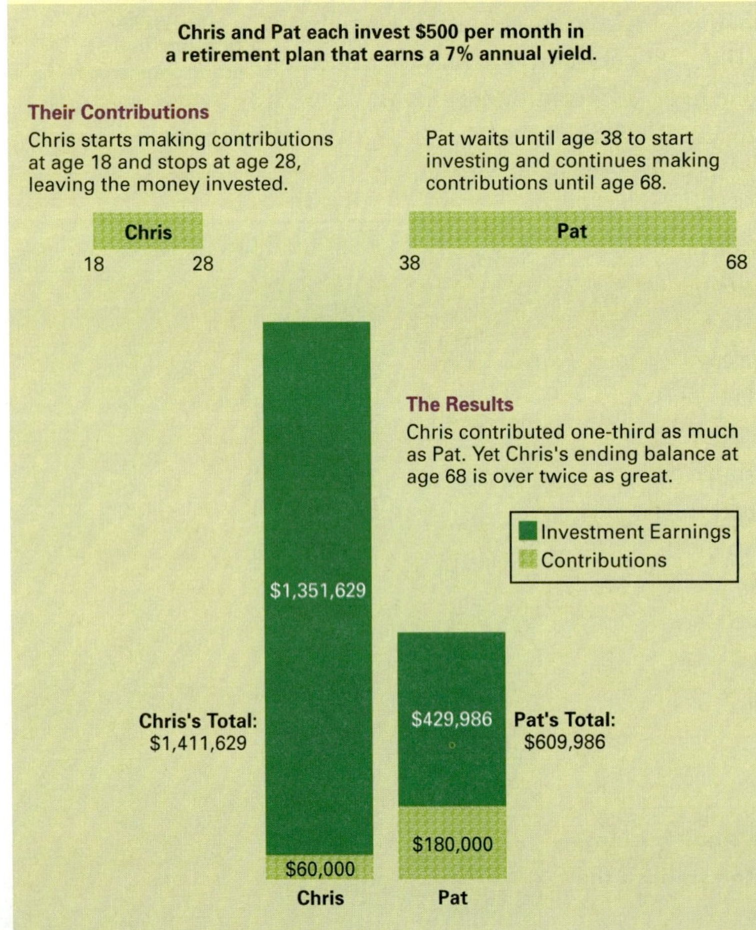

Start Early

When you're just beginning your career, you have a key advantage when it comes to retirement planning: Time is on your side. The final balance in your retirement account is determined not so much by the total amount invested, but by the number of years the investment is allowed to grow. For an example that illustrates this point, take a look at Figure 13-9.

Class Activity. Have students write an essay explaining how each type of investment (Social Security, pension plan, personal savings) plays an important role in retirement planning.

13-9

Time is a major factor affecting how an investment grows. **Name two others.**

Research Activity. Have students search online for retirement planning tools. Have them use one such tool to compare the results of investing two different amounts each month or of investing for two different periods of time, as shown in Figure 13-9.

As the figure shows, someone who starts early will come out ahead of someone who invests a larger sum but starts later. Why? Even after contributions stop, the amount already invested continues to earn money over the life of the account. Of course, the account could grow even more if contributions don't stop. In the example shown, if Chris kept contributing $500 a month for another 40 years, the ending balance would be over $2.7 million! Although inflation will affect its future purchasing power, that sum is definitely much better than Pat's results.

Review Your Plan Regularly

Once you have a retirement investment plan, review it on a regular basis. You can consult a financial advisor or use retirement planning tools found in financial software and on the Web.

- **Set your goals.** Decide when you want to retire and how much monthly income you want in retirement. Identify about how long this income will need to last.
- **Make estimates and calculations.** Estimate the monthly amount you'll receive from Social Security and defined-benefit plans. Subtract that amount from your desired monthly retirement income to find how much income you'll need from other sources. Calculate the balance needed in your retirement fund when you retire in order to provide the necessary income. Finally, estimate the future balance of your retirement fund based on how much is in it now, your projected contributions, and an estimated investment yield. Don't forget to factor in inflation.
- **Adjust your plan if needed.** If your anticipated needs exceed your anticipated retirement fund, you can increase the amount you're setting aside for retirement or look for ways to get a higher return on your investment. You also could consider retiring later or working part-time during retirement. By reviewing your retirement plan once a year, you can identify a potential shortfall while there's still plenty of time to make adjustments.

Answer Key. Answers to the Section Review questions are provided in the Section Lesson Plan located in the *Teacher Resource Guide.*

Section 13.2 Review

CHECK YOUR UNDERSTANDING

1. What's the main difference between a defined-benefit plan and a defined-contribution plan?
2. How are traditional and Roth IRAs different?
3. Why is it important to begin investing early for retirement?

CONSUMER APPLICATION

Starting a Retirement Plan Imagine that you've just started your first full-time job after college. You'll be eligible to contribute to your employer's 401(k) plan after one year. What steps could you take in the meantime to start a retirement investment plan?

The Stock Market

For those who are investing with long-term goals in mind, the stock market is worth considering. Stock prices will always rise and fall, but careful management can reduce the risks.

Objectives

After studying this section, you should be able to:

- Explain basic concepts of stock ownership and the stock market.
- Evaluate the risks involved in stock ownership.
- Describe how to research stocks.

Key Terms

stock
shares
shareholders
stock exchange
stock market
dividend
stockbroker

STOCK MARKET BASICS

Suppose that a corporation needs money for expansion or product development. Instead of borrowing from a bank, it might decide to raise the money from investors by selling **stock**—ownership interest in the corporation. It does this by making **shares**, or individual units of ownership, available for purchase. Investors who purchase shares of stock are called **shareholders**. Shareholders are actually part-owners of the company. They have the opportunity to make money if the company does well, but they also bear the risk of losing money if the company is unsuccessful or the economy experiences a downturn.

How Stocks Are Traded

When a company first issues stock, investors buy shares directly from the company in an *initial public offering*. After that, investors usually buy the stock from other investors who own it and wish to sell it.

Research Activity. Have students use newspaper or Internet stock listings to track the prices of five companies' stocks for a week. Have them create a line graph showing the stocks' daily ups and downs. At the end of the week, have them calculate each stock's price range—high, low, and average.

The organized trading of stocks is known as the **stock market**. It works much like an auction. Those people interested in purchasing stock bid on it, offering the price they want to pay. If someone who owns the stock is willing to sell it at the offered price, the transaction is made.

Stocks may be traded at a **stock exchange**, a central location where stocks are sold on a trading floor. Historically, Wall Street, in Manhattan, has been the center of stock trading activities. It is the home of the oldest stock exchange, the New York Stock Exchange (NYSE), where many of the largest and wealthiest companies in this country trade. See Figure 13-10. The second-largest stock exchange is the American Stock Exchange (AMEX), where stocks of many smaller and medium-sized companies are traded. Stocks that meet the requirements for being traded on a particular stock exchange are said to be *listed* on that exchange.

Stocks that are not listed on any stock exchange are called *over-the-counter* (OTC) stocks. Instead of being bought and sold on a trading floor, they are traded by phone and computer through global electronic networks. The largest such network is the Nasdaq (NAZ-dak) Stock Market. In addition to handling trades of over-the-counter stocks, Nasdaq also lists stocks.

Regulating the Stock Market

The Securities and Exchange Commission (SEC) is the federal agency that protects the interests of investors by regulating companies that sell stock. The SEC requires these companies to publicly disclose honest and accurate information about their financial health. It can bring lawsuits against companies that make fraudulent statements about their financial transactions. The SEC also oversees the activities of stock exchanges, OTC stocks, investment advisors, and anyone else who is involved in the buying and selling of stocks. Although the NYSE, AMEX, and Nasdaq regulate themselves, the SEC is the final authority over their activities.

13-10

The trading floor of the New York Stock Exchange may seem chaotic, but it's actually a highly organized system.

Research Activity. Ask students to search online to find out roughly what percentage of stocks pay dividends.

Returns on Stocks

Investors who own shares of stock may receive returns in two forms.

- **Dividends.** Owners of stock may periodically receive a **dividend**, a payment to shareholders that represents a portion of the company's net profits. Dividends are usually paid four times a year in the form of a check or additional shares of stock. Not all stocks pay dividends. See Figure 13-11.
- **Capital gains and losses.** If you buy shares when their value is low and sell them when their value is high, your profit is called a *capital gain.* On the other hand, if you sell shares for a lower price than you paid for them, you lose money and suffer a *capital loss.*

Point Out. If you have a capital gain, you must pay capital gains tax. Capital gains are taxed at a different rate from ordinary income.

Working with a Stockbroker

A **stockbroker** is an individual or firm that will buy and sell stock for clients according to their instructions. Other terms for stockbroker include *broker* and *brokerage.*

If you're looking for a stockbroker, consider how much service you want. Some people prefer to pay more for *full-service brokers,* who provide investment advice in addition to handling stock transactions. *Discount brokers* offer a more basic service and are substantially less expensive.

Many brokers offer services over the Internet. Clients who sign up for the online service can make trades using a personal computer. Online brokers often make research materials available on their Web sites to help clients choose stocks and make trading decisions.

Critical Thinking. ***Ask:*** Why is the cost of a stockbroker's services an important consideration to an investor?

13-11

Companies use news releases to announce the amount of their dividends. How might the size of the dividend affect the price of the company's stock?

Critical Thinking. ***Ask:*** How can an individual investor evaluate the health of a company? What might be some signs that a company is doing well?

Other Ways to Buy Stock

It's possible to invest in the stock market without going through a broker. Money in a 401(k) plan might be entirely or partly invested in stocks, for example, or an employee might own company stock through an ESOP. Mutual funds, which you will read about in Section 13.4, are another option.

It may also be possible to buy a company's stock directly from the company through a *direct stock plan.* Although there may be a fee for participating in such a plan, the cost is less than paying a broker. Most plans allow participants to invest small amounts and to automatically reinvest dividends.

THE RISKS OF OWNING STOCK

Much of the risk involved with stocks comes from their volatility. Stock prices can move up or down in value every day, sometimes dramatically.

Why Stock Prices Change

In simple terms, stock prices go up and down because of supply and demand. The greater the number of people who want to own a particular stock, the higher its price will be. The fewer people who want to own that stock, the lower its price.

InfoSource. Have students consult the Web site of the Securities and Exchange Commission for more information about direct stock plans.

Many factors can influence the number of investors who want to own a stock, and therefore the stock's price. They include:

- **The company's health.** Investors and brokers study financial statistics that indicate how well a particular company and its stock are doing. Indications that the company is well managed and thriving encourage investors to buy more stock. This increase in demand causes the stock price to rise. If there are signs that the company is in a decline, the stock value is likely to go down.
- **Industry trends.** Investors and brokers also consider trends that might affect the health of an entire industry. For instance, if the federal government were to impose additional health and safety regulations on the poultry industry, costs for poultry producers would go up and profits would go down. The value of poultry industry stocks would probably decline for a time.
- **Economic factors.** For many reasons, stock prices can be affected by the state of the economy. For instance, low interest rates on loans are good for businesses and encourage investors to buy stock.

Direct Stock Plans

To find companies that offer direct stock plans:

- Try typing "direct stock plans" into a Web search site. You'll probably find links to sites that provide databases of companies offering direct stock plans.
- Look for investor information at the Web sites of specific companies of interest.

Research Activity. Ask students to read a report on the overall performance of the stock market over the past year. Have them make note of specific events or economic factors that affected the price of stocks overall and the price of stocks in certain industries.

That's one reason the stock market tends to go up when interest rates go down. During a recession, stocks tend to fall.

- **National and world events.** The election of a new leader, the passage of trade legislation, the start or end of a war—these and many more events can cause stock prices to go up or down, depending on how investors feel the event will affect businesses. See Figure 13-12.

Tracking the Stock Market

Every day, some stocks go up in price and some go down. Indexes are a way to measure overall price changes in the stock market. For example, the Nasdaq Composite Index tracks the prices of more than 5,000 domestic stocks traded on the Nasdaq system. The Dow Jones Industrial Average tracks 30 stocks of large, well-known companies in industries such as financial services, technology, retail, entertainment, and consumer goods. The Standard & Poor's 500 measures the average performance of 500 prominent industrial, transportation, financial, and utility stocks.

Discussion. ***Ask:*** What events have caused stock fluctuations in recent years? How might the long-range direction of stock prices be affected?

13-12

Major world events can cause stock prices to dip and investors to become nervous. However, in the long run, stock indexes such as the S&P 500 have continued to move upward. What would you advise long-term investors to do during a national or global crisis?

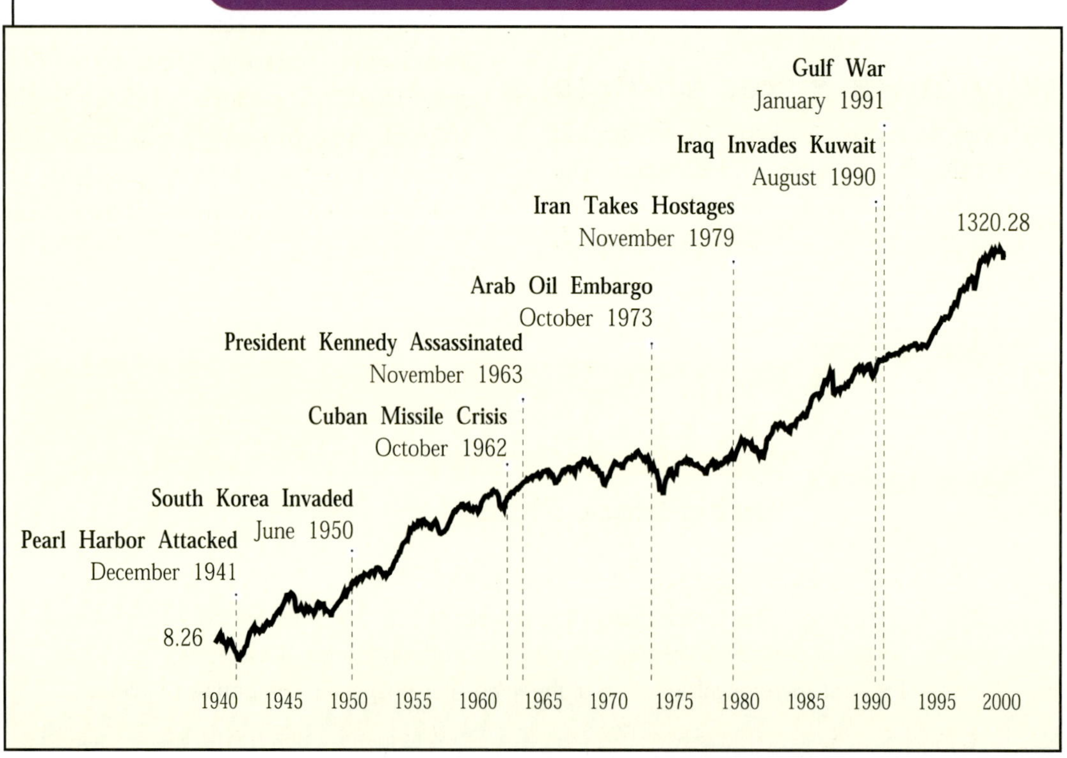

Critical Thinking. ***Ask:*** Why might some investors choose to invest in stocks that they know to be high risk?

Types of Stock and Their Risks

All stocks involve risk, but some more than others. Being able to recognize differences in risk will help you choose stocks that are appropriate for your investment strategy.

Two types of stock may be issued by a single company: *common stock* and *preferred stock.* Common stock entitles shareholders to vote on any matter affecting the company, while preferred stock does not give shareholders voting rights. Preferred stock has less risk because the dividend rate is fixed. With common stock, dividends vary, increasing both risk and potential return. See Figure 13-13.

13-13

Most shares of stock are common stock. The "par value" shown on a stock certificate is usually a small amount that has no relationship to the market price.

NUMBER 0000000

SHARES 100

ORGANIZED UNDER THE LAWS OF THE STATE OF ILLINOIS

ZZZ CORPORATION

This Certifies That Sam A. Shareholder is the owner of One hundred COMMON SHARES $1.00 per share PAR VALUE OF full paid and non-assessable transferable on the books of the Corporation in person or by duly authorized Attorney upon surrender of this Certificate properly endorsed.

In Witness Whereof the said Corporation has caused this Certificate to be signed by its duly authorized officers and sealed with the Seal of the Corporation.

this 25th day of September A.D. 20 05

Cynthia Carter, SECRETARY

Kathryn Thompson, PRESIDENT

No. 914

Jump$tart. Discuss with students the possible reasons why stocks tend to yield higher returns than other investments. *(Saving & Investing)*

Stocks of large companies with a proven track record of reliable earnings and dividends are called *blue chip* stocks. They're considered lower in risk than other stocks because it's unlikely that such solid companies will fail. On the other hand, *growth stocks*—those of companies that are growing rapidly, often because they are new and innovative—carry more risk. *Penny stocks,* those costing less than a dollar per share, should be avoided because of their extremely high risk.

Minimizing the Risks

Despite their risks, stocks have a place in most investment portfolios. Over any ten-year period, stocks have consistently offered higher returns than any other form of investment. You can minimize your risk by keeping these points in mind.

- Consider stocks a long-term investment. Because of its volatility, the stock market isn't the place for money that you'll need in the next five years.

Point Out. One way for investors to buy stocks is to put money into an index fund. Rather than buying the stock of an individual company, they spread their investment out across every stock in a given index, such as the S&P 500. This diversifies their investment and reduces risk.

- Invest in stocks only as part of a diversified portfolio. Make sure the stocks you hold come from not only different companies, but several different industries. Balance higher and lower risk stocks in keeping with your investment goals.
- Make sure you're willing either to spend time researching and monitoring your stocks or to pay a competent financial advisor to do it for you. If you don't have the resources to keep track of your portfolio, consider a mutual fund, discussed in Section 13.4.
- Try not to become overly concerned with day-to-day ups and downs in stock prices. If you find yourself wanting to make frequent stock trades in reaction, reconsider your investment strategy. Investing in stocks requires discipline to ride out short-term volatility.

RESEARCHING STOCKS

Before investing in a particular stock, learn as much as you can about the company. One way to start is with firsthand experience. Have you used the company's products or shopped in its stores? What did you think of them? Does the company seem popular with consumers?

However, you'll need to do more research to learn whether the company is well managed and has a history of delivering good financial results. One important source of information is the company's annual report. It provides a summary of the company's goals and results for the previous year, as well as detailed financial data. Many companies make their annual reports available on their Web sites.

Discussion. ***Ask:*** Why might you need to take your temperament into account when choosing an investment strategy?

Translating Stock Quotations

52-week Hi	52-week Lo	Stock	Sym	Div	Yld %	PE	Vol 100s	Hi	Lo	Close	Net Chg
95^{44}	69^{88}	ZZZ Corp.	ZZZ	1.76	2.1	43	17535	85^{10}	83^{25}	84^{80}	$+1^{81}$

52-week Hi Lo: The highest price ($95.44) and lowest price ($69.88) paid for the stock in the last 52 weeks.

Stock: The name of the company, often abbreviated.

Sym: The stock's ticker symbol.

Div: The annual dividend per share ($1.76 in this example). Not all stocks pay dividends.

Yld %: The yield, or dividend yield. It is calculated as the annual dividend divided by the most recent closing price. In this example, the yield is 2.1% (1.76 ÷ 84.80 = 0.021).

PE: The price/earnings ratio, a basic measure of a stock's value. It represents the ratio of the stock price to the annual earnings per share.

Vol 100s: The daily volume, or number of shares traded on the most recent trading day, in multiples of 100. In this example, 1,753,500 shares of ZZZ were traded.

Hi Lo: The highest price ($85.10) and lowest price ($83.25) paid for the stock during the most recent trading day.

Close: The closing price (price for the last trade) on the most recent trading day.

Net Chg: The net change, or difference between the most recent closing price and the previous closing price.

13-14

Newspaper stock quotes vary but may include some or all of the information shown here. Similar information is available from online sources. Find a stock quote in a newspaper or online and interpret its information.

Research Activity. Have students read the annual report of a company that interests them and write an evaluation of the company's financial health.

Answer Key. Answers to the Section Review questions are provided in the Section Lesson Plan located in the *Teacher Resource Guide.*

13-15

A trend of rising stock prices is known as a *bull market,* while a trend of falling prices is called a *bear market.*

What would you do if the price of a stock you owned was falling during a bull market? During a bear market?

Stock quotes can be found in most large daily newspapers. Figure 13-14 shows an example and explains what information it includes. Many financial Web sites provide similar stock information. A series of one to five letters called a *ticker symbol* uniquely identifies each stock.

Reading daily and weekly business magazines and newspapers is helpful to any investor. Look for information about not only specific companies, but industry trends and the overall economic climate. For example, you'll be better able to interpret changes in the price of a stock that you own if you know whether the market in general is going up or down. See Figure 13-15.

After you choose and purchase a stock, continue to monitor the company's economic health. If it appears that a decline in dividends or stock value is due to chronic problems within the company, you might want to cut your losses by selling your shares. Vigilance—along with knowledge and patience—is a key to successfully investing in the stock market.

Section 13.3 Review

CHECK YOUR UNDERSTANDING

1. Name several possible influences on a stock's volatility.
2. What is the difference between common stock and preferred stock?
3. Describe how you would research a stock before investing in it.

CONSUMER APPLICATION

Investment Advice Todd wants to make as much as he can from his investments. He was told that investing in the new XYZ Company would lead to very large returns. He's thinking about placing all of his money in XYZ stock. Write a letter to Todd explaining the risks of his approach.

Objectives

After studying this section, you should be able to:

- Distinguish between different types of bonds.
- Explain the advantages of mutual funds.
- Describe insurance investment products.
- Evaluate the risks of investing in real estate, commodities, and collectibles.

Key Terms

bonds
mutual fund
prospectus
annuity
real estate
commodities

SECTION 13.4

Other Investments

Besides stocks and retirement accounts, many kinds of investments might have a place in a well-planned portfolio. Each has its own risks and potential for returns.

BONDS

Corporations and governments can obtain funds by issuing certificates of debt called **bonds**. For the group that issues it, a bond is a way to borrow money. For the person that buys it, a bond is an investment. The buyer gives money to the bond issuer, who promises to repay the debt plus an additional amount by a certain date, called the *maturity date.*

Bonds provide a return in one of two ways. Some bonds pay interest at stated intervals, such as twice a year. Other bonds don't provide regular interest payments, but instead are purchased for less than their face value. The investor receives the full face value—also known as the *par value*—at maturity.

Types of Bonds

Investors can choose from several types of bonds. They make choices based on the amount they want to invest, how much risk they're willing to assume, and the return they want.

Class Activity. Have students create a chart or other visual comparing the features of different types of bonds.

- **Savings bonds.** U.S. savings bonds, discussed in Chapter 12, are considered so safe and reliable that many people think of them as a form of savings rather than investment.

- **Treasury securities.** In addition to savings bonds, the U.S. Treasury issues three other types of bonds, known collectively as *Treasury securities.* Like savings bonds, Treasury securities are safe investments because they're guaranteed by the U.S. government. Another advantage is that earnings are not subject to state or local taxes. The government issues Treasury securities by selling them at auction. A bank or broker can help you place a bid. It's also possible to buy Treasury securities from other investors in much the same way that you might buy stocks. Figure 13-16 describes the three types of Treasury securities.

Community Activity. Have students consult a local bank to find out whether it is possible to invest in Treasury securities or corporate bonds there.

- **Municipal bonds.** Bonds issued by local and state governments are known as *municipal bonds.* They can be purchased through brokers or dealers. Interest earned on municipal bonds is free from federal income tax and, in some cases, state and local taxes. This tax advantage usually makes up for the lower returns municipal bonds provide.

- **Corporate bonds.** Bonds issued by corporations can be purchased through brokers or banks, normally in minimum amounts of $1,000. They generally have higher rates of return than government bonds but carry more risk.

Bond Ratings

A bond's level of risk depends on the issuer's ability to repay the debt with interest. Rating services, including Standard & Poor's Rating Service and Moody's Investor Service, assign ratings to bonds based on the financial condition of the issuer. Both services use similar rating scales. The highest rating, AAA or Aaa, is for bonds with the lowest risk.

13-16

The U.S. Treasury can decide which of these types of securities to issue at any given time. Find out which ones are currently offered.

Types of Treasury Securities

	MATURITY PERIOD	MINIMUM PURCHASE AMOUNT	FORM OF RETURN
Treasury bills	13 to 52 weeks	$1,000 (face value)	Difference between purchase price and face value paid at maturity
Treasury notes	1 to 10 years	$1,000	Semiannual interest payments
Treasury bonds	More than 10 years	$1,000	Semiannual interest payments

Team Activity. Give each student an index card with the name of a stock or bond (real or fictitious) and its rate of return (positive or negative). Then have small groups pool their resources into "funds" and average together the returns listed on their cards. Ask how many students did better by diversifying.

Highly rated bonds are referred to as *investment-grade bonds.* Those with low ratings are known as *high-yield bonds,* because of their high rate of return, or *junk bonds,* because of their high risk.

MUTUAL FUNDS

A **mutual fund** is a group of investments that is held in common by many individual investors. Individuals purchase shares in the mutual fund. They might invest only a few thousand dollars each, but when their money is combined, it can add up to millions. An investment company uses the money to purchase and manage various *securities*—stocks, bonds, and similar types of investments. Earnings are divided among the fund's investors.

Compared to individual stocks and bonds, mutual funds have two key advantages.

- **Diversification.** A single fund may hold securities from hundreds of different companies—something few investors could accomplish on their own. This broad diversification significantly reduces risk. See Figure 13-17.
- **Professional management.** Few individual investors have the knowledge, time, dedication, or resources to select stocks and bonds and continually track their portfolios. Mutual funds are managed by experienced, professional financial experts. They have access to extensive research, market information, skilled analysts and traders, and technology to help them make investment decisions.

Mutual Fund Styles

Each mutual fund has an objective. Funds with similar objectives can be placed in groups, or *styles.* Here are a few examples of the many available mutual fund styles.

13-17

Because it includes a mixture of investments—such as various stocks and bonds, for example—a mutual fund provides diversity that can help shield investors from risk.

Critical Thinking. ***Ask:*** What are the advantages and disadvantages of investing in mutual funds rather than individual securities?

Point Out. Their low fees give index funds a better rate of return, on average, than most managed mutual funds.

- **Money market funds** are restricted by law to certain types of short-term investments. As a result, money market funds are among the lowest in both risk and return. The objective for money market investors is to maintain the value of their investment amount.
- **Bond funds** are sometimes called fixed-income funds. Their risk and return vary widely depending on the types of bonds in which they invest.
- **Stock funds** are further categorized into types. *Aggressive growth funds* normally hold the highest risk. These funds do not produce much interest income or dividends but usually grow in value. *Growth funds,* like aggressive growth funds, seek stocks whose prices are expected to rise. However, growth funds are lower risk than aggressive growth funds. *Equity income* funds are for investors who want current income from their funds. The fund managers choose stocks that are expected to pay high dividends rather than stocks that are expected to grow in price. *Index funds* invest in the stocks that are included in an index such as the Standard & Poor's 500. They tend to have lower management fees than other mutual funds.

Economic Impact & Issues. ***Ask:*** What does an increase in new home construction mean for the economy?

Economic Impact & Issues

Economic Indicators and the Stock Market

As you've read, economic indicators are like thermometers—they give clues to the economy's health. Investors in the stock market are especially watchful of leading indicators, because a change may foretell a new economic trend. New home construction and the unemployment rate are two examples of leading indicators. As predictors of the economy's direction, leading indicators can detect trends that will affect certain types of companies more than others. In turn, the companies may become more profitable—or less so—in the future.

For example, suppose the Federal Reserve announces it is selling government securities. Knowing this will raise interest rates, you might avoid buying shares in a company that relies on consumer borrowing to sell their products, such as a steelmaker. A steelmaker provides materials for automobiles, large appliances, and commercial buildings, and consumer borrowing helps drive these businesses.

In fact, you might think twice about buying any stocks at all. Higher interest rates discourage businesses from borrowing, too. The harder it is to get credit, the harder it is for a company to expand.

As the example shows, the stock market is itself a leading economic indicator. A lack of investing shows a lack of optimism about the economy. In contrast, enthusiastic trading usually foretells an economy on the upswing, as confident investors try to take advantage of expected economic growth.

FIGURE IT OUT

Imagine that three fast-food chains have announced slow sales for two straight months. Write a dialogue between an investor and a stockbroker that shows how this news might affect an investment strategy.

Jump$tart. Ask students to read the prospectus of a mutual fund and write a summary of the types of information it provides. *(Saving & Investing)*

- **International funds** invest in either the stocks of foreign corporations or the bonds of foreign governments or agencies. Although their performance can be difficult to predict, international funds can help diversify investment portfolios.

Choosing a Mutual Fund

Magazine articles that list and compare mutual funds can help investors narrow down their choices. Before making a final decision, further investigation is needed.

- **Read the prospectus.** A **prospectus** is a legal document that provides potential investors with information about a mutual fund or other security. It describes the fund's objectives and management. The prospectus also includes facts and figures about the fund's past performance. Remember, however, that how well a fund did in the past doesn't necessarily indicate how well it will do in the future. The factors that helped bring about previous returns may have changed or be about to change.
- **Check out the fees.** Management fees help pay for the fund's management, advertising, and other costs. In addition, investors may have to pay a *load*, or sales charge, when they make a fund transaction. The load is a percentage of the transaction amount. *No-load funds* have no sales charges, but other fees may be higher or investors may be required to hold shares longer.

Caption Answer. Endowment insurance ensures that your goal will be met.

INSURANCE AS AN INVESTMENT

Usually the primary purpose of insurance is to protect against financial loss. Two types of insurance products, however, are purchased with investment as the main goal.

Insurance is explained further in Chapter 14.

Endowment Insurance

An endowment insurance policy might be purchased with a specific investment goal in mind, such as education expenses or retirement. After making payments for a certain number of years or until a certain age, the purchaser receives a benefit equal to the face value of the policy. If, however, the person dies before then, the benefit is paid to those named in the policy. See Figure 13-18.

13-18

Endowment insurance can be a way to invest for a specific goal. What advantage does it offer compared to other investments?

Community Activity. Ask students to find out how local property values have changed over the past ten years.

Annuities

An **annuity** is a contract purchased from an insurance company. The contract guarantees to provide payments at regular intervals in the future, usually after age 59½. If the annuity holder dies before payments start, a benefit is paid to survivors. Annuities generally don't pay high returns, but they provide safe, guaranteed income and tax advantages.

Fixed annuities offer a fixed rate of return guaranteed by the insurance company. *Variable annuities* pay variable rates of return, depending on how well investments made by the insurance company have performed. *Equity-indexed annuities* offer a guaranteed minimum return with the possibility of higher returns based on the performance of a stock market index.

Caption Answer. Possible answers include the condition of the property, its location, the state of the economy, and interest rates.

MORE INVESTMENT OPTIONS

Retirement funds, stocks, bonds, and mutual funds are among the most common types of investments, but they are not the only options. Some people choose to make substantial investments in real estate, the commodities market, and collectibles.

Real Estate

Many people invest in **real estate**—land and any structures on it—by owning their own homes. In addition, some people purchase property such as apartment buildings, office and retail space, or parcels of unused land. Some real estate investors earn income by renting their property to others. Most hope their property will go up in value so it can be resold for a profit. Investing in real estate offers a good hedge against inflation, since property values typically rise in step with other price increases. See Figure 13-19.

13-19

Real estate can be a good investment if the property continues to grow in value. What factors might affect the value of property?

Research Activity. Ask students whether they have ever collected anything. Find out what types of items students collected. Then tell students to visit an online trading site, such as eBay, to find out what types of prices are available for these collectibles today.

One drawback of real estate is that it's not as liquid as many other investments. If you need to sell real estate, you may have to wait weeks or months to get a fair price. In addition, it can be time consuming and expensive to maintain the property. Finding reliable renters is not always easy, and dealing with unreliable ones can cause many headaches. It can also be difficult to diversify real estate investments.

Commodities

Wheat, corn, iron ore, natural gas, and precious metals are examples of **commodities**, or basic economic goods bought and sold in quantity. An agreement to deliver a particular commodity at a specific price at a certain date in the future is called a *futures contract.* The terms of the contract also spell out the quantity and quality of goods to be delivered. At a commodities or futures exchange, these contracts are bought and sold on a trading floor. The Chicago Board of Trade is the largest commodities exchange in the United States. The Commodities Futures Trading Commission (CFTC) regulates trading in commodities.

Commodities trading requires relatively little in the way of an initial investment and has the potential for high returns. However, it is very risky. Even experienced investors can easily lose money.

Answer Key. Answers to the Section Review questions are provided in the Section Lesson Plan located in the *Teacher Resource Guide.*

Collectibles

People collect all sorts of things as a hobby. Some collect items that they hope are, or might someday be, considered rare and valuable—art, antiques, books, stamps, coins, gems, even old toys and comic books. If the items increase in value over time, they might be sold at a profit. However, few such items actually go up in value very much. Even if they do, there's no guarantee of finding a buyer willing to pay what they're worth. It's usually best to focus on the enjoyment a collection brings rather than its possible value as an investment.

Section 13.4 Review

CHECK YOUR UNDERSTANDING

1. How is a Treasury bill different from other types of Treasury securities?
2. What advantages do mutual funds have over investing in individual stocks?
3. Name one advantage and one disadvantage of investing in real estate.

CONSUMER APPLICATION

Local Municipal Bonds Research whether your community, or one nearby, has issued municipal bonds within the last 20 years. What type of project were the bonds issued to fund? What face value and interest rate did they have? For how long were the bonds issued?

SECTION 13.5

Estate Planning

Few people like to think about estate planning. However, having a plan for how assets and debts will be managed after death can bring peace of mind.

Objectives

After studying this section, you should be able to:

- Explain the benefits of estate planning.
- Describe the purpose of a will and other estate planning documents.
- Compare ways to plan for funeral expenses.

Key Terms

estate
estate planning
will
executor
beneficiary
intestate
living trust
power of attorney
living will

WHAT IS ESTATE PLANNING?

Most adults have a variety of assets and liabilities, such as savings accounts, investments, a home, personal property, and unpaid loans and bills. The assets and liabilities left behind by a deceased person are that person's **estate**. Settling the estate involves paying off liabilities and distributing assets in accordance with the law. **Estate planning** is the process of making legal and financial arrangements for how one's property should be administered before and after death.

Estate planning is important for several reasons. It helps people provide financially for loved ones or for a favorite organization or cause. It can reduce the time and legal complications involved in settling the estate and minimize the amount of taxes that must be paid. In addition, an estate plan can address what happens if a person, although still living, becomes incapable of making financial and health decisions.

Steps in Estate Planning

The first step in estate planning is to review your assets and liabilities by creating a balance sheet, as explained in

Class Activity. Have students practice writing out wills in class, either for themselves or for some fictitious person. Remind them to include all the elements of a will discussed in the textbook: an executor, guardians for children, and instructions for assets and liabilities.

Section 9.1. Next, think about your objectives and gather information that can help you make decisions about how to dispose of your estate. You may want to enlist the expertise of a financial professional who can help you understand your options. Books about estate planning also can be helpful. The final step is to prepare the necessary legal and financial documents, usually with the help of an attorney or other appropriate professional. However, you may be able to create legally valid documents using self-guided, do-it-yourself forms or software.

PREPARING A WILL

The most essential part of an estate plan is a **will**, a legal document in which a person directs how his or her estate is to be distributed after death. In most states, a person must be at least 18 years old to prepare a will.

The Functions of a Will

A will should provide detailed and specific instructions about how you want your estate to be administered. See Figure 13-20. Typically, a will should fulfill at least the following four basic functions.

- **Identify an executor.** An **executor** is the individual who is in charge of handling the affairs of an estate. The executor handles such tasks as taking an inventory of assets, settling debts, and paying taxes.

  Some people designate an attorney or financial advisor as their executor; others choose a responsible family member or friend.

- **Identify a guardian for children, if needed.** A person who has children younger than 18 years of age should designate a legal guardian to care for them in the event of the death of both parents. The person named should be consulted first and agree to fulfill this important responsibility.

- **Give instructions for liabilities.** Any outstanding debts or obligations must be paid before the remaining assets can be distributed.

13-20

Wills have been used for thousands of years. This is an excerpt from the will prepared by George Washington. Give possible reasons why people developed the custom of making wills.

(Detail. Conservation of Art on Paper, Inc.)

Community Activity. Ask students to find out what laws apply in your state to the cases of people who die intestate.

- **Give instructions for assets.** A person or group designated to receive some or all of a deceased person's assets is called a **beneficiary**. A spouse, children, siblings and other relatives, friends, and favorite organizations are typical choices. Each beneficiary may be given a set dollar amount, specific assets (such as a home or shares of stock), or a percentage of the estate. See Figure 13-21.

If There Is No Will

A person who dies without a valid will is said to die **intestate**. In this case, state law will determine how the estate is to be settled. This process can be very time consuming and expensive, and the outcome may not reflect the deceased person's wishes. In some cases, property in the estate is owned by more than one person. If so, the other owners inherit the property by right of survivorship.

After Preparing the Will

Wills must fulfill certain legal requirements. Most states require that wills be typewritten, and they must be signed and dated. Witnesses—who cannot be beneficiaries—must watch as you sign your will, and they must sign and date the document as well.

Critical Thinking. *Ask:* Why shouldn't you keep your original will in your safe deposit box?

Your signed will should be kept in a place accessible to your executor. Keep a copy of your will—*not* the original—in a safe deposit box.

As your circumstances change, you might find that you want to change the terms of your will. You may be able to do so by preparing a document called a *codicil*, which is a legal amendment to a will. However, in many cases it's best to prepare a new will and specify that it replaces any prior wills you made.

13-21

Some people choose to support an organization by naming it as a beneficiary in their will. For example, when Lydia Moss Bradley died in 1908, she left her estate to the educational institution that she had founded some years before, which is now known as Bradley University. (Bradley University/ Duane Zehr)

Research Activity. Ask students to search online for information about preparing your own will and other end-of-life documents.

Discussion. ***Ask:*** Under what circumstances might someone choose to create a living trust or a durable power of attorney?

PREPARING OTHER DOCUMENTS

In addition to making a will, regularly review and update the beneficiaries you've selected for assets that aren't covered in wills. These include pension plans, IRAs, 401(k) plans, life insurance policies, and annuities. You may also need other legal documents to successfully manage your estate. Originals of these documents should be stored in a safe place with other important papers.

- **Living trust.** A **living trust** is a legal arrangement that can serve as an alternative to a will. It transfers control of a living person's assets to a *trustee*, someone who holds and manages assets for someone else. The trustee can be a person, such as an attorney, or an institution, such as a bank. If you were to set up a living trust, you would continue to make use of your assets while you are alive. Upon your death, they would be transferred to your beneficiary without having to go through *probate*, the legal process involved in filing a will.
- **Durable power of attorney.** A **power of attorney** is a legal document assigning someone the right to act on a person's behalf. Despite "attorney" in the name, you can grant this power to anyone you choose. "Durable" means that if you become incapable of making decisions—including the decision to revoke the power of attorney—it will still remain in force. Some people prepare two separate power of attorney documents, one for financial decisions and another for health care decisions. Others combine both designations in a single document. The person given the right to make decisions is often referred to as an agent or proxy. Preparing a power of attorney helps ensure that someone you trust will be able to make decisions for you if necessary.

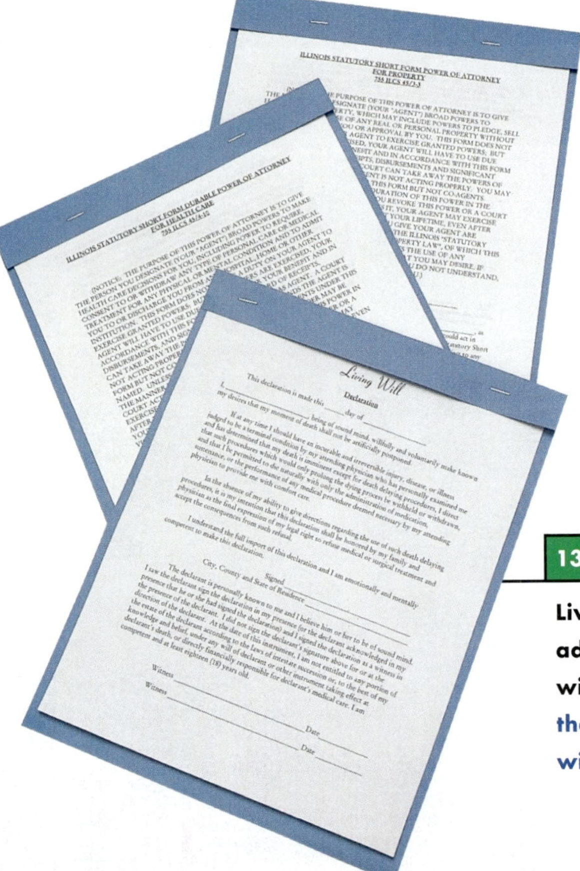

13-22

Living wills and other documents address needs not met by traditional wills. Why is it important to discuss the provisions of these documents with family members?

Community Activity. Explain to students that funeral and memorial societies are another funeral planning option. These cooperative groups help relatives deal with funeral planning and can negotiate lower rates on funeral services. Ask students to find out about memorial societies located in your area.

- **Living will.** A **living will** is a legal document that outlines a person's wishes for medical treatment under specific circumstances. A typical living will directs physicians and loved ones to discontinue artificial life support if the person is near death with no hope of recovery and is unable to communicate his or her wishes at the time. A copy of the document should be kept in the person's medical file. The person's physician, family members, and the agent named in a health care power of attorney (if any) should be made aware of the living will and its details. See Figure 13-22.

FUNERAL PLANNING

The average cost of a funeral is close to $10,000. It's just as appropriate to use consumer skills to help control funeral expenses as it is to plan any other major purchase.

The FTC Funeral Rule requires funeral homes to disclose their prices over the telephone on request. They must also provide itemized price lists outlining the options available and their costs.

Prepaid Funerals and Other Options

Some people arrange and pay for their funeral in advance. By prepaying, consumers can pay today's prices instead of inflated future prices. They can also plan exactly the type of funeral service they desire, sparing family members the responsibility of making those decisions at a difficult time.

However, consider the disadvantages of prepaying. The money is tied up for years and earns no interest. If you move, you may not be able to transfer your funeral arrangements to another location. You also take a risk that the funeral home or cemetery you contract with could go out of business in the meantime.

Instead of paying in advance, you can plan to cover funeral expenses with an insurance policy or other investments. Specific desires for your funeral arrangements can be spelled out in a letter of final instructions. Such a letter can also include personal messages to relatives and friends, as well as helpful information such as a list of financial accounts, locations of important documents, and names of legal and financial advisors. Make sure the letter is accessible to a close family member, and give a copy to the executor of your will.

Answer Key. Answers to the Section Review questions are provided in the Section Lesson Plan located in the *Teacher Resource Guide.*

Section 13.5 Review

CHECK YOUR UNDERSTANDING

1. What are the benefits of estate planning?
2. What is the purpose of a will? A living will? A living trust?
3. What are the advantages of paying for funeral expenses through an insurance policy rather than a prepaid contract?

CONSUMER APPLICATION

State Succession Law Find out how assets are divided if a resident of your state dies without a will. Summarize the results for someone with and without a surviving spouse and child.

CHAPTER 13

Review & Activities

CHAPTER SUMMARY

- Investments are judged on return, liquidity, volatility, and risk. You can learn to invest wisely. (13.1)
- Retirement income can come from varied sources. Retirement planning should begin early. (13.2)
- Stock is a way to share in the ownership of a business. With a careful approach, you can reduce stock risks. (13.3)
- Bonds, mutual funds, and other investments, which differ in risk, can diversify a portfolio. (13.4)
- Creating an estate plan provides security and protection. (13.5)

Get Rich—Quick! Two new members of Sarah's informal, online investment club are urging everyone to buy stock in a new company they just "discovered." The club tracked the stock for two weeks. Its price rose considerably. Everyone is eager to buy before it goes higher, but Sarah has doubts. What arguments can she make for delaying investment in the company? (13.1)

Reviewing Key Terms and Ideas

1. What is the relationship between **return** and **risk**? (13.1)
2. Why should inflation be a consideration when evaluating investments? (13.1)
3. Describe three basic investment strategies. (13.1)
4. Explain why **diversification** is a wise investment strategy. (13.1)
5. Name four ways to learn more about investing. (13.1)
6. How does a **401(k) plan** differ from an **IRA**? (13.2)
7. Why should you take an active role in planning for retirement? (13.2)
8. What should be done when reviewing a retirement plan? (13.2)
9. Basically, how does the **stock market** work? (13.3)
10. Explain the function of a **stock exchange**. (13.3)
11. How might you earn **dividends**? (13.3)
12. To minimize risk in the stock market, what points should you keep in mind? (13.3)
13. Compare corporate and municipal **bonds**. (13.4)
14. Why might some people prefer a **mutual fund** over other investments? (13.4)
15. What is an **annuity**? (13.4)
16. What is the risk when trading in **commodities**? (13.4)
17. What are the four basic functions of a **will**? (13.5)
18. What happens when a person has no will? (13.5)
19. Why might you draw up a **power of attorney**? (13.5)

Answer Key. Answers to the Chapter Review & Activities are provided in the Teacher's Manual in the *Teacher Annotated Edition* of the text.

Thinking Critically

1. **Analyzing Consequences:** To what extent do you think the government, employers, and employees should go to ensure that employees have an adequate income after retirement? What are the consequences to individuals, businesses, and society if that need is not met? (13.2)
2. **Drawing Conclusions:** Some employees fail to enroll in available 401(k) plans, even when the employer matches contributions. Why do you think they don't sign up? What are the drawbacks to not enrolling? (13.2)
3. **Making Comparisons:** What are pros and cons of trading stocks online instead of trading through a broker by phone? (13.3)
4. **Analyzing Economic Concepts:** When the federal government runs a deficit, it issues Treasury securities. How might this affect the national debt? (13.4)

Building Consumer Skills

1. **Investment Strategies:** Investigate and list ways to invest for income, growth, and tax reduction. (13.1, 13.3, 13.4)
2. **IRA Choices:** Learn about the IRAs offered by a local financial institution. What investment options are available? What are the terms and restrictions of the accounts? (13.2)
3. **Risk Evaluation:** Create a diagram that classifies different types of investments as low, medium, and high risk. Include stocks, bonds, real estate, commodities, and collectibles. If necessary, break the types into subtypes. Explain the specific risks of each investment and why you categorized it as you did. (13.1, 13.3, 13.4)
4. **Researching Stocks:** Using at least three different sources, gather information about a particular company's stock. Compare the kinds of information provided by the sources and explain the value to investors. (13.3)
5. **Funeral Costs:** Calculate the costs of a funeral, including cremation versus burial. Compare the pros and cons of two ways a family can prepare for these expenses. (13.5)

CONSUMER CONNECTIONS

- **Family:** Ask family members whether they have prepared a will, a durable power of attorney, and a living will. Discuss the benefits of having these documents. (13.5)
- **Community:** Find out whether an investment club is active in your community. If so, talk to a member about how the club works. Summarize your findings. (13.1)

CHAPTER 14

Insurance

Reading with Purpose

- Write down the colored headings in this chapter.
- As you read the text under each heading, visualize what you are reading.
- Reflect on what you read by writing a few sentences under each heading to describe it.
- Reread your notes.

SECTION 14.1

How Insurance Works

Objectives

After studying this section, you should be able to:

- Describe the role of insurance in managing risk.
- Explain basic insurance concepts.
- Give guidelines for choosing insurance.

Key Terms

liability
insurance
policy
exclusion
endorsement
premium
claim
deductible
co-insurance

Life is full of risks. If you play a sport, you risk being injured. If you own a car, you risk having it stolen or getting in an accident. While insurance can't prevent a sports injury or a stolen car, it can minimize the financial impact of these and other events.

MANAGING FINANCIAL RISK

Many events can cause financial losses. They fall into three broad categories of risks.

- **Property risks.** You risk financial loss if your property is damaged, destroyed, or stolen. Examples range from the theft of a pair of shoes to a fire that completely destroys your home.
- **Personal risks.** Illness, injury, disability, or death of a family member can result in the loss of that person's income, as well as added expenses such as medical bills and funeral costs.
- **Liability risks.** Suppose you run a red light and cause a traffic accident in which someone is injured. You could be responsible for paying the person's medical bills. **Liability** means legal responsibility to pay someone who has suffered an injury or loss caused by you.

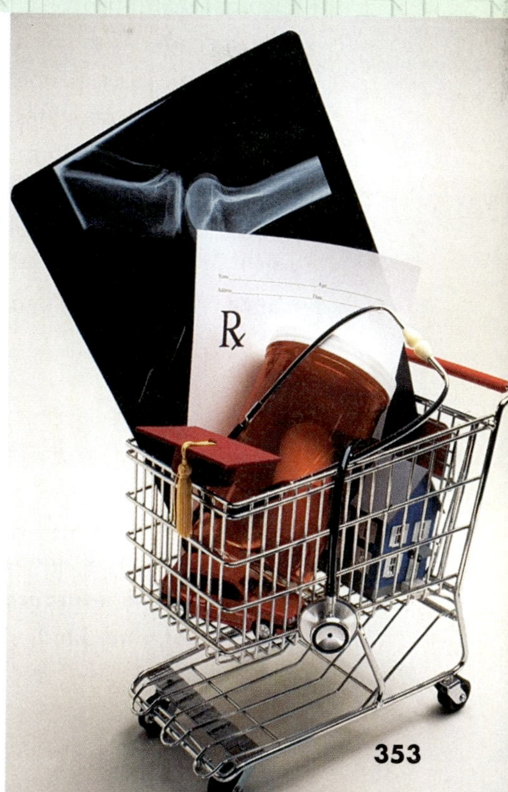

Jump$tart. List the three categories of risk on the board. Ask students how each type of risk could result in financial loss. Then ask them to name some strategies (in addition to buying insurance) for managing each category of risk. *(Money Management)*

Insurance and Risk Management

All of these potential risks must somehow be managed. Your choices for managing risk include reducing risk, avoiding it, or retaining it. For example, keeping your car locked and installing antitheft devices will help reduce the risk that it will be stolen. Still, some risk remains. The only way to completely avoid the risk is not to have a car at all. You can retain the risk by accepting the fact that if the car is stolen, you'll use your own money to buy another one.

Insurance provides another way to manage risk. **Insurance** is purchased protection that guarantees to pay you in the event of certain specified losses. It is a way of limiting any one person's financial risk by sharing the risk among a large group of people. This is called *transferring* risk. Through the services of an insurance company, many people pay into a common fund. The few who actually do have losses draw on that money. In other words, many people pay a little so that no one person has to pay a lot.

In some cases, people are required to have insurance. Most states, for example, have laws requiring minimum auto insurance. However, even if there were no such laws or rules, most people would still want the protection against financial hardship that insurance provides. See Figure 14-1.

Two Basic Insurance Principles

Insurance is based on the principle of *indemnity*, which means restoring the insured person to the financial position he or she was in before the loss occurred. In other words, insurance is not designed to leave people better off after a loss than they were before.

To buy insurance, you must have an *insurable interest* to protect, meaning that you have a financial stake in the life or property being insured. You can't buy insurance on your friend's car, for example, since its loss would not cause financial hardship to you.

14-1

Families risk financial ruin if they don't purchase insurance to protect their home. **What other kinds of property should you protect?**

Class Activity. Ask students to make a list of risks they might face as young adults. Then have them prioritize the risks according to the importance of insuring against loss. Remind them that when prioritizing, they should consider both the likelihood and the potential costs of each risk.

Prioritizing Risk

Purchasing insurance to protect against every possible loss would be very expensive. Consumers must decide which risks they can afford to retain and which they cannot. Suppose you could buy insurance that would replace your clothing if it became stained or torn. Would such insurance be worth the price? Consider the opportunity cost of the items you'd have to give up to pay for the insurance. You might decide that you can easily manage the risk of damaged clothing in other ways. In contrast, if you lost all your possessions in a fire and had no insurance, how would you recover financially? Insurance to protect against that type of financial loss is more necessary and valuable.

UNDERSTANDING INSURANCE TERMS

Before acquiring insurance, it helps to know the meaning of some basic terms used in the insurance industry.

- The **policy** is the written agreement between the policyholder—the consumer who purchases insurance—and the insurance company. The rights and obligations of each are spelled out in the policy, which is a legal contract. The policyholder agrees to make regular payments to the insurance company. In return, the insurance company agrees to pay the policyholder if certain events occur, such as a fire or theft.
- **Exclusions** are specific risks not covered by a policy, such as normal wear and tear or damage caused intentionally.
- **Endorsements**, sometimes called *riders*, are attachments to a standard insurance policy that add or take away coverage. For example, an endorsement might add coverage for a valuable collection. See Figure 14-2.
- **Premiums** are payments insured people make to the insurance company in exchange for coverage.
- A **claim** is a request for payment of a loss. If your TV set were stolen, you would file a claim with your insurance company.

14-2

A collection of valuable items might not be covered by a standard policy. An endorsement could provide added protection. Name other possessions that might require an endorsement.

Critical Thinking. ***Ask:*** Why is a deductible an incentive to take precautions against loss?

Eonomic Impact & Issues. Have students research insurance costs and create a graphic organizer on high-risk versus low-risk areas.

- Many insurance policies have a **deductible**, a set amount the insured person must pay per loss before the insurer will pay benefits. For example, if a kitchen fire caused $1,000 worth of damage and your home insurance policy had a $250 deductible, the insurance company would cover only $750 of the damages. Insurance companies have deductibles to help keep their costs down and to give the policyholder an incentive to take precautions against loss. Often, the higher your deductible, the lower your premiums.
- **Co-insurance** is an arrangement in which the insurance company and the insured person share the costs of claims after the deductible is met. For example, if you file a claim for a dentist's bill, the insurance company might subtract the deductible and then pay 80% of the remainder. You would be responsible for the other 20% as well as the deductible.

UNDERSTANDING INSURANCE COSTS

Premiums provide an insurance company with money for operating expenses and payment of losses, plus a profit. Since insurance companies can't know in advance how much policyholders will claim for losses, they estimate the amount based on what they have paid out in other years and set insurance rates accordingly. If losses are increasing, premiums go up. If losses are decreasing, premiums may go down.

Economic Impact & Issues

Insuring Against Disaster

Floods, wildfires, and other natural disasters make an obvious impact on an area's physical landscape. They can also affect the availability of insurance, which can shape the region's economy.

One reason insurance companies stay in business is that they pay relatively few claims at one time. After a natural disaster, however, tens of thousands of policyholders may be entitled to payment for property damage. As a result, some companies no longer offer catastrophe insurance in disaster-prone areas—flood insurance along low-lying coastlines, for example, or fire insurance in the "interface" between cities and forests. Those that do offer such insurance often charge very high premiums.

As you might imagine, high insurance premiums can dampen economic growth. Businesses in disaster-prone areas may need disaster insurance to get a loan. Costly premiums keep new businesses from starting up and discourage existing ones from expanding. Homeowners often find that policies don't cover the ever-rising costs of repairs or rebuilding, so some simply leave their property uninsured and assume all of the financial risks of a natural disaster.

FIGURE IT OUT

Locate an article on possible solutions for the problem of insuring property in high-risk areas. Discuss the advantages and disadvantages of each proposal in class.

Critical Thinking. ***Ask:*** Is it fair for insurance companies to base an individual's premiums on characteristics that are not under his or her control, such as gender, age, or location? Why or why not? Can you think of another way to assign risk that would be fair to both individuals and insurance companies?

Rates are not the same everywhere. Each state is divided into rating territories, such as a city, a part of a city, a suburb, or a rural area. Insurance companies collect figures for each territory showing how much they paid out in claims. They base their rates on these figures.

If two policyholders in the same area purchase the same amount and type of coverage from the same insurance company, their premiums may differ. That's because insurance companies base their premium rates on statistical analysis of the risks posed by different groups of people. For example, statistics show that males under age 25 pose the highest risk for vehicle insurance, since they have more accidents than any other defined driving group. Consequently, their insurance premiums are the highest among the groups.

CHOOSING INSURANCE

Most people need at least the following four basic types of insurance. Each provides protection in specific situations. See Figure 14-3.

- **Auto insurance** can compensate you if your vehicle is stolen or if it's hit by a falling tree limb, for example. In case of a traffic accident, auto insurance can provide payment for damage to vehicles and other property and injuries to you or others.

14-3

Auto, home, health, and life: It's crucial that you protect yourself and your family by carrying each type of insurance. Which risks—property, personal, and liability—would you want to be protected against in each case?

Team Activity. Have students work in groups to create posters or collages that illustrate the four basic insurance needs: auto, home, health, and life insurance. Suggest that they look at Figure 14-3 as a starting point for choosing images to illustrate each of the four needs.

- **Home insurance** protects you in case your possessions are stolen or damaged, even if the loss occurs away from home. For homeowners, the structure of the home is also covered against damage or destruction. Home insurance usually includes liability coverage that protects you if, for example, a guest is injured in your home.
- **Health insurance** coverage varies. Minimal coverage may include only medical emergencies. Extensive coverage may include everything from routine doctor visits to elective surgeries.
- **Life insurance** pays a benefit to designated people if the insured person dies. Thus, it protects families from loss of income. It can also be used as an investment.

As you read about each type of insurance in the rest of this chapter, you'll gain information to help you choose the right coverage. No matter which type of insurance you're looking for, shop around for the coverage and service you need at an economical price. Studies show that many Americans are either underinsured (don't have enough protection) or are paying more than they should for insurance.

Sources of Insurance

Health and life insurance can be obtained through individual or group policies. Most group insurance is offered to people through their employers, who often pay part of the premiums as a benefit. The cost to employees is much lower than if they bought insurance on their own. When looking for a job, consider the insurance benefits carefully.

People who want to purchase individual coverage often contact an insurance agent. The agent may be independent (selling many kinds of insurance for a number of different companies), employed by a particular insurance firm, or a combination of both. See Figure 14-4.

Instead of working with an agent, you may choose to apply for an insurance policy over the phone, through the mail, or on the Internet. At some Web sites you can get

Research Activity. Ask students to consult recent news articles for statistics on how many Americans are uninsured or underinsured. As a class, discuss the reasons for this problem.

14-4

Some people purchase insurance through an agent because they prefer the direct contact and personal relationship they can develop. What are some other advantages of purchasing coverage through an insurance agent?

InfoSource. Have students search online to find out what factors rating services use to rate insurance companies.

Answer Key. Answers to the Section Review questions are provided in the Section Lesson Plan located in the *Teacher Resource Guide*.

quotes from several insurance companies, then apply for the policy of your choice. You probably won't receive personal service or have the benefit of an agent's knowledge, but as a result of lower overhead costs, you may receive discounts or other savings.

Whether you work with an agent or not, choose your insurance company carefully. If the company goes broke, you'll be left without protection. At the library or on the Internet, you can find out how long the company has been in business and whether it is licensed in your state. A number of services rate insurance companies based on their financial strength and other factors.

Find out how the company's premiums compare with those offered by others for the same coverage. Special benefits or services, such as a nationwide claims service that can help you when you're away from home, may be important to you as well.

Applying for Insurance

When you apply for insurance, be prepared to answer many detailed questions. If you apply for auto insurance, for instance, the company will want to know whether you've had citations or accidents in the past. Your answers help the company determine whether it considers you insurable and if so, what risk category you fit into.

Once you have an insurance policy, you may not always be able to receive benefits immediately. For example, a health insurance policy might have a one-year waiting period before claims relating to pre-existing medical conditions will be paid. Like deductibles, a waiting period helps reduce the insurance company's share of risk.

Section 14.1 Review

CHECK YOUR UNDERSTANDING

1. How does insurance manage and limit financial risk?
2. Describe three factors that affect insurance costs.
3. What should you consider when selecting an insurance company?

CONSUMER APPLICATION

Managing Risk Is it worthwhile to pay $200 a year for a home insurance policy with a $250 deductible to insure $1,000 worth of property? Explain.

InfoSource

Insurance Companies

To find information about specific insurance companies, use library and Internet resources to:

- Contact your state insurance department.
- Read the periodic reports on insurance coverage featured in consumer magazines such as *Consumer Reports.*
- Consult one of five major ratings services in the United States: A.M. Best, Duff & Phelps, Moody's, Standard & Poor's, and Weiss.
- Study the Web sites of individual insurance companies.

Objectives

After studying this section, you should be able to:

- Analyze the need for various types of auto insurance coverage.
- Compare the pros and cons of no-fault insurance.
- Describe factors that affect auto insurance rates.
- Explain what to do in case of a traffic accident.

Key Terms

no-fault insurance
depreciation
assigned-risk pool

SECTION 14.2

Auto Insurance

Driving an automobile can give you a sense of freedom and independence. With this freedom comes responsibility—not only to drive safely and obey traffic laws, but also to carry adequate auto insurance.

THE NEED FOR AUTO INSURANCE

The automobile is one of society's greatest sources of economic risk. Motor vehicle crashes are the leading cause of death in the U.S. and carry an economic cost of more than $150 billion a year. Car theft is also costly. Statistics from the National Insurance Crime Bureau report almost 1.1 million vehicles stolen in a recent year. Many are found later, but most are damaged or stripped of parts.

Most states require that drivers carry certain minimum auto insurance coverage. Typically, you will be asked for proof of insurance if you get a ticket or are in an accident. In some states, you can't register your car and receive license plates without proof of insurance.

SYSTEMS OF AUTO INSURANCE

In most states, auto insurance is based on a traditional fault system. Insurance companies pay claims according to each person's degree of fault, or responsibility for causing an accident.

Discussion. ***Ask:*** Do you agree that no-fault insurance might discourage negligent drivers from changing their driving habits? Why or why not?

In contrast, some states use a **no-fault insurance** system. Under this system, no fault or blame is assigned in the event of an accident. All parties involved collect from their own insurance companies for losses up to their coverage limits. The no-fault system limits the right to sue other drivers for damages. Individuals still have the right to sue if there is permanent injury or disfigurement, death, or very high property loss.

In the traditional fault system, expensive and lengthy court cases are often required to determine fault. No-fault insurance greatly reduces the need to go to court. People who favor the no-fault system say that it results in more affordable insurance for everyone. On average, however, the rates in no-fault states have been higher than in other states.

No-fault insurance has several drawbacks. Not all medical conditions resulting from an accident are covered, and there is a strict monetary limit above which no payments are made. Some people believe that since negligent drivers cannot be sued for causing an accident, they will have no incentive to change their driving habits.

Caption Answer. Coverage requirements may reflect accident statistics, the results of lawsuits, and certain ethical standards.

TYPES OF COVERAGE

An auto insurance policy includes a number of different kinds of coverage—some required, some optional. Each provides insurance protection for specific situations. Figure 14-5 summarizes the basic kinds of coverage.

14-5

Each type of auto insurance coverage addresses different needs. What reasons might states and lenders have for requiring certain coverage?

Types of Auto Insurance Coverage

TYPE OF COVERAGE	WHAT IT PROTECTS AGAINST	REQUIRED OR OPTIONAL?
Collision Coverage	Damage to your own vehicle due to a traffic accident	May be a requirement of getting a new car loan Optional otherwise
Comprehensive Physical Damage Coverage	Loss or damage to your own vehicle due to noncollision causes such as theft, vandalism, fire, hail	May be a requirement of getting a new car loan Optional otherwise
Liability Coverage	Injury or damage that you cause to other people or their property	Required in most states
Medical Payments Coverage or Personal Injury Protection	Injury to you or your passengers due to a traffic accident	Required in certain no-fault states
Uninsured/Underinsured Motorists Coverage	Injury or damage to you, your passengers, or your vehicle caused by a driver without adequate insurance	Required in some states

Critical Thinking. ***Ask:*** Is it worthwhile to carry collision coverage on an old car that is not worth much? Why or why not?

Collision Coverage

Collision coverage pays for the repair or replacement of your own vehicle after a traffic accident. For example, if your car rolls over after hitting an icy patch in the road, collision coverage will help pay for repairs.

In most cases, the insurance company will pay no more for repairs than the current value of the vehicle—that is, its value just before the accident. For most vehicles, the current value is less than what you paid for the vehicle because items go down in value over time. Age, normal wear and tear, and the fact that used items are less valuable than new ones all contribute to this **depreciation**, or loss in value over time.

Suppose you have an old car. Although you paid $3,000 for it, it's now worth only $1,200. If it's damaged in an accident and the repair estimate is $2,300, the insurance company will pay you $1,200 minus your deductible. The car is said to be *totaled*, or damaged beyond reasonable repair.

Point Out. Explain to students that collision coverage generally protects drivers when they rent a car; they don't need to buy separate coverage from the rental company.

Community Activity. Ask students to talk to a friend who owns a car and find out how much liability coverage drivers are required to carry.

Comprehensive Physical Damage Coverage

Comprehensive physical damage coverage protects your own vehicle against risks unrelated to traffic accidents, such as fire, hail, theft, and vandalism. As with collision coverage, the most an insurance company will pay under comprehensive coverage is not the original cost of the vehicle, but its actual, depreciated cash value at the time of the loss. See Figure 14-6.

Liability Coverage

Liability coverage steps in when a covered driver causes injury or damage to other people or their property. It's required in almost all states, whether they use a traditional or no-fault system. There are two parts to liability coverage. *Bodily injury liability* covers expenses related to injuries suffered by others. *Property damage liability* covers damage not only to vehicles, but also to buildings,

14-6

Comprehensive physical damage coverage provides protection for damage caused by vandalism, such as a broken windshield. What do you think you should do if you discover such damage?

Critical Thinking. ***Ask:*** Why are unlicensed drivers not covered by liability coverage? Who would pay if an unlicensed driver had an accident?

trees, lawns, telephone poles, and so on. Liability coverage pays not only for damages but also for court costs and legal fees, up to the policy's limits.

Liability coverage applies to any accident involving the policyholder's vehicle, as long as it was driven by either the policyholder, a member of the immediate family, or someone who had permission to use the vehicle. The driver must have been licensed at the time of the accident.

Medical Payments Coverage and PIP

Under certain circumstances, you may need or want to purchase either medical payments coverage or personal injury protection (PIP) as part of your auto insurance. If you live in a no-fault state, one or the other is likely to be required by law. Since these two types of coverage are similar, it's not necessary to have both.

Point Out. Explain to students that medical payments coverage and PIP may also cover policyholders riding in another person's car.

- **Medical payments coverage.** If you, members or your immediate family, or relatives living with you are injured in an auto accident, this coverage would pay for immediate, short-term medical treatment costs. If the accident involves your vehicle, any passengers are also covered. Medical payments coverage can be especially helpful if someone riding in your car does not have health insurance. See Figure 14-7.
- **Personal injury protection.** Like medical payments coverage, personal injury protection (PIP) covers medical expenses for the policyholder and other passengers in the policyholder's vehicle. In addition, PIP policies in some states provide at least partial coverage of injury-related expenses such as lost wages, rehabilitation, and home nursing care. For example, if you were injured in an auto accident and as a result couldn't work for two months, personal injury protection might pay you an amount equal to two months' wages.

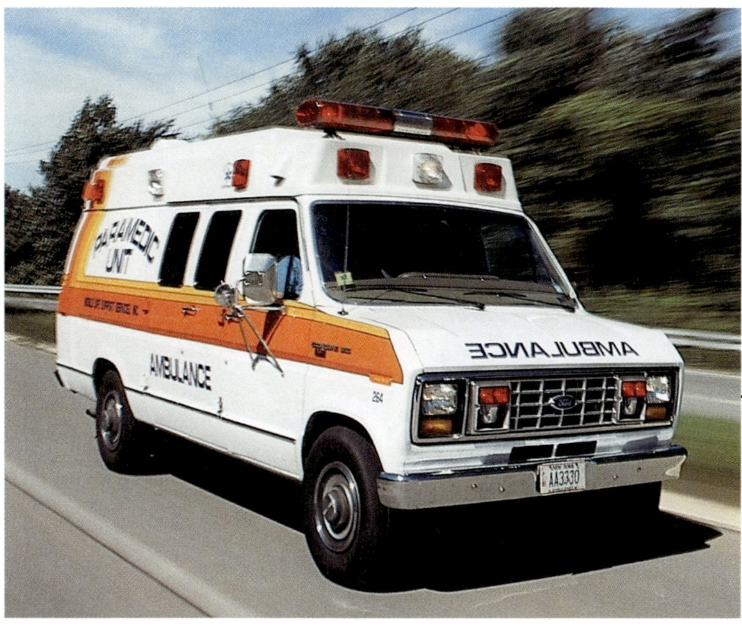

14-7

Medical payments coverage would pay for treatment at the scene of an accident. **Find out whether this coverage is required in your state.**

Critical Thinking. *Ask:* Is it fair for drivers to be required to carry uninsured/underinsured motorist coverage? Why or why not?

Uninsured/Underinsured Motorists Coverage

Some states require drivers to carry uninsured/underinsured motorists coverage. This coverage provides protection in situations such as these:

- A hit-and-run driver leaves the accident scene and can't be identified.
- You're in an auto accident caused by someone who does not have insurance.
- The other driver in an accident has too little insurance to cover your losses.

In the first two examples, your insurance company would pay for your losses. In the third example—an underinsured motorist—your policy would pay the difference between what you can collect from the other driver's insurance company and the losses you suffered.

Although coverage varies, in many cases only injury-related losses are covered, not property damage. Uninsured/underinsured motorists coverage applies to you and all the members of your immediate family, whether they are riding in a vehicle (your own or someone else's) or walking. It also applies to passengers in your vehicle.

Point Out. Consumers can also get emergency road service by joining an auto club, such as the American Automobile Association.

Other Types of Coverage

In addition to the basics, you might decide to add some optional types of coverage to your auto insurance policy. For example, emergency road service coverage pays for towing and labor costs if your car breaks down. Rental car reimbursement provides coverage for the cost of a rental car while your vehicle is being repaired. Some companies offer new-car coverage that pays for total repair or replacement costs, even if they exceed the current value of the car. Each of these options adds to the cost of the policy, so you must weigh whether the benefits are worth the additional premiums.

Most auto insurance policies won't cover you while you're driving a motorcycle. A separate motorcycle insurance policy is required. See Figure 14-8.

14-8

Motorcycles are considered high-risk vehicles, so insurance is costly. Taking a safety course and maintaining a good driving record can reduce the premiums.

Class Activity. Ask how many students would be willing to double their premiums in order to double their coverage. List the response on the board. Then ask how many would be willing to pay 75 percent more, 50 percent more, and so on. Draw conclusions about when higher coverage is a good deal.

ASSESSING YOUR COVERAGE NEEDS

Before you shop around for auto insurance, determine the types and amount of coverage you need. The most important consideration is how much liability coverage to purchase.

The amount of liability coverage usually is described in three numbers. For example, 50/100/25 means that the policy limits for any one accident are:

- $50,000 for the injuries of any one person.
- $100,000 for all injured parties (two or more).
- $25,000 for property damage.

The minimum required coverage varies from state to state. In most cases, the minimum amount would not be enough if you had to file a claim, particularly because of the high cost of medical care and the possibility of a lawsuit. Many insurance companies and consumer publications recommend coverage amounts of at least 100/300/50 to cover most possible expenses. Although more coverage means higher premiums, increasing the coverage to two, three, or even four times the minimum will probably not raise your rates very much.

What about collision and comprehensive coverage? These are worthwhile for valuable vehicles, since even minor damage can be very costly to repair. See Figure 14-9. If you get a loan to buy a new car, the lender will probably require collision and comprehensive coverage.

As a vehicle gets older and its value decreases, collision and comprehensive coverage should be re-evaluated. For a vehicle that's very low in value, they may not be worthwhile and can be dropped altogether. Remember, the insurance company won't pay you more than the current value of the vehicle. You could easily end up paying more in premiums than you would receive if you made a claim. Some companies will not even sell collision coverage on older vehicles.

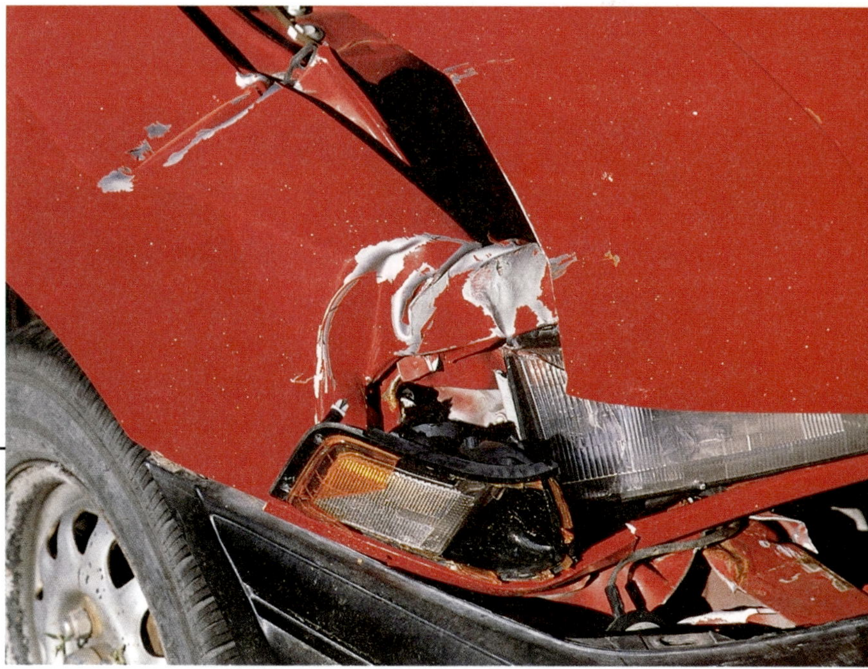

14-9

Even a "fender bender," a minor auto accident, can result in high repair costs.

Dollars and Sense. Ask students to choose a particular model and year of vehicle. Have them follow the steps listed to choose insurance for that type of car. Students should explain to insurers that they are doing a project for school and not actually shopping for insurance.

Also consider what size deductible you want. Most policies have a $250 or $500 deductible on collision and comprehensive physical damage coverage. The higher the deductible, the lower the premium.

AUTO INSURANCE RATES

In addition to the amount of coverage and the deductible, auto insurance rates are affected by the following factors.

- **Age.** Drivers under age 25 pay higher premiums. Statistics show that this age group has more accidents than any other group.
- **Gender.** Men likely will pay more for auto insurance because statistics show that they have more accidents than women.
- **Marital status.** Drivers who are married have statistically fewer accidents and therefore lower premiums.
- **Driving record.** A safe driver—someone who has had no accidents and no serious traffic violations for at least three years—probably will have lower insurance rates.
- **Type and age of vehicle.** Vehicles that are newer, more expensive, or more costly to repair will have higher auto insurance premiums. Models that are more frequently stolen will also cost more to insure.
- **Vehicle use.** The more miles you drive, the greater the chance of having an accident. Rates are usually higher for people who drive more than 15,000 miles a year for work or business.
- **Place of residence.** People in large cities usually pay more for auto insurance than people in suburban or rural areas do. More accidents occur in urban areas, and medical care, legal services, and car repairs are more costly in cities.
- **Number of drivers on the policy.** Putting additional drivers on an insurance policy raises the premium. Still, it costs less to add a driver under age 25 to his or her parents' policy than to purchase a separate policy.

DOLLARSandSENSE

Three Bids for Auto Insurance

Choosing auto insurance can be complicated because of the wide range of options. Before you buy a policy:

- Choose three companies that have a good reputation. Ask for recommendations from friends and family members, then research the companies to make sure they're financially sound.
- Determine the amount of coverage that seems right for you, based on reading articles or talking to an agent.
- Get a price quotation in writing from each company. Make sure each bid uses the same specifications.
- Make your decision based on reputation as well as price.

Research Activity. Ask students to consult auto insurance Web sites to find discounts available for teens and summarize them in the form of a chart.

Many insurance companies offer discounts on auto policies. For example, you could earn a discount for maintaining good grades or for having taken a driver education course. Consumers may receive discounts for using seat belts, having antitheft devices such as car alarms, insuring two or more vehicles under the same policy, having both auto and home insurance with the same company, or simply for being long-time customers.

Options for Problem Drivers

People with very poor driving records have difficulty finding auto insurance. Insurance companies don't want to take the risk of insuring them. A person who has been turned down three times for insurance becomes eligible to apply for insurance from the **assigned-risk pool**. This is a group of drivers within a state who are unable to obtain auto insurance on their own.

Once in the assigned-risk pool, a driver is assigned randomly to an insurance company. Companies generally must insure their high-risk drivers for at least three years. Usually, only minimum liability coverage is offered. Rates are generally 25% to 50% higher than for other drivers.

Caption Answer. You should give your name, your location, an explanation of what happened, and information about any injuries.

If you're in the assigned-risk pool, pay your premiums promptly and try to improve your driving record. This will make it easier for you to eventually get insurance on your own and reduce your premiums.

IN CASE OF AN ACCIDENT

No one expects to have an accident, but you should know what to do if you find yourself in this situation. Safety is the first priority. Pull off the road if possible. In a serious accident, however, let the vehicles remain where they are. Turn on your flashers to warn other vehicles.

Police should be called if the accident is serious or involves property damage, a traffic violation, or intoxication. If anyone appears to be injured, ask for medical assistance as well. See Figure 14-10.

14-10

In many locations, you can call 911 to summon emergency help. What information should you give when you call?

Community Activity. Have students contact a local auto repair shop to find out whether it offers discounts for people insured by a particular company.

Answer Key. Answers to the Section Review questions are provided in the Section Lesson Plan located in the *Teacher Resource Guide.*

While you're waiting for help to arrive, stay on the scene. If necessary, and if you can safely do so, set up flares or warning triangles and try to direct traffic away from the accident. Be cautious, however—you could be hit by oncoming traffic.

Don't discuss the details of the accident with anyone other than the police. Do, however, exchange information with other drivers, including name, insurance company, policy number, driver's license number, and name of the owner of the vehicle. Write down the license numbers of the vehicles involved. If there are witnesses to the accident, ask for their names and phone numbers.

When the police arrive, an officer will take statements from all parties involved and write a police report. Be honest about what happened. Don't admit fault or assign blame—stick to the facts. Ask for the officer's name in case you have questions or need to track down the report.

Filing a Claim

Call your insurance company as soon as possible after the accident. You'll be contacted by a claims adjuster who will handle your claim. Follow his or her instructions. You may be asked to submit paperwork or to take your vehicle to a claims center or repair facility for a damage estimate.

Ask the adjuster for a copy of your complete claim file for your records. If you don't receive one, file a complaint with your state's department of insurance. Here are some additional consumer tips for handling an auto insurance claim:

- **Choose your own repair facility.** Some repair shops sign agreements with insurance companies to perform repair work at discount prices in exchange for business. Don't let yourself be pressured into using one of these shops if you're not confident that it will do quality work.
- **Seek appropriate medical care.** Your insurance company can't tell you where to seek medical care. However, it will ask questions if it feels you sought unnecessary treatment. Be prepared to justify any treatment you receive.
- **Get legal help if needed.** You may want to hire an attorney if you're involved in an accident with substantial damages or if you have not been able to collect any insurance benefits within 30 days of filing a claim.

Section 14.2 Review

CHECK YOUR UNDERSTANDING

1. What is the purpose of automobile insurance liability coverage? How much coverage is recommended?
2. Name five factors that affect auto insurance rates.
3. If you are in a traffic accident, what should you tell the other driver?

CONSUMER APPLICATION

Required Coverage Investigate your state's requirements for auto insurance coverage. You might check publications in the library or search the Web sites of your state's department of insurance or department of motor vehicles. Do you live in a fault or a no-fault state? What minimum coverage is required? When must you show proof of auto insurance? Write a paragraph explaining the results of your research.

SECTION 14.3

Home Insurance

Think of all the items found in a typical home. Clothing, furniture, electronic equipment, appliances, cookware, dishes, books, tapes—the list is almost endless. How could a family afford to replace all these items if they were damaged or stolen? Home insurance is there to help.

Objectives

After studying this section, you should be able to:

- Analyze the need for various types of home insurance coverage.
- Describe factors affecting home insurance rates.
- Explain the purpose of a household inventory.

Key Terms

personal property
appraisal
household inventory

HOME INSURANCE NEEDS

Like other forms of insurance, home insurance is designed to protect policyholders from serious financial loss. Most people choose a package policy that combines two types of coverage: property and liability.

- **Property coverage** insures against risks such as fire and theft. Depending on the policy, this coverage can be extended to both real property and personal property. Real property is a structure such as a house or garage. **Personal property** is property that can be moved, such as furniture, appliances, clothing, and jewelry.
- **Liability coverage** provides financial protection against certain losses caused to others. For example, it pays for medical bills if someone is injured while visiting your home.

Class Activity. Have students write a short story about someone whose home is affected by one of the perils listed in Figure 14-11. Their stories should show how having or not having insurance affects the outcome of the situation for the homeowner.

Home insurance is sometimes referred to as a *homeowner's policy*. That name is misleading because home insurance is important for renters as well. Unlike homeowners, renters don't need to insure the structure. The owner of the property carries insurance for that. However, the property owner's insurance policy does not cover renters' personal property, nor does it provide liability coverage for injuries that occur inside the rental unit. Therefore, renters should obtain their own home insurance protection.

PROPERTY COVERAGE

In a home insurance policy, the types of property protected and the number of risks, or perils, covered depend on the form of the policy. The most common forms include:

- **Basic form (HO-1).** This policy covers the home and personal property against damage from 11 specific perils.
- **Broad form (HO-2).** This policy covers more perils than HO-1. Figure 14-11 shows the perils covered by HO-1 and HO-2.
- **Special form (HO-3).** This policy, the most common form of home insurance, is meant for the homeowner who wants extensive protection. It covers the house, all additional structures, and personal property against almost any peril except earthquake, flood, war, and nuclear accident. In case of a dispute, it's up to the insurance company to prove that damage is *not* covered under the policy. This differs from a policy such as HO-1 or HO-2, in which the policyholder must prove that damage was caused by one of the named perils.
- **Tenants form (HO-4).** This policy, sometimes called the *contents form,* covers the renters' personal property only. Covered perils are generally the same as those on the HO-2 form.

HO-1 and HO-2 Perils

HO-1

Covers the following 11 perils:

- Lightning or fire
- Theft
- Hail or windstorm
- Explosion
- Civil uprising or riot
- Smoke
- Aircraft
- Vehicles
- Damage by glass or safety glazing material that's part of a building
- Volcanic eruption
- Vandalism

HO-2

Covers all perils included under HO-1 plus:

- Water-related damage caused by utility or appliance problems
- Electrical surge problems
- Falling objects
- Building collapse due to weight of snow, ice, or sleet

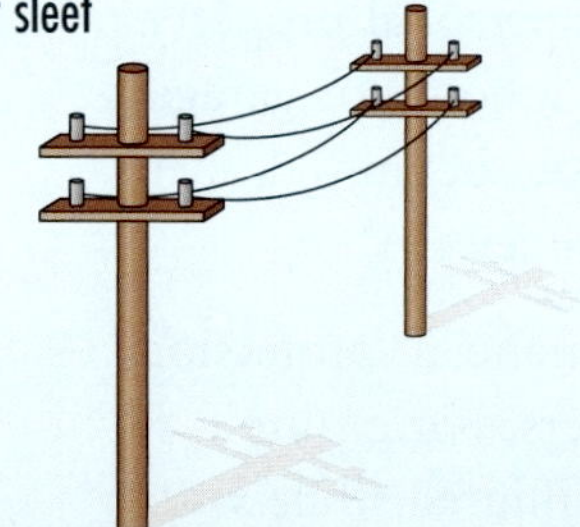

Critical Thinking. ***Ask:*** Why are earthquakes, floods, wars, and nuclear accidents not covered by standard home insurance policies?

14-11

Both the HO-1 and HO-2 forms identify specific perils that are covered. Which perils do you think might be most likely to occur?

Class Activity. On the board, make two columns labeled "Replacement" and "Actual Cash Value." Ask students what reasons people might have for choosing replacement-value insurance versus actual-cash-value insurance. List the reasons they give in the appropriate columns.

- **Condominium owners form (HO-6).** This policy was developed for people who own an apartment or other housing unit through the condominium form of ownership. The policy insures only those parts of the structure that are the individual owner's responsibility.

TEXTLINK

For an explanation of condominium ownership, see Section 23.1.

Replacement Versus Actual Cash Value

Suppose you purchased a new bicycle four years ago. If you decided to sell your bike to someone today, you would receive much less than what you paid for it. After all, it's now a used, four-year-old bike, not a brand new one. Similarly, if your bike were stolen, most insurance policies would pay you only its current value—not what you paid for it, and not what it would cost to buy a new bike today. Insurance coverage that uses this method is called *actual cash value coverage.*

For a higher premium, some insurance policies provide *replacement coverage.* This type of coverage pays the cost of replacing items with comparable new ones. If a fire destroyed your home, replacement coverage would pay the current cost to build a home of similar size and quality. However, it won't pay more than the value of the policy. See Figure 14-12.

Amount of Coverage

If you have a home loan, the lender will require a certain amount of home insurance coverage. However, the required amount is seldom enough. Insurers generally recommend that homeowners insure their homes for 100% of full replacement value.

Discussion. ***Ask:*** As a homeowner, how would you decide whether to pay for actual cash value coverage or replacement coverage?

14-12

Whether or not you choose replacement coverage, be sure to purchase an adequate amount of insurance so that losses will be fully covered. How might you determine the cost of replacing a home and its contents?

Class Activity. Ask students to make a list of factors to consider when shopping for a home insurance policy. These might include factors that would affect the amount of coverage, the type of policy, and the decision to purchase or not to purchase additional coverage.

Your insurance agent should be able to calculate what it would cost to replace the home, or you can hire someone to do a detailed appraisal. An **appraisal** is an estimate of value made by a qualified person. For insurance purposes, this estimate should be based on the value of only the home and its contents, not the land on which the home sits. That's because risks such as theft, fire, and wind damage generally don't affect the land.

A home insurance policy covers the house and an attached garage. Depending on the policy, other structures such as a tool shed, guest house, or detached garage may also be covered.

Personal property insurance covers all household items and other belongings owned by family members, except vehicles. Items are covered while at home or away from home. In a standard home insurance policy, the amount of personal property coverage is usually 50% of the amount of coverage on the structure. Additional coverage can be purchased if needed. If you're unsure of the value of your possessions, check with your insurance agent or consider having your personal property appraised.

About every three years, check the value of the home and personal property, then update the amount of insurance if needed. Some insurance policies have an inflation guard endorsement that automatically increases policy limits each year.

Additional Coverage

Many home insurance policies also provide coverage for temporary living expenses. If the insured home is damaged so much that it can't be inhabited, this coverage pays for rent and certain other expenses until the home is repaired or another one is purchased.

Endorsements—attachments to the policy—can add coverage for specific hazards not normally included in a standard home insurance package. You can also purchase endorsements to cover valuable items such as antiques, artwork, jewelry, or other items not specifically covered under the original policy.

14-13

Many homes that suffer flood damage are located in areas considered to be at low to moderate risk of flooding.

Community Activity. Ask students to find out whether flood insurance or earthquake insurance is recommended in the area where they live.

Flood insurance must be purchased as a separate insurance policy, not through an endorsement. You're eligible to purchase flood insurance if you live in a community that participates in the National Flood Insurance Program. This program is a partnership between insurance companies and the Federal Emergency Management Agency (FEMA). You can check with FEMA or with your insurance agent to determine whether you can buy flood insurance. Rates are based on the level of flood risk in different areas, as mapped by FEMA. If the home is in a high-risk zone, flood insurance may be required when you apply for a home loan. Even in a zone with low or moderate risk, flood insurance may be a wise purchase. See Figure 14-13.

Critical Thinking. ***Ask:*** How would the value of your assets affect the amount of liability insurance you need?

Earthquake insurance also requires a separate policy. Such policies are offered by most insurance companies. Premium rates are generally based on the likelihood of an earthquake occurring in a given area. In the United States, earthquakes strike hardest and most often along the Pacific Coast, but they can happen anywhere.

LIABILITY COVERAGE

The standard level of liability coverage for home insurance is around $300,000. Higher amounts of coverage are recommended for policyholders with more assets. Liability coverage under a home insurance policy gives protection against claims in three areas:

- **Personal liability coverage.** This coverage protects you from lawsuits arising from property damage or bodily injury. For example, it would provide coverage if a visitor to your property slipped, suffered a head injury, and sued you for damages.
- **Medical payments coverage.** This coverage protects you, your family, and your guests from accident-related medical bills.
- **Physical damage coverage.** Minor damage that you or someone in your family causes to another's property is paid for by physical damage coverage. It protects against such risks as hitting a baseball through a neighbor's window. See Figure 14-14.

14-14

Oops! The liability coverage of a home insurance policy will pay for damage you cause to other people's property. Give another example of liability coverage.

Point Out. Between 2000 and 2004, the average home insurance claim was just over $5,000.

Umbrella Policy

A *personal liability umbrella policy* is a separate insurance policy that supplements the liability coverage provided by your home and auto insurance. For example, suppose a lawsuit holds you liable for $1 million, but your home insurance policy has a liability limit of $300,000. If you had an umbrella policy, it would cover the amount over $300,000 up to its own limit, minus a relatively small deductible. An umbrella policy may also cover certain types of claims that are not covered by most home and auto policies. The cost is relatively low.

HOME INSURANCE RATES

Several factors can cause home insurance rates to be higher or lower for the same amount of coverage.

- **Deductible.** The standard deductible amount for most home insurance policies is $250. Increasing the deductible to $500, $1,000, or more will significantly reduce your premiums.

Discussion. *Ask:* How might knowing the factors that affect the cost of home insurance influence your choice of a place to live?

- **Local firefighting capability.** Insurance companies look at factors such as the distance to the nearest fire station and hydrants, whether the local fire department is professional or volunteer, and the amount of equipment it has. Better firefighting capabilities mean lower home insurance rates.
- **Construction materials.** Rates are lower for homes built of concrete or brick, for example, because they have less risk of being destroyed in a fire than homes built of wood.
- **Preventive measures.** Insurance companies offer discounts to homeowners who have alarm systems, smoke detectors, fire extinguishers, and deadbolt locks.

FILING A CLAIM

After a loss, contact your insurance company as soon as possible. You'll probably be asked to fill out a claims form. If the claim is for damage to your home, a claims adjuster will inspect the damage and submit a report to the company. See Figure 14-15. Once the insurance company has this verification and an estimate for the cost of repairs, it will pay your claim.

Critical Thinking. *Ask:* Why do you think it's a good idea to file a claim very soon after a loss?

14-15

Claims adjusters are trained to assess damage. They authorize the amount of payment you will receive for your claim.

Class Activity. Challenge students to create a household inventory for their room at home. If they share a room, the inventory should include their own belongings and any items that are shared, such as furniture. Have them take their inventories home and check to see how much they remembered.

Answer Key. Answers to the Section Review questions are provided in the Section Lesson Plan located in the *Teacher Resource Guide.*

14-16

Household inventory forms are available from insurance agents, or you can create your own. Without looking, try listing the contents of your bedroom. Can you remember every item?

Sample Household Inventory

LIVING ROOM

NO. OF ITEMS	ITEM	DESCRIPTION	DATE PURCHASED	PURCHASE PRICE	CURRENT VALUE
2	Armchairs	upholstered	10/2/01	$800	$600
5	Art/frames	prints	–	800	700
100	Books		–	1500	800
2	Bookcases	walnut	3/5/02	1200	1000
1	Cabinets and contents	entertainment center, videotapes	1/25/03	1500	1400
1	Closet contents	coats, hats	–	1200	900
1	Desks	oak – antique	family	–	400
3	Drapes/curtains/blinds	linen – floor length	10/15/01	750	600
4	Lamps	1 floor – iron 3 table – ceramic	8/5/02	350	250
1	Rugs	9x12 wool	6/17/02	900	700
1	Sofa	damask	10/2/01	1200	800
3	Tables	walnut	10/2/01	750	650
1	TV	15"	9/15/01	500	250
1	VCR		9/15/01	200	50
			Total	$11,650	$9,100

Household Inventory

When it comes to your personal property, proving the amount of loss is up to you. If your home were burglarized, would you be able to list all of the items stolen and the value of each? Most people would have a hard time remembering those details, especially under stress. Prepare ahead of time by keeping a **household inventory**, or detailed list of personal belongings.

List the belongings for each room of the home, including everything you would need to replace if it were damaged or stolen. Don't forget the contents of garages, sheds, and other storage areas. Include the quantity and description of each item, the date it was purchased, and the original price. Be as specific as you can. If possible, estimate the current cash value. Figure 14-16 shows an inventory of items in a living room.

It's also a good idea to photograph or videotape your personal property and to keep purchase receipts. Keep the inventory, pictures, and receipts in a safe place *outside* the home, such as in a safe deposit box. Update the inventory periodically, perhaps every six months, to record new items and remove those that are no longer in your possession.

Section 14.3 Review

CHECK YOUR UNDERSTANDING

1. How do the insurance needs of a homeowner and a renter differ?
2. What steps can consumers take to reduce their home insurance rates?
3. Why is it helpful to maintain a household inventory?

CONSUMER APPLICATION

Weighing Options Your insurance agent tells you that you can receive a 25% discount on your premiums. In order to qualify for the discount, however, your yearly deductible will need to be increased from $250 to $750 per year. What are the pros and cons of such an offer?

Objectives

After studying this section, you should be able to:

- Analyze the need for various types of health insurance coverage.
- Identify sources of health care benefits.
- Compare managed care and traditional health plans.
- Describe government-sponsored health care programs.

Key Terms

fee-for-service plan
managed care plan
primary care physician
co-payment
HMO
POS
PPO
Medigap policies
Medicaid
workers' compensation

SECTION 14.4

Health Insurance

The cost of health care is extremely high, making it hard for the average person to afford regular medical care. A major illness could wipe out most families' savings. Health insurance is an essential part of a personal financial plan.

THE NEED FOR HEALTH INSURANCE

People need health insurance because it's impossible to predict future medical expenses. Routine care as well as medical emergencies easily can cost thousands of dollars. Health insurance protects consumers from the high costs of medical bills that might ruin them financially.

Medical research, new drugs and treatments, and advanced technology have helped provide better health care, but also drive up costs. In addition, health care professionals and hospitals must purchase insurance to protect themselves against medical malpractice lawsuits. The costs of this insurance are passed on to consumers. Since medical care and treatment costs will no doubt continue to rise, it's vital to have a basic understanding of health insurance options.

Team Activity. Have students work in pairs to determine which types of health insurance a young adult would be likely to need. Have them prioritize their lists and share them with the class. Note whether most students agreed on which types of insurance are most important for young people.

KINDS OF COVERAGE

Health insurance policies often are referred to as health care plans. Before choosing a health care plan, it's helpful to understand the kinds of coverage that may be included in one. Sometimes the different types of coverage are part of an overall package, while in other cases you must sign up for each separately.

- **Medical benefits** pay a large share of hospital and surgical expenses. Coverage for other medical care, such as routine doctor visits and prescription drugs, is often provided as well. See Figure 14-17.
- **Major medical coverage** is for catastrophic illnesses such as a heart attack or cancer. It pays the high costs involved in long hospital stays and multiple surgeries. Coverage begins after the limits on basic medical benefits have been reached.
- **Dental benefits** may cover services such as routine examinations, cleanings, X rays, fillings and other repairs, and oral surgery.
- **Vision benefits** may pay part or all of the cost of eye exams, glasses, and contact lenses.
- **Disability insurance** provides weekly or monthly payments to people who can't work because of illness or accident. It replaces part or all of the income they would normally receive from paychecks. Most policies have a waiting period between the first day of disability and the day benefits begin. During this waiting period, some workers receive sick-leave pay or other kinds of income from their employers.
- **Long-term care insurance** is designed to cover costs of an extended nursing home stay. Home health care and other forms of assistance may be covered as well. Many health insurance plans do not cover these costs or provide very limited coverage, so a separate long-term care insurance policy may be needed.

Caption Answer. Coverage begins after the limits on basic medical benefits have been reached.

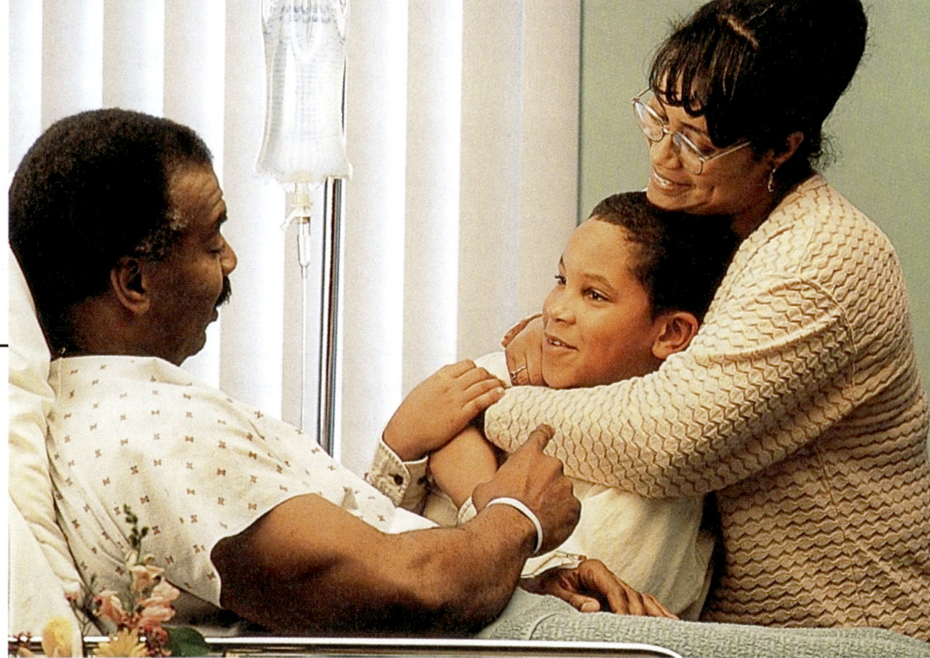

14-17

Medical benefits might include room and board, routine nursing care, and other services needed while in the hospital. **When does major medical coverage begin?**

Discussion. ***Ask:*** If you had a pre-existing condition, how might your decisions about health insurance be affected?

Exclusions from Coverage

Exclusions are specific conditions not covered or services not paid for by health insurance. Typical exclusions might be cosmetic surgery, laser surgery to correct vision, and other elective (optional) surgery. Pre-existing health problems may be covered only after a waiting period or not at all.

Most plans have rules to prevent receiving duplicate benefits from more than one source. When people are covered under two health insurance plans—their own and their spouse's, for example—the two insurance providers will work together to coordinate their benefits.

SOURCES OF COVERAGE

Once you've considered the types of coverage you may need, how can you obtain it? There are several sources.

- **Group policies.** Most people with health insurance are covered under group plans through their employers or other organizations. The cost of group health insurance is lower than that of individual plans because some high-risk people are excluded from the group. Some companies or groups pay the premiums as a benefit for their employees or members. More commonly, however, the two share the premium costs. See Figure 14-18.
- **COBRA.** If you leave your employer and would not otherwise have health insurance for several months, you may be eligible for continued medical benefits under the Consolidated Omnibus Budget Reconciliation Act (COBRA). This federal law states that under certain circumstances, workers and their families can keep their previous group coverage, at their own expense, for up to 18 months.

Community Activity. Have students contact an insurance agent in their community to find out what types of policies are available for individuals.

14-18

Employees may have health coverage through a group plan provided where they work. **How is the cost of such plans handled?**

Research Activity. Ask students to read an article about managed care plans. Have them write a paragraph summarizing the article's main points about the advantages and disadvantages of such plans and how they compare with fee-for-service plans.

- **Individual policies.** Those not covered under a group plan, or who want additional coverage, can obtain an individual policy. In addition to being more expensive, individual policies differ from group plans in many ways. With group plans, the level of benefits is fixed by the terms of the plan. With individual plans, the applicant chooses benefits, and each family member is enrolled separately.

- **Government programs.** Some people are eligible for federal government health insurance programs such as Medicare and Medicaid. You'll read more about these programs later in this section.

TYPES OF HEALTH CARE PLANS

Whatever their source, health care plans are broadly categorized as fee-for-service plans or managed care plans. The type of plan you choose will depend on the options you prefer and what you're willing to pay.

Fee-for-Service Plans

A **fee-for-service plan** is a plan under which you are charged for each medical service you receive, and your insurance plan pays a portion of that fee. Sometimes called *indemnity plans*, fee-for-service plans give you the widest range of choices of doctors and hospitals of any health care plan. You can choose the doctor you want, change doctors at any time, and see a doctor as often as you wish. However, hospital expenses may need to be pre-approved prior to admission.

In a fee-for-service plan, you are largely responsible for keeping track of the paperwork associated with your care. In a typical situation, you would pay the doctor's office at the time of your visit, file a claim with your insurance company, and then wait for partial reimbursement. See Figure 14-19.

Critical Thinking. ***Ask:*** Who would be most likely to buy an individual health insurance policy?

14-19

Using a fee-for-service plan means filling out paperwork and waiting to be reimbursed for charges you've already paid. **What is a significant advantage of having a fee-for-service plan?**

Class Activity. Have students create a two-column chart comparing the pros and cons of fee-for-service plans and managed care plans.

Fee-for-service plans have a yearly deductible, such as $500 for an individual or $1,000 for family coverage. After you've paid the deductible for the year, the insurance company will share the costs of care in a co-insurance arrangement. For example, 80/20 co-insurance means the insurance company will pay 80% of costs after the deductible. Most plans set an *out-of-pocket maximum*, which is an upper limit to the total amount you pay for deductibles and co-insurance in any one year.

In general, fee-for-service plans cost more than other types of health plans and involve more paperwork. However, they can be a good choice for people who want the fewest possible restrictions on care and can afford to pay extra for that freedom.

Managed Care Plans

When fee-for-service plans were the only type of health coverage, large numbers of claims created high costs for insurance companies. A **managed care plan** is a health care plan that is designed to lower costs for both the insurer and the consumer while maintaining a high standard of care.

Managed care plans are not all alike, but they have several characteristics in common. Each involves a network of selected health care providers, such as doctors and hospitals, that meet the plan's standards for quality care. These health care providers agree to provide care for specified fees, thus controlling the plan's costs. Patients have a strong incentive to seek care within the network, since the plan pays lower benefits or no benefits for care provided outside the network.

Caption Answer. Your PCP knows your medical history, your insurance coverage, and which specialists to recommend.

Another way for managed care plans to lower their costs is by emphasizing wellness and encouraging preventive care. Many plans pay most or all of the cost of routine exams, for example. The idea is to prevent health problems before costly treatments become necessary.

Most, but not all, managed care plans require members to choose a **primary care physician**, a physician who coordinates care. Patients are encouraged or required to visit the primary care physician first for any type of medical problem or concern. The primary care physician then decides whether the patient should see a specialist. This, too, helps control costs. See Figure 14-20.

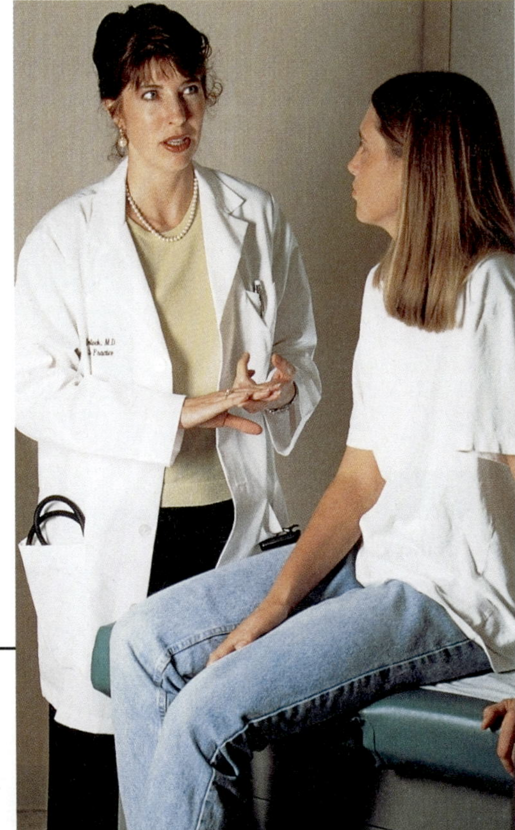

14-20

Under a managed care plan, your primary care physician serves as your first access to medical care. Why is it important that your PCP coordinate your care with specialists?

Class Activity. Hand out copies of a health insurance policy summary. Have students make a list of questions about the coverage that the summary does not answer. Ask them what sources they might consult to find the answers to these questions.

Consumers pay a yearly or monthly fee to join a managed care plan. The plan typically pays the health care provider directly for any services provided to covered individuals. For some services, the plan member may not have to pay anything. For others, the plan member is responsible for part of the cost in the form of a flat fee, called a **co-payment**, given to the health care provider at the time of service. Most co-payments are relatively small, such as $10 to $20. Since the plan member does not need to be reimbursed, there are no claim forms to fill out.

Several types of managed care plans exist. As Figure 14-21 shows, they vary in cost and flexibility.

- **HMO.** A **health maintenance organization (HMO)** is a health care group that offers medical care to members for a prepaid fee and small co-payments. Compared to other health plans, HMOs generally are the least costly to the consumer but have the most restrictions. For example, the choice of physicians is limited to those within the HMO. An HMO's health care providers are typically paid a fixed amount per patient per year, regardless of how often the patient seeks services. Some critics say this gives physicians a financial incentive to take on more patients while providing less service to each.

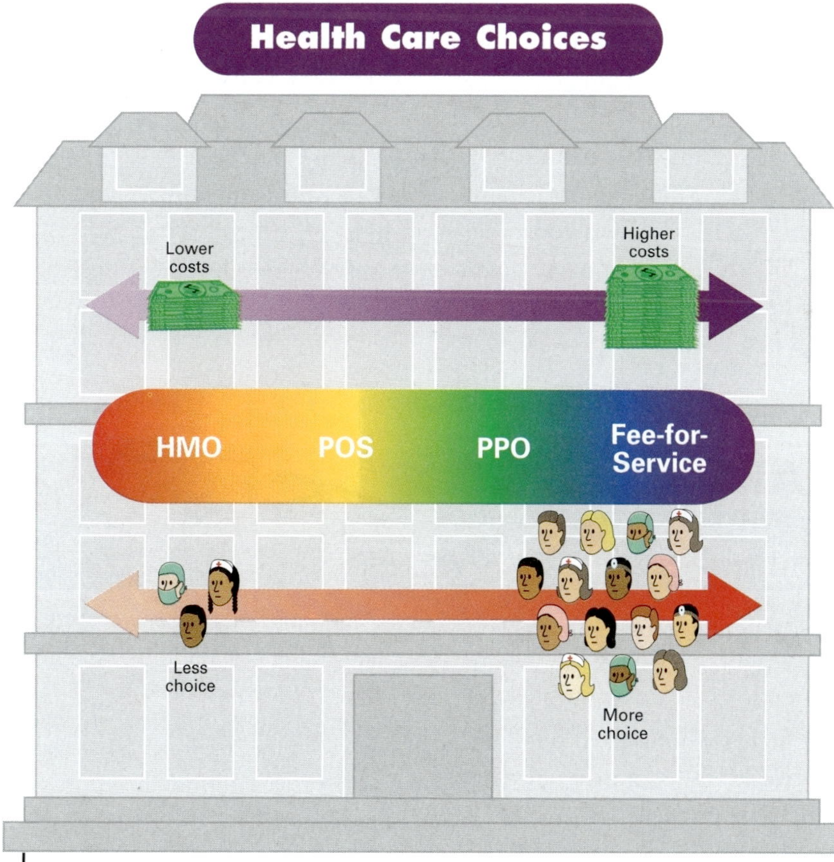

14-21 **In general, health care plans that offer more choice tend to cost more.** Which type of plan most appeals to you? Why?

Team Activity. Have students work in groups to develop a consumer brochure outlining the features of HMO, POS, and PPO managed care plans.

- **POS.** After the introduction of HMOs, several variations on managed care were developed that allow more freedom of choice. One type is the **point-of-service plan (POS)**, a managed care plan that provides the option of using health care providers outside the plan's network. If you stay within the network, the plan functions much like an HMO. If you receive care outside the network, it works more like a fee-for-service plan, and the cost to you is higher.
- **PPO.** Another type of managed care is the **preferred provider organization (PPO)**, a group of medical doctors, hospitals, and other health care providers who have agreed to extend services at reduced rates through an insurer or third-party administrator. For the consumer, the features of a PPO are similar to those of a point-of-service plan. The main difference is that many PPOs do not require that a primary care physician coordinate care. An EPO, or *exclusive provider organization*, is similar to a PPO.

Dollars and Sense. Ask students to make a list of the five criteria that would be most important to them personally in choosing a health care plan.

Within each of these categories, many variations have developed as companies attempt both to serve the needs of patients and remain profitable. As plans evolve, the differences between categories seem to diminish. Health care reform and changes in health care markets are expected to lead to other forms of managed care in the future.

GOVERNMENT HEALTH CARE PROGRAMS

The health insurance plans discussed thus far normally are purchased through private companies. Some consumers, however, are eligible for health insurance coverage under programs offered by federal and state governments.

Medicare

Medicare, a federal health insurance program, provides coverage for U.S. citizens age 65 or older and some people under age 65, such as those who are disabled. The Medicare plan has three parts.

DOLLARSandSENSE

Choosing a Health Care Plan

No single health care plan is best for everyone. When faced with a choice, carefully research the available plans so you understand exactly what is covered and for what cost. If possible, ask others who have used the plans you're considering about their experiences. Then ask yourself questions such as:

- Am I satisfied with my current doctors? Would they still be available to me? Am I willing to switch to save money?
- In a fee-for-service plan, can I afford the deductibles and co-insurance up to the yearly maximum?
- Are there prescription medications I take regularly? What would they cost under each plan?

Community Activity. Ask students to visit a local pharmacy and find out what kind of help it offers seniors signing up for Medicare drug coverage.

- **Hospital insurance (Part A).** Most eligible people do not have to pay a premium for this coverage. It helps pay for hospitals and certain other facilities, as well as for some home health care. See Figure 14-22.
- **Medical insurance (Part B).** This optional coverage helps pay for services not covered by Part A, such as doctor visits, lab tests, and therapy care. Those who enroll in Part B pay a monthly premium.
- **Prescription drug coverage.** People choose from different plans that typically pay about half of their prescription drug costs. They pay a monthly premium.

People can get Medicare coverage in different ways. The original Medicare plan is a fee-for-service plan that covers many health care services and allows care by any doctor or hospital that accepts Medicare. In some areas, private companies work with Medicare to offer other plans. These include managed care plans that may limit services to certain doctors and hospitals.

Research Activity. Have students search online to find out the eligibility requirements for Medicaid and for disability benefits under Social Security.

Since some expenses are not covered by the original Medicare plan, many consumers buy **Medigap policies**, health insurance policies purchased from private companies to supplement Medicare coverage. There are twelve standardized Medigap plans. Each plan is the same from company to company and in most states, but premiums vary. It pays to shop around for a Medigap policy.

Medicaid

The federal and state governments share the cost of medical aid to low-income families under a program known as **Medicaid**. Benefits go to families who are near the poverty level and have no other means to pay for their medical care.

Each state has its own Medicaid program, so programs and benefits vary. All states, however, must cover those people receiving public assistance and must pay for services such as hospital bills, doctors' services, home health care, and long-term nursing home care. States have the option to cover additional services such as visits to clinics, prescription drugs, and vision care.

Social Security Disability Benefits

Workers who have paid into the U.S. Social Security system and who develop conditions that prevent them from working may receive Social Security disability benefits. To be eligible, they must be under age 65 and meet certain other requirements. Benefits begin at the sixth full month the person is disabled and continue as long as the disability lasts.

14-22

A stay in a skilled nursing facility would be covered under Medicare Part A.

Caption Answer. *Many health problems and accidents are unrelated to your work; some workers' comp plans don't provide full coverage.*

WORKERS' COMPENSATION

Under state-regulated **workers' compensation** programs, employees are insured against injuries that occur on the job, no matter who or what caused the injuries. Job-related illnesses and death also are covered. Although each state administers a workers' compensation plan, it is not a government program. Employers pay premiums to insurance companies or state agencies to provide coverage to their workers. See Figure 14-23.

Workers' compensation benefits vary from state to state and employer to employer. Some plans cover all necessary expenses for treatment of an injury. Others pay for expenses up to a certain amount. After a waiting period, injured employees who are unable to work may also receive income benefits that partially replace their lost wages. Workers who have health insurance coverage are still eligible for workers' compensation benefits.

Employees who receive workers' compensation are prohibited from suing their employers because of their injuries. Workers' comp payments, in other words, are considered a full discharge of the employer's responsibilities.

Answer Key. *Answers to the Section Review questions are provided in the Section Lesson Plan located in the Teacher Resource Guide.*

14-23 Although some occupations are more hazardous than others, injuries and deaths can occur in any workplace. Why is it necessary to have health insurance even though you're covered by workers' compensation?

Section 14.4 Review

CHECK YOUR UNDERSTANDING

1. If your health plan provides coverage for medical benefits, why might you also want to have major medical coverage? Disability insurance?
2. Name an advantage and a disadvantage of having an HMO as your health plan.
3. Who is eligible for Medicare coverage? For Medicaid?

CONSUMER APPLICATION

Figuring Your Cost Suppose you receive a medical bill for $6,000. Your fee-for-service health plan has 80/20 co-insurance with a $250 deductible and a $10,000 out-of-pocket maximum. Assuming this is your first medical claim for the year, how much of the cost would be your responsibility? Explain your answer.

SECTION 14.5

Life Insurance

Nobody really wants to think about life insurance, but it's something that many people can't afford *not* to think about. Without life insurance, those left behind after the death of a family member may face financial hardship. Some types of life insurance can be helpful before death, too.

Objectives

After studying this section, you should be able to:

- Analyze the need for various types of life insurance coverage.
- Distinguish between insurance and investment features of life insurance policies.
- Explain factors to consider when purchasing life insurance.

Key Terms

term life insurance
permanent life insurance
cash value

REASONS FOR HAVING LIFE INSURANCE

In its most basic form, life insurance is insurance coverage that pays benefits to a designated person in the event of the insured's death. Many people buy life insurance to replace income that stops when they die. If their income supports a family, life insurance proceeds can be used to continue that support.

Besides replacing income, life insurance can provide money for other purposes. It can pay for funeral expenses as well as medical bills that were not covered by health insurance. It can make it possible for surviving family members to pay for services, such as housekeeping, previously performed by the insured. Life insurance policies can also be used to guarantee a loan. If the insured borrows $5,000, for example, and dies before repaying it, the insurance repays the loan. In addition, as you will see, some forms of life insurance may be purchased as an investment.

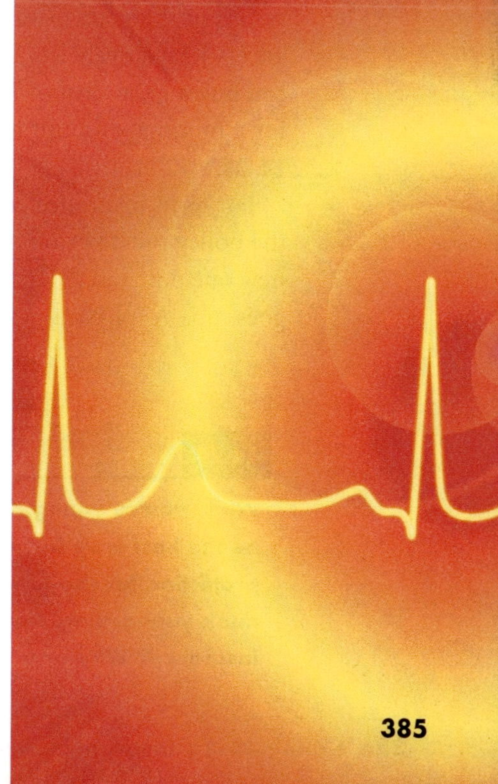

Critical Thinking. ***Ask:*** What is the primary advantage of each type of term life insurance?

TYPES OF LIFE INSURANCE

Life insurance policies fall into two main categories. One type provides insurance protection for a limited period of time. The other type provides coverage for one's entire life and also includes an investment feature.

Term Insurance

Life insurance that gives protection for a specific period of time—for example, one year, five years, or ten years—is called **term life insurance**. If the policyholder dies within that period, the policy pays a death benefit to the person or persons named in the policy. The benefit is equal to the amount of coverage purchased. If the policyholder lives until the end of the term and does not renew coverage, the policy expires without paying a benefit.

Unlike some kinds of life insurance, term insurance has no investment element; it simply provides insurance coverage. While this may sound like a disadvantage, it actually results in the main advantage of term insurance—its relatively low cost. A young person can buy a great deal of insurance protection for a minimal amount of money. See Figure 14-24.

For term insurance coverage to continue, the policy must periodically be renewed or a new one purchased. Each time, the premium goes up. A physical examination may be required as well. Any serious health problems that develop could add to the costs of premiums or even cause the insurance to be denied.

Point Out. Emphasize that the main advantage of term life insurance is its low cost. This may make it a particularly good choice for young people.

Several types of term insurance are available, including:

- **Level term.** This is the most common type of term life insurance. Premiums remain the same over the period of coverage, as does the death benefit.
- **Decreasing term.** With this type of policy, premiums are fixed, but the death benefit is gradually reduced over the life of the policy. This type of insurance is sometimes used to cover debts that are paid off over time, such as a home loan.

14-24

While you're young, term insurance might be the best way for you to get maximum protection for the lowest premiums. Do you think young, single people need life insurance? Why or why not?

Class Activity. Hold a debate in class on the relative merits of term life insurance and permanent life insurance. Divide the class into two teams and have each team summarize the advantages of one form of life insurance. Afterward, have students vote on which type they think is better.

- **Renewable term.** Some policies guarantee you the right to renew your coverage without having another physical examination. Many experts believe that a renewable term policy best serves the needs of most life insurance buyers.
- **Convertible term.** This type of policy allows you to change from term to permanent coverage without having a physical examination. This feature is important to people who want the flexibility of choosing a different type of policy later. However, the premiums are generally higher than for nonconvertible term insurance.

Permanent Insurance

Insurance that gives a person protection for his or her entire lifetime is called **permanent life insurance**. Because it also includes an investment component, it is sometimes called *cash value life insurance*. Each premium includes not only the cost of the actual insurance coverage, but an additional amount that is put into an investment account. This additional amount, which grows over time as premiums and investment earnings accumulate, is called the policy's **cash value**. If the insured cancels the policy, he or she may be entitled to some or all of the cash value. The insured can also borrow funds from the accumulated cash value without risk of cancellation of the policy. The cash value is different from the policy's *face value*, which is the amount of insurance coverage payable as a death benefit. See Figure 14-25.

Permanent life insurance is offered in several forms, including:

- **Whole life.** Also called *straight-life* or *ordinary-life* insurance, a whole-life policy provides life insurance protection for your entire life as long as premiums are paid. The amount of the premiums is set when the policy is bought and remains the same.
- **Limited-payment life.** With this form of insurance, you pay premiums for a set number of years or to a certain age, and then stop. Coverage, however, continues for the rest of your life. Premiums are higher than for a whole life policy.

Face Value and Cash Value

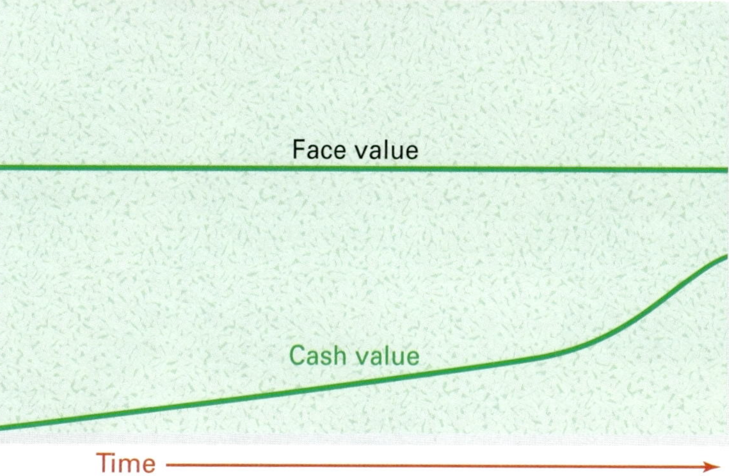

14-25

The face value of a permanent insurance policy remains the same over time, but the cash value increases.

Critical Thinking. *Ask:* For what kind of person would each type of life insurance described in this chapter be the best choice?

- **Universal life.** A universal life policy provides a guaranteed minimum rate of return on its investment component and has flexible features. You may reduce or increase the face value of the policy as your insurance needs change. If you want to invest an additional amount in the policy, you can pay a higher premium or an extra lump sum. When you're short of cash, you may be allowed to pay less than the usual premium. The difference is taken out of the cash value of the policy.
- **Variable life.** In a variable life policy, you have control over how the cash value is invested. The cash value of your policy will change with your investment results, so there is no guaranteed cash value amount. There is, however, usually a minimum face value guarantee. Some variable life policies have a fixed schedule, in which premiums are paid at specific times and in specific amounts. Some allow flexible premiums, so that the amount and payment dates may be changed as the policyholder's needs change.

Discussion. *Ask:* Would you choose permanent life insurance as a way to invest for the future? Why or why not?

Which Type for You?

Consumers must decide whether term or permanent insurance best suits their needs. Term insurance costs far less than permanent insurance for the same amount of coverage. For instance, if you choose term insurance, less than $200 per year might buy you the same amount of coverage as permanent insurance that costs more than $2,000 per year. For someone on a tight budget, a term policy may be the only way to afford adequate insurance protection.

Of course, the extra money you pay for permanent insurance doesn't disappear—it builds cash value. However, it may be hard to tell what portion of the premium is being invested and what rate of return the investment is actually earning.

Many consumer advocates suggest that consumers who can afford permanent insurance would be better off to buy term insurance, pay lower premiums, and put the difference into investments that they control. Of course, this plan requires that they have the

14-26

People have different needs for life insurance at different life stages. What factors should this couple consider when choosing between term and permanent insurance?

Critical Thinking. ***Ask:*** Why is it important to read a life insurance policy before you sign it? What could happen if you did not do so?

Class Activity. Ask students to make a list of major life events that might require a policyholder to update his or her list of beneficiaries.

discipline to save and invest on their own. Some consumers appreciate having savings and investment done for them through their insurance choices. See Figure 14-26.

POLICY FEATURES AND PROVISIONS

You can obtain life insurance through your employer or an association to which you belong, such as a credit union. You can also buy an individual policy through a life insurance agent. However you obtain life insurance, read the policy before you sign it. If you don't understand it, ask your agent or someone who is knowledgeable about insurance to explain it to you. Knowing some of the common provisions and features of policies will help you choose a policy and understand its terms.

- **Premiums.** Annual premiums usually cost somewhat less per year than paying semi-annually, quarterly, or monthly. The policy may allow a grace period—usually about a month—to pay the premium after it is due. If you don't pay during this period, the policy lapses and your coverage ends. To get it re-instated, you may have to have a physical examination.
- **Dividends.** Some life insurance policies may pay you a *dividend*, which is a share of the company's surplus. A policy that pays dividends is called a *participating policy* and is issued by a *mutual* life insurance company—one owned by its policyholders. Dividends are not guaranteed, but are paid only if the company has a surplus due to lower costs or higher investment earnings than anticipated. Dividends can be paid in cash, left in the policy to accumulate, used to pay part of the premiums, or used to purchase additional insurance. A *nonparticipating policy*, which does not pay dividends, generally has lower premiums. However, when you factor in the dividends, participating policies may cost less in the long run.
- **Beneficiaries.** The *beneficiary* is the person or group to whom death benefits will be paid. Although it can be anyone or any group, most people name a member of the family. See Figure 14-27. Be sure to update your list of beneficiaries as needed. If you should die and none of your beneficiaries are still living, the insurance proceeds will go into your estate.

14-27

People often designate their children or other dependents as beneficiaries of their life insurance. Why might you designate different beneficiaries over time?

Research Activity. Ask students to find an online life insurance calculator. Have them use it to calculate the amount of insurance coverage needed by a 37-year-old who is the sole wage earner for a family of four, including two school-age children. Then have them research the cost of such a policy.

- **Benefits.** When the insured dies, the beneficiary must make a claim to the insurance company in order to receive the benefits of the policy. Beneficiaries can usually choose how they would like to receive benefits, such as in one lump sum or a certain amount each month. Benefits are typically not subject to income tax.

HOW MUCH LIFE INSURANCE?

Your needs for life insurance will change over the course of your life. A single adult who lives alone and does not contribute to anyone else's support probably needs little, if any, life insurance—perhaps just enough to cover funeral expenses. On the other hand, a parent who is the sole support of two toddlers will need enough life insurance to feed, clothe, shelter, and educate those children until they reach adulthood. After the children are grown, the amount of insurance needed generally will decrease. See Figure 14-28.

Your insurance agent can help you determine the amount of life insurance you need. Other means for determining your insurance needs include financial software packages and calculators on insurance-related Web pages. These calculators typically ask you to estimate anticipated future financial needs, along with your available financial resources, and use a formula to calculate your recommended coverage amount.

Social Security Survivors' Benefits

When assessing life insurance needs, remember to consider Social Security survivors' benefits. After a worker covered by the Social Security system dies, these benefits are paid to the surviving spouse and any children. You can find out the anticipated amount by checking your annual Social Security statement or contacting the Social Security Administration. Income from survivors' benefits will decrease the amount of life insurance coverage needed.

14-28

When determining the amount of life insurance coverage needed, remember to consider long-range goals, such as providing for a child's education or wedding.

Critical Thinking. ***Ask:*** Why do insurance companies base premium amounts on risk factors? Do you think it is reasonable for them to do so?

FACTORS AFFECTING COST

Life insurance costs can vary widely, so compare quotes from several companies. The premium amount depends on the type of insurance and the face value of the policy. In addition, insurance companies look at the following risk factors.

- **Insured's health.** A person in poor health will pay higher premiums than someone in good health. Smokers pay higher premiums than nonsmokers.
- **Family health history.** A person whose family has a history of heart disease, cancer, or other serious illness with a genetic component might pay higher premiums.

14-29

If you plan to take up skydiving, be prepared to pay higher life insurance premiums. Why would insurance companies charge more for life insurance to someone whose occupation or hobby is hazardous?

Answer Key. Answers to the Section Review questions are provided in the Section Lesson Plan located in the *Teacher Resource Guide.*

- **Occupation or hobbies.** A person's job or hobby and its hazards can affect the cost of premiums. See Figure 14-29.
- **Gender.** In general, the average life expectancy for women is longer than for men. Therefore, women pay less for life insurance.
- **Age of insured.** People will pay more for life insurance as they get older, since the chances of dying become statistically higher.

Section 14.5 Review

CHECK YOUR UNDERSTANDING

1. How does term life insurance differ from permanent life insurance?
2. What is a cash value policy?
3. What should you consider when deciding how much life insurance to purchase?

CONSUMER APPLICATION

Life Insurance Strategy Suppose you are a 37-year-old with three children under the age of 12. You earn $45,000 a year, and your spouse earns $39,900. You want to make sure all of your children receive a postsecondary education and to provide for them in the event of your death or your spouse's, so you'll need to supplement your current savings and investments. Develop a strategy to purchase life insurance for you and your spouse, using what you know about life insurance options.

CHAPTER 14

Review & Activities

CHAPTER SUMMARY

- Insurance manages financial risk by sharing it among a large group. Choose insurance companies and policies carefully. (14.1)
- You need enough required and optional auto insurance coverage. Take safety steps after an accident and file a claim correctly. (14.2)
- Home insurance provides property and liability coverage. A household inventory can help you file a claim. (14.3)
- Health care plans protect against high medical bills and determine the choices you have in medical care. (14.4)
- Life insurance pays death benefits and may be an investment tool. The amount of coverage needed changes over a lifetime. (14.5)

THE $avvy Consumer

Double Coverage: When Jen started college, she signed up for the school's health insurance plan. Then an older student pointed out that she bought a short-term policy from a private company in order to be assured of getting better care. The student suggested that Jen do the same. What facts does Jen need to know in order to decide whether buying the extra coverage is worthwhile? (14.4)

Reviewing Key Terms and Ideas

1. How does **insurance** transfer risk? (14.1)
2. What is the difference between an **endorsement** and an **exclusion**? (14.1)
3. Name one advantage and one disadvantage of **no-fault insurance**. (14.2)
4. Name three kinds of auto insurance coverage. Why is each necessary? (14.2)
5. What is **depreciation**? How does it relate to insurance coverage? (14.2)
6. For auto liability coverage, what do these numbers mean: 50/100/25? (14.2)
7. What is the advantage of having a home insurance policy with replacement coverage? (14.3)
8. How might an **appraisal** of your home affect your insurance rates? (14.3)
9. Name three protections with liability coverage under a home insurance policy? (14.3)
10. Describe four influences on home insurance rates. (14.3)
11. Describe three categories of coverage that might be in a health plan. (14.4)
12. Name four sources of health care benefits. (14.4)
13. Explain the basic differences between **fee-for-service** and **managed care plans.** (14.4)
14. Describe the differences between two government-sponsored health care programs. (14.4)
15. Does **cash value** relate to a policy's insurance or investment aspect? Explain. (14.5)
16. Why do many consumer advocates recommend **term life insurance**? (14.5)

Answer Key. Answers to the Chapter Review & Activities are provided in the Teacher's Manual in the *Teacher Annotated Edition* of the text.

Thinking Critically

1. **Supporting Your Position:** Insurance companies base their premiums on such factors as age, gender, and marital status. Instead, should insurance rates be the same for everyone? Which approach would be more fair to consumers? Why? (14.1)
2. **Drawing Conclusions:** Why do you think young drivers have more automobile accidents than older age groups? What could be done to reduce the number? (14.2)
3. **Understanding Cause and Effect:** Managed care evolved as a way to reduce the medical claims paid by insurance companies. Which specific features of the managed care approach would likely result in fewer and smaller claims? Why? (14.4)
4. **Analyzing Economic Concepts:** How might competition affect the managed care plan market? (14.4)

Building Consumer Skills

1. **Choosing Insurance:** Research the financial strength and customer satisfaction ratings of three companies that offer auto insurance. Compare their rates for identical coverage. Explain which company you would choose and why. (14.1)
2. **Auto Insurance Discounts:** Investigate auto insurance discounts offered to teens by various insurers. Write an article explaining your findings. (14.2)
3. **Auto Accident Guidelines:** Create a booklet to keep in a vehicle for use in case of an auto accident. Include important phone numbers, steps to take, forms for recording information at the scene, and guidelines for filing a claim. (14.2)
4. **Long-Term Care Costs:** Investigate the costs of nursing home care. Then research the cost of long-term care insurance. Summarize your findings. Would you recommend long-term care insurance? Why or why not? (14.4)
5. **Life Insurance Needs:** Create a hypothetical case in which a person would be wise to purchase term insurance. Do the same for permanent insurance. Explain your reasons. (14.5)
6. **Factors Affecting Life Insurance:** Make a checklist of at least six personal factors that consumers should consider when choosing a type and amount of life insurance. Explain how each factor might affect the decision. (14.5)

CONSUMER CONNECTIONS

- **Family:** Discuss with family members the purpose and benefits of a household inventory. Create or update an inventory for one or more rooms in your home. (14.3)
- **Community:** Looking at maps (state and national), locate your area. What perils that home insurance can cover are possible where you live? Gradually expand your focus to areas farther away, including other parts of your state and then the country. Identify perils in various locations and the kinds of insurance that people would need. For example, where would Nation Flood Insurance be important? (14.3)

CHAPTER 15

Persuasion in the Marketplace

Reading with Purpose

- As you read this chapter, create an outline using the colored headings.
- Write a question for each heading to help guide your reading.
- Write the answer to each question as you read the chapter.
- Ask your teacher to help with answers you cannot find in the text.

SECTION 15.1

The Role of Advertising

Objectives

After studying this section, you should be able to:

- Identify forms of advertising.
- Analyze the impact of advertising.
- Explain how advertising is regulated to protect consumers.

Key Terms

direct mail advertising
infomercials

How do you feel about ads? Are commercials a nuisance because they interrupt programs, or are they more entertaining than the programs themselves? Whether you love them or hate them, advertisements are here to stay.

FORMS OF ADVERTISING

Although some forms of advertising have been around for centuries, advertisers continue to develop innovative approaches that are often based on new technology. Here are some examples of advertising methods. You can probably think of others that you've seen.

- Print ads in newspapers, magazines, telephone directories, and other publications.
- **Direct mail advertising**—printed advertising sent through the mail directly to consumers' homes. Examples include catalogs, flyers, and promotional newsletters.
- Radio and TV commercials. Even some gas pumps show commercials on miniature video screens.
- **Infomercials**—TV or radio ads that run 30 minutes or longer and are designed to resemble programming. Some infomercials use a talk-show format, with a celebrity host surrounded by an enthusiastic studio audience. Others

Discussion. ***Ask:*** Which form of advertising do you believe to be the most effective? What makes it more effective than other forms of advertising?

Critical Thinking. ***Ask:*** How might the world be different if there were no advertising at all? Do the benefits of advertising outweigh the drawbacks?

seem like investigative reports or documentaries and are hosted by actors who are supposed reporters or experts.

- Ads that appear on Web pages, pop up in a separate window, or in email messages.
- Billboards and signs, whether outdoors, in a subway car, on the sides of buses and trucks, or in other places.

THE IMPACT OF ADVERTISING

The primary purpose of advertising is to convince consumers to spend money on goods and services. With so much competition for consumers' dollars, companies must advertise products in order to sell them.

Advertising strongly influences the choices that consumers make. Sometimes it may seem as though consumers are so consistently surrounded by advertising that they just ignore it. However, the impact, whether obvious or subtle, is there. Companies wouldn't spend so much money on advertising if they didn't believe it works. Advertisers select a particular advertising tool because of its cost—which usually is based on how many people the ad is likely to reach—and its effectiveness in reaching the right audience for a particular product or service. See Figure 15-1.

From the advertiser's point of view, advertising clearly has benefits. What about from your point of view? For consumers, advertising has both benefits and drawbacks.

Benefits for Consumers

By making it easier for you to compare prices and find out about sales, advertising helps you save money. Advertising can save you time as well—you can check a newspaper ad, for example, to find out a store's hours and prevent a wasted trip.

Some advertisements provide information to help you make better consumer choices. Without such ads, you might never

15-1

Advertisers spend millions of dollars each year developing innovative ways to get your attention. Ad agencies are often the creative force behind the ads. How do you respond to ads directed at teens?

Research Activity. Challenge students to find three ads that sound too good to be true. Have them circle statements that appear false or misleading.

Economic Impact & Issues. Have students research the growing use of product placement. How does it compare to traditional advertising?

know about the beneficial features of a product, new types of products that might interest you, or the services offered by businesses in your area. Public service ads promote health and safety by encouraging actions such as wearing seat belts.

Advertising also plays a role in making it possible for newspapers, commercial television stations, Web sites, and other media to provide information and entertainment at low or no cost to consumers. That's because much of the expense of publishing and broadcasting is paid for through the sale of advertising.

Drawbacks for Consumers

Some aspects of advertising can pose problems for consumers. For one thing, people sometimes find ads annoying, as when a blaring commercial interrupts a favorite program or a billboard spoils a beautiful view.

Another drawback is related to advertising's power of persuasion. Advertisements can lead consumers to spend money on items they don't truly need or want, or to select a product that's not really a wise choice. Some ads are deceptive; they omit or misstate information, harming consumers as a result. Most advertising is not deceptive, but a careful consumer should be on the alert for ads with false or misleading statements.

TEXTLINK

Examples of deceptive advertising are found in Section 1.4.

Economic Impact & Issues

Keeping Sales Up When Times Are Slow

In a slow economy, falling sales can force some businesses to scale back their budgets, including their marketing costs. You might expect to see fewer ads, but ironically you may see more—with a difference.

When business is slow, every sale is important to keep a company afloat. Cutting back on advertising can decrease sales further. Businesses may try to advertise smarter. Flashy, high-tech—and high-priced—graphics might be replaced with clever, low-tech creativity. For example, which ad might generate more sales when gas prices are very high, a costly eye-popping ad that grabs the attention of people who love large vehicles or a simpler ad for a small car that gets good gas mileage? Even with the less expensive ad, the smart seller might generate more sales by carefully directing the appeal.

You may also see ads in different places and media time slots as sellers focus their budget to reach the largest target audience for the money. Advertising time and space may be offered at lower rates since media outlets are also likely to be hurt by slow sales. (Remember that advertising provides newspapers and radio and TV stations with much of their income.) This allows businesses to buy premium spots that are otherwise unaffordable.

FIGURE IT OUT

Choose an ad that uses an expensive technique, such as a paid celebrity endorsement or an exotic setting. Design a lower-cost replacement ad. Be creative. Use humor if you like.

Research Activity. Have students watch an hour of children's television programming on a Saturday morning. Ask them to list the products they see advertised during that hour and make note of any claims in the commercials that seem exaggerated. Have them share their findings in class.

REGULATION OF ADS

The Federal Trade Commission (FTC) regulates advertising to help ensure that ads are fair and accurate. The FTC defines advertising standards for publishers and broadcasters, and it makes those standards available to advertisers and the public.

Advertisements that make claims about health or safety receive the most attention. Health or safety claims must be supported by tests, studies, or other scientific evidence that has been evaluated by qualified experts. The FTC also pays special attention to advertisements aimed at children, since children are more vulnerable to the effects of advertising. See Figure 15-2.

The FTC monitors only national advertising. If it determines that an ad is making inaccurate or false claims, it orders the company to discontinue the advertisement. It also can order that monetary damages be paid to consumers. By regulating advertising, the FTC protects both consumers and legitimate businesses from the unfair tactics of a few dishonest advertisers.

15-2 **Advertisers are not supposed to take unfair advantage of children's limited ability to detect exaggeration. For example, a commercial should not make it seem as though a toy can do something it can't.**

Section 15.1 Review

CHECK YOUR UNDERSTANDING

1. What is direct mail advertising?
2. How does advertising benefit consumers?
3. What does the FTC do to combat deceptive advertising?

CONSUMER APPLICATION

Informative Ad Find an example of a highly informative ad. Identify the types of information provided and how the information would be helpful to consumers. What other information about the product might consumers need? How could they obtain it?

Answer Key. Answers to the Section Review questions are provided in the Section Lesson Plan located in the Teacher Resource Guide.

SECTION 15.2

Evaluating Advertisements

Objectives

After studying this section, you should be able to:

- Recognize methods of persuasion used in advertising.
- Use critical thinking skills to evaluate ads.

Key Terms

puffery
endorsement
testimonial

Consider two different ads for the same brand of jeans. The first ad points out their popularity—millions of people wear them. The second ad emphasizes how wearing these jeans will help you express yourself as an individual. Even though the same product is advertised, the messages are very different—yet both may be effective.

METHODS OF PERSUASION

Advertisers know that many consumers make purchasing decisions based on their feelings rather than facts. Therefore, ads often try to appeal to consumers' emotions. They may boast that a product will make your life easier, happier, healthier, or safer. They appeal to your hopes, desires, and fears.

Familiarity with the strategies advertisers use will help you exercise better judgment as a consumer. Start by learning to recognize the difference between factual information and persuasive techniques. Here are some common methods of persuasion. See how many of them you can spot in ads.

Class Activity. Ask students to give examples of claims that might be made about products. List the claims on the board. Then ask the class to identify the claims as subjective or objective. Ask them to explain their reasoning. Mark the claims with either an S for subjective or an O for objective.

Positive Images

Have you ever noticed how most models in ads always look great and appear to have perfect lives? The implication is clear: Using this product will make you as happy as the people in the commercial. Ads may encourage you to transfer positive feelings about any number of things—a fun party, a beautiful beach, an attractive person—to whatever product is being pitched. In fact, some ads that rely heavily on this technique don't even show the product.

Puffery and Subjective Claims

Exaggeration in advertising is so common that there's a special name for it. **Puffery** refers to exaggerated claims or descriptions intended to increase a product's reputation or appeal. For example, a commercial might show an athlete eating an energy bar, then jumping over a tall building. The Federal Trade Commission would not consider this ad deceptive. Both the advertiser and the FTC assume consumers will understand that the exaggeration is not to be taken seriously.

Subjective claims such as "Great tasting" or "Gives your hair incredible shine" are also frequently found in advertising. They are subjective because they're matters of opinion, not fact. Advertisers are not required to provide proof of such statements. In contrast, an objective claim such as "Leaves your hair 30% shinier than the other leading brand" must be backed up with evidence.

Before-and-After Comparisons

Print advertisements often use before-and-after pictures to show the supposed results of a product or service. The designers of such ads can use certain tricks to ensure that the "after" picture looks better than the "before" picture. For instance, an ad for a weight-loss product may show a blurry black and white snapshot of a tired-looking woman in unflattering clothing. The "after" picture, in full color, shows her looking happy and energetic, with perfect hair and makeup and a bright, appealing outfit. See Figure 15-3.

Endorsements

An **endorsement** is an advertising message that appears to reflect the opinions, beliefs, findings, or experience of a person or group other than the advertiser. Ads often make use of celebrity, expert, or consumer endorsements. An endorsement may take the

Critical Thinking. ***Ask:*** How do puffery and subjective claims differ from deceptive and fraudulent advertising?

15-3

Before-and-after comparisons can be misleading. Why might you be skeptical of this comparison?

Class Activity. Ask volunteers to name products that they have seen endorsed by celebrities (but without naming the celebrities). Then ask the rest of the class to name the celebrity endorser of each product. Discuss what their ability to do so implies about the effectiveness of celebrity endorsements.

form of a **testimonial**, which is a positive statement made by an endorser about a product or service—"This movie is hilarious! I loved it!" Endorsements can also consist of a product demonstration; the use of a person's name, likeness, or signature; or an organization's name or seal.

The Federal Trade Commission sets rules governing endorsements. Words attributed to endorsers must reflect their honest opinions. If they claim to use the product, they must actually use it. Advertisers must be able to show proof that endorsers who claim to be experts are legitimate. When a group endorses a product, the endorsement must reflect the collective judgment of the organization.

If the endorser has a connection to the seller, such as owning stock in the company, that connection must be made known to consumers. If the "ordinary consumer" in the ad is in fact an actor or model portraying a consumer, that too must be disclosed. However, advertisers are not required to say that celebrity endorsers have been paid. Unless the ad specifically says that the celebrity was not paid, you should assume that he or she was. See Figure 15-4.

Humor, Slogans, and Jingles

Television and radio commercials frequently use humor to sell products. Ads that make consumers laugh generally leave a lasting impression. Likewise, advertisers often use slogans, repetitive phrases, rhymes, and jingles (short, catchy songs) in the hopes that they will help people remember the product.

Other Emotional Appeals

Advertisers try to persuade consumers in countless ways. Here are some examples of additional techniques designed to appeal to your emotions.

- **Bandwagon.** Some ads attempt to sell you a product by convincing you that everyone is "jumping on the bandwagon" to enjoy this product. For example, a commercial might show crowds of people rushing to the store to buy the advertised item.

Team Activity. Have students work in small groups to create a slogan or jingle for a fictitious product. Have each group recite its slogan or jingle to the class. Ask the other students whether each jingle would help them remember the product name.

15-4

Many athletes are highly paid to endorse products in ads. What rules must such ads follow?

Critical Thinking. *Ask:* What groups of people do advertisers target with each type of emotional appeal? What makes this strategy effective?

- **Group identification.** Ads may imply that using their product will help you fit in with a particular group. A soft drink ad might show a group of teens wearing trendy clothing and having a great time together. The implication is that teens who choose that drink are hip and popular. See Figure 15-5.
- **Trendsetter.** The trendsetter tactic, on the other hand, encourages you to stand out from the crowd by being one of the first people to try something new. High-tech gadgets and daring fashions might be promoted this way.
- **Hidden fears.** Sometimes advertisers play on the fears of consumers. An ad for breath mints might suggest that you'll be embarrassed if you don't use the product.

Team Activity. Have students work in small groups to develop fictitious advertisements that use one or more of the strategies described in this section.

- **Traditional values.** A commercial for lemonade might show children sitting with their grandmother on the porch swing of an old-fashioned farmhouse. The advertiser knows that traditional values associated with home and family are appealing to many people.

RECOGNIZING ADS

It's not always easy to recognize when someone is trying to sell you something. Ads are sometimes deliberately hard to distinguish from the content provided by publishers and broadcasters. An infomercial may look like a talk show; a magazine ad may look like an article; a newspaper ad may resemble an editorial. What about that message in the corner of the Web page you're browsing—is it part of the site's content, or an ad?

Recognizing ads is an essential consumer skill. That's because the way you evaluate and interpret information should depend on, among other things, whether or not someone is trying to sell you something. For instance, watching a group of people enthusiastically praise a piece of exercise equipment might impress you—until you realize they're all being paid to do so.

Point Out. Another type of emotional appeal is cause-related marketing, in which a company promises to contribute some of its profits to a charitable cause.

15-5

Some ads imply that using a certain product will make you "one of the team." What types of products might be advertised in this way?

Class Activity. Bring in a copy of a print advertisement. Have the class analyze the ad, using the critical thinking questions on this page.

How can you recognize ads in disguise? First, look for disclosures, such as "paid advertisement" in fine print on a magazine or newspaper page. Infomercials are often described as "paid programming" in TV listings and identified as paid commercial presentations at the beginning of the broadcast. Beyond that, use your critical thinking skills. If pitching a particular product seems to be the focus of the presentation, you're probably viewing an ad.

THINKING CRITICALLY ABOUT ADS

As you encounter advertisements that interest you, put them through some tests before making a decision. Ask yourself these questions:

- Which elements of this advertisement caught my attention—music, color, the setting, a model or actor, a slogan? What connection do those elements have to the actual product being promoted?
- In what ways is the ad trying to influence me? How is it trying to reach my emotions?
- Am I being given all of the facts? What does the advertisement *not* tell me about the product?
- What does the fine print say?
- Does this advertisement sound too good to be true? What specific claims does it make? How can I research them to find out if they're accurate?

By using your critical thinking skills, you can benefit from ads without being overly swayed by their powers of persuasion. See Figure 15-6.

Answer Key. Answers to the Section Review questions are provided in the Section Lesson Plan located in the *Teacher Resource Guide.*

15-6 **Stop and think about the techniques used in ads and whether their claims are legitimate. What other questions might you want to ask about ads?**

Section 15.2 Review

CHECK YOUR UNDERSTANDING

1. What is an endorsement?
2. Describe three other persuasive techniques used by advertisers.
3. How can you use critical thinking to evaluate ads?

CONSUMER APPLICATION

Analyzing an Ad Choose a magazine ad that uses one or more of the persuasive techniques identified in the text. Explain which techniques are used and in what ways. Do you feel they would be effective in persuading you to buy? Why or why not?

Objectives

After studying this section, you should be able to:

- Describe how to benefit from sales, coupons, and other promotions.
- Recognize subtle ways sellers encourage consumer spending.
- Explain consumer rights regarding telemarketing and door-to-door sales.

Key Terms

loss leader
incentive
rebate
trading up
telemarketing

SECTION 15.3

Promotional and Sales Tactics

People who sell products and services are fishing for customers. They lure them with sales, coupons, and other enticements. Unlike fish, consumers can benefit in this situation—if they know how to take advantage of special purchase opportunities.

PRICE PROMOTIONS

So far in this chapter you've read about advertising, but that's just one of the promotional techniques that marketers use. *Promotion* is any form of communication used to inform people about a product or service or persuade them to make a purchase. In turn, promotion is just one component of *marketing*—the process of developing, promoting, and distributing products.

A particularly effective way to encourage the purchase of a product or service is to make its price attractive to consumers. Understanding sales and other price promotions can help you be a more effective consumer.

Sales

Most shoppers love sales—and retailers know it. That's why so many retailers advertise sales, which are temporary price reductions, so frequently. Sales appeal to consumers not

Point Out. Some stores make a business of going out of business, reopening under a new name, and then repeating the process.

only because of the actual savings, but because buying an item on sale makes people feel they are successful bargain hunters.

However, not all sales offer equal savings. A truly wise shopper understands the different types of sales and how best to take advantage of them.

- **Clearance sales.** To reduce the existing level of inventory, or unsold merchandise, a retailer may decide to hold a *clearance* or *inventory reduction* sale. These sales are often related to the change of seasons. Although the selection is often limited, clearance sales are one of the best opportunities for significant savings.
- **Other seasonal sales.** Due to competition, or in some cases tradition, retailers often reduce prices on certain items at a particular time of year. Back-to-school sales are an example. Many department stores have "white sales" for towels and bedding in January. If you know the cycle of such sales, you may save money by timing your purchases accordingly. See Figure 15-7.
- **Going out of business sales.** A store can use this phrase only if it is really going out of business. Another term often used is *liquidation sale,* because the entire inventory is being *liquidated,* or converted into cash. You may find some great deals.

Community Activity. Ask students to visit a store in their area and note how many items are offered on sale or at a special price.

- **Holiday and miscellaneous sales.** Sales frequently coincide with holidays, such as Labor Day, but at times they may seem to be held for no special reason. While some bargains can be found, these sales usually do not represent the best opportunities for overall savings.

If the store runs out of an advertised sale item, ask for a *rain check*—a certificate that will allow you to purchase the item later at the sale price. If you prefer, ask whether the store is offering a substitute for the out-of-stock item.

Other Price Reductions

A retailer can't legally refer to a "sale" price unless it has recently sold the same item at a higher price. Therefore you may see items advertised as a "special value" or "special purchase." This usually means the retailer has shipped in a limited quantity of low-priced merchandise that it does not regularly carry. Such merchandise is often of lower quality than the regular stock.

15-7

Merchants try to draw business away from competitors by offering low prices on items that consumers are likely to be shopping for. When might you find these gardening tools on sale?

Discussion. ***Ask:*** Some consumers shop at several stores to buy only loss leaders. Would you try this strategy? Why or why not?

Some retailers choose not to have sales at all, but instead advertise that their prices are always low. These retailers may still promote an item as a "special value" or call attention to its "new low price."

Some items are marked down in price because they're flawed or damaged. A sign or price tag saying "as is" signals that the item is imperfect in some way and that you won't be able to return it for a refund. In addition, the item might not be covered by the product's regular warranty.

Loss Leaders

If a store is advertising an extremely low price on a specific item, it may be a loss leader. A **loss leader** is an item priced below the retailer's cost in order to attract customers to the store. Although retailers lose money on the sale of loss leaders, they hope to make up for it by selling additional, more profitable items to the customers who come in. Keep in mind that the prices of other items in the store may be marked up to compensate for the loss leader. In some states, using loss leader pricing is unlawful because it is considered unfair competition. In other states, it's a legal marketing tool.

Dollars and Sense. Ask students to choose a specific product and compare prices for it from at least three stores or vendors.

Price Comparisons

When you're shopping, you may see signs on store shelves such as "Elsewhere $5.99—Our Price $3.99" or "Only $12.99—Comparable Value $15.00." When you encounter such comparisons, pay attention to exactly what is being compared. The first example implies that the very same item is sold at other stores for a higher price. In the second example, the "comparable value" could be a competing brand of similar quality.

Retailers may also compare their price for an item with the manufacturer's suggested retail price. By law, manufacturers can only suggest a retail price; they can't force retailers to set their price at that level. It's common for retailers to sell items for less. Thus, stores boasting that they sell goods below the suggested retail price are not necessarily offering an unusual bargain.

DOLLARSandSENSE

Tips for Bargain Hunters

If you like to look for a sale rather than pay the regular price, you're not alone. To make sure you're really getting a bargain:

- Compare the unit price, or the price per item, pound, or other measure. To calculate the unit price, divide the cost by the number of units.
- Pay attention to what's on sale and what's not. Retailers hope that once they've lured you in with bargains, you'll make additional full-price purchases.
- Check items carefully for flaws. Ask about return and exchange policies.

Team Activity. Have students work in groups to come up with an incentive they think would persuade teens to buy a product.

Caption Answer. If you don't need the product, buying it is a waste of money regardless of the price.

INCENTIVES

Many manufacturers and retailers offer incentives to consumers. An **incentive** is a reward offered to encourage a particular behavior, such as buying a product. For example, free gifts, "bonus with purchase" items, and frequent flyer miles are incentives used to attract consumers' interest. So are coupons, rebates, and sweepstakes.

Coupons

A coupon entitles its bearer to savings on a product, such as 50 cents off, 20% off, or two for the price of one. In most cases, a coupon must be used within a limited period of time. Newspapers, magazines, and countless mailed flyers are loaded with coupons. In some stores, the cash register prints coupons for products similar to some that were just purchased. Internet advertisers also feature coupons that can be used on their sites or printed and used in their stores.

Some coupons are issued by retailers to attract business and can be used only for items purchased from that retailer. Other coupons are offered by product manufacturers to encourage people to try their products or to remain loyal to their brand. Most manufacturer's coupons can be used at any store that accepts them. The manufacturer reimburses the retailer for the coupon amount. Some stores advertise that they will double or triple the value of manufacturer's coupons. Since the manufacturer reimburses only the face value, the rest comes out of the retailer's pocket—or perhaps from customers' pockets, if the store raises prices to make up for the loss.

Coupons can offer you great savings if you use them wisely. That means using them only for items that you really need, not as an excuse to make impulse purchases. Also consider whether you can save more money by choosing store brand or generic items instead of using coupons to buy name-brand products. If you decide to save coupons, organize them by category and keep track of when they expire. See Figure 15-8.

15-8

A few moments spent clipping coupons can result in significant savings at the store. Why should you use coupons only for items that you really need?

Discussion. ***Ask:*** Under what circumstances would you consider it worth the work of applying for a rebate? How big would the payoff have to be?

Rebates

Manufacturers or retailers may offer rebates on specific items. A **rebate** is a partial refund of an item's purchase price. The consumer applies for the rebate by mailing in a form and proof of purchase. After the rebate is processed, the consumer receives a check for the rebate amount.

If you're motivated to choose a product because of its rebate, ask yourself whether you're willing to take the time to apply for it. Companies count on the fact that not everyone will bother to mail in the form. When applying for a rebate, follow the instructions exactly. Keep a photocopy of the form and proof of purchase for your records. The form usually includes instructions for where to write or call if you haven't received the rebate after a reasonable time.

Research Activity. Have students read and summarize the rules for entering a sweepstakes or contest offered at a store, in a magazine, or online.

Sweepstakes and Contests

"You could be the lucky winner of $20,000 or a brand new car!" Sweepstakes promotions are an effective way to grab the attention of consumers. See Figure 15-9.

While most sweepstakes are legitimate, some are frauds designed to take your money. How can you tell the difference? Legitimate sweepstakes never require you to make a purchase or pay a fee. In contrast, fraudulent sweepstakes almost always require that you spend money to enter or to claim your prize. You might be asked to pay a "handling fee," for instance, or to call a 900 number that ends up adding $50 to your phone bill. If you fall for the bait, the fraudulent sweepstakes promoter will keep your money. You get nothing at all in return, or at best, a "prize" worth much less than the amount you paid.

It's legal for contests that are based on skill, such as solving a puzzle or writing a poem, to require that you make a purchase, payment, or donation to enter. Still, it's wise to be wary. Some contests lure entrants into a series of increasingly difficult tasks, with higher entry fees at each round. By law, terms and rules of skills contests must be clearly disclosed.

15-9

Dramatic sweepstakes promotions that offer huge prizes generate lots of excitement. Even though a legitimate sweepstakes says "no purchase required," many consumers will buy the featured product anyway.

Community Activity. Ask students to visit a store in their community and look for examples of subtle tricks used to influence consumers' choices, such as end cap displays or grouping related products together. Have them take notes on what they see and share their observations with the class.

SUBTLE WAYS OF SELLING

Advertisements, sales, and coupons are easy to identify as promotional techniques. However, some of the other methods used by marketers to encourage you to buy might surprise you. Stores, Web sites, catalogs, and products themselves are often designed with the goal of influencing the customer's frame of mind and shopping behavior. Here are some examples.

- Items that are purchased most frequently—like bread and milk in a food store—are usually found in the farthest corner of the store. The retailer hopes that as you walk by all the other merchandise to get there, you'll find something else to buy.
- Items that are most profitable for the merchant are given prominent positions, such as an eye-level shelf or a display that partially blocks an aisle. Small, high-profit items are placed at checkout lanes to encourage impulse buying.
- The decor of a store is designed to project an image and attract a particular type of customer. A teen clothing department, for instance, might feature pulsing music, neon lights, and a giant video screen. See Figure 15-10.
- Music in some stores is slow and relaxing, encouraging shoppers to browse longer. At a fast-food restaurant, up-tempo music might be played so that people will eat faster and make way for the next batch of customers. Stores and restaurants may be decorated in certain colors for the same reasons.

In using these tactics, retailers are simply doing their job of trying to increase sales so that they can stay in business and make a profit. You might even appreciate some of these techniques because they make shopping a more pleasant experience. However, don't let them distract you from your job of making wise consumer decisions. The more you're aware of the subtle ways in which marketers try to influence you, the more likely that you'll make decisions based on what's best for you, not the marketer.

Class Activity. Have students interpret this quotation from Nicholas Johnson, former FCC commissioner: "It used to be that people needed products to survive. Now products need people to survive."

15-10

Stores are designed to appeal to certain groups of shoppers. If you ran this store, who would be your target audience? How would you try to attract those customers?

Discussion. ***Ask:*** How might you respond if a salesperson tries to convince you to trade up on a product?

PERSONAL SELLING

Making purchases in a store, over the phone, or from someone who comes to your door involves interaction with a clerk or salesperson. Smart consumers are able to benefit from salespeople without being pressured into overspending.

Salespeople in Stores

When you visit a store, salespeople are there to help you. They can answer questions and help you locate an item that may be particularly hard to find. See Figure 15-11.

Many salespeople are paid on commission. The more you spend, the more they get paid. There's no problem with that as long as you remember your own priorities and budget. Don't let a salesperson talk you into a purchase that you'll later regret.

Suppose you're shopping for a DVD player. When the salesperson sees you looking at a $300 machine, she points out the additional

Point Out. Another sales technique involves suggesting add-ons, such as socks or shoe polish for a customer who is buying shoes.

features found on a $400 model. Convincing customers to buy a higher-priced item than they originally intended to buy is a sales technique known as **trading up**. Remember, you can always try to negotiate a lower price.

There's a difference between trading up and illegal *bait and switch* practices. Suppose a salesperson tells you that an advertised item is not actually available or is of poor quality, then steers you to a higher-priced one. This is bait and switch, and it should be reported to your local or state consumer protection agency.

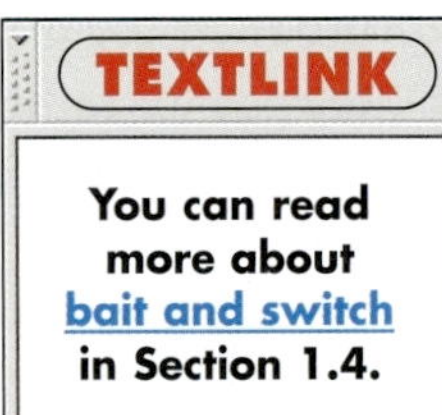

Telemarketing

Marketing goods and services by telephone is known as **telemarketing**. Telemarketers are required by law to make it clear they are selling something, give the name of the company they're representing, and avoid all forms of deception. Limits are set on the hours during which they may call consumers. See Figure 15-12.

If you're not interested in what a telemarketer is offering, politely say so. If necessary, simply hang up the phone. If you don't want to receive marketing calls on behalf of that seller in the future, tell the caller to put you on the seller's "do not call" list. The telemarketer must honor your request and refrain from calling you again, or else face a penalty

15-11

When you need assistance while shopping, seek out salespeople who know their merchandise and answer questions satisfactorily. Name some types of purchases that would require knowledgeable assistance from a salesperson.

Team Activity. Have pairs of students role-play scenes in which a person at home must deal with a door-to-door salesperson. Scenes may demonstrate techniques the salesperson uses to pressure the homeowner into buying and techmiques the homeowner uses to resist.

under the FTC's Telemarketing Sales Rule. Some states have a statewide "do not call" list. State lists and the National Do Not Call Registry apply to all telemarketers.

While most telemarketers are legitimate, some are fraudulent. Be wary of giving out your credit card number, Social Security number, or other personal information to a stranger who has called you. If you're interested in a telemarketer's offer, play it safe. Instead of agreeing to anything on the spot, ask for more information to be sent to you. When you receive it, verify that the company is legitimate before deciding whether to go ahead with the purchase.

Answer Key. Answers to the Section Review questions are provided in the Section Lesson Plan located in the *Teacher Resource Guide.*

15-12

Telemarketers might be calling to offer products or services that could be useful to you. What can you do to make sure that a company is legitimate?

Door-to-Door Sales

Like telemarketing, door-to-door sales is a technique used by both legitimate and fraudulent companies. If a door-to-door salesperson offers a product or service that appeals to you, ask for a business card for future contact. This will give you an opportunity to check out the person's company as well as time to think about your purchase.

In response to concerns about high-pressure tactics of some door-to-door salespeople, the Federal Trade Commission issued the Cooling-Off Rule. It allows consumers three business days to cancel purchases of $25 or more made in their own homes or in a location outside the seller's normal place of business. The seller must advise consumers of their right to cancel and provide them with a cancellation form.

Section 15.3 Review

CHECK YOUR UNDERSTANDING

1. Explain three guidelines for using coupons effectively.
2. Give an example of how a store manager might arrange merchandise to increase sales.
3. What is a "do not call" list? How does it affect telemarketers?

CONSUMER APPLICATION

Sale Pros and Cons From reading newspaper ads, you learn that two stores have the item you want. One store is going out of business. The other is having a season-ending clearance sale. What benefits and drawbacks associated with each kind of sale would you want to consider before you go shopping?

CHAPTER 15

Review & Activities

CHAPTER SUMMARY

- Advertising has benefits and drawbacks for consumers and strongly influences their decisions. The primary purpose of most advertising is to sell a product, but by law it cannot be deceptive. (15.1)
- Advertisers use many methods of persuasion that appeal to emotions. Think critically about advertisements and how they try to influence you. (15.2)
- Subtle merchandising techniques encourage consumers to buy. Wise consumers know how to use sales, coupons, and other promotions to their advantage, and they exercise their rights regarding telemarketing and door-to-door sales. (15.3)

Just Like the Pros: Maria wants to play professional basketball. She spends a lot of money on the shoes worn by her favorite player. When her friend Beth points out that the player is paid to endorse them, Maria replies, "I know, but she wouldn't wear them in a game unless she thought they were the best." How might Beth respond to that argument? (15.2)

Reviewing Key Terms and Ideas

1. Identify five forms of advertising. What does an advertiser consider when deciding which to use? (15.1)
2. How are **infomercials** similar to regular programming? How are they different? (15.1)
3. Describe two ways advertising benefits consumers. (15.1)
4. Explain two ways advertising can be a drawback for consumers. (15.1)
5. How does the FTC regulate advertising? (15.1)
6. What is **puffery**? Why do advertisers use it? (15.2)
7. What might need to be disclosed in an ad that includes an **endorsement**? (15.2)
8. What might a **testimonial** help to sell a product? (15.2)
9. How does a bandwagon appeal differ from a trendsetter appeal? What do they have in common? (15.2)
10. Give two examples of ads in disguise. (15.2)
11. Why should you be cautious about buying a marked-down item? (15.3)
12. What is a **loss leader**? (15.3)
13. How does a **rebate** work? (15.3)
14. How can you distinguish between a legitimate sweepstakes and a fraudulent one? (15.3)
15. What occurs when a salesperson uses the **trading-up** technique? (15.3)
16. Explain the Cooling-Off Rule. (15.3)

Answer Key. Answers to the Chapter Review & Activities are provided in the Teacher's Manual in the *Teacher Annotated Edition* of the text.

Thinking Critically

1. **Supporting Your Position:** Give your opinion of these statements and explain your reasoning: **a**) "What an ad says doesn't matter. The important thing is to just get people to remember a brand name." **b**) "Television has too much advertising." (15.1)
2. **Distinguishing Fact from Opinion:** Suppose an ad says, "Our easy-to-use software will save you time and effort." Is this a statement of fact or opinion? Would the advertiser have to prove this claim? Why or why not? (15.2)
3. **Analyzing Economic Concepts:** Explain how the concepts of demand, supply, and equilibrium price (discussed in Section 5.2) relate to clearance sales. (15.3)
4. **Coupon Savings:** Collect ten manufacturer's coupons. After researching prices, create a graph comparing the cost of buying items with the coupons versus buying equivalent store brand or generic products. What else would influence your decision to use coupons? (15.3)
5. **Price Negotiation:** Imagine you're buying a DVD player. The salesperson shows you a different DVD player that costs $100 more. With a partner, enact a scene in which you try to negotiate a lower price for the more expensive item. (15.3)

Building Consumer Skills

1. **Ad Regulations:** Research the FTC's guidelines regarding one of these: endorsements, use of the word "free," advertising on the Internet, or deceptive pricing. Give examples of ad content that would not meet the guidelines and explain why. (15.1)
2. **Teen-Targeted Ads:** Analyze the ads on a weekly TV program that you like. Are the products targeted to teens? Why or why not? What persuasive techniques are used? Discuss the impact the ads might have on teens' purchasing decisions. Repeat this activity with a program aimed at young children. (15.1, 15.2)
3. **Salesmanship:** Think of a product or service you would like to sell. Simulate a sales situation, with a partner acting as the customer. Demonstrate how you would use sales techniques to assist and advise the "customer." Analyze where the line is drawn between pressuring or manipulating a customer and selling appropriately. (15.3)

CONSUMER CONNECTIONS

- **Family:** Ask adult family members about experiences they've had with telemarketers and door-to-door salespeople. Were the experiences positive or not? Discuss the rights that consumers have regarding these sales methods. (15.3)
- **Community:** With a team of students, choose a few items that you buy, such as magazines, DVDs, clothing, and shoes. Identify stores that sell the items and decide who will visit each store. Visit the stores and take notes on how the items are marketed. Note store atmospheres, displays, arrangement of merchandise, and prices. Compare team notes and draw conclusions about the relationship between marketing and spending. (15.3)

CHAPTER 16

Shopping Skills

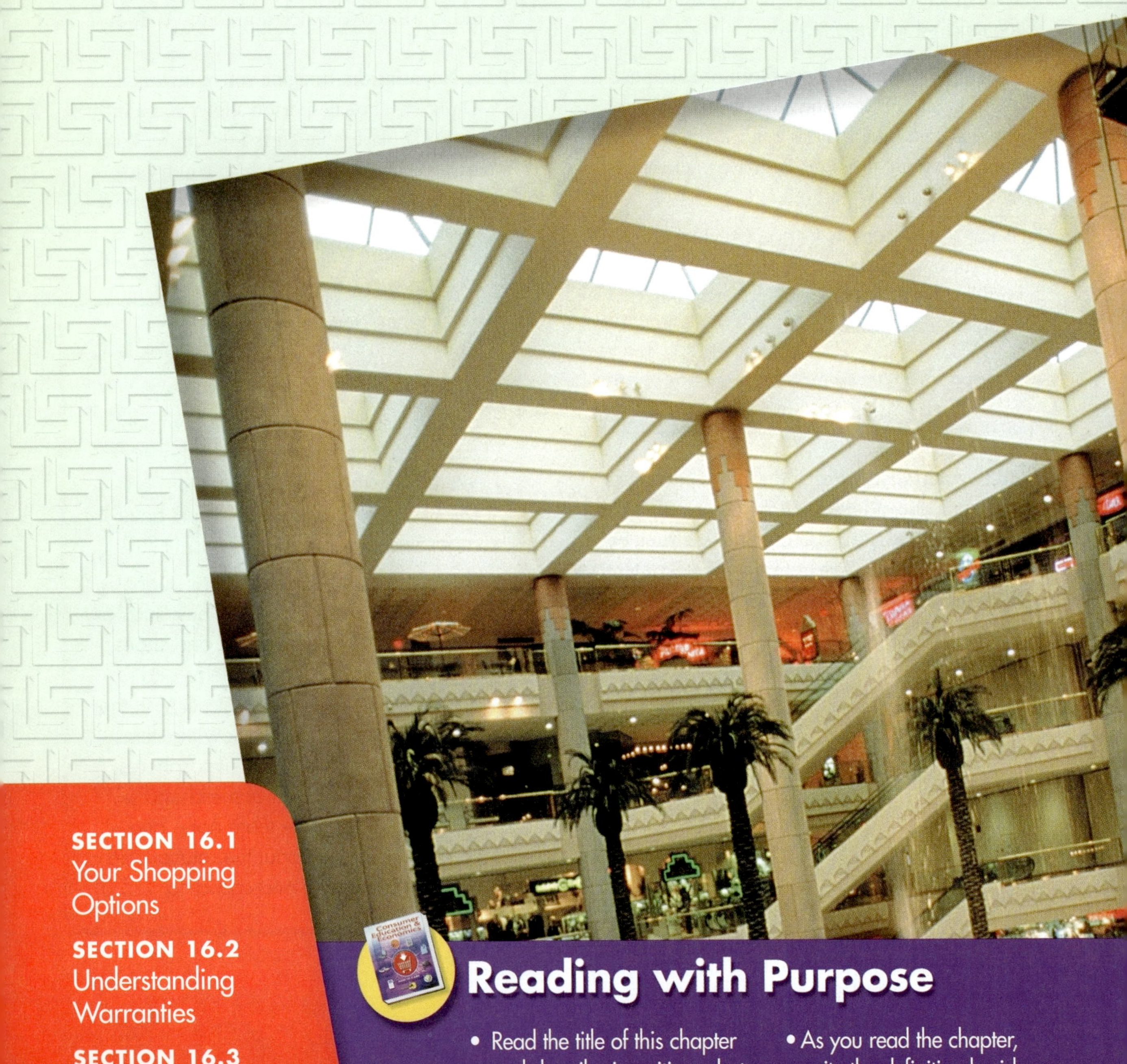

SECTION 16.1
Your Shopping Options

SECTION 16.2
Understanding Warranties

SECTION 16.3
Finding the Best Buys

SECTION 16.4
Shopping for Services

Reading with Purpose

- Read the title of this chapter and describe in writing what you expect to learn from it.
- Write down each key term, leaving space for definitions.
- As you read the chapter, write the definition beside each term.
- After reading the chapter, write a paragraph describing what you learned.

SECTION 16.1

Your Shopping Options

When you're shopping for that special something, do you cruise the mall, scan the catalogs, or browse the Web? Shopping is more exciting now that you can buy almost anything from almost anywhere.

Objectives

After studying this section, you should be able to:

- Compare and evaluate different types of retailers.
- Describe pros and cons of shopping from home.
- Explain guidelines for bidding in an Internet auction.

Key Terms

warehouse clubs
outlet stores
factory seconds

COMPARING RETAILERS

You have many choices of where and from whom to buy merchandise. Sometimes you might buy from an individual—at a garage sale or flea market, in an online auction, or by responding to a classified ad, for example. Most of your purchases, however, will be made from retailers, merchants who are in business to sell to consumers.

Many different retailers can meet your shopping needs, whether they offer goods in local stores, in a catalog, on the Internet, or through some combination of the three. Choosing a retailer can be just as important as choosing the product itself. Retailers differ from one another in:

- **The types of products sold.** Some retailers specialize in a certain category, such as clothing, office supplies, or auto parts. Others sell a broader range of merchandise.

Class Activity. Have students make a chart comparing the advantages and disadvantages of different types of retailers.

- **The variety and assortment of items offered.** If you're looking for a toaster, one retailer might offer dozens of brands and models; another only two or three.
- **Prices in comparison with other retailers.** Some merchants emphasize everyday low prices. Others have higher prices, but consumers can find bargains during sales and promotions.
- **The level and quality of service provided.** Receiving a higher level of service may require paying higher prices, but there are exceptions to this general rule.

Types of Retailers

Retailers range from small outfits run by a few people to huge national chains. As the marketplace continues to evolve, it becomes more difficult to categorize different types of retailers. Consider department stores, for example. There are upscale department stores, discount department stores, and varying levels in between. Each wants to be perceived as unique, fulfilling certain wants and attracting certain types of customers. The best way to get to know specific retailers is to shop at them and make comparisons yourself.

InfoSource. Have students visit the Web site of the Better Business Bureau to find out where their local office is located.

You can probably give examples of department stores, discount stores, and large or small specialty stores in your area. Other types of retailers may be less familiar to you. **Warehouse clubs** sell products to customers who pay a membership fee. Most of the products are sold in bulk quantities at significant savings. Selection and customer service, however, are very limited. **Outlet stores**, also called *factory outlets*, sell merchandise from only one manufacturer, generally at less than full retail price. Often the merchandise is excess stock. You may also find **factory seconds**, products that may have slight defects that do not affect the performance or appearance of the product. Such items are sometimes marked "irregular."

Evaluating Retailers

Reliability is an important consideration when selecting a retailer. Anyone can make the claim "satisfaction guaranteed or your money back"; only reputable businesses will back up that claim. You'll want to choose retailers that have a record of stability and satisfactory customer service. If you're considering a retailer that you're not familiar with, investigate its record before you buy.

Retailer Reliability

You can find out how long a retailer has been in business by contacting your local Better Business Bureau (BBB). In addition, the BBB or your state or local consumer protection office can tell you if they have received complaints against the retailer and how the company responded to those complaints. At online shopping sites, look for a symbol that indicates the site has been verified by a third party.

Community Activity. Ask students to visit a retailer in their community and evaluate it, using the checklist provided on this page.

In addition to reliability, you should evaluate several factors related to service:

- The ease or difficulty of locating items, whether in a store or online.
- Payment methods accepted, such as credit card or personal check.
- Policies regarding returns, refunds, shipping methods and costs, and privacy of personal information.
- Helpfulness and knowledge of sales staff or customer service representatives. See Figure 16-1.
- Special services offered, such as gift wrap or special orders.
- Service provided after the sale, including assistance with questions or problems you might have and maintenance or repair of products.

16-1

A locally owned store may charge more than a chain store, but it may offer better service from more experienced employees. For what kinds of items might you choose a locally owned store over a chain store?

Critical Thinking. *Ask:* For what types of merchandise is it better to shop in person instead of at home?

SHOPPING AT HOME

Many retailers give you the opportunity to shop and buy without leaving home. Shopping at home—whether by phone, mail, or the Internet—has several advantages. It may provide a much wider selection of merchandise than you could find locally. You can place an order without leaving home. In many cases you can shop 24 hours a day. Using the Internet, you can compare the selection and prices offered by several retailers in a matter of minutes, saving you the time and trouble of going from store to store. In some cases, you can get better deals from a catalog or online than you can at a store.

On the other hand, shopping at home has drawbacks. Looking at a picture of an item is not the same as being able to touch it, inspect it for quality, and try it on. Although you can shop anytime, you must wait for purchases to be delivered, which might take days or weeks. With most online purchases you have to pay the cost of shipping. When the merchandise arrives, it may not be quite what you thought it would be. If you return the item, you may have to pay additional shipping costs.

FCCLA. Have teams of students use the Consumer Clout unit of Financial Fitness to develop a smart shopping video for consumers. Videos may offer advice on how to shop for a specific product or service, or they may provide general shopping strategies. If possible, have students make their videos available to the public through a local library or community center.

Critical Thinking. ***Ask:*** Why is it important to keep a record of your transactions when you shop at home?

Tips for At-Home Shopping

When shopping from a catalog, a TV shopping channel, or over the Internet, follow these tips. They'll help you maximize the benefits of home shopping and minimize the drawbacks.

- Guard against impulse purchases. It's easy to get carried away when you can shop by mouse click or phone call.
- Before placing an order, identify the company and assess whether it's reliable. Make sure online orders use a secure site.
- Study product descriptions and pictures carefully. Note details such as the dimensions of the item, what it's made of, and care instructions. If the description is unclear or incomplete, call a customer service representative and ask questions before you order. See Figure 16-2.

TEXTLINK

Review the guidelines for safeguarding your privacy in Section 1.3.

Point Out. Note that some cards offer temporary credit card numbers to use for online purchases as a way to protect your real card number from theft.

- Compare prices—including all shipping and handling charges—with those of other retailers.
- Find out the company's return and refund policy. Who pays return shipping charges?
- Find out how long delivery is expected to take. If you need the item by a certain date, place the order well in advance.
- Pay by credit card if possible. As explained in Chapter 11, the Fair Credit Billing Act gives you important protection when you do.
- Keep a record of your transactions. For an online transaction, print out the address of the site and a copy of your order and transaction number. Many businesses will send a confirmation of your purchase.
- Check your order promptly when it arrives. Notify the company immediately if there is a mistake or damage.
- If the item isn't delivered on schedule, contact the company. The FTC's Mail or Telephone Order Merchandise Rule, which also applies to Internet purchases, states that a company must ship your merchandise within the time promised or offer to refund your money. If no shipping time is promised, the company generally has 30 days to ship your order.

16-2

Shopping from home can save you time and money if you're careful about ordering. What are some ways in which at-home shopping might cost you more than shopping in a store?

Caption Answer. You could research a product by checking local merchants, catalogs, and other Web sites to decide on the highest price you would pay.

Answer Key. Answers to the Section Review questions are provided in the Section Lesson Plan located in the *Teacher Resource Guide.*

16-3

Online auctions may be enticing, but are you really getting a good deal? Explain how you could research a product before bidding.

Internet Auctions

At an auction Web site, you can find a wide variety of new and used goods for sale. Typically, a description of each item is posted on the auction site for a certain number of days. During that time, registered users can place bids. At the end of the auction, the highest bidder and the seller arrange for payment and delivery. This system is based on mutual trust—buyers and sellers who don't keep up their end of the bargain are barred from further trading at that site.

Buyers who want more assurance may use a third-party *escrow service.* For a fee, the escrow service will accept payment from the buyer and hold it. After the buyer has received and approved the merchandise, the escrow service will release the payment to the seller.

Before you bid on an item in an Internet auction:

- Check out the seller's feedback rating and comments from other buyers (if available). Look for signs that the seller describes auction items honestly and ships them promptly.
- Read the description carefully. See Figure 16-3. Contact the seller if you have questions about the item or the terms of the auction. Request proof of authenticity for any item that might be a fake or an illegal copy.
- Consider your bid amount carefully, and make sure you understand the auction rules. Once you place a bid, you usually can't retract it.

Section 16.1 Review

CHECK YOUR UNDERSTANDING

1. What factors should you consider when evaluating the service offered by different retailers?
2. Name three advantages and three disadvantages of at-home shopping.
3. How can you protect yourself when participating in an online auction?

CONSUMER APPLICATION

Online Purchases Name a product you would buy online and one you would not. Explain your answer.

Objectives

After studying this section, you should be able to:

- Explain the purpose of a warranty.
- Analyze the terms of different types of warranties.
- Evaluate the need for a service contract.

Key Terms

warranty
implied warranty
full warranty
limited warranty
service contract

SECTION 16.2

Understanding Warranties

Two weeks ago, you purchased a portable CD player and have really enjoyed it. Today, it just quit working! You saved a long time for this product and can't afford to buy another one. Is your purchase protected?

THE PURPOSE OF WARRANTIES

When you buy a product, especially an expensive product, you want to be sure it will work properly and last a reasonable length of time. When you hire someone to perform a service, you want to know that the job will be done right and that any problems will be corrected. This type of assurance is best provided by a **warranty**, a guarantee of the soundness of a product or service. Warranties protect consumers against faulty products and poor workmanship. Wise shopping includes finding out whether a product or service carries a warranty and understanding its terms.

IMPLIED WARRANTIES

A warranty that is legally in effect even though it is not in writing is called an **implied warranty**. It's created by state law rather than by company or store policy. Implied warranties include the following:

Point Out. Sometimes an implied warranty covers a product even when the written warranty doesn't.

- **Merchantability.** This is an implied promise that every product sold is in proper condition and does what it is intended to do. For example, a can opener must open cans. If the product does not perform its intended use, the seller must replace it or allow you to return it for a refund. See Figure 16-4.
- **Fitness for a particular purpose.** This type of warranty takes effect when the seller advises a customer that a product can be used for a special purpose. Suppose a customer asks for hiking boots that are waterproof. The sales clerk recommends a certain pair of boots, and the customer buys them on the strength of that recommendation. If it turns out that the boots leak, the seller must take them back and refund the customer's money.

Discussion. ***Ask:*** If you bought a portable CD player at a store, what qualities would you expect to be guaranteed by its implied warranty?

WRITTEN WARRANTIES

Many manufacturers, sellers, and service providers go beyond the implied warranty by providing a written warranty. For example, a written warranty might state that a wireless phone is warranted against any defects in materials and workmanship for two years. Certain items may be excluded from coverage, such as batteries, accidental damage, or charges for labor if repair is needed. However, a written warranty can't negate the coverage provided by an implied warranty.

Magnuson-Moss Warranty Act

Written warranties are regulated by the Magnuson-Moss Warranty Act, passed in 1975. The act, which applies to goods but not services, does not require that manufacturers or sellers provide a written warranty. However, it protects consumers against deceptive warranties and provides for legal recourse if a warranty is not honored. Under the terms of the act, a written warranty for a product must include:

- A clear description of exactly what is covered and, if necessary, what is not covered.
- What the manufacturer or seller will do if the product is defective.
- Who is eligible for the warranty.

16-4

An implied warranty carries a promise that a product, such as this lawn mower, will do what it is intended to do. What rights does a buyer have if a product does not work?

Class Activity. Ask students to bring in written warranties from different products they or their families have purchased. With the class, examine these warranties to determine which are full and which are limited. Note whether each one includes the information required under Magnuson-Moss.

- When the warranty becomes effective and how long it is in effect.
- Steps the owner must take in order to get a product repaired or replaced while it is under warranty.
- What the owner should do if he or she has a complaint about the warranty.

Full and Limited Warranties

The Magnuson-Moss Warranty Act also spells out the difference between a "full warranty" and a "limited warranty." A **full warranty** meets five federal standards for comprehensive warranties as specified in the Magnuson-Moss Warranty Act. A **limited warranty** does not meet one or more of these standards, but it still provides valuable protection. Figure 16-5 shows the standards that a full warranty must meet in comparison to a limited warranty.

Note that "full warranty" does not necessarily mean the warranty has no restrictions. A warranty that has a time limit or excludes certain items from coverage can still be called a "full warranty" if it meets the five standards listed in Figure 16-5.

A product or service may have more than one warranty. For instance, there may be a full warranty during the first year after purchase and a limited warranty for the next two years.

16-5

Unless a warranty meets all five of the tests listed in the left column, it is a limited warranty. Which type of warranty guarantees a replacement or refund if the product can't be fixed?

Full and Limited Warranties

FULL WARRANTY	LIMITED WARRANTY
The warranty is extended to anyone who owns the product during the warranty period.	The warranty might be limited to the original owner.
There is no cost to the consumer for warranty service.	The consumer might have to pay something for service.
The consumer does not have to do anything to receive service other than notify the company about the problem.	The consumer might have to fulfill a requirement such as returning a warranty card.
If the company is unable to repair the product after a reasonable number of attempts, the company must either give the consumer a refund or provide a new product or part.	A refund or replacement might not be offered.
The warranty does not limit the duration of implied warranties.	The warranty might limit implied warranties to the time period of the written warranty.

Point Out. Explain that warranty cards often ask for personal information that the manufacturer can sell to marketing firms. For privacy reasons, some consumers choose not to return the cards. Unless otherwise specified, the warranty will still apply even if the product is not registered.

GETTING THE MOST FROM A WARRANTY

The time to begin thinking about a warranty is *before* you make a purchase. Find out what type of warranty is offered on any goods or services you are considering. For products costing over $15, sellers are required by federal law to make any written warranties available to consumers before purchase. Read warranties carefully so you know exactly what is covered and for how long. You may decide to pay more for a product or service with a stronger warranty.

After your purchase, follow these steps to get the most out of your warranty.

- Register the product if the warranty requires it. You might have to mail in a card or register on a Web site. See Figure 16-6.
- File the warranty information in a safe place. Attach your receipt, which verifies when and where you purchased the item. If applicable, record the date of installation.
- Use the product according to directions and only for its intended purpose. Using a flashlight as a hammer probably will void your warranty.
- Maintain the product by performing required or suggested maintenance and inspections.

Caption Answer. The receipt proves your ownership of the product and provides a record of the date and place of purchase.

If You Have a Problem

If the product breaks or is defective, or if you are unhappy with a service that was performed, first look at your warranty. Find out whether the problem is covered and make sure the warranty is still in effect. If it is, follow the warranty's instructions for obtaining service.

If you follow the steps specified in the warranty but the problem is not resolved, write a letter of complaint to the manufacturer, following the guidelines explained in Section 1.5. If you still do not receive adequate service, contact your state consumer protection agency for assistance.

16-6

Registering ownership of a product is often the first step in making the most of a warranty. Why should you also keep the receipt?

Critical Thinking. *Ask:* Do you agree or disagree that service contracts are seldom necessary? In what situations might they be worth the extra cost?

SERVICE CONTRACTS

When you buy a product such as a major appliance, a computer, or electronic equipment, you may be asked whether you'd like to buy a service contract. A **service contract**, sometimes called an *extended warranty*, is an optional service agreement that may be purchased to provide protection beyond the warranty. If you don't buy one at the time you purchase the product, you may be contacted later, a few months before the original warranty runs out.

Many consumer experts advise that service contracts are seldom necessary. That's especially true if you've chosen a quality product with a good reputation and a strong warranty. A service contract may buy you extra peace of mind, but it can increase your costs in the long run. When deciding whether to buy a service contract, ask yourself these questions:

- What coverage does the service contract provide that the warranty does not? For how long is each in effect?
- Would the service contract cost more in the long run than paying for repair service if needed?
- Is this type of product likely to require expensive repairs? Remember, defects are likely to show up early, during the original warranty period.
- How long do I plan to keep this product? If you typically buy a new computer printer every three years, then buying a five-year service contract isn't a good idea.

Answer Key. Answers to the Section Review questions are provided in the Section Lesson Plan located in the *Teacher Resource Guide.*

Point Out. Note that some service contracts, such as those on cars, may require the consumer to pay a deductible each time the product is serviced.

- If I buy the service contract, how will I get service if I need it? Service that you can get only at a local store may not be helpful if you move.
- If the service contract includes or requires periodic maintenance, is such maintenance really necessary? Will I remember to have it done on schedule?
- What is the initial cost of the service contract? Are there any additional costs?
- Who is backing the service contract? What is the reputation of that company?

If you think a service contract would be worthwhile, find out if you can wait until the warranty expires to purchase it. You will not use a service contract while your warranty is in effect, so why pay for one until you need it?

Section 16.2 Review

CHECK YOUR UNDERSTANDING

1. What purpose do warranties serve?
2. What are the two main types of written warranties? How are they different?
3. Why should you think carefully before deciding whether to buy a service contract?

CONSUMER APPLICATION

Service Contract Decision You just bought a new stereo receiver for $250. The warranty covers labor and parts for one year and parts for an additional two years. The salesperson offers you a three-year service contract covering labor and parts for $75. Would you buy the service contract? Explain your answer.

SECTION 16.3

Finding the Best Buys

Getting the most for your money can be a challenge. However, by planning within your budget and researching your options, you can make wise purchasing decisions.

Objectives

After studying this section, you should be able to:

- Explain guidelines for planning purchases.
- Identify steps in researching a product.
- Describe strategies for comparison shopping.

Key Terms

comparison shopping
national brands
store brands
generics

PLAN BEFORE YOU SHOP

Sometimes you enjoy shopping just for fun. It's a great way to spend time with friends, to get ideas for future purchases, or even to dream a little. At other times, you're on a mission for a specific item. Your experience can still be fun, but you need to plan so that you can make the best selection at the lowest price. Follow these guidelines to achieve your goal.

- **Identify needs and wants.** Before you begin shopping, decide what you intend to buy. Think about your needs and wants in relation to each specific item you want to buy. What features and characteristics, such as color, size, quantity, or performance, are you looking for? You might not know all the answers immediately, but you can continue refining your needs and wants throughout the shopping process.
- **Consider your budget.** Determine a price range for this purchase—that is, what you're willing to pay. Take your overall budget into consideration, as well as the amount of debt you have. Also consider factors such as

Jump$tart. Have students read an article in a consumer magazine about things to look for when choosing a specific product. *(Spending & Credit)*

how important the item is to you, whether you want it to last a long time, and how often you'll use it. You might be willing to pay a higher price for an item that you expect to use for many years.

- **Plan when to shop.** Wise shoppers try to time their purchases to get the most for their money. In certain circumstances, it may be wiser to put off a purchase. For example, instead of buying on credit and paying finance charges, you might decide to wait until you've saved enough to pay cash. You may also be able to save money by waiting for a sale.

PRODUCT RESEARCH

If you're shopping for a major purchase, such as a personal computer or a bicycle—or any type of product that you're not familiar with—some research is in order before you start shopping. By gathering all the information you can about a product, you can learn what your choices are, how different features affect the cost, and how to judge price and quality more effectively.

Dollars and Sense. Challenge students to use this checklist to compare several brands of a specific product and choose the best buy.

- Talk to people who have purchased the product you are looking for. Are they happy with it? Where did they get it? What are its particular features? Was the cost reasonable?
- Check your library or the Internet for consumer information regarding the product you want. In publications such as *Consumer Reports*, *Consumers' Research*, and *Consumer Guide*—as well as magazines on specialized topics such as computers or automobiles—you can find product ratings and information on consumer satisfaction that will help you narrow your choices. Take notes on your findings so that you can use the information when shopping.
- Call stores or look online to find prices and features of the product you want. Many Web sites provide detailed information about products, including reviews by people who have used them and price comparison charts.

DOLLARSandSENSE

Do Your Research

As you research specific products made by different companies, consider these questions about each:

- Is the product sturdy and well made? Is it safe? Is it easy to use?
- Do products made by this company have a record of reliability?
- Does the product perform well compared to others?
- Does it have all the features you consider important?
- What type of maintenance does it require? How does that affect the long-term cost?
- Overall, does the product's quality seem worth the price?

Point Out. One way to comparison shop for groceries is to compare different forms of foods, such as fresh, frozen, canned, and dried.

- Visit stores to examine the products available. Read labels, tags, instruction books, and warranties. Ask salespeople how different products compare, how features work, and what they recommend. If appropriate, ask for a demonstration of the product or try it yourself.

COMPARISON SHOPPING

You often can save money by **comparison shopping**, or checking several alternatives to make sure you are getting the best price on an item. Depending on what you're shopping for, your alternatives might include different retailers, different brands or styles of a product, different size packages, and so on. You can comparison shop by visiting local stores, checking ads and catalogs, and searching Internet retail sites. Sometimes a combination of all three strategies is most effective. See Figure 16-7.

When you're in a hurry, you might be tempted to skip comparison shopping and

Community Activity. Have students visit a supermarket and compare the prices of different-sized packages of the same product.

buy the item as soon as you find it. However, comparison shopping doesn't necessarily take long, and you might be surprised at how much you can save.

Sometimes comparison shopping is fairly straightforward. If two local stores carry identical clock radios, but one sells it for $10 less, the decision is easy. Often, though, price must be weighed along with other factors. If you're shopping for a blue shirt, for example, you'll probably find several choices that are slightly different. You might choose a higher-priced shirt because it has the style you want or because it seems better in quality. On the other hand, you might decide that a lower-priced shirt will do just fine. Compromises must often be reached among needs, wants, quality, price, and other factors.

Be wary of prices that seem too good to be true, especially when offered by unfamiliar businesses or unknown individuals. You won't save money in the long run if the product is unsatisfactory or is not delivered as promised.

Class Activity. Conduct a class taste test to compare different brands of a specific food. Include at least one national brand, one store brand, and one generic version of the food. Do not allow the testers to see which brand is which. Ask them to evaluate each brand on a scale of one to ten (low to high). Afterward, reveal the name and price of each brand. Ask students which brand they would choose, based on its evaluation and price.

16-7

Comparison shopping is particularly important when you're buying large items. How can this shopper make sure she's getting the best deal?

Class Activity. Ask students to develop lists showing how long they would consider it reasonable to comparison shop for different items.

National Brands, Store Brands, and Generics

When comparison shopping for some items, you can choose from:

- **National brands**—products with well-known, nationally advertised trade names.
- **Store brands**—products that are marketed only in a particular chain of stores and thus have lesser-known trade names. Store brands are also called *private labels.*
- **Generics**—"plain label" products that do not have a brand name.

Store brands are generally less expensive than national brands, and generics often cost even less. Makers of national brands buy costly advertising on television networks, in major magazines, and in newspapers across the country. The cost of advertising is passed on to the consumer.

You can save money by not limiting yourself to national brands. In many cases, the quality of store brands and generics is hard to distinguish from that of national brands. They may even be made by the same company. Instead of assuming that national brands are better, try the alternatives and decide for yourself.

MAKE YOUR SHOPPING COUNT

Planning your shopping, researching products, and comparing prices can save you money, but require time and effort in exchange. Weigh the amount of time it takes you to find the best deal against how much money you can potentially save. If you spend an hour comparison shopping and save $50, that's time well spent. However, if you spend three hours and save only $5, you might be better off paying a little extra and saving yourself the time.

Answer Key. Answers to the Section Review questions are provided in the Section Lesson Plan located in the *Teacher Resource Guide.*

Also consider the importance of your purchase. If you're buying a car, it would be reasonable to spend several weeks researching your choices before making a decision. Not only is a car one of the more expensive purchases you'll ever make, but also your safety is at stake, and you'll depend on the car for years. The same amount of research effort would not be worthwhile for a notebook or a kitchen towel. Still, if you develop the habit of keeping a sharp eye out for good quality at the lowest possible prices, you may know just where to find the best buy on a notebook when you need one. Even pennies saved on small, everyday purchases add up over time.

Section 16.3 Review

CHECK YOUR UNDERSTANDING

1. Explain how timing your purchases can help you save money.
2. How can you research a product before you buy it?
3. Give three examples of ways to comparison shop.

CONSUMER APPLICATION

Researching a Purchase Choose a purchase you've been thinking about making. Describe the specific steps you would take to research and buy the product. Explain the purpose of each step.

SECTION 16.4

Shopping for Services

Consumers are spending more than ever on services. Some services, such as haircuts and dry cleaning, are fairly routine; others, such as building an addition to a home, are major, one-time projects. The cost of services can range from a few dollars to tens of thousands. How can you get your money's worth?

Objectives

After studying this section, you should be able to:

- Explain how shopping for services differs from shopping for goods.
- Give guidelines for choosing a service provider.
- Describe what a contract for services should include.

Key Terms

bonded
contract

A DIFFERENT KIND OF SHOPPING

When buying services, just as when buying products, you want to get the most value for your money. However, there are several differences between buying products and services. For example:

- Most products have a clearly identified price. The price of services may be harder to determine, which makes it more difficult to comparison shop.
- Quality, too, may be harder to determine. If you're shopping for a product, you can check reviews and ratings of specific brands. With services, performance is more variable. The quality of a paint job, for instance, depends on the type of paint used, the skill of the painter, how the surface was prepared, and even the weather on the day the painting was done.

Class Activity. Ask students to brainstorm a list of services they might pay for. Then ask how they would find a good provider for each service listed.

Jump$tart. Ask students whom they would ask for recommendations when looking for a service provider. *(Spending & Credit)*

- When you buy a product, the transaction is usually fairly simple. Buying a service often involves estimates, contracts, and other paperwork.
- If you're not happy with a product, in many cases you can return it for a refund. Once a service has been performed, however, it can't be "undone." Dissatisfaction must be resolved by other means.

CHOOSING A SERVICE

As with any kind of shopping, think about your needs, wants, and budget before you look for someone who provides a service. You may also need to do some research so that you can ask knowledgeable questions. For example, if you want to hire a landscaping service to create a pond in your backyard, you might want to learn something about ponds: What kinds of pond plants and fish are particularly suited to the climate in your area? How much care will you need to provide after the pond is in place? Getting answers to questions ahead of time will help you better understand what you'll need from the service provider.

Identify Candidates

Start your search by making a list of people or businesses that you might hire to perform the desired service. If there are many possibilities in your area, you'll need to narrow them down. Rather than picking some at random, ask friends or family members for recommendations. Have they hired someone to do similar work? Were they pleased with the results? You can also try contacting professional associations for a list of names to consider. See Figure 16-8.

Check Their Qualifications

Once you've identified several people or businesses that you might hire, the next step is to screen them by checking their qualifications. Your goal is to eliminate unsuitable candidates and identify the best choices among those that remain, based on skill, reliability, professional ethics, and similar characteristics. Here are some strategies you might use to screen candidates:

16-8

Friends and family can suggest names of reputable service providers. The Better Business Bureau can tell you whether complaints have been filed against a business.

Team Activity. Have pairs of students role-play scenes in which a shopper is interviewing a potential service provider.

- Interview them. For example, parents who are choosing a child care provider would ask many questions about a candidate's background, experience, child care philosophy, discipline techniques, and so on.
- Ask to see a sample or pictures of the company's or person's work. If you're looking for a house painter, ask for the addresses of other local houses the crew has painted and take a look at them.
- Ask for a list of *references*, people who can attest to the qualifications of the candidate. Many businesses will provide, on request, the names of current or former customers who are willing to be contacted. Talk to several about the service they received. Find out what problems occurred, if any, and how they were resolved.

Caption Answer. You will know the final cost ahead of time, and the service provider cannot exceed it without your authorization.

- Make sure the company or person is licensed (if a license is required). For example, plumbers and hair stylists should be licensed, generally by the state. You can ask to see the license and then verify with the appropriate agency that it's legitimate.
- Verify that a service provider is bonded and insured, if necessary. A service provider who is **bonded** carries insurance to cover financial loss caused by a third party. If, for example, you hire a moving service, you'll want assurance that you'll be protected if an employee steals from you. The provider should also carry liability insurance for personal injury, property damage, and workers' compensation. Ask the provider for proof of bonding and insurance, and verify the coverage.
- Check with the Better Business Bureau or professional associations to see whether any complaints have been filed against a company or person you are considering.

Get Estimates

Before you agree to have work done, ask for an estimate of how much it will cost. It's common to receive estimates for services such as home and car repairs, for example. See Figure 16-9. After getting an estimate, you can choose whether or not to have the

Class Activity. Ask students to assume they work in the service industry. Have them choose a field and summarize in writing what they would do to provide top-notch service in order to be hired again and recommended to others.

16-9

Estimates should include charges for parts or materials as well as labor. Why is it advisable to get an estimate before you authorize work to be done?

Critical Thinking. *Ask:* Is it always a good idea to hire the service provider with the lowest estimate? Why or why not?

Class Activity. Ask students to prepare a sample contract for a service that includes all the information listed on these two pages.

service performed by that person or company. Estimates are helpful for several reasons: They allow you to compare prices, they give you a chance to meet a representative of the company, and they reduce surprises when you get the final bill.

Many businesses provide free estimates. Others charge a small fee, which is usually deducted from the final bill if you decide to have the service performed.

Ask for a written estimate that spells out exactly what will be done. Check it carefully to be sure it includes everything you want. If you're getting estimates from several service providers, make sure they all follow the same specifications so you can make a fair comparison.

Ask what will happen if the actual cost exceeds the estimate. Will you pay only the estimated amount, or will extra charges be added? If the final cost differs from the original estimate, ask for an explanation and an itemized list of additional costs.

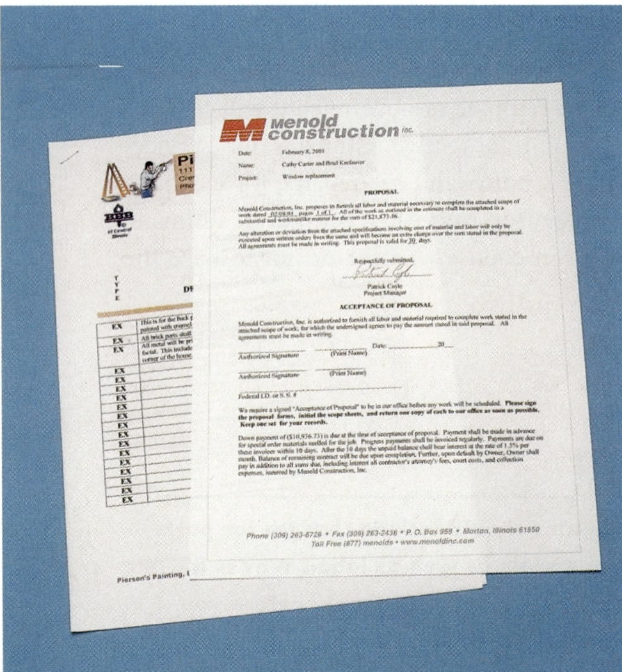

16-10

A signed contract protects both the service provider and the consumer.

WORK ORDERS AND CONTRACTS

For some services, you'll sign a work order or contract after selecting someone to do the job. A *work order* is simply a request for work to be done. For example, if you take your car in for repairs, you may be asked to sign a work order that describes the service you want performed. By signing the work order, you authorize the repairs to be done and agree to pay for them. The work order may also spell out how you will be charged.

For major jobs, such as a home repair or remodeling job costing several thousand dollars, a contract is needed. A **contract** is a legally binding agreement between two or more parties. You should have a written contract, agreed to and signed by both you and the person or business providing the service, to protect both parties in case there is a dispute about services or payment. See Figure 16-10.

For your protection, before you sign a contract for a service, make sure it includes the following information:

- The name, address, telephone number, and license number (if required) of the person or business providing the service.
- A detailed description of the work to be done. If appropriate, it should include an itemized list of all the materials that will be used and their specifications. Responsibilities such as getting permits and cleaning up after the project should also be spelled out.

Research Activity. Some Web sites provide references for different types of service providers. Ask students to find and evaluate one such site.

- An estimated start and completion date.
- The total cost of the project and, for larger projects, a payment schedule that specifies when payments are due and in what amounts. For example, the contract might call for one-third of the cost to be paid before work begins and the remainder once it is completed. Never agree to provide full payment in advance.
- Any warranties or guarantees on the services performed or materials used.
- Anything the contractor has promised verbally. Putting promises in writing ensures that you'll be able to enforce them.

Under some circumstances, you can cancel a contract after signing it. If you sign a contract in a location other than the seller's place of business (in your home, for example), the Federal Trade Commission's Cooling-Off Rule, giving you the right to cancel within three business days, may apply. The Cooling-Off Rule does not apply in certain situations, including home maintenance and repairs. However, if the contract includes a credit transaction for which your home is pledged as security, the Truth in Lending Act's *right of rescission* (discussed in Section 11.4) gives you at least three business days in which to cancel.

USING AND EVALUATING THE SERVICE

During the time that the service provider is working for you, make every effort to maintain positive communication. Be open to questions from the provider and ask questions if you don't understand what's being

Answer Key. Answers to the Section Review questions are provided in the Section Lesson Plan located in the *Teacher Resource Guide.*

done. Try to be flexible—sometimes problems arise that weren't anticipated, and it's best if everyone works together to resolve them.

When you're evaluating a service, consider more than just the finished product. The kind of customer service you receive will influence whether you use that provider again. For example, if an auto mechanic is efficient, friendly, and charges a fair price, you probably will continue to use his or her services.

If you're dissatisfied with the service you've received, contact the service provider and explain the problem. Sometimes the suggestion that you might take your business elsewhere is enough to get results. Service providers, like other businesspeople, want satisfied customers, repeat business, and good references. If the provider will not resolve the problem, contact your local or state consumer protection office for advice.

Section 16.4 Review

CHECK YOUR UNDERSTANDING

1. In what ways is shopping for services different from shopping for a product?
2. How should a consumer go about screening service provider candidates?
3. What information should a contract for a remodeling job include?

CONSUMER APPLICATION

Buying a Service You bought a watch a few years ago, but it has stopped working and is no longer covered by its warranty. The watch is expensive enough that you want to get it fixed by a jeweler. What should you keep in mind when preparing to get the watch fixed?

CHAPTER 16

Review & Activities

CHAPTER SUMMARY

- To make the best shopping choices, evaluate types of retailers and follow the guidelines for at-home shopping. (16.1)
- Warranties protect you against faulty products and services. A service contract can extend the benefits of a warranty. (16.2)
- To help you find the best buys, plan and research before you shop and use comparison-shopping techniques. (16.3)
- Shopping for services is more complex than shopping for products and takes additional work and skills. To ensure the best service, learn how to choose a service provider and understand contract provisions. (16.4)

THE $avvy Consumer

Cutting Costs or Cutting Corners?
Isaac's family is thinking of updating their kitchen. Some friends said they had a good experience with a professional kitchen designer: "She saved us from making mistakes and got supplies for a lot less than we would have paid." Isaac's family had thought theirs was a do-it-yourself project. How can they decide whether hiring a designer would be money well spent? (16.4)

Reviewing Key Terms and Ideas

1. Under what conditions could you save money when buying at a **warehouse club**? (16.1)
2. What are **factory seconds**, and where might you find them for sale? (16.1)
3. List four guidelines for shopping from your home. (16.1)
4. What guarantee does a **warranty** provide? (16.2)
5. Define **implied warranty** and explain its components. (16.2)
6. What items must a written warranty for a product include? (16.2)
7. What is a **service contract**, and what is its relationship to a warranty? (16.2)
8. Summarize the guidelines for planning purchases. (16.3)
9. How does **comparison shopping** save you money? (16.3)
10. Describe how you would go about comparison shopping for a digital camera. (16.3)
11. Explain the primary difference between **national brand** and **generic** products. (16.3)
12. What should a **contract** for service include? (16.4)
13. Explain two ways in which the process of hiring someone to remodel your bathroom would be different from the process of purchasing the supplies yourself. (16.4)
14. What should you do if you are dissatisfied with the service you've received? (16.4)

Answer Key. Answers to the Chapter Review & Activities are provided in the Teacher's Manual in the *Teacher Annotated Edition* of the text.

Thinking Critically

1. **Making Predictions:** Describe how and why shopping might be different 100 years from now. (16.1)
2. **Making Comparisons:** Think of two kinds of service that would require a contract. How might the contracts differ? Name an element in one contract that might not be needed in the other. (16.2)
3. **Evaluating Information:** Suppose you're buying a hair dryer for about $20. The seller offers an extended warranty (for two years instead of one) as an add-on cost. Would you pay for it? Why or why not? (16.2)
4. **Identifying Alternatives:** Assume that you've saved enough money to buy a new bicycle and have identified the model you want. What are your options for locating the bicycle you've chosen? (16.3)
5. **Analyzing Economic Concepts:** Many cultures barter, or trade, for goods. How might large-scale bartering affect a local economy? (16.3)

Building Consumer Skills

1. **Shopping Choices:** Create a chart identifying the advantages and disadvantages of shopping at stores compared to at-home shopping. (16.1)
2. **Warranty Terms:** Assume you are buying a portable CD player. Explain the steps you would take before and after the purchase to be sure you have warranty service on the product. (16.2)
3. **Contract Investigation:** Investigate three types of contracts, such as a movie rental, cellular phone, and lending contract. What are the legal responsibilities of each? (16.2)
4. **Buying Recommendations:** Think of an appliance or electronic item that you might buy when you're on your own. Check *Consumer Reports* for buying recommendations. If you were buying now, what brand would you choose, and why? (16.3)
5. **Weighing Costs:** Suppose you need to buy a pair of boots. The ones you want cost $60 in a nearby store. You can get them for $48 at a discount store in another part of town. However, you would have to take an hour off from your job, losing $8 in pay, and you'd have to spend $3 each way for transportation. Which is the best deal? (16.3)

CONSUMER CONNECTIONS

- **Family:** Ask family members about their experiences with Internet auctions. Have they been favorable or not? Prepare guidelines that family members can use when buying from Internet auction sites. (16.1)
- **Community:** With a partner, think of a service that you could offer in your community, such as lawn care, home organization, or catering. Discuss and make notes on what customers would expect from you. Write a pledge that describes your commitment to good service. Then create a contract to use in your business. Finally, "sell" your service to another partnership in the class. (16.4)

CHAPTER 17

Technology Products

Reading with Purpose

- Write down the colored headings in this chapter.
- As you read the text under each heading, visualize what you are reading.
- Reflect on what you read by writing a few sentences under each heading to describe it.
- Reread your notes.

SECTION 17.1

Managing Technology Choices

Many consumers are fascinated by the latest high-tech gadgets—everything from handheld computers to video game systems to digital cameras. Shopping for items like these can be fun but challenging.

Objectives

After studying this section, you should be able to:

- Analyze how technological advances affect consumer decisions.
- Describe ways to overcome the challenges of shopping for technology products.

Key Terms

obsolete
planned obsolescence

THE PACE OF CHANGE

Technology is continually making new consumer products available. Think of all the methods that have been developed for recording and playing music over the years—from the earliest wax cylinders to vinyl records, tapes, CDs, MP3 files, and beyond. Each time the format changed, consumers had to decide whether to adopt the new technology or stick with the old. Those who switched had to learn a new lingo, invest in equipment, and start building their music collections all over again. Changes like these won't stop in the future—they'll just come faster.

Some consumers react by craving every new gadget that comes along. Dazzled by the glitter and hype, they make costly impulse purchases. Others are so overwhelmed by new technology that they give up, missing out on developments that could make their lives easier and more enjoyable. Smart consumers are able to avoid both extremes. The key is to understand and adapt to the rapid pace of technological change.

Class Activity. Ask students to choose a high-tech product they'd be interested in owning. Then have them answer the questions on these two pages to determine whether the purchase would be wise. If they decide that it would not, ask them what alternatives they might choose.

Obsolescence

New developments can sometimes make old technology—like those wax cylinders—obsolete. A product that is **obsolete** is so out of date that it's no longer useful. However, sellers of consumer products may define "obsolete" more loosely. They want consumers to think that a product is obsolete as soon as something newer has been introduced. They hope to increase sales by convincing consumers to replace old products with new ones.

For example, perhaps every year a software company releases a new version of a popular program. While the new version may have many improvements, that doesn't necessarily make the old version obsolete. There's nothing wrong with continuing to use the previous version if you're still satisfied with it. See Figure 17-1.

Some manufacturers go a step further. They use a strategy called **planned obsolescence**, purposely designing products to have a short life so that consumers will be forced to replace them. Suppose a manufacturer discontinues a certain model of computer printer and stops supplying replacement parts for it. If even one small part breaks down or wears out, consumers will be forced to buy a whole new printer. This strategy can backfire, however, if frustrated consumers decide to switch to another brand of printer instead.

Ready or Not?

In spite of marketing pitches designed to make previous products seem obsolete, wise consumers buy new technology only when they're ready. They base their decision on their own priorities and budget. Before you buy a high-tech product, ask yourself:

- How will it improve my life?
- How often will I use it?
- Do I want it just because my friends do?

17-1

Technology products that are several years old don't necessarily belong on the junk heap. They might still work well enough for you. What organizations might accept donations of used computers?

Class Activity. Hold a class debate on whether it's better to make high-tech purchases sooner or later. Afterward, have students vote on the issue.

Dollars and Sense. Ask students to search store circulars or Web sites for high-tech products that are on sale because new models are coming out.

- What are some potential drawbacks of owning this product?
- Are the benefits worth the costs?
- What are the alternatives to buying this product?

After answering these questions, you may find that the "must-have" product you've been wanting isn't that important to you after all. On the other hand, you may end up with a more clearly defined sense of why you want to make the purchase.

Timing the Purchase

Assuming you decide to shop for a high-tech item, there's still the question of *when* to buy. Whether it's better to make the purchase sooner rather than later depends on the situation.

Technology products that are brand new—especially software packages—might have bugs or defects. The first consumers to buy the product may pay a high price in problems and frustration. Waiting a few months gives the company time to fix any initial flaws.

Waiting may also save you money due to the effects of supply and demand. When a product is first introduced, the price is usually greatest. As more products are manufactured by competitors, the price often comes down. In general, advances in technology tend to result in lower prices and improved features over time.

On the other hand, waiting isn't always the best answer. Suppose a family is having problems with their TV, which is quite old. Although they can afford a new one, they keep putting off the purchase. They've heard that new technology will improve the picture quality on models coming out in a year or so. In this situation, waiting may not bring much benefit. Will the new technology really make a difference to this family? Is the quality of the TVs available now good enough? Remember, technology will always be improving—there will never be a perfect version of a product. Consumers who are always waiting for the next new development miss the opportunity to use and enjoy what's currently available.

CHALLENGES FOR TECH SHOPPERS

Whenever you shop, you face tasks such as sorting out the options, sticking to your budget, and choosing quality products. When it comes to technology products, those tasks can become even more challenging.

Wait . . . and Watch Prices Fall

Have you put off a high-tech purchase so long that a newer model is about to hit the shelves? If so, you may be able to get a great bargain. Manufacturers and retailers often drop the price of older models to make room for the new. Just make sure the product you buy has the features you want and is still covered by a warranty.

Class Activity. Ask students to list the features they would want in a specific high-tech product and rank them in order of importance.

Techno-Talk

If you're shopping for a type of product that's new to you, it can be hard to know what to look for. Even experienced consumers might not understand all the technical details and jargon. If the salesperson says a digital camera has a resolution of 6 megapixels, what does that mean? Is it necessary for your purposes or not?

Before you shop, do your homework. Check out magazine articles and product reviews. Talk to someone you know who has the type of product you're interested in. The more you learn before you shop, the less likely you are to be swayed by advertising hype or deliberately confusing sales pitches.

Expensive Temptations

Sticking to your budget is another challenge of high-tech shopping. It's tempting to upgrade to a model with more options, more buttons, and more programmable features. To keep your spending in bounds, prioritize your wants and set a price range before you shop. Ask yourself how often you'd really use the features found on more expensive models. Are they worth the extra cost, or would a simpler model do?

Hitches and Glitches

Besides saving money, there's another benefit to choosing models without unnecessary features. The more features a product has, the more complicated it will be to use. If your new purchase gathers dust because learning to use it is too difficult or time-consuming, you've wasted money. In addition, more features can mean more chances for something to go wrong.

Not all products have user-friendly designs, and some don't work as reliably as they should. With this in mind, shop defensively. Ask to try out items if possible. Learn about warranty, customer service, and technical support policies. When you read product reviews, look for information about usability and reliability. Visit Web sites where you can view comments from people who have already purchased and used the product.

If you end up with a product that's frustrating to use or doesn't work, take advantage of any service and support options that are offered. If you don't get satisfaction, make your voice heard. Call or write to the company and let them know about the problem. You may help make it possible for future consumers to enjoy better products.

Answer Key. Answers to the Section Review questions are provided in the Section Lesson Plan located in the *Teacher Resource Guide.*

Section 17.1 Review

CHECK YOUR UNDERSTANDING

1. What is the strategy behind planned obsolescence?
2. Explain the pros and cons of buying a high-tech product as soon as it comes out on the market.
3. Why should you learn as much as you can about technology products before you shop?

CONSUMER APPLICATION

Product Research Find an informative advertisement and an objective review about a recently released high-tech product. Write a paragraph comparing and contrasting the two sources. What information is included in each? How is the information presented? Draw conclusions about the benefits and drawbacks of each source of information.

SECTION 17.2

Choosing Phone Service

Keeping in touch with friends and family might seem effortless, but first you've got to wade through an ocean of phone plans to find the one that's best for you. Whether you're shopping for wireless or home phone service, do your research before you buy.

Objectives

After studying this section, you should be able to:

- Give guidelines for choosing and using wireless phone service.
- Describe options available in home phone service.
- Explain ways to fight telephone service fraud.

Key Terms

roaming charge
home coverage area
slamming
cramming

WIRELESS PHONE SERVICE

Some people don't find it necessary to carry a phone with them, but others wonder how they ever got along without one. If you're in the market for wireless phone service, start by asking yourself how you intend to use it. Do you want a phone mainly for emergencies or for everyday calls? About how many minutes of use will the phone get in a month? Will most calls take place during weekdays, evenings, or weekends? Where will you be when using the phone, and where will you call—across town or across the country? Do you want to send text messages, read email, or access the Web from your phone?

In addition, think about your budget. How much are you willing to spend up front? What about each month after that?

Since so many plans and phones are available, having a clear idea of your priorities will help you narrow the choices. Then you can shop carefully to find the right combination for you. Select a service plan first, then a phone.

Critical Thinking. ***Ask:*** What are the pros and cons of prepaid phone service? For what kind of users might this type of service be a good choice?

Types of Service

Consumers who are shopping for wireless phone service should start by considering two basic choices.

- **Analog or digital?** Analog cellular service was at one time the main technology for mobile phones. Later it was joined by digital cellular and digital PCS technology, which quickly grew in popularity. Aside from technical details, how do they differ? Analog service costs less but is becoming obsolete. Digital service provides more security and better voice quality, and it also supports Internet features.
- **Contract or prepaid service?** Most wireless phone users sign a one- or two-year contract. Prepaid service—which lets you buy minutes as you go, without a long-term commitment—is another option. Per-minute rates are generally higher for prepaid service, and you'll still have to purchase a phone separately. Nevertheless, you might choose prepaid service if you want to try out a service provider and get a feel for how quickly you'll use up minutes. Prepaid service might be your only option if you don't have a credit record.

InfoSource. Have students search online to find out what wireless phone services are available in your area and compare pricing for two different plans.

Comparing Service Plans

Wireless phone service plans vary widely, and there are seemingly dozens in any given area. You'll need to understand their differences in order to choose a plan that's right for you.

- **Included minutes.** With most plans, the monthly fee includes a certain number of minutes of phone usage—called *airtime*—per month. The more minutes you sign up for, the higher the monthly fee, but the lower the cost per minute. Choose a plan that gives you at least as many minutes as you expect to use. If you go over the limit, the extra time will be billed by the minute at a higher rate. Many plans offer a separate, higher allowance of airtime minutes for nights and weekends. Unused minutes generally expire at the end of the month.
- **Roaming and home coverage.** Most plans specify a **roaming charge**, a per-minute cost for using the wireless phone while you're outside a specific geographic area. Inside this area, which is called the **home coverage area**, wireless calls don't incur roaming charges. The home cover-

InfoSource

Wireless Service

The Internet can make shopping for wireless phone service easier. At the Web sites of most wireless phone companies, you can enter your home zip code, then view the service plans available in your area. Maps of coverage areas and information about pricing are usually provided. You can compare the plans offered by several wireless service providers without leaving home.

Jump$tart. Have students compare three wireless service plans. Ask them which one would best meet their needs and why. *(Spending & Credit)*

age area might be a certain area within your state, a region that spans several states, or the entire country.

- **Long distance.** In some plans, you'll also be charged a per-minute rate for long distance calls—those in which the person you're talking to is outside a local calling area. This local calling area may differ from the home coverage area used to determine roaming.
- **Special features.** Many service providers offer features such as call waiting, caller ID, text messaging, roadside assistance, and so on. Some features may be included in the basic monthly fee, while others cost extra. Look for the package that includes the most features you will really use for the lowest price.
- **One-time fees.** When you sign up for the plan, you might have to pay an activation fee. If you end the contract early, a termination fee is usually charged. Find out whether these fees apply if you decide to change plans while remaining with the same provider.

Choosing a Wireless Phone

Once you've chosen a wireless service plan, the provider will probably show you a selection of phones that you can purchase.

Point Out. Tell students that many companies and charitable organizations will accept used cell phones—working or not—for recycling.

Sometimes a free or discounted phone is offered as part of a package or special promotion. If you buy a phone elsewhere, make sure it's compatible with your service plan.

No matter where you buy the phone, shop carefully. Ask to see and try out a working phone rather than a nonworking display model. Evaluate its ease of use and, if possible, the clarity of calls. Look for an estimate of battery life, and find out what accessories are included. Product reviews in magazines or online can help you compare phones. See Figure 17-2.

Since wireless phones are small and portable, they can be damaged easily. Find out what the warranty covers. For an extra monthly fee, the wireless service provider may offer an extended warranty or insurance plan.

17-2

Size, cost, and ease of reading the display are important features to consider when comparing wireless phones. What else would you want to consider?

Critical Thinking. ***Ask:*** Do hands-free wireless phones solve the problem of driver distractions? Why or why not?

Wireless Phone Safety and Courtesy

Using a wireless phone while driving is distracting and can lead to accidents. Some states prohibit the use of wireless phones while driving or require the use of a hands-free model. Whether or not such laws apply, it's safest to pull off the road before making or answering calls.

In some places—such as hospitals, gas stations, and airplanes—wireless phone usage may be restricted due to potential hazards. Turn off the phone if instructed by a sign or announcement.

Point Out. In some places, booths for cell phone use are provided. They allow privacy for your call and courtesy toward others who don't want to listen.

Practice courtesy as well as safety. In places where incoming calls will disturb others, such as a movie theater or library, turn off the phone or set it to vibrate or flash instead of ring. When using the phone around others, keep your voice down and your call brief. See Figure 17-3.

HOME PHONE SERVICE

Choosing home phone service requires plenty of comparison shopping. You'll want to find the combination of local and long distance service that's right for you.

Local Service

Local telephone service providers generally offer a choice of monthly plans. Each plan includes a charge for the basic service of simply having a phone line. Beyond that, you may have a choice of paying by the minute for each local call or paying a flat rate each month for unlimited calls. When you order service, make sure you understand what each package includes.

Providers also offer options at extra cost. Some options, such as call forwarding and caller ID, add a set monthly charge to every phone bill. Others, such as automatic callback, might be charged on a pay-per-use basis. Either way, special features can add a considerable amount to your monthly bill,

Community Activity. Have students investigate the choices of telephone service available where they live. Ask them to find out the price of basic service, the range of optional services available, and the cost of these extras, and to draw conclusions about which service is the best buy.

17-3

When talking on a wireless phone in public, speak quietly so you don't disturb others. Be discreet—don't discuss private matters around strangers.

Dollars and Sense. Ask students to check a copy of their home phone bill to see how rates are stated and what restrictions apply.

so think about whether they're worth the cost. For instance, it would probably cost less in the long run to buy an answering machine than to pay for voice mail each month.

Local Toll Service

Some calls are not long distance, yet are made to places outside your local calling area. These calls may be known as local toll, regional toll, local long distance, short distance, or intra-LATA calls. They are usually billed at a per-minute rate. Traditionally, local telephone companies have provided and billed for local toll service. However, you may be able to select a different company to provide this service instead. Shop around and compare rates before deciding.

Long Distance Service

Most long distance carriers offer a variety of rate plans. They can be based on a flat monthly rate, a per-minute charge, or a combination. Per-minute rates often vary depending on the day of the week and the time of day or night. In addition, calls to cities within your state (*intrastate*) are charged at a different rate than calls to other states (*interstate*) or to international locations.

Research Activity. Have students compare the rates offered by dial-around plans and prepaid cards with those of traditional long-distance carriers.

If you choose a carrier but don't sign up for a specific rate plan, you'll generally be charged the company's highest rates. Check the different plans offered by the carrier to see which one best fits your calling pattern. If you see ads from other companies offering lower rates, ask your current service provider for a rate plan that's as good or better.

Whether or not you've subscribed to a specific long distance carrier, you have two other choices for long distance service.

- **Dial-around plans** require using a toll-free number or a prefix—such as "10-10" followed by three digits—before dialing a long distance number. Rates vary widely and may include restrictions.
- **Prepaid cards** for long distance calling can be purchased online and at many stores. The card gives you a certain number of long distance minutes and includes directions for using them. Since they can be used anywhere, prepaid cards can be a good option for travelers.

DOLLARSandSENSE

Shopping for Home Phone Service

Whether you're shopping for local, local toll, or long distance service, keep these tips in mind.

- Study past phone bills to determine how many calls you typically make, where you call, and when. Then calculate what your calls would have cost under different rate plans, including any monthly fees.
- Pay attention to how rates are stated. If you're charged $1.00 for all calls up to 20 minutes, that includes calls lasting only *one* minute.
- Watch for restrictions. Do the low rates apply only to calls placed at certain times, on certain days, or within certain areas?

Community Activity. Have students contact the local phone company to learn about procedures for avoiding slamming and cramming.

Answer Key. Answers to the Section Review questions are provided in the Section Lesson Plan located in the *Teacher Resource Guide.*

17-4

Read the fine print before signing a check or a sweepstakes entry form. You might be authorizing a change in your phone service. Why do you think companies usually provide this explanation in small type?

TELEPHONE SERVICE FRAUD

Be alert for two deceptive practices related to phone service. **Slamming** is switching a consumer's phone service to a different company without permission. **Cramming** means adding charges to a consumer's phone bill for services that were not ordered or received, such as calling cards or club memberships. Both slamming and cramming are illegal. Dishonest companies use these techniques anyway, hoping consumers won't notice.

Take steps to combat slamming and cramming. Ask your phone company to send you a form to sign stating that your service can't be changed unless you request it in writing. Monitor your monthly bills carefully. If you find any unfamiliar charges, call the phone company or the company whose name appears on the bill and ask what the charges are for. If they're not legitimate, ask that they be removed from the bill.

Some companies try to trick consumers into authorizing phone service changes or charges. For example, they may send you a check in the mail. The fine print states that if you endorse and cash the check, you've given permission for your long distance service to be changed. See Figure 17-4.

Section 17.2 Review

CHECK YOUR UNDERSTANDING

1. When should you avoid using a wireless phone for safety reasons?
2. What is a dial-around plan?
3. What should you do if you find unauthorized charges on your phone bill?

CONSUMER APPLICATION

Wireless Plans Create a table that could help a consumer compare features and costs of wireless phone service plans.

SECTION 17.3

Choosing Internet Service

How can a consumer get convenient, reliable Internet service at the best possible price? It takes three pieces to solve the Internet connection puzzle—hardware, a connection method, and a service provider.

Objectives

After studying this section, you should be able to:

- Compare options available in Internet service.
- Describe guidelines for choosing Internet service.
- Explain how to resolve Internet service problems.

Key Terms

modem
dial-up access
broadband
DSL
Internet service provider (ISP)

HARDWARE OPTIONS

If you want only occasional access to the Web and email, and don't mind leaving home to get it, it's not necessary to invest in a home computer and Internet service. You may be able to use computers at the public library or an Internet café at little or no cost.

For Internet access from home, there are alternatives to using a personal computer. For example, some manufacturers offer devices designed strictly for Internet functions such as using email. They're really just computers with limited features. These devices cost less than full-fledged computers and are generally smaller and easier to use. Another alternative is a device that connects to a television. Some game consoles also offer the ability to access the Internet. However, each of these devices has limitations.

Since personal computers have more capabilities, they will probably remain the most common Internet access device. To connect to the Internet, a personal computer

Economic Impact & Issues. Have students identify technological advances brought about by economic factors.

Team Activity. Have students work in small groups to create a glossary of terms related to Internet-based businesses.

requires a **modem**, a device that enables it to send and receive data over telephone lines or other communications lines. Modems can be built-in or external.

CONNECTION METHODS

Several types of connections can link a home computer to the Internet. The standard method for many years has been **dial-up access**, which means Internet access through a regular telephone connection. It's generally the most economical method, but it has several drawbacks. Connecting to the Internet requires the computer to dial a phone number and wait for the connection to be made. Access can be hampered by busy signals and dropped connections. If you have only one phone line, you can't use the telephone while you're connected to the Internet. The connection quality is not always good, and transmission is relatively slow.

As a more expensive alternative to dial-up connections, consumers can choose from several types of **broadband**, or high-speed Internet access. Just as more water can flow through a fire hose than a drinking straw, broadband allows more electronic data to be transmitted through the connection. There's no need to dial a number to access the Internet—a broadband connection is active whenever the computer is on.

Broadband access is available through several means:

- **Cable.** Some companies offer Internet access through the same cable that brings TV signals to the home. For many people, this is the easiest way to get broadband access.

Economic Impact & Issues

Steering the Course of Technology

The development of any technology says something about the economy of the times. Consider the wok, a pan that is indispensable to Asian chefs. The wok was developed in China about 2,000 years ago, when firewood for cooking was scarce. The wok's shape allows heat to spread quickly and evenly to all the food and provides plenty of room for tossing and stirring. With this simple technology, a little firewood went a long way.

The modern-day auto industry finds itself in a similar situation. Because of consumer concern over gas prices, automakers are developing technology that will allow cars to get more miles per gallon.

The rising price of gas may also help expand some technologies used to shop over the Internet. For example, some supermarkets have seen more customers using online delivery services. These shoppers save money by having groceries delivered to their door rather than driving to get them.

FIGURE IT OUT

Put on your entrepreneurial cap. What service that uses Internet technology could you provide to help people save gas? Assume you have the needed resources. Write a description of your idea.

Point Out. Note that although cable connections reach higher maximum speeds than DSL, their speed suffers when there are many users online.

- **DSL.** Digital subscriber line, or **DSL**, is technology that provides high-speed Internet access over ordinary telephone lines. A single phone line can be used for voice calls and Internet access.
- **Satellite connection.** One type of technology sends Internet data from a satellite to a home receiver dish. Another sends signals from towers to home antennas.
- **Wireless broadband.** Connecting to the Internet without plugging in a computer is known as a wireless, or wi-fi, connection. People can purchase wireless routers to create wireless connections in their home. In some cities, people use wi-fi connections in *hot spots*—areas that offer wireless access. Hot spots can be office buildings, restaurants, and even city parks.

INTERNET SERVICE PROVIDERS

An **Internet service provider (ISP)** is a company that provides Internet access and related services to consumers and businesses. ISPs include local, regional, and national companies. The providers that you can choose from will depend on what connection method you're interested in. Some ISPs offer several types of service, such as dial-up and DSL, and different rate plans.

Community Activity. Have students check out ISP services in your area. Ask them to show a comparison of the services in a chart format.

Before signing up for Internet service, get information from the company and, if possible, talk to current users. Compare factors such as:

- **Cost.** Some rate plans offer unlimited use for a flat monthly fee. Others give you a limited number of hours per month and charge by the minute or hour after that. Pick the plan that best suits your predicted pattern of use.
- **Extra services.** Does the ISP offer storage space for your own Web site? Can you have multiple email addresses? Is there an extra charge for such services? See Figure 17-5.
- **Dial-up access numbers.** If you're going with a dial-up connection, look for an ISP with an access number that's a local call for you. Otherwise you could rack up huge long distance bills. Multiple access numbers make it easier to connect during high-traffic times.

17-5

When several family members share an Internet account, they might like to have multiple email addresses. What do you think are the advantages of this?

Critical Thinking. ***Ask:*** For what kind of users might Internet to go be considered a necessity? For whom would it be a luxury?

Answer Key. Answers to the Section Review questions are provided in the Section Lesson Plan located in the *Teacher Resource Guide.*

17-6

A PDA can serve as an electronic organizer and run a variety of software. Some are equipped for Internet access. What might be the pros and cons of using a PDA?

- **Reliability.** Other users may be able to tell you whether they've had difficulty getting and staying online. Have there ever been service disruptions?
- **Technical support.** Will the ISP assist you in setting up your new service? Do they offer free telephone support? Is it available anytime or only during certain hours?

Once you've chosen an ISP, evaluate your service every six months or so. If your usage patterns have changed, then another rate plan might suit you better.

Handling Service Problems

If your service is disrupted, call the ISP to report the problem. Check the details of your service plan to see whether you'll get a refund for downtime. If you find an error in a bill, write to the company, following the guidelines in Section 1.5, to dispute the incorrect charges. If a problem is not corrected in a reasonable amount of time, you can file a complaint with the Federal Communications Commission (FCC) or your state attorney general's office.

INTERNET TO GO

Some consumers want the convenience of being able to access the Internet while they're on the go. With a properly equipped handheld device and a wireless service plan, they can read and send email from almost anywhere. They may also be able to access weather and traffic reports, stock quotes, sports scores, news headlines, and movie times, for example.

Internet access from a handheld device requires paying a monthly fee to a service provider. Devices that can be equipped for Internet access include digital wireless phones and personal digital assistants (PDAs). See Figure 17-6.

Section 17.3 Review

CHECK YOUR UNDERSTANDING

1. What advantages does a broadband connection have over dial-up access?
2. Describe three factors to compare when choosing between different ISPs.
3. To whom should you complain if an Internet service problem is not resolved?

CONSUMER APPLICATION

Broadband Comparison Research the pros and cons of cable and DSL Internet service. Write a paragraph comparing and contrasting the two.

SECTION 17.4

Choosing a Home Computer

A home computer is not a necessity of life, but many families find it useful. Although computer technology changes rapidly, consumers who understand basic computer concepts and do their research should be able to steer their way through the maze of choices.

Objectives

After studying this section, you should be able to:

- Explain factors to consider when shopping for a computer.
- Describe lower-cost ways to gain computer assess.

Key Terms

microprocessor
RAM

BASIC CONSIDERATIONS

The first step in choosing a home computer is to decide what tasks it will be used for. If family members will share the computer, consider how each person will want to use it. All new computers, and many older ones, are capable of basic tasks such as word processing, budgeting, email, and browsing the Web. Specialized tasks—such as editing digital video—may require paying more for a computer equipped to handle them. Prioritize your wants in case they can't all be met within your budget.

Once you've identified the tasks you want to perform, think about two basic questions:

- **Laptop or desktop?** Laptops take up less space and are portable, so they can be taken on the road or used in different areas of the home. However, desktop computers offer a bigger screen that's easier to read and a larger keyboard that makes typing more convenient. Desktop

Community Activity. Have students conduct a school survey to find out how many families own computers. For those that do, have them find out what model they use and which operating system they run. Have students display the results of their surveys in a graph.

models also tend to be less expensive than laptops, both to purchase and to repair or upgrade.

- **Which operating system?** All personal computers come with an *operating system*, the basic program that allows the computer to run. Several competing operating systems have been developed. Knowing which operating system you prefer will narrow your choice of a computer. If you're not sure, try different operating systems by taking a class or using a friend's computer. Software that you purchase later must be compatible with the operating system, so check into the variety of programs that are available.

EVALUATING COMPUTER FEATURES

Once the preliminary decisions are made, you'll be ready to start comparing the features of different computer systems. See Figure 17-7. Whether you shop in stores, by catalog, or online, here are some of the most important features to evaluate.

17-7

When buying a computer, it pays to compare features and try them out. Why would knowing computer terminology also be useful?

Processor Speed

The **microprocessor** is the electronic circuitry that tells the computer how to process information. Think of it as the brains of the computer. Although other factors are also involved, in general, a computer with a more powerful microprocessor will perform tasks faster.

One way of comparing microprocessors is by their *clock speed*, measured in megahertz (MHz) or gigahertz (GHz). You might expect that a computer with a 1.7 GHz microprocessor will run faster than one with a 1.5 GHz microprocessor. That's often true, but not always. To learn which computers are actually fastest, read product reviews that include speed tests.

Memory

Another important consideration is memory, which you might think of as a computer's electronic workspace. **RAM**, which stands for *random access memory*, is the main memory used by the computer to run the operating system and active programs. The amount of RAM in a computer determines its ability to run large, complex programs and to have several files and programs open at one time. It also affects how quickly programs run.

Research Activity. Ask students to read a product review of a computer system and evaluate how well it would meet their personal needs.

Team Activity. Ask students to rank the computer add-ons listed, basing the rankings on which ones they consider most useful. Then have pairs of students exchange and compare their lists. Have them note any differences and discuss the reasons why their computing needs might differ.

Memory is typically measured in megabytes (MB) or sometimes gigabytes (GB). (A gigabyte is just over a thousand megabytes.) Research how much RAM is required by the operating system and applications you'll be using. Then make sure the system you're considering includes more than enough and allows for future expansion.

Storage

When you save a document on a computer, it's placed in storage. The computer's main storage area is its hard drive, and the larger it is, the more documents and programs you can store. Many hard drives can accommodate several gigabytes of data.

As you compare different computers, also take note of what other types of disk drives are provided. Zip® disks, CDs, and DVDs are among the options for storing data if the computer is equipped with the appropriate drives.

Components

If the processor speed, memory, and storage are satisfactory, take a careful look at the visible parts of the computer system. Are the keyboard and mouse comfortable to use? Is the display uniformly clear and sharp, with good color and a screen large enough for easy viewing?

If devices such as modems and disk drives aren't built in, they can usually be added as external components that plug into the computer. You'll probably want to have a printer as well, and perhaps other devices, such as a scanner. See Figure 17-8.

Some extra components may come bundled with the computer system. If not, and you want to add them, plan for the additional costs. If you purchase external devices separately, make sure they're compatible with the computer. Pay special attention to the type of connection required.

Class Activity. Ask one or more volunteers who have computer expertise to demonstrate aspects of computer use for the class (for example, hooking up a digital camera or using a scanner or printer).

17-8

Photos taken with a digital camera can be stored on a home computer. How would you get printed copies of the photos?

Class Activity. Have students create a checklist of factors to consider when selecting software for a home computer.

InfoSource. Instruct students to look for examples of shareware and freeware on the Internet. Have them download and evaluate one such program.

Cards are electronic circuitry that can be added inside the computer to expand its features. For example, a sound card can improve a computer's sound quality and make it possible to connect stereo speakers and a microphone. Video cards make it possible to watch video streamed over the Internet. Ask whether the functions you want require adding cards that are not included in the basic model. Also find out how much capacity the computer has for adding cards in the future.

Software

Many computers come bundled with software programs. A typical package might include word processing, spreadsheet, presentation, email, and games software.

If you want additional software, compare prices and features and make sure that programs are compatible with your computer. Commercial software is usually available on CD-ROMs or other disks. Some can be downloaded from the Internet. Software companies often provide demo versions, which allow you to try the software on a limited basis before deciding whether to buy.

To save money, look for *shareware*, low-cost software that typically is developed by individuals rather than large companies. Most shareware can be tried out for free. If you like the software and want to keep using it, you're asked to voluntarily pay a fee to the developer. To save even more, try public domain software, also called *freeware*—it's available at no cost.

LOWER-COST ALTERNATIVES

If your budget doesn't permit buying a new computer, consider these lower-cost alternatives.

- **Use free computers.** Computers are available to use at no cost at many schools and public libraries. Usage may be regulated or supervised, but you can't beat the price. See Figure 17-9.
- **Rent computer time.** Commercial copying and printing centers often have computers that customers can use. Internet cafés offer access to email and the Web. Even though you'll be charged an hourly fee, you can save money if you don't use a computer often.
- **Buy used.** Manufacturers and retailers sometimes provide deals on refurbished

Freeware and Shareware

Looking for free or low-cost software? Freeware and shareware can usually be downloaded from the Internet. Use "freeware" or "shareware" as a search keyword, or check out Web sites of computer magazines or user groups. Remember to pay for any shareware that you decide to continue using.

Research Activity. Have students research the cost of one of the alternatives to buying a new computer and evaluate its cost-effectiveness.

Answer Key. Answers to the Section Review questions are provided in the Section Lesson Plan located in the *Teacher Resource Guide*.

17-9

Internet cafés exist around the world. Are there any in your area? How do people use them?

Discussion. ***Ask:*** What problems might you encounter when attempting to upgrade an old computer? Under what circumstances would you consider it worth the effort to upgrade?

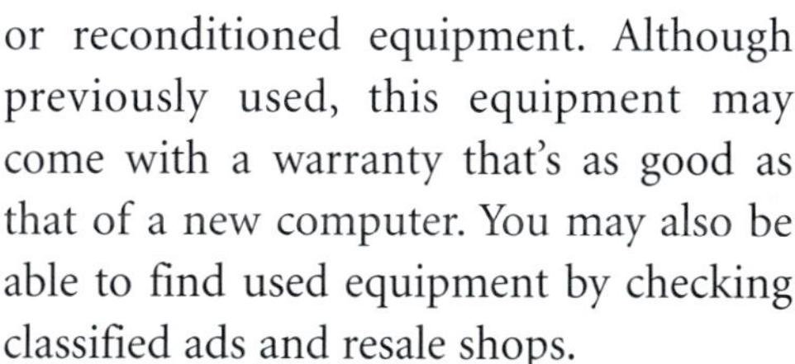

or reconditioned equipment. Although previously used, this equipment may come with a warranty that's as good as that of a new computer. You may also be able to find used equipment by checking classified ads and resale shops.

- **Lease.** Leasing is similar to renting. Instead of spending a large amount of cash up front, you pay to use the equipment over time. You won't own the equipment when the term of your lease expires, but you might be able to purchase it at a reduced rate.
- **Upgrade.** If you have an old computer, consider upgrading it. For example, you might be able to add RAM, replace the hard drive with a larger-capacity one, add other drives, and install cards that improve speed or add functions. Weigh the expense of buying and installing upgrades against the cost of a new system.

Section 17.4 Review

CHECK YOUR UNDERSTANDING

1. Why is it important to establish your priorities before shopping for a computer?
2. What is the difference between computer memory and storage?
3. Describe two lower-cost alternatives to buying a new computer.

CONSUMER APPLICATION

Computer Budgets Make a list of features and components you'd like to have in a computer system. Use catalogs, newspaper ads, or the Internet to compare the prices and features of several available models. Which of the wants on your list could be met with a budget of $500? With a budget of $1,000?

CHAPTER 17

Review & Activities

CHAPTER SUMMARY

- Technology changes so quickly that knowing when to buy can be difficult. When making technology purchases, be realistic about your priorities and budget. (17.1)
- Shop carefully for wireless and home phones and service plans. Be aware of slamming and cramming fraud. (17.2)
- Internet connections require hardware, a connection method, and a service provider. You can shop for an ISP after you choose a connection method. (17.3)
- Before buying a computer, determine who will use it and for which tasks. Learn to compare systems and additional components. (17.4)

THE $avvy Consumer

Out of the Loop: All of Anna's closest friends have a cell phone or PDA—except Anna. Her friends often chat with one another or send text messages. By the time Anna hears what's new, her friends are tired of talking about it. She often feels left out of the loop. Although it would strain her budget, Anna is willing to buy one of these devices if that's what it takes to keep her friendships. Should she buy one? What other approaches to the situation could Anna take? (17.1)

Reviewing Key Terms and Ideas

1. What are some ways in which consumers might react to technological advances? (17.1)
2. When is a product **obsolete**? (17.1)
3. What are four questions to ask yourself before buying a high-tech product? (17.1)
4. What can you do to minimize the possibility of purchasing a high-tech product that's frustrating to use? (17.1)
5. Name three factors to consider when researching wireless phone service. (17.2)
6. Compare analog and digital services. (17.2)
7. How do **roaming charges** differ from long distance charges? (17.2)
8. What choice do you have in regard to local toll calls? (17.2)
9. What is **slamming**? What can consumers do about it? (17.2)
10. What is the purpose of a **modem**? (17.3)
11. What is the difference between **broadband** and **dial-up access**? (17.3)
12. What factors should you take into account when choosing an **Internet service provider**? (17.3)
13. List the steps you should take if your Internet service is disrupted. (17.3)
14. What is a **microprocessor**? (17.4)
15. Why is the amount of **RAM** in a computer an important consideration? (17.4)
16. Name three lower-cost alternatives to purchasing a home computer. (17.4)

Answer Key. Answers to the Chapter Review & Activities are provided in the Teacher's Manual in the *Teacher Annotated Edition* of the text.

Thinking Critically

1. **Recognizing Consequences:** Kid's toys have become increasingly high-tech. What are some positive and negative consequences for young children and their parents? (17.1)
2. **Supporting Your Position:** Overall, do you think the popularity of wireless phones has changed everyday life for better or worse? Why? (17.2)
3. **Analyzing Economic Concepts:** What is deregulation? Find out when long distance or local telephone service was deregulated. How has that affected consumers? (17.2)
4. **Understanding Cause and Effect:** When each new generation of home computers is introduced, it seems to do everything you could want. In just a few years, however, many people feel they "need" a better model. What drives this cycle? (17.4)

Building Consumer Skills

1. **Technology Terms:** Work with your class to create a glossary of "Technology Terms for Consumers." Include terms and definitions that people need to understand when shopping for technology devices. Share the glossary with friends and family. (17.1)
2. **Wireless Phone Guidelines:** Working with a team, create a skit or video to demonstrate safe and considerate wireless phone use. (17.2)
3. **Local Services:** Investigate connection methods and ISPs available in your area. Compare services, fees, contract obligations, and technology required. Report your findings. (17.3)
4. **Handheld Technology:** Investigate handheld wireless Internet technology. What kinds of products and services are available? Write an article on the subject for your school newspaper. (17.3)
5. **Computer Shopping:** Using catalogs and online sources, research features and prices of both laptop and desktop computers. Are there businesses in your area that sell used or refurbished computers? Create a chart that compares the prices and available options for each type of computer. (17.4)

CONSUMER CONNECTIONS

- **Family:** Do any older or younger members of your family need help in learning to use a computer or another technology device? If so, volunteer to spend some time working with the person. You could strengthen a bond and make a difference in someone else's life. (17.1)
- **Community:** Find out whether your community offers any of the following: **a)** public computer use for little or no cost; **b)** in-home computer repair and troubleshooting; **c)** training for people who need basic knowledge of computer use; **d)** education programs for those who want to work in the computer field. Check the Yellow Pages of the telephone directory and other resources to learn what's available. (17.4)

CHAPTER 18

Clothing and Grooming

Reading with Purpose

- As you read this chapter, create an outline using the colored headings.
- Write a question for each heading to help guide your reading.
- Write the answer to each question as you read the chapter.
- Ask your teacher to help with answers you cannot find in the text.

SECTION 18.1

Planning Clothing Purchases

Think about the last clothing item you bought. Why did you choose it? Knowing what influences your clothing decisions will help you make wise choices to meet your needs and wants.

Objectives

After studying this section, you should be able to:

- Analyze factors that influence clothing decisions.
- Describe the steps involved in wardrobe assessment.
- Give examples of economical ways to build your wardrobe.

Key Terms

wardrobe
accessories
fashion
classics

INFLUENCES ON CLOTHING DECISIONS

Every day you have to decide what to wear. While some people look forward to that choice, others are less enthusiastic. The secret to enjoying clothing choices is a well-planned wardrobe. Your **wardrobe** is the collection of clothes, shoes, and accessories that you own. **Accessories** are items that complete an outfit, such as scarves, ties, jewelry, belts, and hats.

A well-planned wardrobe meets your clothing needs and wants and reflects careful buying decisions. To make the best decisions, you should be aware of the physical, psychological, and social factors that influence you.

Physical Factors

One of the influences on your daily clothing choices is the weather. In cold weather, warm clothes help your body retain heat. On a rainy day, a raincoat can help you stay dry.

Depending on your activities, you may choose clothing that can help protect you from injury. If you're going hiking in the woods, long pants and a long-sleeved shirt

Class Activity. Ask students to name some things that influence their decisions about what to wear. List their responses on the board. Then ask students to sort the list into two groups: physical factors and psychological factors. Ask them which group they think affects their clothing choices more.

can protect you from scratches and insect bites. If you're going biking, you'll want to wear a helmet.

Comfort is another consideration. Comfortable, well-fitting shoes make the most sense if you expect to be on your feet all day. Loose clothing that allows you to move freely is the best choice if you're going out to shoot baskets.

Psychological Factors

Clothing can affect the way you feel about yourself. When you feel good about your clothing choices, you're likely to feel more attractive and more confident. However, individual preferences vary. Some people want to wear the latest styles, while others choose more traditional clothes. You may like to wear dark colors, but your best friend might prefer bright colors. Your goal may be to blend in or to stand out from the crowd. See Figure 18-1.

Social Factors

Other people and the society in which you live also influence your clothing choices. Recognizing these influences can help you to make more appropriate clothing decisions.

- **Family.** You begin to learn about clothing within the family setting. The adults in your family guide your clothing choices as well as teach by their own example.

18-1

Everyone has unique clothing preferences. In what kinds of clothes and colors do you feel most comfortable?

Class Activity. Have students name situations and events they experience. List them on the board, and ask students to describe appropriate outfits for each.

Team Activity. Have students work in groups to brainstorm specific examples of messages the media send about clothing. Have them use this list to develop a three-column chart showing the medium (television show, print ad, etc.), the message, and how the message might affect teens' clothing purchases.

- **Peers.** The influence of classmates and friends is particularly powerful during the teen years. Many teens prefer clothing styles similar to those of their peers.
- **Media.** Television, movies, magazines, and other media send powerful messages about clothing. A television show or movie can inspire a clothing trend. A sports figure endorses a brand of sneakers, and suddenly everyone wants to wear that brand. Advertisers create demand for new clothing items by suggesting that you'll be more attractive and more popular if you dress in a certain way.

Discussion. ***Ask:*** What clothing items are currently considered status symbols? How do status symbols affect people who cannot afford them?

- **Fashion.** **Fashion** is a look or style that is popular at a particular time. Fashion tends to change rapidly. Long leather coats may be popular one year. The next year, leather is out and woolen hooded coats are in. See Figure 18-2.
- **Status.** Certain clothing items are viewed as status symbols. They send a message that you can afford a particular brand name or that you shop at a particular store.
- **Other social factors.** The opinions of others may influence some of your decisions about clothing. People often choose clothing based on what is considered appropriate for a certain occasion. If an employer asks you to follow a dress code, you may have to buy clothes that you would not normally choose.

ASSESSING YOUR WARDROBE

"My closet's packed, but I can't find a thing to wear." If this complaint sounds familiar to you, it's time for some wardrobe planning. Wardrobe planning involves assessing, maintaining, and acquiring clothes and accessories that meet your needs and wants. Here's how.

1. **Sort garments.** Look through your closet and drawers. Take out every item that you don't wear.

18-2

If you're influenced by fashion trends, you're likely to choose clothes that reflect the latest styles and colors.

Critical Thinking. ***Ask:*** How can taking time to assess your wardrobe save time and energy in the future?

2. **Identify problems.** For each item that you don't wear, ask why. Is it stained, wrinkled, or worn? Does it need repair? Is it out of fashion? Is it too large or too small? Do you dislike the look or the color? Do you need something to go with it? Had you forgotten about it?

3. **Find solutions.** For any problem that has a solution, take action. Wash and iron garments or take them to the cleaners. Make needed repairs. See Figure 18-3. For every solved problem, put the item back in the closet.

4. **Clear out unwanted garments.** Give away or sell items that you no longer want, but that are in good shape. Some service organizations and charities accept donations of clothing for those in need. Recycle worn garments by cutting them up for fabric projects or cleaning cloths.

Team Activity. Have groups of students draw posters illustrating a creative way to adapt or recycle an unwanted garment.

5. **Identify items to add.** To complete the process, determine what items you need or want to add in order to round out your wardrobe.

BUILDING YOUR WARDROBE

Once you've identified your needs and wants, you can begin to build your wardrobe. Save money by using your resources and by learning ways to stretch your wardrobe.

Using Your Resources

You don't need a large budget to build your wardrobe if you think creatively. You might, for example, be able to trade clothes with a friend. Consider giving a new look to a garment by altering the length, shortening the sleeves, adding colorful buttons, or using fabric paints, dyes, or embroidery. Convert torn jeans into a pair of shorts.

You can also expand your collection of clothes by buying used clothing. Many people love to look for bargain clothes at thrift shops, secondhand stores, flea markets, and garage sales. You might find used clothing that you can wear as is or that you can alter to a new style.

18-3

Making needed repairs makes it possible to wear a garment again. What would be the best time to make such repairs? Why?

Class Activity. Set up a dummy (or student model) in the classroom dressed in a basic outfit, such as jeans and a white shirt. Have students attempt to create a variety of effects by combining this outfit with different accessories. If possible, take photos of their more successful efforts for a bulletin board display.

18-4

Accessories can bring an outfit to life. **What items do you use to change the look of an outfit?**

Answer Key. Answers to the Section Review questions are provided in the Section Lesson Plan located in the *Teacher Resource Guide.*

Stretching Your Wardrobe

Stretching your wardrobe involves getting more use out of the clothes you have. It's a matter of choosing the right items and using techniques to introduce variety. Here are some suggestions:

- **Build with classics.** **Classics** are fashions that don't go out of style. A simple white shirt or straight black pants, for example, will last from year to year.
- **Look for multipurpose items.** Avoid buying clothes that will have limited use. Instead, look for garments that will be suitable for different kinds of occasions.
- **Try new clothing combinations.** Look for varied ways to use garments in your wardrobe. Pairing a vest with a different shirt, for example, can give it a new look.
- **Focus on a few colors.** If you base your wardrobe on two or three colors, you'll find it easier to coordinate new purchases with your existing collection. You also have more opportunity to mix and match garments in different combinations.
- **Accessorize.** Accessories can change the look of a garment. Try adding new accessories and using them in different ways. See Figure 18-4.

Section 18.1 Review

CHECK YOUR UNDERSTANDING

1. Give examples of physical, psychological, and social factors that affect clothing decisions.
2. What can you do with items from your wardrobe that you no longer want?
3. Describe three inexpensive ways to add to your wardrobe.

CONSUMER APPLICATION

Wardrobe Assessment Follow the steps listed in the text to assess your wardrobe. Write a paragraph summarizing the steps you took and what you discovered.

Objectives

After studying this section, you should be able to:

- Compare places to buy clothing.
- Explain how to evaluate garments.
- Describe different types of fibers, fabrics, and finishes.
- Analyze the information given on clothing labels.

Key Terms

consignment shops
natural fibers
manufactured fibers
blends
finishes
hangtags

SECTION 18.2

Shopping for Clothing

Consumer skills can't ensure that you'll find the perfect item of clothing at a great price. However, they can increase your chances of being satisfied with the clothing purchases you make.

WHERE TO SHOP

When deciding where to shop for clothes, weigh factors such as the range and quality of goods offered, price, convenience, and the level of sales assistance. Different stores satisfy different needs and wants.

- **Department stores** generally carry a wide range of clothing and accessories. Prices may be higher than at most other stores, but quality of service may be higher, too.
- **Specialty clothing stores** focus on a particular group of customers, type of clothing, or both. For example, there are specialty stores that sell menswear, sportswear, or petite or large sizes.
- **Discount stores** may offer the same brands as department stores but at lower prices, or they may focus on less expensive brands. Most discount stores are self-service.
- **Outlet stores** can sell a particular brand of merchandise at a reduced price because the items come directly from the manufacturer. Some products sold at outlet

Class Activity. On the board, list various places where clothing can be purchased. Ask students to identify advantages and disadvantages of each type of store, and list their responses on the board. Then ask students which type of clothing store they consider the best choice overall.

stores are irregulars or seconds, meaning that they have flaws and imperfections. Others are simply surplus goods.

- **Thrift shops and consignment shops** sell used clothing. Thrift shop items have been donated, while **consignment shops** give part of the sale price to the original owner. You may be able to find inexpensive clothing in good condition at both kinds of stores.
- **Catalog and Internet shopping** offer the convenience of shopping at home. Prices vary, and you have to pay for shipping. Because you can't actually see or feel the garments, or try them on before ordering, you risk being dissatisfied when they arrive. See Figure 18-5.

Sales and Markdowns

Many clothing stores offer marked-down prices several times a year. The most common times for sales are at the end of each season, when stores want to make room for new merchandise. Watch for sale ads and discount coupons in local newspapers.

When buying a garment that's on sale, check it over carefully. Look for tears, scratches, snags, stains, missing buttons, a broken zipper, poor workmanship, or any other flaw. Find out if the sale is final, which means you won't be able to return the item. Even a sale price is no bargain if you buy something you can't wear.

EVALUATING GARMENTS

How do you decide whether or not to buy? When you're considering a purchase, try on the garment and ask yourself these questions.

- **Does it fit?** Selecting a garment in your size doesn't guarantee that it will fit. Sizes vary from one manufacturer to another. When you try on the garment, don't just stand in front of the mirror. Walk, sit, bend, crouch down, stretch, and fold your arms. Is the garment comfortable? Does it move and give where it should? Examine how each part of the garment fits, checking for any bulging or wrinkling.

18-5

With a computer and an online service, you can check out clothing from a variety of sources without leaving home. What are the main advantages and disadvantages of Internet shopping?

Critical Thinking. ***Ask:*** Which types of garments are most important to have well made? For which types is quality less important? Explain why.

- **Does it look good?** Think of an outfit that has brought you many compliments. What makes it work for you? Most people find that certain colors and styles bring out their best features. Choose colors that go well with your hair and skin tone. Remember that dark colors tend to make people look more slender, while light colors can make them look heavier. Vertical lines tend to add height, while horizontal lines add width.

- **Does it go with other items?** If you're trying on pants, think about how they'll team up with shirts that you already have. You'll save money if you choose garments that fit in rather than having to buy a complete outfit every time. Think about whether you have the right shoes and accessories, too.

Class Activity. Bring in a garment to pass around the class. Have students evaluate it, using the list of questions in Figure 18-6.

- **Is it well made?** Quality is more important for some garments than for others. For example, a heavy coat that you will wear often over several seasons should be well made and of sturdy material. Inexpensive shorts to wear at the beach need not be so well made. Figure 18-6 lists points that can help you judge a garment's quality.

18-6

Carefully checking garment construction will help you to evaluate clothing before you purchase it. Do you think that higher-priced clothing is always higher in quality? Why or why not?

Judging Garment Quality

To determine whether a garment is well made, pay attention to the details.

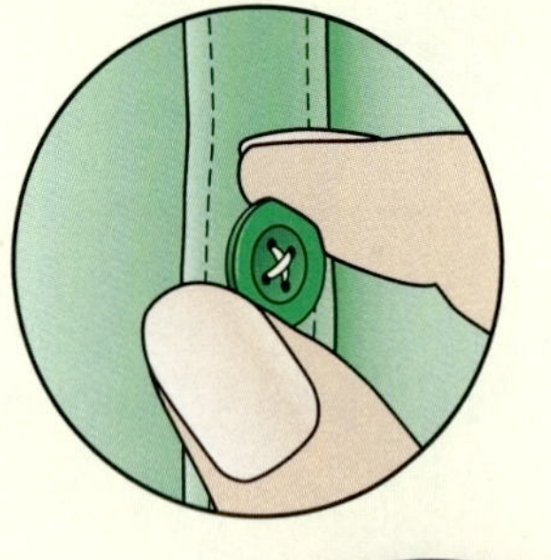

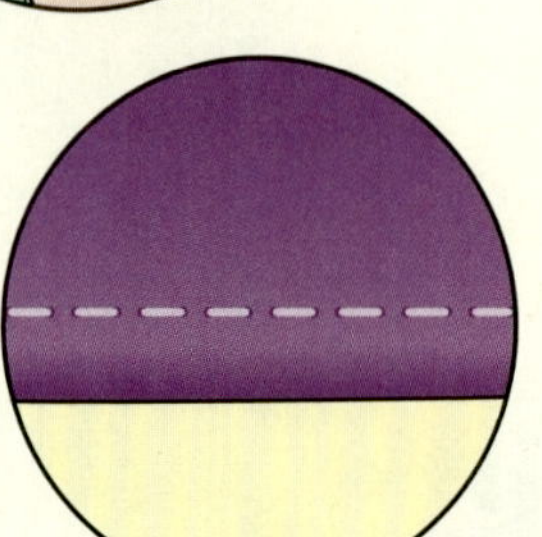

- Are seams flat and unpuckered?
- Are seam edges finished to prevent unraveling?
- Are buttons sewn on securely?
- Are buttonholes correctly placed and the correct size?
- Are hooks, eyes, and snaps securely stitched?
- Does the collar lie flat?
- Do fabric designs match at the seams?
- Are pockets sewn on straight?
- Are pocket corners reinforced?
- Are belt hooks reinforced?
- Does the zipper slide up and down easily?
- Is the hem straight and even?

Economic Impact & Issues. Have students identify the pros and cons of knock-offs to consumers and manufacturers.

- **Is the price right?** Consider how the price relates to the quality of the item. Some people prefer to pay more for one quality item than to buy several low-cost items of lower quality.
- **What care does it need?** Check the label. Can it be machine-washed? Washing by hand takes time, and cleaning bills can be expensive.

FIBERS, FABRICS, AND FINISHES

Clothes are made of fabrics, and fabrics in turn are made of fibers. Fibers come from many sources and have different characteristics. Learning about fibers, fabrics, and finishes will help you choose garments.

Discussion. ***Ask:*** Which are your favorite fibers? What do you like about them? Are there any that you don't like? Why?

Types of Fibers

Fabrics are made of natural fibers, manufactured fibers, or blends. **Natural fibers** come from natural sources such as plants or animals. Cotton, wool, linen, and silk are the most common natural fibers used in clothing. **Manufactured fibers** are made from substances such as wood pulp and petroleum. Nylon, rayon, acetate, and polyester are examples of manufactured fibers. Figure 18-7 on the next page lists the characteristics and typical uses of some commonly used fibers.

Blends are combinations of different fibers. They take advantage of each fiber's positive qualities. For instance, cotton and polyester is a blend that combines the comfort and absorbency of cotton with the strength and wrinkle resis-tance of polyester.

Economic Impact & Issues

High Fashion at Low Costs

Knock-offs are mass-produced garments that mimic high-fashion designs. Making and selling these less expensive imitations is common in the fashion world. It's also legal, since separate elements of a design cannot be copyrighted, although the design itself can. For example, anyone can put letters on a shirt. A particular set of initials in a certain lettering style, however, is legally protected intellectual property.

The growing appeal of knock-offs is changing the economics of the clothing market. It's giving competition to "second line" collections. These are the more conventional, mass-marketed clothes that some fashion designers create and that knock-offs may closely resemble. Designers are pressured to turn out these affordable collections quickly.

The need to keep up with the latest fashions is also shifting the focus from getting products to market cheaply to marketing them quickly. Some manufacturers will pay more to have clothes made near the target audience rather than wait a few days to have them shipped from another country where production costs are lower. Producers and consumers in the countries involved feel the impact of this decision in the job market.

FIGURE IT OUT

Investigate trends in other types of merchandise copying, legal and otherwise, such as song swapping and video piracy. What is the financial impact on each industry? Who benefits and who is hurt?

Class Activity. Pass around a magnifying glass so that students can observe how the different fabrics in the clothes they are wearing are constructed. Ask them what they observe about each type of fabric. Have each student make a sketch showing how a given type of fabric looks close up.

Know Your Fibers

	FIBERS	CHARACTERISTICS	TYPICAL USES
NATURAL	Cotton	Plant fiber; strong; durable; soft; absorbs moisture; wrinkles easily; can shrink	Shirts, sweaters, dresses, jeans, underwear, socks
	Flax	Plant fiber; made into fabric called linen; stronger than cotton; absorbs moisture; dries more quickly than cotton; wrinkles easily; shrinks unless treated	Suits, pants, shirts
	Ramie	Plant fiber; silk-like luster; very strong but stiff and brittle; poor resiliency and elasticity; often combined with other fibers such as flax and cotton	Sweaters, knitted tops, shirts
	Wool	Comes from sheep fleece; versatile; durable; resists wrinkling; warm; easily damaged by moths; shrinks and mats; may pill	Coats, suits, slacks, sweaters, socks
	Silk	Comes from silkworm cocoons; natural luster; strong yet lightweight; smooth; may yellow with age; may show water spots	Scarves, ties, dresses, shirts
MANUFACTURED	Acetate	Silk-like appearance; soft; dries quickly; may wrinkle; often made into taffeta and satin	Shirts, dresses, pants
	Acrylic	Soft; wool-like but not as warm as wool; resilient; quick-drying; often made into fleece fabrics	Sweaters, pants, outerwear
	Nylon	Strong; lightweight; resilient; doesn't stretch or shrink; often uncomfortable in hot and cool weather	Pantyhose, swimsuits, outerwear
	Polyester	Wrinkle resistant; strong; dries quickly; blends well with other fibers; absorbs stains; low absorbency of moisture	Shirts, blouses, pants
	Spandex	Excellent elasticity; strong; lightweight	Underwear, swimwear, active sportswear

18-7 **Compare the characteristics of these fibers.** **How do their uses relate to their characteristics?**

Point Out. Other types of natural fibers used in fabric include ramie and hemp. A common synthetic fabric is rayon, made from cellulose.

Types of Fabrics

Fibers are twisted into yarns, which are then woven or knitted to make fabrics. Woven fabrics are made from two sets of interlaced yarns. Knitted fabrics are made by looping yarns together in interlocked rows. The method used to put yarns together, as well as the type of fibers used, influences what a fabric is like. For example, woven fabrics tend to be stiffer and stronger than knitted fabrics.

Types of Finishes

Finishes are treatments applied to fabrics to produce a certain look, feel, or performance. A newly woven fabric is often a limp, dull, off-white color. A finish adds color, design, and texture. Some finishes are dyes, applied in a variety of ways to produce patterns. Others improve the texture and comfort of the fabric. The finish may enable the fabric to resist wrinkles, mildew, flames, moths, stains, water, or shrinkage.

LABELS AND HANGTAGS

All clothing must have one or more attached labels that provide certain information for consumers. Often these labels are sewn into side seams or center backs of garments. The information required by law includes:

- Identification of the manufacturer or store, or the brand name of the product.

Answer Key. Answers to the Section Review questions are provided in the Section Lesson Plan located in the *Teacher Resource Guide.*

Critical Thinking. *Ask:* Why are clothing labels required by law to include certain information? How does this information help consumers make choices?

- The percentage of fiber content by weight, such as "100% Cotton."
- The country of origin.
- Care instructions indicating how to wash, dry, iron, or otherwise care for the garment. They may include such warnings as "No bleach" or "Wash bright colors separately."

Other information, such as the size, may be given on attached labels or on **hangtags**, removable tags attached to clothing. Labels and hangtags provide useful information. Make a habit of reading them before you buy a garment.

Section 18.2 Review

CHECK YOUR UNDERSTANDING

1. What is the difference between a specialty store and an outlet store?
2. What six factors should you consider when evaluating a garment?
3. How do woven and knitted fabrics differ?

CONSUMER APPLICATION

Garment Labels Read the sewn-in labels on five garments found in your home or in a store. Make a chart that categorizes and compares the information on the labels. If you were shopping for these garments, how might the label information influence your purchasing decisions?

Objectives

After studying this section, you should be able to:

- Discuss the benefits of caring for clothing.
- Explain basic procedures for clothing care.

Key Terms

launder
dry cleaning

SECTION 18.3

Caring for Clothing

You'll get more mileage from your clothing budget if you take good care of your clothes. Keeping garments clean and in good repair, and storing them with care, will help prolong their life.

ROUTINE CARE

Clothing care begins with daily routines. At the end of the day or whenever you change your clothes, check them over quickly. Does anything need to be mended? If possible, make needed repairs right away. Otherwise, put clothes to be mended together in one place so you can repair them later. Before putting dirty clothes in a hamper or laundry bag, empty all pockets and check for stains. If you notice a stain, try to attend to it immediately. A quick rinse with cold water can remove many stains from washable fabrics. Remember that the longer a stain stays on a fabric, the harder it is to remove.

Some garments don't need to be washed or cleaned after every wearing. Let them air out, brush off any hair or lint, and then put them away. Get in the habit of hanging clothes in a closet or folding and placing them on shelves or in drawers when you're not wearing them. That way they'll be easy to find and ready to wear when you want them.

Class Activity. Ask students to brainstorm a list of clothes that might be found in a family's laundry. List these items on the board. Then ask students to sort these garments according to how they should be washed (by machine, or by hand, in hot or cold water) and dried (by machine, dried flat, or hung).

DOING LAUNDRY

When you **launder** a garment, you wash it by hand or machine using water and a soil-removing product. With careful laundering, clothes last longer. Doing the laundry is part of every family's routine. In some families, one person might sort and wash clothes while others fold and iron. Taking turns doing the laundry is another way to share the task.

The care label that is sewn into the garment describes proper washing and cleaning methods. The information on the label will enable you to sort washable garments into those that can be machine-washed and those that need to be washed by hand.

Machine Washing

For best results, follow these guidelines when washing clothes by machine.

- **Check care labels.** Check the label for the correct water temperature to use. Also note whether a delicate, permanent press, or regular wash cycle is recommended.
- **Sort items.** Sort clothes by water temperature and wash cycle. Also sort by color—the dyes in some dark or brightly colored clothes can bleed onto white and lightly colored fabrics. Heavily soiled garments should be washed separately, as should fabrics that might leave lint on others.

Research Activity. Assign each student a common type of clothing stain, such as grass or blood. Have them search library and Internet resources to learn how to remove this type of stain from clothing.

- **Treat stains.** Before washing, treat stains on garments with a stain remover. Follow the directions on the container. A heavily stained garment may need to be presoaked. See Figure 18-8.
- **Load and set the machine.** Avoid overloading. If clothes are crammed together, they won't clean well and will wrinkle more easily. Load the machine evenly, distributing the weight around the drum so it stays in balance. Adjust the water level for the load size. Set the machine for the desired cycle.

18-8

Most stain removal products are formulated to work on a variety of common stains. Apply the product directly to the stained area.

Critical Thinking. *Ask:* What are the advantages and disadvantages of hanging clothes outdoors rather than tumble-drying them?

Dollars and Sense. Have students compare the cost of dry cleaning a garment with the cost of using a home dry-cleaning kit.

- **Add cleaning agents.** Follow package directions for using laundry detergent and other products. Bleach or fabric softener may need to be diluted, put in a dispenser, or added at a certain time in the cycle.

Hand Washing

Hand washing is recommended for delicate fabrics such as silk and wool. Fill a basin with water and add a mild detergent. Place the garments in the basin and gently squeeze the sudsy water through them. Rinse the clothing in cool water until the water runs clear. Then roll the garments in a clean towel to remove as much water as possible before laying them out to dry.

Drying Methods

Different fabrics need to be dried in different ways. Always follow the drying instructions on the care labels. Here are the main drying methods.

- **Tumble dry.** Set the dryer for high, medium, low, or no heat, as specified on the garment care label. Most manufactured fibers need to be dried at a lower temperature than natural fibers. Avoid overloading the dryer. If it is overloaded, the clothes will take longer to dry and will be more wrinkled. Be sure to remove all of the lint from the lint filter after each use.
- **Hang to dry.** Some fabrics shrink or lose their shape when tumbled dry. If a label says, "Hang to dry," place the garment on a hanger over an area where it can drip-dry.
- **Dry flat.** Some garments should be dried flat to avoid stretching. Lay the garment flat on a drying rack or on a surface that won't be damaged by moisture.

Ironing and Pressing

Some garments come out of the dryer wrinkle-free and ready to wear. Others need ironing or pressing to remove wrinkles. Ironing is done by moving the iron back and forward. Pressing is done by raising and lowering the iron from one area to the next. For fabrics that stretch easily, or to make sharp creases, press rather than iron.

Irons have different temperature settings, which are usually labeled with the names of fibers. Cottons and linens generally need to be ironed at high temperature settings, while most manufactured fibers need to be ironed at lower settings. Many irons can be set to

DOLLARSandSENSE

The Costs of Clothing Care

Which is the better buy: a $15 shirt that needs to be dry-cleaned or a $25 shirt that can be machine washed? At $4 a cleaning, the cheaper shirt will have cost an additional $12 after just three cleanings. If you're tempted to save money by washing clothes that should be dry-cleaned, think again. Chances are the garments will shrink or the colors will run. You can, however, try do-it-yourself dry cleaning.

Class Activity. Demonstrate to students how to perform a simple clothing repair, such as replacing a button. Then have students try it for themselves.

produce steam for removing wrinkles and setting creases. Follow the manufacturer's directions for adding water to a steam iron. Distilled water is usually recommended to avoid mineral buildup.

DRY CLEANING

Dry cleaning is a process that cleans fabrics using special liquids instead of water. If you take garments to a professional dry cleaner, point out stains and their causes. The cleaner will know which cleaning agents to use and can give the stain special attention. If you want to try dry cleaning garments yourself, you can use a coin-operated machine or products that are made to work in a tumble dryer.

MAKING MINOR REPAIRS

There's an old saying, "A stitch in time saves nine." In other words, making a simple repair right away usually saves making a larger one later and keeps the garment wearable.

Minor repairs are quick and easy to do. You can sew a loose seam shut with tiny hand stitches or with machine stitching that overlaps the existing seam. Attach a loose button as soon as you notice that it's loose. It takes only a few minutes and will prevent you from losing the button. If a garment has a small hole or tear, cover the hole with a patch. You can buy sew-on or iron-on patches in many different colors.

Answer Key. Answers to the Section Review questions are provided in the Section Lesson Plan located in the *Teacher Resource Guide.*

Point Out. Although cedar blocks and chips are widely believed to repel moths, they actually work by covering up the smell of wool.

STORING CLOTHES

Proper storage helps keep garments in good shape so they're ready to wear when you want them. Garments made from woven fabric can be hung in a closet. Knitted items, such as sweaters, should be folded and placed on shelves or in drawers so they don't stretch out of shape.

Avoid stuffing garments into an overcrowded closet or drawer. Doing so can cause wrinkles and make it hard to find what you want. Organize closets and drawers by grouping similar clothing together. Hanging short items together in your closet creates extra storage space below.

In climates where seasons change, you may want to free up closet and shelf space by placing out-of-season clothes in garment bags, boxes, or chests. Clean or wash all garments before you put them away for the season. Soiled fabrics might attract moths and other insects that eat holes in fabrics. Moths are particularly attracted to soiled woolen clothes.

Section 18.3 Review

CHECK YOUR UNDERSTANDING

1. Why is it a wise consumer practice to care for clothing properly?
2. Why do you need to check care labels before washing clothes in a machine?
3. Explain how to store clothes properly.

CONSUMER APPLICATION

Laundry Guidelines Prepare a list of guidelines for doing laundry that you can keep with your family's laundry supplies.

Objectives

After studying this section, you should be able to:

- Explain how grooming products are regulated by the FDA.
- Evaluate the information found on grooming product labels.
- Give guidelines for using grooming products safely.

Key Terms

hypoallergenic
dermatologist
noncomedogenic

SECTION 18.4

Choosing Grooming Products

In bathroom cabinets everywhere, half-empty containers of shampoos, shaving lotions, moisturizers, and makeup sit unused and unwanted. The consumers who bought them discovered that many grooming products are not as effective as they seem in the ads.

REGULATION OF GROOMING PRODUCTS

All sorts of grooming products, from hair gel to mouthwash to hand cream, are regulated by the Food and Drug Administration (FDA). However, different rules apply depending on whether the FDA considers the grooming product to be a drug or simply a cosmetic.

Grooming products that claim to affect the structure or function of the body must follow rules that apply to drugs. That is, they must be proven safe and effective before they can be sold. Examples of such products include fluoride toothpastes, dandruff shampoos, antiperspirants, and preparations containing sunscreen.

Grooming products that do not claim to affect the structure or function of the body are considered to be cosmetics and not drugs. They can use ingredients without approval and do not have to prove their performance claims.

Research Activity. Ask students to study the labels of several grooming products. Have them note which products claim to affect the structure or function of the body and whether these products list their active ingredients. Also ask them to look for the words and phrases listed on this page.

However, if a product or ingredient is found to be harmful after it's on the market, the FDA can take action to halt its sale.

LEARNING FROM LABELS

Grooming products are required to have an ingredients list on the label. The ingredients must be listed in descending order of quantity. The only ingredients that need not be listed are specific fragrances, flavors, and "trade secrets."

If the grooming product is considered to be a drug, the ingredients list is divided into two categories: "active ingredients" and "other ingredients." The active ingredients, which must be listed first, are the chemicals that make the product effective.

The names of many ingredients are difficult to decipher. However, by studying ingredients lists, you can determine whether products contain ingredients that you want to avoid. You can also find out whether competing brands contain the same ingredients. See Figure 18-9.

Labels also include words or phrases carefully chosen to sell the product. Consumers should think critically when they see terms such as the ones listed below. Don't just assume that these terms mean the product is better than others.

- **Natural.** This term suggests that the ingredients come directly from plants or animal products as opposed to being produced artificially. However, no regulations govern the use of this term—it can mean whatever the manufacturer wants it to mean. In any case, there is no scientific evidence that natural ingredients are better.
- **Hypoallergenic.** In theory, a **hypoallergenic** product is less likely to cause an allergic reaction. In practice, manufacturers are not required to back up this claim with scientific evidence.
- **Dermatologist-tested.** A **dermatologist** is a physician who specializes in treating the skin. The manufacturer does not have to provide information about who tested the product, what tests were conducted, or what the results were.
- **Fragrance-free.** This term doesn't necessarily mean that the product contains no fragrance ingredients. A small amount of fragrance may have been added to cover up the odor of other ingredients.

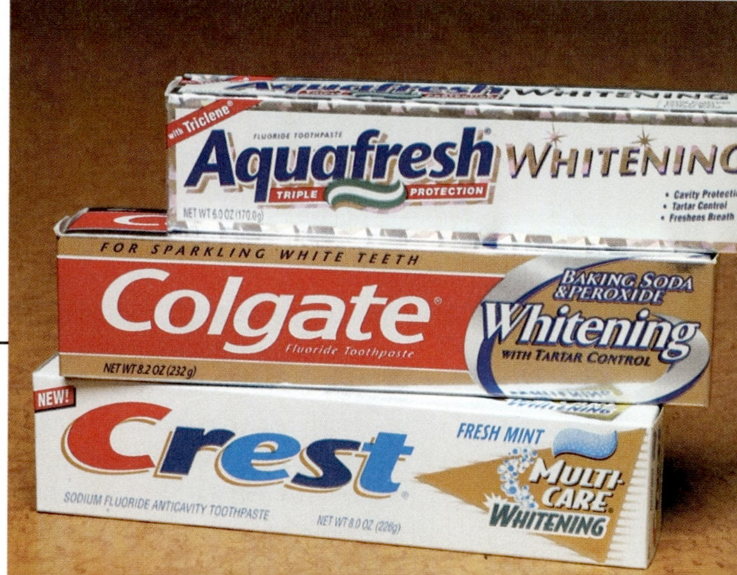

18-9

You may find that different brands contain the same active ingredients in the same amounts. If that's the case, how would you choose which product to buy?

Discussion. ***Ask:*** What products have you tried based on recommendations from others? Did the products work as well for you as you expected?

- **Noncomedogenic.** The term **noncomedogenic** (non-koe-mee-doe-jeh-nik) suggests that the product will not clog pores and lead to acne. Again, the claim does not have to be proven.
- **Vitamin-enriched.** Although vitamins in food can be healthful, there is no clinical evidence that adding vitamins to grooming products has any beneficial effect.

MAKING INFORMED DECISIONS

One way to choose grooming products is to ask for recommendations. Friends and family members may have ideas to share about what has and hasn't worked for them. Keep in mind, though, that the grooming needs of others may be different from yours. For example, a conditioner that works well on thick, curly hair may not be right for fine, straight hair. A moisturizer that works well for dry skin may not be suitable for oily skin. Compare hair and skin types when you evaluate recommendations.

When comparing similar grooming products, some consumers assume that a higher price means better quality. That may be true, if higher-quality ingredients were used in the product. However, sometimes the price difference is due to packaging and advertising costs. In addition, some marketers use "prestige pricing" to imply that a product is valuable. The high price is intended to improve the product's image. The quality may actually be no better than that of a lower-priced product.

InfoSource. Have students use the sources listed to research and write a report on a specific grooming product.

SAFETY AND GROOMING PRODUCTS

You probably don't associate grooming products with any kind of risk, but injuries and allergic reactions can result from their use. Protect yourself by reading the directions before using any product. Some labels carry helpful advice and warnings. For example, you might be instructed to test a product on a small patch of skin. If your skin reacts to the product, don't use it.

Most grooming products have the potential to cause an allergic reaction, even when they are labeled "allergy tested" or "hypoallergenic." The first signs of a reaction are redness and irritation. See Figure 18-10. If you experience these symptoms, stop using

InfoSource

Grooming Products

You can use electronic and print sources to gather information about grooming products.

- *Consumer Reports* frequently tests and rates grooming products.
- Health-related publications and Web sites may include articles about grooming products and their ingredients.
- The FDA and the National Institutes of Health (NIH) provide consumers with information about the safety and contents of grooming products.

Critical Thinking. ***Ask:*** What might happen if you do not follow the instructions and warnings on grooming product labels?

Answer Key. Answers to the Section Review questions are provided in the Section Lesson Plan located in the *Teacher Resource Guide.*

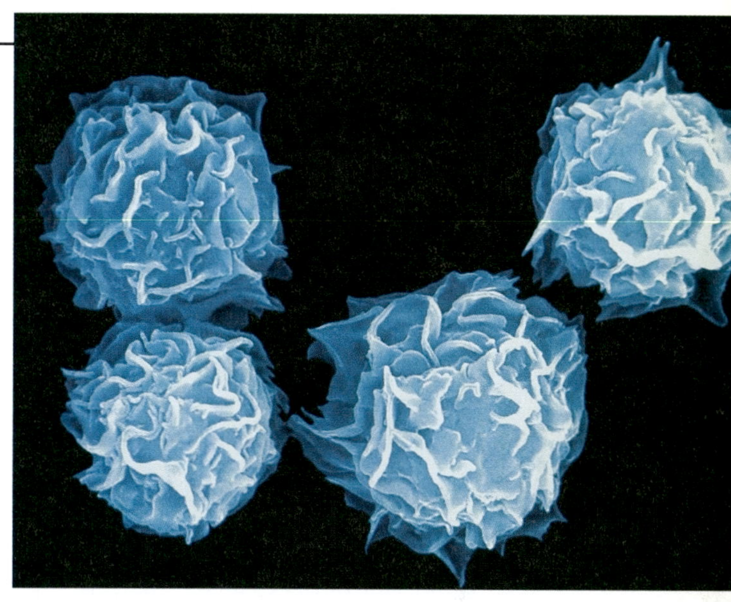

18-10

Mast cells like these are found in your skin tissues. When they react to an allergy-causing substance, the result is often an itchy red rash.

Team Activity. Give student pairs a dollar amount to "spend" on grooming products. Have them choose an array of grooming products for a person who has none, looking for best prices in order to get the most for the assigned amount of money. Compare results.

the product. If you're prone to reactions, pay careful attention to the labeled ingredients. You may be able to identify the substance that causes the reaction.

Labels will also inform you if a product is flammable. Using an aerosol product, such as hair spray, near heat or fire is dangerous because the product can ignite. Nail polish products are also highly flammable.

Following some common-sense guidelines will help protect you from infection and injury associated with grooming products. Here are some tips to remember:

- Wash your hands before using grooming products.
- Don't share grooming products with others. Avoid using testers at makeup counters.
- Don't use eye makeup if you have an eye infection.
- Keep grooming products tightly closed to preserve freshness. Store them out of sunlight. Light and heat can break down preservatives.
- Throw away any product that changes color or develops a bad odor, or is past its expiration date. Replace mascara every three months.
- Never apply makeup while driving.

Section 18.4 Review

CHECK YOUR UNDERSTANDING

1. What determines whether the FDA regulates a grooming product as a drug? Why is this significant?
2. If a product is labeled "natural," what does that tell you about the product? Explain.
3. Give four guidelines for using grooming products safely.

CONSUMER APPLICATION

Comparing Labels Choose a grooming product that you use regularly. Compare the labels on three brands. How are they similar and different? Summarize your findings in a brief report that you can share with others.

CHAPTER 18

Review & Activities

CHAPTER SUMMARY

- Physical, psychological, and social factors influence clothing decisions. Assessing and building your wardrobe can help you make the most of your clothing budget. (18.1)
- Different types of stores sell clothing. When shopping, read clothing labels and evaluate garments carefully. (18.2)
- Clothing requires routine care and repairs, regular laundering or dry cleaning, and proper storage. (18.3)
- Some grooming products are regulated as drugs. Consumers should make informed decisions about grooming products and use them safely. (18.4)

I've Got to Be Me: The clothing styles that are popular with many teens don't interest Nate. He can't afford to spend much on clothing, yet he wants a look of his own. Nate would like his personality to show, but he does not want to stand out in a negative way. How can he make a personal statement with his appearance that addresses all of these concerns? (18.1)

Reviewing Key Terms and Ideas

1. What are **accessories**, and what part do they play in a **wardrobe**? (18.1)
2. What steps should you take when assessing your wardrobe? (18.1)
3. How can **classics** help you stretch your wardrobe dollar? (18.1)
4. What is the best way to determine whether a garment fits properly? (18.2)
5. How do **natural fibers** differ from **manufactured fibers**? (18.2)
6. Describe two ways in which fibers can be turned into fabrics. (18.2)
7. What are fabric **finishes**? Give examples of their various uses. (18.2)
8. What information can be found on a clothing label? (18.2)
9. Describe how to **launder** clothes in a washing machine. (18.3)
10. What is meant by **dry cleaning**? (18.3)
11. What is the benefit of making clothing repairs as soon as possible? (18.3)
12. Why is it helpful to store clothes properly? (18.3)
13. Explain the differences between the FDA's two classifications of grooming products. (18.4)
14. What does the term **hypoallergenic** suggest? (18.4)
15. List three guidelines to prevent infections from the use of grooming products. (18.4)

Answer Key. Answers to the Chapter Review & Activities are provided in the Teacher's Manual in the *Teacher Annotated Edition* of the text.

Thinking Critically

1. **Analyzing Economic Concepts:** Fashions go through cycles that start when they're introduced and continue as consumer interest grows, peaks, and declines. Some cycles are short (fads), and some are long (classics). How do you think prices are affected during these cycles? (18.1)
2. **Understanding Cause and Effect:** What influences your clothing choices the most? Why? How might this change in the future? (18.1)
3. **Drawing Conclusions:** When should you consider other people's opinions as you select clothing? Why? (18.1)
4. **Identifying Evaluation Criteria:** Think of a new grooming product that you want to try. What would you consider before purchasing the product? (18.4)

Building Consumer Skills

1. **Wardrobe Planning:** Assume that you are starting a new career and need a basic wardrobe right away. You want to buy several versatile items, and add more as money allows. What would you buy if you had the following to spend: a) $100 or less; b) $200; c) $300? List the items and costs for each option. Include alternatives to spending, as needed. (18.1)
2. **Retailer Comparison:** Choose two specific clothing retailers in different categories, such as a local discount store and a specialty clothing Web site. Compare the retailers in terms of selection, price, convenience, and service. (18.2)
3. **Clothing for Family Members:** Develop clothing selection guidelines for one of the following: a) infants; b) preschool children; c) older adults with limited dexterity. (18.2)
4. **Sorting Laundry:** Choose 12 garments from home. After reading the care labels, sort the items as you would for laundering. What determines how the clothes are sorted? (18.3)
5. **Clothing Care Costs:** How much does clothing care cost? With a partner, determine what a family with two employed adults, a teen, and a young child might spend on average per month. Create your own family description. Include laundry products, dry cleaning, and tailoring in the calculations. (18.3)
6. **Grooming Product Claims:** Analyze the use of vague or unproven claims (such as "natural") on the labels of ten different grooming products. Explain why consumers should be skeptical of such claims. (18.4)

CONSUMER CONNECTIONS

- **Family:** Talk with family members about how responsibilities for clothing care and repair are handled. Are responsibilities shared? Do some people feel overburdened? If your family wants to make some changes, create a schedule that assigns responsibilities reasonably. (18.3)
- **Community:** Find out what local organizations accept donations of used clothing. Create an ad campaign to encourage donations. (18.1, 18.2)

CHAPTER 19

Transportation

Reading with Purpose

- Read the title of this chapter and describe in writing what you expect to learn from it.
- Write down each key term, leaving space for definitions.
- As you read the chapter, write the definition beside each term.
- After reading the chapter, write a paragraph describing what you learned.

SECTION 19.1

Transportation Options

Every day, millions of Americans are on the move—traveling to work or school, going shopping, keeping appointments, meeting friends. To get around, they might use a car, train, bus, or bicycle. When you're choosing a form of transportation, consider your options carefully.

Objectives

After studying this section, you should be able to:

- Evaluate the pros and cons of using mass transit.
- Evaluate the pros and cons of using one's own vehicle.
- Summarize factors to consider when choosing transportation.

Key Terms

mass transit
exhaust emissions

USING MASS TRANSIT

When it comes to transportation, your choices will depend largely on where you live. **Mass transit**, transportation systems designed to carry large numbers of people, may be an option. In many cities, people can travel by bus or subway. Suburban residents may use commuter trains.

The fares paid by users don't cover all the costs of operating mass transit systems. Tax money subsidizes, or supports, the systems. Most mass transit systems receive support from federal funding, but are operated by local government agencies.

Benefits

Mass transit offers the following benefits to individual passengers and to society as a whole.

- **Economy.** Public transportation fares can be less than the cost of gas, tolls, and parking.

Critical Thinking. ***Ask:*** What other steps could transit officials take to reduce consumer resistance and increase ridership?

- **Convenience.** Bus and train passengers can read, work, make phone calls, or relax while riding.
- **Energy savings.** Many passengers can be moved for a fraction of the energy required to move them individually.
- **Less pollution. Exhaust emissions**—pollutants such as hydrocarbons and carbon monoxide that are released when gasoline is burned—are a major threat to the environment. When fewer vehicles are driven, exhaust emissions are reduced, thereby reducing air pollution.

Point Out. Note that some transit systems allow patrons to bring their bikes on board so they can ride them at either end of their commute.

- **Less congestion.** By cutting down on the number of vehicles entering a city, public transportation systems reduce traffic congestion in downtown areas. See Figure 19-1.

Overcoming Resistance

For all its benefits, mass transit often meets with consumer resistance. Some people dislike having to plan their time around the transit system's schedules. Some protest that facilities are dirty and poorly maintained. Some dislike crowded conditions. Fear of crime is another reason some people stay away.

Transit officials try to respond to consumer resistance in order to increase ridership. Some of the steps taken include modernizing equipment, improving cleanliness, and increasing security. Some transit systems reduce fares for older adults or offer incentives to local businesses that subsidize transit fares for their employees.

USING YOUR OWN VEHICLE

As shown in Figure 19-2, the majority of Americans continue to rely on their own transportation to get to work. Some have no choice. Their jobs may require them to have

19-1

Taking public transportation allows you to use your time productively or just enjoy the ride. In what ways does society benefit when more people use mass transit?

Research Activity. Ask students to research the cost of using public transit for all the traveling they might do in the course of a month. Then have them figure out the cost of driving a car for the same trips (including all the costs listed on this page). Have them display their findings in chart form.

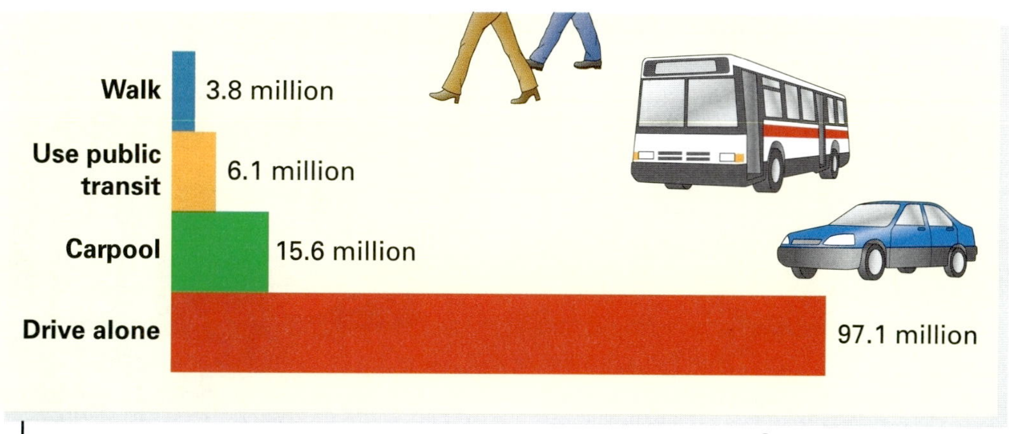

19-2 **The number of Americans who use public transportation is tiny compared with those who drive alone or with others.** **What could be done to persuade more people to switch to mass transit?**

a vehicle, or their community might not be served by a public transit system. Others could use mass transit, but prefer the comfort, independence, and flexibility that driving provides. They don't have to wait for trains or buses, and they can run errands or work late if they wish.

Using one's own vehicle has disadvantages, though. Cars and other vehicles are expensive. In addition to monthly loan or lease payments, drivers must pay for fuel, licenses, insurance, maintenance, repairs, and parking.

People who drive to work may experience more stress than those who use public transportation, especially when bad weather creates difficult driving conditions. Drivers have to deal with traffic jams, road repairs, and other aggravating circumstances. Unlike mass transit commuters, drivers must remain alert at all times.

The use of automobiles and other vehicles has a social cost, too. Commuters' vehicles contribute greatly to air pollution. They also add to the need for well-paved streets and highways that are expensive to build and maintain. More traffic on the roads means more accidents. Traffic accidents cost billions of dollars and claim more than 40,000 lives every year.

CHOOSING TRANSPORTATION

Consider the following questions when deciding which type of transportation to use.

- Where do you go most often, and how far away are those places?
- How much will transportation cost you? Investigate and compare the costs of using mass transit, owning a vehicle, or using other forms of transportation.

Community Activity. Ask students to find out where it is possible to park in their area. Have them label a local map with notes showing the location of each parking facility, its type (meters, parking lot, garage, etc.), and its cost, including daily or monthly rates (if they are available).

19-3

There are many options when it comes to getting around. What other methods might work for you?

Research Activity. Have students learn about high-speed rail service and report to the class. Where is it in use? What are the pros and cons?

- Where are your local mass transit terminals or stations located? Can you walk to these locations?
- If you use your own vehicle, where will you park? Is parking available near both your destination and your home?
- What safety concerns do you have? Taking mass transit may be safer than driving on busy highways and streets. On the other hand, driving your own car may be preferable to waiting for a bus in an unsafe neighborhood.
- What other choices are available? If you can't afford a vehicle and don't have access to mass transit, perhaps you could join a carpool, ride a bike, walk, skate, or use a scooter. See Figure 19-3.

When weighing your options, be sure to talk with others who travel the same route as you. You may discover options you hadn't considered before. Everyone has to make choices about transportation, and you can benefit from the experience of others.

Answer Key. Answers to the Section Review questions are provided in the Section Lesson Plan located in the *Teacher Resource Guide.*

Section 19.1 Review

CHECK YOUR UNDERSTANDING

1. In what ways do individuals benefit from using public transportation?
2. What reasons do people give for driving their own vehicles, even if mass transit is available?
3. What factors should you consider when choosing your main method of transportation?

CONSUMER APPLICATION

Public Transportation Research the public transportation systems that serve your community or one nearby. Find out what destinations the systems serve, when they are available, and what they charge. Prepare a brief summary of your findings.

SECTION 19.2

Understanding Vehicle Financing

Suppose you've decided to get a vehicle of your own. Now what? How much can you afford to spend? Should you buy or lease? Researching your payment options will help you make wise decisions.

Objectives

After studying this section, you should be able to:

- Distinguish between buying and leasing a vehicle.
- Describe factors to consider when choosing vehicle financing.
- Explain costs involved in leasing a vehicle.

Key Terms

lease
title
lessee
capitalized cost reduction

WHAT CAN YOU AFFORD?

Few people can afford to buy a vehicle outright. Most enter into a deal that involves monthly payments spread over a period of time. Your first task, therefore, is to figure out what you can afford to spend on a vehicle each month. Review your budget, or create a budget if you don't already have one. Decide how you can adjust other expense categories to make room in your budget for vehicle expenses. Be realistic. Once you obtain a vehicle, the expenses that come with it will continue month after month, so set a limit that won't be a financial burden.

Keep in mind that the amount you budget for vehicle expenses must cover more than just monthly payments. You'll also have to pay insurance premiums and operating expenses, such as gas, parking, maintenance, and repairs not covered by a warranty. These costs vary, depending on factors such as the age of the vehicle, the cost of gasoline, and the amount of driving you do. If you go over the

Team Activity. Have students work in small groups to develop brochures that help consumers decide between buying and leasing a vehicle. If possible, have them include a comparison of the costs of buying a specific vehicle and leasing the same vehicle.

figures with an experienced driver, you should be able to estimate how much to allow for insurance and operating expenses and what monthly payments you can afford.

BUY OR LEASE?

Unless you can afford to pay cash for a vehicle, you have two financing options:

- **Buying with a loan.** Most consumers who buy a vehicle make a down payment and take out a loan for the remaining amount. The loan is repaid in monthly installments. Once you have repaid the loan, the vehicle belongs to you. You can keep it and make no more payments; you can sell it; or you can trade it in for a newer vehicle.
- **Leasing.** When you **lease** a vehicle, you make monthly payments in exchange for exclusive use of the vehicle for a specified period of time. You do not own the vehicle. At the end of the leasing period, you must return the vehicle, unless you decide to buy it at that point.

How Do You Decide?

Leasing applies to new vehicles only. If you're looking to acquire a used car, leasing is not an option.

What if you want a new car? To decide whether to buy or lease, you'll want to know which costs less overall. Monthly lease payments are usually lower than monthly loan payments. However, in the long run, leasing may be more expensive than buying a vehicle. The only way to be sure is to estimate and compare the total costs of a specific loan and lease for a specific vehicle. However, several questions can help provide an indication of whether buying or leasing is a better choice for you.

19-4

The way a family plans to use a vehicle can be an important factor in deciding whether to buy or lease. Under what circumstances does leasing make the most sense?

Point Out. Tell students that in some cities, an alternative to buying or leasing is car sharing. Drivers who need a car only occasionally can join a car-sharing service and pay by the hour or the day whenever they want to use one of the cars owned by the service.

- **How much wear and tear will you put on the vehicle?** Most lease agreements require that you pay an extra charge if the vehicle has excessive wear and tear when you return it. If you haul a lot of belongings in your vehicle or if you tend to drive off-road and in rough terrain, leasing may not be right for you. Of course, if you buy a vehicle, it's still wise to keep it in good condition so that you'll get a good price when you trade it in or sell it. See Figure 19-4.
- **How much will you drive the vehicle?** Most leases include a mileage limit. At the end of the lease period, you must pay a certain amount (between 10 and 20 cents) for every mile over the limit. If you drive more than 12,000 to 15,000 miles a year, a lease probably isn't the way to go.
- **How long do you want to keep the vehicle?** In the long run, the least costly option usually is to buy a vehicle and keep it as long as you possibly can. However, for consumers who want a new vehicle every two or three years, leasing may cost less than frequent buying.

Class Activity. Have students calculate the difference in the monthly payment between a 36-month loan and a 60-month loan at 5 percent.

SHOPPING FOR A VEHICLE LOAN

If you decide to buy a vehicle, you'll need to shop for a loan. A wise consumer puts as much effort into getting good loan terms as into finding the right vehicle. You can obtain a loan from a financial institution or from a car dealer.

In general, the goal of loan shopping is to find the lowest interest rate. Remember, though, that the total amount you pay depends on the length of the loan as well as the interest rate. As Figure 19-5 shows, a low-interest rate loan stretched over a longer period of time can actually cost you more than a loan at a higher interest rate over a shorter period of time.

Before you start shopping for a loan, make a quick check of your personal finances. Know how much money you have saved, how much debt you have, and how much you can afford in monthly payments. Know your credit history. If you have a history of using credit cards wisely and making payments on time, you're more likely to be approved for a loan.

19-5

You'll pay more if you borrow at 4% for 48 months than you will if you borrow at 5% for 36 months. Why do some people choose a longer loan period in spite of the higher cost?

Comparing Car Loans

If you borrow $12,000 at a rate of...	for...	you'll pay back $12,000 PLUS
4%	36 months	$ 754.36 interest
4%	48 months	$1,005.53 interest
4%	60 months	$1,259.88 interest
5%	36 months	$ 947.43 interest
5%	48 months	$1,264.88 interest
5%	60 months	$1,587.33 interest

Research Activity. Have students shop online for a new vehicle loan. Ask them to compare different loan options and rates offered by different sellers.

Dollars and Sense. Ask students to check out an ad for a special loan deal offered by a car dealer and find out what its terms are.

Many lenders have Web sites that enable people to shop for loans online. Some sites include a calculator that enables you to compare different loan options. This is a convenient and easy way to explore different financing arrangements.

Whether you shop online, visit lenders personally, or call them, the same precautions apply. Before you sign anything, make sure you understand exactly what you will owe and what the repayment terms will be.

The Down Payment

The amount of the down payment is a percentage of the vehicle's price. Typically, the minimum is 10%. However, if you are a first-time buyer with no credit history, or if you have a poor credit history, you may be asked to pay a higher percentage.

Keep in mind that the larger the down payment, the less money you'll have to borrow and the less you'll pay in monthly finance charges. Make your down payment as large as possible, but don't use up all your savings. You should keep enough in reserve to cover possible emergencies.

A down payment does not have to be in cash. If you have a vehicle to trade in, the value of that vehicle can count toward the down payment. So can a manufacturer's rebate—a return of part of the price you pay for the vehicle—which you might be offered if you buy a new car. If the amount of the trade-in or rebate is high enough, you may not have to pay cash at all.

Monthly Payments

Monthly payments depend on the amount borrowed, the interest rate, and the length of the repayment period. Your monthly payments will remain the same throughout the loan period. However, the amount that goes toward the interest will gradually decrease and the amount going toward the principal will increase.

Until the loan is paid in full, the lender is the owner of the vehicle and keeps the title. The **title** is a legal document that shows who owns the vehicle. You should receive a copy

DOLLARSandSENSE

Is Dealer Financing a Good Deal?

New car dealers sometimes offer loan terms that seem too good to pass up. Before you sign on the dotted line, check for hidden catches. For example, the loan with 0% interest might require a large down payment, while the no-down-payment deal socks you with a high interest rate. To qualify for special financing, you might have to pay the full sticker price. In many cases, you'd be better off to negotiate a lower price on the vehicle and shop around for financing at financial institutions.

Critical Thinking. ***Ask:*** Where is a safe place to keep the title to your car? Why would it be unwise to keep the title or a copy inside the car?

of the title for your use in the meantime. If you fail to make your payments, the lender has the right to repossess the vehicle.

LEASING A VEHICLE

Vehicle leases are arranged through new car dealers. The person who leases the vehicle is the **lessee**.

When looking into the possibility of leasing, be sure to learn about all the costs in advance so that you can compare the benefits of leasing versus buying. Include figures for insurance, taxes, and operating expenses, because you'll be responsible for these even if you are leasing.

Leasing costs fall into three main categories:

- **Up-front costs.** The first month's payment must be made when signing the lease. Other costs may also have to be paid up front, such as a refundable security deposit, taxes, registration fees, an acquisition fee, and various other charges. Sometimes the lessee pays a **capitalized cost reduction**—a payment, similar to a down payment, that results in a lower monthly fee.
- **Monthly payments.** By making monthly payments, the lessee pays for the vehicle's depreciation—the difference between the vehicle's original value and its projected value at the end of the lease period. The monthly payment also includes an additional amount, similar to interest, that is paid to the leasing company in return for the use of their vehicle.

Jump$tart. Ask students to evaluate the benefits and costs of leasing. Under what circumstances would they consider leasing to be a better deal than buying a new car? *(Spending & Credit)*

Answer Key. Answers to the Section Review questions are provided in the Section Lesson Plan located in the *Teacher Resource Guide.*

- **End-of-lease costs.** At the end of the lease period, you may have to pay a disposition fee to cover the leasing company's expense of "disposing" of the vehicle. You may also have to pay charges if you exceed the mileage limit, or if there is significant wear and tear to the vehicle. Remember, too, that if you decide to end a lease early, you may have to pay a considerable penalty.

Find out before you sign a lease agreement what all the charges and fees will be. If you want the option to buy the vehicle when the lease expires, make sure that's included in the contract. You may also want to find out whether the lease can be extended. However, it's not advisable to lease a vehicle for a longer term than its warranty. Once the vehicle is out of warranty, you will be responsible for repairs.

Section 19.2 Review

CHECK YOUR UNDERSTANDING

1. What is the difference between buying and leasing a vehicle?
2. Describe factors that can affect the size of the down payment on a vehicle.
3. What three kinds of costs are involved in leasing a vehicle?

CONSUMER APPLICATION

Buy or Lease? Suppose that you are considering buying or leasing a new car. Describe the steps you would take to determine which option is best for your situation.

Objectives

After studying this section, you should be able to:

- Describe information to gather when shopping for a vehicle.
- Explain how to evaluate a vehicle.
- Give guidelines for negotiating and finalizing the purchase of a vehicle.

Key Terms

book value
invoice price
base price
options
MSRP
sticker price
lemon laws

SECTION 19.3

Shopping for a Vehicle

Whether you're looking for a used car or a new one, gather as much information as you can. An informed consumer is more likely to get the right vehicle at the right price.

SETTING PRIORITIES

As you consider what type of vehicle you'll buy, think about how you'll use it. If you'll mainly travel between home and school or work, look for an economical and reliable vehicle. If you plan to carpool regularly or if you have a large active family, you'll want something roomier.

Consider where you live, too. Driving on snow-covered mountain roads requires a vehicle designed for such conditions. Extremely hot weather calls for powerful air-conditioning. There are vehicles to meet every want and budget, from traditional sedans and coupes to minivans to SUVs and pickup trucks. Determine which will best suit your budget and priorities.

New or Used?

Should you shop for a used vehicle or a new one? If you're like most people, you'll start with a used vehicle and perhaps eventually buy a new one. Used vehicles are generally less expensive than new ones. For the same amount of money, you might be able to choose between a small, cheaply made new car and a larger three-year-old car that

Class Activity. Ask students to make a list of the factors they would consider most important when choosing a vehicle. Have them assign a number of points, from one to five, to each factor. Discuss how they could use this list to help them evaluate cars they might consider buying.

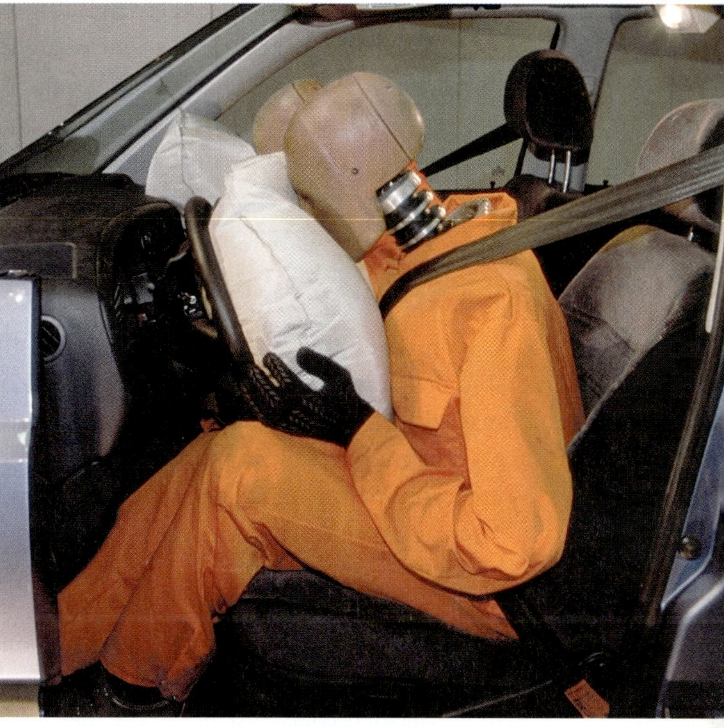

19-6

Crash-test ratings can help you select a safe, reliable make and model. Why would it be a good idea to check several sources for crash-test results?

Class Activity. Have students make a table comparing the advantages and disadvantages of buying a new vehicle and a used vehicle.

is more solidly built. Whether you decide on a new car or a used car, you still have a lot of research ahead of you.

RESEARCHING MAKES AND MODELS

Once you've determined the price you can pay and the general type of vehicle you want, research and compare different makes and models. Is there a particular manufacturer that you prefer? Is there a special model and year that interests you? Do you just want to browse through some possibilities? Useful information is readily available, both online and in print.

Important factors to consider when you do your research include:

- **Safety.** Braking and emergency handling are important elements for accident avoidance. Airbags and head restraints provide protection in the event of a crash. See Figure 19-6.
- **Reliability.** Some manufacturers and some specific models of vehicles get high marks for quality and reliability. You might have to pay a little more for a reliable model, but you'll save on repairs and aggravation.
- **Fuel economy.** In general, the larger or more powerful a vehicle is, the more gas it uses. Some vehicles require premium fuel, which is more expensive. If you want to control your fuel costs, look for a vehicle that runs on regular gas and gets good mileage.
- **Power and performance.** Depending on how you plan to use your vehicle, you'll need to keep in mind such factors as how well it can accelerate to highway speeds or handle steep hills.
- **Comfort and convenience.** Some vehicles have more headroom and legroom or can hold more cargo than other vehicles of similar size.

InfoSource. Ask students to read a review of a specific vehicle in one of the sources listed here. Have them share their findings with the class.

- **Insurance.** The vehicle you choose can affect what you pay for insurance. Once you know which vehicles interest you, call your auto insurer and find out what your premiums would be. You can also use the Internet to compare quotes from various insurance companies.

Road Tests and Reviews

Compare different vehicle models by studying road test results and reviews in magazines and online. Road tests are practical tests conducted by professional drivers to judge the performance of new-model cars. They report on features such as handling and braking, acceleration, convenience and comfort, and fuel economy.

You also can find extensive information about how older vehicles have performed over time. Detailed charts list problems that have occurred in particular models and will help you pinpoint the best years for that model. Some sources also provide frequency-of-repair reports on older vehicles.

Research Activity. Have students look up the book value of a specific make, model, and year car. Ask whether it was more or less than they expected.

RESEARCHING PRICES

Suppose you see an ad for a used car in your local newspaper. How do you know if the seller is asking a fair price? Check the vehicle's book value. The **book value** is the estimated value of a given make, model, and year of vehicle. It's based on factors such as the condition of the vehicle, mileage, overall condition, and even the part of the country in which the vehicle is being sold. You can look up the book value of a vehicle online or in the Kelley *Blue Book.* Not only can you then judge if the asking price is fair, but you'll also have a bargaining tool.

New Car Prices

If you're shopping for a new car, you'll want to know some basic pricing terms.

- The **invoice price** is the price the dealer pays the manufacturer for the vehicle. The dealer usually won't tell you the invoice price, but it's available from sources such as *Consumer Reports* and several Web sites. It's a good idea to obtain the invoice price

InfoSource

Online Vehicle Research

Web sites associated with magazines such as *Consumer Reports, Road and Track,* and *Car and Driver* provide information on many aspects of buying a vehicle. Look for:

- Road test reports, vehicle reviews, and comparisons.
- Safety features and ratings.
- Prices for new and used cars.
- Leasing information.
- Vehicle history reports for used cars.

Class Activity. Ask students to list options that might be added on to a new car. List their responses on the board. Then have students vote on which five options they would consider most important to have on a car. Discuss which types of options were most popular and why.

19-7

A label showing the MSRP and the fuel economy of the vehicle is required by law on all new vehicles. What is the advantage of knowing a vehicle's fuel economy?

because it will help you negotiate a deal. Note that the invoice price is often higher than the price the dealer actually pays, because manufacturers offer various rebates and discounts that lower the dealer's cost.

- The **base price** is the price of a vehicle with its standard equipment—features that every model comes with. It does not cover various **options**, which are features available at extra cost. For example, a basic radio system may be standard equipment, while a CD player is an option. Examples of other possible options are a sunroof, tinted windows, and leather seats. A feature that's an option on one vehicle may be standard equipment on another.
- The **MSRP** is the manufacturer's suggested retail price. It includes the base price, the price of options installed by the manufacturer, and the manufacturer's transportation charge. See Figure 19-7.
- The **sticker price** is the dealer's initial asking price, as marked on the sticker affixed to the vehicle's window. It is the sum of the MSRP plus the price of dealer-installed options, dealer preparation, and additional dealer markup and profit. The dealer preparation fee covers the cost of cleaning the vehicle, handling paperwork, filling the tank with gas, and completing other tasks before turning the vehicle over to you.

Use consumer magazines and relevant Web sites to determine not only the dealer's invoice price but also the typical price for that vehicle in your area. The more information you gather up front, the easier it will be for you to negotiate a fair price.

Research Activity. Ask students to find an ad for a used vehicle being offered for sale by a private owner. Then have them check the cost of a similar vehicle at a used car dealer. Have them share results in class. Draw conclusions about how much buyers can save by purchasing directly from sellers.

19-8

Searching for a vehicle on the Internet can save time. Some buyers also prefer to make an offer for a vehicle this way rather than negotiating face-to-face.

FINDING VEHICLES

You've narrowed your choices to a few specific makes and models. The next step is to find actual vehicles. That means connecting with sellers. Some of your options are:

- **Private owners.** People who want to sell their used vehicles often place classified ads in newspapers or other publications. You can usually get the best price by buying directly from an owner. However, a private owner will not offer a warranty.
- **Dealers.** Some dealers sell only used cars. New-car dealers sell vehicles made by specific manufacturers, and may also sell a variety of used cars.
- **Internet.** Many dealers have Web sites that let you compare what you're looking for with what they have in their inventory. Some sites allow buyers to list the price they're willing to pay for a vehicle. Dealers look over the offers and decide whether they're willing to meet the buyer's request. See Figure 19-8.

EVALUATING A VEHICLE

Once you locate a vehicle that interests you, take as much time as you need to evaluate it thoroughly. The process you follow will depend on whether you are buying a used or a new vehicle, and on whether you buy from a dealer or from a private individual.

Inspect the Vehicle

A thorough inspection is most important when you buy a used vehicle from a private seller, since the responsibility for future repairs and service work will be entirely in your hands. Inspecting the vehicle can keep you from making someone else's problems your own. When inspecting a used car, check the following:

Community Activity. Ask students to contact a local repair shop and find out what the mechanics check when inspecting a used vehicle for a buyer.

Critical Thinking. *Ask:* What is implied when the VIN on the owner's title does not match the one on the dashboard?

19-9

When inspecting a used car, be sure to check the odometer. What else should you be concerned about?

Class Activity. Ask students what the odometer reading is in Figure 19-9 (68,319 miles). Ask them what is registering in the space to the right of this number (fractions of a mile).

- **Odometer.** This is the instrument on the dashboard that tells you how many miles the vehicle has been driven. See Figure 19-9. The more miles a vehicle has been driven, the more likely it is to need major repairs in the near future. When you buy a used vehicle from a dealer, the dealer must supply you with a disclosure form revealing the true mileage.
- **Tires.** Examine the depth of the tire tread on all four tires. Uneven wear can indicate a number of problems.
- **Interior.** Check the brake and accelerator pedals, as well as the upholstery, for wear—a clue to the vehicle's age and use. Check for signs of leaks or flooding, including water marks on the upholstery, trim, or floor and swelling or buckling of interior trim panels.
- **Exterior finish.** Check for signs of rust or pitting. Remember, some people try to mask such problems with a coat of paint. Check along window moldings as well.
- **Heating and electrical systems.** With the engine running, test the heating and cooling systems, lights and signals, wipers, radio, and CD or tape player.
- **Mechanical systems.** Check for fluid leaks by looking under the hood and under the vehicle. Test the steering, brakes, and transmission. Problems could signal the need for a major repair.
- **Body and frame.** Look for new or improperly fitting parts, mismatched paint, or suspension problems that might signal that the vehicle has been in a major accident. Some states require this information to be disclosed in all used-car sales.

Before making an offer on a used vehicle, arrange to have a reliable technician conduct a thorough check of the vehicle. You should also make sure the Vehicle Identification Number (VIN) on the owner's title matches the one on the vehicle's dashboard.

Community Activity. Challenge students to identify a good route in their neighborhood for test-driving a car. Tell them to choose a route that includes both city streets and a segment of highway, as well as a hill on which to test acceleration. Have them trace their proposed route on a map.

An inspection of a new car is less critical, since it will be under warranty. Still, it's a good idea to check for any damage or defects and to make sure that all items listed on the sticker have been provided.

Read the Sticker

Any car that you buy from a dealer will have a sticker. The sticker tells you what is standard equipment and what options have been installed on that particular vehicle. Read the list carefully to make sure it includes the features that you want.

Dealers who sell used vehicles are required to attach a Buyers Guide sticker to the window of each vehicle they offer for sale. The Buyers Guide tells customers the warranty terms or whether the vehicle is sold "as is," without a warranty. See Figure 19-10.

Check the Warranty

All new vehicles come with warranties, but the terms vary. For example, one warranty may guarantee vehicle parts and systems for 36 months or 36,000 miles, whichever is reached first. Another may offer coverage for 36 months without the mileage limit. Some used cars come with limited warranties. Read the warranty carefully and make sure you know what it covers.

Take a Test Drive

If you're interested in a vehicle and are satisfied with the visual inspection, take it for a test drive. The test drive should be long enough to give you a good sense of the vehicle's operation. If possible, choose a route that includes both city streets and highway driving. As you drive, give special attention to braking, shifting, acceleration, handling, comfort, and ease of operation. Be alert for knocks, noises, and rattles, all of which can signal malfunctions. Make sure you can

Critical Thinking. ***Ask:*** Why should a route for a test drive include both city streets and highway driving?

19-10

In addition to giving warranty information, the Buyers Guide on a used car reminds buyers to get all promises from the seller in writing. Why is this valuable advice?

Team Activity. Have pairs of students play a negotiation game. Tell them the invoice and sticker prices of a fictitious car. The buyer gets a point for each dollar below the sticker price; the seller gets a point for each dollar above the invoice price. If they do not reach a deal, no one gets any points.

19-11

A test-drive is essential when buying a car, but you may need more help in judging a car's condition. If you're not knowledgeable about the inner workings of a car, you can hire a reliable mechanic to look for possible problems.

reach all the controls comfortably, and pay attention to whether you have enough headroom and legroom.

If you're considering a new vehicle that has to be ordered, drive a demonstrator to get an idea of what that make and model is like. However, before you actually sign a contract, drive the specific vehicle you want to purchase. See Figure 19-11.

NEGOTIATING THE DEAL

When you buy a vehicle, you usually have an opportunity to negotiate the price. Be aware, though, that it's up to you to take the initiative. Even though you may find the idea of negotiating unpleasant, you could save a lot of money by making the effort.

Discussing Price

When buying a new car, you'll be in a better position to negotiate price if you know the invoice price—the price the dealer paid for the vehicle. Remember that dealers have to make a profit to stay in business, but most are willing to accept less than the sticker price. Here are some guidelines.

- Negotiate up from the invoice price rather than down from the sticker price.

Discussion. ***Ask:*** What should you do if you don't understand all of the information in the purchase agreement when you read it?

- Don't discuss trade-in or whether you are buying or leasing. These are not relevant when determining a fair price for the vehicle.
- Leave any manufacturers' rebates out of the discussion. The rebate comes directly to you and doesn't cut into the dealer's profit.

If you plan to lease a vehicle, you still need to pay attention to price. Some dealers may imply that price is not negotiable in a lease, but this is not true. It's in your best interest to negotiate a lower lease price.

Completing the Deal

Once you and the dealer have agreed on a price, you can discuss buying or leasing arrangements. If you have a vehicle to trade in, ask what the dealer will give you for it. The amount of money dealers offer for a trade-in is usually less than book value, so you might consider selling it yourself.

Get everything in writing. Make sure the purchase agreement states the correct price of the vehicle and lists all the options you asked for. Before you sign any documents, make sure you understand them. Use a calculator to check that all numbers have been totaled correctly. Make sure you are given a copy of everything you sign.

When you pick up your vehicle, check to see that all the options and accessories you ordered are included. Inspect the vehicle thoroughly and test-drive it. If you are buying a used vehicle, assure yourself that all asked-for repairs have been made. If you are buying or leasing a new vehicle and find a defect, have the dealer sign an agreement to correct it. At this point in the purchasing process, you are in the best position to have any problems corrected.

Answer Key. Answers to the Section Review questions are provided in the Section Lesson Plan located in the *Teacher Resource Guide.*

Lemon Laws

Once you accept delivery, the vehicle is yours. If you are unhappy with the vehicle, you can't return it to the seller and ask for a refund, as you can for most other purchases. However, all 50 states do have **lemon laws**, laws that protect buyers of vehicles with serious defects. These vehicles are known as "lemons" because they are a sour deal for buyers. Although state laws vary, a lemon is usually defined as a vehicle that has not been successfully repaired after four attempts for the same defect or that has been out of service because of defects for 30 days during one year. Lemon laws typically require dealers to replace such a vehicle or to refund the customer's money.

Section 19.3 Review

CHECK YOUR UNDERSTANDING

1. What are some factors you should take note of when researching makes and models of vehicles?
2. How can knowing the invoice price of a vehicle help you?
3. At what point in a negotiation should you discuss a trade-in? Why?

CONSUMER APPLICATION

Evaluating a Vehicle Suppose a friend has found a used car for sale and comes to you for advice about purchasing it. Make a checklist of the steps your friend should take in order to evaluate the car's condition.

SECTION 19.4

Owning a Vehicle

Vehicle ownership brings added independence, but also added responsibilities. If you took out a loan or a lease, you are responsible for making monthly payments. You also must insure the vehicle. Keeping the vehicle running well and driving safely are also among your responsibilities.

Objectives

After studying this section, you should be able to:

- Explain guidelines for maintaining a vehicle.
- Describe how to choose and use vehicle service facilities.
- Give examples of responsible driving habits.

Key Terms

maintenance schedule
rebuilt
reconditioned
recall

VEHICLE MAINTENANCE

Regular maintenance helps your vehicle last longer and reduces the money and time spent on repairs. A vehicle that gets regular maintenance is safer, uses less fuel, and causes less pollution, too.

Every new vehicle comes with an owner's manual that provides a guide to the car's features. The manual also contains a **maintenance schedule**, which is a timetable for routine servicing and for checking or replacing parts. If you buy a used vehicle, try to obtain a copy of the owner's manual. If it is not with the vehicle, check with the manufacturer. The manufacturer may be able to send you a manual or may have a Web site that provides maintenance schedules.

You can save money by learning to do some routine maintenance tasks yourself. Remember, though, that working

Class Activity. Show students a diagram of a car's engine. See whether they can locate the battery and the reservoirs for various fluids.

on or around a vehicle can be dangerous. Do only those procedures for which you have knowledge and the right equipment.

Here are some items that should be checked regularly:

- **Windshield washer fluid.** Check the level each time you refuel the vehicle.
- **Engine oil.** Keeping your vehicle's oil at the proper level helps keep the engine lubricated and running well. Check the oil level each time you refuel, and replace the oil and oil filter at recommended intervals.
- **Transmission fluid.** Transmission fluid lubricates the transmission gears. In some cars, the fluid rarely, if ever, needs to be changed, but check the fluid levels when you change the engine oil.

Critical Thinking. ***Ask:*** How can taking care of routine vehicle maintenance save you money in the long run?

- **Brake fluid.** Brake fluid is essential to the proper operation of your braking system. Brake fluid usually does not need to be changed, but check the fluid level when you change the engine oil to make sure it's not leaking.
- **Tire pressure.** Low inflation causes tires to wear out faster, reduces fuel efficiency, and can cause accidents. Overinflation causes a bumpy ride. Check tire pressure once a month and keep it at the level specified in your owner's manual. See Figure 19-12.
- **Radiator coolant/antifreeze.** This fluid helps keep your engine at a safe operating temperature. Check the coolant/antifreeze level once a month to ensure that it continues to protect your engine. Replace it every few years or more often if needed.

Class Activity. Bring in a tire gauge and demonstrate how to use it and read it. A bicycle tire may be suitable for this demonstration. Invite students to practice this skill for themselves.

19-12

Taking care of car tires is critical for safety and good mileage. Along with maintaining tire pressure, be sure to have tires rotated routinely so that the tread wears evenly. Replace worn tires to prevent a blowout while you are driving.

Community Activity. Have students ask family members and friends who are car owners if they could recommend a good service facility in the area. Have them keep a list of facilities and the number of recommendations each one gets, along with notes about the good qualities of each place.

19-13

When you take your vehicle in for service, explain as thoroughly as possible any problems that you're having. Why is finding a dependable service facility so important?

Class Activity. Have students tell about car-repair experiences their family and friends have had, both positive and negative. List "Points to Learn" on the board as the experiences are described.

- **Lights.** Once a month, check to make sure the headlights, tail lights, signal lights, brake lights, hazard warning flashers, and interior lights work properly.
- **Battery.** Newer batteries are maintenance-free. If your car has an older battery, inspect it once a month. Check the water level and add more if needed. Clean and tighten the terminals if needed.

Your vehicle's dashboard has warning lights and gauges designed to alert you to situations such as low fuel level, low oil pressure, an overheated engine, low brake fluid, and other problems. By responding quickly, you may avoid a breakdown and high repair costs.

SERVICE FACILITIES

How can you choose a service facility for maintenance and repairs? You have many options, including dealerships, service stations, independent garages, specialty centers (such as muffler, brake, or transmission shops), and large retail facilities. All offer various levels of service at various prices.

If the car is under warranty, take it to the dealership. Otherwise, ask for recommendations from friends or family members. Then call several shops to compare prices. Find out if they charge a flat per-hour rate or for actual time spent working on your vehicle. Ask about warranty policies, too. Make sure the facility's business hours are convenient for you, and ask whether they provide transportation or a loaner vehicle while your vehicle is in the shop. See Figure 19-13.

Dollars and Sense. Have students do research to find out what types of vehicles actually require premium gasoline and why.

You'll want to make sure that the facility you choose is trustworthy. Check the facility's current license if your state requires one. Look for technicians who are certified. Contact the Better Business Bureau or your attorney general's office to see if the facility has a satisfactory record.

Getting Estimates

Once you've chosen a service facility, explain what work you want done. Ask for a written estimate of the costs for the work, including both labor and parts. Sometimes technicians can give you an estimate when you take the vehicle in. You'll probably be asked to sign an estimate form before work can begin.

The shop cannot exceed the written estimate without your permission. If you can't wait at the shop while the vehicle is being repaired, leave a phone number where you can be reached. The technician can call if he or she has questions, finds additional problems, or needs your approval to proceed with repairs that exceed the original estimate.

Discussion. ***Ask:*** What are some other ways to be a responsible driver? How many of the drivers you see on the road seem to be responsible?

Replacement Parts

There are two options for replacing vehicle parts. One is to use new parts that are made to the manufacturer's specifications. The other, usually less expensive, option is to use rebuilt or reconditioned parts. The terms **rebuilt** and **reconditioned** are used interchangeably and describe used parts that have been restored to a good working condition. When the repairs made to your vehicle are under warranty, find out whether your warranty covers the use of new parts or rebuilt ones.

Recalls

When manufacturers discover a problem with one of their vehicle models, they may issue a recall of that model. A **recall** is a manufacturer's request for owners to take their vehicle to a dealership for repair. Most recalls are made for safety reasons. Recall notices are usually mailed directly to owners. If you are notified of a vehicle recall, take the vehicle to a dealer for repair as soon as possible. You do not have to pay the cost of repairing the vehicle defect.

DOLLARSandSENSE

Is Premium Worth the Price?

Premium gas has a higher octane rating than regular gas and costs more per gallon. Many people think that they are doing their engine a favor by buying premium. Not so. An engine won't function better with premium fuel if it doesn't require it. To make sure you're not paying too much at the pump, check the owner's manual to see what octane level your vehicle requires. Only about 5% of the cars sold in the United States today need premium gasoline.

Point Out. Make sure students know that children must ride in the back seat away from air bags. Children under eight should use booster seats.

Answer Key. Answers to the Section Review questions are provided in the Section Lesson Plan located in the *Teacher Resource Guide.*

19-14

When you're driving, keep your full attention on the road. If you need to make a phone call, read a map, or take care of other tasks, pull over first.

RESPONSIBLE DRIVING

When you drive, you're responsible for your safety and for the safety of passengers and other people on the road. Good driving habits also can save energy and prolong the life of your vehicle.

Driving is a serious responsibility. You need to be alert at all times and aware of road conditions, weather conditions, and other drivers. Here are some guidelines to remember.

- Know and obey traffic rules. They were developed to make driving safer and more efficient for everyone.
- Stay focused. Many accidents occur because the driver becomes distracted—by other passengers, by phone conversations, or by activities such as eating. See Figure 19-14.
- Stay sharp. Don't drive if you are not alert and thinking clearly.
- Buckle up. Always wear a safety belt and insist that passengers do, too. If young children are riding in the car, make sure they are in approved safety seats.
- Drive smoothly. Sudden starts and stops waste fuel, cause wear and tear on the vehicle, and increase pollution.

Section 19.4 Review

CHECK YOUR UNDERSTANDING

1. Why is it important to follow a maintenance schedule?
2. Why should you get an estimate before getting a vehicle repaired or serviced?
3. Give five guidelines for safe driving.

CONSUMER APPLICATION

Maintenance Tasks Imagine that you've just bought your first car. List the maintenance tasks you already have the knowledge to perform. Then list those you think you could do if someone showed you how.

CHAPTER 19

Review & Activities

CHAPTER SUMMARY

- All forms of transportation have advantages and disadvantages. Several factors influence transportation choices. (19.1)
- Consumers have the option of either buying or leasing a vehicle. Whether taking out a loan or a lease, consider all costs involved in vehicle financing. (19.2)
- Shopping for a new or used vehicle involves researching and evaluating available choices. The purchase or lease price of a vehicle can usually be negotiated. (19.3)
- Maintaining and repairing a vehicle will keep it running efficiently. Drivers have an obligation to develop safe, responsible driving habits. (19.4)

THE $avvy Consumer

Look Before You Leap: Tori is shopping for her first car. She plans to keep it for a few years, until she can afford a nicer one. She is looking at a low-priced older car that someone advertised in the newspaper, and it seems acceptable. What actions should Tori take in order to avoid unwanted surprises? (19.3)

Reviewing Key Terms and Ideas

1. Explain two advantages and two disadvantages of using **mass transit**. (19.1)
2. Explain two advantages and two disadvantages of using your own vehicle. (19.1)
3. How can using mass transit reduce **exhaust emissions**? (19.1)
4. What should a person consider when choosing among different modes of transportation? (19.1)
5. Name three ways in which buying and **leasing** a vehicle differ. (19.2)
6. Explain at least two factors to consider when deciding whether to buy or lease a vehicle. (19.2)
7. When you have a vehicle loan, why does the lender hold the **title**? (19.2)
8. When and why might someone pay a **capitalized cost reduction** fee? (19.2)
9. What information can you obtain from road tests and reviews of vehicles? (19.3)
10. What is the difference between **invoice price** and **sticker price**? (19.3)
11. Name five specific things to look for when evaluating a used vehicle. (19.3)
12. What are **lemon laws** designed to do? (19.3)
13. Why might you receive a notice of **recall** from the manufacturer of your vehicle? (19.4)
14. Describe three responsible driving habits. (19.4)

Answer Key. Answers to the Chapter Review & Activities are provided in the Teacher's Manual in the *Teacher Annotated Edition* of the text.

Thinking Critically

1. **Making Predictions:** Review Figure 19.2. What might happen if the number of Americans who drive alone decreased to 15.6 million, and the number who carpool increased to 97.1 million? Consider economic, safety, and environmental factors. (19.1)
2. **Drawing Conclusions:** Why do you suppose lemon laws were created? (19.3)
3. **Analyzing Economic Concepts:** How do you think the cost of fuel impacts vehicle sales in general? In turn, what is the effect on the economy? (19.3)
4. **Analyzing Behavior:** How can you tell whether a car salesperson is trustworthy? Describe what you would look and listen for. (19.3)
5. **Understanding Cause and Effect:** Give two examples of how neglect of car maintenance can create a safety hazard for you and other people on the road. (19.4)

Building Consumer Skills

1. **Interest Costs:** Using current interest rates, calculate the costs of taking out a $5,000 loan for a used vehicle with terms of 36, 48, and 60 months. Show your results with a bar graph. If you were buying a vehicle, how would these interest costs affect your decisions about financing? (19.2)
2. **Buy or Lease?** Research and calculate the total costs of buying and leasing a specific vehicle. In what situations might buying be a better choice? When might leasing be a better choice? (19.2)
3. **Internet Shopping:** Investigate how the Internet can be used when shopping for a vehicle. Write a report about the tools that are available and how effective they are. (19.3)
4. **Closing the Deal:** Work with a partner to create a script that describes the process of negotiating and finalizing a car deal. Then perform a skit based on the script. (19.3)
5. **Maintenance Plan:** Based on the manufacturer's recommendations, develop a plan to maintain a particular vehicle model for one year. Create a chart that includes the types of maintenance to be done, a timetable to follow, and the estimated costs. Identify any tasks you could perform yourself. Calculate an estimated annual cost of all maintenance. (19.4)

CONSUMER CONNECTIONS

- **Family:** With family members, discuss how your family could save on transportation expenses. Choose one or more techniques to try out for a period of time. Then evaluate the results of your experiment. Will you continue the practice? Why or why not? (19.1)
- **Community:** Create a consumer's guide to the vehicle service facilities in your area. Include any information that you think would help consumers choose and use these facilities. In a separate paragraph, explain why you provided the information you did. (19.4)

CHAPTER 20

Recreation

SECTION 20.1
Planning Your Leisure Time

SECTION 20.2
Managing Recreation Expenses

SECTION 20.3
Planning a Vacation

Reading with Purpose

- Write down the colored headings in this chapter.
- As you read the text under each heading, visualize what you are reading.
- Reflect on what you read by writing a few sentences under each heading to describe it.
- Reread your notes.

SECTION 20.1

Planning Your Leisure Time

It's getting harder and harder to find free time. The demands of work or school, household tasks, and other commitments leave few hours in the week for relaxation and enjoyment. That makes it all the more essential to build free time into your schedule and plan how to use it.

Objectives

After studying this section, you should be able to:

- Explain the benefits of recreation.
- Describe factors that affect the use of leisure time.
- Give suggestions for effectively managing leisure time.

Key Terms

recreation
leisure time
hobby

THE REWARDS OF RECREATION

Recreation is any activity that you find pleasurable and rejuvenating. Riding your bike or reading a book, playing a sport or a quiet game—these activities can be beneficial and rewarding in several ways.

- **Mental health.** Meaning "to give new life," recreation is a good word to describe how rest, relaxation, and pleasurable activity affect your mind and emotions. By reducing stress and recharging your mental batteries, you can return to your tasks with a fresh outlook. Some recreational activities offer opportunities for personal growth through creative expression.
- **Physical health.** Many kinds of recreation involve physical activity, such as exercise or playing sports. Being physically active can improve your health and boost your energy. At the same time, it reduces tension and stress and helps you relax.

Class Activity. Ask students to name some of their favorite recreational activities and explain why they find each one rewarding. List their responses on the board. Then ask the class to identify the opportunity costs of each activity listed.

- **Social health.** Through group recreation, you can meet people with similar interests. These activities also give friends and families a chance to become closer by having fun together. You can learn teamwork and sportsmanship, important in all areas of life, through recreation with others.
- **Extra income.** Sometimes a recreational activity can double as a way to earn a little extra money. A person who enjoys creating watercolor paintings might be able to sell them at art shows, for example.
- **Helping others.** Recreation can be combined with volunteering. If you like music, you could reach out to nursing home residents by singing or playing an instrument. Putting a smile on someone's face can be as rewarding for you as it is for the other person.

TEXTLINK

To learn more about volunteering, see Section 3.2.

INFLUENCES ON LEISURE TIME

Leisure time is time that you have available to do whatever you choose. Just like any other choice involving resources, deciding how you spend leisure time requires you to consider *opportunity cost*—what you give up when you choose one alternative instead of another. For example, deciding to play volleyball might mean missing a chance to catch a movie and vice versa.

People spend their leisure time in many different ways. They base their choices on factors such as:

- **Interests.** Just about anything you like to do can become a **hobby**, an activity outside of a regular occupation that is pursued for enjoyment. Examples of hobbies are sewing, woodworking, cooking, gardening, hiking, reading, biking—anything that interests you. See Figure 20-1.
- **Abilities.** You might choose a recreational activity, whether it's writing poetry or swimming, because you have ability in that area. You can also develop a brand new skill. Try it—learning something new can be fun, and you may discover a hidden talent.

20-1

Spending your leisure time pursuing a hobby can be both relaxing and productive. What is your favorite hobby? How much time are you able to devote to it?

Discussion. *Ask:* Which of the factors listed here have the most influence on how you choose to spend your leisure time?

Critical Thinking. *Ask:* How might your educational goals influence your decisions about what recreational activities to pursue?

20-2

Many families make sure that they spend at least some of their recreational time together. If you had more recreational time with your family, what would you like to do?

- **Profession.** Some people spend leisure time doing something that's related to what they do for a living—a carpenter might enjoy building birdhouses. Others prefer recreational activities that provide a change of pace from their workday routine.
- **Budget.** Some recreational activities cost little or nothing; others involve buying or renting equipment or paying fees. Section 20.2 examines ways to manage the costs of recreational activities.
- **Schedule.** You might have to bypass some recreational choices because they occur at times that conflict with school, work, or other scheduled activities. Fortunately, many recreational activities can be enjoyed whenever you choose and don't require large blocks of time.
- **Goals.** Your use of leisure time may be influenced by your desire to meet certain goals, such as making a gift for a friend's birthday or spending more time outdoors. See Figure 20-2.

Although people make individual choices about how to spend their leisure time, patterns can be seen in the recreational activities of Americans as a whole. Some trends, such as an increase in the number of people who work long hours or have two jobs, result in less leisure time. Trends such as a general increase in discretionary income or a greater emphasis on physical fitness have an effect on how leisure time is spent. Technology, too, can influence how people use their free time by providing options such as video games and the Internet.

Class Activity. Consider your class list of leisure activities. Ask students to classify them as passive or active, mental or physical, social or solitary.

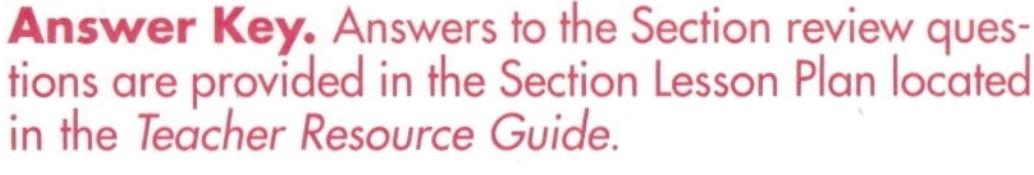

Answer Key. Answers to the Section review questions are provided in the Section Lesson Plan located in the *Teacher Resource Guide.*

20-3

Taking a class can introduce you to a hobby before you invest in equipment and supplies.

MANAGING LEISURE TIME

Have you ever spent a lazy afternoon flipping TV channels, only to find yourself becoming restless and bored instead of relaxed and refreshed? At the end of a weekend or summer vacation, have you ever felt disappointed that you didn't spend more time doing what you truly enjoy? These are signs that you could benefit from managing your leisure time more effectively.

If you put off recreation until you're not busy, you may never get to it. Instead, set aside time for yourself or to spend with friends or family, even if you have to make appointments. Then plan how best to use this time in recreation that you find fun or rewarding. For some activities, such as a bike ride with friends, you may need to set aside several hours. However, many activities—such as playing an instrument, weight lifting, or sewing—are easy to fit into smaller segments of time. Try to have any needed materials and equipment organized and ready. See Figure 20-3.

As you plan to use your leisure time, remember to balance your recreational activities. For example, try to include activities that are passive, such as listening to music, as well as those that are active, such as playing the piano. If you balance mental activities, such as reading, with physical activities, such as basketball, you'll benefit more from both. You'll benefit socially from spending some time in team sports and group activities, but also choose some solitary activities.

Be flexible. Your plans for leisure time might have to change if you take a part-time job or are invited to a movie on the spur of the moment. If you leave some flexibility in your schedule, you can adapt your recreational activities to fit new circumstances and goals.

Section 20.1 Review

CHECK YOUR UNDERSTANDING

1. How can recreation benefit mental, physical, and social health?
2. Explain how opportunity cost relates to managing leisure time.
3. What strategies can help a busy person find time for recreation?

CONSUMER APPLICATION

Leisure Activity Influences Identify three leisure activities you enjoy. What factors influence why these activities appeal to you? What factors influence how often you actually take part in these activities?

SECTION 20.2

Managing Recreation Expenses

Many businesses, from sporting goods stores to theme parks to movie theaters, compete for your recreation dollars. Like all consumer spending, the money you spend on recreation has an impact on your budget.

Objectives

After studying this section, you should be able to:

- Discuss considerations in budgeting for recreation expenses.
- Distinguish between public and private recreational facilities.
- Explain guidelines for choosing recreational facilities and equipment.

Key Terms

discretionary expenses
season tickets

BUDGETING FOR RECREATION

Some recreational activities are practically free, such as going for a walk or writing stories. Others require the purchase or rental of equipment, supplies, or special clothing. For cycling, you need a bicycle, a safety helmet, and some tools. For photography, you need camera equipment.

Recreation costs fall in the category of **discretionary expenses**—expenses that are not absolutely necessary. After you budget for necessities, you can decide how much of your remaining income you wish to spend on discretionary expenses, including recreation.

When deciding how to spend the money you've budgeted for recreation, weigh opportunity cost. Would you rather go to one expensive concert or to several movies or school plays? Would you rather play golf once or go bowling several times?

It's helpful to think about recreation expenses in terms of cost per use. Before purchasing equipment or signing up

Community Activity. Ask students to choose a specific leisure activity that interests them. Have them locate public and private facilities for this activity in their area and research the costs of using them. Then have them write a report on how people in their area can engage in this activity on a budget.

for an activity, think about how often you will participate. Sports or hobby equipment may be a worthwhile expenditure if you'll enjoy using it often, but not if it collects dust. If there's something you really enjoy doing, such as going to ball games or to the local community theater, consider buying season tickets. **Season tickets** enable you to attend a series of events during a specified period for a lower cost per ticket.

USING RECREATIONAL FACILITIES

The recreational facilities in your area may differ greatly in cost and in the recreational opportunities offered. There are two basic types of facilities.

- **Public facilities** are run by the local, state, or federal government and are supported by taxpayer dollars. Examples include national and state parks, community centers, and neighborhood parks, playgrounds, and swimming pools. Local park districts might offer classes or athletics. Many public facilities and activities are free of charge, while others charge small fees. Anyone may use them. See Figure 20-4.
- **Private facilities** are run by private organizations or businesses. Some private facilities are nonprofit but have restrictions on who can use them. For example, a private neighborhood pool might allow only residents of that neighborhood to swim there. Other facilities, such as

20-4

Public recreational facilities are usually inexpensive and available to everyone.
In what ways do these facilities benefit the whole community?

Economic Impact & Issues. ***Ask:*** What factors influence the location of recreational facilities in your community?

Community Activity. Have students use the criteria listed here to evaluate a local recreational facility and write a report of their findings.

Economic Impact & Issues

Recreation in Healthy Times

The options and availability of recreational facilities reflect the state of the economy. Facilities such as health clubs and gyms must keep a close eye on the changing market to survive. Economic trends offer clues on how to tap into a new customer base.

For example, at one time, gyms catered to serious athletes, usually male, and health clubs were thought to be a luxury reserved for only the wealthiest people. However, as adults across the board became more interested in fitness, the demand for health clubs and gyms rose. Health clubs responded by branching out into suburban areas and providing a variety of activities and a welcoming atmosphere in which less fit adults could feel comfortable getting in shape.

Likewise, as more women got involved in physical activities—and began working, which increased their disposable income—health clubs responded. New chains were designed as women-only clubs. Co-ed gyms and health clubs began offering child care services as well as classes that appeal especially to women. Some clubs hope to capture the next generation by offering separate classes for their clients' children.

FIGURE IT OUT

Make a list of public and private recreational facilities in your area. Include those that have been discontinued. For example, think about libraries, swim programs, teen centers, and others. How have the economy and tax base affected the services and operating hours of these facilities?

health clubs, are commercial enterprises operated for profit and are open to anyone willing to pay for use. Fees can be substantial depending on the facility's size, quality, and services.

Choosing a Recreational Facility

If you're thinking about using a public or a private recreational facility, you may need to do some research first. For example, if you're planning a party at a community center, you'll want to ensure that it's well maintained and large enough to accommodate your group. If you decide to take dance lessons, investigate both your park district's classes and private schools or studios in your area.

Take into account the following when choosing recreational facilities.

- Visit the facility at the time you expect to use it. Does it have the equipment and facilities you'll need? Are they kept in good condition? How crowded is the facility?
- Ask about hours of operation. Is the facility available when you're free? For example, you might wind up at a bowling alley when all lanes are being used for lessons.

Community Activity. Have students investigate the services, hours, and costs of two health clubs in the community and create a comparison chart.

- If you'll need instruction, ask about the qualifications of professional trainers or instructors and how long they've worked there.
- What are the fees? Do they cover equipment or supplies you might need?
- Check the facility's reputation. Call your local Better Business Bureau and ask if there have been any complaints. Ask friends about their experiences.

Joining a Health Club

Health clubs provide classes and special equipment for a variety of fitness activities. Before you join a club, take steps to protect your investment.

- Ask about a free trial pass so you can try out the facilities or classes, or buy a trial membership for a few months before you make a long-term commitment.
- Once you decide to commit, see if you can save money by paying a year's dues in advance.
- Ask about special deals. Some clubs have lower-cost memberships limited to off-peak hours. Others have family packages.
- Review the contract carefully before you sign it. Make sure anything the salesperson has promised is written into the contract.

BUYING RECREATIONAL EQUIPMENT

Before spending money on recreational equipment, find out what equipment is recommended, how to judge its quality, how often it needs replacing, and what the cost should be. Read articles or ask advice from instructors or experienced friends. Borrowing or renting equipment is an excellent way

Answer Key. Answers to the Section Review questions are provided in the Section Lesson Plan located in the *Teacher Resource Guide.*

to try out both an activity and different brands or types of equipment. Later you can decide what you want to purchase.

When it's time to make a purchase, check out reviews and ratings in magazines and online, and comparison shop for the best price. Most equipment comes in all price ranges. For recreational use, you don't need top-of-the-line professional equipment.

Used equipment can save you money, but make sure it's in good working condition. For example, if you buy a used bike helmet, look it over carefully to make sure it isn't damaged in a way that would reduce its protection. If you're unsure about an expensive item's condition, ask if you can take it to a repair shop and have it checked out.

Although you should dress appropriately for health and safety, special clothing may or may not be needed. In some cases, it's more fashion than necessity.

Section 20.2 Review

CHECK YOUR UNDERSTANDING

1. What factors should you take into account when budgeting for recreation expenses?
2. Give examples of public and private recreational facilities.
3. What should you do before purchasing used sports equipment?

CONSUMER APPLICATION

Hobby Expenses Choose a specific sport or hobby to analyze. List at least three types of expenses that would be associated with it. What strategies could you use to reduce those costs?

SECTION 20.3

Planning a Vacation

Is there somewhere you've always wanted to go on a dream vacation? Perhaps you've blocked off a long weekend for a special trip. Where will you go? How will you get there? Most important, can you afford it? Planning will help you enjoy your vacation without worry.

Objectives

After studying this section, you should be able to:

- Explain the importance of planning and budgeting for a vacation.
- Evaluate travel options and methods of making travel arrangements.
- Give guidelines for packing for a trip.

Key Terms

bed-and-breakfast
hostels
itinerary
reservations
vacation package

STARTING TO PLAN

Vacation planning starts with a goal. Sometimes the goal is to go away next weekend—it doesn't matter where, as long as it's enjoyable. Another time, the goal might be to visit a particular destination, even if it takes years to save and plan for the trip. Either way, you need to consider your resources—including your budget—as you make a plan for meeting your goal.

When it comes to choosing where and when to take a vacation, keep in mind two basic rules.

- The farther the distance you travel, the more it will probably cost to get there and back.
- The farther ahead you plan, the more money you can save. That's because, with a few exceptions, you can get better deals on transportation and lodging when you make arrangements weeks or months in advance.

Jump$tart. Ask students how a limited budget might affect a family's choice of a vacation spot. *(Money Management)*

Besides saving you money, planning can help ensure a successful trip. What might happen if you took a long-distance trip without adequate planning? You might get to your destination and have no place to stay. You might miss out on some great places and events because you didn't know about them. You might not bring the right clothes for the weather or for your activities. You might even run out of money. With careful planning, you can avoid these problems.

Researching Your Destination

Whether you already know where you want to go or are just looking for ideas, investigating destinations is an essential part of planning a trip. Look for information about:

- Special attractions such as museums, parks, and geographic features.
- Where and when special events are held.
- Available accommodations and their costs.
- Times of year when the destination is most and least crowded or expensive.

InfoSource. Have pairs of students use the sources listed to research a vacation destination and prepare a presentation, with visuals, for the class.

- Typical weather at the time you might travel.
- Whether public transportation is available.
- Local laws, customs, and currency, if you're planning to travel to another country.

Planning for Expenses

The ideal way to pay for a vacation is to save for it rather than accumulating bills you may not be able to cover later. Deposit a certain amount of money from each paycheck into an interest-earning savings account earmarked for your vacation.

How will you know how much money you'll need? You can start exploring what you'd like to do on your vacation well in advance. Estimate what your costs might be for transportation, lodging, food, entertainment, and souvenirs. Set the total as your savings goal. As your vacation nears, create a vacation budget detailing how much you've decided you can spend. Stick to your budget and you'll be able to enjoy your vacation without worrying about money. See Figure 20-5.

Critical Thinking. ***Ask:*** Why is saving up for a vacation a better choice than using credit to pay for it? What steps could families take to help them save for a vacation?

InfoSource

Travel Destinations

For information on travel destinations, try these sources:

- State and local departments of tourism. Most have Web sites.
- The National Park Service Web site.
- Travel guides and magazines in libraries and bookstores.
- Travel agents.
- Web sites for making travel arrangements.
- The American Automobile Association. Members can get guidebooks at a local office or online.

Team Activity. Have students work in small groups to plan a five-day vacation for a family of four. Have them choose a destination and research the options for transportation, lodging, food, and entertainment. Have them outline an itinerary and present it, along with its costs, to the class.

20-5

If you're on a tight budget, consider vacationing close to home. Millions of Americans live within driving distance of state or national parks.

Point Out. Tell students that another lodging option is home exchanges. Networks of people make their houses available to each other for vacation while they are away. Thus, a family from Maine and a family from Colorado could each spend a week staying in the other's house.

Evaluating Travel Options

Once you've selected a destination, you'll need to decide how to get there. You'll enjoy your vacation more, and probably save money, if you decide on travel arrangements before you leave.

- **Transportation.** There are many ways to get to your destination—airlines, trains, buses, rental cars, driving your own vehicle, or a combination. In general, faster modes of travel cost more. Driving is the most flexible option—you can set your own schedule, take side trips if you wish, and carry more with you. On the other hand, driving a long distance takes time, can result in additional costs for food, lodging, and gasoline, and can be more tiring.
- **Lodging.** Motels and hotels range from budget accommodations to luxury resorts, but they aren't your only lodging option. A **bed-and-breakfast** is a privately owned home that offers lodging with the morning meal included in the price. **Hostels** are inexpensive, supervised lodgings, often designed for young travelers. An organization called Hostelling International operates a network of hostels in over 70 countries. Hostels generally have dormitory sleeping accommodations, a recreation room, and a self-service kitchen. Campgrounds are another inexpensive lodging option for those with camping equipment or a recreational vehicle (RV).
- **Food.** If you dine out for every meal, costs can add up fast. To save money, consider packing food to take on the road. Choose lodgings with kitchen facilities and prepare your own meals. Preparing even half of your meals will cut your costs significantly.

Research Activity. Have students visit one or more travel sites on the Internet and compare the services they offer with those of a local travel agency.

MAKING TRAVEL ARRANGEMENTS

One way to arrange a trip is through a travel agency. Travel agents can help you plan your **itinerary**, the route or schedule of a trip. They'll make your **reservations**, arrangements to guarantee that lodgings or travel accommodations will be held for you. They'll provide you with a printed itinerary that includes dates, hotel addresses, and flight numbers and times. A travel agency might charge a small fee.

Many travel sites on the Internet let you search options for air travel, hotel rooms, and car rentals and save tentative itineraries. Once you're satisfied with an itinerary, you can make reservations online with a credit card.

You can also directly contact specific airlines, hotel chains, and car rental companies to make your own reservations. Search for them by name on the Internet or call them. Most have a toll-free telephone number.

Critical Thinking. ***Ask:*** What are the advantages and disadvantages of choosing a vacation package? What can travelers do to minimize problems?

Dollars and Sense. Have students work in small groups to create a similar set of guidelines for finding the lowest lodging costs.

Finding the Best Deals

Comparison shopping and a little know-how can help you find travel bargains. Travel agents, travel Web sites, and consumer or travel magazines can give you tips for saving money on travel. They can also help you find the lowest prices available and keep you informed about sales and special bargains. If you make your own travel reservations, don't hesitate to ask for a lower price than you're initially quoted.

Vacation Packages

A **vacation package** is an arrangement that offers a combination of travel purchases for one price. For example, a package might include transportation, lodging, food, and tickets to parks, museums or other attractions. With some packages, you travel on your own and have some choice of schedules, hotels, or other features. Other packages are group tours with a specific itinerary, led by a guide. Some tours cater to a particular age group or a common interest, such as art history or backpacking. See Figure 20-6.

DOLLARSandSENSE

Finding the Lowest Airfare

When you're shopping for airline tickets, you can save a bundle when you:

- Compare prices of different airlines.
- Compare different routes to your destination.
- Check prices for different airports if you're close to more than one.
- Make reservations at least three weeks in advance.
- Fly in the middle of the week and stay at your destination over a Saturday night.
- Purchase nonrefundable tickets.

Class Activity. Bring in a small bag suitable for a short trip. Have volunteers practice packing it and see what they can fit into it.

Answer Key. Answers to the Section Review questions are provided in the Section Lesson Plan located in the *Teacher Resource Guide.*

20-6

Many high schools make group travel packages available to their students during school breaks. What city or country would be your first choice to visit? Why?

A cruise is a package that includes accommodations and meals aboard a ship. You usually need to arrange your own flight to the city where the cruise begins, but sometimes it's included in the package.

If you find the right package, you can save both money and planning time. Make sure, however, that you understand exactly what is included in a package before purchasing it. Get the itinerary and the cancellation and refund policies in writing.

PACKING

It's almost time to go on your vacation! Keep these tips in mind as you pack.

- Travel light. Bring clothes that you can wear more than once and in different combinations. Pack clothes you can layer in case the weather changes.
- Check with the airline, train, or bus company about how much luggage you can carry on, how much you can check, and which items are not allowed.
- Pack essentials—items that you can't replace or do without, such as prescription medications—in your carry-on luggage in case your checked luggage is delayed.
- Carry identification, credit cards, and money in a safe place, such as a money belt or a pouch worn under your clothing. Carry only small amounts of cash. Consider using traveler's checks (see page 255), which can be replaced if lost or stolen.

Section 20.3 Review

CHECK YOUR UNDERSTANDING

1. What are the advantages of planning a vacation far in advance?
2. Describe three ways of making travel arrangements.
3. What information should you obtain before packing for a plane trip?

CONSUMER APPLICATION

Lodging Options Research the cost of staying at a hostel at a destination of your choice. Compare the cost of the hostel to the price range of motels or other lodgings in the same area. Aside from cost, how would staying at the hostel differ from staying at other lodgings?

CHAPTER 20

Review & Activities

CHAPTER SUMMARY

- Recreation offers a variety of benefits. Although many factors affect the use of leisure time, effective management can help you make the most of it. (20.1)
- Budgeting can help you manage recreation expenses. When choosing recreational facilities and equipment, it is wise to follow consumer guidelines. (20.2)
- Various travel options and methods of making travel arrangements are available. By planning and budgeting, you can have a more satisfying and economical vacation. (20.3)

THE $avvy Consumer

Whirlwind Weekend: Lucas's family is planning a weekend trip to a large city that is two hours from their home. While there, Lucas wants to visit a natural science museum, his sister wants to go to a water park, his mother wants to browse the antique shops, and his father wants to eat at some restaurants that are known for their good food. How can Lucas's family plan their time so that the trip is enjoyed by everyone? (20.3)

Reviewing Key Terms and Ideas

1. What is **recreation**? What benefits can it offer? (20.1)
2. List and give examples of three factors that affect people's use of **leisure time**. (20.1)
3. What are some examples of a **hobby**? (20.1)
4. In what ways should you try to balance your use of leisure time? (20.1)
5. Why is opportunity cost a factor when you're budgeting for recreation? (20.2)
6. How can **season tickets** save a consumer money? (20.2)
7. Name two differences between public and private recreational facilities. (20.2)
8. How would you evaluate a health club before joining? (20.2)
9. What alternatives can reduce the expense of acquiring recreational equipment? (20.2)
10. When researching vacation destinations, what kinds of information should you look for? (20.3)
11. Explain the recommended way to plan for vacation expenses. (20.3)
12. What is a **bed-and-breakfast**? (20.3)
13. Why might a **hostel** be a wise lodging choice? (20.3)
14. Why is it beneficial to have an **itinerary** and **reservations** before you set out on a trip? (20.3)
15. When packing for a flight, where should you put prescription medications? Why? (20.3)

Answer Key. Answers to the Chapter Review & Activities are provided in the Teacher's Manual in the *Teacher Annotated Edition* of the text.

Thinking Critically

1. **Making Comparisons:** Do you think it's more beneficial to schedule leisure time in small time periods throughout the week or in one or two longer segments of time? Why? (20.1)
2. **Making Predictions:** Suppose you're planning a trip to a country that you've never visited. How might your experiences and perceptions differ depending on whether you take a guided group tour, travel on your own, or stay with friends who live there? (20.3)
3. **Analyzing Economic Concepts:** How is the health of the economy affected by consumers' recreation spending and vice versa? (20.1, 20.2, 20.3)

Reviewing Key Terms and Ideas

1. **Hobby Ideas:** What hobbies do you have? Some people have collections (stamps, dried flowers, spoons). Hobbies can also be activities (making jewelry, hiking, raising goats, scrapbooking). Even learning about a topic, such as the history of England, can be a hobby. Share your hobby with the class, either through a presentation or a display. What hobbies that others present would you like to try? (20.1)
2. **Leisure Time:** For a week or two, keep track of how you spend your time. Use a chart that shows the hours of the day. Analyze the results. How was leisure time spent? Could you use leisure time more effectively? Create and implement a plan that shows how to improve your use of leisure time. (20.1)
3. **Fitness Options:** Research the costs, convenience, and advantages of a two-year health club membership. Then research the costs and advantages of home exercise equipment. Create a chart comparing the advantages and disadvantages of each. (20.2)
4. **Vacation Transportation Costs:** Choose a vacation spot and research transportation options. Estimate and compare the costs of two options, keeping in mind that longer traveling times can add to meal and lodging costs. Explain the pros and cons of each option. (20.3)
5. **Travel Arrangements:** Evaluate two travel Web sites for options and ease of use. Using screen shots of the Web sites or multimedia software, present the advantages and disadvantages of each site to the class. (20.3)

CONSUMER CONNECTIONS

- **Family:** Could your family benefit from sharing more recreational time? Talk with family members about this question. What activity that everyone would enjoy could be included in the family schedule? Put a plan into action and evaluate how it worked. (20.1)
- **Community:** In class, identify public recreation facilities available in your area. With a team, choose one facility to evaluate. Develop a list of criteria and rankings, such as 1 to 4 for excellent to poor, to use in your evaluation. As you evaluate, keep notes on why you chose each ranking. Compare results in class. (20.2)

CHAPTER 21

Food and Nutrition

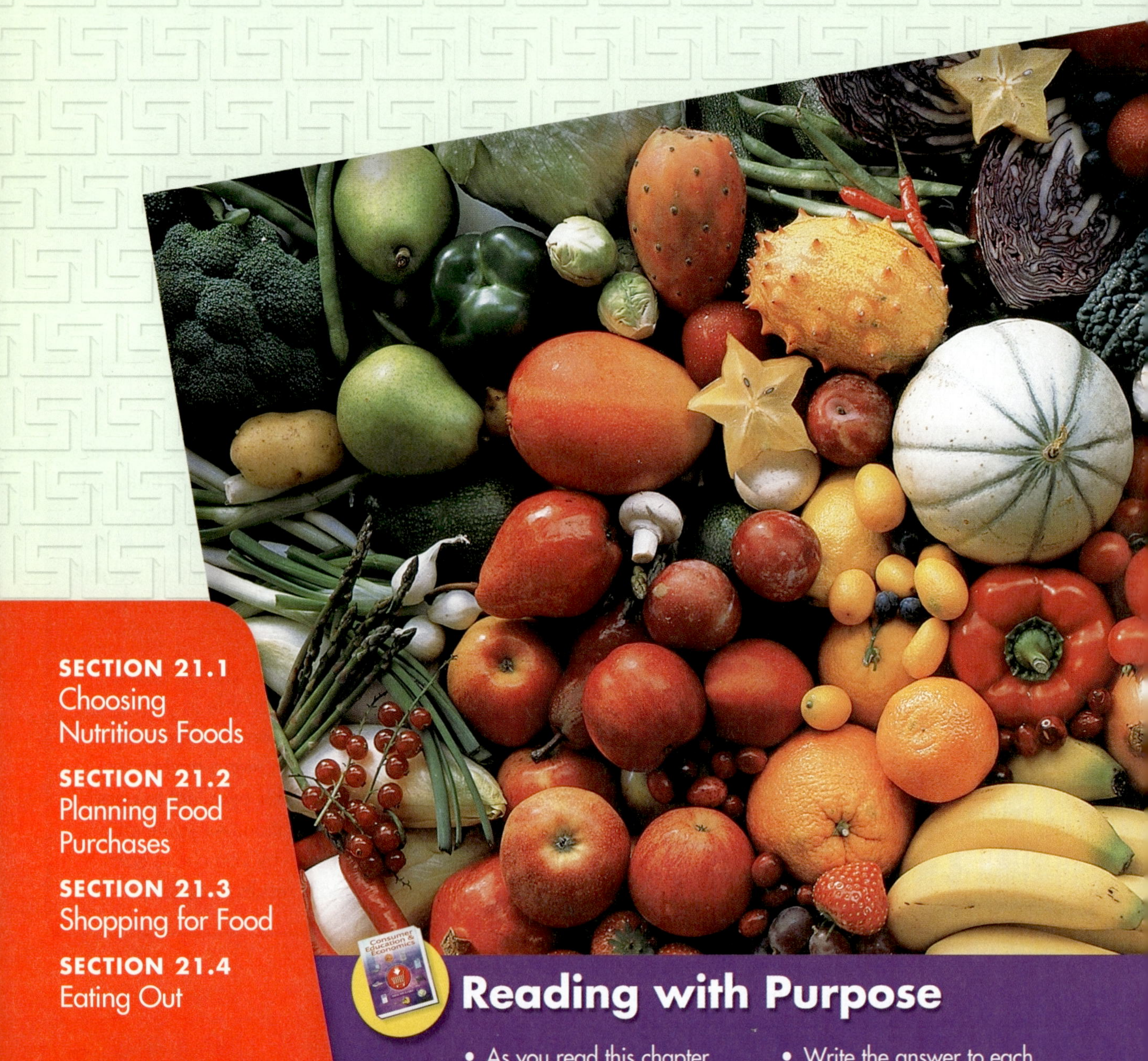

Reading with Purpose

- As you read this chapter, create an outline using the colored headings.
- Write a question for each heading to help guide your reading.
- Write the answer to each question as you read the chapter.
- Ask your teacher to help with answers you cannot find in the text.

SECTION 21.1

Choosing Nutritious Foods

How do you decide what to eat each day? The foods you eat affect the way you look and feel and have an important influence on your health. Knowing about healthful eating will help you make smart choices.

Objectives

After studying this section, you should be able to:

- Discuss influences on food choices.
- Explain the link between nutrition and health.
- Identify functions and sources of nutrients.
- Describe guidelines that encourage wise food choices.

Key Terms

nutrition
nutrients
nutrient density
calorie
Dietary Guidelines for Americans

INFLUENCES ON FOOD CHOICES

Have you ever gone into the kitchen to make popcorn after seeing a popcorn commercial on TV? Advertising is just one of many factors that influence your food choices. Your family and friends influence your food choices, too. You may like certain foods because you grew up enjoying them at home. Your friends might encourage you to try new foods. Some families enjoy particular foods that are part of their cultural heritage.

What you eat is influenced by your family's resources, such as how much money and time you have to spend. Some families may choose fast foods or convenience foods because they don't have time to make meals from scratch. Yet another resource is knowledge. Learning about different types of foods enables you to make food choices that will benefit your health. This knowledge also makes it possible for you to make healthy food choices without giving up family traditions or personal preferences.

Class Activity. Ask students to name foods that are high in carbohydrates. List them on the board. Then ask students to classify the foods listed based on whether they are high in sugars, starches, or fiber, noting that some may fall into more than one group. Discuss which foods are the healthiest choices.

NUTRITION AND HEALTH

Nutrition is the process of using food to nourish your body. It involves **nutrients**, the substances found in food that enable the body to function properly. You need certain types and amounts of nutrients to maintain good health. When you meet your nutritional needs, your body develops and works properly, and you have the energy you need for an active lifestyle. Good nutrition helps you look and feel your best, and it reduces your risk of certain diseases.

Everybody needs the same nutrients. The amounts needed vary depending on factors such as age and level of activity. Teens, for example, are growing rapidly and often are very active, so they need more of most nutrients than adults. Don't be alarmed if you have a large appetite—your body may be sending you an important message. See Figure 21-1.

TYPES OF NUTRIENTS

Food nourishes you with a variety of nutrients. Each nutrient has its own functions, but many nutrients work in teams. All the nutrients are equally important for good health. The many nutrients that are known can be grouped into six categories.

- **Carbohydrates** are sugars and starches, and they are your body's main source of energy. Sugars occur naturally in many foods, such as milk, fruits, and grains. Sugars are also refined, or removed from their natural sources, and then added to foods such as candy and cookies to sweeten them. On food labels, ingredients such as sucrose, dextrose, fructose, corn syrup, and honey are added sugars. Starches are found in breads, cereals, rice, pasta, dry peas and beans, lentils, and starchy vegetables such as potatoes and corn. Many fruits and vegetables contain fiber, plant material that cannot be digested. Fiber is important to good health. It helps food move through the digestive system and protects you against certain diseases.
- **Proteins** are used for your body's growth and repair and to maintain cells and tissues.

Caption Answer. Nutrients in the right amounts are needed to fuel the rapid growth of the teen years.

21-1

Teens need extra nutrients to fuel their growth and give them energy. Why is it particularly important to pay attention to nutrition during the teen years?

Critical Thinking. *Ask:* What problems might result from a diet that does not contain dark green, leafy vegetables?

Proteins also provide energy and help your body fight disease. Good sources of protein include meat, poultry, fish, eggs, dairy products, dry beans and peas, and nuts.

- **Fats** are a concentrated form of energy and are necessary for healthy skin and normal growth. They also carry certain vitamins to places where they are needed in the body. Fats occur naturally in many foods, such as meat, poultry, fish, egg yolks, nuts, and dairy products. Fats are also found in vegetable oil, margarine, and mayonnaise.

Point Out. Milk is fortified with vitamin D to help the body absorb calcium (which is also found in milk) and other minerals.

- **Vitamins** are needed only in small amounts, but are vital for good health. They help your body fight disease, use other nutrients, and regulate body processes. Figure 21-2 lists important vitamins, their functions, and their sources.

Caption Answer. Vitamin A aids night vision.

21-2

Vitamins are needed in very small quantities, yet play a significant role in nutrition. Which vitamin helps your vision in dim light?

Vitamins

VITAMIN	FUNCTIONS	SOURCES
Vitamin A	Promotes healthy skin, hair, bones, teeth; aids vision in dim light; provides resistance to infection	Dark green, leafy vegetables such as broccoli, spinach; deep yellow and orange fruits and vegetables such as carrots, sweet potatoes, cantaloupe; dairy products such as milk and cheese; eggs; liver
Vitamin D	Helps build strong bones and teeth; helps body absorb calcium	Milk fortified with vitamin D; fatty fish such as salmon and mackerel; liver; exposure to sunlight
Vitamin E	Helps form red blood cells and muscles; protects other nutrients from damage	Vegetable oils; margarine; whole grain breads and cereals; dark green, leafy vegetables; nuts and seeds
Vitamin K	Helps blood clot	Dark green, leafy vegetables; wheat bran and wheat germ; egg yolks; liver
B Vitamins (including thiamin, riboflavin, niacin, B6, B12, and folic acid)	Help body produce energy from carbohydrates, fats, and proteins; maintain healthy nervous system; help build red blood cells; protect against infection	Whole grain and enriched breads and cereals; dry beans and peas; nuts; meat, poultry, fish; eggs; dairy products
Vitamin C	Helps maintain bones, teeth, gums; helps heal wounds; aids iron absorption from foods; builds resistance to infection	Citrus fruits such as oranges, grapefruit; broccoli, raw cabbage, brussels sprouts; potatoes; tomatoes; strawberries; mango; cantaloupe

Research Activity. Challenge students to keep a record of the beverages they drink for one day and determine whether they are getting enough water.

- **Minerals** are also needed in small quantities. They become a part of body structures such as bones and teeth, and they regulate certain body functions, such as making red blood cells and helping blood to clot. Figure 21-3 lists important minerals, their functions, and sources.

Caption Answer. Iron helps the blood carry oxygen.

Point Out. Explain to students that caffeine is a diuretic, so drinking caffeinated beverages can actually cause the body to lose fluids.

- **Water** regulates body functions by contributing to many chemical reactions. It also helps keep body temperature within a normal range. Your body uses and loses water constantly, and you need to replace it. Some foods, particularly fruits and vegetables, provide some of the water your body needs. Still, experts generally recommend that you drink at least 8 cups of liquid every day. Choose plain water, fruit or vegetable juices, milk, or soups. Drinks containing caffeine and sodas that are high in sugar are not recommended.

21-3

Minerals help many parts of the body to function properly. Which mineral helps the blood carry oxygen throughout the body?

Selected Minerals

MINERAL	FUNCTIONS	SOURCES
Calcium	Maintains strong bones and teeth; regulates heart, muscle, and nerve function	Milk and milk products; sardines, canned salmon with bones; dark green, leafy vegetables; dry beans and peas
Iron	Helps blood carry oxygen; helps cells use oxygen	Red meats, liver, fish, shellfish; egg yolks; dark green, leafy vegetables; dry beans and peas; dried fruits such as peaches, raisins; whole grain and enriched breads and cereals
Magnesium	Helps nerves and muscles work properly; builds bones; regulates body fluids	Whole grain breads and cereals; dark green, leafy vegetables; dry beans and peas; nuts and seeds
Phosphorus	Works with calcium and vitamin D to build strong bones and teeth; helps body produce energy	Meat, poultry, fish; eggs; milk and milk products; dry beans and peas; whole grain breads and cereals
Potassium	Helps heart, muscles, nerves work properly; helps regulate fluid balance and blood pressure	Oranges, bananas; dried fruit; meats, poultry, fish; dry beans and peas; potatoes
Sodium	Helps regulate body fluids; helps muscle action	Table salt; natural foods that contain salt, such as carrots and spinach; processed foods such as bread, cheese, cereals, and snack foods
Zinc	Helps the body heal wounds, form blood, and make protein; helps body use carbohydrates, fats, proteins, and vitamin A	Meats, liver, poultry, fish, shellfish; eggs; nuts and seeds; dairy products; dry beans and peas; whole grain breads and cereals

Point Out. Bone mass builds up from childhood to young adulthood. Getting enough calcium early can help prevent osteoporosis, a brittle-bone condition.

Nutrition for Teens

During your teen years, you grow at a faster pace than at any time since you were an infant. You need the right nutrients to fuel that growth. Three nutrients—calcium, iron, and zinc—are particularly important at this life stage. Studies show that many teens don't get enough of these nutrients.

Calcium works with vitamin D and phosphorus to build strong bones. Building up bone mass while you're young helps prevent

Critical Thinking. *Ask:* What are some ways to increase your calcium intake if you don't drink milk?

bones from becoming brittle later in life. One reason that many teens don't get enough calcium is that they tend to drink soft drinks rather than milk. If you're one of those teens, do yourself a favor and switch to fat-free or low-fat milk. If you don't like milk, get calcium from other sources. See Figure 21-4.

The need for iron increases in the teen years because of the onset of menstruation in females and rapid growth in both genders. Zinc, essential for healthy growth, also takes on added importance in the teen years.

GUIDELINES FOR HEALTHFUL LIVING

Designing a healthful eating plan is not difficult if you follow certain guidelines. The U.S. government has developed a food guidance system and guidelines to help you make wise daily choices about food and physical activity.

FCCLA. Have the class use the Eat Right unit of Student Body to prepare a Healthy Foods Fair for your school. Have students choose and prepare a variety of healthful foods, including main courses, snacks, and desserts. Then have them set up tables in the school cafeteria and offer samples of their healthful foods, along with printed copies of recipes and menus, to their schoolmates.

21-4

Yogurt is rich in calcium. What other foods are good sources of this mineral?

Class Activity. Have students prepare a sample menu for a day, including meals and snacks. They should be sure to include the appropriate amount of food from each food group for a person of their age, gender, and activity level. Have students share their menus with the class.

MyPyramid

MyPyramid, shown in Figure 21-5, is a symbol and food guidance system developed by the U.S. Department of Agriculture (USDA). Its purpose is to encourage healthful food choices and promote physical activity.

The color bands in MyPyramid represent five food groups (plus oils). How much food do you need each day from these groups? In part, that depends on the number of calories you burn through physical activity. By accessing MyPyramid on the Internet and entering your age, gender, and activity level, you can get an estimate of your calorie needs and the food amounts you should eat from each group. With this information, you can explore how your food choices fit the amounts of food recommended from these food groups:

- **Grain Group.** Bread, pasta, oatmeal, breakfast cereals, tortillas, and grits are examples of grain products. Grains are important sources of dietary fiber, several B vitamins, and minerals, including iron and magnesium.
- **Vegetable Group.** This group includes any fresh, frozen, canned, or dried vegetables, eaten raw or cooked, as well as vegetable juice. Vegetables are important sources of potassium, dietary fiber, folic acid, vitamins A, E, and C, and other nutrients.
- **Fruit Group.** Any fruit or 100 percent fruit juice counts as part of the Fruit Group. Fruits are important sources of many nutrients, including potassium, dietary fiber, vitamin C, and folic acid.
- **Milk Group.** This food group includes milk and many foods made from milk, including yogurt and most cheeses. Foods in the Milk Group provide calcium, potassium, and vitamin D.

21-5 MyPyramid represents a personalized approach to healthy eating and physical activity.

- **Meat & Beans Group.** All foods made from meat, poultry, fish, dry beans, peas, eggs, nuts, and seeds are considered part of this group. They supply many nutrients, including protein, B vitamins, vitamin E, iron, zinc, and magnesium.

Designing an eating plan based on the food groups is easy and flexible. You can adapt your choices to your own food preferences, eating patterns, family circumstances, and cultural traditions. Some foods, such as pizza, include foods from several groups.

Research Activity. Have students use MyPyramid on the Internet to determine the amounts of food they need daily from the food groups.

When choosing foods from each food group, keep these principles in mind:

- **Variety.** All foods contain some nutrients. However, no single food provides all the nutrients you need in adequate amounts. Each food group offers many different foods, so be sure to vary your choices from day to day.
- **Nutrient density.** Some foods are said to be more nutrient dense than others. **Nutrient density** is a comparison of the nutrients in a food to the amount of calories. A **calorie** is a unit of energy. Foods with high nutrient density supply a significant amount of several nutrients, such as vitamins and minerals, in relation to the amount of calories. When choosing foods from the five food groups, focus on those with high nutrient density.

Dietary Guidelines for Americans

The **Dietary Guidelines for Americans**, developed jointly by the USDA and the Department of Health and Human Services, give science-based advice on food and physical activity choices for health. The Dietary Guidelines are revised every five years. Following the steps listed below, which are based on the 2005 Dietary Guidelines, can help you reach your best level of health.

InfoSource. Have students visit the Web site of one of the organizations listed and write a description of the information the site provides.

- **Get enough nutrients within your calorie needs.** Choose a variety of nutrient-dense foods and beverages from the basic food groups. Just be sure that you stay within your daily calorie needs. MyPyramid can help you adopt a balanced eating pattern.
- **Manage your weight.** Maintaining your body weight in a healthy range helps you look and feel better. The key to weight management is to balance the energy you get from foods and beverages with the energy your body uses in daily activities. Both forms of energy are measured in calories. If the food you eat has more calories than your body uses, the extra energy is stored in your body as fat.

InfoSource

Nutrition Advice

For accurate, up-to-date nutrition information, reliable sources include:

- Registered dietitians—nutrition experts who have earned the right to use the R.D. credential.
- The American Dietetic Association and its Web site.
- The Center for Nutrition Policy and Promotion and the Food and Nutrition Information Center. Both are USDA offices that provide consumer information in print and online.

Class Activity. Ask students to name some of their favorite snack foods. Go through the list and ask students which of the foods are high in sugar or fat and low in other nutrients. Mark these with an X. Then ask them to name nutrient-dense foods they could substitute for each of the marked foods.

21-6

Physical activity, as well as nutrition, needs to be built into your daily routine. What kinds of physical activity do you enjoy most?

- **Be physically active each day.** Physical activity includes any activity that keeps you moving. Being active helps you look and feel good, maintain a healthy weight, and manage stress. Physical activity also strengthens your heart and lungs and can help prevent future health problems. Aim to build at least 60 minutes of physical activity into your daily routine. See Figure 21-6.
- **Focus on fruits and vary your veggies.** Fruits and vegetables are naturally low in fat and good sources of fiber. They are also important sources of vitamins and minerals, especially vitamins A and C. Plan to get most of your fruit choices from a variety of fruits rather than fruit juice. Eat more dark green vegetables, orange vegetables, and dry beans and peas.
- **Make half your grains whole.** Whole grains contain the entire grain kernel and all of its nutrients, including fiber. At least half of all the grains you eat should be whole grains. Examples of whole grain foods include oatmeal, whole wheat bread, and brown rice.
- **Get your calcium-rich foods.** Teens need 3 cups of fat-free or low-fat milk per day or equivalent milk products. People who can't consume milk products, or choose not to, should be sure to get calcium from other sources.
- **Go lean with protein.** Vary your protein choices by including beans, peas, nuts, and seeds. Make your meat, poultry, and fish choices lean ones, and bake, broil, or grill them.
- **Limit fats.** For children and teens age 4 to 18, total fat intake should be 25 to 35 percent of calories. Most of the fats you eat should come from sources such as fish, nuts, and vegetable oils. To reduce the risk of heart disease, read the nutrition information found on food labels and choose foods that are low in saturated fats, *trans* fats, and cholesterol.

Class Activity. Ask students to write a paragraph explaining how teens can motivate themselves and each other to be more physically active.

Answer Key. Answers to the Section Review questions are provided in the Section Lesson Plan located in the *Teacher Resource Guide*.

21-7

Using herbs and spices in cooking can reduce your salt intake and add subtle, complex flavors. What are some other strategies for cutting down on salt?

- **Be choosy about carbohydrates.** Choose fiber-rich fruits, vegetables, and whole grains often. Look for foods and beverages low in added sugars. Soft drinks tend to be high in sugar and low in other nutrients. Foods such as candy, cakes, cookies, ice cream, and sweet cereals also have large amounts of added sugars.
- **Reduce sodium (salt) and increase potassium.** Choose and prepare foods with little salt, and eat plenty of potassium-rich foods, such as fruits and vegetables. Most Americans get more sodium—which comes mainly from salt—than they need. Getting too much sodium contributes to high blood pressure, which can lead to a heart attack or stroke. Potassium helps counteract sodium's effects on blood pressure. It's a good idea to get out of the salt habit while you're young. Go easy on salty snacks, such as potato chips and pretzels, and on processed foods that are high in sodium, such as many canned foods. Add less salt during cooking and at the table. Flavor foods with herbs and spices instead. See Figure 21-7.
- **Play it safe with food.** Food that is not handled, stored, or prepared properly can cause illness. Wash your hands before and after handling food. Keep work surfaces clean and always use clean utensils. Keep raw meat, poultry, and fish away from ready-to-eat foods. Cook foods to a safe temperature. Promptly refrigerate foods that spoil easily.

Keep in mind that scientists are continually researching nutrition and making new discoveries. As this process continues, the advice of nutrition experts may change. It's important to stay informed by reading the latest guidelines from reliable sources.

Section 21.1 Review

CHECK YOUR UNDERSTANDING

1. How do resources influence food choices?
2. How does your body obtain and use protein?
3. In addition to advice about food choices, what other topics are addressed in the Dietary Guidelines for Americans?

CONSUMER APPLICATION

Analyzing Your Food Choices List all the foods you ate yesterday and estimate the amounts. About how much food did you have from each food group? What do you conclude?

Objectives

After studying this section, you should be able to:

- Analyze factors affecting food prices and food budgets.
- Give guidelines for planning nutritious meals within a budget.

Key Terms

convenience foods
staples

SECTION 21.2

Planning Food Purchases

Do you know what's for dinner tonight? Planning ahead has many benefits. It saves time and enables you to enjoy more balanced and varied meals. It can also help you save money.

UNDERSTANDING FOOD PRICES

Do you sometimes do the food shopping for your family? If so, you know that prices for some items change from week to week. Managing a food budget can be challenging, but if you understand what affects food prices, you are likely to be a smarter consumer.

Production and Distribution

Food starts with agriculture. Raw materials, labor, and equipment are needed to grow crops or raise animals. After food is harvested, it goes through various types of processing, such as cleaning, sorting, and packaging. From the processing plant, food is transported to distributors and stored in warehouses. Finally, it's shipped to retail stores. All of these steps involve costs passed on to consumers.

Some foods are more highly processed than others. **Convenience foods** are foods processed in ways that make them easier to use. A few examples of convenience foods are

Economic Impact & Issues. ***Ask:*** What resources would people in wealthy countries need to avoid diseases of affluence?

canned soups, instant pudding mixes, packaged shredded cheese, and frozen dinners. Convenience foods tend to cost more than their fresh food counterparts because of the extra processing involved in producing them.

Research and Marketing

The costs of developing and promoting food products are also passed on to consumers. Food companies continually spend money on research and development to come up with new products or to improve on existing ones. Packaging is another major expense. In fact, you sometimes pay more for

Research Activity. Have students go to a supermarket and compare the prices of national, store, and generic brands of a particular food.

the package than for the contents. Food companies also spend money on promoting and advertising their products. That's one reason why national brands cost more than store-brand or generic products, which receive little or no advertising.

Supply and Demand

Food prices fluctuate according to supply and demand. A reduced supply of a food product that's in high demand can result in temporary price increases. When droughts, floods, or unseasonably high or low temperatures damage crops, for instance, the cost of those foods rises. See Figure 21-8 on the following page.

Economic Impact & Issues

Wealth and Health

Nutritionally, the relationship between wealth and health may seem obvious: as a nation becomes more prosperous overall, its people can afford more food, and of a better quality. Wealth brings nutritional problems of its own, however. While impoverished people suffer from deficiency diseases, caused by a lack of nutrients, prosperous societies see an increase in so-called lifestyle diseases. These illnesses, like heart disease and cancer, are partly due to overconsumption, along with the lack of physical activity.

Ironically, these "diseases of affluence," as they are also called, hit the lower economic groups the hardest. Processed foods, which are affordable and easily available, often contain more fat and sodium than fresh foods. Though fresh foods may be cheaper and more nutritious, lower-income families might not have the resources needed to prepare them.

Culture plays a large role in food choices, too. A poor family in China typically eats a traditional, plant-based, low-fat, low-sodium diet. A poor family in the United States is apt to rely on convenience or fast foods.

FIGURE IT OUT

Choose a main dish, such as lasagna, to serve to a family with two adults and two teens. Calculate the costs of preparing the dish, first with fresh ingredients, and second with convenience foods. Figure each cost for the dish as a percentage of these weekly food budgets: $50, $100, and $150. Compare the percentages. What do you conclude? How does the local economy affect each budget situation?

Team Activity. Have teams of students plan a week's worth of meals for a family of four with a weekly grocery budget of $100. Teams can find recipes in cookbooks or online databases and use supermarket fliers to estimate the prices of ingredients. Have each team present its menus.

21-8

A sudden freeze in an area with many orange groves can reduce harvests, leading to an increase in the prices consumers pay for oranges and orange juice.

Class Activity. Have students create scrapbook pages with ideas for saving money on food expenses. Help each student choose a specific idea (for example, using coupons, a low-cost recipe, and not shopping when hungry). Then each student should create a page that presents the idea chosen. Assemble the pages into a money-saving scrapbook for classroom reference.

On the other hand, a plentiful supply leads to lower prices. Many fresh fruits and vegetables are available in large quantities at certain times of the year—the months when they are in season according to their natural growing cycle. You can save money, and get better quality produce, by buying fresh foods when they are in season.

BUDGETING FOR FOOD EXPENSES

On average, about 14% of spending in U.S. households goes toward food. This amount varies, however. In households that have more family members or less income than average, food expenses tend to make up a larger proportion of spending. Individual priorities and preferences are also factors.

TEXTLINK

Planning a budget is explained in Section 9.3.

Food expenses should be planned within the context of the overall household budget. Food is an essential budget item. Other budget categories may need to be cut back in order to allow a food budget that is large enough to meet the family's needs.

Money is one of the most important resources for meeting food needs. However, it's not the only one. When money to spend on food is limited—as it is for most people—other resources can help fill the gap. Knowledge about nutrition and smart food shopping can help you get better nutrition at less cost. Time, energy, food preparation skills, and kitchen equipment can help you prepare more meals at home using inexpensive ingredients. In this way, you can save

Discussion. *Ask:* What other types of main dishes make it possible to cut back on the amount of meat used? What are the benefits of doing so?

money by buying fewer convenience foods and eating out less. You might even use your resources to grow some of your own food in a garden. As you will learn, there are many ways to stretch your food dollars and get the most nutrition for your money.

PLANNING MENUS

It's a good idea to plan menus for meals you're going to eat at home for a week or more at a time. Planning ahead in this way has several advantages:

- **Save money.** By deciding what you will eat before you shop, you'll buy only what you need and will be less likely to waste food. Buying in larger quantities for more meals could save you money as well.
- **Save time.** Planning ahead cuts down on the number of shopping trips you need to make.
- **Better nutrition.** When you plan several meals at a time, you can make sure your overall eating pattern is nutritionally balanced. You can also plan ways to put more variety into your food choices.

Dollars and Sense. Have students compare the price of a restaurant meal with the cost of the ingredients needed to make the same meal at home.

- **Meet special dietary needs.** Some people have special dietary needs, such as a food allergy or a chronic health condition that means avoiding certain foods. If that's true of you or someone in your family, careful menu planning is essential.

Money-Saving Ideas

To maximize the value of your food dollars, follow these guidelines when planning your menus:

- Plan to use leftovers or perishables before food goes bad.
- Pay attention to store ads and fliers in your local newspaper. They give information about special deals and often include coupons. Keep track of how prices change so that you'll recognize a true bargain.
- Base some of your meals on nutritious, inexpensive foods, such as grains and beans.
- In recipes such as stews, try cutting back on the recommended quantities of meat, poultry, or fish. Add more vegetables and grains instead.

DOLLARSandSENSE

Dining Out or In

Eating in a restaurant is almost always more expensive than eating a similar meal at home. Why? When eating out, you pay for not only the food, but also the employees, rent and utilities on the building, and the furnishings, as well as profit for the restaurant owner.

Frequent dining out can quickly become a budget-breaker. When you get in the habit of planning meals, you'll be less likely to use eating out as an emergency solution to the "What's for dinner?" dilemma.

Research Activity. Have students search cookbooks or online recipe listings for dishes that can be prepared in 15 minutes or less.

Low-Cost Convenience

Convenience foods can be a helpful resource for busy families. However, the time saved by using convenience foods comes at a cost. Many convenience foods are not only higher in price than foods you prepare yourself, but also higher in fat and sodium. Some alternatives to buying convenience foods include the following:

- Collect quick and easy recipes, ones that allow you to prepare fast meals.
- Use a slow cooker. Your meal will be cooking while you're away from home and will be ready when you return.
- Prechop vegetables such as green peppers and onions. Grate your own cheese.
- When making a main dish, make twice as much as you need for that meal. Serve half and freeze half for a later meal.

PLANNING YOUR SHOPPING

After you've planned menus for the week, the next step is to plan your food shopping. Having a plan before you go to the store will help you save time and money.

- **Make a shopping list.** To make your list, refer to the menus you've planned and check to see what you already have. If you're running low on any **staples**—basic food items you always want to have on hand, such as rice or flour—add them to the list. Check supermarket ads for items on sale—if you use them often and you have room to store them properly, plan to stock up while prices are low.
- **Shop once a week.** More frequent trips waste time. They also increase the chances that you'll buy extra items you don't really need.
- **Shop when stores are not crowded.** This will give you time to read labels, compare prices, and avoid long lines at the checkout.
- **Don't shop when you're hungry.** Hunger pangs can make almost anything edible look like something you must have.

Point Out. Note that speed-scratch cooking (making meals that contain some prepared ingredients, such as canned soup) can cut the time needed for cooking without costing as much as fully cooked convenience foods.

Answer Key. Answers to the Section Review questions are provided in the Section Lesson Plan located in the *Teacher Resource Guide.*

Section 21.2 Review

CHECK YOUR UNDERSTANDING

1. Why do many convenience foods cost more than other foods?
2. Besides money, what resources can help you meet food needs?
3. Describe four strategies for saving money when planning menus.

CONSUMER APPLICATION

Seasonal Savings Research what fruits or vegetables are currently in season. Choose one and describe three different ways to use it in meals or snacks. Explain the benefits of buying in season.

SECTION 21.3

Shopping for Food

Effective food shoppers know how to use label information and how to judge the quality of different kinds of foods. They use a variety of strategies to save money, starting with their choice of where to shop.

Objectives

After studying this section, you should be able to:

- Evaluate various types of retail food stores.
- Analyze food labels and other consumer information.
- Describe ways to get value and quality when shopping for food.

Key Terms

cooperative
net weight
Daily Values
pull date
expiration date
unit price
bulk foods

CHOOSING FOOD STORES

Supermarkets, the most familiar option to most food shoppers, offer the convenience of a wide range of goods in one location. Doing most of your shopping in one store can save time. However, depending on your needs and preferences, you may decide to shop for food at more than one place. You might go to a specialty store for ethnic foods or to a farmer's market for fresh local produce. If you have space to store large quantities of food, you might find it economical to pay for a membership at a food warehouse club.

Convenience stores, delivery services, and online grocery shopping attract busy consumers. These options can indeed save time, but shoppers usually pay more than they would at a supermarket.

Food cooperatives are an option in some communities. A **cooperative** is a business organization owned and operated by members for their own benefit. Members of a food cooperative usually must contribute either food that they've produced or their time by working, and they may have to pay a fee. In exchange, members benefit from lower prices and, in some cases, a share of profits.

Team Activity. Have each student develop a checklist for evaluating food stores. Then have pairs of students swap and compare their checklists.

When evaluating food stores, check their cleanliness and the quality of the food. Compare the prices and special promotions offered, such as discount cards or double coupons. Also consider the location, hours of operation, and the level of customer service. It's worth doing a little detective work to find the stores that best suit your needs.

USING CONSUMER INFORMATION

Supermarkets are full of information. When shopping for food, allow enough time to study labels, learn about prices, and build other skills that will make you a smart shopper.

21-9

Food labels enable you to determine exactly what you are buying. **Why do you think the name and address of the food company is required?**

Caption Answer. The name and address must be listed so that consumers can contact the company if they're dissatisfied with the products.

Food Labels

One of the responsibilities of the Food and Drug Administration (FDA) is to regulate the labeling of food products. Food labels are required by law to carry certain information for the benefit of consumers. See Figure 21-9. The basic information provided on a food label includes:

- **Statement of identity.** This is the name of the food, such as "Cream of Tomato Soup" or "Shredded Mozzarella Cheese."
- **Quantity.** This may be indicated by the number of items in the package, the volume (such as 2 quarts), or the net weight. The **net weight** is the weight of the product and any liquid in which the product is packed, not including the weight of the container.
- **Ingredients.** These must be listed in order by weight, from the largest amount to the smallest. Something that lists water as its first ingredient contains more water than anything else. By law, ingredients that might cause allergic reactions must be clearly identified on the label.
- **Manufacturer.** The label must give the name and address of the manufacturer, packer, or distributor.

The FDA also regulates the use of descriptive terms such as "light," "reduced fat," and "low sodium." In order for these terms to appear on the label, the food must meet specific requirements.

Class Activity. Ask students to examine the Nutrition Facts label in Figure 21-10 and draw conclusions about how healthful this food is.

Nutrition Facts

Packaged foods must carry a "Nutrition Facts" label, which provides valuable information about the nutrient content of the food. An example is shown in Figure 21-10. You can find the following information on the Nutrition Facts label:

- **Serving size.** The nutrient content of the food is based on this serving size.
- **Calories.** The number of calories per serving is given, as well as the number of those calories that come from fat.
- **Nutrient amounts per serving.** Certain nutrients are listed in grams or milligrams. These include total fat, saturated fat, *trans* fat, cholesterol, sodium, total carbohydrate, fiber, sugars, and protein.
- **Percent Daily Value.** Nutrient reference amounts, called **Daily Values**, have been set by the FDA for use on food labels. The Daily Values help consumers know whether a given amount of a nutrient is a little or a lot. The label shows what percentage of the Daily Value for specific nutrients is provided by one serving of the food.

Class Activity. Have students compute the total daily value for potassium, using the figures on the label. If 310 mg of potassium is 9% of the daily value, what is the total amount recommended for a day? In other words, 9% of what equals 310 mg? (310 ÷ 0.09 = 3,444 mg total; to check, 0.09 of 3,444 = 310 mg. The rounded daily value is 3,500 mg.)

Research Activity. Have students research the USDA's grading system for meats and make a poster showing what each grade indicates.

Grade Labels

Grade labels are indications of quality that may appear on certain food items, such as meats, poultry, eggs, fruits, and vegetables. They are based not on nutritional value but on the food's appearance, taste, and texture. Grade labels might use descriptive terms such as "Grade A," "select," or "fancy," depending on the type of food. Grading is usually voluntary. The service is provided by various government agencies, mainly within the USDA, but paid for by the food producers and processors who request it.

Nutrition Facts

Serving Size 1 cup (228g)
Servings Per Container 2

Amount Per Serving	
Calories 260	Calories from Fat 120
	% Daily Value*
Total Fat 13g	**20%**
Saturated Fat 5g	**25%**
Trans Fat 2g	
Cholesterol 30mg	**10%**
Sodium 660mg	**28%**
Total Carbohydrate 31g	**10%**
Dietary Fiber 0g	**0%**
Sugars 5g	
Protein 5g	
Vitamin A 4%	Vitamin C 2%
Calcium 15%	Iron 4%

*Percent Daily Values are based on a 2000 calorie diet. Your daily values may be higher or lower depending on your calorie needs:

	Calories:	2,000	2,500
Total Fat	Less than	65g	80g
Sat Fat	Less than	20g	25g
Cholesterol	Less than	300mg	300mg
Sodium	Less than	2,400mg	2,400mg
Total Carbohydrate		300g	375g
Dietary Fiber		25g	30g

Calories per gram:
Fat 9 • Carbohydrate 4 • Protein 4

21-10

The Nutrition Facts label makes it easy for you to compare brands. What is the main purpose of this label?

Class Activity. Have students compare the unit price of two boxes of cereal: a 10-ounce box for $2.39 and a 24-ounce box for $3.90.

Product Dates

Some food packages are marked with a date to help you judge quality and freshness. Several types of dates are used, depending on the product.

- **Pull date.** If the date says "Sell by," it's a **pull date**, indicating the last day the manufacturer recommends that the item be sold. Although the product must be pulled off the store shelf after that date, a reasonable amount of time is allowed for home storage and use.
- **Pack date.** A date that indicates when the product was packaged can help you determine how long the food has been sitting on the shelf in the store.
- **Freshness date.** The words "best if used before" often appear before a freshness date. The food will be safe to use after that date but will be past its peak of quality.
- **Expiration date.** An **expiration date** indicates the last day that a product should be eaten. Both federal and state governments regulate the expiration dates for certain perishable foods.

Dollars and Sense. Ask students how they would decide when it is worthwhile to buy large packages of food products.

Unit Pricing

Another source of consumer information is the product's price tag, which is usually found on the store shelf. In many cases, the shelf tag includes the price of the item and also the **unit price**, which is the cost per unit of measurement. Unit pricing makes it easier to compare the prices of different sizes and brands of a product. For example, you can tell whether an 8-ounce jar of peanut butter is a better buy than a 15-ounce jar by comparing the cost per ounce.

SAVING MONEY ON FOOD

Food labels, freshness dates, and unit prices all help you get the most for your money at the supermarket. In addition, you can use these money-saving strategies to make the most of your food dollars.

- Comparison shop and consider alternatives. For example, compare the costs of frozen, canned, and fresh vegetables. Look for bargains on fresh fruits and vegetables that are in season.

DOLLARSandSENSE

Bigger Isn't Always the Best Value

Large packages often have a lower unit price than small packages. Even if the larger size appears to be a bargain, make sure that you'll be able to use all that you buy. Getting a 6-pound bag of apples at a reduced price sounds good, but if half of the apples spoil before you eat them, that's no bargain at all.

Caption Answer. National brands pay to advertise on television, in magazines, and in newspapers; store brands generally do not.

- Consider buying **bulk foods**, which are foods displayed in covered bins from which you can scoop the amount you want into a plastic bag. Nuts and grains are often sold in this way.
- When buying meat, poultry, and fish, keep in mind that some cuts yield more servings per pound than others. For example, boneless chicken breasts may cost more per pound than bone-in chicken breasts, but they will provide more servings per pound.
- Consider buying store brand products. National brands and store brands may be identical in quality. They may even have been packed at the same time by the same processor using comparable ingredients. See Figure 21-11.

Critical Thinking. *Ask:* How do food stores try to encourage impulse purchases? How can consumers avoid these temptations?

- Use coupons wisely. If you use them to buy items you don't need, you're not saving money. Compare prices—you might save more by choosing a different brand instead of using the coupon.
- Food stores try to encourage impulse purchases, so shop defensively. Stick to your shopping list and skip the aisles that don't contain any items on your list. Think twice about tempting gadgets, magazines, or candy placed in the checkout lanes.

CHOOSING QUALITY FOOD

When shopping for food, consider quality as well as price. In general, avoid purchasing any food that looks damaged. Don't buy dented cans or torn bags or boxes. Check that safety seals are intact. Make sure that frozen foods are solidly frozen and are not coated with ice crystals, which could indicate that the product thawed and was refrozen.

21-11

You can find store brands that are the equivalents of national brands for most products in supermarkets. Why do store brands cost so much less than national brands?

Class Activity. Bring in some samples of fresh, ripe fruits and vegetables. Pass them around the classroom so that students can examine them. Ask them to look carefully at their color, feel their texture, smell their aroma, and then use the guidelines on this page to evaluate their quality.

Grain Products

Look for whole grain products by checking ingredients lists. Keep in mind that a loaf labeled "wheat bread" doesn't necessarily contain *whole* wheat unless the ingredients list says so. Products such as white bread and white rice have undergone processing that removes fiber and nutrients. Enriched grain products have had some nutrients added back in.

Fruits and Vegetables

Choose fruits and vegetables that are bright in color and free from damage such as slits and bruises. In general, vegetables should be firm and crisp. Avoid those that are wilted or rubbery. Fruits should feel heavy for their size and, if ripe, yield slightly to pressure. Some fruits, such as pears and bananas, can be purchased unripe and allowed to ripen at room temperature.

Produce that has been prepackaged by the store—such as a shrink-wrapped tray of tomatoes—may include overripe or damaged items. Whenever possible, select fresh fruits and vegetables individually. See Figure 21-12.

Dry Beans and Peas

Beans and peas are an excellent source of protein and fiber. You can buy dry beans and peas in bulk, in bags or boxes, or as canned goods. Canned beans and peas are ready to heat and serve. When buying loose or packaged dry beans and peas, look for bright color, uniform size, and no visible damage.

Meat, Poultry, and Fish

All meat and poultry products are inspected by the USDA to ensure that they meet basic sanitary guidelines. Government inspection of fish is voluntary.

- **Meat.** Check the color—beef should be bright red, pork should be grayish pink, and lamb should be pinkish red. Make sure that any outside fat is white, not yellow. Grades of beef include prime, choice, and select. Of the three, select is the leanest and least expensive.

21-12

When selecting fruits and vegetables, inspect each item carefully. Why is it best to avoid prepackaged produce?

Team Activity. Have students work in small groups to create a booklet for consumers on how to choose high-quality foods. Groups can use information from this section and illustrate it with drawings or photos clipped from magazines.

- **Poultry.** Look for poultry that is meaty and doesn't look dry. If you're buying a whole bird or pieces with skin, the skin should be creamy white or yellow and unblemished.
- **Fish.** Fresh fish should have firm flesh and a mild, fresh aroma, not a pronounced fishy smell. Whole fish should have red gills and bright, bulging eyes.

Eggs

Eggs are classified by size, such as extra large, large, and medium. Large is the size used in most recipes. When buying eggs, open the carton and make sure the eggs are clean and have no cracks. Brown eggs tend to be more expensive than white eggs, even though the color of the eggshell has no effect on nutrition or quality.

Dairy Products

Most dairy products are available with a range of fat content. For instance, you can purchase fat-free (skim), low-fat (1%), reduced-fat (2%), or whole milk. Make sure the milk you buy has been pasteurized to kill harmful bacteria. Be sure to check freshness dates of dairy products.

STORING FOOD

It doesn't matter how good the food is when you buy it if it spoils before you eat it. To prevent spoilage and preserve quality, go straight home after you finish shopping and store the food properly as soon as you get there. Be especially careful to keep refrigerated and frozen foods cold. Pick them up last at the store and put them away first when you get home.

Keep most fruits and vegetables in the crisper section of your refrigerator. Exceptions are potatoes, sweet potatoes, and onions, which you should store in a cool, dark, dry place. In warm, humid weather, keep bread in the refrigerator. Otherwise, store it at room temperature. Store other grain products in covered containers in a cool, dry place. Check the labels of canned and packaged foods to see how they should be stored. Some may be stored at room temperature while unopened but must be refrigerated after opening.

Answer Key. Answers to the Section Review questions are provided in the Section Lesson Plan located in the *Teacher Resource Guide.*

Section 21.3 Review

CHECK YOUR UNDERSTANDING

1. What should you consider when evaluating food stores?
2. Give two examples of money-saving strategies to use when shopping for food.
3. What quality signs should you look for when choosing fresh fruits?

CONSUMER APPLICATION

Comparing Brands Find two competing brands of a canned food, such as soup or vegetables. Compare the unit price and Nutrition Facts of both products. Create a chart to show the differences and similarities. Is one product a better value than the other? Why or why not?

Objectives

After studying this section, you should be able to:

- Discuss strategies for selecting foods when eating out.
- Explain how to pay the bill and tip the server.

Key Terms

entrée
à la carte
gratuity

SECTION 21.4

Eating Out

Every day, millions of Americans eat at least one meal outside the home. They might eat in a fast-food restaurant, a table-service restaurant, or a cafeteria. By following smart consumer strategies when you eat out, you can enjoy healthful eating within your budget.

CHOOSING FROM THE MENU

It's just as important to choose nutritious foods when you eat out as it is when you eat at home. For that reason, it's a good idea to check menus before deciding where to eat. Look for restaurants that offer a wide variety of foods. Use your knowledge of food groups and the Dietary Guidelines to determine if a restaurant can provide the nutrients you need. Over time you will get to know the restaurants in your community that offer the best choices for you.

Americans today take an active interest in nutrition, and many restaurant owners have responded to this interest. Menus might include items with descriptions such as "low-fat" or "heart-healthy." Many fast-food restaurants provide customers with nutrition information that lists the amount of calories and nutrients in their menu items.

Point Out. In 1950, a typical serving of French fries at a fast food restaurant was one-third the size of the largest serving sold today.

Class Activity. Have students measure amounts of food with a food scale or measuring cups to get a sense of how large reasonable portion sizes should be.

When deciding what to eat, think about the foods you have already eaten, or expect to eat, that day. Then make sure that your day's food choices as a whole give you the recommended amount from each food group. If you're short on vegetables, for example, consider ordering a salad.

It's easy to eat too much, or too much of the wrong foods, when you eat out. To prevent this, develop strategies that will limit your intake of fat and cholesterol and increase your consumption of healthful nutrients. Here are some suggestions:

- **Limit portion sizes.** Restaurant servings seem to keep growing in size. To avoid eating more food than you need, ask your server for a smaller portion or order an appetizer instead of a main course. If you're eating with others, consider ordering a dish that you can share. If that's not an option, you can always eat half a portion at the restaurant and take the remainder home for another meal.
- **Ask for broiled or grilled foods.** Fried foods contain a lot more added fat than broiled or grilled foods do. Usually a menu will indicate whether an item is broiled, grilled, or fried. If it does not, ask your server how the food is prepared.
- **Control high-fat toppings.** Ask for butter, sour cream, salad dressings, and sauces to be left off or served on the side, so you can control how much of them you eat. You can also choose low-fat or fat-free alternatives.
- **Choose carefully at the salad bar.** If you choose foods from a salad bar, be aware that many salad bar items, such as pasta salad, potato salad, and vegetables marinated in oil, are high in fat. Look for raw vegetables and fruits instead. See Figure 21-13.

Community Activity. Ask students to check out the items on the salad bar the next time they visit a restaurant that has one. Have them note what percentage of items were actually fruits and vegetables.

21-13

Salad bars are popular because customers can select just the foods they want. How can you use this to your nutritional advantage?

Community Activity. Ask students to pick up copies of takeout menus from local restaurants and bring them to class. Have the class analyze the names and descriptions of some of the dishes offered for clues about their nutritional values.

- **Make your beverage count.** Remember that many soft drinks are high in sugar and low in other nutrients. For a calcium boost, order milk with your meal. If you don't like milk, order water or juice.
- **Be dessert-wise.** Many desserts are high in fat and sugars. If you want a sweet ending to the meal, consider sharing a dessert, ordering a low-fat frozen yogurt, or substituting fresh fruit, either from the menu or later at home.

Understanding Menus

Whether you eat in a fast-food place or at a table-service restaurant, it's important that you understand what you're ordering. For example, would you know the difference between alfredo sauce and marinara sauce? Both are served with pasta. Alfredo sauce has a rich cream base. It's much higher in fat content than marinara sauce, which has a tomato base.

If you are unfamiliar with a term on the menu, ask your server to explain it. It's particularly important to ask questions if you have a food allergy or special dietary restrictions, or want to avoid particular ingredients. The server should be able to tell you what a dish contains and how it's prepared. Be specific if you want to know about a certain ingredient. See Figure 21-14.

Read the menu carefully before you order so that you know exactly what you're getting. At many restaurants, the **entrée** (AHN-tray), or main course, comes with one or more side dishes. If that means you'll get more food than you want, consider ordering à la carte. When you order an item **à la carte**, it's served separately without a side dish. The advantage to this strategy is that you have more control over what you order. The disadvantage is that ordering à la carte is almost always more expensive.

Team Activity. Have pairs or small groups of students role-play scenes for the class that involve ordering a meal in a restaurant.

21-14

Don't hesitate to ask your server to explain a menu item. What types of questions might you want to ask?

Class Activity. Have students calculate a 15% tip for a meal that costs $34.70 and figure out how much the total bill with tip would be.

Controlling Costs

Eating out is generally more expensive than eating at home, but there are ways to control the costs. Here are some suggestions:

- Order only what you want. If you're not particularly hungry, order an appetizer instead of an entrée. Don't let the server tempt you to buy a dessert if you really don't want one.
- Look for lower-cost items. Chicken, for example, is generally less expensive than steak.
- Take note of beverage prices. Some restaurants offer unlimited refills for one price, while others charge for each glass or cup. Consider asking for water instead of a high-priced soda.
- When deciding what to order based on cost, remember to factor in the sales tax and tip.

PAYING THE BILL AND TIPPING

At a fast food restaurant you pay in advance. At most restaurants with table service, you pay when you have finished your meal. At that point, the server leaves a check that lists the items you ordered, their cost, and a total cost for the meal. If you're with a group of people who want to pay separately, ask for separate checks when you order. If separate checks are not possible, arrange for one person to pay the bill and figure out how much each person owes. Always read the check carefully to make sure that everything you ordered is listed and that you were not charged for items you didn't order.

Answer Key. Answers to the Section Review questions are provided in the Section Lesson Plan located in the *Teacher Resource Guide.*

In most restaurants, customers are expected to pay their server a tip, or **gratuity**—money offered for a service that has been performed. How much should you tip a server? The general starting figure is 15% of the cost of the meal. If you're particularly happy with the service you receive, you might pay a higher percentage. Some restaurants automatically add a 15% tip to the total, usually for large groups. If you're not sure whether a gratuity is already included in the bill, ask.

Most restaurants allow you to pay for the meal and tip with either cash or a credit card. If you pay in cash, leave the money for the tip on the table. If you use a credit card, you can write the amount for the tip in the appropriate space, then calculate the total.

Section 21.4 Review

CHECK YOUR UNDERSTANDING

1. Describe three ways to cut down on fat when eating out.
2. What should you do if you can't tell how an entrée is prepared by reading the menu?
3. What is the first thing you should do when you receive a check for a meal?

CONSUMER APPLICATION

Checking Menus Use what you learned in this section to evaluate the menu of a restaurant in your community. Look at the variety of foods offered, the information provided in the menu, and the prices. Prepare a report of your findings that you can share with others.

CHAPTER 21

Review & Activities

CHAPTER SUMMARY

- Foods supply six basic types of nutrients essential to good health. Appropriate guidelines help consumers design a healthful eating plan. (21.1)
- Many factors affect food prices. Planning nutritious meals within a budget is essential for meeting food needs. (21.2).
- Food labels provide valuable consumer information. Reading food labels and carefully planning shopping trips will result in more food value for your money. (21.3)
- Planning and knowledge can help consumers manage costs and select nutritious food when eating out. (21.4)

THE $avvy Consumer

A Shaky Base? Brittany has started including protein bars and meal replacement shakes in her eating. They're relatively expensive, but she likes saving time, cost, and effort in planning, shopping for, and preparing many meals. According to the Nutrition Facts panels, the bars and shakes supply most of her nutrient needs. Brittany is relying on these items more often at mealtimes, saying she fills in any nutrient gaps with "real" food. What factors might Brittany be overlooking? (21.1, 21.3)

Reviewing Key Terms and Ideas

1. Describe four factors that influence food choices. (21.1)
2. What is **nutrition**? (21.1)
3. What are the six basic types of **nutrients**? Give an example of a function and a source for each. (21.1)
4. What are the five food groups that you need food from every day? (21.1)
5. Explain how considering **nutrient density** can help you make wise food choices. (21.1)
6. How much physical activity should you aim for every day? (21.1)
7. What are **convenience foods**? (21.2)
8. Explain how food prices are affected by supply and demand. (21.2)
9. What factors influence the size of a family's food budget? (21.2)
10. How might a supermarket meet a consumer's shopping needs? A specialty food store? (21.3)
11. What information is provided by the **net weight** and the **Daily Values** on labels? (21.3)
12. What is the difference between a **pull date** and an **expiration date**? (21.3)
13. What might be the advantage of buying store brands? (21.3)
14. Give two suggestions for limiting your fat intake when you eat out. (21.4)
15. How can you control costs when eating out? (21.4)
16. Why should you add a **gratuity** when paying your bill at a restaurant? (21.4)

Answer Key. Answers to the Chapter Review & Activities are provided in the Teacher's Manual in the *Teacher Annotated Edition* of the text.

Thinking Critically

1. **Understanding Cause and Effect:** In what ways can peers be a negative influence on food choices? What could you do to be a positive influence on the food choices of your peers? (21.1)
2. **Analyzing Economic Concepts:** How do specialization and international trade affect the variety of foods available to U.S. consumers? (21.2, 21.3)
3. **Making Predictions:** Eating out is on the rise. Do you think this trend will continue? Why or why not? (21.4)

Building Consumer Skills

1. **Nutrition Guidelines:** Write an editorial for the school newspaper, taking a stand on teen health. Include information that teens need to know about the Dietary Guidelines for Americans. (21.1)
2. **Menu Planning:** Imagine that you have a budget of $8 per day to meet your own food needs. Plan a day's menu that includes the recommended amounts for you from each food group. List the foods needed, the quantity you need, and the estimated cost for each. Revise your menu, if necessary, until the cost is within your budget. How easy or difficult was it to meet your budget? What money-saving strategies did you use? (21.1, 21.2)
3. **Food Labels:** Imagine a new food product and design your own label for it. Include all the required consumer information described in the text. Explain how each part of your label would help consumers. (21.3)
4. **Fast-Food Choices:** Choose a fast-food restaurant. List menu items for two meals—one planned with the Dietary Guidelines in mind, the other chosen without regard to nutrition. Using nutrition information obtained from the restaurant or other sources, find out how much fat, sugar, sodium, calcium, and vitamin A is provided by each meal. Create a visual display comparing the meals and their nutritional value. (21.1, 21.4)

CONSUMER CONNECTIONS

- **Family:** Prepare two versions of a main dish, one using a convenience product and the other made from scratch. Calculate the cost, preparation time, and sodium content of each version. Serve the dishes to family members, and have them compare appearance and flavor. What are the advantages and disadvantages of each dish? (21.2)
- **Community:** With a partner, compare the availability, quality, freshness, and prices of five food items at two area food stores. Does one of the stores stand out as the better shopping choice? Why or why not? (21.3)

CHAPTER 22

Health Care

Reading with Purpose

- Read the title of this chapter and describe in writing what you expect to learn from it.
- Write down each key term, leaving space for definitions.
- As you read the chapter, write the definition beside each term.
- After reading the chapter, write a paragraph describing what you learned.

SECTION 22.1

Protecting Your Health

Protecting your health is something to be conscious of every day. Getting into good habits now will enable you to enjoy good health—and reduced medical costs—for years to come.

Objectives

After studying this section, you should be able to:

- Explain the benefits of wellness.
- Give examples of actions that protect health and promote safety.
- Describe the hazards of risky behaviors.

Key Terms

wellness
stress

THE BENEFITS OF WELLNESS

Every day you make consumer decisions—such as how to spend your time or what to eat and drink—that affect your health. For example, going for a walk and then enjoying some fresh fruit is more likely to have a positive effect on your health than playing video games while chewing a candy bar.

Many people make wellness a priority. **Wellness** involves making a conscious effort to achieve an overall state of well-being. Practicing wellness is no guarantee that you'll never have a health problem. However, if you take care of yourself, the chances are good that you'll look and feel better, have more energy and a more positive outlook, and experience fewer health problems.

MAKING HEALTH A HABIT

Wellness starts with developing healthy habits. The teen years are a great time to do that. At this time in your life, you're making decisions for yourself and establishing your

Jump$tart. Ask students how developing healthy habits when young can help to ensure good health and save money in the future. *(Money Management)*

own way of life. If you develop healthy habits, you'll benefit now and for years to come.

- **Healthy eating.** To get all the nutrients you need, follow the nutrition guidelines explained in Section 21.1. Be sure to eat a variety of foods, including plenty of fruits, vegetables, and whole grains. Make sure you get enough fluids, too.
- **Physical activity.** An active lifestyle is an important component of wellness. Being active helps you look and feel better, gives you more strength and energy, and helps reduce stress. You can increase your physical activity through planned exercise and sports or informal activities like walking and biking. Even everyday actions such as climbing stairs can add to your activity level. See Figure 22-1.

Critical Thinking. ***Ask:*** Why are medical and dental checkups important throughout life? What problems might occur if you skip them?

- **Good hygiene.** Hygiene needs to be part of your daily health routine. Brushing and flossing your teeth and keeping your skin and hair clean make you look and feel better and contribute to your overall health.
- **Medical and dental checkups.** Don't wait until you have a problem before seeing a health care professional. Annual wellness checks with a health care provider help prevent disease or injury from developing or getting worse. Regular dental checkups ensure that any problems with teeth or gums are caught and treated early.

MANAGING STRESS

Stress is physical or mental tension caused by events or situations. Most people experience some stress in their daily lives—usually from simple frustrations and annoyances, but sometimes from serious problems. Because stress is a normal part of life, you can't avoid it, but you can learn how to manage it.

Class Activity. Have students name things that cause them stress. List their answers on the board. For each stress problem, have them suggest a way to relieve it. Were any of the stresses named linked to finances? Ask students how financial matters can cause stress for people of various ages and at different stages of the family life cycle. How can such stress be prevented?

22-1

Physical activity can take many forms. Choose whatever activities you enjoy. **How could you increase your level of activity?**

Class Activity. Have students write a short story about a teen experiencing stress. Have them show the cause of the stress and how the teen manages it.

Class Activity. Have students plan a schedule for the coming week, including time for school, homework, rest, excercise, and socializing.

22-2

Having friends who are good listeners can help make problems easier to handle. What kinds of stress management techniques work best for you?

Point Out. Explain to students that while positive stress can motivate you, negative stress can lead to health problems, such as frequent colds, aches and pains, or difficulty sleeping.

- Take care of yourself physically. Eat well, stay physically active, and get plenty of sleep.
- Be realistic about how much you can do. Allow time in your schedule to relax and have fun. Make a to-do list and use it to set priorities.
- Develop a support system of family and friends. Talking with people you trust about what is causing you stress can help. See Figure 22-2.
- Try to keep things in perspective. It's easy to exaggerate a problem when you're stressed out.

STAYING SAFE

Safety is another component of wellness. Most injuries result from carelessness and could have been prevented. Learn to concentrate on what you're doing and to think ahead.

- **Safety on the road.** Safety is a concern any time you're on the road. Car accidents are the biggest cause of injuries to teens, partly because teens are less likely than any other age group to wear safety belts. Get into the habit of buckling up every time you get into a car, and never ride with a driver who has been drinking or using drugs. If you use a bicycle or motorcycle, wear a helmet. More than 70% of deaths from bicycle accidents result from head injuries.
- **Sports and recreational safety.** Before you get involved in any sporting activity, know the risks involved and how to protect yourself. Make sure you have the recommended protective gear.
- **Safety at home.** You may think that home is the safest place to be. In fact, many accidents occur in the home. Section 23.5 provides suggestions for keeping your home safe.

Community Activity. Ask students to make a guide to first-aid classes in their area, including their locations, schedules, and costs.

Answer Key. Answers to the Section Review questions are provided in the Section Lesson Plan located in the *Teacher Resource Guide.*

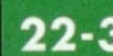

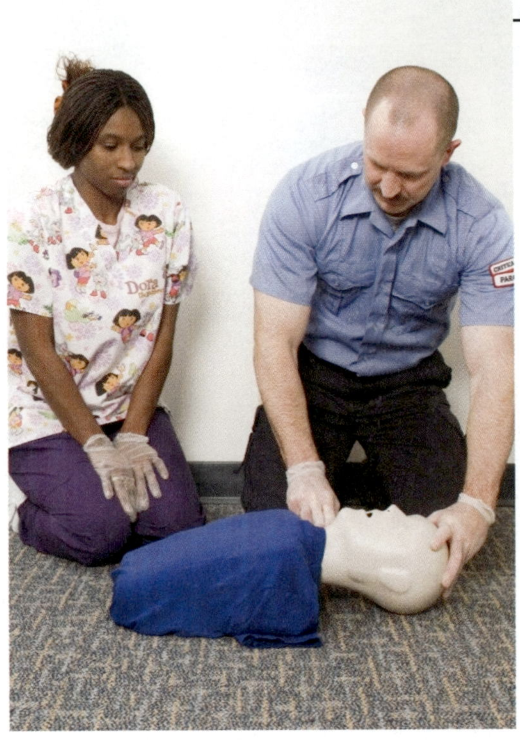

22-3

Taking a course in first aid can give you information and skills that might save your own life or the life of someone else.

- **First aid.** If you were involved in an accident, or came upon an injured person, would you know what to do? Taking the wrong action could do more harm than good. By learning the principles of first aid, you can determine what actions you can take until medical help arrives. See Figure 22-3.

AVOIDING RISKY BEHAVIORS

A healthy lifestyle also involves avoiding substances and behaviors that will harm your health. Here are some examples.

- **Tobacco.** Most people are aware that tobacco, in any form, increases the chance for cancer and heart disease. It contains nicotine, a highly addictive drug, as well as hundreds of other harmful substances.
- **Alcohol.** It's against the law for teens to drink alcohol, and for good reason. Alcohol is a depressant drug that interferes with the functioning of the brain. Alcohol is a factor in almost 50% of traffic fatalities involving young people.
- **Drugs.** If you value your health, you'll say no to illegal and misused drugs. They interfere with your ability to think, cause irresponsible behavior, and can endanger your life.

Section 22.1 Review

CHECK YOUR UNDERSTANDING

1. How can practicing wellness benefit you?
2. Give four examples of healthy habits that contribute to wellness.
3. Explain why alcohol and drugs are dangerous.

CONSUMER APPLICATION

Personal Wellness Inventory Examine your health and safety behavior and determine which areas need improvement. Prepare a list of habits you need to develop.

SECTION 22.2

Buying Health Care Products

Objectives

After studying this section, you should be able to:

- List precautions to take when using medications.
- Explain concerns related to dietary supplements and weight loss products.
- Describe signs of possible health fraud.

Key Terms

prescription drugs
pharmacist
over-the-counter drugs
side effects
generic drug
dietary supplements
fad diets

Americans spend millions of dollars on health care products every year, and the makers of these products spend millions of dollars to advertise them. Because these products affect your health, you should choose and use them wisely.

MEDICATIONS

Americans today have access to a wide variety of medications. Before you take any medication, you need to know something about it. There are two main categories of medications:

- **Prescription.** Some medications, while effective and beneficial to the people who need them, can cause serious harm if used unnecessarily or by people with certain health conditions. To control the availability of such medications, the U.S. Food and Drug Administration (FDA) classifies them as **prescription drugs**. These drugs can be sold only with a written order from a health care professional. They can be obtained only from a **pharmacist**, a person who has been trained and licensed to prepare and sell medicines.

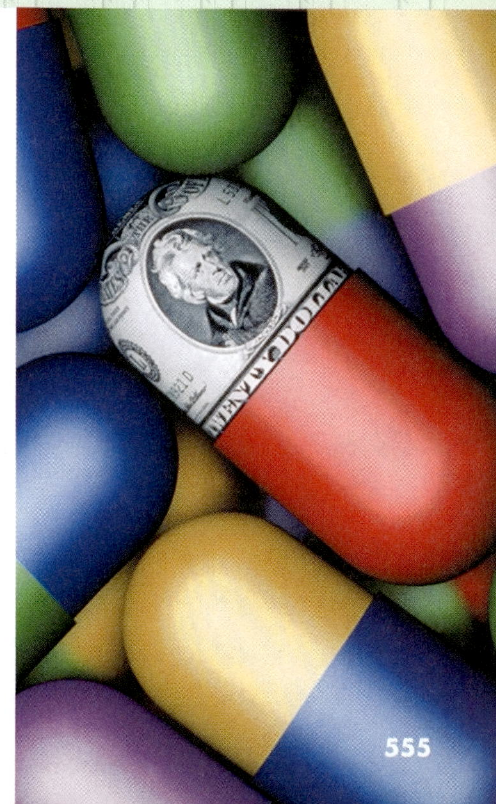

Class Activity. Ask students to name some medications they have heard of. List them on the board. Then break down the list into prescription and over-the-counter medications. Draw conclusions about what medications are more likely to be familiar to teens and why.

- **Over-the-counter.** Medicines that can be purchased without a prescription are called **over-the-counter drugs**. Thousands are sold in the United States. Although they have fewer potential hazards than prescription drugs, over-the-counter drugs can still cause harm if not used as directed.

Using Medications Safely

In the case of over-the-counter medications, it's up to you to decide which products are safe and appropriate for you to use. Before choosing a product, carefully read the information on the outer packaging. It should explain what the product is for, how it should be used, and who should not use it. For example, the label might say the drug should not be taken by children, pregnant women, people with certain allergies, those who are taking specific prescription drugs, and so on. If you're not sure what over-the-counter medicine to choose, ask a pharmacist for guidance.

Prescription medications, too, come with information about who should not use the drug. It may be found on the package or on an information sheet provided by the pharmacy. To be safe, always check this information. If any statement makes you think you should not take the drug, bring it to the attention of the pharmacist or your health care provider. See Figure 22-4.

Before you start taking any medication, make sure you understand exactly how it is to be used. Discuss the directions for use with the health care provider when you receive a prescription and again with the pharmacist when filling it. Whether it's a prescription or over-the-counter medication, read both the outer label information and any leaflet provided inside the package. Be sure to learn the answers to the following questions:

- How much should you take and at what times of the day? Note any special instructions, such as taking the medication with or without food.

22-4

When having a prescription filled, ask the pharmacist to explain precautions and directions for use. Be sure to tell the pharmacist about any other medications or supplements you're taking.

Research Activity. Ask students to research the cost of a name-brand drug (prescription or over-the-counter) and its generic equivalent. Have them report their findings in class. Compare the results obtained for different drugs and calculate the average percentage savings of choosing a generic drug.

- When should you stop taking it? In some cases, it's important to keep using the medication for a certain length of time, even if you feel better before then.
- What are the possible side effects? **Side effects** are reactions to a drug other than the intended effect. You may need to adjust your daily activities because of them. Some drugs, for example, cause drowsiness.

Store medications in a safe place where children cannot get to them. If you won't need the medications anymore, or if they're past their expiration date, get rid of them by flushing them down the toilet. Under no circumstances should you allow someone else to use your prescription drugs. They are prescribed for you alone, with your illness and your medical history in mind. It could be dangerous for someone else to take your medications.

Controlling Costs

Medications, especially prescription ones, can be quite expensive. You may be able to save money by using a **generic drug**, a medication that is chemically identical to a brand-name drug but costs less. Ask your doctor or the pharmacist if there is a suitable generic drug for your condition.

If you receive a prescription, you'll need to decide where to get it filled. Taking it to the local pharmacy is one option. You may also be able to use a mail order service that sends prescription drugs to you after you order them online or by mail or telephone. Your decision may depend on the type of drug you have been prescribed and the kind of health plan you have. If you have an ongoing condition for which you need prescriptions to be refilled regularly, you may find that the mail order option is cheaper and more convenient.

DIETARY SUPPLEMENTS

Dietary supplements are products taken by mouth for the purpose of increasing one's intake of nutrients or other dietary substances. Supplements may take the form of pills, capsules, liquids, powders, teas, or bars. Some supplements provide vitamins, minerals, protein, or fiber. Others are herbal products, such as echinacea, ginkgo, and ginseng, which claim to offer a number of benefits. Many Americans routinely take dietary supplements in the belief that the supplements will improve their health in some way. See Figure 22-5.

22-5

Americans spend millions of dollars every year on dietary supplements. How would you judge whether claims made about supplements are reliable?

InfoSource. Have students visit the Web site of one of these organizations and note what types of information it provides about dietary supplements.

For several reasons, you need to be cautious about using dietary supplements.

- Dietary supplements are not tightly regulated. They do not have to go through the premarketing approval process that is required for prescription and over-the-counter drugs. The FDA will take action only if it receives reports of problems caused by a specific supplement.
- Too much of some nutrients can cause unpleasant side effects or serious health problems.
- Experts disagree on the effectiveness of dietary supplements. If the product is not effective, you are wasting your money.
- Herbal remedies can cause allergic reactions and other side effects in some people.
- Supplements of any kind can interfere with the effectiveness of prescription drugs. Serious side effects might result from combining supplements with medications or from combining different supplements.

Critical Thinking. ***Ask:*** Why are some weight loss plans actually dangerous? How can you identify plans that could be dangerous?

Most people get all the nutrients they need by eating a variety of foods. If you think you need dietary supplements, check with your health care provider or with a nutritionist to find out if you have a nutrient deficiency. If you do take dietary supplements, be sure your doctor knows about them, especially when the doctor prescribes or recommends medications.

WEIGHT LOSS PRODUCTS

Americans spend millions of dollars every year on all sorts of weight loss programs and products. Some are legitimate, safe, and effective. Others can be a waste of money or even dangerous. To protect themselves, consumers should:

- Find out from reliable sources whether they really need to lose weight. Remember, it's natural for growing teens to put on pounds and inches.

InfoSource

Reliable Health Information

Among the best sources of reliable health information are these U.S. government agencies, which you can visit on the Web:

- Department of Health and Human Services (HHS). Their Healthfinder site on the Web provides extensive information and links to other reliable sources.
- Centers for Disease Control and Prevention (CDC).
- National Institutes of Health (NIH).
- Food and Drug Administration (FDA).

Class Activity. Bring in a copy of a magazine ad for a health care product, such as a weight loss product or a dietary supplement. Have students analyze the ad and note whether it contains any of the signs of fraud listed. Ask them what they could do if they wanted to learn more about this product.

- Check with their physician before taking any weight loss drugs or supplements.
- Avoid weight loss plans that call for losing more than 2 pounds per week or eating less than 1,500 calories per day, unless their physician approves.
- Make sure that any weight loss plan followed calls for eating a variety of foods from the five food groups and being more physically active.
- Be skeptical of ads that make exaggerated claims about weight loss. Most are scams.
- Check out the qualifications of staff members before signing up for a weight loss program, and get all fees in writing.

Fad diets are weight loss plans that are based on misinformation and are not healthy or beneficial. They promise quick weight loss with very little effort. Most of these diets don't work, and some are actually dangerous. Stay away from one-food diets, liquid diets, and diet pills. They don't provide the nutrients you need for growth and health and cannot be maintained for a lifetime.

RECOGNIZING HEALTH FRAUD

Health fraud involves the sale of worthless products that are claimed to prevent or cure diseases and other health problems. "Miracle cures" for arthritis and other chronic diseases are examples of health fraud, as are many diet aids and weight loss products. To protect yourself from fraud, you need to develop a healthy degree of skepticism and to recognize the signs of fraud. For example, be skeptical of:

- Any product that says it is based on a "secret recipe" or an "ancient secret."
- Products that claim instant, or incredibly fast, results.
- Products that claim they can treat, cure, or prevent a particular disease for which there is no conventional treatment.
- Products whose advertisements consist of testimonials from "satisfied customers." These people are usually paid.

If you would like more information about a health care product, contact the manufacturer directly. A legitimate manufacturer will answer your questions and provide the information you request.

Answer Key. Answers to the Section Review questions are provided in the Section Lesson Plan located in the *Teacher Resource Guide.*

Section 22.2 Review

CHECK YOUR UNDERSTANDING

1. What should you find out about a medication before taking it?
2. What types of problems could possibly result from using dietary supplements?
3. Name three possible signs of health fraud.

CONSUMER APPLICATION

Reading the Label Visit a store and select a commonly used over-the-counter medication. Read the label carefully. What is the drug for? Are any side effects listed? Are there any other warnings? Summarize your findings in a brief report to share with your classmates.

Objectives

After studying this section, you should be able to:

- Compare different types of health care providers and facilities.
- Explain how to choose health care providers.
- Give guidelines for communicating effectively with a health care provider.

Key Terms

primary care physician
specialists
private practice
group practice

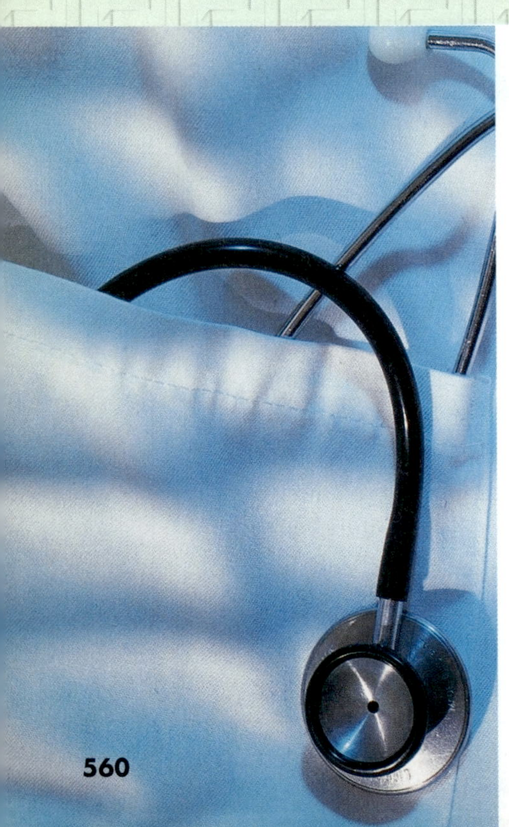

SECTION 22.3

Using Medical Services

The best time to choose a health care provider is when you're well, not when you're sick. Choosing health care providers in whom you have confidence, and maintaining good communication with them, will help ensure that you get the care that you need.

TYPES OF HEALTH CARE PROVIDERS

Most people visit at least three types of health care professionals on a regular basis: a **primary care physician**, who coordinates your health care and provides general medical care; a dental care provider; and a vision care provider. At times, you may need or want to visit additional **specialists**, health care professionals with training and experience in specific types of care.

Primary Care Physicians

Your primary care physician is the doctor you see for checkups and general medical care. Most primary care physicians are family practitioners, internists, or pediatricians. *Family practitioners* are trained to treat a wide variety of conditions in people of all ages. *Internists* specialize in internal medicine, which involves the diagnosis and treat-

Critical Thinking. ***Ask:*** What are the pros and cons of choosing a family practitioner as your primary care physician?

Point Out. Doctors recommend that all women over age 18 have regular yearly examinations by a gynecologist.

ment of common diseases. *Pediatricians* focus on the treatment of children and adolescents. In addition to overseeing the general care of their patients, primary care physicians refer them to specialists when specialized care is needed.

Dental Care Providers

Dental care providers help patients care for their teeth and gums, and they provide treatment to correct and prevent dental problems. *Dentists* are trained in general dentistry, which includes filling cavities, extracting teeth, and replacing lost teeth. Many dentists are assisted by *dental hygienists*, licensed professionals who are trained to take X rays, clean teeth, and teach patients how to care for their own teeth. *Orthodontists* specialize in straightening teeth that are out of alignment. *Oral surgeons* perform surgical procedures such as extracting wisdom teeth. *Periodontists* are concerned with gum disease. See Figure 22-6.

Vision Care Providers

Vision care providers are concerned with diagnosing, treating, and correcting eye and vision problems. The three main types of vision care providers are distinguished by the amount of training they receive and the extent of services they can offer. *Ophthalmologists* are physicians who specialize in treating diseases of the eye and performing eye surgery. *Optometrists* specialize in prescribing and fitting glasses and contact lenses. *Opticians* fill prescriptions for glasses and contacts by making lenses and helping people choose eyewear.

Other Specialists

Some people might see a specialist on a regular basis for particular needs. For example, many women arrange periodic examinations by a *gynecologist*, a physician who specializes in women's reproductive systems. Others see specialists on an as-needed basis.

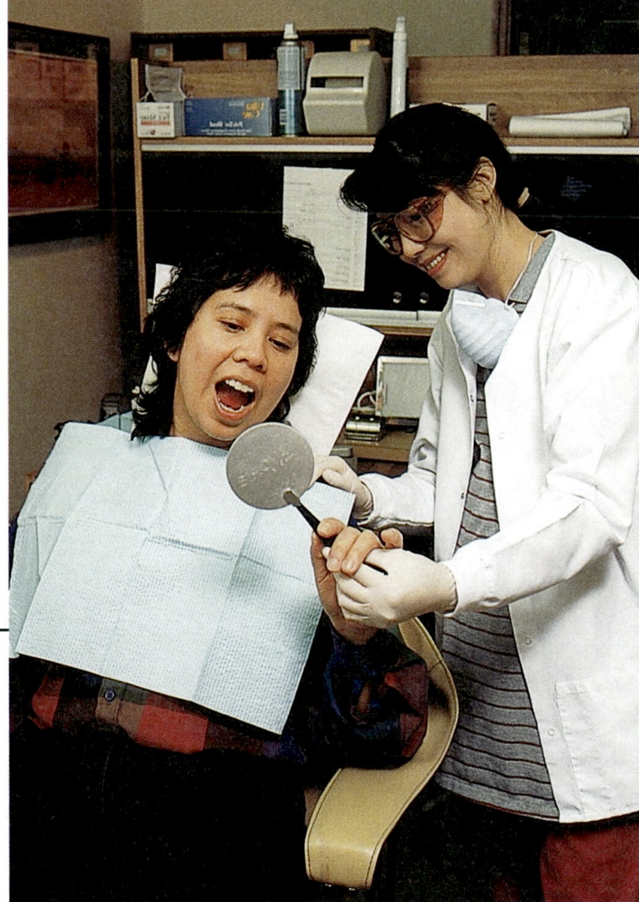

22-6

Proper dental care is important not only for your smile, but for your general health. The type of dental care provider you see will depend on the care you need.

Class Activity. Have students prepare charts comparing the pros and cons of each health care setting.

Caption Answer. Possible answers: less flexible scheduling, reliance on one doctor's availability, and familiarity with your medical history.

Examples of specialists include *dermatologists*, who specialize in disorders of the skin; *allergists*, who treat people with serious allergies; and *sports medicine doctors*, who specialize in sports-related injuries.

WHERE HEALTH PROVIDERS PRACTICE

Health care providers practice in a variety of settings. These include:

- **Private practice.** Some primary care physicians and specialists work in a **private practice**. This is an arrangement for providing medical care in which the physician works for himself or herself. Patients have the advantage of seeing only one physician, and of building trust and confidence in him or her over time. See Figure 22-7.
- **Group practice.** In a **group practice**, two or more physicians join together to offer health care in a single location. The physicians in a group practice share the cost of office space, equipment, and support staff. Patients' records are centralized. If one of the physicians is unavailable, patients may receive treatment from another physician in the practice.
- **Clinics.** Community clinics offer free or low-cost medical services for low-income patients who do not have health insurance or who are underinsured. The clinics often rely on local or state government funding or on donations and volunteer support from religious organizations or community groups.
- **Student health centers.** Many colleges and universities have health centers that offer medical care to students. In many cases, services are provided free; student fees cover the costs. Student health centers offer preventive health care as well as checkups, counseling services, and treatment for diseases and minor emergencies. Many include a pharmacy.
- **Urgent care centers.** These facilities are a convenient option for sudden illnesses and minor emergencies. They're generally open from early in the morning

22-7

Many patients prefer private practice physicians because they want to build a relationship with one doctor. What might be some disadvantages of private practice?

Research Activity. Have students contact a physician referral service to find out what services it provides and what criteria it uses for its referrals.

Discussion. ***Ask:*** Why is it desirable to meet each physician you are considering and ask your questions in person? What else might you ask?

until late at night, and you don't need an appointment. Some patients may select a personal or family physician from the clinic staff and visit that practitioner for routine medical care.

SELECTING A HEALTH CARE PROVIDER

Before you can choose health care providers, you need to know what your family's health care plan covers. Some plans specify which providers you may use if you want the services to be covered by insurance. Depending on how the insurance program is set up, you may be able to choose any physician or you may have to choose from a list of physicians provided by the insurance plan.

TEXTLINK

Types of health care plans are discussed in Section 14.4.

Physicians in private practice who accept payment from specific health care plans are listed in the plan's directory of participating providers. Plan members should consult this directory to determine whether they can use a particular physician.

Get Recommendations

When you have the necessary information, you can ask friends, relatives, coworkers, or neighbors for recommendations. They may have used the services of physicians in your community and may be willing to share their experiences with you. If you're moving to a new location and must choose a new physician, your current health care provider may be able to recommend one. In addition, many hospitals and health organizations offer physician referral services over the phone and on the Internet. See Figure 22-8.

22-8 **Physician referral services can provide the names of qualified health care providers in a particular specialty, such as pediatrics.**

Investigate Further

Once you have identified two or three physicians who are conveniently located, call each physician's office to speak to the office manager. Explain that you are a prospective new patient and would like to ask a few questions. If possible, arrange a brief visit so that you can meet the physician and ask your questions in person. Asking questions such as the following can help you narrow your choices:

- What are the office hours? What arrangements can be made for care outside those hours or when the physician is away?

Team Activity. Ask students to consider the list of questions on pages 563 and 564. Have them rank these factors in order of importance when choosing a health care provider. Then have pairs of students exchange and compare their lists.

- Does the health care provider emphasize preventive health care? Does he or she conduct wellness checks?
- What are the physician's credentials? You have a right to know about his or her education, training, and membership in professional associations.
- With what hospitals is the physician affiliated? The physician should be connected with at least one nearby hospital with a reputation for quality care.
- In a group practice, would you be assigned to one health care provider, or to any of the providers who are on duty at a particular time? You may prefer to see one doctor only.
- What is the fee for a first-time examination? For a regular checkup? Remember, the highest fee does not necessarily mean the best service.

Dollars and Sense. Ask students to check out community bulletin boards or other resources to learn about low-cost medical services in their area.

- How long would you have to wait for an appointment for a routine checkup?

Make an Initial Visit

Once you've made your choice, arrange for a wellness check or routine examination. That way you can meet the physicians and their staff and determine whether the practice meets your needs. After your checkup, evaluate the service you received:

- In the office, how long did you have to wait to be seen?
- Was the office clean and pleasant? Were the office staff pleasant and helpful?
- Did you find it easy to talk to the health care provider? Did he or she answer your questions and make sure you understood the answers? Did he or she seem concerned with your well-being?

DOLLARS and SENSE

Controlling Your Health Care Costs

Many families are finding that medical expenses are taking more and more of their budget. They have to contribute greater amounts to their health care plans and pay more out-of-pocket expenses. Here are some steps you can take to help keep medical costs down.

- Follow the principles of wellness.
- Take advantage of free or low-cost medical services in your community, such as immunizations and screenings.
- If you change physicians, arrange to have the results of any diagnostic tests, such as X rays, forwarded rather than having the tests again.
- Get itemized bills for all medical procedures and examine them carefully for errors.

Team Activity. Have pairs of students act out scenes in which a patient visits a doctor. Scenes should illustrate good communication between doctor and patient, as described in the list of tips on pages 565 and 566.

22-9

Sometimes it can be difficult to absorb all the information provided during a visit to the doctor. Why might it be helpful to have someone else with you?

Discussion. ***Ask:*** Why is it a good idea to make your first visit to your new health care provider a wellness check or routine examination?

- Was the examination unhurried? Was it thorough? Did the health care provider explain the medical procedures clearly?

If you're not satisfied with the service you received, you may be able to check other recommendations you received and switch to another practice. Be aware, though, of your health plan's policy on choosing and switching doctors. With some plans, you're allowed to switch primary care physicians only during an annual enrollment period. With other plans, you can switch at any time. Whenever you change physicians, contact your previous physician's office and ask for your medical records to be sent to the new one.

MAINTAINING GOOD COMMUNICATION

The key to getting the most from your visits to health care providers is communication. You need to express yourself clearly, make sure that all your questions are answered, and make sure you understand the advice or directions you are given. Here are some tips for communicating effectively with your health care provider:

- Before your visit, prepare a list of questions you want to ask. If you are going for a checkup, write down any information that will be helpful to the health care provider. If you're sick, write down your symptoms and note any actions you have taken to treat those symptoms. Also write down the names and dosages of any medications you have been taking.
- Take notes during your visit to make sure you don't forget any information your doctor gives you. You might want to ask a family member or friend to come along and take notes for you. See Figure 22-9.
- If you don't understand something your health care provider tells you, ask him or

Point Out. Hospital emergency rooms are required by law to accept all patients, whether or not they have insurance. As a result, they often become a source of routine care for people who lack health insurance or who cannot find doctors willing to treat them.

her to explain it again until you understand it completely.

- At the end of your visit, review the questions you brought with you and make sure they have been answered. Then briefly repeat your understanding of the action you have been advised to take next. This will ensure that you have understood everything and haven't missed an important directive.

If you believe that you need a referral to a specialist, discuss the matter with your doctor and ask for recommendations. If you have any doubts about your doctor's diagnosis or suggested treatment plan, you may wish to see another doctor to get a second opinion.

HOSPITAL CARE

If you need treatment in a hospital, how do you decide which hospital to go to? Your decision may be governed by your family's health plan or by the available options in your area. If you would like the physician you have been seeing to perform the procedure, you must go to a hospital with which the physician is affiliated.

If you do have a choice of hospitals, you can do some research to determine which one is best for you. Find out, for example, if one of the hospitals has particular expertise in the branch of medicine that is relevant to you. Ask around to discover what reputation the hospitals have. You can also contact consumer groups to determine how the hospitals compare with one another in terms of performance and patient satisfaction.

Answer Key. Answers to the Section Review questions are provided in the Section Lesson Plan located in the *Teacher Resource Guide.*

The majority of hospitals in the United States are general hospitals, which accept all kinds of medical cases and treat both outpatients and inpatients. *Outpatients* receive treatment on the day they're admitted and then return home. *Inpatients* need to stay in the hospital for one or more nights. Some general hospitals are also teaching hospitals. In addition to treating patients, they provide undergraduate and postgraduate training for medical professionals.

A specialized hospital, in contrast, focuses on one kind of disease, on one part of the body, or on a particular population. Some hospitals specialize in the treatment of cancer, for example; others are eye hospitals or dental hospitals; still others treat only children or older people.

Section 22.3 Review

CHECK YOUR UNDERSTANDING

1. What three types of physicians most often provide primary care? How do they differ?
2. What is the main advantage of a community clinic? Of an urgent care center?
3. Name at least four topics you should ask about when checking out a potential health care provider.

CONSUMER APPLICATION

Communication Checkup Use the guidelines you've learned in this section to evaluate your way of communicating with your current health care providers. Write down the changes you might make to communicate more effectively next time you have an appointment.

SECTION 22.4

Child and Adult Care Services

Many families make arrangements for their young children to be cared for by others during the day. Increasingly, families with older family members who need care also look for outside help. Strong consumer skills help such families find the options that best suit their needs.

Objectives

After studying this section, you should be able to:

- Describe care options for children and older adults.
- Discuss considerations in choosing child and adult care services.
- Explain ways to manage the costs of these services.

Key Terms

nanny
flexible spending account
home health aides

CHILD CARE

Families use child care for all kinds of reasons. Working parents often need someone to care for their children during part of the day. Some parents arrange for child care so that their children can socialize with other children. Others look for facilities that provide education as well as care. They may believe that their children will adapt more easily to school if they have been exposed to an early education setting first.

Options for Child Care

There are several possible approaches to child care. They vary in setting, structure, and opportunities to interact with other children. Here are some of the choices that may be available.

Community Activity. Ask students to use the telephone directory and local newspapers to identify child care services available in your community. Have them create a chart showing the different child-care options and which category of care they fall into (in-home, preschool, etc.).

- **In-home care.** Parents may arrange to have someone come to their home to take care of their children. In some cases, the caregiver lives in the home; in others, the caregiver comes and goes each day. The level of training for caregivers varies. Some parents hire a **nanny**, a professional who has received training in child care and provides care in the child's home. Another option is an au pair (oh PARE), a young person from a foreign country who cares for children in exchange for room and board. Au pairs generally have little or no training in child care.

- **Family child care.** Under this arrangement, parents take their children to the provider's home to receive care. See Figure 22-10. Each state has guidelines specifying the number of children who may be in the home, depending on the size of the home, the number of caregivers, and the ages of the children.

- **Child care center.** These facilities provide child care in a setting similar to a small school. Some child care centers have several classrooms and group children by age. Because of their size, child care centers can generally offer a greater variety of facilities and activities than a home-based arrangement.

- **Corporate child care.** Some large corporations offer child care facilities for their employees. This arrangement has benefits for employers and employees. Employers can attract and keep employees who need child care arrangements. Employees can see their children during the day and answer any questions caregivers might have.

- **Preschool.** Preschool may be an option for three- to five-year-old children. Schedules for preschool classes vary, but typically they meet two or three days a week for two to four hours. Different preschools follow different teaching philosophies.

FCCLA. Have students work as a class to develop a resource to connect parents with child care services in your community. Possible types of resources include a bulletin board on which child care providers can advertise their services, a Web site, or a newsgroup through which parents and care providers can contact each other. Have the class submit this project as a Focus on Children STAR Event.

22-10

Family child care offers small-group interaction in a home setting. What are some possible disadvantages of family child care?

Community Activity. Arrange for the class to visit a preschool or after-school program. Have them observe how children interact with caregivers and take notes on the types of activities provided for the children. In class, discuss the benefits of this type of child care for children and parents.

22-11

Visiting a child care facility helps parents determine whether it's right for their child. What might they look for on such a visit?

- **Parent co-op.** In a co-op arrangement, children attend a child care center or preschool in which parents work as volunteer aides, assisting the paid staff of the facility. The parents work a set number of days each month. One advantage of this situation is that it reduces the cost parents must pay for child care. Another is that parents participate in the care their children receive.
- **School-age child care.** Many school-age children need a place to go before and after school hours and on school holidays. Facilities that offer care for school-age children include community centers, YMCA/YWCA centers, and family child care providers, as well as some public and private schools.

Factors to Consider

Before making a decision, parents should check the credentials of any child care options they are considering. Most states have licensing requirements for child care establishments. To receive a license, the facility must meet certain health and safety regulations, and child care providers must complete courses in first aid, health, and safety.

There are also various assessment and accreditation programs for individuals who work in child care. Some people earn a Child Development Associate (CDA) credential, for example. Individuals who earn this credential have demonstrated that they are able to meet the needs of children and nurture their development.

Most parents explore several options and visit several facilities before selecting child care. Factors to consider include the general environment, the kinds of activities, the ratio of staff to children, the number of children, the training and experience of the staff, and the cleanliness and safety of the facility. See Figure 22-11.

Critical Thinking. ***Ask:*** Why should parents carefully research child care expenses before setting up a flexible spending account?

Discussion. ***Ask:*** How do you think older adults would feel about needing a caregiver? How could their feelings and concerns be addressed?

Managing Child Care Costs

Costs, of course, are another major factor affecting child care decisions. Some options may have to be eliminated if they are out of financial reach. Professionally trained nannies are generally the most expensive child care option. Costs for group child care vary widely.

Paying for child care often requires careful budgeting. Some working parents can take advantage of a **flexible spending account** (FSA), a benefit in which a predetermined amount from each paycheck is set aside to be used for qualified expenses. One type, a dependent care FSA, can be used to reimburse child care expenses. The money set aside in an FSA is not subject to income tax, but is forfeited if not used by the end of the year. Eligible families with children should also investigate income tax deductions and credits that can help offset child care costs.

Parents who need child care but who cannot afford the fees may be able to apply for financial assistance from state or local authorities. They may also wish to explore low-cost options. Some communities offer publicly funded child care facilities, and public school programs for school-age children are generally inexpensive.

22-12 **Senior Meals and Services is one of the programs that makes it possible for older people to live in their own homes.** **What other services might be helpful?**

Class Activity. Have students suggest needs that older adults living alone might have. List ideas on the board (include basic contact with other people). How can students help?

ADULT CARE

Just as the demand for child care has grown rapidly in recent times, so too has the demand for adult care. People today live longer, healthier lives. Many older people are active and independent until well into their eighties or nineties. At some point, though, they may need assistance with some aspects of daily living. When family members are not able to provide that assistance, they can turn to a variety of facilities and services.

In-Home Assistance

Older people who can continue to function in their own homes are generally encouraged to do so. They can receive various types of assistance. Those who can no longer prepare meals for themselves can take advantage of Meals on Wheels, a service that delivers hot meals, using volunteers to make the deliveries. See Figure 22-12.

Community Activity. Have students contact a local home health aide to find out about the services he or she provides and their costs.

Team Activity. Have students work in small groups to make posters comparing the different residential options described on pages 571 and 572.

22-13

Spending time with young friends can improve the outlook of older adults. In what other ways do the adults and children benefit from interaction?

Older people who need help with personal care and dressing may arrange for a home care aide to visit. Those who need help with medications, or who need other health-related services, may get regular visits from a home health aide. **Home health aides** are health care professionals who come into a person's home to provide needed health-care assistance. The level of aid provided depends on the individual's needs.

Adult Day Care Centers

Adult day care centers offer a safe environment and supervision for older people who can't be left alone at home during the day. The centers organize social activities and provide meals and personal care. Some are intergenerational centers, providing both child care and adult care. The centers usually have separate areas for each group, along with a central area where the two groups can interact. See Figure 22-13.

Residential Options

For older adults who can no longer live alone or with family members, a variety of residential options is available. The choice will be influenced by the individual's health, by the amount of care needed, and by what the person can afford.

- **Retirement communities** consist of apartments or small houses restricted to older adults. Services such as shopping trips and transportation are generally available. Residents continue to live independently, but may choose to share meals with other residents in a communal dining room and participate in social activities.
- **Adult family care** is an arrangement in which older adults who need care or supervision live with a host family in a private home. The host family provides assistance with daily living and opportunities for interaction.

Community Activity. Have students visit an assisted living facility in their community and find out what services and levels of care it provides.

InfoSource. Ask students to find out which types of residential care are available in your community and how much each one costs.

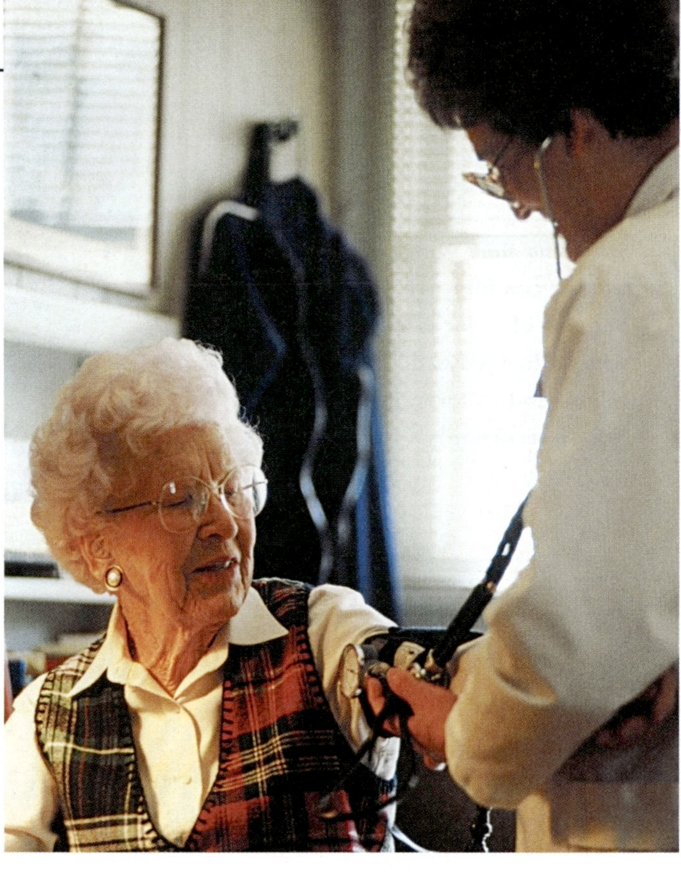

22-14

A hospice program can arrange for medical equipment, medication, nursing care, and other services to be provided in the home. How might remaining at home benefit the patient?

- **Assisted living facilities** are for people who need assistance with day-to-day activities but who do not require round-the-clock care. Residents live in apartments or rooms and meet for meals. They receive assistance with bathing, dressing, and other aspects of personal care, and may be provided with transportation to shopping and medical facilities.
- **Nursing homes**, also called extended care facilities, provide continuous monitoring and nursing care for people who have severe health problems. Nursing homes are staffed by specially trained health care professionals.
- **Continuing care facilities** offer a combination of independent living apartments, assisted living units, and nursing home facilities. As a resident's needs change, he or she can move to the level of

InfoSource

Adult Care Facilities

To find out about services for older adults in your community, start with your telephone directory. Look in the government pages for a Guide to Human Services. Then check under Senior Citizens, Health Care Services, and In-Home Services.

Research Activity. Ask students to research long-term care insurance. Have them write a report explaining how it works and what it costs.

Answer Key. Answers to the Section Review questions are provided in the Section Lesson Plan located in the *Teacher Resource Guide.*

care that is required. This flexible arrangement enables married couples with different health needs to remain in the same facility, and is less disruptive to individuals who experience declining health.

- **Hospice programs** offer care for people who are terminally ill. In some cases patients move into a hospice building, where they receive care and comfort from trained professionals. In other cases, they remain at home, and the hospice workers provide the needed care in that setting. See Figure 22-14.

Factors to Consider

It's important to check credentials when considering adult care facilities. Most states have licensing requirements for facilities that offer housing and care for older people, and state health departments conduct routine checks. Families might also check into accreditation from a nationally recognized organization such as the American Association of Homes and Services for the Aging.

Other factors to consider include the services offered by the facility, the staff-to-resident ratio, the qualifications and experience of staff members, and the costs. Family members will want to arrange a tour of any facility they are considering. The tour will enable them to get a feel for the environment and perhaps talk to some of the residents as well as to members of the staff. Some facilities are willing to let potential new residents stay for a few weeks initially before they make a commitment.

Managing Adult Care Costs

Managing the costs of adult care means being well informed about the older person's financial situation, the costs of different facilities, and sources of financial assistance. Some older people have insurance that covers part or all of the cost of their care. Long-term care insurance, which is purchased specifically to help with the costs of nursing homes and other care options, has been gaining in popularity as more and more people have become aware of the need for it. Medicare and Medicaid will cover nursing home care for a limited time if a person meets specific requirements. Families should also find out what assistance their community or state offers. As with child care, people who are paying the costs of care for an older family member should look into tax deductions, tax credits, and the use of flexible spending accounts.

Section 22.4 Review

CHECK YOUR UNDERSTANDING

1. Describe the differences between family child care and a child care center.
2. What types of assistance are available to older adults who live in their own homes?
3. Name three strategies that can help families manage the costs of child or adult care services.

CONSUMER APPLICATION

Tour Checklist Imagine that you will be touring a specific type of care facility that you're considering for a child or older adult in your family. Make a checklist of questions to ask on the tour. Explain how your questions would help you reach a decision.

CHAPTER 22

Review & Activities

CHAPTER SUMMARY

- Wellness has lifelong benefits. You can practice wellness by developing healthy habits, managing stress, preventing injuries, and avoiding risky behaviors. (22.1)
- Medications, dietary supplements, and weight loss products require consumer caution. Look for signs of fraud when purchasing health care products. (22.2)
- Researching your options can help you find health care providers and facilities that meet your needs. You need to communicate effectively with health care providers. (22.3)
- Although a growing number of child and adult care services are available, consumers face challenges in finding quality care and managing the costs. (22.4)

THE $avvy Consumer

Strong Medicine: Ben's friend Martin was describing his new doctor: "He has a nasty way with patients. At my first visit, he told me I was out of shape and that my eating habits were terrible. Now he's warning me about drugs and cigarettes, without even asking if I use the stuff. I'm going to look for someone who's easier to get along with." What might Ben suggest that would be helpful? (22.3)

Reviewing Key Terms and Ideas

1. What does **wellness** mean? Why should you make it a priority? (22.1)
2. Name three ways to manage **stress.** (22.1)
3. List two ways to prevent injuries when you're a driver or passenger. (22.1)
4. What should consumers do before choosing an **over-the-counter drug**? Why? (22.2)
5. What is the advantage of using **generic drugs**? (22.2)
6. What are **dietary supplements**? Why should consumers be cautious about using them? (22.2)
7. What precautions should you take before using a weight loss product? (22.2)
8. What is the difference between a **primary care physician** and a **specialist**? (22.3)
9. How could you get health care as a college student? (22.3)
10. What steps should you take when choosing a health care provider? (22.3)
11. What can you do to ensure effective communication with your heatlh care provider? (22.3)
12. Describe three types of child care. (22.4)
13. What factors should be considered when choosing a child care facility? (22.4)
14. How can a **flexible spending account** help families manage child or adult care expenses? (22.4)
15. What services might a **home health aide** perform? (22.4)
16. Contrast assisted-living facilities with retirement communities. (22.4)

Answer Key: Answers to the Chapter Review & Activities are provided in the Teacher's Manual in the *Teacher Annotated Edition* of the text.

Thinking Critically

1. **Supporting Your Position:** Do you think today's teens are under more stress than teens of previous generations? Provide reasons to support your opinion. What can be done to help teens cope with stress? (22.1)
2. **Recognizing Assumptions:** What assumptions do some consumers make about herbal products? Do you think these assumptions are justified? Why or why not? (22.2)
3. **Analyzing Economic Concepts:** If people in a country don't get adequate health care, what impact do you think that has on the country's economy? What countries of the world are affected by this situation? (22.3)
4. **Analyzing Alternatives:** Compare the benefits and drawbacks of a parent co-op versus a child care center. How might each option affect a parent or guardian's resources? (22.4)

Building Consumer Skills

1. **Wellness Promotion:** Create a cartoon, song, or poem to teach other teens about the benefits of wellness and ways to practice it. Present your creation to the class. (22.1)
2. **Risky Behaviors:** Develop a public service advertisement to discourage teens from using tobacco or alcohol. Include information about health risks. (22.1)
3. **Weight Loss Ad:** Analyze an advertisement promoting a weight loss product. Does the information in the ad seem reliable? Why or why not? What evidence in the ad leads you to think that the product is safe or unsafe? Do you suspect any claims in the ad might be fraudulent? Why or why not? (22.2)
4. **Medical Sources:** Investigate health care services available locally at little or no cost. Create a poster that can be displayed at school to inform students about these options. Include the location, phone number, hours of service, and types of services provided. (22.3)
5. **Costs of Care:** Choose a career that interests you and find out the average starting salary in your area. Then research the cost of child care at a local facility. Calculate the percentage of your salary you would have to apply to child care if you were a working parent. What conclusions can you draw about the cost of child care? (22.4)

CONSUMER CONNECTIONS

- **Family:** Discuss stress with family members. What kinds of stress do different family members feel? Are there ways that you can support each other better? (22.1)
- **Community:** Find out about volunteer programs that provide services to children or older adults in your community. Identify any volunteer opportunities that might fit into a teen's schedule. Then plan a campaign to recruit volunteers from your school. (22.4)

CHAPTER 23

Housing and Furnishings

Reading with Purpose

- Write down the colored headings in this chapter.
- As you read the text under each heading, visualize what you are reading.
- Reflect on what you read by writing a few sentences under each heading to describe it.
- Reread your notes.

SECTION 23.1

Housing Options

How much can you afford to spend on housing? What kind of home do you want? What location would best suit you? Should you rent or buy? These are just a few of the questions to consider when choosing a place to live.

Objectives

After studying this section, you should be able to:

- Describe factors that affect housing choices.
- Distinguish between different types of housing.
- Compare the pros and cons of renting and buying a home.

Key Terms

duplex
row houses
townhouse
condominium ownership
cooperative ownership
tenants
landlord

HOUSING NEEDS AND WANTS

The search for a home begins with you. Before you start to narrow down your housing options, think about what needs and wants you expect your home to fill.

A place to live is one of life's basic necessities. Not only does a home provide the physical needs of shelter and safety, but it can also satisfy psychological needs. It can be a place where you relax in privacy, share meals and the events of the day with your family, and entertain friends. Your home, and the way you furnish and decorate it, can also be an expression of your individuality.

While some basic needs are common to everyone, specific housing requirements and preferences vary. They depend on factors such as the number of people in a family, the stage in the family life cycle, and how people prefer to spend their time. A growing family needs more space than an older couple whose children have left home. Working people need a home within commuting distance

Point Out. Note that the average American family spent about a quarter of its income on housing in one recent year. However, this percentage varied widely by income level. For those in the lowest quintile (one-fifth of the population), it was nearly 74 percent. It also varied by region of the country.

of their workplace. Retired people may look for a housing complex that provides convenient services. People who have little free time would probably prefer a home that requires little maintenance.

As you begin to search for a home, think about your own and your family's stage of life and how it affects your housing requirements. Also consider your preferences for a location, a style of home, and so on. You should realize, however, that most people have to compromise. It's fun to imagine your dream home, and doing so can help you clarify your desires and future goals. At some point, though, you must realistically look at your resources and set priorities.

23-1 **For someone with the right skills, buying a "fixer-upper" can save money and provide satisfaction. What are some disadvantages of choosing such a home?**

HOUSING AND YOUR RESOURCES

Housing is a major expense. Income and savings usually determine the kind of housing a family can afford. For most families, about one-third of total spending goes toward housing. Housing expenses include rent or home loan payments, taxes, utilities, furniture and equipment, and housekeeping supplies. By far the largest expense, accounting for more than half of the total, is rent or home loan payments.

In addition to money, consider how other resources can help meet housing needs. Someone who has time, tools, and skills in areas such as carpentry—or who is willing to acquire them—can save money by selecting a home in need of repair and working to fix it up. See Figure 23-1.

Discussion. ***Ask:*** What are the advantages and disadvantages of sharing housing with friends? What decisions should be made beforehand?

Sharing Housing

Another way to reduce housing costs is to share a home with others. Many young people start out by sharing with one or more friends. This arrangement has many financial advantages, but requires cooperation and communication from all those involved. People who share a home need to agree on

Team Activity. Divide the class into four groups. Assign each group an area of the country: South, West, Midwest, or Northeast. Have each team research the cost of housing in its assigned region. Have teams compare their results. As a class, make a graph comparing housing costs for different areas.

rules for sharing expenses, space, food, and supplies. They also need to respect each other's privacy and be willing to resolve any disputes fairly and courteously.

EVALUATING LOCATIONS

The first decision to make when looking for a place to live is the location. The region of the country that you live in is often guided by family tradition or by career choice. The location you choose within that region may affect the price of housing—some areas are more expensive than others. Location also has a major impact on quality of life.

City, suburban, and rural locations are quite different from one another. Cities offer a greater variety of housing types, a faster-paced lifestyle, and more entertainment. Suburban areas have more space while still offering a variety of shops and restaurants within a short drive. Rural locations allow a quieter, more private lifestyle. Location preferences vary and may change over time. Some people might prefer city life while they are young and single, for example, but move to the suburbs when they start a family. See Figure 23-2.

Discussion. *Ask:* What other questions might you ask yourself when choosing where you would like to live?

Neighborhoods and communities offer a variety of facilities and services that influence a person's choice of home. How far is it to the nearest shopping center? Where is the public library? Is there public transportation? What kinds of recreational facilities are offered? What level of police and fire protection is provided? These are just a few of the questions home seekers might ask themselves.

TYPES OF HOUSING

When it comes to choosing a type of housing, consider both the type of structure and the type of ownership. Each type of housing satisfies different needs and wants.

23-2

The location you choose will affect the price you pay for housing and the quality of your life. What aspects of location are particularly important to you?

Team Activity. Organize the class into five teams. Assign each team one of the dwelling types listed. Have each team create a poster illustrating the characteristics of this type of dwelling and comparing its advantages and disadvantages. Arrange all posters side by side as a bulletin board display.

Single- and Multiple-Family Dwellings

Almost every type of housing imaginable can be found in the United States. The terms used for different types of housing may vary from region to region. Whatever names they go by, the following types of dwellings are common.

- **Single-family detached.** A dwelling that has no shared walls and that is designed to be used by one household is a single-family detached home. These homes come in all sizes and can be old or new. Examples include a four-bedroom, two-story, modern colonial house; a single-story, 40-year-old ranch; and a manufactured (or "mobile") home. A single-family detached home offers more privacy than any shared dwelling.
- **Duplex.** A building that contains two separate living units is a **duplex**. The units may be attached side by side or one above the other. Each has its own entrance. A duplex has most of the advantages of a single-family detached home, though it offers less privacy. Variations on the duplex concept—such as a triplex, consisting of three units—have been developed.
- **Row house.** As the name suggests, **row houses** are houses that are attached at the side walls. Usually row houses are similar in design and owned independently. Many row houses are older, multiple-story buildings located in cities. See Figure 23-3.
- **Townhouse.** In appearance, townhouses can be similar to row houses. The term **townhouse** refers to a dwelling of two or three stories that is usually (but not always) attached at the sidewalls to other units in a multiple-family complex. Townhouses are often similar in size but may have unique designs. Some townhouse complexes provide such facilities as a swimming pool or tennis courts for residents to use. Row houses don't usually have these.

23-3

Row houses are making a comeback in some cities. What are some advantages and disadvantages of this type of dwelling?

Community Activity. Ask students to interview either a condominium owner or someone who owns a share in a cooperative in their area. Have them ask about the pros and cons of the arrangement and whether the person is satisfied overall. Have students discuss their findings in class.

- **Apartment.** Apartment buildings range from an older house divided into three or four units to a high-rise building containing hundreds of units. Apartments vary in size from one-room units, called *efficiency apartments* or *studio apartments*, to large units with several bedrooms and bathrooms. *Garden apartments* are located in low-rise buildings surrounded by landscaped grounds. Some apartments have their own outside entrances, while others are entered from a shared inner hallway.

Types of Ownership

All of the types of housing just described may be rented or owned. When people buy a single-family detached home, they own the building and the land, and they are responsible for the upkeep and maintenance. That is the traditional type of home ownership. When people buy a unit in a multiple-family complex, such as an apartment or townhouse, they enter into a type of shared ownership. There are two main types.

- **Condominium. Condominium ownership** involves individual ownership of a unit and shared ownership of common areas such as hallways and exterior grounds. Individual owners are responsible for maintaining their own units. Maintenance of common areas is the responsibility of the condominium association, made up of residents and representatives of a management company, and is paid for by a monthly homeowner's fee. See Figure 23-4.
- **Cooperative. Cooperative ownership** involves ownership of shares in a corporation that owns the entire property. Those who buy shares in a cooperative receive exclusive rights to a specific unit. Members of the cooperative appoint a board of directors, which takes responsibility for maintenance and services.

23-4 **Since condominium owners don't have to take care of outdoor maintenance, they have more time for other activities. Who might find condominium ownership especially appealing?**

RENT OR BUY?

Both renting and owning a home have advantages and disadvantages. Most people start out by renting, partly because it's easier to manage financially than buying. Some people look upon renting as a stepping stone toward home ownership. Others find that the advantages of renting outweigh the responsibilities of home ownership. For people who can't afford to buy a home, renting may be the only option.

Point Out. With every mortgage payment they make, home buyers increase their equity, or the portion of the property's value that they own. Renters, by contrast, must make payments every month without building any equity.

Advantages of Renting

Rental housing is available in all sizes and price ranges, and may be furnished or unfurnished. Some advantages of renting over buying include:

- **Limited responsibility.** **Tenants**, people who rent property, generally don't have to be concerned about major repairs and maintenance of the property. If the roof leaks or the sink backs up, the tenant reports the problem and it becomes the owner's responsibility. An owner of rental property is often called a **landlord**. In most rental agreements, the landlord is also responsible for yard work, exterior painting, snow removal, and the like.
- **Predictable costs.** Tenants know what their monthly rent payments will be and don't have to worry about unexpected costly repairs. This enables them to budget more efficiently and to save money that might otherwise be spent on repairs and maintenance.
- **Greater flexibility.** Renting makes sense for people who expect to move frequently, are not ready to make a commitment to home ownership, or are still undecided about where to settle. A tenant must give notice or wait until a rental agreement expires before moving, but does not have to worry about selling a home.

Disadvantages of Renting

While renting has a number of advantages, it also has disadvantages. They include:

- **Limited control.** Renters have to abide by the landlord's rules. They might not be permitted to keep pets in their home or make changes to the decor. They have little control over the way the building is managed and maintained. Some rental properties have rules that restrict the hours when guests may visit. See Figure 23-5.
- **Financial limitations.** Unlike money spent on home loan payments, money spent on rent does not contribute to ownership of a property. Renting offers no tax benefits either. Renters may find that their rent increases each year. They must either agree to pay the higher rent or find another place to live.

23-5

When renting, you may not be able to have pets, or you may have to pay a separate deposit to cover potential damage. What are some other disadvantages of renting?

Discussion. *Ask:* What skills can homeowners develop to help reduce their home maintenance costs?

- **Fewer conveniences.** While the situation varies depending on the type of housing, renters often have access to fewer conveniences than homeowners. For example, while many homeowners have their own laundry equipment, renters may have shared laundry facilities or none at all.

Advantages of Buying

Like renting, owning a home has both advantages and disadvantages. Here are some of the advantages of home ownership.

- **Independence.** When you own a home, you are usually free to make changes to it as you wish. You may plant a garden or add a patio or deck. Some people remodel their home as their family grows or as their needs change. This freedom to adapt a home to suit personal needs and wants is highly valued by most homeowners.

- **Investment opportunity.** Buying a home is an investment in real estate. If the economy is healthy, property that is well cared for will probably grow in value over time. As a result, the homeowner should be able to sell the property for more than he or she paid for it.

- **Tax advantages.** Homeowners enjoy definite tax advantages. Interest on home loans and property taxes paid to local governments are deductible from federal income tax.

- **Feeling of security.** Many people don't feel they have settled down permanently until they have purchased a home of their own. Owning a home gives them a feeling of security—a sense that they will always have a roof over their head.

Answer Key. Answers to the Section Review questions are provided in the Section Lesson Plan located in the *Teacher Resource Guide.*

Disadvantages of Buying

Home ownership is not right for everyone. Disadvantages of home ownership include:

- **More maintenance.** Most homeowners are fully responsible for the maintenance and upkeep of their property, inside and out. They must either spend time on yard work, painting, and other chores or pay someone else to do the work.

- **Unplanned expenses.** Homeowners can budget for routine expenses of running a home, but some expenses occur without warning. Fixing a leaky roof or a faulty furnace can be costly.

- **Reduced flexibility.** Homeowners have less flexibility than renters when it comes to moving from one place to another. The costs of buying and selling a home can be high, and selling a property may take several months.

Section 23.1 Review

CHECK YOUR UNDERSTANDING

1. Why do different families have different housing requirements?
2. How does a townhouse differ from a single-family detached home?
3. What are the main advantages that renting has over buying a home?

CONSUMER APPLICATION

Sharing a Home Imagine that you're about to start sharing an apartment with two friends. List the topics you'll want to discuss with your friends to help prevent misunderstandings and conflicts related to your housing arrangement.

Objectives

After studying this section, you should be able to:

- List guidelines for searching for a rental unit.
- Summarize the information contained in a standard lease.
- Identify rights and responsibilities of tenants and landlords.

Key Terms

lease
security deposit
sublet
evict

SECTION 23.2

Renting a Home

The first home you choose on your own is likely to be a rental unit. You'll need to make many decisions before you move in. Once you become a tenant, you'll learn to handle new responsibilities.

FINDING A RENTAL HOME

Locating a suitable rental home takes research and thorough planning. Start by taking stock of your resources, making a list of what you're looking for in a home, and identifying locations that might offer the kind of housing you need. These preliminary steps will enable you to narrow your options and focus your search.

Where to Look

Once you determine what you're looking for, you can start to find out what is available. Sources of information about available rental units include:

- **Newspaper advertisements.** Look in the classified section under "Apartments for Rent" or "Houses for Rent." To save space and money, advertisers often use abbreviations. Some common abbreviations used in housing ads are explained in Figure 23-6 on the next page.
- **Outdoor signs.** Visit the area where you want to live, looking for "For Rent" signs. Check the bulletin boards at local convenience stores, too.

Community Activity. Have students use one or more of the resources listed here to locate rentals in their neighborhood. Ask them to report their findings in class, including what resources they used and how many rentals they found. Draw conclusions about which resources are most useful.

23-6

To understand classified ads for rental units, you need to know commonly used abbreviations. What does "2 br apt c/a d/w $650 + util" mean?

Caption Answer. Two-bedroom apartment with central air conditioning and dishwasher. Tenant pays $650 a month plus the cost of utilities.

Rental Ad Abbreviations

ABBREVIATION	WHAT IT MEANS
a/c	air conditioning
apt	apartment
br	bedroom
bth	bathroom
c/a	central air conditioning
cpts & drps	carpets and drapes
d/w	dishwasher
fpl	fireplace
furn	furnished
gar	garage
lr	living room
mbr	master bedroom
pvt entr	private entrance
refs req'd	references required
w/d	washer and dryer
w/w cpt	wall-to-wall carpeting
+ util	utilities to be paid in addition to rent

- **Online listings.** Some real estate services and newspapers place listings on the Internet. You can search for available properties by entering the desired location, number of bedrooms, and price range.
- **Agencies and services.** Some real estate agencies keep lists of rental properties, and some communities offer apartment-finding services. You may have to pay a fee for these services.
- **Family and friends.** If you have family members or friends in the area where you want to live, let them know what you're looking for.
- **Organizations.** Types of organizations that might keep lists of vacancies include student housing offices at colleges and universities, labor union offices, chambers of commerce, and human resources offices at local companies.

Making Inquiries

As you look for rental property, obtain as much information as possible by telephone. That will save you the trouble of visiting places that are clearly not suitable for you. Before making any calls, make a list of the topics you want to cover, such as location, number of rooms, rent and what the rent includes, what furnishings or appliances are provided, whether pets are allowed, and additional costs that must be paid before moving in. If you call several people about different rental units, make a separate information sheet for each one. Arrange to visit any places that seem to meet your needs.

Team Activity. Have students examine the checklist in Figure 23-7 and rate each item listed on a 1-to-5 scale based on how important they would consider this factor when choosing a place to rent. Have pairs of students compare their ratings and discuss reasons for any differences in their choices.

Inspecting Rental Units

Before you begin inspecting rental units, prepare an on-site inspection checklist. This will help you compare the features of different units and keep track of what you see at different locations. Make copies of your checklist, and fill out a copy for each apartment or house you inspect. Note any outstanding features as well as potential problems. Don't be shy about making a thorough inspection and asking questions. Figure 23-7 suggests items you might want to include in your inspection checklist.

Be sure to ask the manager or landlord about correcting unsatisfactory conditions, such as a broken window or a dripping faucet. If you're seriously interested in a particular unit, explain that you will agree to rent the unit only if specific repairs are made.

Critical Thinking. ***Ask:*** Why is it impossible to get all of the information that you need about a rental property by telephone?

23-7

Use a checklist like this when inspecting rental units. What additional items might you add to your checklist?

Checklist for Evaluating Rental Units

EXTERIOR
- ✓ Are the grounds well maintained?
- ✓ Are the grounds and building exterior well lit?
- ✓ Is the building exterior in good condition?
- ✓ Is there a place for you to park a car?
- ✓ Is there parking for guests?

COMMON AREAS
- ✓ Are hallways and other common areas in good condition?
- ✓ Are they well lit?
- ✓ Is there a communal laundry room?
- ✓ Is there a secure place for tenants to store items other than in their units?
- ✓ Where is mail delivered?

SAFETY AND SECURITY
- ✓ Is access to the building controlled?
- ✓ Are sturdy locks installed on doors and windows?
- ✓ Is there a smoke detector in each unit?
- ✓ Are there fire sprinklers?
- ✓ Is easy exit possible in case of a fire?

INSIDE THE UNIT
- ✓ Are the size and number of rooms adequate?
- ✓ Is the layout of rooms practical and pleasing?
- ✓ Are floors and walls in good condition?
- ✓ Do windows open and close properly?
- ✓ Are window coverings provided?
- ✓ Are furnishings, if any, sturdy and in good condition?
- ✓ Is there enough storage space?
- ✓ What major appliances are provided? Are they clean and operating properly?
- ✓ Is the unit clean? Are there signs of pests?
- ✓ Can you hear much noise from other apartments or the street?

UTILITIES AND SYSTEMS
- ✓ Does the heating system work well?
- ✓ Is there air conditioning? Does it work well?
- ✓ How is the temperature controlled?
- ✓ Are there enough electrical outlets?
- ✓ Does the plumbing work properly?
- ✓ Is there enough water pressure?
- ✓ Are light fixtures adequate?
- ✓ Is there a cable TV hookup?

Class Activity. Distribute copies of a sample rental application to the class and have students fill them out. Discuss what personal information they were required to provide and what application fee, if any, was called for. Ask students how sure they would want to be about a rental before applying for it.

Final Steps

After you've visited several units and created a checklist for each one, you can begin to narrow your choices. Review the checklists and set aside those that are clearly not suitable. Then compare the pros and cons of those that remain and decide which one you prefer.

Next, contact the owner or manager of the unit you've selected. You may be asked to complete a rental application. A typical application asks for information such as your previous addresses and the phone numbers of previous landlords. A potential landlord may call these people to find out if you were a trustworthy tenant. You may also be asked to provide personal references and details about your income, bank accounts, and any loans you may have. Some landlords perform a credit check, and you may have to pay a rental application fee to cover its cost. If your application is accepted, you're on your way to becoming a tenant. See Figure 23-8.

23-8

The information you provide on a rental application helps the landlord judge whether you'll be a reliable tenant. Why might a landlord check your credit record?

Fair Housing Act

People looking for a home are protected from discrimination by the Fair Housing Act. This act prohibits discrimination because of race, color, national origin, religion, gender, family status, or disability. The law applies to both rental and privately owned property. One exception to this rule applies to housing for older people, which is allowed to require that residents be above a certain age. If you feel you've been discriminated against, contact the HUD (Housing and Urban Development) office nearest you and file a complaint.

UNDERSTANDING LEASES

Before you move into a rental unit, you and the landlord will probably sign a lease. A **lease** is a legal contract that specifies the rights and responsibilities of the tenant and landlord. Most landlords require you to sign a lease for one year, although some will rent to tenants on a month-to-month basis. Some landlords have a verbal agreement with tenants and don't require a written lease. Most people recognize, though, that it's wiser to have a written agreement that protects the rights of both the tenant and the landlord.

If you're a first-time renter with no rental history, you may need a cosigner on your rental agreement. The cosigner accepts responsibility for the rent if you fail to pay it.

Class Activity. Have students draw up a sample lease for a fictitious rental property. The lease should cover all the points listed on this page.

Critical Thinking. *Ask:* How can you ensure that your security deposit will be refunded?

Terms of the Lease

Before signing a lease, read it carefully and make sure you understand what it says. If necessary, ask someone who has experience with such documents to explain it to you. See Figure 23-9.

A typical lease includes the following information:

- Address of the rental unit.
- Starting and ending dates of the lease.
- Amount of monthly rent, date of the month on which rent is due, and fee for late payment of rent.
- Amount of security deposit the renter pays and conditions for getting it refunded. A **security deposit** is a sum of money that the landlord holds until the tenant moves out, to cover the cost of any damages caused by the tenant. The security deposit is often equal to one month's rent or more.
- Any other deposits or initial payments that must be made. For example, the tenant may have to pay a special deposit in order to keep pets in the unit. Some leases require payment of both the first and last month's rent in advance.
- Description of the utilities included in the lease.
- List of contents if the unit is furnished.
- Statement about responsibility for repairs and maintenance.
- Rules regarding pets, visitors, noise, hanging pictures, and so on.
- Amount of notice a tenant must give before moving out.
- The penalty for breaking the lease.
- Rules about subletting. To **sublet** a rental unit, a renter allows another tenant to take over the unit and pay the rent. This is also called subleasing. If, for example, you got a job in another town and needed to move, you might be able to sublet your unit to someone else until your lease

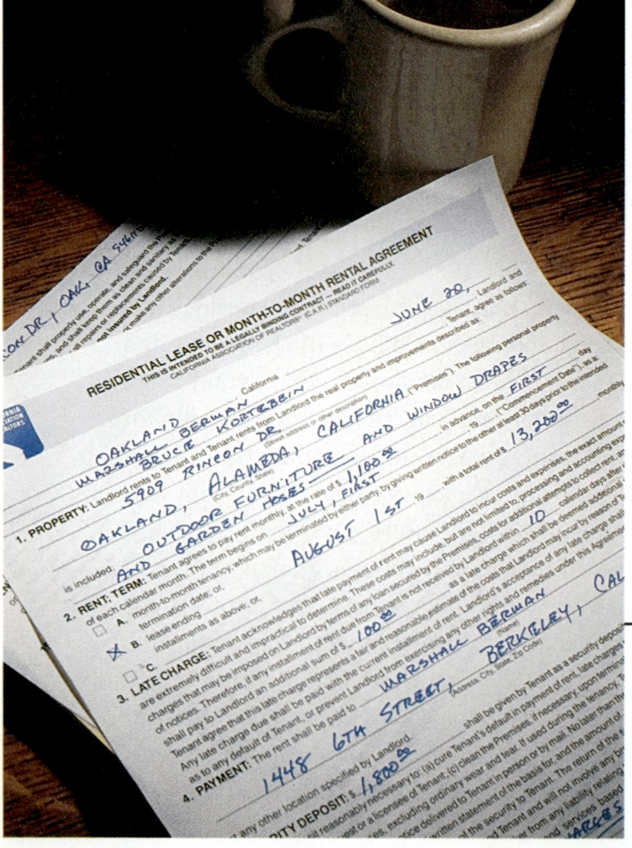

23-9

A typical lease is a detailed document with a lot of small print. Why is it important to read and understand everything before you sign?

Point Out. Note that renters can protect themselves by taking pictures of existing damage before moving in and having two prints made—one for the landlord and one for their own files (signed and dated by the landlord). That way, if the damage is questioned later, they can prove it was there beforehand.

expires. You would still be legally responsible for the unit and the rent, because your name would still be on the lease.

If you disagree with any terms in the lease, you may ask for changes before you agree to sign. The landlord may or may not agree to make the changes you request. Don't rely on spoken promises or make assumptions. For example, if the lease says that no pets are allowed, but you see that another tenant has a dog, don't assume that you, too, will be able to keep a pet.

Any damage in the rental unit, such as cracked tiles or a chipped mirror, should be recorded in the lease or on a check-in form to be completed when you take possession. That way you won't be charged for the damage when you move out. If the landlord has agreed to make certain repairs or to replace certain items, do a follow-up inspection to make sure they were done before you sign the lease.

SUCCESSFUL RENTING

When you rent a home you accept certain responsibilities. The way you handle those responsibilities will determine how well you get along with your landlord and with other renters. Successful renting starts with careful planning.

Moving In

When you move to a new place, you may need to arrange for utilities—such as gas, electricity, water, telephone, and cable TV—to be turned on or connected and for accounts to be set up in your name. Don't wait until the last minute, because these arrangements can take some time.

Dollars and Sense. Have students contact a local truck rental company to find out the costs and terms of renting a moving van.

DOLLARSandSENSE

Moving Costs

Moving your belongings into a new home need not be expensive. Here are some options to consider.

- Depending on how much you have to move, you may be able to move everything in a few car trips.
- If that's not an option, rent or borrow a truck. Ask some friends to help.
- If you plan to hire a moving company, get recommendations and ask for cost estimates. Hiring a moving company is more expensive than moving yourself, but it saves time and effort.

Team Activity. Have students work in groups to produce a consumer handout outlining the responsibilities of both landlords and tenants.

Research Activity. Have students find out what sources of help are available to tenants whose landlords do not take care of their responsibilities.

23-10 Being a responsible tenant means showing consideration to your neighbors by keeping music low and other noise to a minimum. What are some other ways you can be a responsible tenant?

Rights and Responsibilities

In return for paying rent, you have the right to live in the unit, provided you abide by the terms of the lease. You also have the right to privacy. That means that the landlord may enter only for legitimate reasons, such as to make needed repairs. Except in case of emergency, the landlord must come at a reasonable time and request permission to enter.

Although renting carries fewer responsibilities than owning a home, you still have your fair share of obligations. In return for the use of the property, you are expected to take reasonable care of it and to keep it clean and safe. You should also respect the rights of other tenants and avoid disturbing them with excess noise or other activities. See Figure 23-10.

Landlords have the right to receive regular rent for their property and to enter the property to make repairs and inspections. If a tenant causes excessive damage, doesn't pay the rent, or breaks the terms of the lease in some other way, the landlord may start proceedings to evict the tenant. To **evict** is to legally force a tenant to vacate a rental unit before the lease has expired.

Landlords have a number of responsibilities. They must make sure that the property meets certain minimum standards set by the local government. For example, there may be local regulations concerning fire escapes or safety bars on windows. Specific responsibilities of the landlord might include:

- Ensure that electrical, plumbing, and heating systems are safe and work properly.
- Keep common areas of the rental units clean, safe, and free of insects and other pests.

Critical Thinking. ***Ask:*** Why is it important to make repair requests in writing and to keep a copy? How can taking notes after calls be beneficial?

- Provide garbage cans for disposal of household trash.
- Provide enough hot water and make sure heat is available during the cold season.

Repairs

If anything in your rental unit needs repair, notify your landlord promptly. Many apartment complexes and other rental units have a procedure to follow when a repair is needed. Following the procedure exactly will help ensure that your repair is made in a timely manner. Your repair request should be in writing, and you should keep a copy. Make notes after any telephone calls about the repair and keep any written correspondence for your records.

Maintaining Good Relations

If you have a problem with your landlord, try to resolve it by communication and negotiation. Your landlord is more likely to be helpful if you show respect and understanding. If an air conditioner quits working, for example, recognize that it may take several days to arrange for repair or replacement.

Moving Out

A tenant also has several responsibilities when moving out of a rental home. Here are some tips to help make your move a smooth one.

- Provide at least as much notice as the lease requires.
- Clean the rental unit thoroughly. If you had put any nails in the walls, remove them and patch the holes.

Answer Key. Answers to the Section Review questions are provided in the Section Lesson Plan located in the *Teacher Resource Guide.*

- Arrange with the landlord for a final inspection after you've moved out. Landlords should not subtract money from your security deposit for normal wear and tear. They will, however, keep money back for repairing any damage that you caused. Landlords generally have up to 30 days to return your security deposit.
- Leave a forwarding address with the landlord. Doing so ensures that your security deposit and any other mail will reach you.
- If you have a good relationship with the landlord, ask for a letter of recommendation. The letter might help persuade future landlords that you are a good tenant.

Section 23.2 Review

CHECK YOUR UNDERSTANDING

1. Where can you find out about available rental units?
2. What is a lease and why is it an important document?
3. Under what circumstances would a landlord be entitled to keep part of a tenant's security deposit?

CONSUMER APPLICATION

Apartment Search Assume that you're looking for a one-bedroom apartment as close as possible to where you currently live. Using newspaper ads or other sources, compare available apartments. How many did you find? What is their price range? What factors might account for differences in price?

Objectives

After studying this section, you should be able to:

- Explain the costs of buying a home and the options for financing it.
- Describe the process of finding a home to buy.
- Summarize the steps involved in the home purchasing process.

Key Terms

mortgage
closing costs
escrow account
points
earnest money
contingency

SECTION 23.3

Buying a Home

Buying a home is the most costly and significant purchase that most people ever consider making. Deciding how to finance this purchase is just one of many steps buyers take along the road to home ownership.

UNDERSTANDING HOME FINANCING

Very few people have the cash to buy a house outright. Most home buyers take out a **mortgage**, or long-term home loan. Understanding the financial aspects of purchasing a home helps make the process go more smoothly.

Costs of Buying a Home

Preparing for home ownership requires an understanding of the costs involved. Some are one-time costs paid at the time of purchase, while others are continuing costs.

- **Down payment.** The down payment is the part of the purchase price that is paid in cash up front. It might range from 5% to 20% or more of the purchase price. The larger the down payment, the smaller the loan.
- **Closing costs.** The term **closing costs** refers to various fees that must be paid by the buyer or the seller at the

Research Activity. Have students do research to find out what percentage of each mortgage payment is applied toward the principal over the life of the loan. Have them create a graph showing how the buyer's equity in the home increases over time (assuming a 20 percent down payment to start).

Closing Costs

Many types of costs must be paid at the closing. They vary slightly from state to state. Here are a few examples.

FEE	DESCRIPTION
Origination fee	Paid to the lender to cover the expense of processing the loan application.
Title search	Pays for an investigation to ensure that the property belongs to the seller and that nobody else has any claims against it.
Survey	A surveyor is paid to map the property lines and produce a report so the buyer will know the exact boundaries of the property.
Credit report	The lender passes along all costs incurred in investigating the buyer's credit history.
Appraisal	Fee to cover the cost of appraising the property to determine its fair market value.
Filing or recording fee	The transfer of property from one owner to another must be recorded in the public records. A fee is charged for this service.

23-11 Buyers receive a list of closing costs a few days before the closing. What does the origination fee cover?

time the purchase is finalized. The total amount of the buyer's closing costs varies, but may add up to several thousand dollars. Figure 23-11 identifies some of the closing costs that buyers typically must pay.

- **Monthly loan payments.** At first, most of each monthly mortgage payment goes to pay interest on the loan. Only a small amount goes toward paying back the *principal*, or original amount borrowed. With each payment, the portion that is applied toward the principal increases.
- **Other continuing costs.** Homeowners must pay property taxes, based on the value of the home, to their local government. Property tax rates vary considerably from area to area. Insurance is another expense of home ownership. Lenders generally will not issue a mortgage without proof of home insurance. Some homeowners must pay other costs, such as condominium association fees.

In some cases, property taxes and home insurance are paid by adding an extra amount to each monthly mortgage payment. The lender puts the extra funds in an **escrow account**, a bank account in which money is

Class Activity. Have students calculate the maximum monthly mortgage payment for a couple with a gross income of $55,000 per year.

Caption Answer. The sale is less likely to be delayed due to problems the buyers may have in obtaining a loan.

held in trust. When the taxes and insurance come due, they are paid from the escrow account. The lender may require an escrow account if the down payment is less than 20%.

23-12 In a tight market, buyers who prequalify for a mortgage may have an advantage over those who don't. Why would a seller prefer a prequalified buyer?

What Can You Afford?

To determine how much they can afford to pay for a home, prospective home buyers should look at their income, savings, and debt. Many lenders use a general rule of thumb that housing expenses—including principal, interest, property taxes, and insurance—should not exceed 29% of gross income (income before taxes are deducted). Consumers must decide whether they would be comfortable devoting that much of their budget to housing expenses. If buyers have too little savings or too much other debt, lenders might not approve a loan as high as the 29% figure suggests.

TEXTLINK

Guidelines for qualifying for credit can be found in Section 11.2.

Potential home buyers are wise to talk to lenders early in the process, just as they're starting to look for a home. Many lenders are willing to *prequalify* buyers. The buyer provides information about income, assets, and debt. The lender then calculates how large a loan is likely to be approved and provides a letter stating the amount. This process helps the buyer know what price range to focus on when searching for a home. A letter of prequalification does not obligate the buyer to get a loan from that lender, nor does it guarantee that the lender will approve the loan. It does, however, indicate willingness to extend a loan. For that reason, sellers are more likely to accept an offer from buyers who have a letter of prequalification. See Figure 23-12.

Types of Mortgages

There are three main types of mortgages:

- **Conventional (fixed rate) mortgage.** The interest rate and monthly payment amount remain the same for the life of the loan. Borrowers may pay a higher rate for this type of mortgage, but they know that their monthly costs will not change.
- **Adjustable rate mortgage.** The interest rate changes to reflect changes in the economy. Rates may change each year,

Critical Thinking. *Ask:* What are the advantages and disadvantages of each type of mortgage? Under what circumstances might each be a good choice?

InfoSource. Have students use newspapers and Web sites to compare interest rates on mortgage loans available from different lenders.

usually for a period of five years, with a limit on how high they can go. The initial rate is usually lower than that for a conventional mortgage. The disadvantage is that buyers don't know whether their monthly payments will increase or by how much.

- **Graduated payment mortgage.** Payments start out low and increase in the later years of the loan. This type of mortgage appeals to people who expect their income to increase and who like to know in advance how much they will pay each month.

Special Loan Programs

Special loans are available to people who might not be able to obtain a traditional mortgage. Homes purchased under these programs may have to meet certain requirements, and there may be a limit to the amount of the loan. Among the loan programs that have helped millions of Americans buy their own homes are:

- **FHA loans.** The Federal Housing Administration (FHA) insures loans to low- and moderate-income families who might not otherwise qualify for a mortgage.
- **VA loans.** The Department of Veterans Affairs insures loans to people who have served in the armed forces. These loans are often made without any down payment.
- **Loans for rural home buyers.** People wishing to buy homes in rural areas may be able to obtain a loan through the Department of Agriculture's Rural Housing Service.
- **First-time buyer programs.** Some lenders have special programs that help first-time buyers by offering lower down payments and easier access to a loan.

Comparing Mortgage Terms

Mortgages can be obtained through many different lenders, including banks, credit unions, and mortgage companies. It's a good idea to compare various loan options from different lenders. Researching the best loan is well worth a buyer's time.

InfoSource

Mortgage Rates

When applying for a mortgage, you're not limited to local lenders. These information sources can help you find the best rates:

- Newspapers with weekly charts that list the rates offered by various lending institutions.
- Web sites that list rates from many different lenders. Try using "mortgage rates" as a search term. If you find a rate you like, some lenders allow you to begin the application process online.

Research Activity. Have students use an online mortgage calculator to figure out the monthly payments on a $100,000 loan over 15 years and over 30 years and how much the buyer would pay altogether over the life of each loan. Discuss reasons buyers might choose a shorter- or longer-term loan.

One of the most important factors in comparing loans is the interest rate. Interest rates change frequently according to general economic conditions, and they vary somewhat from lender to lender. Since mortgages are long-term loans, finding an interest rate that's even a fraction of a percentage point lower can save thousands of dollars in interest over the years.

Another important factor is the length of the loan term. Most buyers take out a loan for either 15 or 30 years. Those who opt for a 15-year mortgage get a lower interest rate and pay significantly less interest overall, but have to make higher monthly payments. Many people prefer to take out a 30-year loan to keep their monthly payments down. They usually have the option to pay it off faster by making additional payments toward the principal without penalty.

When comparing mortgages, buyers also need to compare the number of points. **Points** are one-time finance charges paid at the beginning of a loan. Each point is 1% of the loan amount. For example, if a lender charges three points on a loan of $100,000, the borrower would have to pay $3,000 in addition to other interest and fees. Loans with points are usually offered at lower interest rates than those without points.

23-13 Many factors must be considered when searching for a home. Other than price, which factors might be most important to you?

Discussion. ***Ask:*** What would you consider more important when buying a home: the house or the neighborhood where it is located? Explain why.

FINDING A HOME

Finding a home to buy takes time and patience. The search is easier for buyers who can be specific about their needs, wants, and priorities. They start with a clear idea of their price range, based on their budget and discussions with lenders. Next, they think about the characteristics of the home they want—a single-family house or a condominium apartment? Older or newer? How large? Then they identify possible areas where they might live. When evaluating areas, buyers consider the types and prices of homes available there, the distance to work or school, and the availability of shopping and other conveniences. They must also consider the future resale value. An attractive home in a desirable area is more likely to gain in value. See Figure 23-13.

Once buyers have their requirements and preferences in mind, they can begin their search. Here are some places they might start.

Community Activity. Have students search classified ads and Internet listings for homes available for sale in your area. Have them note what information the listings provide about the features of the house and the characteristics of the neighborhood.

- **Classified ads.** Most major newspapers have a section devoted to homes, often on Saturday or Sunday. The majority of ads are placed by real estate agencies.
- **Open houses.** During an open house, people can walk through a home that's for sale and ask questions about it. Most open houses are held on Saturday or Sunday.
- **Internet.** Many real estate companies have their own Web sites with listings. The sites make it easy to search for homes by price range, location, number of bedrooms, or other characteristics. Some sites provide pictures or virtual tours of the homes.

Working with an Agent

Real estate agents are professionals in the business of buying and selling homes. They can be very helpful to potential buyers. Most agents have access to a multiple listing service (MLS), which is an electronic listing of homes offered for sale by various real estate agencies in the area. Real estate agents can find a selection of homes that fit the buyer's requirements. They can organize tours of the homes and guide the buyer through the purchasing process. See Figure 23-14.

Typically, a potential buyer does not have to pay a fee to work with a real estate agent. Agents receive commissions from sellers. However, since this commission is usually included in the asking price of the home, the buyer indirectly pays for the services of any real estate agents involved in the sale. People who want a real estate agent to help them buy a home can ask friends or relatives for recommendations or call two or three agencies and arrange meetings. They should choose an agent who is familiar with the area where they want to live.

Evaluating Homes

Viewing homes helps buyers narrow down what they like and dislike. However, it can also become overwhelming as buyers try to remember what they've seen. To make the process easier, buyers can obtain an evaluation sheet from a real estate agent or from an online source and complete a copy of the sheet for each home that they view. The sheet will help them remember details such as the layout of the home, the number of rooms, and any special features. Later, they can use their completed sheets to compare different homes and narrow down their choices.

23-14

A real estate agent can help make the home-finding process easier. What qualities would you look for in a real estate agent?

Economic Impact & Issues. Have students research three types of mortgages and explain their relationship to the economy.

COMPLETING THE PURCHASE

Once buyers identify a home that they want and can afford, they can begin the purchasing process. To understand the documents they are signing, many home buyers consult an attorney for legal advice.

Making an Offer

The first step is to make an offer. The offer does not have to be as high as the asking price of the home. Sellers often set an asking price that is higher than the price they expect to get, in anticipation of bargaining.

To make an offer, the buyers have their real estate agent or attorney draw up an offer-to-purchase contract. This document

Critical Thinking. ***Ask:*** Why are contingencies often included in an offer-to-purchase contract? How do such contingencies protect the buyer?

states the property they want to purchase, the price they're offering, the date they wish to assume ownership, and other details.

The offer is submitted to the seller along with a check. This payment is **earnest money**, a deposit to prove that the buyer is serious about purchasing the home. The amount of earnest money required varies, but may be 1% to 10% of the offered price. If the buyer doesn't buy the home, the seller has the right to keep the money. If the transaction is completed, the earnest money is applied to the down payment.

The offer may include a number of contingencies. A **contingency** is a condition that must be met in order for the sale to occur.

Economic Impact & Issues

The Cost of Mortgages

When choosing between a fixed rate and an adjustable rate mortgage (ARM), the power to forecast the nation's finances as well as your own would be useful.

If you foresee robust growth in the economy and in your own career field, you might decide on a fixed rate mortgage. The interest rate may be higher than for an ARM, but your income will be growing. If the Federal Reserve raises interest rates to cool an overheating economy, your rate won't be affected.

An ARM might be appealing if you predict only mild growth. The Federal Reserve probably wouldn't raise interest rates, for fear of stifling the economy further. Thus, the interest rate on your ARM is also less likely to rise. In addition, the index on which the rate is based, such as the interest rate on Treasury bonds, would remain steady. In a very active market, the rate change could be less predictable. Budgeting for other major expenses can be more difficult when your mortgage payments change periodically.

FIGURE IT OUT

Find out what these ARM terms mean: teaser rate; rate adjustment periods; and mortgage payment cap. Then write a response to this situation: If you were a young employed parent who wants to buy a home now, would you prefer a fixed rate or an ARM? Why? How would your specific situation and the economy affect your choice?

Class Activity. Have students create a glossary of terms associated with home buying. Discuss how understanding these terms can help buyers.

For example, the buyer might request that the sale be contingent, or dependent, on:

- Ability to obtain financing.
- Satisfactory reports from professional inspectors. Certain inspections may be required by state law, but the buyer can ask for additional ones. Examples include inspections for termites, lead, asbestos, radon, and structural defects.
- The completion of certain specified repairs by the seller.
- Attorney approval of the contract. Some states require this.

Reaching an Agreement

The seller can either accept the buyer's offer, reject it, or make another offer in return, called a *counteroffer*. For example, if the home was listed for $145,000 and the buyer offered $140,000, the seller could make a counteroffer of $142,500.

When both buyer and seller agree on a price and sign the offer, it becomes a legally binding sales contract. The earnest money is deposited in an escrow account until the sale becomes final. Once the seller accepts the earnest money, he or she may not sell the home to anyone else. However, the sales contract can be amended at any time if both seller and buyer agree to the amendment.

Obtaining a Loan

Even if the buyer prequalified for a loan, the actual loan application can't be completed until the sales contract is signed. After the application is made, it usually takes several days or weeks for the lender to obtain the information and documents necessary to finalize the loan. The lender completes a credit check if it was not done earlier. At

Answer Key. Answers to the Section Review questions are provided in the Section Lesson Plan located in the *Teacher Resource Guide.*

some point in this process, the lender explains the terms of the loan and gives the buyer a chance to "lock in," or finalize, an interest rate. After the interest rate is locked in, it will not change before the deal is completed, even if prevailing interest rates change.

Closing the Deal

The final step in the home-buying process is the *closing*, a meeting at which the property sale becomes final. Typically, the buyer and seller attend, along with the lender's representative, the real estate agents involved, and possibly others, such as attorneys for the buyer and seller. Ahead of time, the buyer receives a written statement itemizing the down payment and closing costs and showing the total amount to be paid. The buyer obtains a cashier's check in this amount to bring to the closing. After many legal documents are signed and money changes hands, the buyer is finally the proud owner of a new home.

Section 23.3 Review

CHECK YOUR UNDERSTANDING

1. What are the one-time costs of buying a home? The continuing costs?
2. Why might prospective home buyers want to work with a real estate agent?
3. If you find a home to buy, what step comes next? Describe how it's done.

CONSUMER APPLICATION

Mortgage Rates Use print or Internet sources to compare mortgage rates from different lenders. Make a chart showing the rates offered for 30-year and 15-year mortgages and the number of points charged. What patterns do you see?

Objectives

After studying this section, you should be able to:

- Give guidelines for planning the purchase of furnishings.
- List features to look for when buying furniture.
- Describe how to select large appliances.

Key Terms

floor plan
traffic patterns
case goods
particleboard
veneer
EnergyGuide label
Energy Star label

SECTION 23.4

Furnishing a Home

You have a new place! Now comes the fun part—furnishing your home. Because home furnishings can be expensive, you'll want to plan and shop carefully to avoid making costly mistakes.

FURNISHING ON A BUDGET

When it comes to furnishing a home, most people start slowly. Few can afford to furnish every room with new items. Many start out with borrowed and secondhand items and build from there. Keep that in mind as you begin planning how to furnish your home.

First determine what furnishings you already have. If you're moving out of your parents' home, find out what they expect, or will allow, you to take. You may be pleasantly surprised! If you already have furnishings of your own, take inventory. Make a list of all the pieces you have and identify those that need to be replaced sooner rather than later.

Next, take a realistic look at your budget, current savings, and savings plan. How much can you can spend on furniture right now? How much can you set aside each month for future purchases? Keep your financial resources in mind as you think about what furnishings to add or replace. Since you probably can't afford to buy everything you'd

Dollars and Sense. Have students search home decorating magazines for creative, low-cost ideas for home furnishings and share them with the class.

like right away, set priorities. You could manage without a coffee table, for example, longer than you can without a mattress.

Credit or Cash?

While furniture and appliance stores often offer generous credit plans, you'd be financially wise to use them sparingly. If you can save up for purchases instead of using credit, you'll eventually enjoy a well-furnished home without the burden of heavy debt. Use credit as needed for purchases that you really can't postpone, such as a refrigerator.

You may come across promotions that offer "no down payment, no interest, and no payments" until a certain date. The idea of getting new furniture or appliances without having to pay anything for months may be very tempting. However, read the financing contract carefully. If you don't pay the cost of the item in full by the specified date, you may be charged interest that is backdated to the time of purchase. This kind of deal is favorable only to those who are able to pay the debt in full when it comes due.

Research Activity. Have students investigate the cost of rent-to-own furniture and appliances and compare it with the cost of buying similar items.

The Rental Option

Renting furniture and appliances is an alternative to buying them. Rental companies offer items ranging from televisions and refrigerators to complete rooms of furniture. They deliver items to the home and pick them up when the rental agreement ends. Renting may be worth considering as a temporary solution for people who are just starting out or who move frequently.

Some consumers enter into "rent-to-own" agreements. If they make weekly or monthly payments on a rented item for a certain length of time, they assume ownership of the item. Before entering into such an agreement, consider the drawbacks. The total cost of all the payments is often much higher than the cost of buying from a retail store, and the quality of the item may be lower.

DOLLARSandSENSE

Creative Low-Cost Furnishings

When it comes to furnishing your home, creativity is almost as good as cash. Try these ideas:

- Think of clever substitutions. A set of inexpensive plastic crates can take the place of an end table, bookcase, or dresser. Over time, you can gradually replace makeshift items with the real thing.
- Check local thrift shops, secondhand stores, and garage sales for inexpensive furnishings. If needed, give them a "makeover" by repainting, refinishing, or adding slipcovers.
- Buy unfinished furniture and stain or paint it yourself. You might even try building a few simple pieces from scratch.

Team Activity. Have students work in small groups. Have each group draw a floor plan of a living room or bedroom, as shown on this page. Then have them decide what items they would choose to furnish this room and use templates to show how they would arrange the furniture.

PLANNING ROOM BY ROOM

It's usually easier and more satisfying to focus your decorating efforts on one room at a time. Start by considering the way the room will be used and the overall look you want to achieve. Gather information and ideas by reviewing books, magazines, and catalogs or by visiting furniture stores. Think about how to combine what you already have with new pieces to create a room that is comfortable and inviting.

Plan the furniture arrangement by developing a **floor plan**, a scale drawing showing the size and shape of a room. You can use graph paper or a design software program, or you can find a Web site that helps you draw a plan. Place shapes to represent pieces of furniture on your floor plan. Experiment with different types and sizes of furniture pieces and different ways of arranging them. Consider **traffic patterns**—the paths people take as they move through a room. Take into account the activities that will occur in the room. In a living room, for example, arrange a seating area so that it's easy for people to make eye contact and carry on a conversation. See Figure 23-15.

23-15

A floor plan enables you to move items around until you find the arrangement that works best. Where are the traffic patterns in this room?

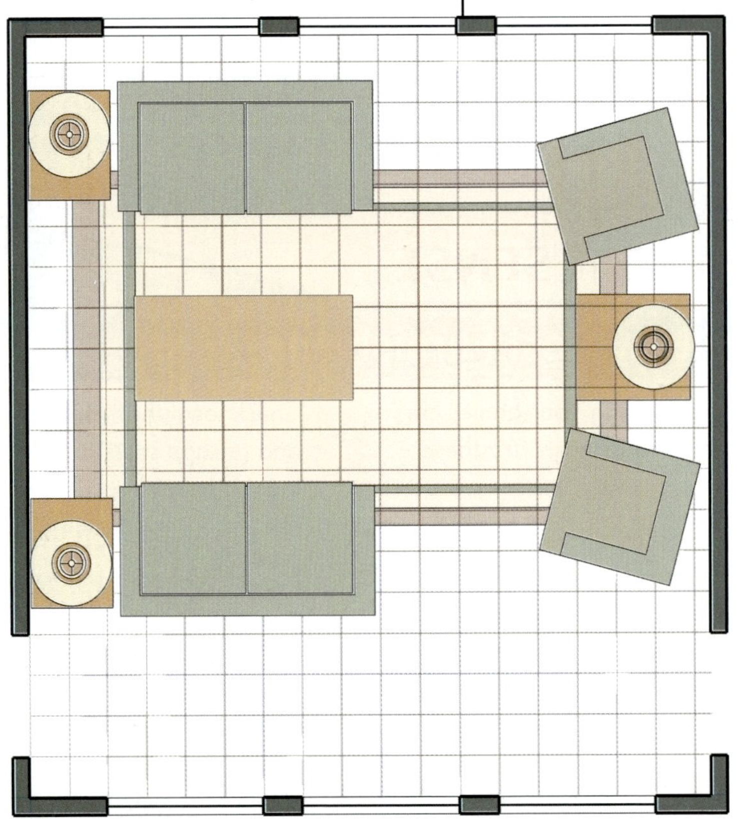

Team Activity. Have teams of students clip pictures from magazines to create a collage of items they would use to furnish a bedroom or living room area.

Discussion. ***Ask:*** What features would you look for when shopping for furniture? Which would you consider most important: quality, looks, or cost?

Checking for Quality in Case Goods

- Sturdy; doesn't wobble.
- Drawers open and close smoothly.
- Drawer stops to prevent drawers from pulling free.
- Smooth corners.
- Back panels screwed firmly in place.
- Doors meet evenly.
- Doors close correctly.
- Handles and hinges firmly attached.
- No scratches or other damage.

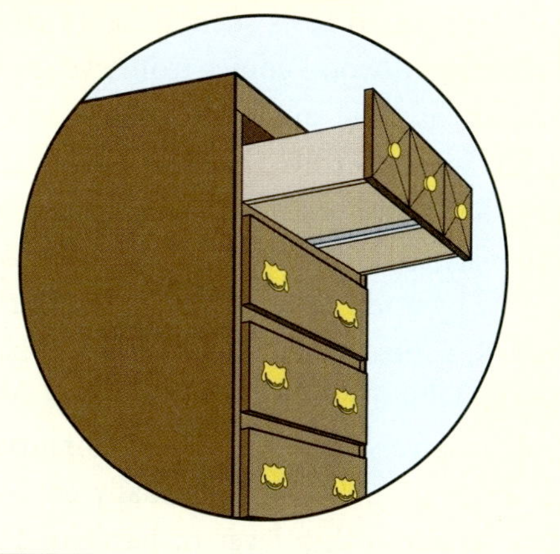

23-16 **Well-built case goods have these characteristics. Why should you open and close all drawers?**

CHOOSING FURNITURE

Once you have a plan for what items you want to buy and your price range, you're ready to go shopping. Take your floor plan measurements with you. Also check the measurements of any areas that might cause problems when items are delivered, such as low ceilings or narrow doorways. If you want the new furniture to coordinate with items you already have, bring along samples of their colors and fabrics.

As you shop for furniture, keep in mind your stage of life, family situation, and way of life. For example, if you expect to move from place to place before you settle down, you might decide to look for versatile furniture that can be taken apart and reassembled easily. Families with children should look for items that will wear well and clean easily.

Unless you're looking for an inexpensive item for short-term use, remember that you might have a piece of furniture for a long time. To ensure that you'll be happy with your purchase in years to come, follow these guidelines:

- Look for designs that are practical and won't become dated.
- Select items that are comfortable. When shopping for a chair, for example, check that the angle formed by the seat and back feels right to you. A chair that a tall person finds comfortable may be very uncomfortable for a short person.
- Make sure items are sturdy and well made.

Before you buy any furniture, learn how to check for quality. The signs of quality to look for depend on the type of furniture: case goods, upholstered furniture, or beds.

Case Goods

Case goods are items of furniture that have no padding, fabric, springs, or covering. Examples include tables, dressers, and desks. They may be made of wood, metal, or plastic. Figure 23-16 explains how to check for quality in case goods.

Community Activity. Tell students to visit a furniture store in the area and check the quality of at least three pieces of case goods and/or upholstered furniture, using the checklists on pages 603 and 604. Have them note how, if at all, the quality correlated to the price of each piece.

The most expensive wood furniture is made from solid wood. Hardwood comes from broad-leafed trees such as oak, maple, and cherry. Softwood comes from evergreen trees such as pine and cedar. Softwood is generally less expensive than hardwood, and it scratches more easily. It is often used for country-style furniture that is not made unsightly by a few scratches or nicks. **Particleboard**, a substance made from wood particles and adhesives bonded together, is even less expensive than softwood. Furniture made from particleboard is usually covered with a **veneer**, a thin layer of hardwood or softwood that gives a pleasing appearance.

Upholstered Furniture

Upholstered furniture has a wooden frame, padding, and springs on the inside, and fabric and cushions on the outside. Sofas and chairs are the most common types. Upholstered furniture is harder to check for quality than case goods because much of the construction is hidden. A salesperson may be able to answer your questions about the interior construction. Also look for the signs of quality listed in Figure 23-17.

Beds

You spend one-third of your time sleeping, so it makes sense to buy a well-made, comfortable bed. The most popular type of bed is a mattress and box spring with a bed frame for support. A firm mattress offers more back support than a soft mattress and is usually recommended. You can lie on different beds in stores to judge their relative firmness.

The overall quality of mattresses and box springs is determined by the size, number, and quality of the springs they contain. Knowledgeable salespeople or store displays may provide this information. Some stores have cutaway models that show the construction of different brands.

Critical Thinking. ***Ask:*** Why is price not necessarily a guarantee of quality when choosing furniture?

23-17

Examine upholstered furniture carefully, and test how it feels when you sit on it. Why is a sturdy frame particularly important?

Checking for Quality in Upholstered Furniture

- Strong frame; no movement or squeaks.
- Thick, even padding.
- Durable, stain-resistant fabric.
- Matching pattern at visible seams.
- Even hems and pleats.
- Snugly fitting cushions.
- Protective covers for arms.
- Reinforcing braces at points of stress.

InfoSource. Have students compare at least two models of a major appliance, using Web sites and such publications as *Consumer Reports*.

Class Activity. Hold up pictures of various models of large appliances (from ads and catalogs). Have students identify features and make comparisons.

InfoSource

Appliance Ratings

When researching major appliances, check out the ratings in published reports and on the Internet.

- Consult publications such as *Consumer Reports* for ratings based on rigorous testing by experts.
- Look for Web sites that provide ratings based on user input. Although some of the information supplied by users may be unreliable, these sites can provide you with clues about customer satisfaction.

SELECTING APPLIANCES

When choosing large appliances such as a refrigerator, range, or dishwasher, it makes sense to shop carefully. These are expensive items, and you want to make sure you choose appliances that have the features that are right for you.

Research

Start by researching the quality and features of different brands and models. In addition to checking published and online sources, ask friends and relatives which brands they recommend. You might also ask people who repair appliances for their input. As you do your research, take note of the size of appliances. Check to see whether you can not only fit them in the available space, but get them through doorways and stairways on the way.

Comparison Shopping

Once you have some brands and models in mind, you can check out appliances in different stores. When you compare prices, calculate the total cost of the purchase. The total cost includes the selling price, the cost of delivery, and the installation fee, along with the cost of a service contract if you choose to have one. For a major appliance such as a refrigerator, you'll probably want to compare the total cost from two or three different stores.

If you can't afford to buy a new appliance, look into purchasing a reconditioned model. This is a used appliance that has been overhauled to restore it to good working condition.

Don't make a decision based on price alone. Two different stores may carry the same appliance at the same price, but one of them may offer a more comprehensive warranty or a better service contract. Check to see if any of the stores or manufacturers offer rebates. Ask about delivery and installation charges and financing arrangements. One store may offer more favorable terms than another.

For more about warranties, refer to Section 16.2.

Class Activity. Ask students to compare two refrigerator models: a standard model that uses 500 kWh per year, and an Energy Star model that uses 350 kWh per year. Have them calculate how much energy and money the more efficient model would save over 20 years at a rate of 6 cents per kWh.

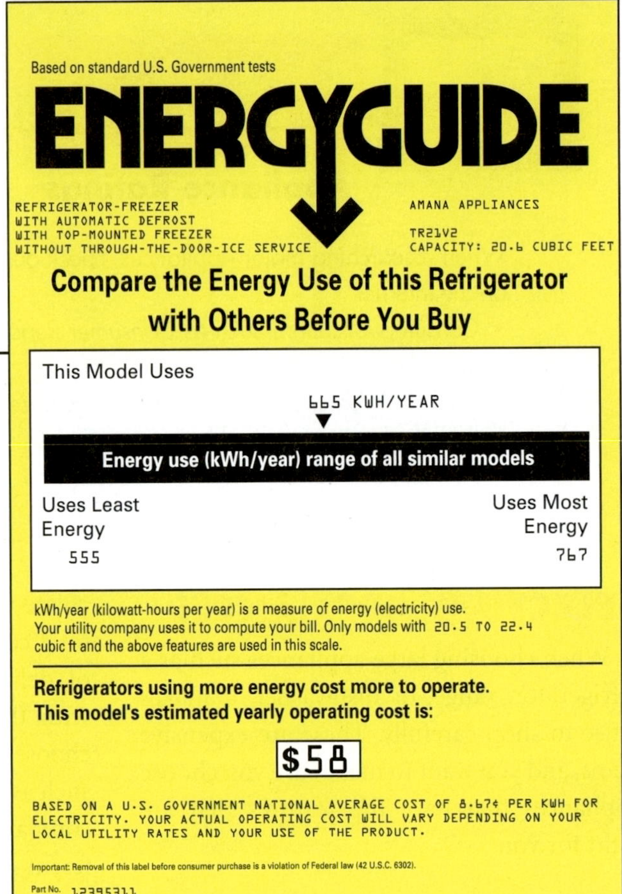

23-18

The EnergyGuide label enables you to compare the energy efficiency of different appliance models. What is the estimated annual energy consumption for the model shown here?

Caption Answer. The estimated annual energy consumption for this model is 665 kilowatt-hours per year.

Energy Efficiency

When purchasing a major appliance, look for energy-efficient features. A feature that saves energy will save you money in the long run. Identifying energy-efficient appliances is made easier by two label programs.

- **EnergyGuide.** An **EnergyGuide label**, as shown in Figure 23-18, is a black and yellow label that gives information about energy consumption. It is required by law on new major appliances such as refrigerators, freezers, dishwashers, and clothes washers. The label shows the estimated annual energy consumption for the model it is attached to, the range of energy use for similar models, and the estimated yearly operating cost.
- **Energy Star.** An **Energy Star label** is a green and blue label indicating that a product has outstanding energy efficiency. See Figure 23-19. Energy Star labels are awarded by the Environmental Protection Agency and the Department of Energy. Only products that meet certain energy efficiency standards receive an Energy Star label. Products that may earn the label include not only refrigerators, dishwashers, and other large appliances,

Class Activity. Have students develop a form that families could use to keep records of appliance service or repairs.

Answer Key. Answers to the Section Review questions are provided in the Section Lesson Plan located in the *Teacher Resource Guide.*

23-19

An Energy Star label tells you that a product meets certain energy efficiency standards. How might you benefit from choosing an appliance that carries this label?

but TVs, VCRs, light fixtures, and computers. The label is also given to new homes and other buildings that have outstanding energy efficiency ratings.

Keeping Records

When you purchase an appliance, keep all documents relating to the purchase. These include the sales receipt, the warranty, and any manuals or instruction booklets. Before using the appliance, study the operating instructions carefully. Failure to do so could result in injury and lead to costly repairs. Damage caused by misuse is excluded from warranty protection. See Figure 23-20.

23-20

If you have the appliance serviced or repaired, keep the service records. They will be useful if you need to document a recurring problem and justify a replacement.

Section 23.4 Review

CHECK YOUR UNDERSTANDING

1. Why is it a good idea to make a floor plan before shopping for furniture?
2. Name three signs that indicate that a sofa is well constructed.
3. What should you keep in mind when comparing the prices of major appliances?

CONSUMER APPLICATION

Appliance Investigation Investigate the refrigerators offered at a local appliance store or an online shopping site. Find the model that uses the least energy and the one that uses the most energy. Compare their features, selling prices, and estimated operating costs. What conclusions can you draw?

Objectives

After studying this section, you should be able to:

- Describe the benefits of home maintenance.
- Explain how to prevent accidents, fires, and poisonings in the home.
- Give examples of ways to promote energy efficiency in the home.

Key Terms

home maintenance
preventive maintenance

SECTION 23.5

Maintaining a Home

Whether you rent or own a home, you'll want to keep it clean and in good repair. The key to efficient home maintenance is to develop systems that work. Safety and energy efficiency are important aspects of running a home, too.

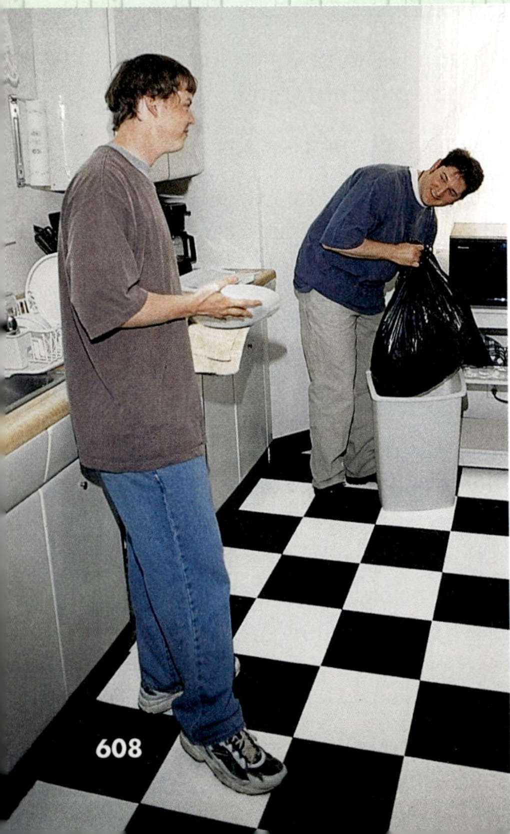

THE BENEFITS OF MAINTENANCE

Home maintenance involves tasks performed to keep a home in good condition. It includes regular cleaning and preventive care. The benefits of good maintenance include:

- **A clean and pleasant environment.** Wouldn't you prefer to return to a clean and tidy home at the end of the day? With regular maintenance, you can enjoy having a home that is welcoming, and you can take pleasure in inviting others into your home.
- **A healthy and safe environment.** Cleanliness protects your health. By cleaning up food scraps and keeping the kitchen clean, you prevent the growth of bacteria and avoid attracting insects and other pests. Cleaning also prevents mold and mildew from developing. A clean and well-maintained environment is a safer

Critical Thinking. ***Ask:*** What are the potential dangers of failing to keep a home in good condition? What are the potential costs?

environment. When you clean up spills and store items in safe places, you help to prevent accidents in the home.

- **Reduced wear and tear.** Keeping furniture clean and polished helps it look better and last longer. Maintaining appliances and other equipment helps them work more efficiently and reduces the cost of repairs and replacement.
- **A more valuable home.** When you invest in a home of your own, you hope that its resale value will increase over the years that you own it. Taking care of your home will help ensure that people will want to buy your home and pay a good price for it.

Maintenance is an important responsibility, but it doesn't have to be overwhelming. The key is to establish systems, schedules, and routines that are workable and efficient.

Class Activity. Have students develop a cleaning schedule for their future family, based on the suggested time frames for cleaning in Figure 23-21.

CLEANING

Don't wait until you can't stand the dirt any longer before you start cleaning! The best way to approach the task is to establish a regular schedule. Some routine cleaning tasks need to be done daily, others weekly, and others monthly or less often. Use Figure 23-21 as a guide for developing your own cleaning schedule.

Cleaning Efficiently

Like any task, cleaning is easier and faster when you approach it systematically. Learn which tools and products to use for different

23-21

Although standards about cleaning vary, most people would agree that some tasks need to be done more often than others. **Which of the tasks listed do you tend to neglect?**

Suggested Time Frames for Cleaning

DAILY:
- Wash dishes.
- Wipe kitchen counters, sink, and cooktop.
- Make beds and straighten rooms.
- Take out garbage.

WEEKLY OR AS NEEDED:
- Vacuum, sweep, or mop floors.
- Dust furniture.
- Clean bathroom sink, shower or tub, and toilet.
- Clean cooktop and other frequently used kitchen appliances.
- Change bedding.
- Do laundry.

MONTHLY OR AS NEEDED:
- Clean refrigerator and freezer.
- Clean oven.
- Wash windows.
- Vacuum or wash window coverings.
- Dust or clean window blinds.
- Straighten and clean kitchen shelves, cupboards, and drawers.
- Straighten closets.

EVERY SIX MONTHS OR AS NEEDED:
- Clean drapes.
- Clean woodwork and walls.
- Wash blankets and bedspreads.
- Clean closets.

Research Activity. Ask students to research a method for performing a basic household cleaning task and demonstrate the technique in class.

Class Activity. Have students develop a plan that a family could use to keep its home clutter-free in ten minutes a day.

tasks and how to use them without wasted motion and effort. Many books, magazine articles, and Web sites offer tips for efficient cleaning.

Good habits can reduce the amount of cleaning that needs to be done. To keep clutter from building up, put away items such as clothes, shoes, books, and CDs when you finish using them. Sort the mail each day and throw away any that you don't want. Follow the rule: "A place for everything and everything in its place."

Clean as you go. If you spill something, wipe it up right away. After brushing your teeth, rinse and wipe the sink. As you prepare a meal, place dirty utensils in soapy water or the dishwasher. To keep floors from getting dirty, place a sturdy doormat outside and inside every entrance and use it to wipe your shoes.

PREVENTIVE MAINTENANCE

A home does not take care of itself. Throughout the year you need to perform certain preventive maintenance tasks to keep things running smoothly. **Preventive maintenance** involves taking actions to prevent problems from occurring or to prevent minor problems from becoming major ones. Paying attention to preventive maintenance can save you money in the long run.

Some preventive maintenance tasks, such as checking the furnace filter and replacing it when necessary, need to be done each month

23-22

You can adapt this schedule to the type of home you have and to the area where you live. Which of these tasks might renters need to perform?

Suggested Preventive Maintenance Schedule

SPRING	SUMMER	FALL
• Remove storm windows and install screens. • Have air conditioning system professionally serviced. • Inspect roof for damage from ice and snow. Repair as necessary. • Make sure gutters and downspouts are clear. • Repair winter damage to sidewalks and driveways. • Change batteries in smoke alarms and carbon monoxide detectors. • Check attic for adequate ventilation.	• Repair any damage to porches, decks, and patios. • Check outside faucets for leaks and repair if necessary. • Apply caulking around windows and doors where needed. • Check outdoor recreation equipment for damage. Repair as necessary.	• Have heating system professionally serviced. • Empty gasoline from lawn mower so that it can be safely stored for the winter. • Remove screens and install storm windows. • Have chimney inspected and cleaned. • Change batteries in smoke alarms and carbon monoxide detectors. • Check attic for adequate insulation. • Clear gutters and downspouts. • Insulate pipes to prevent freezing.

Critical Thinking. ***Ask:*** Which home maintenance tasks could older children and teens do? What supervision might they require?

Team Activity. Have small groups of students make a list of home maintenance tasks and use one of the methods suggested for managing them.

23-23

If you move into a home that has high shelves, one of your first purchases should be a sturdy step stool. What's wrong with standing on a chair or another piece of furniture?

or every few months. Others need to be done in the spring, summer, or fall to prepare your home for the coming season. Homes in different parts of the country have different maintenance needs, depending on the climate. Figure 23-22 suggests some projects that you might place on your preventive maintenance schedule.

DELEGATING MAINTENANCE TASKS

In many households, home maintenance is a shared responsibility. Pitching in gives everyone the satisfaction of contributing, and more can be accomplished in a shorter time. Together, make a list of tasks and decide how to assign them. You might let people choose the tasks they prefer, draw tasks at random, or work out a rotating schedule. Keep in mind that some people may not be physically able to do certain tasks. Once you agree on the assignments, post the list so there can be no arguments over who is responsible for what.

If you'd rather spend money than time, you may decide to recruit paid help, such as a home cleaning or lawn care service. Ask family members, friends, or neighbors for recommendations. Make sure you know exactly what services you're paying for. You can usually adjust the frequency or extent of service to suit your budget. If any service is not what you expected, speak up. The company may be eager to remedy the situation. If not, you can try another company.

HOME SAFETY

Thousands of serious injuries occur in homes every day. The most common types of injuries result from falls. Other types of home injuries include burns, electrical shocks, and poisonings. An important part of home maintenance, then, involves keeping your home safe.

Preventing Accidents

Most falls occur in kitchens and bathrooms and on stairs. To prevent falls in the home, wipe up spills immediately, use nonskid rugs, and keep stairways well lighted and free from clutter. To avoid tripping over something at night, keep a lamp beside the bed and install nightlights in hallways. If you need something that's out of reach, don't stand on a chair—use a sturdy step stool or ladder. See Figure 23-23.

Class Activity. Have students develop a home safety checklist based on the guidelines in this section of the textbook. Suggest that they use this checklist to evaluate the safety of their own homes and suggest any needed improvements to adults in the family.

23-24 Smoke detectors save lives and property. Many safety experts recommend installing new batteries twice a year. Do you have enough smoke detectors in your home?

To prevent scalds and burns, set your water heater thermostat to 120°F or below. When cooking, make sure that pot handles are turned inward so they won't accidentally be bumped. Use potholders and oven mitts when handling hot containers. Place guards or screens around fireplaces and wood-burning stoves.

Prevent electrical shocks by replacing any broken or frayed electrical cords. Keep all electrical appliances away from water and cover unused electrical outlets with safety covers.

Preventing Fires

Many home fires are caused by careless behavior. To prevent fires in the home, keep matches and lighters out of the reach of children. Make sure that anyone who uses smoking materials extinguishes them correctly. Prevent grease fires by keeping cooktops and ovens clean. Keep potholders and towels away from the range. Never use flammable substances, such as aerosols, near a source of heat. Keep space heaters away from fabrics such as drapes or sheets. Have fire extinguishers handy in areas such as the kitchen and garage, and learn how to use them correctly. To help ensure that everyone gets out if there is a fire, install at least one smoke detector on each level of your home and test the smoke detectors regularly. See Figure 23-24.

Community Activity. Have students contact their local utility company to find out whether it offers home energy audits for homeowners.

Preventing Poisonings

Young children are curious and can't read labels. The best way to prevent poisonings is to keep all poisonous products out of their reach or locked away. Store cleaning products on a high shelf, not under the sink. Store all medicines in child-resistant containers in a locked cabinet. Prevent carbon monoxide poisonings by having furnaces checked regularly and by installing carbon monoxide detectors. Keep the number of the nearest poison control center next to the telephone so that you can call and get advice if there is an emergency.

Preparing for Emergencies

No matter where you live, there's always the possibility that some type of emergency may strike. The power may be out for an extended time, or you may have to take shelter from a severe storm. You can prepare for these and other events by having emergency supplies at hand. Basic supplies include a flashlight, battery-operated radio, extra batteries, candles, bottled water, canned food, and a first aid kit. Check with an organization such as the Red Cross to see how they recommend that you prepare for various types of emergencies.

THE ENERGY EFFICIENT HOME

In addition to keeping your home safe, you'd be smart to keep it energy efficient. Energy efficiency is good for the environment, and it saves money. If you buy new appliances, make sure they are energy efficient. In addition, follow these energy-saving tips:

Answer Key. Answers to the Section Review questions are provided in the Section Lesson Plan located in the *Teacher Resource Guide*.

More tips for conserving energy can be found in Section 3.3.

- Install weather stripping around doors and windows to help reduce heat loss in winter and to keep warm air out in summer.
- Wrap your water heater in an insulating jacket.
- Make sure the attic has enough insulation.
- Install programmable thermostats so that you can set the temperature lower (in winter) or higher (in summer) when you're sleeping or not at home.
- Use a humidifier in the winter. Humid air feels warmer, so you can set the thermostat lower.

Section 23.5 Review

CHECK YOUR UNDERSTANDING

1. How does preventive maintenance save money?
2. Give three examples of ways to prevent falls in the home and three examples of ways to prevent fires.
3. How do programmable thermostats help you save energy and money?

CONSUMER APPLICATION

Energy Efficiency Make a list of measures that could be taken to improve the energy efficiency of the home where you live now.

CHAPTER 23

Review & Activities

CHAPTER SUMMARY

- Many factors influence people's decisions about choosing a home. Various types of housing are available to rent and to buy. (23.1)
- Finding a rental home requires a thorough search and evaluation. Before renting, learn about leases, rights, and responsibilities. (23.2)
- Prospective home buyers must learn about costs and financing and follow specific steps. (23.3)
- Develop a plan to furnish your home over time, and then shop carefully. (23.4)
- Regular maintenance adds to the comfort and value of a home. Safety and energy efficiency are important considerations. (23.5)

THE $avvy Consumer

Sight Unseen: Alicia went to look at a rental unit in a large apartment complex. The manager told her that the unit to be rented was being painted, but she could show Alicia an identical apartment in another building. What value, if any, would this be to Alicia? Should Alicia rent the apartment based on seeing the identical one? What other options does she have? (23.2)

Reviewing Key Terms and Ideas

1. Explain five factors that affect housing choices. (23.1)
2. How are **duplexes, row houses**, and **townhouses** similar and different? (23.1)
3. How does **condominium ownership** differ from traditional home ownership? (23.1)
4. What are the financial advantages and disadvantages of owning a home? Of renting a home? (23.1)
5. Why should you inspect a rental unit before signing a contract? (23.2)
6. What is the purpose of a **lease**? Give five examples of the information it typically includes. (23.2)
7. What are two rights and two responsibilities of tenants? Of landlords? (23.2)
8. How do a conventional **mortgage** and an adjustable rate mortgage differ? (23.3)
9. Describe the process of finding a home to purchase. (23.3)
10. Why must home buyers pay **earnest money**? (23.3)
11. Could a home sale involve multiple **counteroffers**? Explain. (23.3)
12. What are the drawbacks to renting furniture and appliances? (23.4)
13. Explain how to plan what furnishings to buy for a new apartment. (23.4)
14. What are some examples of **case goods**? (23.4)
15. What does **home maintenance** include? Why is it beneficial? (23.5)
16. Name three ways to make a home more energy efficient. (23.5)

Answer Key. Answers to the Chapter Review & Activities are provided in the Teacher's Manual in the *Teacher Annotated Edition* of the text.

Thinking Critically

1. **Analyzing Economic Concepts:** Suppose you invest in a home. How can the value of your home be affected by nearby properties? (23.1, 23.3)
2. **Identifying Alternatives:** If your furniture budget is small, what low-cost items might you substitute for a dining table, a desk, an entertainment center, and a sofa? (23.4)
3. **Negotiating Decisions:** Explain how you would handle these disagreements with a spouse: **a**) You like city life, but your spouse wants a house in the country. **b**) Your spouse wants to pay more than you planned for a great house, and you want to stick to the financial limit you set. **c**) Your spouse takes on very few responsibilities for household care and maintenance. (23.1, 23.3, 23.5)

Building Consumer Skills

1. **Location, Location:** Imagine that you're searching for a place to live. Create a checklist for evaluating neighborhoods and communities based on your own priorities. (23.1)
2. **Rental Search:** Make a list of available one-bedroom rental units in a neighborhood or community of your choice. Explain what sources you used to find the rental units. Calculate the average monthly rent for furnished and unfurnished units. Compare information in class. (23.2)
3. **Figuring Expenses:** Find the rent on an apartment you might choose as a young single person. Estimate the move-in costs and the total cost per month to live there. What income would you need to have? (23.2)
4. **Purchasing Process:** Draw a diagram that shows the sequence of steps from the time buyers find a home to the time they become owners. Include alternative paths to show how the steps might vary. (23.3)
5. **Evaluating Furnishings:** Evaluate the quality of one large furniture item for sale new or used, such as an entertainment center or sofa. Explain what you observed. How would you rate the quality of this item? Why? (23.4)
6. **Safety Tips:** Choose one of the common causes of injuries in the home. Create a poster or other visual presentation that illustrates tips for preventing those injuries. (23.5)

CONSUMER CONNECTIONS

- **Family:** Would your family like to share household maintenance and cleaning tasks more equitably? With family members, create a list of tasks, and decide how to divide responsibilities. Include daily, weekly, monthly, and seasonal chores. (23.5)
- **Community:** What rental options would someone who uses a wheelchair have in your community? Do buildings have elevators and ramps? Are sidewalks accessible? Is transportation available? What improvements, if any, would you suggest? (23.2)

GLOSSARY

401(k) plan. A type of defined-contribution pension plan to which the employee contributes on a pretax basis. **(13.2)**

A

acceleration clause. A provision in an installment loan contract that gives the seller the right to declare the whole balance due if the buyer misses even one installment payment. **(11.4)**

accessories. Items that complete an outfit, such as scarves, ties, jewelry, belts, and hats. **(18.1)**

accredited. Officially recognized as maintaining standards that will qualify students for additional education or for work in their chosen profession. **(4.3)**

add-on clause. A loan contract provision that allows purchases to be added to an existing installment loan, with earlier purchases used as security for later ones. **(11.4)**

à la carte. A term describing menu items ordered and priced separately. **(21.4)**

allowances. Factors on IRS Form W-4 that affect the amount of income tax withholding. **(8.3)**

annual percentage yield (APY). The actual annual rate at which interest is earned, including the effects of compounding. **(12.3)**

annuity. A contract purchased from an insurance company that guarantees to provide payments at regular intervals in the future, usually after age 59½. **(13.4)**

antitrust laws. Laws designed to regulate unfair business practices that reduce competition. **(5.3)**

appraisal. An estimate of value made by a qualified person. **(14.3)**

apprenticeship. A training program that combines classroom instruction with paid on-the-job experience under the guidance of a skilled worker. **(4.3)**

APR. Annual percentage rate; the annual rate of interest that is charged for using credit. **(11.3)**

aptitudes. Natural talents. **(4.2)**

APY. *See* **annual percentage yield**.

arbitration. A procedure in which a neutral person or panel listens to both sides of a dispute, weighs the evidence, and reaches a decision. **(1.5)**

archive. To put documents in long-term storage in an area that is not immediately accessible. **(9.4)**

assets. Items of value that you own, including money. **(9.1)**

assigned-risk pool. A group of drivers within a state who are unable to obtain auto insurance on their own. **(14.2)**

ATM. Automated teller machine; a computer terminal that gives bank customers electronic access to their accounts at any time through the use of a specially coded card. **(10.2)**

B

bait and switch. A deceptive practice in which a retailer advertises a product that it has no intention of selling, hoping to persuade customers to buy a higher-priced product. **(1.4)**

balance of payments. An accounting of all of a nation's financial transactions that involve other countries during a particular time period. **(7.1)**

balance of trade. The difference between the value of a nation's exports and its imports. **(7.1)**

balance sheet. A statement of what you own and what you owe. **(9.1)**

balloon payment. A final loan payment that is much larger than the other installments. **(11.4)**

bankruptcy. Legal relief from repaying certain debts. **(11.5)**

bartering. Exchanging goods or services with another person. **(2.2)**

base price. The price of a vehicle with its standard equipment. **(19.3)**

bed-and-breakfast. A privately owned home that offers lodging with the morning meal included in the price. **(20.3)**

beneficiary. A person or group designated to receive some or all of a deceased person's assets. **(13.5)**

bias. A preference that might prevent impartial judgment. **(2.4)**

biodegradable. Able to decompose naturally in the environment. **(3.3)**

blends. Combinations of different fibers. **(18.2)**

bonded. Carries insurance to cover financial loss caused by a third party. **(16.4)**

bonds. Certificates of debt. **(13.4)**

book value. The estimated value of a given make, model, and year of vehicle. **(19.3)**

broadband. High-speed Internet access. **(17.3)**

budget. 1. An estimate of anticipated income and expenses for a certain period of time. **(6.2)** 2. A plan for spending and saving based on income and expenses. **(9.1)**

budget deficit. An amount by which spending exceeds revenue. **(6.2)**

budget surplus. An amount by which revenue exceeds spending. **(6.2)**

bulk foods. Foods displayed in covered bins from which customers can scoop the desired amount into a plastic bag. **(21.3)**

business cycles. The ups and downs of the economy. **(6.1)**

C

calorie. A unit of energy. **(21.1)**

canceled check. A check that is stamped and perforated by a financial institution to show that it's been paid. **(10.3)**

capital. Machines and technology used in the production of goods and services. **(5.2)**

capitalized cost reduction. An up-front payment, made when leasing a vehicle, that results in a lower monthly fee. **(19.2)**

career. A series of related jobs or achievements through which a person progresses in a particular field. **(4.1)**

case goods. Items of furniture that have no padding, fabric, springs, or covering. **(23.4)**

cashier's check. A check issued and guaranteed by a bank. **(10.4)**

cash value. In a permanent life insurance policy, the accumulated value of the additional amounts paid in premiums beyond actual insurance coverage and of investment earnings on those amounts. **(14.5)**

certificate of deposit (CD). A certificate issued by a financial institution to indicate that money has been deposited for a certain term. **(12.4)**

certified check. A check from a personal checking account that has been stamped by the bank to guarantee that there are sufficient funds in the account to cover it. **(10.4)**

chain letter. A message sent by postal mail or email that instructs the recipient to send copies to a certain number of other people. **(1.4)**

citizenship. The way you respond to being a member of a community or other group. **(3.2)**

claim. A request made by the holder of an insurance policy for payment of a loss. **(14.1)**

class action suit. A lawsuit filed on behalf of a group of people who all have the same complaint. **(1.5)**

classics. Fashions that don't go out of style. **(18.1)**

closed-end credit. A one-time extension of credit for a specific amount and time period. **(11.1)**

closing costs. Various fees that must be paid by the buyer or the seller at the time the purchase of a home is finalized. **(23.3)**

co-insurance. An arrangement in which the insurance company and the insured person share the costs of claims after the deductible is met. **(14.1)**

collateral. Property that is pledged to guarantee repayment of a loan. **(11.1)**

collection agency. A business that collects unpaid debt for others. **(11.5)**

command economy. An economic system in which decisions about what to produce, how, and for whom are decided by a central government. **(5.1)**

commercial banks. Financial institutions owned by shareholders and operated for their profit. **(10.1)**

commission. A fixed percentage or amount of profit given to an employee in exchange for making a sale. **(8.1)**

commodities. Basic economic goods bought and sold in quantity, such as wheat, corn, iron ore, natural gas, and precious metals. **(13.4)**

comparison shopping. Checking several alternatives to make sure you are getting the best price on an item. **(16.3)**

competition. Rivalry between two or more businesses that offer similar goods or services. Each tries to win a larger share of the market. **(5.2)**

compound interest. Interest calculated on both deposits made and prior interest earned. **(12.3)**

condominium ownership. A form of home ownership that involves individual ownership of a unit and shared ownership of common areas such as hallways and exterior grounds. **(23.1)**

conservation. The careful management and protection of valuable natural resources to ensure their quality and longevity. **(3.3)**

consignment shops. Stores that sell used items and give part of the sale price to the original owner. **(18.2)**

conspicuous consumption. Purchasing goods or services to impress others. **(2.3)**

consumer. Someone who uses goods and services. **(1.1)**

consumer action panels. Groups formed by trade associations to address consumer complaints. **(1.2)**

consumer advocates. People or organizations who work on behalf of consumers. **(1.2)**

consumer affairs departments. Departments (of businesses) that communicate with customers about their rights and needs as consumers. **(1.2)**

consumer finance companies. Businesses that specialize in making small or personal loans. **(11.4)**

consumer price index (CPI). A measurement of the change in prices over time of a specific group of goods and services. **(6.1)**

contingency. A condition that must be met in order for the sale of a home to occur. **(23.3)**

contract. A legally binding agreement between two or more parties. **(16.4)**

convenience foods. Foods processed in ways that make them easier to use. **(21.2)**

cookies. Small files stored on a computer that enable a Web site to "remember" information about a visitor. **(1.3)**

cooperative. A business organization owned and operated by members for their own benefit. **(21.3)**

cooperative ownership. A form of home ownership that involves ownership of shares in a corporation that owns the entire property. **(23.1)**

co-payment. A flat fee given to a health care provider at the time of service. **(14.4)**

corporation. An organization that is owned by many people but treated by law as a single entity separate from its owners. **(5.2)**

cosigner. A person with a strong established credit history who signs a credit application and contract along with the borrower. **(11.2)**

CPI. *See* **consumer price index**.

cramming. Adding charges to a consumer's phone bill for services that were not ordered or received. **(17.2)**

credentials. Licenses, certifications, or degrees that indicate knowledge and experience in a certain subject area or qualification to perform a certain service. **(2.4, 9.5)**

credit. The supplying of money, goods, or services at present in exchange for the promise of future payment. **(11.1)**

credit bureau. A firm that collects information about the credit worthiness of consumers. **(11.2)**

credit counseling. Guidance provided by trained people who help consumers learn to live within their means. **(11.5)**

credit history. A pattern of past behavior in regard to repaying debt. **(11.2)**

credit limit. The maximum amount of credit that a creditor will extend to a borrower. **(11.3)**

creditor. A business or organization that extends credit. **(11.1)**

credit rating. An evaluation of a consumer's credit history. **(11.2)**

credit report. A record of a particular consumer's transactions and payment patterns. **(11.2)**

credit score. A numerical rating, based on credit report information, that represents a person's level of credit worthiness. **(11.2)**

credit union. A nonprofit financial institution owned by its members. **(10.1)**

critical thinking. Applying reasoning strategies in order to make sound decisions. **(2.4)**

D

Daily Values. Nutrient reference amounts set by the U.S. Food and Drug Administration for use on food labels. **(21.3)**

debit card. A card that allows the user to subtract money from a bank account in order to obtain cash or make a purchase. **(10.2)**

debt consolidation loan. A loan that combines all existing debt into a new loan with a more manageable payment schedule. **(11.5)**

deceptive advertising. Advertising that is likely to mislead consumers through false statements, omitted information, or other unfair means. **(1.4)**

deductible. A set amount an insured person must pay per loss before the insurer will pay benefits. **(14.1)**

deduction. On a paycheck, anything that is subtracted from gross pay. **(8.2)** *Also see* **tax deduction**.

default. Failure to fulfill the obligations of a loan. **(11.5)**

deficit spending. The practice of spending more money than was received in revenue. **(6.2)**

delinquent. Overdue. **(11.5)**

demand. The quantity of a particular good or service that consumers are willing and able to buy at a given price. **(5.2)**

dependent. Someone who is supported by a taxpayer's income. **(8.3)**

depreciation. Loss in value over time. **(14.2)**

depression. A major economic slowdown, longer lasting and more serious than a recession. **(6.1)**

dermatologist. A physician who specializes in treating the skin. **(18.4)**

dial-up access. Internet access through a regular telephone connection. **(17.3)**

Dietary Guidelines for Americans. Guidelines developed jointly by the U.S. Department of Agriculture and the Department of Health and Human Services to offer advice about food and physical activity choices for health. **(21.1)**

dietary supplements. Products taken by mouth for the purpose of increasing one's intake of nutrients or other dietary substances. **(22.2)**

direct deposit. An arrangement in which pay is electronically transferred directly into the recipient's bank account. **(8.2)**

direct mail advertising. Printed advertising sent through the mail to consumers' homes. **(15.1)**

discount rate. The interest rate that banks pay when borrowing money from the Federal Reserve Bank. **(6.3)**

discretionary expenses. Expense categories that are not absolutely necessary, such as vacations or entertainment. **(9.3, 20.2)**

discretionary income. The amount of available income after taxes and necessary spending for food, clothing, and shelter. **(12.2)**

distance education programs. Educational programs that use various methods—such as the Internet, videotape, audio and video conferencing, and print materials—to teach students who are not present on campus. **(4.3)**

diversification. A strategy of making a variety of investments in order to reduce exposure to risk. **(13.1)**

dividend. A payment to shareholders that represents a portion of the company's net profits. **(13.3)**

down payment. A portion of a purchase price paid by cash or check at the time of purchase. **(11.4)**

dry cleaning. A process that cleans fabrics using special liquids instead of water. **(18.3)**

DSL. Digital subscriber line; technology that provides high-speed Internet access over ordinary telephone lines. **(17.3)**

duplex. A building that contains two separate living units. **(23.1)**

E

earnest money. A deposit to prove that a buyer is serious about purchasing a home. **(23.3)**

ecology. A science that deals with the relationships between living things and the environment. **(3.3)**

economic indicators. Measurements used to monitor the health of the economy. **(6.1)**

economics. The social science that examines how societies use scarce resources to produce and distribute goods and services that satisfy peoples' wants and needs. **(5.1)**

economic system. The way a society uses resources to satisfy its peoples' needs and wants. **(5.1)**

electronic funds transfer (EFT). The movement of funds by electronic means. **(10.2)**

embargo. A government order prohibiting trade. **(7.2)**

endorsement. 1. A signature on the back of a check that entitles the payee to either receive payment or transfer it to someone else. **(10.3)**
2. An attachment to a standard insurance policy that adds or

takes away coverage. Sometimes called a *rider.* **(14.1)** 3. An advertising message that appears to reflect the opinions, beliefs, findings, or experience of a person or group other than the advertiser. **(15.2)**

EnergyGuide label. A black and yellow label, found on major appliances, that gives information about energy consumption. **(23.4)**

Energy Star label. A green and blue label awarded by the Environmental Protection Agency and the Department of Energy to products with outstanding energy efficiency. **(23.4)**

entrée. (AHN-tray) Main course of a meal. **(21.4)**

entrepreneur. (on-truh-pruh-NOOR) Someone who owns a business or assumes the financial risk for a business. **(4.2)**

escrow account. A bank account in which money is held in trust. **(23.3)**

estate. The assets and liabilities of a deceased person. **(13.5)**

estate planning. Making legal and financial arrangements for how one's property should be administered before and after death. **(13.5)**

ethics. Values about right and wrong that serve as guidelines for human behavior. **(3.1)**

evict. To legally force a tenant to vacate a rental unit before the lease has expired. **(23.2)**

exchange rate. The cost of one currency expressed in terms of another currency. **(7.1)**

exclusions. Specific risks not covered by an insurance policy. **(14.1)**

executor. The individual who is in charge of handling the affairs of an estate. **(13.5)**

exhaust emissions. Pollutants that are released when gasoline is burned. **(19.1)**

expiration date. Date on a food package indicating the last day that the product should be eaten. **(21.3)**

export. A product sent to a foreign country for sale. **(7.1)**

F

factory seconds. Products that may have slight defects that do not affect performance or appearance. **(16.1)**

fad diets. Weight loss plans that are based on misinformation and are not healthy or beneficial. **(22.2)**

fads. Interests, products, or styles that people take up with exaggerated enthusiasm for a brief time. **(2.3)**

family life cycle. The series of stages through which a family passes. **(2.1)**

fashion. A style that is popular at a particular time. **(18.1)**

FDIC. Federal Deposit Insurance Corporation; a federal agency that insures deposit accounts in most banks and savings associations. **(10.1)**

federal funds rate. The interest rate at which banks lend money to one another overnight. **(6.3)**

Federal Reserve Board. The governing body of the Federal Reserve System. **(6.3)**

Federal Reserve System. The central bank of the United States. **(6.3)**

fee-for-service plan. A plan under which you are charged for each medical service you receive, and your insurance plan pays a portion of that fee. **(14.4)**

finance charge. The cost of using credit, including interest and any fees. **(11.1)**

finishes. Treatments applied to fabrics to produce a certain look, feel, or performance. **(18.2)**

fiscal policy. The federal government's use of taxing and spending policies to help stabilize the economy. **(6.3)**

fixed expenses. Regular payments that don't vary in amount. **(9.3)**

flexible spending account. A benefit in which a predetermined amount from each paycheck is set aside to be used for qualified expenses. **(22.3)**

flextime. A system that allows flexible work hours. **(4.1)**

floor plan. A scale drawing showing the size and shape of a room. **(23.4)**

fossil fuels. Energy sources formed in the earth, such as coal, oil, and natural gas. **(3.3)**

fraud. Deceitful conduct designed to manipulate another person for some gain. **(1.4)**

free enterprise. An economic system in which individuals are free to own and control business enterprises that compete for profit with a minimum of government regulation. **(5.1)**

free trade. A government policy of minimizing trade restrictions. **(7.2)**

full warranty. Warranty that meets five federal standards for comprehensive warranties as specified in the Magnuson-Moss Warranty Act. **(16.2)**

G

garnishment. The legal withholding of a specified sum from a person's wages in order to collect a debt. **(11.5)**

GDP. *See* **gross domestic product.**

generic drug. A medication that is chemically identical to a brand-name drug but costs less. **(22.2)**

generics. "Plain label" products that do not have a brand name. **(16.3)**

goals. Targets for what you want to accomplish. **(2.1)**

goods. Physical objects that are produced for consumers. **(1.1)**

grace period. Period of time during which the balance on a credit card may be paid in full to avoid finance charges. **(11.3)**

gratuity. Money offered for a service that has been performed; a tip. **(21.4)**

gross domestic product (GDP). The total dollar value of goods and services produced in a country during the year. **(6.1)**

gross income. The total amount of money earned before taxes and other paycheck deductions. **(9.3)**

gross pay. On a paycheck, the total amount of money earned for working during the pay period. **(8.2)**

group practice. An arrangement in which two or more physicians join together to offer health care in a single location. **(22.3)**

H

hangtags. Removable tags attached to clothing. **(18.2)**

health maintenance organization (HMO). A health care group that offers medical care to members for a prepaid fee and small co-payments. **(14.4)**

hobby. An activity outside of a regular occupation that is pursued for enjoyment. **(20.1)**

home coverage area. The geographic area in which wireless phone calls don't incur roaming charges. **(17.2)**

home health aides. Health care professionals who come into a home to provide needed health care assistance. **(22.4)**

home maintenance. Tasks performed to keep a home in good condition. **(23.5)**

hostels. Inexpensive, supervised lodgings, often designed for young travelers. **(20.3)**

household inventory. A detailed list of personal belongings. **(14.3)**

hypoallergenic. Less likely to cause an allergic reaction. Used to describe grooming products. **(18.4)**

I-J-K

identity theft. The illegal use of an individual's personal information. **(1.3)**

implied warranty. A warranty that is legally in effect even though not in writing. **(16.2)**

import. A product brought in for sale from a foreign country. **(7.1)**

import quota. A government limit on the quantity or value of a certain imported product. **(7.2)**

impulse purchase. A purchase made on a whim, without planning. **(2.3)**

incentive. A reward offered to encourage a particular behavior, such as a purchase. **(15.3)**

individual retirement account. *See* **IRA.**

inflation. A general, prolonged rise in the prices of goods and services. **(6.1)**

infomercials. Television or radio ads that run 30 minutes or longer and are designed to resemble programming. **(15.1)**

installment. A set portion of a loan amount that the borrower must pay at regularly scheduled intervals. **(11.1)**

insurance. Purchased protection that guarantees to pay you in the event of certain specified losses. **(14.1)**

interest. A fee paid for the opportunity to use someone else's money over a period of time. **(6.1, 10.1)**

Internet bank. A financial institution that operates exclusively over the Internet using online banking. **(10.1)**

Internet service provider (ISP). A company that provides Internet access and related services to consumers and businesses. **(17.3)**

internship. A paid or unpaid short-term job offered to a student interested in entering a particular field. **(4.3)**

interview. A formal meeting that employers use to evaluate prospective employees. **(4.4)**

intestate. Without a valid will. **(13.5)**

investing. Committing money for the purpose of making a profit over time. **(12.1)**

investment club. A group of people who meet regularly to learn about investing and to make investments together. **(13.1)**

invoice price. The price the dealer pays the manufacturer for a vehicle. **(19.3)**

IRA. Individual retirement account; a personal savings plan that enables workers and their spouses to set aside money for retirement. **(13.2)**

ISP. *See* **Internet service provider.**

itemized deductions. On a tax return, a listing of the amounts actually spent on tax-deductible expenses during the year. **(8.3)**

itinerary. The route or schedule of a trip. **(20.3)**

Keogh plan. (KEY-oh) A federally approved, defined-contribution, tax-deferred retirement plan designed specifically for self-employed people. **(13.2)**

L

landlord. An owner of rental property. **(23.1)**

launder. To wash garments or other items by hand or machine using water and a soil-removing product. **(18.3)**

law of demand. Principle stating that when the price of a product goes down, demand for that product will generally go up; when the price goes up, demand will generally go down. **(5.2)**

law of supply. Principle stating that when the price of a product goes up, the supply will generally go up; when the price goes down, the supply will generally go down. **(5.2)**

leadership. The ability to inform and guide others. **(3.2)**

lease. 1. To make monthly payments in exchange for exclusive use of a vehicle for a specified period of time. **(19.2)** 2. A legal contract for renting a home that specifies the rights and responsibilities of the tenant and landlord. **(23.2)**

leisure time. Time that you have available to do whatever you choose. **(20.1)**

lemon laws. Laws that protect buyers of vehicles with serious defects. **(19.3)**

lessee. The person who leases a vehicle or other merchandise. **(19.2)**

liabilities. Debts or obligations owed to others. **(9.1)**

liability. Legal responsibility to pay someone who has suffered an injury or loss caused by another. **(14.1)**

lien. A claim upon property to satisfy a debt. **(11.5)**

limited warranty. A warranty that does not meet one or more of the standards of a full warranty but still provides valuable protection. **(16.2)**

liquidity. The ease with which savings or investments can be turned into cash to be spent. **(12.4)**

living trust. A legal arrangement that can serve as an alternative to a will. It transfers control of a living person's assets to a *trustee*, someone who holds and manages assets for someone else. **(13.5)**

living will. A legal document that outlines a person's wishes for medical treatment under specific circumstances. **(13.5)**

loan sharks. Unlicensed lenders who operate outside the law and charge excessive interest. **(11.4)**

loss leader. An item priced below the retailer's cost in order to attract customers to a store. **(15.3)**

M

maintenance schedule. A timetable for routine servicing and for checking or replacing parts. **(19.4)**

managed care plan. A health care plan that is designed to lower costs for both the insurer and the consumer while maintaining a high standard of care. **(14.4)**

management. The process of using resources effectively to reach goals. **(2.2)**

manufactured fibers. Fibers made from substances such as wood pulp and petroleum. **(18.2)**

market economy. An economic system in which decisions about what to produce, how, and for whom are decided by individuals acting in their own self-interest. **(5.1)**

marketplace. All of the goods and services available for sale to the general public. **(1.1)**

mass transit. Transportation systems designed to carry large numbers of people. **(19.1)**

media. Channels of mass communication, such as newspapers, magazines, radio, television, and related Web sites. **(1.2)**

mediation. A process in which two parties try to resolve a dispute with the help of a neutral third party. **(1.5)**

Medicaid. A program under which the federal and state

governments share the cost of medical aid to low-income families. **(14.4)**

Medicare. A program that pays some of the costs of medical and hospital care for people who are 65 and older and for some people under 65, such as those who are disabled. **(5.3)**

Medigap policies. Health insurance policies purchased from private companies to supplement Medicare coverage. **(14.4)**

mentor. An experienced coworker who acts as a guide or informal teacher for new employees. **(4.5)**

microprocessor. The electronic circuitry that tells a computer how to process information. **(17.4)**

minimum wage. The lowest hourly rate an employer may legally pay most workers. **(8.1)**

mixed economy. A combination of the command and market economic systems. **(5.1)**

modem. A device that enables a computer to send and receive data over telephone lines or other communication lines. **(17.3)**

monetary policy. Efforts by the Federal Reserve Board to stabilize the economy by regulating the money supply. **(6.3)**

money market account. A type of savings account in which deposits are invested by the financial institution to yield higher earnings. **(12.4)**

money order. A purchased certificate used to pay a specified amount to a particular payee. **(10.4)**

money supply. The total amount of money in circulation at any given time. **(6.3)**

monopoly. A situation in which a single company controls the supply of a good or service for which there is no close substitute. Also known as a *trust.* **(5.3)**

mortgage. Long-term home loan. **(23.3)**

MSRP. Manufacturer's suggested retail price; for a vehicle, it includes the base price, the price of options installed by the manufacturer, and the manufacturer's transportation charge. **(19.3)**

mutual fund. A group of investments that is held in common by many individual investors. **(13.4)**

mutual savings banks. State-chartered financial institutions operated by trustees for the benefit of depositors. **(10.1)**

N

NAFTA. *See* **North American Free Trade Agreement**.

nanny. A professional who has received training in child care and provides care in the child's home. **(22.4)**

national brands. Products with well-known, nationally advertised trade names. **(16.3)**

national debt. The total amount of money that the federal government owes. Also known as the *public debt.* **(6.2)**

natural fibers. Fibers that come from natural sources such as plants or animals. **(18.2)**

naturalization. The process by which a foreign-born person becomes a citizen. **(3.2)**

needs. Things you must have in order to live. **(2.1)**

net income. The amount of money you expect to receive after paycheck deductions. **(9.3)**

net pay. The amount of pay an employee is left with after taxes and other deductions are subtracted from gross pay. **(8.2)**

net weight. The weight of a product and any liquid in which the product is packed, not including the weight of the container. **(21.3)**

net worth. The difference between your assets and liabilities. **(9.1)**

no-fault insurance. A system under which no fault or blame is assigned in the event of a traffic accident, and all parties involved collect from their own insurance companies for losses up to their coverage limits. **(14.2)**

noncomedogenic. (non-koe-mee-doe-jeh-nik) Will not clog pores and lead to acne. Used to describe grooming products. **(18.4)**

nonrenewable resources. Natural resources that cannot replace themselves. **(3.3)**

North American Free Trade Agreement (NAFTA). A wide-ranging regional trade agreement between the United States, Canada, and Mexico. **(7.2)**

nutrient density. A comparison of the nutrients in a food to the amount of calories. **(21.1)**

nutrients. The substances found in food that enable the body to function properly. **(21.1)**

nutrition. The process of using food to nourish your body. **(21.1)**

O

obsolete. Out-of-date and no longer useful. **(17.1)**

online banking. Conducting business with financial institutions over the Internet. **(9.2)**

online bill payment. Paying bills electronically over the Internet. **(9.2)**

online bill presentment. Receiving bills electronically over the Internet. **(9.2)**

online profiling. A practice in which companies collect information about the Web sites a consumer visits, then use that information to predict what the consumer may buy in the future. **(1.3)**

open-end credit. Credit that can be used repeatedly. Sometimes referred to as a *line of credit.* **(11.1)**

opportunity cost. The value of the best alternative you give up when you decide to use resources one way rather than another. **(2.2)**

options. Features available on a vehicle at extra cost. **(19.3)**

outlet stores. Stores that sell merchandise from only one manufacturer, generally at less than full retail price. Also called *factory outlets.* **(16.1)**

outstanding. Refers to transactions received by the bank after the closing date of your bank statement. **(10.3)**

overdraft. Lack of sufficient funds to cover the full amount of a check. **(10.3)**

over-the-counter drugs. Medicines that can be purchased without a prescription. **(22.2)**

overtime. Work in excess of 40 hours per week. **(8.1)**

P-Q

particleboard. A substance made from wood particles and adhesives bonded together. **(23.4)**

payee. The one to whom a check is made out. **(10.3)**

pension plan. Any retirement plan offered to a company's employees. **(13.2)**

permanent life insurance. Insurance that gives a person protection for his or her entire lifetime. **(14.5)**

personal property. Property that can be moved, such as furniture, appliances, clothing, and jewelry. **(14.3)**

pharmacist. A person who has been trained and licensed to prepare and sell medicines. **(22.2)**

piecework. Work for which wages are based on the number of items or pieces produced. **(8.1)**

PIN. Personal identification number; a secret code that protects the security of accounts. **(10.2)**

planned obsolescence. The practice of purposely designing products to have a short life so that consumers will be forced to replace them. **(17.1)**

point-of-sale transaction. The act of paying for an item by making an electronic funds transfer at the place of purchase. **(10.2)**

point-of-service plan (POS). A managed care plan that provides the option of using health care providers outside the plan's network. **(14.4)**

points. One-time finance charges paid at the beginning of a loan. Each point is 1% of the loan amount. **(23.3)**

policy. The written agreement between a consumer who purchases insurance and the insurance company. **(14.1)**

portfolio. Collection of investments. **(13.1)**

POS. *See* **point-of-service plan**.

power of attorney. A legal document assigning someone the right to act on a person's behalf. **(13.5)**

preferred provider organization (PPO). A group of medical doctors, hospitals, and other health care providers who have agreed to extend services at reduced rates through an insurer or third-party administrator. **(14.4)**

premiums. Payments insured people make to the insurance company in exchange for coverage. **(14.1)**

prepaid cards. Cards sold in specified dollar amounts that can be used to purchase products or services. **(10.4)**

prescription drugs. Drugs that can be sold only with a written order from a health care professional and can be obtained only from a pharmacist. **(22.2)**

preventive maintenance. Taking actions to prevent problems from occurring or to prevent minor problems from becoming major ones. **(23.5)**

primary care physician. A physician who coordinates health care and provides general medical care. **(14.4, 22.3)**

principal. Original amount borrowed. **(11.1)**

priorities. Judgments about the relative importance of alternatives. **(2.1)**

private practice. An arrangement for providing medical care in which a physician works for himself or herself. **(22.3)**

pro bono. At no charge; refers to free legal services provided to clients who face extreme financial hardship. **(9.5)**

procrastinate. To put off taking action. **(2.2)**

productivity. A measure of the efficiency with which goods and services can be produced. **(5.2)**

profit. Earnings after all costs of production have been paid. **(5.2)**

progressive tax. A tax that takes a larger percentage of the income of high-income people than of low-income people. **(5.4)**

proportional tax. A tax that takes the same percentage out of everyone's income. **(5.4)**

prospectus. A legal document that provides potential investors with information about a mutual fund or other security. **(13.4)**

protectionism. A policy of using trade restrictions to protect domestic businesses from foreign competition. **(7.2)**

puffery. Exaggerated claims or descriptions intended to increase a product's reputation or appeal. **(15.2)**

pull date. Date on a food package indicating the last day the manufacturer recommends that the item be sold. **(21.3)**

pyramid scheme. An illegal get-rich-quick plan. Each participant pays a sum of money to join, then recruits several other people. Those people in turn pay a fee and recruit others. **(1.4)**

R

RAM. Random access memory; the main memory used by a computer to run the operating system and active programs. **(17.4)**

real estate. Land and any structures on it. **(13.4)**

rebate. A partial refund of an item's purchase price. **(15.3)**

rebuilt. Restored to good working condition; refers to used vehicle parts. **(19.4)**

recall. A manufacturer's request for owners to take a vehicle to a dealership for repair. **(19.4)**

recession. A period of significant decline in the economy, usually lasting six months to a year. **(6.1)**

reconcile. To bring a bank statement and your own record of transactions into agreement. **(10.3)**

reconditioned. Restored to good working condition; refers to used vehicle parts. **(19.4)**

recreation. Any activity that you find pleasurable and rejuvenating. **(20.1)**

redress. Remedy for a wrong or a loss. **(1.2)**

references. People who will recommend an applicant to an employer on the basis of character or ability. **(4.4)**

regressive tax. A tax that takes a larger percentage of the income of low-income people than of high-income people. **(5.4)**

renewable resources. Resources that replace themselves by natural cycles over time, such as plants, trees, water, soil, and air. **(3.3)**

repossession. Taking away property due to failure to make loan or credit payments. **(11.5)**

reservations. Arrangements to guarantee that lodgings or travel accommodations will be held for you. **(20.3)**

reserve requirement. The percentage of a bank's deposits that it must keep on hand. **(6.3)**

resources. Anything that is useful or helpful in the process of achieving goals or solving problems. **(2.2)**

résumé. (REH-zuh-MAY) A personal data sheet that describes a job seeker to prospective employers. **(4.4)**

retailers. Those who sell goods and services directly to consumers. **(1.1)**

return. The income that an investment produces. **(13.1)**

revenue. Money collected or received by a government for public use. **(5.4)**

right of rescission. The right, provided by the Truth in Lending Act, that gives borrowers up to three business days to cancel a loan or other credit transaction for which their home is pledged as security. **(11.4)**

risk. The possibility of variation in the return on an investment. **(13.1)**

roaming charge. A per-minute cost for using a wireless phone while outside a specific geographic area. **(17.2)**

Roth IRA. An IRA in which contributions are not tax-deductible; however, earnings accumulate tax-free. **(13.2)**

row houses. Houses that are attached at the side walls. **(23.1)**

S

safe deposit box. A locked box that can be rented in a secure area of a bank. **(9.4)**

salary. A set amount of money earned by an employee per

year or other fixed length of time. **(8.1)**

saving. Setting aside money for future use. **(12.1)**

savings and loans. Financial institutions that originally specialized in providing funds to home buyers, but now provide a variety of financial services. **(10.1)**

savings bonds. Nontransferable debt certificates issued by the U.S. Treasury. **(12.4)**

savings plan. A step-by-step approach for putting money aside in savings. **(12.2)**

scarcity. An economic principle stating that because of limited resources, an economic system can't possibly produce all the goods and services that people want; therefore, choices must be made about how the limited resources will be used. **(2.2)**

season tickets. A package deal that enables the purchaser to attend a series of events during a specified period for a lower cost per ticket. **(20.2)**

secured credit. Credit that is backed by a pledge of property. **(11.1)**

secure site. A Web site that uses safeguards to protect information from theft during transmission. **(1.3)**

security deposit. A sum of money that the landlord holds until the tenant moves out, to cover the cost of any damages caused by the tenant. **(23.2)**

service contract. An optional service agreement that may be purchased to provide protection beyond the warranty. Sometimes called an *extended warranty*. **(16.2)**

services. Actions that are performed for someone. **(1.1)**

severance package. Bonus pay or special benefits offered to laid-off workers. **(4.5)**

shareholders. People who have purchased shares of stock in a corporation and are therefore part-owners of the company. **(5.2, 13.3)**

shares. Individual units of ownership in a corporation. **(13.3)**

shoplifting. The theft of merchandise from stores. **(3.1)**

side effects. Reactions to a drug other than the intended effect. **(22.2)**

simple interest. Interest calculated only on money deposited, not on prior interest earned. **(12.3)**

slamming. Switching a consumer's phone service to a different company without permission. **(17.2)**

small claims court. A court of law in which disputes involving sums under a certain amount are resolved by a judge. **(1.5)**

Social Security. An insurance program that is sponsored by the federal government and pays benefits to qualified people. **(5.3)**

Social Security number. The unique nine-digit number used by the Social Security Administration to keep track of a person's earnings. **(1.3)**

specialists. Health care professionals with training and experience in specific types of care. **(22.3)**

standard deduction. On a tax return, a set amount that the IRS allows as a tax deduction without the need to list actual expenses. **(8.3)**

standard of living. The way you live as measured by the kinds and quality of goods and services you can afford. **(4.1)**

standards. Established levels of quality or quantity to measure against. **(2.1)**

staples. Basic food items kept on hand. **(21.2)**

status symbols. Possessions or activities by which social or economic prestige is measured. **(2.3)**

sticker price. The dealer's initial asking price for a vehicle. **(19.3)**

stock. Ownership interest in a corporation. **(13.3)**

stockbroker. An individual or firm that will buy and sell stock for clients according to their instructions. **(13.3)**

stock exchange. A central location where stocks are sold on a trading floor. **(13.3)**

stock market. The organized trading of stocks. **(13.3)**

store brands. Products that are marketed only in a particular chain of stores. Also called *private labels*. **(16.3)**

stress. Physical or mental tension caused by events or situations. **(22.1)**

sublet. When a renter allows another tenant to take over a rental unit and pay the rent. Also called *sublease*. **(23.2)**

supply. The quantity of a particular product that producers are able and willing to make available for sale at a given price. **(5.2)**

T

tariff. A tax on imports. **(7.2)**

tax. A required payment to a local, state, or national government. **(5.4)**

tax credit. On a tax return, an amount subtracted directly from the amount of tax owed. **(8.3)**

tax deduction. An expense that reduces the amount of income that is taxed. **(8.3)**

telecommute. To work from home using communication links to the workplace. **(4.1)**

telemarketing. Marketing goods and services by telephone. **(15.3)**

tenants. People who rent property. **(23.1)**

term. A period of time during which money must be kept on deposit. **(12.4)**

term life insurance. Life insurance that gives protection for a specific period of time. **(14.5)**

testimonial. A positive statement made by an endorser about a product or service. **(15.2)**

tips. Money given to an employee by customers in exchange for performing a service. **(8.1)**

title. A legal document that shows who owns a vehicle. **(19.2)**

townhouse. A dwelling of two or more stories that is attached at the side walls to other units in a multiple-family complex. **(23.1)**

trade deficit. A negative balance of trade, which occurs if a country spends more on imports than it receives for exports. **(7.1)**

trading up. A sales technique used to convince customers to buy a higher-priced item than they originally intended to buy. **(15.3)**

traditional economy. An economic system in which decisions about what to produce, how, and for whom are based on traditional customs and beliefs of the society. **(5.1)**

traffic patterns. The paths people take as they move through a room. **(23.4)**

traveler's checks. Documents that function as cash but can be replaced if lost or stolen. **(10.4)**

U-V

unemployment insurance. A joint federal and state plan designed to provide income to workers who have lost their jobs. **(4.5)**

unit price. The cost per unit of measurement. **(21.3)**

vacation package. An arrangement that offers a combination of travel purchases for one price. **(20.3)**

values. Strongly held beliefs and principles about what is worthwhile. **(2.1)**

vandalism. The deliberate destruction of property. **(3.2)**

variable expenses. Expenses that normally increase or decrease. **(9.3)**

veneer. A thin layer of hardwood or softwood applied over another material to give a pleasing appearance. **(23.4)**

vested. Entitled to some or all of one's money in a retirement plan when leaving a company. **(8.1)**

volatility. The degree to which an investment's return or value may change. **(13.1)**

volunteer. A person who offers services to a worthwhile cause for no pay. **(3.2)**

W-X-Y-Z

wages. Employee earnings that are paid by the hour, day, or item. **(8.1)**

wants. Things you desire but that are not necessary to live. **(2.1)**

wardrobe. The collection of clothes, shoes, and accessories that a person owns. **(18.1)**

warehouse clubs. Businesses that sell products to customers who pay a membership fee. Most of the products are sold in bulk quantities at significant savings. **(16.1)**

warranty. A guarantee of the soundness of a product or service. **(16.2)**

wellness. The practice of making a conscious effort to achieve an overall state of well-being. **(22.1)**

will. A legal document in which a person directs how his or her estate is to be distributed after death. (13.5)

wire transfer. A financial transaction that electronically moves funds from one bank to another. **(10.4)**

workers' compensation. State-regulated programs that insure employees against injuries that occur on the job, job-related illnesses, and job-related death. **(14.4)**

work ethic. A sense of responsibility to do a job well. **(4.5)**

World Trade Organization (WTO). An organization that governs over 140 member nations. **(7.2)**

CREDITS

Design: Squarecrow Graphics
Cover Photos: Corbis RF, Corbis/Estelle Klawitter, Corbis/Marianna Day Massey; Getty Images: davies & starr, Thomas Northcut, Siede Preis, Masterfile RF, Squarecrow Graphics

Imagestate/Michael Agliolo **5**, Getty Images/V.C.L. **5**, Imagestate/Michael Agliolo **5**, Imagestate/Wayne Aldridge **6**, Getty Images/Jim Linna **6**, PhotoResearches Inc./Tom & Pat Leeson **7**, Corbis/Mark Gamba **7**, SuperStock **8**, Getty Images/Al Cohen **9**, Getty Images/Gary Buss **10**, Getty Images/Malcom Piers **10**, Imagestate/Jeff Smith **11**, Getty Images/Sparky **11**, Corbis/Sanford Agliolo **12**, Getty Images/Wides + Holl **12**, Index Stock/Walker Bibikow **13**, Corbis/SM/Michael Keller **14**, Getty Images/Tanya Constantine **14**, Getty Images/Michael Shay **15**, Index Stock/Diaphor Agency **15**, Corbis/James Marshall **16**, Corbis/George B. Diebold **16**, StockFood/Newedal **17**, Corbis/William Whitehurst **17**, Imagestate/Janis Schwartz **18**, Corbis/Don Mason **20**, Corbis/George B. Diebold **21**, Corbis/George B. Diebold **22**, Corbis/Tom Stewart **23**, Corbis/Gareth Brown **24**, Dana White **25**, Better Bus. Bureua, Arlington, VA **27**, Corbis/Marci Brennan **28**, Glencoe **29**, Glencoe **30**, William Taufic **33**, Otto Rogge **34**, Articulate Graphics **35**, Corbis/LWA **36**, Corbis/Ed Bock **37**, Corbis/Jeff Zaruba **38**, Corbis/Firefly Productions **40**, Corbis/Glen McGlaughlin **41**, Articulate Graphics **42**, Corbis/Jose L. Pelaez Inc. **45**, Corbis/Charles Gupton **46**, Glencoe **48**, Getty Images/Ron Chapple **49**, Getty Images/Michael Simpson **52**, Getty Images/Mark Scott **53**, Corbis/Don Mason **54**, Getty Images/Chris Noble **55**, Michael Herron **56**, Getty Images/Emmanual Favre **57**, Corbis/Tom Stewart **58**, Corbis/Tom Stewart **59**, Getty Images/Michael Krasowitz **61**, Getty Images/Rob Gage **62**, Getty Images/Christian Michaels **63**, Ann Garvin **64**, Getty Images/Ryan McVay **65**, William Whitehurst/StockMarket **67**, Photoresearchers Inc./Laurent & Herrera **68**, PhotoResearchers Inc. Vignali Vision **69**, Dana White **71**, Getty Images/Pat LaCroix **74**, Ken Karp **75**, Getty Images/Mel Yates **76**, Corbis/David Sailors **77**, Cheryl Fenton **78**, PhotoResearchers/J. Jargaux **79**, Corbis/Mug Shots **80**, Roger Bean **81**, Jenny Thomas **82**, Greenpeace **83**, Corbis/Reuters News Media Inc. **84**, Picturesque/Jeff Lepore **85**, Corbis/Tom Young **88**, Articulate Graphics **89**, Corbis/Francesco Cascioli **92**, Mishima **93**, Corbis/Cesar E. Paredes **94**, Eric Manning **95**, Corbis/Mug Shots **96**, Getty Images/Bill Losh **97**, Getty Images/Tom Stewart **98**, Corbis/Ariel Skelley **99**, Articulate Graphics **101**, Corbis/Steve Chenn **102**, Articulate Graphics **103**, Corbis/Roy Morsch **104**, Corbis/Chuck Savage **105**, Corbis/Jose L. Pelaez **106**, Corbis **107**, V.C.L **110**, Articulate Graphics **111**, Corbis/Jon Feingersh **112**, Getty Images/Triangle Images **115**, Corbis/Darama **116**, FEEO **117**, Timothy Fuller **118**, Corbis/Jose Luis Pelaez Inc. **119**, Corbis **120**, Corbis/Rob Lewine **121**, Corbis/Brownie Harris **122**, Robert Cattan **126**, Erwin B. Nielsen **127**, David Frazier **128**, Corbis **129**, David Frazier **130**, Corbis/George B. Diebold **132**, Corbis/Mike Clemmer **133**, Corbis/Charles Gupton **134**, Corbis/Dann Tardif **135**, Articulate Graphics **136**, Articulate Graphics **137**, Getty Images/Walter Hodges **138**, Corbis/Lester Lefkowitz **140**, Getty Images/John Rizzo **141**, Corbis/Ariel Skelley **143**, Corbis/Firefly Productions **144**, Getty Images/Steve Taylor **145**, Corbis/Al Francekevich **146**, Articulate Graphics **147**, Roger B. Bean **148**, Articulate Graphics **149**, Articulate Graphics **150**, Corbis/Theirry Cariou **154**, Corbis/Peggy and Ronald Narnett **155**, Articulate Graphics **156**, Corbis/Marci Brennan **157**, Corbis/Jose L. Pelaez **158**, SuperStock/Brian Munich **159**, Corbis/Lee Snider **162**, Articulate Graphics **163**, Corbis **164**, Washington Convention & Vistors Assn. **165**, Corbis/Chuck Savage **166**, Corbis/Lester Lefkowitz **167**, Getty Images/Justin Guariolia **168**, Corbis/Paul Chmielowlec **170**, Corbis/Kevin Dodge **171**, Corbis/Masami Sano **174**, Getty Images/Garry Hunter **175**, Articulate Graphics **176**, Corbis/Richard T. Nowitz **177**, Corbis/Photomorgana **178**, Articulate Graphics **180**, Articulate Graphics **181**, Articulate Graphics **182**, Corbis/Denis Scott **183**, Getty Images/PicturePress **184**, Corbis **185**, Corbis/Lester Lefkowitz **186**, Getty Images/Elizabeth Simpson **190**, Corbis/Jose L. Pelaez **191**, Corbis/Mug Shots **192**, Getty Images/bread & butter **194**, Corbis/Rand M. Ury **196**, Articulate Graphics **197**, Ashland Oil Inc./Chris Jones **198**, Getty Images/Mark Adams **199**, Getty Images/Elizabeth Simpson **200**, IRS **201**, Corbis/David Raymer **202**, IRS **203**, Corbis/Lester Lefkowitz **204**, Getty Images/Gail Shumway **208**, Getty ImagesAntony Nagelman **209**, Corbis/Chuck Savage **210**, Articulate Graphics **211**, Getty Images/Frederic Tousche **212**, Corbis/Rob Lewine **213**, Getty Images/Flying Colours Ltd. **215**, Corbis/Jon Feingersh **216**, Corbis/Mug Shots **217**, Corbis/Tom Stewart **217**, Corbis/Jose L. Pelaez **218**, Corbis/Brad Gaber **219**, Corbis/Rob Lewine **220**, Articulate Graphics **222**, Articulate Graphics **223**, Corbis/LWA **225**, Articulate Graphics **226**, Corbis/Chuck Savage **227**, Corbis/Jon Feingersh **229**, Corbis/Tom and Dee McCarthy **230**, Corbis/Jon Feingersh **230**, Corbis/William Taufic **230**, Corbis/Paul Barton **232**, Corbis/Chuck Savage **236**, Getty Images/Ken Reid **237**, Getty Images/John-Francis Bourke **238**, FDIC **239**, Corbis/Cameron **241**, Corbis/David Stoecklein **242**, Corbis/Tim Bird **244**, Corbis/Jon Feingersh **245**, Getty Images/Jim Linna **246**, Dana White **248**, Articulate Graphics **249**, Articulate Graphics **250**, Articulate Graphics **251**, Articulate Graphics **252**, Ken Karp **254**, Ann Garvin **255**, Dana White **256**, Getty Images/Jack Hollingsworth **257**, Imagestate/Michael Lichter **260**, Getty Images/Steve Smith **261**, Corbis/Mug Shots **263**, Articulate Graphics **264**, Corbis/Mug Shots **265**, Getty Images/Richard Price **266**, Corbis/Mug Shots **267**, Articulate Graphics **268**, Corbis/Chuck Savage **271**, Articulate Graphics **272**, Corbis/Firefly Productions **275**, Corbis **276**, Articulate Graphics **277**, Jon Feingersh **279**, Jennifer Leigh Sauers **280**, Corbis/George B. Diebold **281**, Index Stock Images, Inc./Bartomeu Amenquai **282**, Corbis/Jose L. Pelaez, Inc. **283**, Getty Images/DCA Productions **284**, Dana White **285**, Corbis/Richard Price **286**, Corbis/Alan Schein **287**, Corbis/Rob Lewine **288**, Corbis/Jon Feingersh **289**, Corbis/Tom Stewart **291**, Corbis/Randy M. Ury **294**, Corbis/Jose L. Pelaez Inc. **295**, Corbis/Jose L. Pelaez inc. **296**, Corbis **297**, Getty Images/Stephen Simpson **298**, Corbis/Peter Steiner **300**, Corbis/Owaki-Kulla **301**, Corbis/Michael Keller **302**, Corbis/Myron J. Dorf **304**, Articulate Graphics **305**, Articulate Graphics **305**, Getty Images/Kevin Laubacher **306**, Articulate Graphics **307**, Articulate Graphics **308**, Corbis/Peter Beck **309**, Corbis/Steve Prezant **310**, Articulate Graphics **312**, Bureau of the Dept. of the Treasury **313**, SuperStock/Jesse Ceballos **316**, Corbis/George B. Diebold **317**, Articulate Graphics **318**, Kevin May **319**, Corbis/Joe Bator **320**, Articulate Graphics **322**, Corbis/John Henley **323**, Corbis/Sanford & Angliolo **324**, Corbis/Jose L. Pelaez Inc. **325**, Corbis/Jose L. Pelaez Inc. **326**, Picturesque/Vedros & Assoc. **327**, Articulate Graphics **328**, David Pollack **330**, SuperStock/Charles Orrico **331**, Articulate Graphics **332**, Articulate Graphics **334**, Articulate Graphics **335**, Articulate Graphics **336**, Corbis/DiMaggio & Kalish **337**, Kevin May **338**, Articulate Graphics **339**, Articulate Graphics **340**, Corbis/Michael Keller **342**, Corbis/Doug Handel **343**, Corbis/Charles Krebs **345**, Conservation of Art on Paper Inc. **346**, Bradley University/Duane Zehr **347**, Mishima **348**, Corbis/Roger Ball **352**, Corbis/Peggy & Ronald Barnett **353**, Getty Images/Richard H. Johnson **354**, Getty Images/Richard J. Johnson **355**, Picturesque/Don Johnston **357**, Picturesque/Steve Murray **357**, Getty Images/Gregg Adams **357**, Picturesque/Vedros & Assoc. Inc **357**, Corbis/Paul Barton **358**, Getty Images/Steve Fitchett **360**, Articulate Graphics **361**, Corbis **362**, Photo Researchers/Larry Mulville **363**, Corbis/Steve Kaufman **364**, Imagestate/Patti McConville **365**, Corbis/Peter Steiner **367**, Imagestate/Warren Faidley **369**, Articulate Graphics **370**, Corbis **371**, Corbis/Phillip Wallick **372**, Corbis/Mug Shots **373**, Corbis/Charles Gupton **374**, Articulate Graphics **375**, Corbis/Michael Barley **376**, Corbis/George Disario **377**, Corbis/Brownie Harris **378**, Dana White **379**, Photo Researchers/Will and Demi McIntyre **380**, Articulate Graphics **381**, Proctor Endowment Home/Randy Sutter **383**, SuperStock/Bill Barley **384**, PhotoResearchers/M. Kulyk **385**, Corbis/Ronnie Kaufman **386**, Articulate Graphics **387**, Corbis/Jose L. Pelaez **388**, SuperStock/Adamsmith **389**, John E. Kelly **390**, Corbis/Tom Sanders **391**, Corbis/Kunio Owaki **394**, Getty Images/Ken Chernus **395**, Corbis/Paul Barton **396**, The Stock Market/Rob Lewine **398**, Andre Lichtenberg **399**, Corbis/Bo Zaunders **400**, Corbis/David Woods **401**, Roger Bean **402**, Ann Garvin **403**, Getty Images/Kimball Hall **404**, Corbis/Ed Bock **405**, Corbis/Michael Keller **407**, Corbis/Gerhard Steiner **408**, Corbis/Chuck Savage **409**, Corbis **410**, Corbis/Charles Gupton **411**, Getty Images/Ian McKinnel **414**, Getty Images/Tanya Constantine **415**, Ken Karp **417**, Claude Cartier **418**, Getty Images/Steve Smith **419**, Corbis/Jeff Zaruba **420**, Corbis/Tom Stewart **421**, Articulate Graphics **422**, Ken Karp **423**, Ken Karp **425**, Corbis/Mug Shots **427**, Corbis/Steve Terrill **429**, Corbis/Rick Gomez **430**, Corbis/Charles Gupton **431**, Mishima **432**, Corbis/William Schlielz **436**, Imagestate/Michael Agliolo **437**, Imagestate/Patti McConville **438**, Corbis/Myron J. Dorf **441**, Corbis **443**, Corbis/Peter M. Fisher **444**, Art MacDillo's/Gary Skillestad **446**, Corbis/Chuck Savage **447**, Corbis **449**, Corbis/Jose L. Pelaez Inc. **450**, Corbis/Jeff Zaruba **451**, Corbis/Charles Gupton **452**, Corbis/Morgan David de Lossy **453**, Getty Images/Jonathan Storey **455**, Corbis/zefa/Erica Shires **458**, Getty Images/David Sacks **459**, Dana White **460**, Dana White **460**, Corbis/Peter M. Fisher **461**, Ann Garvin **462**, Getty Images/Adrian Weinbrecht **463**, Tom & Theresa Stack **464**, Corbis/John Henley **465**, Articulate Graphics **466**, Articulate Graphics **468**, Ken Karp **470**, Ken Karp **471**, Corbis/Norbert Schafer **474**, Kevin May **475**, Stem Gems/Photoresearchers Inc. **477**, SuperStock **480**, Imagestate/Patti McConville **481**, Picturesque/Roger Ball **482**, Articulate Graphics **483**, Ann Garvin **484**, Corbis/Mug Shots **485**, Corbis/Darama **486**, Articulate Graphics **487**, Corbis/Robert Tinney **490**, SuperStock **491**, Kevin May **493**, Corbis/Jose L. Pelaez Inc. **494**, Kevin May **495**, Kevin May **496**, Getty Images/Nick Daly **497**, Corbis/Paul Barton **499**, SuperStock/Ingram Publishing **500**, Corbis/Chris Sorensen **501**, Corbis/Anthony Redpath **503**, Corbis/David Lawrence **506**, SuperStock **507**, Ken Karp **508**, SuperStock/Kwami Zukomo **509**, Corbis/Peter Beck **510**, Corbis **511**, Kevin May **512**, Corbis/Alan Schein **515**, Picturesque/Stephen McBride **517**, SuperStock **519**, Stock Food/Maximilian **522**, Mark Romine **523**, Stock Food/Renata Marcialis **524**, Articulate Graphics **525**, Articulate Graphics **526**, Ann Garvin **527**, Articulate Graphics **528**, SuperStock **530**, Getty Images/Image Source **531**, Corbis/George Disario **532**, StockFood/Eising **534**, Corbis/Jose L. Pelaez **537**, Joe Mallon **538**, Joe Mallon **539**, Brent Phelps **541**, Ken Karp **542**, Corbis/William Whitehurst **544**, Ken Karp **545**, Dana White **546**, Corbis/Denis Scott **550**, PhotoResearchers Inc./V. Habbick **551**, Corbis/Ed Bock **552**, Jenny Thomas **553**, Scott M. Thompson/ICC **554**, Corbis/Dennis Meyler **555**, Corbis/Jose L. Pelaez, Inc. **556**, PhotoResearchers, Inc./B. Rauch **557**, PhotoResearchers, Inc./Saturn Stills **560**, Keith Berry **561**, Corbis/Jose Luis Pelaez Inc. **562**, Corbis/Paul Barton **563**, Imagestate/Patrick Ramsey **565**, PhotoEdit/Merrit Vincent **567**, Arnold and Brown **568**, Dana White **569**, David R. Frazier Photolibrary Inc. **570**, Kevin May **571**, Getty Images/Chronis Jons **572**, Imagestate/Patti McConville **576**, Corbis/Ray Juno **577**, Luther Linkhart/SuperStock **578**, Corbis/Mug Shots **579**, Corbis/Craig Tuttle **580**, Luis Delgado **581**, Corbis/Charles Gold **582**, Kevin May **584**, Articulate Graphics **585**, Articulate Graphics **586**, Luis Delgado **587**, Marshall Berman **588**, Corbis/Jose L. Pelaez Inc. **590**, Corbis/Ed Bock **592**, Articulate Graphics **593**, Corbis **594**, Getty Images/David Gaz **596**, Getty Images/Stockdisc **597**, Timothy Fuller **600**, Donald Wardlaw Architect AIA **602**, Articulate Graphics **603**, Articulate Graphics **604**, Articulate Graphics **606**, J.J. Stoecker **607**, Corbis/Chuck Savage **607**, Dana White **608**, Articulate Graphics **609**, Articulate Graphics **610**, Kevin May **611**, Dana White **612**

INDEX

INDEX

D

E

INDEX

G

H

I

INDEX

N

P

INDEX

Q

R

S

INDEX